Time Out Guides Limited
Universal House
251 Tottenham Court Road
London W1T 7AB
Tel + 44 (0)20 7813 3000
Fax + 44 (0)20 7813 6001
Email guides@timeout.com
www.timeout.com

Editorial
Editor Jan Fuscoe
Deputy Editor Emma Howarth
Copy Editor Elizabeth Winding
Researchers Cathy Limb, Fiona Shield
Proofreader Tamsin Shelton
Indexer Cathy Limb

Managing Director Peter Fiennes
Financial Director Gareth Garner
Editorial Director Sarah Guy
Series Editor Cath Phillips
Editorial Manager Holly Pick
Accountant Ija Krasnikova

Design
Art Director Scott Moore
Art Editor Pinelope Kourmouzoglou
Senior Designer Josephine Spencer
Graphic Designer Henry Elphick
Junior Graphic Designer Kei Ishimaru
Digital Imaging Simon Foster
Ad Make-up Jodi Sher

Picture Desk
Picture Editor Jael Marschner
Deputy Picture Editor Tracey Kerrigan
Picture Researchers Helen McFarland, Troy Bailey

Advertising
Sales Director & Sponsorship Mark Phillips
Sales Manager Alison Wallen
Advertising Sales Ben Holt
Advertising Assistant Kate Staddon
Copy Controller Declan Symington

Marketing
Group Marketing Director John Luck
Marketing Manager Yvonne Poon
Sales & Marketing Director, North America
Lisa Levinson

Production
Group Production Director Mark Lamond
Production Manager Brendan McKeown
Production Coordinator Caroline Bradford

Time Out Group
Chairman Tony Elliott
Financial Director Richard Waterlow
TO Magazine Ltd MD David Pepper
Group General Manager/Director Nichola Coulthard
Managing Director, Time Out International
Cathy Runciman
TO Communications Ltd MD David Pepper
Group Art Director John Oakey
Group IT Director Simon Chappell

Contributors
London Jan Fuscoe, Emma Howarth, with thanks to contributors to *Time Out London*; **Canterbury to the Coast** Ronnie Haydon; **Hastings to Dungeness & Romney Marsh** Yolanda Zappaterra; **Brighton** Peterjon Cresswell; **Chichester & Around** Charles Godfrey-Faussett; **Isle of Wight** Yolanda Zappaterra; **South Hams** Kate Fuscoe; **Falmouth & the Roseland Peninsula** Helen Gilchrist; **Isles of Scilly** Simon Coppock; **Padstow & Rock** Hayley Lawrence; **Mendips** Simone Baird; **Bristol** Jessica Eveleigh; **Malmesbury & Tetbury** Anna Norman; **South-west Cotswolds** Jonathan Cox; **Woodstock to Burford** Cathy Limb; **Brecon Beacons** Jessica Eveleigh; **Ludlow** Will Fulford-Jones; **Orford to Southwold** Dominic Earle; **Bury St Edmunds to Lavenham** Lesley McCave; **North Norfolk Coast** Phil Harriss; **Manchester** Anna Norman; **Harrogate** Jill Turton; **Helmsley & Harome** Charles Godfrey-Faussett; **Windermere & Ambleside** Roopa Gulati; **Edinburgh** Keith Davidson; **Glasgow** Keith Davidson; **Mid Argyll & Bute** Keith Davidson; **Speyside** Keith Davidson; **Strangford Lough** Caroline Workman; **Mid Kerry** Caroline Workman.

Additional reviews Sarah Guy, Cath Phillips. **Thanks to** Angela Haley of Ards Borough Council, Daisy Collins, Francis Gooding, Nadia Menuhin, Charlie Simonds.

Maps JS Graphics (john@jsgraphics.co.uk)

Cover photography Prestonfield Edinburgh
Back cover photography by Sam Robbins and Sandy Young.

Photography by pages 3, 108, 109 Walter Weber; pages 11, 12, 14, 241, 244, 247, 248, 252, 253, 263, 265, 267, 268, 269, 275 Sam Robbins; page 15 Henry Godfrey; pages 25, 56, 57, 60 Tove Breitstein; page 26 (left) Ed Marshall; pages 26 (right), 27 Andrew Brackenbury; pages 32, 41 Britta Jaschinski; page 39 Ming Tang Evans; page 43 Angela Moore; pages 45, 47 Elsam; pages 50, 54, 55 Kent Tourism; page 59 Richard Harris/ www.thelittlewhitebox.co.uk; page 68 Rob Greig; page 76 Alys Tomlinson; pages 77, 81 Scott Wishart; page 87 www.visitbrighton.com; page 95 Gaston Duval; page 98 (right) Isle of Wight Tourism; pages 99, 103, 104, 105, 107 Paul Murphy; pages 101, 123, 127, 309 English Heritage Photo Library; pages 112, 113 Richard Downer; pages 114, 115 www.discoverdevon.com; page 125 Peter Cade; page 126 Dawn Runnals; page 128, 135, 403 Michelle Grant; pages 136, 137, 140, 144 Simon Coppock; pages 146, 150 The Cornwall Folk Festival; page 147, 214 Alamy; page 149 Four Corners; pages 154, 196, 197, 205 Alex Ramsay; pages 168, 169 The Chapter of Wells; page 172 South West Tourism; page 173 Destination Bristol; page 176 Mandy; page 179 Jamie Woodley; page 187 Mark Bolton/ Superstock; page 190 Paul Groom; page 207 Steven Woodman; page 209 Blenheim Palace and Jarrold Publishing; pages 200, 201 South Cerney Outdoor Education; page 216 (left) Cadw (Crown Copyright); page 216 (right) Finn Beales; page 217 Getty Images; pages 221, 222, 223 www.breconbeaconstourism.co.uk; page 227 Nathan Morgan; page 230 South Shropshire District Council; pages 231, 236 www.foodestival.com; page 234 Tim King; pages 240, 243 WDC Image Library; page 256 St Edmundsbury Borough Council; pages 276 (left), 280, 289 Simon Buckley; pages 276 (right), 277, 286, 287 John Oakey; page 283 Tim Otley; pages 290 (left), 294, 300, 305, 307, 308 Roger Scruton; pages 290 (right), 299, 303 Harrogate International Centre; page 304 Mark Danton; page 310 Ian Stuart; pages 322, 323, 327, 329, 330, 331, 333, 334, 335, 336, 337, 342, 344, 345, 346, 348, 349, 351 Olivia Rutherford; pages 352, 353, 356, 359, 362, 000 Sandy Young; page 369 www.visitscotland.com; pages 374, 375 Chivas Brothers Ltd.; pages 376, 377, 380, 381 Northern Ireland Tourist Board.

The following images were provided by the featured establishments: pages 17, 18, 19, 21, 23, 24, 36, 44, 48, 63, 66, 68, 69, 74, 75, 78, 79, 84, 88, 89, 91, 92, 98 (left), 116, 118, 121, 122, 129, 130, 132, 133, 152, 153, 158, 160, 161, 164, 165, 178, 182, 185, 186, 189, 191, 192, 195, 199, 203, 204, 206, 208, 226, 238, 248 (mid- left & bottom), 251, 257 (top), 258, 260, 261, 262, 271, 272, 273, 291, 296, 312, 313, 317, 321, 328, 364, 365, 370, 382, 385, 386, 387, 390, 391, 393, 394.

Weekend Breaks

IN GREAT BRITAIN & IRELAND

timeout.com

Published by Time Out Guides Ltd, a wholly owned subsidiary of Time Out Group Ltd.
Time Out and the Time Out logo are trademarks of Time Out Group Ltd.

© Time Out Group Ltd 2007
Previous editions 2005.

10 9 8 7 6 5 4 3 2 1

This edition first published in Great Britain in 2005 by Ebury Publishing
A Random House Group Company
20 Vauxhall Bridge Road, London SW1V 2SA

Random House Australia Pty Limited 20 Alfred Street, Milsons Point, Sydney, New South Wales 2061, Australia
Random House New Zealand Limited 18 Poland Road, Glenfield, Auckland 10, New Zealand
Random House South Africa (Pty) Limited Isle of Houghton, Corner Boundary Road & Carse O'Gowrie,
Houghton 2198, South Africa

Random House UK Limited Reg. No. 954009

For further distribution details, see www.timeout.com

ISBN 10: 1-84670-020-5
ISBN 13: 978184670 0200

A CIP catalogue record for this book is available from the British Library

Printed and bound by Firmengruppe APPL, aprinta druck, Wemding, Germany

The Random House Group Limited makes every effort to ensure that the papers used in our books are made from
trees that have been legally sourced from well-managed and credibly certified forests. Our paper procurement
policy can be found on www.randomhouse.co.uk.

Contents

Great Value
UK car hire

Drive a bargain

▶ All inclusive rates

▶ Delivery and collection available

▶ One-way rentals

▶ Unlimited mileage

It's so quick and easy to hire from Alamo, one of the UK's leading car hire companies. Rentals can start from 12 noon on Friday and end 10am Monday, so you can really make the most of your long weekend away.

Just book and enjoy the drive.
Call 0870 400 4565

alamo.co.uk

About the guide

This book is divided into 30 breaks, starting in London and moving out towards the further reaches of Great Britain and Ireland. (If you're looking for a particular hotel or restaurant, see the index *pp404-420*.) Each of the breaks has something special about it, but absolutely central to each one are life-enhancing hotels, restaurants and pubs.

The details

Booking accommodation in advance is always recommended: most of the places we feature in this guide are very popular, and at least several weeks' (and often months') notice is required. We've tried to indicate where children and/or dogs are welcome (or not) – but it's always best to discuss this first with the establishment in question. Unless otherwise stated, breakfast is included in room prices. Some hotels offer special rates for weekends, often including dinner. It's always worth asking about such deals when you book.

The maps featured in this book are intended (with the exception of the town plans) for general orientation, and you will need a road atlas or other detailed map to find your way around.

The listings

• Throughout this guide we have listed phone numbers as dialled from within the country in question, but outside the particular village, town or city.
• The times given for dining are those observed by the kitchen; in other words, the times within which one can order a meal. These can change according to the time of year and the whim of the owners. Booking is always a good idea, and essential on Fridays and Saturdays, or if you're travelling any distance.
• Main course prices are given as a range, from the cheapest to the most expensive – obviously, these prices can and will change over the life of a guide.
• Where credit cards are accepted, the following abbreviations have been used: AmEx (American Express); DC (Diners Club); MC (MasterCard); V (Visa).

The reviews

The reviews in this guide are based solely on the experiences of *Time Out* reviewers. While every effort has been made to ensure the accuracy of the information contained in this guide, the publishers cannot accept any responsibility for errors it may contain. Opening times, owners, chefs, menus and other details can change at any time.

Let us know what you think

We hope you enjoy this book and welcome any comments or suggestions you might have. Email us at guides@timeout.com.

SPONSORS & ADVERTISERS

We would like to thank our sponsor, MasterCard, for its involvement in this guide. However, we would like to stress that sponsors have no influence over editorial content. The same applies to advertisers. No attraction, hotel, restaurant or pub has been included because its owner advertised in the guide: an advertiser may receive a bad review or no review at all.

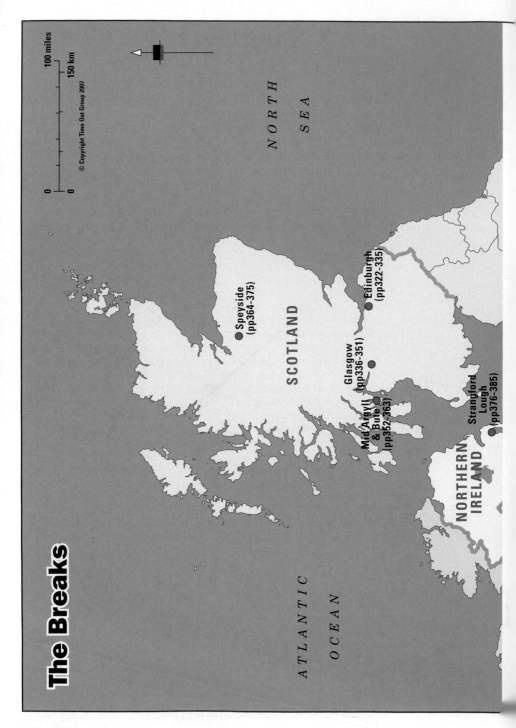

The Breaks

100 miles

150 km

© Copyright Time Out Group 2007

NORTH SEA

Speyside
(pp364-375)

SCOTLAND

Edinburgh
(pp322-335)

Glasgow
(pp336-351)

Mid Argyll
& Bute
(pp352-363)

Strangford
Lough
(pp376-385)

NORTHERN
IRELAND

ATLANTIC

OCEAN

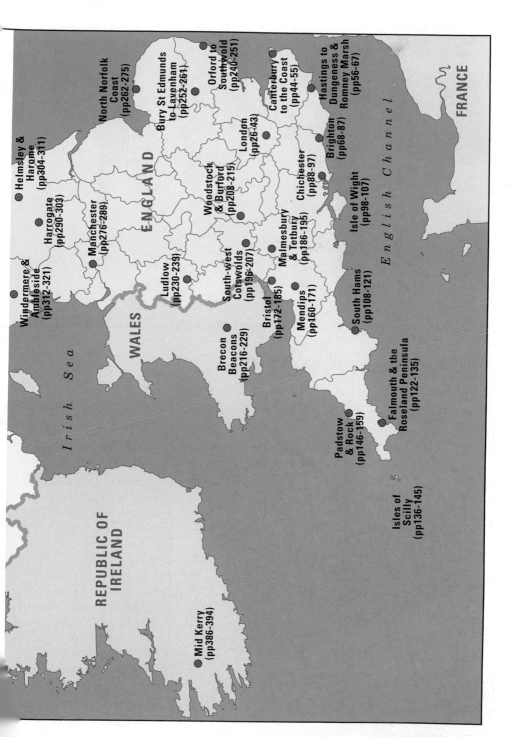

REPUBLIC OF
IRELAND

Mid Kerry
(pp386-394)

Irish Sea

WALES

ENGLAND

FRANCE

English Channel

Windermere &
Ambleside
(pp312-321)

Helmsley &
Harome
(pp304-311)

Harrogate
(pp290-303)

Manchester
(pp276-289)

North Norfolk
Coast
(pp262-275)

Bury St Edmunds
to Lavenham
(pp252-261)

Orford to
Southwold
(pp240-251)

London
(pp26-43)

Woodstock
& Burford
(pp208-215)

Canterbury
to the Coast
(pp44-55)

Hastings to
Dungeness &
Romney Marsh
(pp56-67)

Brighton
(pp68-87)

Chichester
(pp88-97)

Ludlow
(pp230-239)

South-West
Cotswolds
(pp196-207)

Malmesbury
& Tetbury
(pp186-195)

Isle of Wight
(pp98-107)

Bristol
(pp172-185)

Mendips
(pp160-171)

South Hams
(pp108-121)

Brecon
Beacons
(pp216-229)

Falmouth & the
Roseland Peninsula
(pp122-135)

Padstow
& Rock
(pp146-159)

Isles of
Scilly
(pp136-145)

Take time out...

...with **15%** off your car hire.*

Whatever your requirements; a small economy car, a large family MPV or something a little special, Europcar has the right vehicle for you!

So, don't just sit there – the open road awaits. Call us on **0870 607 5000**, or visit **www.europcar.co.uk**, and quote promotional code *45122094* to receive you discounted rental.

Europcar

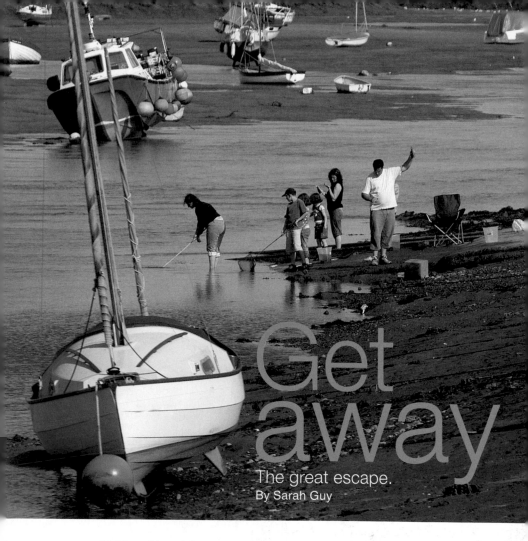

Get
away

The great escape.
By Sarah Guy

This guide celebrates the joys of a few days away, and to that end we've gathered together a selection of the loveliest places to stay in Great Britain and Ireland, some of which can compete with the best in the world. But while we don't want to rain on our own parade, we can't pretend that enjoying a weekend away is always as easy as we'd like. It's hard – and in many areas impossible – to get around the countryside without a car. And our objection to this isn't only a green attitude – for many people a weekend can't be truly relaxing if it involves driving for hours on a traffic-clogged road. At weekends, public transport outside the major cities often seems to be little more than a poor joke. Many services (bus and rail) don't even run on a Sunday (the day most people might want to don their hiking boots), even in some of the most scenic and well-trodden parts of the country (try catching a bus in and around North Yorkshire, for example). And even forgetting Sundays, transport systems never seem to be 'joined up': having caught a main-line train, it's not unusual to wait for an hour or more for a branch-line or bus connection.

And don't even think about taking your bicycle – unless you have a folding one (accepted without reservation) or are able to book well in advance. Reservations are now free on all National Rail services, but many local trains only accept up to two bicycles.

For example, First Great Western – covering Bristol, the Cotswolds, South Wales and the west of England – can carry up to six on high-speed trains, but fewer on other trains (and those at the discretion of the conductor). For the full picture, download the *Cycling by train* leaflet from www.nationalrail.co.uk.

We've tried to include as many car-free breaks as possible, though the fact remains that too much of the countryside is inaccessible to anyone without a vehicle. But take comfort from the fact that once you've reached many of our most luxurious retreats, you won't want to wander too far from the grounds.

CLOSED FOR THE WINTER

We're also shut out from most of the nation's stately homes and historic houses for much of the winter – precisely the season when rainy-day activities are called for. The National Trust, being the owner of so many properties, bears the brunt of most complaints. We asked the Trust why the seasonal shutdown occurs, and were told it was 'to enable the important conservation work that needs to be carried out with often fragile historic houses'. Though we understand the need for conservation work, we can't believe that conservation requirements are the same

Wells & Walsingham Railway

throughout every single property, but the Trust says, 'Obviously, each property is unique and the level of work does vary, but there is often more involved than people realise.' In order to give people some insight into this conservation work, the Trust runs a series of 'putting to bed' events – for details see www.nationaltrust.org.uk or call 0870 458 4000.

'What's wrong can really be summed up as a 'can't do' attitude.'

The few properties that are open in the off-season are the ones that are financially sustainable during this period, such as (parts of) Beningbrough Hall and Gardens in North Yorkshire, or the Red House in Bexleyheath. Otherwise, you're left with a range of gardens and parks for inclement-weather sightseeing trips.

English Heritage (different from the National Trust in that it is a public body partly funded by the government) has 308 properties and places of interest open during the winter (see www.english-heritage.org.uk for more details). Obviously, some of these are ruins or other open-air sites, but many are houses or castles – the Royal Pavilion in Brighton or Osborne House on the Isle of Wight, for example. As an organisation it is actively involved in trying to increase visitor numbers in the off-season, and so tries to balance conservation requirements with visitors' needs.

NEGATIVE ATTITUDE

The rest of what's wrong can really be summed up as a 'can't do' attitude. From the familiar story of the malicious glee with which pub and restaurant owners announce that the kitchen is shut at 2.01pm, to the fact that many places won't accept bookings for just one night at weekends, it all too often feels as though the answer to any request will be 'no'. 'Hospitality' can be hard to come by too – arriving at a hotel and being made to feel unwanted or inappropriate is a frequent occurrence. We've left several well-known places out of this guide on those grounds. And why is food and drink still the Achilles heel of so many establishments? Picture-postcard pubs with no real beer (or real food for that matter), hotels where the in-room milk is UHT or the coffee instant, children's meals that are nothing but junk – all crop up with dismal regularity.

THE FUTURE'S LOOKING BRIGHTER

A different, more consumer-friendly breed of hoteliers and restaurateurs is gradually becoming more prevalent, however. People are increasingly making a special hotel, spa or restaurant the focus of a weekend away, rather than the scenery or the recreational activities, so it pays to be one of those establishments that get it spot on. From the cosmopolitan chic of Babington House through to the rural charm of the Star Inn in Harome, these places are destinations in their own right.

The new range of boutique hotels – which includes excellent chains such as Hotel du Vin (*see p402* **Useful addresses**), as well as one-offs – deserves particular praise. Many of them have breathed new life into moribund areas, for example the George in Rye (*see p63*). And nowadays some even have green credentials (*see p15* **How green is my valley?**).

Another welcome development is the reinvention of the country-house hotel as an adult playground, with stuffiness removed – the roll-call includes Barnsley House and Cowley Manor (*see p202*), Calcot Manor (*see p191*), Whatley Manor Hotel (*see p192*) and, of course, Babington House (*see p165*). These places are so inviting that it really doesn't matter what the weather does – who cares if it's sleeting if you can hunker down in a screening room or sink into a hot tub?

The answer to a perfect weekend at any time of the year? – choose your hotel carefully. The new breed of hoteliers offers a beguiling mix of cool design, warm welcome, comfortable beds, good food and little luxuries, banishing forever the memory of unlovely B&Bs and shielding guests from the remaining irritations of British life.

Snettisham Park Farm

How green is my valley?
The eco option. By Lisa Ritchie

You've made the decision to leave a lighter carbon footprint by forgoing a budget flight in favour of a short break on home soil (and you may even be taking the train to reduce emissions further). Well done. But are you ready to move on to the next level of environmental awareness? 'Eco' is the current travel buzzword – and not only in far-flung, developing countries. An area comprising Counties Fermanagh, Leitrim, West Cavan, North Sligo, South Donegal and North West Monaghan has become Ireland's first designated ecotourism destination. Embracing a variety of leisure-related businesses that conform to a set of environmental standards, the Greenbox region (www.greenbox.ie) offers a green health farm, Ard Nahoo, overlooking Lough Nahoo near Dromahaire, County Leitrim, and the Gyreum near Riverstown, Sligo – a circular structure made from renewable sources that functions as arts centre, alternative 'church' and hostel-style eco-lodge. If that sounds a little too New Age for your taste, the options are widening for a luxury break combined with impeccable green practices.

GREEN ROOMS

'People think you have to sacrifice quality for environmental awareness, but they actually sit side by side,' says Vanessa Scott, who owns Strattons (4 Ash Close, Swaffham, Norfolk PE37 7NH, 01760 723845, www.strattons-hotel.co.uk, £150-£175 double; £200-£225 suite) with her husband Les. 'The best food is local food.' The Scotts run their ten-room, 18th-century luxury guest house according to a strict environmental code that is rewritten each year and extends to every aspect of the business. 'The ethos is to only use local artists, local artisans, local food producers. I know everybody's banging the drum about that, but you can go up to the coast and see people advocating local produce and then there's foie gras on the menu.' All staff are thoroughly involved in the process, including going on field trips to suppliers so that they can answer questions from customers.

'An accumulation of small things make a big difference.'

The hotel, secreted down a narrow lane behind a row of shops in attractive market town Swaffham, shatters the perception of eco-accommodation as spartan. Restored over a period of 17 years, using conservation materials and regional building techniques, the house mixes traditional and modern decor with contemporary art ('My husband and I met at art college and the hotel is a bit like a great big canvas,' says Scott). Each of the stylish rooms is unique; choose, for example, the manor-house opulence of the Red Room (which once sheltered a Fatwa-threatened Salman Rushdie) with its sumptuously curtained and carved four-poster bed, fireplace and private cobbled courtyard, or the modern Edie suite (named after local artist Linda Roast's wonderful large-scale portraits of her dog) with clean-lined leather headboard and glass bricks separating the tiled bathroom. The dramatically decorated Stalls and the Opium room are in separate buildings in the grounds. A life-size indigenous red-deer stag made from recycled agricultural iron by Rachael Long stands guard in front of the house, embodying the Scotts' ethical trinity of creativity, locality and environmental awareness.

Far from being shoved down your throat (apart from notes on provenance on the menu and a polite request not to keep the tap running while brushing your teeth in the bathroom), the environmental action goes on behind the scenes and doesn't intrude on the guests' experience. Staff sort rubbish for recycling and there's a compost, so only two per cent of waste goes into landfill. All waste – water, food scraps, packaging – is weighed as

Strattons

it leaves the premises in kilos, so they can devise strategies for improvement. The newer rooms are on a separate circuit controlled by a single switch, so the housekeepers don't have to rush up and turn off all the lights and appliances. 'Grey' water is used to water the garden, which provides some of the ingredients for the restaurant, guest newspapers are made into paper bricks for the fire or shredded for bedding for the free-range chickens, who can be seen clucking around the grounds. Even doing away with luxury bathroom miniatures in favour of refillable dispensers saved over 150 kilos of soap being chucked away. It's an accumulation of small things that make a big difference.

Since they opened, back in 1990, the Scotts had always run the business with a certain degree of environmental awareness, but it wasn't until 1997, when they participated in a waste minimisation project with the University of Hertfordshire that they realised their approach was too ad hoc and got the technical advice they needed to come up with a practical policy.

Swaffham itself is a bit of an eco-destination – down the road from the hotel, groups of schoolchildren tour the town's EcoTech Centre; since a second wind turbine was erected in 2003, it supplies 75 per cent of the town's electricity, saving 3,500 tonnes of CO_2 emissions each year. Often overlooked by visitors in favour of the coast, the wildlife-rich heath and woodland of the Brecks is great walking territory.

'Most of the products, from the jams to the handmade natural soaps, are produced locally.'

A 'tool box' in your room contains useful local leaflets and specially devised maps for nearby walks or cycle rides (of around four to six miles) from the hotel. Long-distance ramblers can pick up the Peddars Way to the coast.

The undisputed ecocentre of England as the home of the Eden Project and other green industries, Cornwall has several options for the environmentally conscious visitor – the Cornwall Sustainable Tourism Project (CoaST; www.cstn.org.uk) aims to encourage and

develop sustainability in the local industry. Recipients of a Gold Award from the Green Tourism Business Scheme, the Primrose Valley Hotel (Porthminster Beach, St Ives, Cornwall TR26 2ED, 01736 794939, www.primroseonline.co.uk, £85-£145 double; £160-£225 suite.) in an Edwardian villa overlooking the lovely Porthminster Beach in Cornwall, has ten airy, updated rooms. As well as extensive recycling, electricity supplied by green company Ecotricity, low-energy lighting and environmentally friendly cleaning products, the hotel supports the Marine Conservation Society and the Cornwall Wildlife Trust. All the fish served in its restaurant comes from sustainable sources and most of the products, from the jams, cheeses and air-dried salami to the handmade natural soaps in the bathrooms, are produced locally.

Further south, the Old Chapel Forge, near Chichester and the South Downs (Lower Bognor Road, Lagness, Chichester, West Sussex PO20 1LR (01243 264380, www.oldchapelforge.co.uk, £50-£70 double; £60-£110 suite) is a superior B&B run according to sustainable principles. It has solar-powered heating, food sourced from local farms and is the holder of a Green Tourism Business Scheme Gold Award. Choose from one of two suites in a converted 1611 chapel, or a self-contained cottage ideal for a large family, whose two en suite doubles can also be booked separately.

SUSTAINABLE SPAS
Indulge in a bit of guilt-free pampering. Titanic Spa (Low Westwood Lane, Linthwaite, Huddersfield HD7 5UN, 01484 843 544, www.titanicspa.com), on the edge of the Pennines in West Yorkshire's Colne Valley, is billed as the country's first 'eco-spa'. One of the area's many defunct mills – housing the spa, plus an apartment complex and hotel – has been converted with the aim of being entirely carbon neutral. Work on the massive industrial building is still underway, but when complete at the end of 2007, all the complex's heating and electricity will be provided by a CHP (combined heat and power) unit, fuelled by chippings from sustainable wood sources, and

Pollaughan Farm

How green is my valley?

solar panels in the roof. In true spa tradition, the famously soft water (largely responsible for the textile boom in these parts as it was ideal for washing wool) is supplied by the complex's own 100-metre-deep bore hole. Although the apartment we stayed in was more Barratt Home than five-star hotel and seemed hastily finished, the loft-style space was attractively modern and comfortable (currently ten apartments are available for spa guests, but a further 16 hotel suites are being added). The spa facilities, however, are extensive and excellent, with a spacious relaxation room complete with a bean bag 'pit', 15-metre salt-filtered pool, gym and whirlpool bath, hair salon, a lengthy menu of Elemis and Decléor face and body treatments and a modern bistro. You could easily spend a weekend wallowing in the Titanic Heat Experience – a series of hot, cold and other sensory conditions – that is the highlight of the spa. As well as the usual sauna and steam rooms, there is the saunarium for those who prefer a gentler level of heat, an aromatherapy room and a menthol-infused ice room, where you can cool yourself down with crushed ice. You can also book hydrotherapy, body treatments performed on a plinth in a hammam, and couples can slather each other with mud in a private steam chamber. Packages start from £99 for use of the spa facilities, one night's accommodation, lunch and dinner in the bistro and continental breakfast/snacks in your apartment. However, should you want to venture outside, there is some beautiful walking country nearby in the National Trust's Marsden Moor Estate, and some decent restaurants, including the popular Olive Branch in Marsden (62 Manchester Road, 01484 844487, www.olivebranch.uk.com).

How green is my valley?

Primrose Valley

In Cornwall, the Budock Vean Hotel (*see p131*), on the Helford River, sees itself as custodian of this Area of Outstanding Natural Beauty (AONB) and a Special Area of Conservation (SAC). Affirmed by a Green Tourism Business Scheme Gold Award, it is committed to conservation, recycling, and using natural (organic where possible) products in its health spa. The Cowshed at Babington House, Somerset (*see p165*) was a pioneer of green pampering with products made from herbs grown in the on-site walled garden.

COTTAGES WITH A CONSCIENCE

A number of purpose-built eco-cottages have sprung up around the country. Slumbering in a secluded valley about 15 miles outside Ludlow (*see pp230-239*), Ecocabin (contact Kate Grubb, Langdale Cottage, Obley, Bucknell, Shropshire SY7 0BZ, 01547 530183, www.ecocabin. co.uk, £90-£105, max four people, min two nights) proves that sustainability can be stylish. Constructed from local Douglas fir and larch, insulated with sheep's wool, and furnished with organic and recycled materials, it exudes a clean-lined Scandinavian simplicity that is a world away from the crusty, hippyish stereotype – you'd never know the kitchen work surface is made from recycled yogurt pots. Everything is geared towards energy efficiency and minimal waste: solar panels supply the hot water, a wood-pellet stove the heating, and waste is disposed of via a worm-assisted compost and recycling collection. True to its principles, there's no TV or CD player, but a wind-up radio, library and board games are provided – so you can rediscover the pleasures of simple pastimes. The cottage sleeps four and you can arrange to have a

selection of local foodstuffs delivered on your arrival. There are also opportunities to participate in local crafts courses or (subject to demand) an 'eco-writing' class with environmental poet Helen Moore – see the website for details.

Pollaughan Farm, on the Roseland Peninsula (Portscatho, Truro, Cornwall, TR2 5EH, 01872 580150, www.pollaughan.co.uk, from £180, two people, three nights) has a collection of cheerfully furnished cottages, converted barns and a farmhouse, which sleep between two and six people. Because of the demand for week-long lets in summer, short breaks are only available between end of October and early March. Valerie Penney, who converted the properties with her husband Tim, is a director of CoaST (*see p18*). As well as emphasising recycling and conservation through insulation and energy-saving light bulbs, the Penneys have introduced a water

Ecocabin

Yurtworks

catchment system that pipes all roof water from the cottages, house and buildings to a wildlife lake that is accessible to the public. They have also provided tree-planting space for a local carbon-emission offset scheme. Children can get up close and personal with farm animals such as donkeys and Dorset ewes, and there is a 'pick your own' vegetable and flower patch – how's that for promoting local produce?

BEAUTIFUL SITES

The original eco-option, camping is now cool – and the options have never been more chic. Yurtworks (Cornish Yurt Holidays, Greyhayes, St Breward, Bodmin, Cornwall PL30 4LP, 01208 850670, www.yurt works.co.uk, from £50 for two, min three nights) started as a sideline of Tim Hutton's tree-planting and coppice management business after he was inspired by seeing one of the circular dwellings (used by nomadic peoples of Central and East Asia) in Alaska, of all places. 'The yurt represented a human presence that was not at odds with its wilderness surroundings,' he

says. 'It is simple, beautiful, round, and touches the earth lightly; I hope some of the visitors feel something like it when they come to stay.' Incredibly, it could also stand up to the Alaskan climate. Encouraged by this, Hutton built one of the structures in Cornwall, and lived in it for a year. Now, as well as making the yurts from sustainable local wood, finished with organic oils (for sale or to hire), he offers holidays in exotically furnished models (Oriental rugs, richly hued cushions, Moroccan lanterns) in a secluded setting on the edge of Bodmin Moor. Heating and cooking are provided by a stove, fuelled by wood thinnings from Hutton's coppice and waste from yurt-making and a local sawmill. The bathroom yurt features a rolltop tub supplied by a wood-burning water heater and a new solar panel – there's even a compost toilet yurtlet. Organic sausages, burgers and eggs from the site's own hens are available.

Winner of the Tourism in Norfolk's Sustainable Tourism Award 2006, Deepdale Farm (Deepdale Farm, Burnham Deepdale, Norfolk PE31 8DD, 01485 210256, www.deepdale farm.co.uk, £40-£60, min two nights) offers a campsite and stylish hostel with great green credentials (a high level of recycling, and waterless urinals and solar panels in the toilets, for example) on the North Norfolk coast (see pp262-275). Sioux Native American tipis, with open fires, are available from March to October. Facilities include an information centre and café as well as the usual campsite necessities. The farm also offers conservation weekends (over 21s only).

So, an environmentally responsible break doesn't have to be spartan, and these breaks can only be the first of many.

The Breaks

London

Bright lights, big city.

Historic and happening, grungy and glamorous, chaotic and constantly evolving, the sheer scale of what London has to offer can be a daunting prospect for the weekend visitor. Rest assured, though, that even the briefest of London encounters can be both rewarding and exhilarating. Embrace the possibilities of fine international dining, glitzy bars and high culture. Indulge in the homely comforts of old-fashioned caffs and proper pubs. Live life on the cutting edge at the city's finest clubs and music venues. Take a whirlwind tour of the sights, dance till the sun comes up or simply saunter the city's markets (*see p40* **Market value**), shops and parks at your leisure. London is a city of endless possibilities and half the fun is deciding which are the ones for you. And remember that If – or should we say, when – you decide to come back for more, the annual *Time Out London Guide* is an invaluable source of information and ideas for a longer stay. For listings information while you're here, pick up a copy of the weekly *Time Out* magazine from any newsagent.

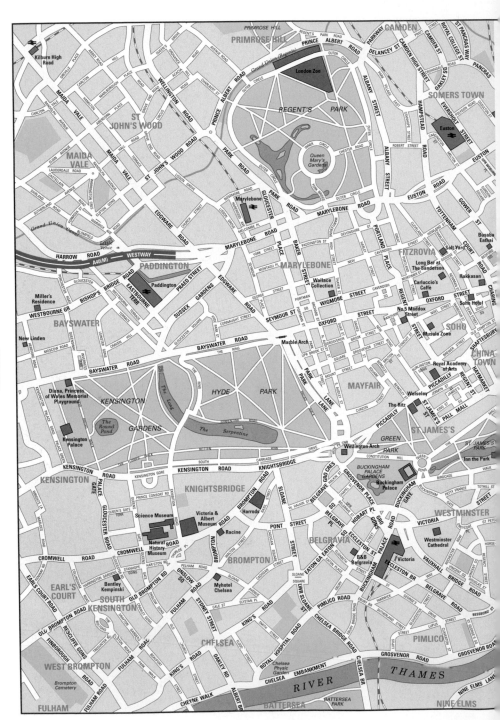

London

DISCOVER THE WILDER SIDE OF LONDON

Explore the London Wetland Centre and discover the beautiful wildlife that lives here. Centre includes lakeside restaurant, discovery centre, gift shop and adventure area for children.

Open 7 days a week from 9.30am to 6pm
T: 020 8409 4400   Visit wwt.org.uk/london

WWT London Wetland Centre, Queen Elizabeth's Walk, Barnes, SW13 9WT
Alight at Barnes Station or take the no. 283 Duck Bus from Hammersmith Tube

Registered charity no. 1030884

Accommodation	★★★★★
Food & drink	★★★★★
Nightlife	★★★★★
Shopping	★★★★★
Culture	★★★★★
Sights	★★★★★
Scenery	★★✩✩✩

WHERE TO STAY

London may be one of the world's top tourist destinations, but its hotels have a bad rep (tiny, overpriced, badly decorated rooms matched by inept service). However, over the last few years there have been signs of change. The luxury hotels have started offering special deals, the budget hotels are making an effort to smarten their decor, and there's a bumper crop of discount hotel websites. But the most encouraging trend is the appearance of designer hotels at prices mortals can afford; we list a selection here, alongside a few of London's admittedly expensive but unmissable gems.

B&B Belgravia

64-66 Ebury Street, SW1W 9QD (7823 4928/ www.bb-belgravia.com). Victoria tube/rail. **Rates** £107-£117 double; £137-£147 family room. **Credit** AmEx, MC, V.
B&B Belgravia is one of the most attractive B&Bs we've seen, almost to *Elle Deco* levels, and it's liveable as well as lovely: there's a laptop equipped with free internet connection, a high-tech coffee machine, games and toys for the kids and a collection of DVDs. Bedrooms are chic and predominantly white, with flat-screen TVs and sleek bathrooms with power showers. Breakfasts are cooked in front of you in the open-plan kitchen and organic ingredients are used where possible.

Bentley Kempinski

27-33 Harrington Gardens, SW7 4JX (7244 5555/www.thebentley-hotel.com). Gloucester Road tube. **Lunch served** noon-2pm Mon-Fri. **Dinner served** 6.30-9.30pm Tue-Sat. **Main courses** £28. **Set dinner** £49 5 courses; £75-£80 tasting menu. **Rates** £450 double; £600-£4,000 suite. **Credit** AmEx, DC, MC, V.

One of London's most opulent boutique hotels, the Bentley offers chandelier-swinging glamour at its best. There are certainly plenty of them: twinkly crystals sparkle in the lobby and the bedrooms, and you can even shave under one in the bathrooms. Elsewhere Louis XV-style furniture, gilt mirrors and marble abound. Bedrooms have thick carpets, luxurious gold satin bedspreads and whirlpool/jacuzzi tubs; the spa features gold-laced mosaics and a Turkish hammam. There's a glitzy restaurant, 1880, which serves extravagant multi-course grazing menus. And for after dinner, the hotel's Malachite Bar is a dim, decadent hideaway ideal for sinking into after a day's shopping and sightseeing. But the real showpiece is the lobby's sweeping staircase – perfect for grand entrances.

Great Eastern Hotel

40 Liverpool Street, EC2M 7QN (7618 5000/ www.london.greateastern.hyatt.com). Liverpool Street tube/rail. **Rates** £305-£345 double; £455-£630 suite. **Credit** AmEx, DC, MC, V.
Once a faded railway hotel, the Great Eastern is now a mammoth urban style mecca, with a design sympathetic to the glorious Victorian building. Bedrooms wear the regulation style-mag uniform: Eames chairs, chocolate shagpile rugs and white Frette linens. And you'll never go hungry or thirsty – the hotel has seven restaurants and bars, of generally impressive quality, though they're no longer Conran-run. The hotel has recently become a Hyatt.

Hoxton

81 Great Eastern Street, EC2A 3HU (7550 1000/www.hoxtonhotels.com). Old Street tube/rail. **Lunch served** noon-4pm daily. **Dinner served** 5.30-10.30pm Mon, Tue, Sun; 7.30-11pm Wed-Sat. **Main courses** £8-£22. **Rates** £59-£149 double. **Credit** MC, V.
The Hoxton, courtesy of Pret a Manger co-founder Sinclair Beecham, opened in September 2006 amid a manic flurry of excitement – it was offering rooms for just £1 (and sometimes still does: sign up online for information). Even without a crazily cheap special rate this is a hotel with plenty going for it. Weekend prices come in below £70 and rooms, although small, offer chic touches such as Frette linen and flat-screen TVs. A free light Pret breakfast is included in the price but there are plenty of more substantial options for the taking in the bar and restaurant downstairs.

Miller's Residence

111A Westbourne Grove, W2 4UW (7243 1024/www.millersuk.com). Notting Hill Gate or Westbourne Park tube. **Rates** £176-£217 double; £270 suite. **Credit** AmEx, MC, V.
Antiques expert Martin Miller's discreet little B&B is possibly London's most romantic hotel. The unmarked red door off Westbourne Grove doesn't look particularly promising, but the interior is an Aladdin's cave: rooms – named after great English poets such as Blake, Byron and

London

SHOPPING

London is brimming with vast department stores, quirky boutiques, atmospheric markets and specialist shops selling everything from door handles to left-handed scissors. Whether you're up for flashing some serious cash or just whiling away an afternoon window-shopping, in the consumption stakes London always comes out on top. Listed below are some of London's best shopping streets. *See also p40* **Market value**.

NEW BOND STREET, W1
Great for designer labels; handy for Fenwicks.

CARNABY STREET, W1
Great for funky fashion and gifts; handy for Liberty.

COVENT GARDEN PIAZZA, WC2
Great for gifts and mainstream and street fashion; handy for Thomas Neal centre.

KING'S ROAD, SW3
Great for high-street fashion; handy for Peter Jones.

KNIGHTSBRIDGE, SW1
Great for designer and high-street fashion; handy for Harrods.

MARYLEBONE HIGH STREET, W1
Great for food, designer homewares, books and one-off gifts; handy for the Conran Shop.

TOTTENHAM COURT ROAD, W1
Great for electronics, home accessories and furniture; handy for Heal's.

WESTBOURNE GROVE, W11
Great for classy homewares and upmarket-but-boho fashion; handy for Portobello Road.

Browning – are dripping in gilt, chandeliers and ornate mirrors. You'll find 18th-century furniture straight out of a period drama, shiny candelabra, baubles and gewgaws. Despite the antique treasures, it's not at all stuffy: there's a casual, bohemian feel, with well-worn, comfy sofas, old Persian rugs and a relaxed sense of occasion. In the salon, help yourself to whisky and curl up by the massive oak fireplace. Ordinary name, extraordinary place.

myhotel chelsea

35 Ixworth Place, SW3 3QX (7225 7500/ www.myhotels.com). South Kensington tube. **Rates** £250 double; £355 suite. **Credit** AmEx, DC, MC, V.

Sister venue to the Bloomsbury original (11-13 Bayley Street, WC1B 3HD, 7667 6000), this is a sleek, fashion-conscious boutique hotel. There's a feminine feel to the place with feng shui touches, an aquarium in the lobby and lots of crystals and candles scattered about. The designers call the look 'traditional English meets *Sex and the City*', which translates as dusty pinks and purples, lush fabrics (cashmere throws) and velvet cushions. Rooms come with New Agey accessories – herbal wellness/hangover kits and the like – and Wi-Fi. Chill-out places include the spa (with fantastic Aveda treatments), Cape Cod-influenced bar and conservatory-style lounge.

New Linden

59 Leinster Square, W2 4PS (7221 4321/ www.newlinden.co.uk). Bayswater tube. **Rates** £79-£140 double; £120-£190 family room. **Credit** MC, V.

The New Linden is a bit of a budget showpiece and popular with it. Rooms are simply but pleasingly designed with wooden floors and marble-tiled bathrooms (some with deluge shower heads), and flat-screen TVs and CD players come as standard. A Viennese buffet breakfast is included in the price, and the location – between Notting Hill and Kensington Gardens – offers easy access to some of London's finest shopping, eating and drinking destinations.

No.5 Maddox Street

5 Maddox Street, W1S 2QD (7647 0200/ www.living-rooms.co.uk). Oxford Circus tube. **Rates** £260 1-bed suite-£640 3-bed suite. **Credit** AmEx, DC, MC, V.

A fantastically located and discreet boutique hotel: blink and you'll miss the unassuming entrance. Decor throughout is chic and serene: bamboo floors and Far Eastern furniture are mixed with fake fur throws and the obligatory crisp white sheets. Rock 'n' roll images of swinging London add a stylish vibe to the suites (many of which have balconies). Alternatively, you can head out to nearby Soho and experience the real thing for yourself. Patara, the Thai restaurant situated below the hotel, makes a great dinner choice, though suites are equipped with kitchens if you prefer to whip up your own creations. A 'Big Bar' facility offers 'good' and 'bad' treats (organic pasta sauces for the good, vodka and jelly babies for the rest of us). Careful attention to detail throughout is all part of the service here.

One Aldwych

1 Aldwych, WC2B 4RH (7300 1000/www.one aldwych.com). Covent Garden or Temple tube/ Charing Cross tube/rail. **Meals served** *Axis* noon-2.45pm Mon-Fri, 5.45-10.45pm Mon-Fri;

5.45-11.30pm Sat. *Indigo* noon-3pm, 6-11.15pm Mon-Fri; 12.30-2.30pm, 6-11.15pm Sat, Sun. **Main courses** *Axis* £14.50-£27.50. *Indigo* £16-£23. **Set meals** *Axis* (lunch, 5.45-7.15pm, after 10.15pm Mon-Sat) £17.50 3 courses; £20.50 3 courses. *Indigo* (6-7pm, 10-11.15pm Mon-Sat) £16.75 2 courses, £19.75 3 courses. **Rates** £360-£435 double; £575-£1,450 suite. *All* **Credit** AmEx, DC, MC, V. R

One look at the glamorous lobby, with its sculpture of a hunched oarsman and sprays of flowers, and you'll understand why this is one of London's most talked-about hotels. A real modern classic, One Aldwych combines the traditional and the contemporary with consummate ease. It's housed in an Edwardian bank building but the streamlined, minimalist rooms all have up-to-date gadgetry (and original artworks). The elegant Lobby Bar is popular with Londoners, the gym is well equipped and there's even a private cinema. But the pièce de résistance is undoubtedly the shimmering 18m pool, complete with music piped into the water.

Portobello Hotel

22 Stanley Gardens, W11 2NG (7727 2777/ www.portobello-hotel.co.uk). Holland Park or Notting Hill Gate tube. **Rates** £180-£300 double; £350 suite. **Credit** AmEx, MC, V.

This swanky Notting Hill mansion has a bohemian rock 'n' roll vibe that's played host to Kate Moss and Alice Cooper (though not at the same time) among others. The elegant rooms ooze colonial romance: potted palms, ceiling fans, wooden shutters and oriental antiques. Some are poky, but some are truly spectacular, featuring four-poster or circular beds, claw-foot bathtubs and loads of seductive cushions and rugs. After a day of shopping locally, you can drink in the hotel bar or soothe aching muscles in one of the many jacuzzi tubs.

Rookery

12 Peter's Lane, Cowcross Street, EC1M 6DS (7336 0931/www.rookeryhotel.com). Farringdon tube/rail. **Rates** £205-£265 double; £495 suite. **Credit** AmEx, DC, MC, V.

Tucked away in a row of converted 18th-century houses, the Rookery is a fabulously atmospheric place to stay. It's stuffed with glorious antiques (gothic-looking oak beds, plaster busts and claw-foot bathtubs) and modern creature comforts (Egyptian cotton sheets and plush towels on heated towel racks). There's a relaxed, intimate feel with touches that are particularly appealing in winter – open fires and cosy corners. Sister hotels Hazlitt's (6 Frith Street, 7434 1771, www.hazlittshotel.com) and the Gore (190 Queen's Gate, 7584 6601, www.gorehotel.com) are similarly classy places.

Soho Hotel

4 Richmond Mews (off Dean Street), W1D 3DH (7559 3000/www.firmdalehotels.com). Leicester Square or Tottenham Court Road tube. **Meals served** noon-11.30pm Mon-Sat; noon-10.30pm

HAMPSTEAD VILLAGE GUESTHOUSE

We never planned to start a hotel in our family home but, when life changed, it was a natural development for the house, which had always welcomed a steady stream of visitors, to become a Guesthouse.

Whilst preserving the Victorian character of the house, all rooms have good writing tables, free wi-fi access and guests can use a laptop and mobile phone at no extra charge. Most important for families is the fridge and kettle in each room and, for general use, there are baby monitors, cots, high chairs, changing mat and a selection of toys which most children make a beeline for.

We have a beautiful garden which is a haven in summer. Hampstead Heath, which is very nearby, is an ideal place for children, with a playground just at the bottom of the road and paddling pool within walking distance. Kentish Town City Farm, also a wonderful place for children, is nearby.

"the family atmosphere made us feel welcome"   *"...this is heaven"*

Peaceful setting, close to
Hampstead Heath, yet in the heart
of lively Hampstead Village

~

Close to underground and bus.
Centre of London in 15 minutes.

~

Large rooms full of character, plus
modern amenities: TV, fridge, kettle
and direct-dial telephone.

~

Breakfast in the garden,
weather permitting

~

Accommodation from £50

~

No smoking

"you made our stay very happy"

Sun. **Main courses** £16-£28. **Set meal** £19.95 3 courses. **Rates** £255-£315 double; £370-£2,500 suite. **Credit** AmEx, MC, V.

Kit Kemp really is taking over London. Her seventh property – the Haymarket Hotel – was set to be unveiled at the time of writing, and if it's anything like the rest of her empire, expect to be impressed. Here at the edgy Soho Hotel there's a classy but contemporary feel. Public rooms feature colours like shocking pink or acid green; huge bedrooms are kitted out in soft neutrals, bold pinstripes and traditional florals. Refuel, the loungey bar and restaurant, has an open kitchen and a car-themed mural. Downstairs, there are two screening rooms for movie moguls and treatment rooms for stressed execs. For the other hotels, including the slightly more affordable Number Sixteen (16 Sumner Place, SW7 3EG, 7589 5232), see the website.

Threadneedles

5 Threadneedle Street, EC2R 8AY (7657 8080/www.theetoncollection.com). Bank tube/ DLR. **Meals served** *Bonds Restaurant* noon-2.30pm; 6-10pm Mon-Fri. **Main courses** £14.95-£22. **Set lunch** £19.50 2 courses, £24.50 3 courses. **Rates** RO £347-£417 double; £564 suite. **Breakfast** £14-£19. **Credit** MC, V.

Occupying the former HQ of the Midland Bank, Threadneedles successfully integrates modern design with a monumental space, complete with an exquisite stained-glass ceiling dome in the lobby. The decor is soothingly neutral, with Korres toiletries in the serene limestone bathrooms. Stress-busting comforts include a scented candle lit at turn-down and a 'movie treats' menu of popcorn, ice-cream and Coke (albeit at a price that may raise your blood pressure). There's also a great restaurant and plenty of weekend deals to tempt non-execs.

Trafalgar

2 Spring Gardens, SW1A 2TS (7870 2900/ www.hilton.co.uk/trafalgar). Charing Cross tube/rail. **Rates** £198-£270 double; £441 studio; £515 suite. **Credit** AmEx, DC, MC, V.

Part of the Hilton group, the Trafalgar has dropped the branding in favour of funky designer decor. The building is imposing, but the mood inside is young and dynamic. The rooms have a masculine feel, but the bathtubs are made for sharing; full-size aromatherapy-based toiletries are a nice touch. The location is its biggest draw: corner rooms overlook Trafalgar square and the small rooftop bar has lovely panoramic views. Ground-level bar Rockwell offers over 100 bourbons.

Zetter

St John's Square, 86-88 Clerkenwell Road, EC1M 5RJ (7324 4444/www.thezetter.com). Farringdon tube/rail. **Brunch served** 11am-3pm Sat, Sun. **Lunch served** noon-2.30pm Mon-Fri. **Dinner served** 6-11pm Thur-Sat; 6-10.30pm Mon-Wed, Sun. **Main courses**

£16.50-£18.50. **Set meal** £18-£35 3 courses; £55 6 courses. **Rates** £127-£330 double. **Credit** AmEx, DC, MC, V.

Clerkenwell's hippest hotel pushes all the right buttons with its buzzy contemporary restaurant, popular cocktail bar and edgy, converted warehouse setting (complete with a dazzling atrium). The bedrooms, all done up in creams and greys, are small but stylish. Their ecological credentials are impeccable: if you open a window, the air-con goes off; water comes from the hotel's own well. Instead of minibars, each vending machines in the corridors dispense gin and tonics, champagne and cappuccinos. The rooftop suites have fantastic wooden decks (and, of course, the best views in the house). The location is also perfect for taking in the topnotch eating, drinking and clubbing possibilities of one of London's most fashionable neighbourhoods.

WHERE TO EAT

In addition to the restaurants mentioned below, the Carluccio's Caffè (8 Market Place, 7636 2228, www.carluccios.com) and Busaba Eathai (22 Store Street, 7299 7900) chains make great choices for a casual lunch or dinner. The former offers quality Italian cooking (antipasto, great pasta and risotto, meat and fish mains) and is also very child-friendly; the latter is a London mini-chain serving up modish food in an equally stylish canteen setting. For an in-depth look at London's restaurant scene, see *Time Out's Eating & Drinking in London* or *Cheap Eats in London*.

Barrafina

54 Frith Street, W1D 4SL (7813 8016/ www.barrafina.co.uk). Leicester Square or Tottenham Court Road tube. **Open/tapas served** served noon-3pm, 5-11pm daily. **Tapas** £4-£9. **Credit** MC, V.

This British-run tapas bar serves simple and traditional tapas, in the best sense. The nibbles include almonds, olives and pan con tomate (tomato-rubbed bread), but it's best to move on swiftly to the cold meats, such as slivers of cured jabugo ham cut from a whole leg behind the counter. A mound of crushed ice displays the fresh seafood: three types of huge prawns, clams, mussels, a vast chunk of raw tuna used to make tuna tartare. The 31 wines by the glass are very well-chosen, but be warned that in combination with this sort of grazing menu, wine can push the bill right up.

Hakkasan

8 Hanway Place, W1T 1HD (7907 1888). Tottenham Court Road tube. **Bar Open** noon-12.30am Mon-Wed; noon-1.30am Thur-Sat; noon-midnight Sun. *Restaurant* **Lunch served** noon-2.45pm Mon-Fri; noon-4pm Sat, Sun. **Dinner served** 6-11pm Mon-Wed, Sun; 6-12pm Thur-Sat. **Dim sum** £3-£18. **Main courses** £10.50-£140. **Credit** AmEx, MC, V.

London

Sleek, stylish and oh-so-sexy: myhotel Cheslea.

You can't deny the glamour of an evening spent at Hakkasan. As you descend the green slate staircase you are greeted by the smell of incense and flowers. Enter the subtly lit space divided by dark latticed screens and you can't fail to feel the buzz of one of London's most happening venues. Hakkasan breaks the Chinatown mould by offering fine, pricey Chinese food in a setting that satisfies both western and oriental tastes. The dim sum is unrivalled in London. Come at lunchtime for crisp triangular pastries stuffed with venison; translucent, emerald green dumplings filled with prawn and fragrant Chinese chives; and light as a-feather deep-fried snacks – stick to tea and it'll cost around £25 a head. There's a fine wine list and enticing cocktails, and service is helpful. Booking is essential.

Inn The Park

St James's Park, SW1A 2BJ (7451 9999/ www.innthepark.com). Green Park or Piccadilly Circus tube. **Lunch served** noon-4pm daily. **Tea served** 3-5pm daily. **Dinner served** 6-9pm daily. **Main courses** £13.50-£18.50. **Set lunch** (noon-4pm Sun) £22.50 2 courses, £27.50 3 courses. **Credit** AmEx, MC, V.
Fantastically located to the north-east of the lake in St James's Park, this striking Oliver Peyton venture is a fine showcase for British talent. The wooden building, partly covered by a turf roof, was designed by Michael Hopkins, while the chic, sauna-like interior is by Tom Dixon. The all-day café menu caters for leisurely breakfasts (full English, crumpets, kippers, an array of different types of bacon) and indulgent afternoon teas, as well as offering a selection of 'grab and go' sandwiches and snacks. For lunch and dinner the place becomes a full-blown restaurant serving produce-led British dishes such as Dorset crab with green apple or belly pork with parnsip mash. Neal's Yard cheeses and prawn cocktail are also hits.

J Sheekey

28-32 St Martin's Court, WC2N 4AL (7240 2565/www.j-sheekey.co.uk). Leicester Square tube. **Lunch served** noon-3pm Mon-Sat; noon-3.30pm Sun. **Dinner served** 5pm-midnight Mon-Sat; 6pm-midnight Sun. **Main courses** £10.75-£35. **Set lunch** (Sat, Sun) £24.75 3 courses. **Credit** AmEx, DC, MC, V.
Securing a table at J Sheekey can be difficult – you need to book well in advance – but it's worth the effort. This elegant fish restaurant shares many things with its sister restaurant, the Ivy: classy design, simple but sublime food and superior celebrities. The menu offers everything from dressed crab to oysters, with excellent main courses including pan-fried cod with crab risotto or steamed smoked haddock with poached egg and colcannon. Desserts are great and service is always spot on. While it's easy to spend a lot of money here (watch those side dishes), it's also possible to keep the bill down. The average main course is under £20 – great value with such superior cooking, especially on the weekend set lunch.

Masala Zone

9 Marshall Street, W1F 7ER (7287 9966/ www.realindianfood.com). Oxford Circus tube. **Lunch served** noon-3.30pm Mon-Fri; 12.30-3.30pm Sun. **Dinner served** 5.30-11pm Mon-Fri; 6-10.30pm Sun. **Meals served** 12.30-11pm Sat. **Main courses** £6.95-£11.95. **Thalis** £7.40-£11.95. **Credit** MC, V.
The popular Masala Zone mini-chain is a fine spot for Indian food. The great-value menu encompasses crisp Bombay beach snacks, meal-in-one plates, rare regional dishes, well-made curries and satisfying thalis. Though there's a canteen vibe, fast throughput and (sometimes) queues, the authenticity survives. For dinner, a combination thali is a good way to go, allowing a choice of any two pots of curry from the menu, plus a starter, two vegetable curries, raita, dahl, kuchumber (diced tomato and cucumber salad), popadoms and chutneys, a chapati and rice.

Moro

34-36 Exmouth Market, EC1R 4QE (7833 8336/www.moro.co.uk). Farringdon tube/rail. **Bar Open** 12.30-11.45pm Mon-Sat (last entry 10.30pm). *Restaurant* **Lunch served** 12.30-2.30pm Mon-Sat. **Dinner served** 7-10.30pm Mon-Sat. **Tapas served** 12.30-10.30pm Mon-Sat. **Main courses** £14.50-£18. **Credit** AmEx, DC, MC, V.
Sam and Sam Clark opened Moro in 1997 and continue to impress diners with their use of top quality authentic ingredients. In fact, Moro has pretty much set the standard for restaurants offering an imaginative English take on Mediterranean food – in this case, Spain and North Africa. There's a wood-fired oven and charcoal grill, both of which are made good use of for the main courses (the likes of char-grilled mackerel with cabbage and caraway salad or wood-roasted pork with Canary Island potatoes) and there's an excellent tapas menu for low-key snacking. Service is seamless, but the place can be noisy and there are few cheap wines. Still, with endless praise, a top-selling cookbook and near-permanently busy tables, this is one to watch.

Racine

239 Brompton Road, SW3 2EP (7584 4477). Knightsbridge or South Kensington tube. **Lunch served** noon-3pm Mon-Fri; noon-3.30pm Sat, Sun. **Dinner served** 6-10.30pm Mon-Sat; 6-10pm Sun. **Main courses** £13-£20. **Set meal** (lunch, 6-7.30pm) £16.50 2 courses; £18.50 3 courses. **Credit** AmEx, MC, V.
A slice of Parisian chic in the middle of very English Knightsbridge. Racine is an atmospheric place to enjoy a decadent lunch or dinner. There's an upmarket, sophisticated air and the place is decked out with mirrors, deep-green banquettes, sleek leather and fresh, white tablecloths. The French bourgeois food is excellent, focusing on rustic-style cooking and prime-quality ingredients. Tasty and well-presented meat and fish dishes are the mainstays. A deservedly popular restaurant.

London

Salt Yard

54 Goodge Street, W1T 4NA (7637 0657/ www.saltyard.co.uk). Goodge Street tube. **Open/ tapas served** noon-11pm Mon-Fri; 5-11pm Sat. **Meals served** noon-3pm, 6-10.30pm Mon-Sat. **Tapas** £3.50-£8.25. **Credit** MC, V.

This stylishly pared-down tapas bar-restaurant is dotted with elegant design features (a striking wooden bar top, a mirrored stairwell) and has a sophisticated, restrained air. The food is as impressive as the decor, delivering classic Spanish dishes with a distinctive (often Italian-influenced) twist. Tuck into chorizo in red wine, tuna carpaccio with broad beans, stuffed courgette flowers or a selection of top-notch charcuterie. An excellent choice for vegetarians too.

St Alban

4-12 Regent Street, SW1Y 4PE (7499 8558/www.stalban.net). Piccadilly Circus tube. **Lunch served** noon-3pm daily. **Dinner served** 5.30pm-midnight Mon-Sat, 5.30-11pm Sun. **Main courses** £9.25-£26. **Credit** MC, V.

St Alban's phone line is hotter than a night out in Cuba because it's from Chris Corbin and Jeremy King, the duo who run the Wolseley (and before that the Ivy). They can't open a new restaurant without creating a snowstorm of media interest, followed by the pick of London's high society dropping in. Once you secure a table, you're treated with the utmost charm and efficiency. The dining room is large but low-ceilinged, and clever seating and elegant, contemporary murals soften the

CLASSY COCKTAILS AND PROPER PINTS

For an expertly mixed cocktail in a stylish setting try one of London's many hotel bars. The Long Bar at the Sanderson (50 Berners Street, W1, 7300 1400, www.sandersonlondon. com) is a dreamy, Philippe Starck-designed oasis of silver, white and glass. Claridge's Bar (55 Brook Street, W1, 7629 8860, www. claridges.co.uk) is the last word in Mayfair elegance: classy 1930s decor, immaculate cocktails and sophisticated service. The art deco American Bar at the Savoy (Strand, WC2, 7836 4343, www.the-savoy. com), where the martini was invented, is a paean to the golden age of the silver shaker. The tasteful Lobby Bar at One Aldwych (*see p33*) is notable for its arched windows and striking modern art, and for a totally OTT South Pacific extravaganza, go to Trader Vic's at the Hilton (22 Park Lane, W1, 7208 4113, www.tradervics.com). Otherwise, try Hakkasan (*see p35*) where the stunning bar combines warehouse chic with Chinese exoticism and LA glam. The kitsch Trailer Happiness (177 Portobello Road, W11, 7727 2700) is renowned for its killer cocktails. Shoreditch hotspot Loungelover (1 Whitby Street, E2, 7012 1234) is a rare breed: a camp straight bar, with flamboyant lighting and furniture. In central London, Crazy Bear (26-28 Whitfield Street, W1, 7631 0088, www.crazybeargroup. com) is super-stylish with excellent cocktails and must-see, though rather disorientating, loos.

If proper pints and cosy snugs are more your style, head straight for one of London's atmospheric old boozers. The small but perfectly formed Dog & Duck (18 Bateman Street, W1, 7494 0697) in Soho oozes traditional style and dates back to 1734. Also worth disappearing into for the evening are the beautifully restored Lamb (94 Lamb's Conduit Street, WC1, 7405 0713), which has the bonus of a patio for outdoor drinking, and the candlelit Jerusalem Tavern (55 Britton Street, EC1, 7490 4281). Try also the tiny Seven Stars (53 Carey Street, WC2, 7242 8521) for its great food and gregarious proprietress Roxy Beaujolais.

Crazy Bear

space. The menu is up-to-the-minute Modern Mediterranean, and the pasta is exceptional. Seafood takes prominence on the menu. Sicilian rabbit stew showed a Moorish influence, while slow-roasted black pig was a triumph. The wine list is a dream, with diverse, well-chosen wines from many of the less obvious regions of Spain and Italy to complement the dishes. Book well ahead.

St John

26 St John Street, EC1M 4AY (7251 0848/ 4998/www.stjohnrestaurant.com). Farringdon tube/rail. Bar **Open** 11am-11pm Mon-Fri; 6-11pm Sat. **Food served** noon-11pm Mon-Fri; 6-11pm Sat. *Restaurant* **Lunch served** noon-3pm Mon-Fri. **Dinner served** 6-11pm Mon-Sat. **Main courses** £13.50-£22.50. **Credit** AmEx, DC, MC, V.

St John's simple yet effective nose-to-tail eating concept (which makes a point of using every part of the animal) has won it many an accolade. The whitewashed walls and steel kitchen counters are similarly no-nonsense. The daily menu doesn't bother with dish descriptions, preferring instead to simply state ingredients: ox heart and lentils or roast lamb and mint sauce, for example. Save room for desserts such as rhubarb crumble cake or lemon posset and shortbread and make sure you try some of the carefully sourced cheese. Friendly service and excellent wines complete the picture, making this a fine choice for a taste of British cooking at its best. The Spitalfields branch at 94-96 Commercial Street, 7251 0848, is more casual and open all day.

Smiths of Smithfield

67-77 Charterhouse Street, EC1M 6HJ (7251 7950/www.smithsofsmithfield.co.uk). Farringdon tube/rail. **Open** *Wine room* 11am-11pm daily. **Snacks** £3-£6. *Dining room* **Lunch served** noon-2.45pm Mon-Fri. **Dinner served** 6-10.45pm Mon-Sat. **Main courses** £11.75. *Ground-floor bar* **Open** 11am-11pm Mon-Sat; noon-10.30pm Sun. *Ground-floor café* **Meals served** 7am-5pm Mon-Fri; 10am-5pm Sat; 9.30am-5pm Sun. **Main courses** £3-£8.50. *Top-floor restaurant* **Lunch served** noon-2.45pm

MARKET VALUE

From the Routemaster bus to the local boozer, traditional London is being usurped by modernity. All the more reason, then, to celebrate the dynamism of London's East End Sunday markets.

Start off at Liverpool Street Station; exit to the left on to Bishopsgate, then make a quick right up Petticoat Lane, or Middlesex Street, as the authorities and street signs have been trying unsuccessfully to rename it for 175 years. Old ways die hard here, and the trade in cheap tat and sardonic repartee is much the same as it was a century ago.

After Wentworth Street, take the second (unnamed) street on the left, go right at Goulston Street and you'll come to Tubby Isaacs (established 1919), one of London's last remaining seafood stalls. Buy a £2 seafood mix, sprinkle with vinegar and gulp down a real piece of history.

Go left on Whitechapel High Street and pass Aldgate East tube station. Take a left up Commercial Street and head for Nicholas Hawksmoor's recently restored Christ Church, built between 1715 and 1729 as part of a missionary initiative to 'civilise' the wild East End. Nearby is the Ten Bells pub (84 Commercial Street, E1, 7366 1721), famously patronised by Jack the Ripper's prostitute victims.

Go through the gateway on the west side of Commercial Street to enter the fine cast-iron Victorian structure of Spitalfields Market. Until the late 1980s, this was a wholesale fruit, veg and flower market; when it moved out, an eclectic mix of stalls and local businesses took over.

There's lots of interesting crafty stuff, but, as you move further in, you won't fail to notice some boxy glass protrusions. The market was targeted by City developers: despite widespread protests, the 1930s western wing was demolished in 2005 and replaced by Norman Foster-designed offices and retail units. Successfully? Explore glass-covered Market Street then consider your verdict over born-again British grub at popular Canteen (2 Crispin Place, E1 6DW, 0845 686 1122, www.canteen.co.uk).

Leave Spitalfields through the handsome Lamb Street exit to the north, cross Commercial Street, carry on up Hanbury Street and nip into the edgy Sunday (Up)Market on the left. At the top of Hanbury Street is Brick Lane (known as Banglatown on account of its sizeable Bengali population). On Sundays this is an international free-market zone. Part flea market, part hawker, part recycler of goods of dubious legality.

Take a right off Brick Lane on to lovely Cheshire Street, which holds shops and stalls both cute and conservative. Next, turn left at St Matthew's Row and carry on over Bethnal Green Road on Turin Street to Gosset Street, through Bethnal Green. At Gosset, go right, then left up Barnet Grove to Columbia Road flower market, the garden centre of the East End. Stop off at the Royal Oak (73 Columbia Road, E2, 7729 2220, www.royaloaklondon.com), a classic pub-turned-gastropub where you can people-watch over a proper pint of ale and a £13 roast.

Columbia Road's
Sunday flower market

London

TEASMADE

The English can't live without tea. So you'd be right in assuming we're connoisseurs of the restorative brew? Wrong. In most parts of the country tearooms mean nothing more than a steaming mug of milky stuff, stewed to super-strength from a bag of tea factory leaf sweepings. But fear not. London has woken up to the variety and exhilaration of fine teas.

The fabulous Yauatcha (15 Broadwick Street, W1, 7494 8888) led the way, but our current favourite is Postcard Teas (9 Dering Street, W1, 7629 3654, www.postcardteas.com, open 10.30am-6.30pm Tue-Sat) – a Mayfair tearoom and shop that is a labour of love for owner Timothy d'Offay. The shop sells a score of brews, both online and on-site, but we advise taking to the single shared table, with its ten stools, and sampling some tea in the flesh. The teas cost £1.50 per pot, cheap for varieties of this excellence – black teas (the oxidised or 'fermented' leaves we tend to drink in the West), green teas and oolongs (semi-'fermented' teas). While you're probably familiar with Darjeeling, the Chinese pu-erh is far less well known – what they all share is that d'Offay has a personal connection with all of them; he's visited many of the growers. There are well-matched nibbles too, such as chocolate cake (£2.50 a slice), medjool dates (35p each) and salted almonds (£1).

If what you crave is a proper English tea – with extravagant sandwiches and cakes – there are many options. If money's no object (a set tea costs about £30) and you're happy dressing smart, try afternoon tea at one of London's swanky hotels: perhaps Claridge's (55 Brook Street, W1, 7409 6307, www.claridges.co.uk), the Ritz (150 Piccadilly, W1, 7493 8181, www.the ritzhotel.co.uk) or the Savoy (Strand, 7836 4343, www.the-savoy.com). No less exquisite is tea at Fortnum & Mason (181 Piccadilly, St James's, 7734 8040, www.fortnumandmason. co.uk). A less starchy version of the formal tea can be had at Notting Hill's Tea Palace (175 Westbourne Grove, 7727 2600, www.teapalace. co.uk), and teatime is often when you'll get the best out of the superb Wolseley (see p43).

Nor is afternoon tea all about the brew: London's cakemakers have really upped their game. Macaron (22 The Pavement, SW4, 7498 2636) was the winner of Best Pâtisserie in the 2006 Time Out awards, but little Peyton & Byrne (196 Tottenham Court Road, W1, 7580 2522, www.heals.co.uk), with its fairy cakes, Scotch eggs and fig rolls, is another favourite.

Mon-Fri; 12.30-3.45pm Sun. **Dinner served** 6.30-10.45pm Mon-Sat; 7-10.15pm Sun. **Main courses** £12-£35. *All* **Credit** AmEx, DC, MC, V. Multi-level Smiths has an industrial, New York warehouse feel, with exposed bricks, reclaimed wood, metal tubing and raw concrete (it was formerly a store for nearby Smithfield meat market). Of the four storeys, the ground floor is the most laid-back, serving breakfast, brunch and casual fare. The next level up is a cocktail and champagne bar, with plush red leather booths. The second-floor Dining Room (serving Modern British dishes) is based around a central mesh gallery, overlooking the champers bar; it's noisy. More peaceful is the Top Floor restaurant, which serves quality, posh British food (organic or additive-free where possible).

Wolseley

160 Piccadilly, W1J 9EB (7499 6996/www.the wolseley.com). Green Park tube. **Meals served** 11.30am-midnight daily. **Tea served** 3.30-5.30pm Mon-Sat; 3.30-6.30pm Sun. **Main courses** £9.50-£34. **Credit** AmEx, DC, MC, V. This stunning building was originally a car showroom and makes a grand space for one of London's prized dining spots. The interior recreates pre-war grandeur with vaulted ceilings, grand pillars, polished marble and weighty chandeliers. For all the opulence, the vibe is friendly and the prices are reasonable. It's open from breakfast onwards, and the long menu has something for everyone. The afternoon tea ritual is memorable. Finger sandwiches, filled with smoked salmon and sliced cucumber, are matched by scrumptious but dainty cakes and scones. The excellent macaroons and almond meringues are worth the indulgence too.

NIGHTLIFE

Where clubbing is concerned, London has got it made – and then some. Prime weekend dancefloor spots include the End (18 West Central Street, WC1, 7419 9199, www.endclub.com), which has rolling residencies each Friday and Saturday; Bugged Out!, Layo & Bushwacka!, Chew the Fat and more are here monthly.

For a shot of übercool head east to Farringdon's Fabric (77A Charterhouse Street, EC1, 7336 8898, www.fabriclondon. com), which dishes out leftfield breaks, drum 'n' bass and electro on Fridays and housier techno stuff on Saturdays, or 333 (333 Old Street, EC1, 7739 5949, www.333 mother.com) in Shoreditch. The nearby Legion pub (348 Old Street, EC1, 7729 4441) is owned by the lot who run the Heavenly Social, and has groovy DJs. Further east is Bethnal Green Working Men's Club (42-44 Pollard Row, E2, 7739 2727, www.workersplaytime.net) for friendly, playful mischief and fancy-dress burlesque.

The cluster of clubs around King's Cross is more than a little happening: 3,000-capacity Canvas (King's Cross Freight Depot, off York Way, N1, 7833 8301, www.canvaslondon.net) does monster indie or breaks parties and the occasional enormous glam party; the Cross (Arches 27-31, York Way, N1, 7837 0828, www.the-cross.co.uk), a great brick arches space, is home to mainstream house parties like XPress 2, Fiction, Renaissance, Space, Pukka Up and more; and the Key (Lazer Road, Goods Yard, off York Way, King's Cross, N1, 7837 1027, www.the keylondon.com) is one of the best small clubs, with a kick-ass roster of leftfield clubs and a disco-lit dancefloor.

Turnmills (63B Clerkenwell Road, EC1, 7250 3409, www.turnmills.com) continues to be shockingly popular. Nights lean towards house, hard house and trance, with Friday's Gallery sold out nearly every time. The Chemical Brothers do New Year's Eve here every year, and it's a very odd mix of neo-classical bits and pieces and a big grotty warehouse with lasers.

Bethnal Green Working Men's Club: the only place to be.

Canterbury to the Coast

The pearl of north Kent is just a crab
and a winkle away from the pilgrims' city.

Top of the cathedral city premiership, Canterbury also has the oldest
church in England, is strategically placed between London and the
major seaports, has ludicrously picturesque narrow streets, and a
winsome position on the eastern bank of the River Stour. Canterbury's
compact nature and antique charms make it irresistible to city breakers
and overseas visitors, so it's elbows out on the High Street in high
season (and far from quiet in low). Blessed relief comes via the well-
trodden route to the seaside and the increasingly fashionable, equally
handsome fishing town of Whitstable, just seven miles north of the
city. A gentle walk along the delightfully named Crab and Winkle Way
is a splendid precursor to the best fish supper in England – if you're
an oyster fan, that is.

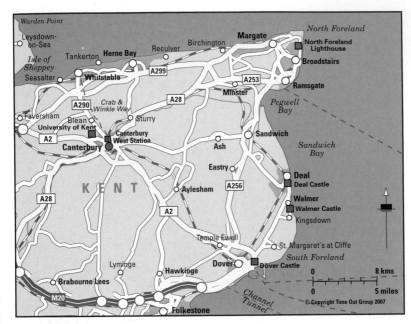

To be a pilgrim

Durovernum Cantiacorum, the Roman settlement built on the River Stour at a crossing point on the long march inland from the east Kent coast, flourished for 400 years. Christianity was practised, but it was the arrival of St Augustine that gave the town its Mother Church status. The rather reluctant Augustine had been sent from Rome by the Pope to convert the pagans and he started at the top, with the Saxon King Ethelbert. Augustine had a willing ally in the form of the king's wife, Bertha, a French Christian who'd been given a Roman building (St Martin's church, see p48) in which to practise her faith as part of a pre-nuptial agreement. The mass conversion to Christianity went well for Augustine and his fellow missionaries, and he established a Benedictine monastery (St Augustine's, see p48).

The cathedral's beginnings are all thanks to King Cuthbert in 758. He built a chapel on the site, which was duly laid waste, with the rest of the city, by the Danes. In 1023 Canute built the Cathedral of the Christ Church, which burnt down 34 years later. Archbishop Lanfranc, the first Norman bishop, had another go in 1070. His building's foundations remain today (go down into the crypt to see the Norman remains).

Canterbury really became a place to flaunt your piety after Archbishop Thomas Becket's horrific murder in 1172. Such was this holy man's status that a guilt-ridden and remorseful Henry II came to Canterbury to be scourged by the monks at the martyr's tomb. After this Canterbury was the country's most important tourist destination for the next 300 years, and pilgrims must have had as much trouble finding lodgings as today's visitors. It pays to book well ahead – we've got no excuse, as most of us aren't taking three days to get here by mule, and we have the internet. There was, of course, a lull in the traffic to Canterbury when Henry VIII accused the long-dead Becket of treason and threatened dire consequences if the ghost did not come out to explain himself. Oddly enough, Becket stayed in his grave and Henry desecrated the cathedral. It suffered further indignities from fanatical Puritans during the Civil War and was the target for Hitler's bombers in the 'Baedeker Raids' of 1942, an attempt to destroy England's heritage sites. The cathedral escaped the worst of the raids, Deo gratia.

The cathedral (The Precincts, 01227 762862, www.canterbury-cathedral.org) is the city's centrepiece, and as such is number one on most tourists' 'to do' list. From the splendour of the 16th-century Christ Church Gate, and the Bell Harry tower soaring heavenward some 250 feet, it is a magical place. It's at its most inspirational just before dusk, especially if there is music going on within and the coach parties are long gone. The nave dates from around 1400, and the must-sees –

lierne vaulting, stained glass, 15th-century quire screen and those spookily indented Pilgrims' Steps – should be viewed in hushed awe (a forlorn hope, given the sheer weight of visitors).

Just down the road from Christ Church Gate, the Royal Museum & Art Gallery (High Street, 01227 452747, www.canterbury. gov.uk/museums) is a monument to high Victorian values. It's set out, with the city library, in a handsome old building and it has a thoughtful diary of frequently changing exhibitions. Permanent ones include the national collection of the art of Thomas Sidney Cooper, the cattle painter, as well as work by Van Dyck, Gainsborough, Sickert and Epstein. There's also a large ceramics collection and the museum of the regiment of the Buffs (Royal East Kent Regiment), or the third regiment of Foot, one of the oldest regiments of the British army (1572). This excellent museum has just received a Heritage Lottery grant to update its galleries, and admission is free. Other cultural collections include those in the Museum of Canterbury (Stour Street, 01227 475202, www.canterbury-museums.co.uk) with its specialist subject, Rupert Bear, and West Gate Towers (St Peter's Street, 01227 789576, www.canterbury-museums.co.uk), just by the river and the beautiful Westgate Gardens. For more contemplative waterside walking, glide over to spooky Greyfriars, just off Stour Street, where the ancient walled

TOURIST INFORMATION
Canterbury
The Butter Market, 12-13 Sun Street, Canterbury, Kent CT1 2HX (01227 378100/www.visitcanterbury.co.uk).
Whitstable
7 Oxford Street, Whitstable, Kent CT5 1DB (01227 275482/www.visit whitstable.co.uk).

Franciscan Gardens and Greyfriars Chapel are all that remain of the first English Franciscan friary built in 1267, during the lifetime of St Francis of Assisi. The gardens are overseen by the community of the Eastbridge Hospital of St Thomas the Martyr (Eastbridge Hospital, 25 High Street, 01227 471688, www.eastbridgehospital.org.uk), also founded in the 12th century (patron: Archbishop of Canterbury). For 800 years the Eastbridge has given shelter to those in need, as well as, more recently, providing a home to a number of elderly people. Visitors can tour the hospital and admire the undercroft with its Gothic arches, the Chantry Chapel, the Pilgrims' Chapel and the refectory with an enchanting early 13th-century mural showing Christ in Majesty (there's only one other like this, in France).

Canterbury Castle (01227 378100, www.canterbury.co.uk), to the west of the city, is a huge Norman stone keep, whose fine brickwork gives a clue to where

Whitstable's sea view

the doorways, dungeons and staircase once stood. This once-great castle was attacked by Wat Tyler and his revolting peasants in 1381.

To delve further into Canterbury's ancient history you have to walk east along the High Street to the Roman Museum (Butchery Lane, 01227 785575, www.canterbury-museums.co.uk), whose underground remains of mosaic floor and hypocaust room have been augmented with reconstructions, computer reconstructions and time tunnels. From here you also get a super view of the cathedral tower. After the Romans comes St Augustine, or at least the ruins of the abbey he had built (Longport, 01227 767345, www.english-heritage.org.uk), now in the capable hands of English Heritage, which has attached a small museum and shop to the site. If you feel the need to keep walking east in search of history, continue past the prison to North Holmes Road and St Martin's Church (01227 768072), the oldest parish church in England where continuous Christian worship has taken place since before 597. It was named after St Martin, Bishop of Tours in France.

Moving on to literature, there's fiction with a smile awaiting at the bizarre Canterbury Tales just off the High Street (St Margaret's Street, 01227 479227), where five of the tales of Chaucer's more colourful pilgrims (including that filthy Miller) are brought to life in mechanised waxworks (spot the bare arse) while you walk around with a headset. Great stuff.

Sights aside, Canterbury commerce keeps you busy. The High Street is a happy marriage of middle of the road fashion chains (Kew, Accessorize, Hobbs etc) and decent, vaguely hippyish independents; then there are the second-hand bookshops and some excellent food shops, delis and cafés. Everything you want to see, do and buy is within walking distance, even the seaside – if you fancy a long walk.

New oyster cult

For car owners, Whitstable is a short drive from Canterbury along the A290. There's also a bus, and an old railway line you can walk along to reach the sea. There is no direct rail link (you change at Faversham), which is ironic because one of the earliest rail routes in Britain was the Canterbury and Whitstable Railway (opened in 1830). Today, it's a much-loved long walk and cycle path that goes by the delightful name of Crab and Winkle Way (*see p52*).

Whitstable is most famous for its oysters, whose devotees wax lyrical about their flavour in magazine food pages across the land. The first person to write in praise of these natives was Juvenal during the Roman occupation of Britain. The little town and its satellites (Seasalter, Tankerton, Reculver) lived off the fruits of the sea for centuries. Queen Elizabeth I granted the famous oyster beds royal protection, and they were leased to local fishermen, who protected them from marauders. The Royal Native Oyster Company, one of the earliest commercial ventures in Europe, was reconstituted as the Whitstable Oyster Fishery Company in 1896. The oyster business went into decline during the early 20th century and was saved from bankruptcy by a pair of prescient businessmen in 1978. These days, Whitstable Oyster Fishery Company controls many thriving businesses and has presided over this picturesque town's gentrification.

Glamorous ABode is Canterbury's original luxury choice.

Talk to Whitstable natives (the people, not the oysters) and you very soon get on to the subject of the DFLs (Down from London). Many love the fact that Whitstable has been so rejuvenated, that there are now trendy restaurants and decent shops. Like all residents of desirable seaside towns (especially one that's only about an hour's fast drive from London), however, they're dismayed by the second homers, whose buying of properties that they leave empty all week forces local folk out of the market. Some are also a bit cynical about the hoopla come July, when the Whitstable Oyster Festival gets going (www.whitstableoysterfestival.co.uk; 21-29 July 2007). For visitors, it's a great beano, even if it is a bad time to eat oysters (there's no R in the month – the creatures should be busily spawning at this time). There's an explanation for the timing – it makes sense for fisherman to hold their festival during closed season for oysters and, in any case, the feast day of St James of Compostella, who became the patron saint of oysters, falls on 25 July. An offshoot of the festival is the sailing and water sports celebration known as the Whitstable Regatta (taking place on the second weekend), which originally consisted of yawl races, rowing races and swimming. The last Oyster Yawl can be viewed at Island Wall, where once were shipyards, sailmakers' sheds and forges. With grants and goodwill, the Favourite Trust helped to rebuild the old boat (www.favourite.org.uk).

More on the history of Whitstable can be found at the friendly Whitstable Museum (Oxford Street, 01227 276998, www. whitstable-museum.co.uk) where there's an exhibition devoted to the town's most famous fan, Peter Cushing, who bought a seafront house here in 1959. The Cushing display at the museum has film stills, props and examples of the actor-turned-painter's art.

Walkers on Whitstable seafront are rewarded at low tide when 'the Street' is revealed – a line of shingle formed by the two currents from the Swale and Thames estuaries. Viewed from a distance, people wandering its length look as though they're walking on water, and many find themselves floundering in it when the tide cuts them off while they are looking out to sea. There's certainly plenty to absorb you on the horizon, such as 30 wind turbines generating electricity for much of the Canterbury area, which turn jauntily in the sea breeze. Towards Herne Bay, the weird Maunsell Forts are just about visible from the shoreline. These *Star Wars*-like structures were built during World War II to defend the south coast from Nazi invasion. They were used in the 1960s by a pirate radio station.

A seaside walk to Herne Bay takes you past Tankerton slopes and its jolly coloured beach huts (such is the demand for these, that new ones that look as though they were bought at B&Q are being shoved up all over the shop). They can be rented (at considerable cost) on an annual licence – another Whitstable moneyspinner.

WHERE TO STAY

Before ABode (*see below*) came on the scene Canterbury's position as an ideal city break destination was severely compromised by the retro chintz nature of its hotels. It's still pretty hard to find anywhere without loads of net curtains and heavily floral walls and carpets. Prices drop once you're outside the city, and carrots – such as heated swimming pools and pretty gardens – pull in the punters (although the decor gets slightly worse). If you're in a car, places like the Ersham Lodge Hotel (12 New Dover Road, CT1 3AP, 01227 463174, www.ersham-lodge. co.uk) and the Ebury (*see p51*), with their own parking and competitively priced rooms, are a safe bet, but their position on the dreary New Dover Road is a drawback. If you're on a tight budget, the city's youth hostel, resplendent in Victorian Gothic, is also on this road (No. 54, 0870 770 5744, www.yha.org.uk) and can give you a double room from just £17.50 per person. More characterful accommodation can be found in Whitstable, where there are any number of old fishermen's and sailmakers' huts and seaside cottages all done up and ready to rent. The Tourist Information Centre's website has a list of self-catering options.

ABode

High Street, Canterbury, CT1 2RX (01227 766266/www.abodehotels.co.uk). Rates £125-£165 double; £175-£325 suite. Breakfast £9.95-£12.95. Credit MC, V.
Bringing a welcome breath of sleek and chic into the cathedral city's hotel collection, this is the third in a small chain of smart hotels created by Andrew Brownsword. Food and drink areas are overseen by Michael Caines and comprise a lavish champagne bar and upmarket Modern British restaurant (*see p54*) located behind the etched glass of the reception – both doing a brisk trade – and an MC Tavern next door. These refreshment options lend

Accommodation	★★★★★
Food & drink	★★★★★
Nightlife	★★★★★
Shopping	★★★★★
Culture	★★★★★
Sights	★★★★★
Scenery	★★★★★

an air of youthful energy. The modish atmosphere is not just a trendy gesture, however – ABode's rooms are a treat. There are 72 of them, ordered by price and size from 'comfortable', through 'desirable' and 'enviable' to 'fabulous' (this last is a penthouse with superior views and a tennis court-sized bed). Rooms have immensely comfortable handcrafted beds with cashmere throws, blonde-wood floors and furniture, enamel baths marooned behind a glass partition (the loo, wet room and a collection of Arran Aromatics toiletries are behind a proper wall), an enormous LCD TV, DVD player and Wi-Fi. A goody basket of locally produced soft drinks, snacks and chocs is also provided in each. Glamorous but markedly unstuffy, ABode is definite cause for celebration in Canterbury.

Canterbury Cathedral Lodge

The Precincts, Canterbury, CT1 2EH (01227 865350/www.canterburycathedrallodge.org). **Rates** £79-£99 double; £139 2-bed apartment (sleeps 3). **Credit** MC, V.
Right inside the cathedral precincts, the accommodation here might not be historic, being only five years old, but the views certainly are. The Lodge offers bright and comfortable accommodation in a private courtyard. Quite plain in decor, the facilities are excellent for the price and location, with specially made toiletries and good showers in the en suites, broadband connection, TV and telephone and a hospitality tray. Continental breakfast is included and the cathedral also has a decent restaurant that places lots of emphasis on fair trade.

Cathedral Gate Hotel

36 Burgate, Canterbury CT1 2HA (01227 464381/www.cathgate.co.uk). **Rates** £58-£130. **Credit** MC, V.
This splendid old hotel was built in 1438 and predates the Christ Church Gate it sits alongside. Its 25 rooms with sloping floors and ceilings are reached via dark narrow corridors and low doorways, so it's undoubtedly atmospheric. The reception area upstairs is furnished with ancient children's toys and accessories, but the antique ambience is marred by the presence of a gigantic soft drinks machine plonked right in front of a carved corner cupboard. The rooms are unpretentious (simply furnished) and you share corridor bathrooms. Ask for rooms called 'Daybreak', 'Cathedral' and 'Joy' (oh joy! it's en suite) as they are the ones with cathedral views. There's a roof terrace under the shadows of Harry Bell tower, where you can take a sunny breakfast.

Duke of Cumberland

High Street, Whitstable, CT5 1AP (01227 280617/www.thedukeinwhitstable.co.uk). **Rates** £70-£90. **Credit** MC, V.
You can't miss the Duke as you come into Whitstable. It's a massive Victorian Shepherd Neame boozer with good cheer glowing from its stained-glass windows. Quality beer and excellent food make it the most popular pub in town. Once the headquarters for the local oyster and dredger men (the 'deluxe' rooms were used as the pay offices), the poor old Duke was rescued a few years ago from an ill-advised incarnation as a nightclub. After this, new tenants moved in and the eight en

Trading up – it's fine local fare all the way at the buzzy Goods Shed farmers' market.

suite guest rooms were neatly refurbished in understated neutral colours. Simply equipped, the rooms have nice soft beds, Neutrogena toiletries in the bathroom, and can be reached by a back door if you don't want to go through the bar. Rates include a cooked breakfast of superior quality (the loaded platefuls of porky or vegetarian full English are made to order, as is the creamy porridge). The (often booked up) restaurant, which is a lovely space with bare floorboards and an ornate skylight, was once the snooker room. The food is highly recommended: locally reared organic chicken, lamb and pork are mainstays of the legendary Sunday roast (usually accompanied by great jazz/blues bands). At other times expect native oysters (sometimes deep fried in beer batter), wild salmon, skate fish cakes and pan-fried organic chicken on the specials board. Last but not least, friendly staff make this a relaxed base from which to explore Whitstable.

Ebury Hotel

65-67 New Dover Road, Canterbury, CT1 3DX (01227 768433/www.ebury-hotel.co.uk). **Rates** £75-£145; £320-£500/wk 2-bed cottage. **Credit** MC, V.
This is quite a grand looking hotel, with a sweeping drive and a Gothic exterior. A large garden and heated indoor swimming pool and spa are added attractions, especially for those on weekend breaks with the kids. The best bedrooms have views of the garden, but most of them are large, light and comfortable. This is a professional, family-run operation with a pretty good restaurant, which is a bonus if you don't fancy the walk into town. The Ebury also has some self-catering flats and cottages to rent, which have been awarded four stars by the English Tourist Council.

Fisherman Huts

Beach Walk, Whitstable, CT5 2BP (01227 280280/www.hotelcontinental.co.uk). **Rates** £100-£175. **Credit** MC, V.
The accommodation here consists of reclaimed fishermen's net-sheds of the 1860s. They've been completely refurbished to be comfortable, but suitably minimalist, so the look is still tongue-and-groove wooden, but with insulation from the sea breezes that tug at the rigging of the boats on the beach just a few feet away. The huts are light and airy, a real tonic for city folk needing a breath of the sea. They have big pine beds, TVs, a little fridge, tea and coffee facilities and a simple bathroom with shower. At breakfast you jog along to the Hotel Continental (*see below*), whose reception administers the huts (for the Whitstable Oyster Fishery Company), for the full works. This is included in the price.

Greyfriars

6 Stour Street, Canterbury, CT1 2NR (01227 456255/www.greyfriars-house.co.uk). **Rates** £55-£100. **No credit cards**.

Unlike many city centre hotels, this one can offer free parking to its guests, but like all the others it's booked up at graduation time and in high season. Although the building dates back to the 12th century, when the first Franciscan monks built Greyfriars House as the gatehouse to their monastery, there isn't much inside to point to its great antiquity, apart from the creaky wonkiness of the stairs and floors. It's a welcoming place, however, where the rooms are clean and simply decorated, with en suite facilities and a full english to look forward to in the morning.

Hotel Continental

Beach Walk, Whitstable, CT5 2BP (01227 280280/www.hotelcontinental.co.uk). **Rates** £70-£145; £150 suite. **Credit** MC, V.
The art deco look and seaside position of this sunny hotel recall those old 1920s advertisements for cruise holidays. The rooms, with their yellow walls, gleaming white bathrooms and basketwork furniture are a pleasure to lounge about in, particularly if you've managed to book one with a balcony and sea view. The Continental is another Whitstable treasure owned by the Oyster Fishery Company, which seems to have the town sewn up, but for visitors it just means that the food in the restaurant is excellent, and that seafood is a speciality (crevettes, oysters, salmon, whole lobster, moules marinière). Breakfast is also a fishy treat if you go in the kipper or haddock direction, otherwise there's a spread of fruit, yoghurts, muesli, croissants and the full English (very full).

Magnolia House

36 St Dunstan's Terrace, Canterbury, CT2 8AX (01227 765121/www.magnoliahousecanterbury. co.uk). **Rates** £95-£125. **Credit** MC, V.
Compact, but highly recommended, Magnolia House treats its guests very well. Most of the rooms are small (with the exception of the grand Garden room, with its four-poster bed), but are clean and well equipped. Each room has a small fridge containing a complimentary half bottle of wine, mineral water and fresh milk for hot drinks. The breakfast is delicious and well worth lingering over. Food is fresh and beautifully presented with plenty of choice. Rolls are warm, toast is crisp, eggs are freshly cooked to your specification and there's a huge variety of cereals, fruit, juices and yoghurts. The breakfast room looks out on to a small and delightfully planted garden and the standard of service is excellent. There is limited parking available, but the best way to savour Magnolia is to come without the motor, as the walk to and from town takes you through peaceful Westgate Gardens.

WHERE TO EAT & DRINK

Michael Caines has brought a touch of Michelin glamour to the Canterbury eating scene, which hitherto was rather pizza and curry heavy. As well as his Fine Dining and beer drinking experiences (*see p54*),

WALK THE CRAB AND WINKLE WAY

In Kent on 3 May 1830, a new means of transportation came into operation that, for its time, was as revolutionary as the space shuttle. The world's first passenger steam railway train ran the distance from Canterbury to Whitstable and consisted of ten wooden, open-box carriages connected by a hook to Stephenson's *Invicta*, a coal-powered locomotive and early version of his *Rocket*. It really was like space travel. The late Georgians, who lined the route, cheering and waving their hats, knew what they were witnessing. There must have been 100 people on board and yet the machine could not only haul them without effort, it could do so at a speed great enough to stiffen the Union Flag on the front carriage, which the mayor and other dignitaries occupied. How proud everyone was. Long live the king.

The new railway line became known as the Crab and Winkle Line, as it was to the shellfish beds at Whitstable that the trains were aimed, and although the railway stopped using the track a century later in 1930, it is now part of the National Cycle Network – and an excellent prospect for a long, but pretty easy bike ride or walk in the country.

It is seven miles from Canterbury to Whitstable and the track is regularly signposted 'Crab and Winkle Way' along its length. The walker or cyclist may pick it up at the Goods Shed farmers' market (*see p53*) by West Station from where it leads through suburban residential streets and across meadows bordering the city up to the campus of the University of Kent. In fact, the line runs through a long (now blocked) tunnel below – which must have been nightmarish for the original passengers. From the tunnel entrance north, the path is impassable to cyclists, who must follow the signs and take the road, but a delight for walkers, who may meet woodpeckers, woodcocks, warblers and tits in the woods on Tyler Hill. From here, looking south, happy pilgrims caught their first sight of the twin towers of Canterbury Cathedral in the haze.

Walkers and cyclists reconvene at the Winding Pond where a group of youths might be found fishing, lighting fires and playing with their mobile phones. In fact, the first engines did not have the power to make it up to the summit unaided – which accounts for the Winding Station. The picnic tables were a later addition. The gradient is gentle down through Blean Woods, across the roaring A299, past Tesco's and on to Invicta Way, which covers the last mile of the route past back gardens to Whitstable Station. You'll find the smell of the sea and the cry of seagulls are now on the wind. Out on the estuary the kitesurfers are leaping, windsurfers are whizzing by and the wind farm is spinning. Everyone seems to be either on holiday or making money in this booming seaside town. It's like the days of steam all over again.

there's a champagne bar in ABode, a modish place in which to clink glasses and pick at delicious vegetables provençale.

Pub wise, Canterbury is in thrall to its students, who take over the West Gate Inn Wetherspoons when they're tired of drinking on campus. Most of the better pubs are Shepherd Neame ones (it's brewed up the road in Faversham), and the best both happen to be in St Dunstan's Street. The Unicorn (No. 63, 01227 463187) is in CAMRA's good books and also has Deuchar's IPA from Edinburgh. The Bishop's Finger (No. 13, 01227 768915), not surprisingly serves Bishops Finger, and attracts both students and more mature clientele. Simple Simon, near the West Gate (01227 762355), is recommended for its choice of ales and strong Biddenden cider. The Cuban, a few doors up from ABode, is quite rowdy and has a dancefloor. There's a nightclub called the Works beyond the city walls (though we can't see that anyone would choose Canterbury for the nightlife).

For a small town, Whitstable has an embarrassment of places in which to eat and drink, but the Old Neptune (Marine Terrace, 01227 272262), with its doorstep lapped by the waves, is the ultimate seaside pub. Another beachfront watering hole is the Whitstable Brewery Bar (01227 280280), which has big windows, sea views and bands. You're spoilt for choice for seafood, of course, and one old established purveyor of seafood worth trying, if you can't get a table at Wheelers or the Oyster Fishery Company restaurant (see p55), is Pearson's (01227 272005), which lies just opposite the latter. The best Indian in town is the courteously staffed Invicta Tandoori (01227 262397).

In Whitstable it helps to know your oysters. Natives (grown in Whitstable, as well as Colchester and Helford) will cost you about £15 per half dozen. If you're only paying about a fiver, however, chances are you're eating the less expensive pacific (also known as rock or gigas), which has a larger, longer shell.

Beau Rivage

101 Tankerton Road, Whitstable CT5 2AJ 01227 272056/www.beaurivage-whitstablerestaurant.co.uk). **Lunch served** noon-2.15pm, **dinner served** 6.30-9.30pm Tue-Sat. **Main courses** £14.95-£19.95. **Set lunch** £13.50 2 courses, £16.50 3 courses. **Set dinner** £16.50 2 courses, £19.50 3 courses. **Credit** MC, V.

This has been Tankerton seaside's bit of posh for well over 20 years, but has been run by the current owners for three. The menu and decor have been updated from 1980s pretensions, but there's still slight overenthusiasm toward drizzling highly coloured jus zigzag style over everything. Zigzags

aside, the food, especially specials such as Romney Marsh lamb, pleasantly pink with rosemary-flavoured jus (ok, but it's lovely jus), and mackerel – firm and moist on the inside and crispily seared and seasoned on the outside – is well cooked and delicious. Local free-range pork and chicken, as well as not always local fish and seafood, make frequent appearances on the regularly changing menu.

East Quay Shellfish

East Quay Harbour, Whitstable, CT5 2AB (01227 262003). **Open** *Oct-Apr* noon-4pm Fri-Sun. *May-Sept* noon-4pm, 6-8.30pm Wed-Sun. **Main courses** £6-£25. **Credit** MC, V.

This self-service restaurant and café bar is in a series of buildings that celebrate the fruits of the sea by means of a little exhibition and a range of tanks displaying, when we visited, a disgruntled looking lobster and some sea bass. There's also plenty to read about Whitstable's oyster dredging history. The food is fab, particularly the fish in beer batter and chips. You can buy half a dozen natives for £13.95 (rock oysters are £6). A big pot of moules marinière with chips is £8.95.

Goods Shed

Station Road West, West St Dunstan's, Canterbury CT2 8AN (01227 459153/ tgsltd@nildram.co.uk). **Breakfast served** 8-10.30am Tue-Sat; 9-10.30am Sun. **Lunch served** noon-3pm Tue-Sun. **Dinner served** Tue-Sat 6-9.30pm. **Main courses** £10-£18 **Credit** AmEx, MC, V.

Six days a week this lofty Victorian building, formerly a railway freight store, buzzes with activity. On a raised wooden platform diners sit at scrubbed tables and choose from the specials chalked up on the board. Only ingredients on sale in the farmers' market below them are used in the restaurant. There are traders from local organic vegetable and fruit farms, apple juice squeezers, a prolific butcher (whole suckling pig, £90), a baker and sandwich-maker, craftspeople, cheese and olive sellers, and many more. For people who care about their food and its provenance, this is heaven. The lunch menu on our visit included perfect leek and potato soup (served with soft, white, slow-baked bread), braised lamb shank, smoked haddock fish cakes or chowder, and a vegetarian platter with spring greens, purple sprouting broccoli, goat's cheese tart, roast potatoes and wild rocket salad. Soft brownies or rhubarb crumble cannot be ignored for dessert. A very good place, this old shed.

JoJo's

209 Tankerton Road, Whitstable, CT5 2AT (01227 274591/www.jojosrestaurant.co.uk). **Lunch served** 1-2.30pm Wed-Sat; 1-3.30pm Sun. **Dinner served** 6.30-9.30pm Wed-Sat. **Main courses** £4.50-£7.50. **No credit cards.**

A diminutive restaurant with lofty principles, JoJo's believes in home-grown, free-range, organic food, locally sourced and simply prepared. It's unlicensed, but would rather customers bringing in their own wine did not bring in one bought from a well-known supermarket giant, as they are 'killing the high street'. The food is gorgeous – freshly prepared and full of Mediterranean sunshine (a big plate of meze to share, quickly fried squid or pollack goujons in beer batter with flavoured mayo, roasted sardines, patatas bravas and stuffed pepper). The restaurant has been fashioned from the proprietor's bedsit (decorated with organic paint and filled with furniture made from reclaimed timber). There's only room for about 20 diners and JoJo's has devoted regulars, so it's not always easy getting a seat. With ingredients coming from the Goods Shed farmers' market and Whitstable fish stalls, lunch here is worth waiting for.

Michael Caines Fine Dining Restaurant

ABode Hotel, 30-33 High Street, Canterbury, CT1 2RX (01227 826684/www.michaelcaines. com). **Rates** £125-£295. **Lunch served** noon-2.30pm daily. **Dinner served** 7-10pm Mon-Sat. **Main courses** £17.50-£19.75. **Set meal** (hotel guests only) £20 2 courses; £58 7-course tasting menu. **Credit** MC, V.

With a young, two Michelin-starred chef at the helm and a modish hotel all around, this is much vaunted as Canterbury's finest dining. It's certainly very smart, and friendly, although the slightly robotic mateyness of the young waiting staff becomes a little wearing by the end of the meal. Soothingly lit and a study in understated, chocolate brown decor, its looks and the elaborate menu are all you would expect. A two-course table d'hôte menu (hotel guests only) for £20 represents good value. The à la carte, with the cheapest starter at £8.50 for jerusalem artichoke soup, is costlier. The breadboard stars spindly own-baked anchovy breadsticks, fluffy floury rolls and little olive tarts – delicious. Courses arrive with much flourish. The tiny quantity of carrot and coriander soup on the set menu is presented in two stages – a sizzling puddle of coriander oil before the soup is poured. It's delicious, but small, like the helpings of risotto, and our other choice of trout cannelloni. The nicest part of our meal was a selection of British cheeses (£11.50), including the creamy norbury blue from Surrey and a goat's cheese called golden cross, served with fig bread, dark oat biscuits and grapes.

Old Brewery Tavern

High Street, Canterbury, CT1 2RX (01227 826682/www.michaelcaines.com). **Open** 11am-11pm Mon-Thur; 11am-2am Fri, Sat; 11am-10.30pm Sun. **Meals served** noon-2.30pm; 6-9.30pm Mon-Thur; noon-3pm, 6-9.30pm Fri, Sat; noon-9pm Sun. **Main courses** £8.50-£17.95. **Credit** MC, V.

Huge black and white prints of grizzled coopers rolling barrels hang on the walls at the Old Brewery Tavern – Michael Caines's nostalgia trip, styled along the lines of what he thinks a tavern should be. The MC OB doesn't look like a

traditional boozer (far too trendy) but it shies away from the gastropub cliché. The food is solid and homely – leek and potato soup, Romney Marsh lamb, fish and chips – but there are lighter numbers, such as fish pie and mixed meze. Beers are many and various (Hoegaarden, Whitstable Brewery, Shepherd Neame, Leffe); the wine list is satisfyingly long.

Samphire

4 High Street, Whitstable, CT5 1BQ (01227 770075). **Meals served** 9am-10pm daily. **Main courses** £10.50-£16. **Credit** MC, V.

Even when Samphire is besieged by weekend crowds attracted to its reasonably priced, unfussy bistro menu, the staff here remain cheerfully friendly. There's no need to book for the big breakfasts of local bacon, sausage and eggs, or brunches and lunches of eggs benedict, stews and soups, but weekend evenings can be very busy. The menu changes about every three months, but expect a choice of around five starters and five mains, featuring unusual British staples such as pigeon breast or beetroot soup, slow-braised lamb, oxtail or venison sausages from the butcher down the road, scallops from Rye Bay and mackerel when available. Dishes are generously proportioned and always accompanied by lots of fresh, seasonal vegetables.

Whitstable

Sportsman

*Faversham Road, Seasalter, Whitstable, CT5
4BP (01227273370/www.thesportsman
seasalter.co.uk).* **Open** noon-3pm, 6-11pm
daily. **Lunch served** noon-1.45pm Mon-Sat;
noon-2.30pm Sun. **Dinner served** 7-8.45pm
Tue-Sat. **Main courses** £13.95-£19.95.
Credit MC, V.

Everything about this isolated Shepherd Neame
pub and restaurant impressed us. It stands
bravely behind the coastal path, a lovely walk
from Whitstable, just beyond the Seasalter caravan parks. It looks a little scarred by the elements so you wouldn't guess, to look at it, that
this is the best place to eat in north Kent. There's
a gallery, a restaurant and a splendid bar, with
a wide choice of ales and a vast chalked-up wine
list and menu. Most of the food is locally produced (you'll see salted hams hanging from the
veranda outside) or caught, and the chef, Stephen
Harris, has a magic touch with it. From the rosemary focaccia and green olives brought with the
drinks, to an antipasti of meats, salads and
native oysters, then on to local wild sea bass,
locally reared organic roast chicken with bread
sauce and brill with razor clams, every dish is
exceptional. Rhubarb sorbet, own-baked brownies
and warm chocolate mousse make fine desserts.
It's all proudly presented by friendly, intelligent

staff. The word on the coast is that trying to book
a table for Sunday lunch is virtually impossible
– so don't leave it too late.

VC Jones

*25 Harbour Street, Whitstable, CT5 1AH
(01227 272703).* **Open** *Summer* 11.30am-8pm
daily. *Winter* 11.30am-8pm Tue-Sun. **Main
courses** £6.20-£8.50. **No credit cards.**

A great traditional chippie that looks like it hasn't
changed much since the 1950s, Jones invariably
has queues outside of an evening. There's a large
choice of fish available for battering and the
chips are perfectly fat and glistening. There's a
little caff behind the glass screen, but a lot of people choose to wander down to the harbour with
their fish supper rather than sit in. It makes a pretty
inexpensive dinner choice too.

Wheelers

*8 High Street, Whitstable, CT5 1BQ (01227
273311/www.whitstable-shellfish.co.uk).* **Meals
served** 1-7.30pm Mon-Sat; 1-7pm Sun. **Main
courses** £16.25-£19. **No credit cards.**

Ask a Whitstable resident where to go for a
decent seafood supper and they'll almost certainly point you in the direction of Wheelers.
Londoners nostalgic for the old St James's oyster bar that closed after what seemed like centuries of trading will be pleased to know that this
Whitstable version was the original – and the
best. It has a small pink and blue shopfront with
a chilled and loaded display of shellfish for diners' delectation. Newcomers may wonder where
they can sit if the two stools in the window are
already occupied. There's a small Victorian parlour at the back that seats about 12 people. Bring
your own wine or beer to accompany your half
dozen oysters (natives or rock), langoustines,
rollmops, smoked haddock and leek tart, snap-
per, roasted cod, or steak, ale and oyster pudding.
There are regular specials on offer too.

Whitstable Oyster
Fishery Company

*Horsebridge, Whitstable CT5 1BU (01227
276856/www.oysterfishery.co.uk).* **Lunch
served** noon-2.30pm Tue-Sat; noon-3.30pm
Sun. **Dinner served** 7-9pm Tue-Fri; 6.30-
9.45pm Sat; 6.30-8.30pm Sun. **Main courses**
£16.50-£21. **Credit** AmEx, DC, MC, V.

Once home to the Royal Native Oyster Stores,
the Oyster Fishery restaurant is renowned for
excellent seafood. To start, you can go native
with Whitstable oysters, pay half as much for
non-natives or just choose the squid, clams,
moules or sardines. Mains include top-notch
organic salmon, sea bass, cod and lobster, and
the dessert list offers the likes of treacle tart,
sticky toffee puddding or chocolate torte. You
can have a drink in the bar upstairs while you
wait for a table (booking is essential). The
Whitstable Brewery beer is worth a try, and
there's also a rather good wine list.

Hastings to Dungeness & Romney Marsh

Expect the unexpected in this quiet, quirky part of the world.

In between the seaside London suburbs of Brighton and Hastings to the west, the sprawling concrete Channel Tunnel town of Ashford to the north and the grey ports of Hythe, Margate and Dover to the east lies a triangle of England that is quite unlike anywhere else. Perhaps it's because it's so difficult to get to (rail links skirt the area at the aforementioned towns), but Romney Marsh and its surrounding area have a sense of other-worldliness that conjures up science fiction scenarios in Tarkovsky movies; you half expect to see Steed and Mrs Peel in an episode of *The Avengers* supping an ale in eerily unchanged villages.

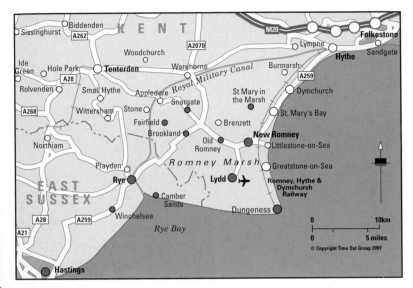

It's a strange but hugely appealing mix of olde-worlde cobbled streets and ancient inns, miles of sandy beaches, a desolate promontory, the world's largest expanse of shingle and as-far-as-the-eye-can-see marshland, criss-crossed by canals and studded with tiny medieval churches and strange concrete defence constructions that date back to post-World War I. The natural strangeness of the place seems to have inspired quirky, man-made additions; here you'll find the world's smallest public railway; houses made out of train carriages and upturned boats, or clad in black rubber; and a power station that hums gently (*see p61*), providing the perfect aural backdrop to the wide open spaces. It's a unique mix that gives this part of Kent and East Sussex a particular charm – and so long as the transport links remain as poor as they are, we suspect (and rather hope) that there won't be any real changes here for decades to come.

Down to the sea in Sussex

Poor Hastings has had a rough ride since its glory Victorian days, when its appeal as a seaside town saw the construction of stunning squares and crescents filled with huge townhouses of such architectural vision that they put near neighbour Brighton to shame. Its sad decline during the 20th century has only recently been halted by a progressive programme that has included refurbishment grants for businesses. The resulting turnaround has been slow but convincing, and the town now makes an ideal starting point for a circular tour that takes in Winchelsea and Rye, the Romney Marshes and Dungeness.

The old town is still the place to hang out, with its towering cliffs scaled by two funiculars, unusual buildings (including the tall, thin wooden net shops), a jumble of second-hand shops and boutiques and the unique Pelham Crescent nestling in the cliffs under what remains of the castle. A wealth of visitor attractions should keep everyone happy – the St Clement's caves (01424 422964, www.discoverhastings.co.uk) in particular are worth a visit, whether you're with kids or not. Heading east out of town towards Rye are a number of lovely little

Accommodation	★★★★☆	
Food & drink	★★★★☆	
Nightlife	★★★★★	
Shopping	★★★★★	
Culture	★★★★★	
Sights	★★★★★	
Scenery	★★★★☆	

TOURIST INFORMATION

Hastings
Queen Square, Hastings, East Sussex
TN34 1TL (0845 274 1001)
Rye
Rye Heritage Centre, Strand Quay,
Rye, East Sussex TN31 7AY (01797
226696/www.visitrye.co.uk).
New Romney
New Romney Station, New Romney,
Kent TN28 8PL (01797 363353/www.
discoverfolkestone.co.uk).

Zanzibar
International Hotel:
where cool comes
as standard.

villages, the best of which – Northiam – is an absolute delight. Its charms include weatherboard houses and a green, a steam train, pleasure boats, a gorgeous medieval church, three pubs and the nearby Great Dixter House and Gardens (see p64 **In an English country garden**), lovingly planted and tended by gardener and garden writer Christopher Lloyd until his death in 2006. A delightful short circular walk around the area gives a wonderful view of the house and gardens, if you can't be tempted in (you can download a PDF of the route at www.winchelsea.net/visiting/guides.htm).

Winchelsea was built on a never-completed medieval grid pattern (laid out by King Edward I) when the 'old' settlement was swept into the sea in the storms of 1287. The place is proud of its status as England's smallest town, but really it's a sleepy village of 400 residents with a wealth of medieval (and later) architecture, a very good pub, a tiny local museum stuffed with bits of broken pottery and old photos, and a tearoom. It's a pleasant place to while away a few hours. Pride of place goes to the church of St Thomas the Martyr, which rises up in the middle of town like a scaled-down cathedral (despite being merely the chancel of the 14th-century original). The church boasts stunning 1920s stained-glass windows designed by Douglas Strachan, along with some fine medieval carvings (including the head of Edward I) and tombs.

A mile or so south-east of here (turn left into Dog's Hill Road) is pebbly Winchelsea Beach, which at low tide reveals not just a sandy strip but also some beautiful, ancient, moss-covered wooden pillars, which are all that remains of old Winchelsea's eastern pier. Lined up like a petrified battalion presenting arms, their strangeness, combined with the silvery, mirror-like rock pools, makes a walk here a must.

Following the national trail that runs alongside the Royal Military Canal (built against the threat of invasion by Napoleon) in the direction of Rye brings you to Rye Harbour village (pick up a picnic at the Rye Harbour Stores, Rye Harbour Road, 01797 226444, which also has maps and walking leaflets for three circular walks) and the extensive Rye Harbour Nature Reserve. This rich and varied triangle of land features natural pits that are a valuable habitat for wetland wildlife, as well as two farms, areas of peaceful woodland and Camber Castle (01797 223862, www.english-heritage.org.uk). The crumbling edifice was built as part of England's coastal defences in the 16th century by Henry VIII, who obviously didn't count on the longshore drift and coastal erosion that have made this coastline the world's largest area of shingle – the castle now lies two miles from the shore.

To the north of the nature reserve lies Rye, a town that's almost too quaint to be true. A photogenic jumble of Norman, Tudor and Georgian architecture, it perches on one of the area's few hills. The narrow, cobbled streets are chock-full of antiques shops, tearooms and pubs, the best of which are the Mermaid Inn and Ypres Castle Inn (for both, see p65). The most rewarding antiques and curio shops are on the High Street, where there's also a

Winchelsea beach hut

great old record shop in the Old Grammar School (built in 1636) and the second-hand bookshop Chapter & Verse (No.105, 01797 222692). Apart from simply wandering the streets, it's worth taking a look at the medieval Landgate gateway and the Castle Museum and 13th-century Ypres Tower (both Gun Garden, 3 East Rye Street, 01797 226728, www.ryemuseum.co.uk). Rye Art Gallery (107 High Street, 01797 222433, www.ryeartgallery.co.uk) offers a changing series of excellent exhibitions, mostly by locals. Architecture fans shouldn't miss St Mary's church (Church Square), dating from 1150. It's capped with a delightfully over-the-top 16th-century clock, decorated with a profusion of baroque touches and two cherubic (and modestly attired) jacks, which curiously strike on the quarter-hour rather than the hour.

From peaceful marshland to golden sands

East from Rye, you can head in two directions; two miles south-east to the coast or north-east into Romney Marsh. The latter is as flat as a pancake and criss-crossed with cycle paths – if you want to head out along the A259 to discover the 14 tiny medieval churches of the marsh, bikes can be hired from Rye Hire (1 Cyprus Place, Rye, 01797 223033). Among the most notable of these gems are St Augustine's at Brookland, with its quite extraordinary detached wooden bell tower, and All Saints (known as the 'Cathedral of the Marsh') at Lydd. North of here is St Thomas à Becket at Fairfield, which many consider to be the epitome of the isolated Romney Marsh church (look for the sign and approach via a causeway). St Clement in Old Romney has a particularly lovely interior, with a magnificent minstrels' gallery. St Mary the Virgin at St Mary in the Marsh, meanwhile, carries the understated gravestone of Edith Nesbit, author of *The Railway Children*, who loved the area and died in the village.

Lydd is also home to a small airport (01797 322411, www.lydd-airport.co.uk, www.lyddair.com) and, while we wouldn't normally recommend an airport as an attraction, this is no ordinary landing spot. Lovely hand-painted 1960s murals adorn the aviation-themed bar and restaurant (*see p65*), and there are scores of tiny planes to watch from a pleasant conservatory or outdoor terrace. If you feel inspired, you can even take a flying lesson or a low-level spin over the area.

Walking on the marsh offers rare pleasures too. The Romney Marsh Countryside Project (01797 367934, www.rmcp.co.uk) organises a good range of walks and events, most of which are free. They're weird enough to do justice to the mood of the area too: evening walks, 'mini-beast' safaris, moth walks, pond-dipping for grown-ups and an introduction to the plants of Dungeness. Walks exploring the marsh's 'listening ears' are among the most interesting. They take place only a few times a year and it's well worth making a special trip to take part. Built in the 1930s as part of an early warning system to detect enemy aircraft approaching from the Channel, these bizarre structures have been the subject of work by various artists, including Tacita Dean. Their presence is another piece of the jigsaw that makes the marsh the unique place it is.

Heading out of Rye along the coast road takes you to the ever-popular Camber Sands, a vast and glittering sandy beach that's a haven for kite-flying, riding, sand-yachting and invigorating walks. Backed by crumbling outbuildings decorated with garishly Billy Childish-style murals, it has an undoubtedly faded charm, but, until last year's arrival of the Place (*see p63 and p67*) there was little reason to stay more than a few hours. It now makes arguably the best weekend base in the area.

To the Point

A thousand years ago, Dungeness Point simply didn't exist. But over the years, longshore drift has slowly built up huge banks of flint shingle, some of them 57 feet deep, which stretch miles out into the sea in a unique promontory. Clustered on the promontory are a lighthouse that offers wonderful views for those prepared to climb the 169 steps, a car park and a good café that offers fish and chips and a Sunday roast alongside the sandwiches.

The light on this remote, gloriously bleak patch of land is odd, reflected from the sea on both sides, and the surreal quality of the landscape is enhanced by the presence of the massive Dungeness nuclear power station that dominates the horizon; at night its lights make it look like the Pompidou Centre in Paris.

While the power station may be the biggest construction on the point, it's by no means the strangest. A wealth of constructed curios make for a fascinating architectural exploration, beginning with film director Derek Jarman's Prospect Cottage. The pretty black and yellow building is typical of the fishermen's cottages that dot the area, but the garden sets it apart. Delicately beautiful, it combines plants straight out of a sci-fi film with driftwood and found materials to create a miniature sculpture park, and has obviously inspired many of the surrounding gardens.

Less aesthetically pleasing but equally worth exploring are shacks constructed from railway carriages dating back to the late 1800s, when the Southern Railway built a station to transport shingle extracted from the beach. When the line went, the carriages remained. The simplest homes retain the sleek, pneumatic shape of the carriages, while others sport sundry outhouses and additions that make them look like relics from the Wild West.

The jewel in the crown, though, is the RIBA award-winning, rubber-clad Vista, a weekend house designed by architect Simon Conder. Constructed from timber and plywood, the house is covered in a wetsuit-like skin, making it reminiscent of an Anish Kapoor sculpture. The flat, matt material seems to form a black hole in the huge, light-filled space, and contrasts wonderfully with the 1930s Airstream caravan that serves as a spare bedroom outside. Conder's masterful use of rubber was no gimmick; picking up on the aesthetic of the area's traditional black pitch cottages, it also does away with the need for exterior drainage and roof guttering.

Such man-made wonders are set against a truly magnificent natural backdrop. The vast expanse of shingle and sea creates an intense feeling of dislocation and disorientation, best experienced by getting out of the car and exploring – and there is plenty of wonderful walking to be done here. The Dungeness RSPB Nature Reserve (Dungeness Road, Lydd, 01797 320588, www.rspb.org.uk) is the best place to experience the fragile ecology of Dungeness Point. Hire binoculars at the visitors' centre, pick up a trail leaflet and head off to explore 2,000 acres housing a quarter of Britain's plant species and 1,550 species of invertebrates, some of which are unique to the area. This is an utterly magical place that, backed by the constant, pervasive hum of the nuclear power station, makes you feel as if you're in an episode of *The Prisoner*. Then, when the miniature Romney, Hythe and Dymchurch Railway train barrels by, you *know* you're in an episode of *The Prisoner*.

Proudly proclaiming to be the 'world's smallest public railway', it is fully functioning but one-third of the standard size. The diminutive train, built by the millionaire racing driver Captain Howey in 1927, even includes a buffet car. Sitting in one of the tiny carriages is a delightfully surreal experience, as you meander from the wide-open shingle of the Point behind back gardens and caravan parks, through woodland and fields to arrive at Hythe, 13.5 miles away. Golfers can stop off at New Romney on the way, where two courses alongside the Channel offer a great day for novices or keen amateurs. Littlestone Golf Club (01797 362310, www.littlestonegolfclub.org.uk) is the

larger championship links course and accommodates a limited number of visitors; the smaller Romney Warren (01797 362231, www.romneywarren golfclub.co.uk) is a pay-and-play course with a practice putting and chipping green.

Finally, a walk along the beach at Littlestone offers a changing landscape that takes in architectural curiosities such as a lovely 120-foot-high red-brick water tower. Now a private residence, it was built in 1890 by local entrepreneur Henry T Tubbs, who hoped to turn the village into a major resort with a pier. Thankfully for fans of this quietly majestic coastline, it never happened.

WHERE TO STAY

Most of the good accommodation in the area is made up of small, independent hotels and award-winning guesthouses clustered around Rye. The smaller ones tend to get reserved weeks ahead, even in the winter months, so book as far in advance as possible.

Wonderfully located on Rye's quaintest cobbled street, the atmospheric 17th-century Jeake's House (Mermaid Street, 01797 222828, www.jeakeshouse.com) has 11 individually decorated rooms; the gold room features an impressive inglenook fireplace in which a lovely wood stove nestles. Little Orchard House (3 West Street, Rye, 01797 223831, www.little orchardhouse.com) has two four-poster bedrooms (one arranged over two levels, one featuring a trompe l'oeil garden) in a delightful Georgian townhouse. Outside there's a large walled garden with an 18th-century smuggler's watchtower and secluded corners for balmy summer days. Winchelsea's New Inn (*see p65*) also has a number of rooms between £55 and £70 for a double.

If you're looking for something on Romney Marsh proper, try the Olde Moat House (Ivychurch, 01797 344700, www.oldemoathouse.co.uk), a medieval property surrounded by its own moat and set in more than three acres of land, or the pretty, three-bedroomed Terry House (Warehorne, Ashford, 01233 732443).

Winchelsea's Strand House in (Tanyard's Lane, 01797 226276, www.thestrand house.co.uk) is a 15th-century house with ten rooms and a delightful garden. Finally, back in Rye, the 16th-century Mermaid Inn (Mermaid Street, 01797 223065) offers olde-worlde tradition at its finest, complete with wood panelling and stone fireplaces, four posters, wonky floors and secret passages, while the quirky Simmons of the Mint (68-69 The Mint, 07776 206203) is an intriguing private house/B&B hybrid, with great breakfasts served by the proprietor, who runs the shop next door.

Fish Café

George in Rye

*98 High Street, Rye, East Sussex TN31 7JT
(01797 222114/www.thegeorgeinrye.com).*
Rates £125-£175 double; £225 suite.
Credit MC, V.

Once one of the scuzziest places to stay in Rye, the George, located bang in the middle of town, has leapt to the top of an already illustrious list of accommodation and restaurants, after a refurbishment programme that cost (depending on who you speak to in town) anywhere from £1m to £2m. We're guessing the upper bracket of that price range, judging by the rooms. Little luxuries include gorgeous Neisha Crosland soft furnishings, mohair throws, inviting 8ft-long squidgy sofas in beautifully soft corduroy, wall-mounted flat-screen TVs, Frette linen on Vi-Spring beds, and Lefroy Brooks bathrooms with two-person walk-in showers or double-size roll-top baths. The loving attention to detail comes courtesy of Katie Clarke, one half of the husband and wife team who took over the 16th-century coaching house, and a former set dresser and prop buyer for TV and film productions. Working with design partner Maria Speake (of chic architectural salvage and design emporium Retrouvius), Clarke has created a hotel that is luxurious, stylish, welcoming and absolutely top of the range. Which begs the question (and the only criticism we can think of): why no bathrobes?

Hope Anchor Hotel

*Watchbell Street, Rye, East Sussex TN31 7HA
(01797 222216/www.thehopeanchor.co.uk).*
Rates £85-£120 double; £110-£145 family room; £95-£170 cottage. **Credit** AmEx, DC, MC, V.

If the tweeness of many of Rye's B&Bs is overly intimate for your tastes but you still want something with character and individuality, the Hope Anchor is a reliable bet. It's set in a lovely location in the heart of town, at the end of pretty, cobbled Watchbell Street. Each of its 12 bedrooms boasts something special, be it stunning views of the town's medieval rooftops, sweet dressing rooms, glorious vistas across the marshes, or hidden passages. All are furnished and fitted to high standards, with lovely bedlinen and a bottle of

sherry on the 'welcome' tea tray. The log lounge or cosy bars are great places to while away a rainy afternoon – but if you really do want to be alone, book either the Hidden Treasure Cottage or the Admiral's Apartment; both are completely self-contained spaces with private terraces and lounges. Children and dogs are welcome.

Place

*New Lydd Road, Camber, Rye, East Sussex
TN31 7RB (01797 225057/www.theplace
cambersands.co.uk).* **Rates** £80-£90 double;
£90-110 triple; £99-£135 family room. **Credit** AmEx, MC, V.

While Rye has more than its fair share of excellent accommodation and food, the coastline heading east of it is as sybaritically bleak as its landscape, barring two places: the Place at Camber Sands and the Romney Bay House Hotel. The two couldn't be more different, but if it's midrange comfort you're after, you won't go far wrong with the Place. Laid out around a ranch-style courtyard, its 18 simply furnished rooms are small but perfectly comfortable, with good beds, tartan blankets and an unusually good free DVD library that ranges from *Guys and Dolls* to *Straw Dogs* (with plenty of kids' movies too). Indeed, the hotel and accompanying brasserie's child-friendly approach may not be entirely to urbane singletons' tastes, particularly as its layout is perfect for kids wanting to tear around while parents keep a watchful eye on them from the lovely outdoor terrace. But don't be put off; this is a relaxing haven in a great location that'll have you hooked from your first visit. The food's top-notch too (*see p67*).

Romney Bay House Hotel

*Coast Road, Littlestone-on-Sea, New Romney,
Kent TN28 8QY (01797 364747).* **Rates** £85-£155 double. **Credit** AmEx, MC, V.

Perched on the seafront, right at the end of the bumpy coastal road, is this ten-bedroom 1920s mansion. It was designed for Hollywood gossip columnist Hedda Hopper by Sir Clough Williams-Ellis, famed for creating the architectural curiosity and *Prisoner* set Portmeirion. With the

IN AN ENGLISH COUNTRY GARDEN

Many rural areas have a vaguely unreal, historical novel feel to them during the hazy days of summer, conjuring up anything from an Austen country-house picnic to Blyton's meddling kids laying waste to the lemonade and hard-boiled eggs. But the counties of Kent and Sussex seem to have this air of languid timelessness all year round – and one of the best ways to experience this sense of time standing still is to visit one of the numerous gardens and country houses.

In this part of the world, there seems to be a National Trust property every couple of yards, including the spectacular Sissinghurst, Nymans Garden and Sheffield Park Garden, as well as the lovely Ightham Mote, Scotney Castle, Chartwell and Bateman's (once home to Rudyard Kipling). To experience a taste of more modern country living (well, 20th century at least), a visit to Great Dixter is a must – and from spring 2007, you can combine an exclusive house-and-garden tour with a cream tea on a steam train. Of course, you can also explore the delights of this superb Arts and Crafts house and gardens on their (and your) own. This place was restored from Tudor decrepitude by Edwin Lutyens at the turn of the 20th century – admire his handiwork and stroll through the gardens, designed by then owner Nathaniel Lloyd and planted by his son, the gardening writer and presenter Christopher Lloyd.

Lloyd junior's wonderful eye and willingness to be bold and experimental in his planting has resulted in something that's much more than a traditional garden; a landscape that marries the best of old-fashioned structuring and planting schemes with the joys of modern garden design. And the icing on the cake? A cream tea taken on a steam train while rolling through the beautiful Rother Valley and High Weald (designated an area of outstanding natural beauty). This is one of the finest ways to taste the English countryside in all its timeless glory.

GREAT DIXTER HOUSE & GARDENS

Great Dixter, Northiam, Rye, East Sussex TN31 6PH (01797 252878/www.greatdixter.co.uk). **Open** Apr-Oct House 2-5pm Tue-Sun. Gardens only 11am-5pm (last admission) Tue-Sun. **Tickets** House & Gardens £7.50; £3 under-16s. Gardens only £6; £2.50 under-16s. **Tour** Gardens & steam train cream tea £18.95 (book in advance). **Credit** MC, V.

sweeping Romney Sands bay at the front and the Littlestone Golf Course on the dunes behind, the hotel is a gloriously peaceful spot where it's impossible to get a room with a bad view. Owners Clinton and Lisa Lovell do everything they can to ensure a comfortable stay, with welcoming, individually styled rooms (two with four-posters), an honesty bar and an upstairs sitting room overlooking the sea for those who don't want to do battle with the prevailing winds outside. If you're looking for lovingly prepared food with an emphasis on locally sourced ingredients, you'd be hard pushed to find a better place to eat on the peninsula. Clinton is the chef, and his classical French training and impeccable culinary pedigree (this is a man with the Ritz on his CV) shine through on the daily changing menu. Fish and seafood, fresh from the boats, play a starring role – whether in the shape of a brandade of cod on toasted brioche, classic lobster thermidor or oriental sea bass. Dinner is an intimate affair, beginning with drinks and hors d'oeuvres in the welcoming drawing room at 7.30pm and moving through the four-course set menu (£37.50) from 8pm in the dining room. The restaurant is open to the public, but only if it's not already taken to full capacity by residents. Afternoon cream teas (£5.95) are deservedly popular – the buttery scones, made by a local baker, are superlative.

White Vine House

24 High Street, Rye, East Sussex TN31 7JF (01797 224748/www.whitevinehouse.co.uk). **Rates** £125-£165 double; £135-£185 family room. **Credit** MC, V.

Its location on the high street means that the White Vine has always been a convenient base for discovering Rye and its surrounding areas, but a total refurbishment has now made it a great place to relax indoors too. Seven individual and tastefully decorated bedrooms with features like rolltop baths and four-poster beds create an air of luxury and quiet calm, giving a sense of an upmarket B&B that is warm, comfy and decidedly atypical of the genre. This mood is carried through into the lovely, 15th-century oak-panelled Elizabethan Room (licensed for civil weddings) and restaurant, which features a full à la carte menu and doubles as a lovely breakfast room for residents. Children and dogs (the hotel arranges for the dogs – not the kids – to be boarded at a local kennel, rather than on site) are welcome.

Zanzibar International Hotel

9 Eversfield Place, Hastings, Kent TN37 6BY (01424 460109/www.zanzibarhotel.co.uk). **Rates** £89-£175 double. **Credit** MC, V.

For years, people have been citing Hastings as the new hot south coast destination, but with no decent places to eat and even fewer places to stay, the faded grandeur of the once-splendid Victorian town was an unappealing prospect. With the Zanzibar, there's now an excellent reason to come here. This tall, thin seafront house, converted from a student hostel, has no reception area; instead, a delightful salon leads to a conservatory honesty bar and garden, making it feel like a private house rather than a boutique hotel. Eight stunning rooms are named after a continent or country, with decor to match. Antarctica is a cool, all-white space, with fittings that include a fake polar bearskin blanket, sauna and steam functions in the shower unit and bright, expansive sea views; Japan is a monochrome delight, featuring an authentic Japanese bathtub and beautiful silkscreen and embroidered artworks; and India is subtly decorated with touches of lush reds and dark furniture. Decor is nicely understated, making rooms individual without turning them into theme parks, and they all share top-of-the-range flat-screen TVs and DVD players, huge comfy beds and crisp linen, state-of-the-art bathrooms and a loving attention to detail that makes leaving the room very difficult. Which, with free papers, a fantastic breakfast (in your room is standard, though you can choose to eat in the lovely salon), free DVDs and a good selection of travel guides to while away the time, is absolutely fine by us.

WHERE TO EAT & DRINK

Really good places to eat used to be few and far between in an area that is still largely reliant on atmospheric medieval pubs serving simply prepared Romney Marsh lamb and locally caught fish and shellfish. But times are changing, and now you'll find some of the finest food on the south-east coast here. The new kid on the block, the George in Rye, is offering real competition to the older guard – the Landgate Bistro and the Fish Café in Rye, the Place at Camber Sands and Romney Bay House Hotel in Dungeness. That's hardly surprising, given that one of its proprietors is Alex Clarke, brother of Sam Clarke of Moro fame.

If fancy isn't your thing, Rye has plenty of simpler eateries. Choose from authentic Italian at Simply Italian (The Strand, 01797 226024), Thai at the Lemon Grass Thai Restaurant (1-2 Tower Street, 01797 222327) or sound pub grub at any number of lovely pubs in town, including the Flushing Inn (4 Market Street, 01797 223292), the Standard Inn (The Mint, 01797 223393), Ypres Castle Inn (Gun Gardens, 01797 223248) and the Ship Inn (Strand Quay, 01797 222233).

The light and informal Fish Café (17 Tower Street, Rye, 01797 222210, www.thefish cafe.com) serves some of the best seafood in Rye. Although the ground-floor café is only open at lunchtime, a more formal dining space upstairs offers a similar, but extended, range of dishes during the evening (booking is highly recommended).

For a dinner with a difference, try the weekend Fly'n'Dine at Lydd Airport (Lydd, Romney Marsh, reservations 01797 322207, www.lyddair.com/flyanddine.html), which consists of drinks and canapés, a low-level 20-minute flight over the Kent coast and a five-course candlelit dinner in the 1960s-style Biggles Bar and Restaurant. At £59 it's quite a bargain, and there's also a lunch option at £39.

The 600-year-old Mermaid Inn (Mermaid Street, Rye, 01797 223065, www.mermaid inn.com) is both pub and restaurant, and oozes quiet confidence and class. In the evening, there's a compulsory minimum charge of £35 per head for the à la carte, offering classic dishes like lobster thermidor or dover sole, or it's £38.50 for four courses from a small but varied set menu. Alternatively, bar offerings of baguettes, platters and sandwiches can be washed down with a fine selection of beers in the lovely bar or small, sunlit garden.

In 1866, Dante Gabriel Rossetti commented on Winchelsea's 'pleasant doziness' from the New Inn (German Street, Winchelsea, 01797 226252), and it's easy to see why. Stepping from the beautiful churchyard into the wonderfully inviting pub, one of just two in town, and you feel as though you've wandered into *The Archers'* Bull pub (pre-computer). Good, hearty bar snacks are there for the taking, and the wide-ranging menu includes traditional dishes such as roasts, succulent gammon steaks and tender fillet steak, own-made pâtés and soups. Specials lean towards locally caught fish and seafood, including Rye Bay scallops with bacon, cream and wine, and rooms are available upstairs should the doziness overwhelm you.

The tiny, multi-award-winning Red Lion (Snargate, Romney Marsh, 01797 344648) is something of a Romney Marsh institution, famed for the fact that its interior hasn't been touched since World War II and its annual one-day beer festival (dates vary). It doesn't do food, but you are welcome to bring your own. If you do, you can unpack your picnic lunch or supper in a pub that dates back to the early 17th century and has been run by the same family for a few years shy of a century. It's an absolute beauty as well, with three tiny rooms featuring a wealth of intriguing memorabilia and photographs: an antique marble counter that makes it look more butcher's shop than bar; tongue-and-groove wall panelling; heaps of games (including nine men's morris and table skittles); and, of course, a range of beers and country wines wide enough to keep you sated and happy for a long time.

Another good option is the Romney Bay House Hotel (*see p63*). It's open to the public for dinner (as long as tables haven't been booked by hotel residents) and also serves afternoon tea until 5pm.

George in Rye

98 High Street, Rye, East Sussex TN31 7JT (01797 222114/www.thegeorgeinrye.com). **Lunch served** 11am-3pm, **dinner served** 7-9pm daily. **Main courses** £12-£16.95. **Set lunch** £13 2 courses, £16 3 courses. **Credit** MC, V.

The small restaurant at the George offers some of the finest dining to be had round these parts. Served in a pleasantly understated setting, the food is scrumptious without being overpriced – the chef is Rod Grossmann, previously a chef at London's Moro. The menu is short; a good thing, seeing as it's all excellent, and choosing is hard enough as it is. Starters of black and white pudding with caramelised apple, and savoy cabbage with roast chestnuts were both delicious, the ingredients fresh and robust without being overpowering. Mains might include oxtail stew with chorizo, roast pork loin and duck breast – and while fish and seafood are well represented, it's a pleasant surprise to find such a determinedly carnivorous menu on the coast. Service is also excellent, with staff on hand to enthusiastically offer wine suggestions and samples if desired, and disappear discreetly if not. It's equally difficult to find fault with the stylish, gorgeously appointed rooms upstairs (*see p62*).

Landgate Bistro

5-6 Landgate, Rye, East Sussex TN31 7LH (01797 222829/www.landgatebistro.co.uk). **Dinner served** 7-9.30pm Tue-Fri; 7-10pm

George in Rye: some of the finest dining around.

Sat. **Main courses** £9.60-£14.50. **Set dinner** (Tue-Thur) £13.50 2 courses, £16.50 3 courses. **Credit** MC, V.

Time was when the Landgate ruled the roost in Rye with its attractive, inventive and pleasingly unfussy dishes. Strong new competition has meant that while this is still a decent choice, it's far from the only one – although it remains a popular spot, and booking is essential. On our last visit, culinary highlights included wonderfully original starters, such as melt-in-the-mouth grilled celeriac with pickled walnuts, and cider and onion soup that was sweet, full of flavour and just the right side of rich and creamy. Mains were more of a mixed bag – grilled dover sole was cooked to perfection and slow-roast belly pork proved suitably succulent and rich, but the partridge was tough, dry and overly salted. The space could also be cosier, and wasn't helped by rather austere lighting. In the new gastronomic haven that Rye is fast becoming, the Landgate may need to sharpen its act if it wants to regain its top spot.

Pilot

Battery Road, Lydd, Dungeness, Kent TN29 9NJ (01797 320314/www.thepilot.uk.com). **Lunch served** noon-2.30pm, **dinner served** 6-9pm Mon-Fri. **Meals served** noon-9pm Sat; noon-8pm Sun. **Main courses** £5.50-£12.50. **Credit** MC, V.

This Dungeness institution serves some of the best fish and chips in Kent. Enormous portions of battered cod, huss, skate, plaice and haddock are as fresh as can be, and the accompanying chips are chunky, crisp and golden. Own-made pies – steak and kidney, steak and ale, chicken and mushroom – are popular too, with a proper baked-with-the-pie pastry crust. Health fans and weight-watchers will welcome the pint of prawns and French bread or decent selection of salads, though they might be tempted to skip dessert (spotted dick and other calorific, wonderfully old-fashioned puds). They'd be missing a treat, however – and besides, there's always the glorious Dungeness Peninsula on which to walk lunch off afterwards.

Place

New Lydd Road, Camber, East Sussex TN31 7RB (01797 225057/www.theplacecamber sands.co.uk). **Lunch served** noon-2.30pm, **dinner served** 6.30-8.30pm daily. **Main courses** £10.25-£17.95. **Credit** AmEx, MC, V.

The Place prides itself on its use of locally sourced and eco-friendly produce (it recently signed up to the Marine Stewardship Council Standard to use stock from well-managed fisheries), but it's what the kitchen does with it that counts. In a laid-back, light-filled brasserie and terrace, the food is easily on a par with the best in the region. The excellent menu changes monthly and offers a carefully selected range of seasonally available dishes, with starters such as griddled Rye Bay scallops wrapped in pancetta and served with black pudding, black bream and chump of Romney Marsh lamb by way

of mains, and glorious puddings of bramley apple crème brûlée and treacle tart with crème anglaise. Portions are perfectly sized, service is superb and a strong wine list rounds things off perfectly.

St Clement's

3 Mercatoria, St Leonards-on-Sea, East Sussex TN38 0EB (01424 200355). **Lunch served** noon-3pm Tue-Sun. **Dinner served** 6-10.30pm Tue-Sat. **Main courses** £10.50-£15.50. **Set lunch** (Tue-Fri) £10 2 courses, £13 3 courses; (Sat) £14.50 2 courses, £17.50 3 courses; (Sun) £20 2 courses, £25 3 courses. **Set dinner** (Tue-Thur) £15.50 2 courses, £18 3 courses. **Credit** MC, V.

Nick Hales, who trained at Le Caprice and L'Odeon, opened the St Clement's two years ago, and has been watching the rave reviews pile up ever since. For the uninitiated, this may seem surprising; at first glance, it looks like the sort of average provincial restaurant that thirtysomething offspring might take their parents to on an anniversary; country cottage pine furniture, magnolia walls, a doorway leading to the pub next door, 20 or so tables… So far, so predictable – so it's a delight to discover that the food is anything but. From a small but appealing menu, a plate of local smoked fish and jerusualem artichoke soup were both excellent, and full of flavour. Mains of cod fillet with garlic mash and lentils and fillet of turbot in parsley and butter sauce were equally successful, as were the puddings (including a chocolate truffle cake that oozed chocolate from its middle), and all for the sort of price you'd pay for a starter at some of Hales' previous restaurants. Given that the ingredients are sourced within a radius of 30 miles and organic wherever possible (although the menu modestly makes no mention of these facts), such a feat is impressive – and still not as impressive as the food.

Woolpack Inn

Beacon Lane, nr Brookland, Kent TN29 9TJ (01797 344321). **Lunch served** noon-2pm, **dinner served** 6-9pm Mon-Fri. **Meals served** noon-9pm Sat, Sun. **Main courses** £4.75-£23.95. **Credit** MC, V.

In the world of CAMRA members and American tourists, all pubs would be like this: low ceilings and original 15th-century beams, sourced, rather enterprisingly, from local shipwrecks. A roaring log fire with settle benches on either side, cheery staff and a selection of own-made dishes that are as mouth-watering as they are big complete the picture. The ploughman's – cheddar, pâté, stilton or ham – come piled high, and specials on a recent visit included winter game dishes of a whole partridge or half pheasant with all the trimmings, and a hefty but delicately flavoured fish pie that (happily, given it was the last one) was substantial enough for two. The menu also offers a good range of salads and a children's meal at £3, while a great selection of local brews makes this an enchanting place to while away an hour or two.

Brighton

The ultimate seaside city break.

Britain's youngest city, England's most popular tourist destination after London, and host of the nation's biggest annual arts festival outside Edinburgh, Brighton has so many new attractions it's hard to know where to start. Top of the list is the i360, the so-called Brighton Eye, a 600-foot observation tower that will both give the city a modern icon and remove the sorry eyesore of the ruined West Pier (*see p86* **Eyeing up Brighton**). Completion is slated for the summer of 2008. By then, work on Frank Gehry's controversial leisure complex on the adjoining Hove seafront should also be under way – a revised proposal was passed by a narrow margin in March 2007, although protestors have vowed to keep fighting.

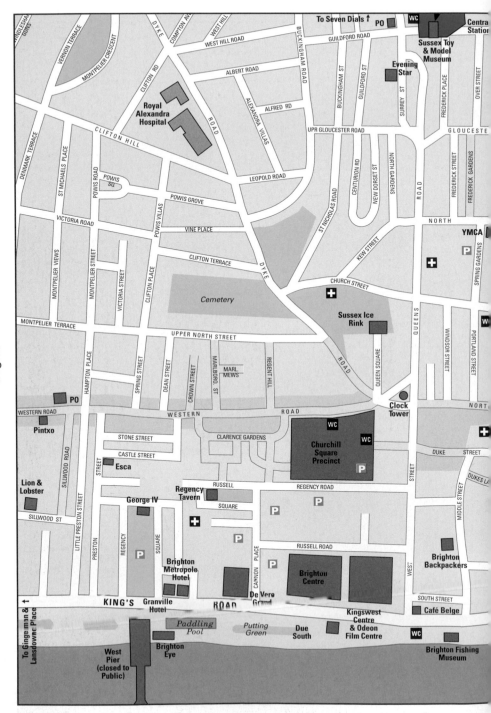

Brighton

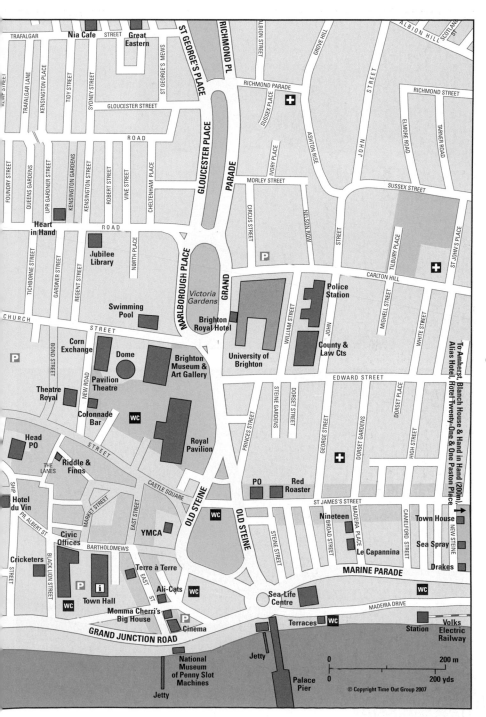

Accommodation	★★★★☆
Food & drink	★★★☆☆
Nightlife	★★★★☆
Shopping	★★★☆☆
Culture	★★★☆☆
Sights	★★☆☆☆
Scenery	★★☆☆☆

The city is falling over itself for destination restaurants and new or revamped boutique hotels – two opened in November 2006 alone. Five major new ones are scheduled for 2007, including a myhotel and a Radisson. Much will be centred on the New England Quarter, currently being constructed between the focal underground scene of the North Laine and the railway station. Those arriving here by the 48-minute twice-hourly fast service from Victoria Station should still see a crown of crane jibs as the train pulls into Brighton. Purring outside the station, growled at by the nearby taxis, will be tuctucs, Europe's first motorised rickshaws (*see p84* **Three wheelin'**), waiting to whisk party-goers down to the lively bar and clubbing scene of the seafront.

A sense of novelty is nothing new to Brighton. A gay hub, a major international student town and child-friendly with it, Brighton still welcomes weekend gaggles of devil-horn-sporting hen parties, ravers, nudists, discerning vegetarians, surfers, sunseekers and wastrels. It practically invented the dirty weekend. Leisure and pleasure? It has them in spades.

Many are satisfied to tumble from station to seafront, calling in at a couple of bars down the hill before plunging on to the pier or the pebbles. But to get the best out of Brighton, seek out its unusual little pockets: the busy gay quarter of Kemp Town, the savage drinking culture of Hanover, the airy terraces of Montpelier, the boho haunts of the North Laine and its tackier if more historic neighbour, the Lanes. Although hilly, all is accessible by an award-winning bus network, with an all-night service on main lines. Some buses terminate at the outskirts of town for easy access to hiking routes over the South Downs, another attraction. Buses bear names of local celebrities (Sir George Everest, Leo Sayer and Ida Lupino), a testament to the improbably random list of personalities Brighton has accommodated and inspired. Walk into any local and you may bump into a bit parter from *Z Cars* or someone from *Crackerjack* in town to do panto.

WHERE TO STAY

There are no more lumpy beds and snarls from grumpy landladies in Brighton these days. Hoteliers are tripping over themselves to convert tatty guesthouses into boutique hotels, squeezing themed rooms into the narrow confines of terraced houses at right-angles to the seafront – three such establishments opened in the second half of 2006 in New Steine alone, Kemp Town's lodgings central. Owners make up for the lack of space by offering as many unique services as they can possibly provide: organic breakfasts delivered to your room, luxuriant bathroom products, comprehensive selections of film and music DVDs. By 2007-08 the focus will shift to the more business-like New England quarter near the station, where a myhotel, a Radisson, a Jury's Inn and an Ibis are all due to be built.

If you're after budget accommodation, there are still guesthouses aplenty. The Tourist Information Centre (*see below*) can make reservations for £1.50 per person per reservation on the day; £5 for advance bookings. For price and location, you could do far worse than the Brighton Royal Hotel (76 Grand Parade, 01273 604182, www.brightonroyalhotel.com), opposite the Pavilion and a hop from the action of Kemp Town. Surprisingly comfortable rooms go for about £20. Regency Square, opposite the West Pier, is another hub of low-cost and mid-range accommodation.

Whatever your budget, certain rules need to be observed. Very few establishments here accept bookings for a Friday or Saturday night only. For the Brighton Festival in May, Pride weekend in August and for any political party conference in September, hotels fill up fast. You'll be lucky to find anywhere for Pride unless you book at least a month in advance.

De Vere Grand (97-99 King's Road, 01273 224300, www.grandbrighton.co.uk, £130-£370 double; £550-£1,300 suite) is, most certainly, Brighton's grandest hotel – from the outside at least. The 'leisure break' weekend tariff is a winner – book two nights in a double sea-view for £130 per person per night; stay for a third night and the price drops by 50%. At these prices, impulsive love affairs can only blossom.

The landmark hotel, wine bar and bistro Hotel du Vin (2-6 Ship Street, 01273 718588, www.hotelduvin.com, £145-£185 double; £250-£405 suite) is perfectly located between the seafront and the Lanes. One of half-a-dozen classy, provincial venues in this beautifully appointed chain, the Brighton branch is set in a jumble of mock Tudor and Gothic revival buildings. High-quality bistro food brings many non-

TOURIST INFORMATION

Royal Pavilion Shop, 4-5 Pavilion Buildings, BN1 1EE (0906 711 2255/www.visitbrighton.com).

guests to the restaurant, and a carefully chosen cellar supplies an equally popular wine bar on the first-floor terrace. Staff are welcoming and very competent.

Alias Hotel Seattle

Brighton Marina, BN2 5WA (01273 679799/ www.aliashotels.com). **Rates** £115-£170 double. **Credit** AmEx, DC, MC, V.

Hip, modern and high-tech, the Brighton branch of the Alias design-hotel chain makes full use of its marina backdrop. Flooded with natural light, cool, comfortable and quirky, its rooms have fabulous touches that will get you scouring the website for another hot deal: white leather headboards, monsoon showers, feather-and-down duvets and smart Italian furniture. Forget tureens of lukewarm egg and beans for breakfast – indulge in Bento in Bed or a box of blueberry muffins and smoked salmon bagels. Seafood predominates at the Mediterranean-inspired Café Paradiso and superior cocktails are served in the candlelit Black and White bar. Families are well catered for, with activity packs, crabbing nets and children's films on offer at reception, plus a baby listening service.

Amherst

2 Lower Rock Gardens, BN2 1PG (01273 670131/www.amhersthotel.co.uk). **Rates** £90-£120 double; £120-£150 suite. **Credit** AmEx, DC, MC, V.

Probably the best bargain among Brighton's new contemporary hotels, combining the most desirable elements of a welcoming B&B with the facilities of a mid-range hotel. Located between Kemp Town and the sea, the neat, fashionable Amherst opened in 2005 and offers two types of room: Junior Suite and Luxury Double, some with sea views. There are differing rates for single or double occupancy and each room is individually styled, featuring feather duvets, Egyptian cotton sheets and widescreen or LCD TV players at the foot of each bed. A full English breakfast is included in the price and brought to your room – if that's not enough, there are complimentary snacks too.

Blanch House

17 Atlingworth Street, BN2 1PL (01273 603504/www.blanchhouse.co.uk). **Rates** £100-£230 double. **Credit** AmEx, MC, V.

Even though they're also busy with their new venture, the Hanbury Club (*see p82* **Night Brighton**), Chris (Groucho Club) Edwardes and Amanda Blanch keep on top of things at this wonderfully conceived hotel, cocktail bar and restaurant. That this unassuming Georgian terrace house should have its dozen rooms themed after snowstorms, roses, rococo decor and '70s disco is all well and good, but that's just for starters. Splendid Fogarty goose-and-duck down duvets and pillows, Relyon pocket-sprung beds, big plasma screens and numerous other thoughtful touches have seen this boutique beauty showered

Alias Hotel Seattle

in praise in broadsheets and style mags. Guests stumping up £125 for the most basic package at this chic retreat will not feel hard done by; those splashing out the full £230 will be well and truly indulged. A full range of therapies and beauty pampering – Indian head massages, reflexology, reiki treatments – is on offer, the cocktail bar cannot fail to hit the spot given the management pedigree, and the Modern European restaurant has diners dashing down from London and beyond. Children and pets are welcome here too.

Drakes

43-44 Marine Parade, BN2 1PL (01273 696934/www.drakesofbrighton.com). **Rates** £95-£300 double. **Credit** AmEx, DC, MC, V.
It's luxury all the way in the latest of Brighton's high-end designer hotels. Snag an expansive bedroom with a view overlooking Brighton Pier and you can sink into a free-standing bath set beside the floor-to-ceiling sea-facing windows. All 20 rooms have been individually created, with sheets of Egyptian cotton, duck-down duvets, LCD-screen TVs and high-speed broadband connections. The concept is to provide the guest with everything so that he need not step out of the door once he arrives – hence the in-house restaurant run by the best chef in town, Ben McKellar of Gingerman fame (*see p79*), the cocktail bar open round the clock to thirsty residents, and the in-room services such as hairdressing and massage.

American visitors will also be delighted to hear that Drakes also offers a full concierge service, for reservation of a romantic restaurant table or VIP entry to a local nightclub.

George IV

34 Regency Square, BN1 2FJ (01273 321196/www.georgeiv.hotel.co.uk). **Rates** RO £60-£120 double; £100-£150 triple. **Breakfast** £4.50-£9. **Credit** AmEx, DC, MC, V.
Opened in 2005, this period townhouse conversion is surely the best bargain with a sea view in Brighton. Set in one of the city's grandest squares, Sue and Steve's welcoming George IV comprises seven rooms, four with fabulous views of the West Pier and surrounding waves. The triple comes with an expansive balcony, ideal for a leisurely room-service breakfast; the solitary single is surprisingly roomy considering its shoebox price of £40-£50. Board games, books and a jukebox provide pastime pleasure in the lounge area, and DVDs and videos can be borrowed from reception, but you're just a short stroll from the seafront and downtown attractions in either direction – get out there and start exploring.

Granville Hotel

124 King's Road, BN1 2FY (01273 326302/www.granvillehotel.co.uk). **Rates** £88-£185 double; £155 suite. **Credit** AmEx, DC, MC, V.

ROYALS AND RUDE PLEASURES

Wander around the shopfronts of lava lamps and naughty knickers in the Lanes today, and you traverse the medieval street pattern of what was once the fishing village of Brighthelmston. Intersected by narrow passageways known as 'twittens' and interspersed with coaching inns and fishermen's cottages, it was transformed in the mid 18th century into a curative retreat by Dr Richard Russell.

Foppish Londoners flocked down in droves. Inns and hotels were built to meet the demand, and bathing machines wheeled out. In 1783 the future George IV rented a farmhouse here, had it converted into a faux-oriental pleasure palace, the Royal

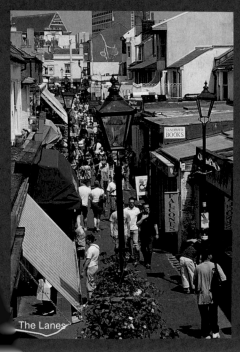

The Lanes

Pavilion, and invited the nation's creative, beautiful and ambitious young things to join him for a life of drinking, womanising and gambling. Suddenly fashionable, the town's population expanded from 3,500 in 1780 to 40,500 in 1831. The train line from London was opened ten years later, but Queen Victoria stripped the Pavilion and snubbed the seaside resort – her stern statue still overlooks the building in disapproval. Brighton has been a quirky, populist escape ever since.

With seven miles of coastline, Brighton is still first and foremost a seaside resort – but its role as an annex of London means that the shopper, the foodie, the bar-hopper and the clubber are well catered for.

Victorian Brighton saw a profusion of eccentric engineering projects, including three piers – only one of which is still standing today. **Brighton** (or **Palace**) **Pier** is a gaudy clutter of hot dog stands, karaoke, games machines and fairground rides; this is the one Raymond Briggs's Snowman flies over in the Christmas cartoon. The superior West Pier was suspiciously firebombed while the funding of major restoration work was being discussed in 2003. The planned **Brighton Eye** (*see p86* **Eyeing up Brighton**) will feature salvaged artefacts such as the pier's original turnstiles. Brighton's shady, sleazy character of lore, enshrined in print, music and film by Graham Greene, Pete Townshend and Ken Russell, is never far away.

The Royal Pavilion

Brighton

Before the Brighton Eye opens, the leading local attraction remains the **Royal Pavilion** (01273 292820, www.royalpavilion.org.uk). George IV's palace – Indian on the outside, dragon-festooned Chinese inside – was transformed into an extravagant party pad when George became Prince Regent in 1811. He had John Nash create a no-expense-spared oriental fantasy, an opulent, camp and spectacular series of rooms recently restored in a £10-million refit. The banqueting room alone, with its extraordinary chandelier, is worth the £7.70 admission fee. Elsewhere, tiny royal beds are embellished with lacquered dragon patterns, and the ballroom and music room exude style. The twin exotic gateways, bulbous domes, turrets and minarets are all Nash's interpretation of what Eastern architecture was meant to be. Queen Vic would have none of it, though, and shipped much of the furniture to Kensington Palace. A 20-minute film tells the whole story.

Billing itself as Brighton's 'original' boutique hotel, the seafront Granville has buckets of personality and imagination. And, considering the location, meticulously conceived two dozen rooms and the quality of buffet breakfast on offer on its summer terrace, it's a bit of a bargain too. The spacious front rooms have unrivalled views of what remains of the West Pier and are surprisingly quiet – all are individually themed. If you're feeling extravagant, opt for an elaborately carved four-poster with en suite jacuzzi; other themed rooms include the art deco Noel Coward Room and the romantic Brighton Rock Room, with its muslin-draped Victorian four-poster. A British menu is offered in the basement restaurant, Fisherman's Rest. During the week, breakfast, either full English, vegetarian or vegan, is included, the £5 weekend/holiday price tag more than reasonable. A recent addition is the sea-facing Brunswick Suite for family groups.

Lansdowne Place Hotel & Spa

Lansdowne Place, BN3 1HQ (01273 736266/ www.lansdowneplace.co.uk). **Rates** RO £130-£160 double; £220-£350 suite. **Breakfast** £13.95. **Credit** AmEx, DC, MC, V.
The latest local restoration job grandly stands near the Hove seafront, a short walk from the West Pier. Guests have been spinning through the stately revolving doors here since 1854 – but now they are treated to contemporary luxuries and a downstairs spa of manifold treatments, massages and facials. All rooms have plasma-screen TVs; most rooms have a sea view and king- or queen-sized beds, mixing period and modern decor. The Emperor Suite is huge (the biggest in town, in fact, over 500sq ft) with floor-to-ceiling windows and a bathtub in the bedroom. All guests can avail themselves of 24-hour room service, the French cuisine in the Grill restaurant and cocktails in the leopard-spotted lounge bar.

Nineteen

19 Broad Street, BN2 1TJ (01273 675529/ www.hotelnineteen.co.uk). **Rates** £80-£250 double. **Credit** AmEx, MC, V.
The most pampering of Kemp Town's boutique hotels, Nineteen goes the whole nine yards when it comes to catering for its visitors. Guests in its eight rooms are treated to breakfast (organic or free-range wherever possible – don't miss out on the smoothies) in bed until 10am weekdays, 11am with a complimentary bloody mary at weekends. Thanks to minimalist decor and light colours, even the smaller rooms feel bright and airy. Beds sit on bases of illuminated, coloured glass bricks, the linen and walls are fresh and white, the latter also adorned with work by local artists – in particular the imaginative photography of Mark Jessey. Luxurious bathrooms come with Molton Brown products and mouthwash, and all rooms have CD and DVD players with a library of items available downstairs. Guests may also help themselves to Penguin biscuits from the kitchen, and

Town House

the honesty fridge filled with quality wines and Czech beers. A range of in-room massages, facials, manicures and pedicures can be ordered – although anyone booked into the prime basement space with its own private courtyard and 500-litre jacuzzi may prefer privacy. Attractive room rates at quiet times of the year.

Sea Spray

25 New Steine, BN2 1PD (01273 680332/ www.seaspraybrighton.co.uk). **Rates** £65-£125 double, £89-£190 suite; £75-£180 family room. **Credit** AmEx, MC, V.
The gimmick of this newly converted themed boutique hotel is the chance to share your bedroom with Elvis, Salvador Dali or Andy Warhol – but this doesn't detract from the comfort of the fluffy bath towels, chic bar and airy breakfast room. Standard 'budget' doubles are also themed – Indian or Japanese – and most things here are executed with a sense of fun (the Hove Actually room refers to a local in-joke). All are equipped with CD players and there are flat-screen TVs in the luxury doubles and suites. There's also a modest treatment room and a late check-out facility until 3pm.

Town House

19 New Steine, Kemptown, BN2 1PD
(01273 607456/www.thetownhousebrighton.
com). **Rates** £85-£150 double. **Credit** AmEx,
DC, MC, V.

The last word in themed boutique hotels, the
(bright red) Town House opened in autumn 2006
under the mantra 'Bespoke – Boutique – Bijou'.
Each of the eight rooms is recherché to the nth
degree – the original Raj map from 1892 and
Lancers' bugle in the Colonial room, the handmade Black Forest cuckoo clock and wooden skis
in the Alpine room – although the ground-floor
Kasbah is the most stunning. The Moroccan
theme will be continued when a marquee is put up
in the back garden for summer 2007. By then, a
basement restaurant and cocktail bar are also
promised. All rooms have LCD TVs and Wi-Fi.

WHERE TO EAT & DRINK

Brighton offers a ridiculous amount of
dining possibilities for a town its size –
nearly 500. Of these, a handful (Blanch
House, One Paston Place, Gingerman)
would hold their head up in any city in the
UK. The rest comprise an attractive global
mix, with plenty of seafood and imaginative
choices for vegetarians; nearly every venue
welcomes children.

New venues open in town almost weekly.
The most talked about arrivals of 2006
have been Riddle & Finns and Pintxo
People – although the most talked-about
establishment per se has been Momma
Cherri's Big House, a lovely success story
with TV stardom to boot.

One Paston Place (1 Paston Place, 01273
606933, www.onepastonplace.co.uk) may
have lost its upmarket French formality, but
it's gained a metropolitan buzz. The food is
exquisite and presented by experienced,
unstuffy staff eager to advise. Gingerman
(21A Norfolk Square, 01273 326688,
www.gingermanrestaurants.com) offers top
quality continental – mainly French – cuisine
at accessible prices.

Meanwhile, award-winning chef Sam
Metcalfe has given Seven Dials (1-3
Buckingham Place, 01273 885555,
www.sevendialsrestaurant.co.uk) – located

ARTS AND ATTRACTIONS

In the Royal Pavilion gardens, the **Brighton Museum and Art Gallery** (01273 292882, www.brighton. virtualmuseum.info) offers an eclectic collection of 20th-century design, ethnic art and local social history; admission is free. A more modern selection can be found at the recently opened **ocontemporary gallery** (80 Trafalgar Street, 01273 698500, www.ocontemporary.com) in the North Laine, with original works by Tracey Emin and David Hockney for sale. The location is significant, as it borders what the local council is at pains to describe as a new cultural quarter, centrepieced by the controversial Jubilee Library, opened in 2005. Opposite is the site of a myhotel scheduled for the end of 2007.

The city also hosts England's biggest arts bash, the **Brighton Festival** (www.brighton-festival.org. uk), for three weeks every May. Almost half a million people attended some 700 events in 2006, the 40th anniversary of its staging. To complement its core elements of theatre, dance, music and art, a fringe festival (www.brightonfestival fringe.org.uk) runs concurrently.

The big anniversary for 2007 is the 200th birthday of the **Theatre Royal** (www.theambassadors.com/theatre royal), with a street party planned for 27 June. The nearby landmark arts venues of the **Joogleberry Playhouse** (www.joogleberry.com), the **Komedia** (www.komedia.co.uk) and, at the main university site in Falmer, the **Gardner Arts Centre** (www.gardner arts.co.uk) provide a year-round artistic agenda. The **Duke of York's Picturehouse** (www.picturehouses. co.uk) is the oldest independent cinema outside London. A similarly well-established hub of artistic activity thrives in the row of private galleries along the seafront near Brighton Pier, the artists' quarter.

For outdoor types, March 2007 will see the launch of the UK's first permanent beach sports venue. **Yellowave** (www.yellowave.co.uk) will be set up on a large rectangle of sand for national volleyball championships, beach soccer and Frisbee. The beach packs out for half the year with barbecues and impromptu parties – free children's playgrounds can be found at the Brighton Pier and Hove Lagoon ends.

Brighton's other child-friendly attractions include the sweet and quaintly tatty **Sea-Life Centre** (Marine Parade, 01273 604234, www.sealifeeurope.com), its Ocean Tunnel below a rickety mock-up of Captain Nemo's *Nautilus* letting you see sharks, rays and Lulu, the ailing giant turtle, swim overhead; and the Volks **Electric Railway** (285 Madeira Drive, 01273 292718,

---

in a former bank – some homely touches, and provided his praiseworthy restaurant with hospitable staff. Two- and three-course deals are a snip considering the quality of fare on offer.Terre à Terre (71 East Street, 01273 729051, www.terreaterre.co.uk) is Brighton's reliably inventive flagship

vegetarian restaurant, and enjoys a reputation that attracts hordes of weekending pan-fried-weary Londoners to its simple space.

Nia Café (87 Trafalgar Street, 01273 671371, www.niacafe.co.uk) is a busy pit stop offering all-day breakfasts to market open Easter-mid Sept) offers a 12-minute ride along the beach from the Sea-Life Centre to the **Marina** (www.brightonmarina.co.uk). There, a mile or so east of Brighton Pier, you will find commercial leisure activities such as bowling, trampolining and a UGC multiplex. Fishing boats, diving trips and sailing excursions can be arranged at the information hut next to the petrol station.

Brighton Museum

browsers. After dark, it dims the industrial lights hanging over its dozen wooden tables and becomes a fully fledged restaurant.

For a sea view, you'll have to stick to chips or standard pizzas, with a couple of honourable exceptions: Café Paradiso (at Alias Hotel Seattle, *see p74*), Due South

(139 King's Road Arches, 01273 821218, www.duesouth.co.uk) and the recently refurbished Alfresco (King's Road Arches, 01273 206523, www.alfresco-brighton. co.uk), in the outstanding setting of the Milkmaid's Pavilion set above the water. The sea-level café is now pretty chic; the Italian food upstairs does a reasonable job of living up to the location. Close to Brighton Pier, there's also the polished, pleasant Terraces Bar, Grill & Dining Room (Unit 8, Madeira Drive, 01273 570526, www.the-terraces.co.uk).

With a dark cellar full of spiky characters, Ali-Cats (80 East Street, 01273 748103, www.myspace.com/alicatsbrighton) is an independent basement bar underneath the Varsity bar-restaurant just in from the seafront – look for the set of steps with cartoon fishbones carved into the concrete – where unusual and cult films are shown, and there are regular happy hours at the start of the week. Brighton Rocks (6 Rock Place, 01273 601139, www.brighton-rocks.com) is Kemp Town's most talked-up bar. It may be modest in size, but makes up for it with a heated terrace, sparkling cocktails and superb organic cuisine.

Colonnade Bar (10 New Road, 01273 328728, www.goldenliongroup.co.uk), adjacent to the Theatre Royal, scores for its civilised and civilising atmosphere and comfy alcoves of intense, arty banter, a world away from all the guzzling and groping going on around any nearby corner.

The low-ceilinged Cricketers (15 Black Lion Street, 01273 329472, www.goldenliongroup.co.uk) is cosy, historic and centrally located in the Lanes, and invariably accommodates gaggles of blokes, clusters of shoppers and local employees on their lunch breaks – and the odd solitary, literary soul, attracted by mention of the place in *Brighton Rock* by former regular Graham Greene.

Evening Star (55-56 Surrey Street, 01273 328931, www.eveningstarbrighton.co.uk) is a rustic haven for real ale types; an independent microbrewery, it has ten hand pumps and a host of unpronounceable Flemish brews by the bottle. Heart in Hand (75 North Road, 01273 683320) is North Laine's classic rock 'n' roll bar, a green-tiled beauty propping up a street corner beside the commercial bustle of the North Laine. A small, vibrant, neighbourhood local, festooned with tatty flyers and posters for past and future gig information, and crowned by a battered jukebox (playing proper old 45s!).

The Lion & Lobster (24 Sillwood Street, 01273 327299) is a wonderful, wonderful little pub tucked away behind Regency Square. It boasts superb beers and ales, fine food (the best Sunday roast in Brighton for £6.50) and occasional live music – but

Brighton

most of all a fine vibe, cool and communal. Roaring fires, seats outside in summer, stills from *Blowup* over the bar, jazz cuttings over the walls and a cosy back room for diners all combine to create a wholesome local. There are even rooms upstairs if you get stuck into a real session and can't tear yourself away.

Behind a grand exterior on a corner of Russell Square right behind the city's main shopping centre, the Regency Tavern (32-34 Russell Square, 01273 325652) hides an interior resembling an explosion in a tinsel factory. Although the staff serve as if performing at a post-war holiday camp, the place is run as a serious business.

NIGHT BRIGHTON

Pier, promenade, Pavilion, pah! Partying is what brings so many down to Brighton from London and points south – a fine tradition upon which the town's very development depended in the days of the foxy Prince Regent.

The key to the town's successful move away from seedy post-pub discotheques to cosmopolitan, quality nightspots has been its dynamic and influential gay community, marginalised in lesser seaside towns – coupled with the phenomenon known as Norman Cook. Launched in 2001, Fatboy Slim's free seafront clubfest, the **Big Beach Boutique**, was put on ice due to security concerns after a quarter of a million people swamped the city centre in 2002. However, its success galvanised the local DJ community and put Brighton on the map as a music capital. When Rio adopted the Big Beach concept in 2003, it was Brighton's name that was evoked. A New Year revival on the first day of 2007 only added to the myth. What Glastonbury is to festivals, Brighton is to clubbing.

Parallel to Fatboy thrives a new wave of private members' bars. The best is the **Hanbury Club**, launched in 2006. Opened by Amanda Blanch and Chris Edwardes of **Blanch House** fame (*see p74*), the Hanbury (83 St

George Road, 01273 605789, www.thehanburyclub.com) is set in an exotic pavilion dating back to the 1850s, revamped in the 1920s. The Hanbury has kept its ornate ceiling and art deco touches, and offers a reasonably priced contemporary cocktail menu. Film nights, burlesque shows and live music events are regular features. As this guide went to press, memberships (annual fee £50) were still available, but numbers are limited. **Koba** (135 Western Road, 01273 720059, www.kobauk.com) and the **Sussex Arts Club** (7 Ship Street, 01273 778020, www.sussexarts.com) are two other centrally located options.

It's not all class in a glass though. Nothing hides the fact that gangs of pissed-up hens in dog-eared devil horns invade the city centre every weekend. West Street at chucking out time is not a pleasant place to be of a Friday night, with young shavers and squawky girlies heading for the bright lights of **Creation** (West Street, 01273 321628, www. creationbrighton.com) and the like.

Five venues, however, do stand out. The intimate, tunnel-like **Funky Buddha Lounge** (King's Road Arches, 01273 725541, www.funkybuddha brighton.co.uk), the vast, high-profile, mainly mainstream **Honeyclub** (214 King's Road Arches, 01273

Brighton

The commendable pub food is a main draw, so much so that bookings are taken for Sunday lunches.

On the downside, downtown Brighton is now so flooded with bars the police want to limit the number of late licences. Throughout the autumn of 2006, half a dozen venues were permitted 24-hour drinking and arrests for assault increased dramatically. Tides of stag and hen parties and unruly weekenders wash over centrally located North Street, West Street and the Lanes. A better barhop is to be had in Kemp Town, on and off the main drag of St James's Street, where the atmosphere is far more relaxed.

202807, www.thehoneyclub.co.uk) and the long-established, back-to-its-old-name **Zap Club** (187-193 King's Road Arches, 01273 202407, www.thezapclub.co.uk) await by the seafront. Nearby is the marvellous **Audio** (10 Marine Parade, 01273 697775, www.audiobrighton.com), an eclectic venue with its digit somewhere near the pulse. If you have one night in town, spend it here.

For something more classy, the three-storey **Ocean Rooms** (1 Morley Street, 01273 699069, www.ocean rooms.co.uk) is the top choice. Entirely and excellently revamped in January 2005, this venue's fabulous sound system and cool upstairs cocktail bar attract world-class DJs into town on a regular basis.

Nights out down here can be accompanied by all manner of stony romping on the beach – followed, when things get a little chilly, by a late supper or early breakfast, with drinks, at 24-hour diner **Buddies** (46-48 King's Road, 01273 323600, www.buddies24hour.net).

Club admission prices being (generally) reasonable around these parts, you should still have enough in your purse to satisfy the munchies. And let's face it, there are worse starts to the day than sunrise over Brighton seafront with a beer and breakfast in front of you.

Most of the above clubs put on at least one gay night (look out for Wild Fruit and Vavavavoom!), but that's only the tip of the iceberg. Landmark Kemp Town funhouses such as the sleek **Charles Street** (8 Marine Parade, 01273 624091, www.charles-street.com), with the inventive Pool club upstairs, and the trashier but mega popular **Revenge** (32-34 Old Steine, 01273 606064, www.revenge.co.uk) are the biggest gay clubs on the south coast. For a few drinks before a night out on the tiles, Marine Parade, now lined with trendy new gay bars, is always a good bet.

Such is Kemp Town's successful crossover mix, however, that key nightspots such as the **Volks** (3 The Colonnade, Madeira Drive, 01273 682828, www.volksclub. co.uk), Audio and the **Funky Fish Club** (New Madeira Hotel, 19 Marine Parade, 01273 696961, www.funkyfishclub.co.uk) attract music lovers across the board.

Every tranny in town – amiably accompanied by goths, drag queens, geezers and lezzers – turns the Danny LaRue-inspired **Harlequin** (43 Providence Place, 01273 620630, www.harlequin-brighton.co.uk) into the living embodiment of what might loosely be termed the Brighton ethic: live it up and let live.

Brighton

THREE WHEELIN'

When you arrive at Brighton station, you'll notice a fleet of growling taxis in the forecourt outside. Discreetly nearby, by the trademark green sign deliberately set away from any bus stop, will be the brightly themed buggies you may have seen in TV travel shows: the tuctuc. Ready and waiting to whisk you to the seafront, marina or any of the 20 hop-on, hop-off stops all the way to Hove, for the snip of £2.50 (day passes £3), Europe's first motorised rickshaw service (www.tuctuc.co.uk) whirrs into action, chugging through traffic and earning stares and waves from passers-by. Vehicles run every ten minutes, 18 hours a day – you're bound to see one. What you can't do is flag one down. According to local law, tuctucs must operate as ordinary transport rather than as a taxi service.

Dominic Ponniah first saw tuctucs on a backpacking gap year in India. Seeing a business opportunity, he bought a fleet of 12 from the Bajaj works in Pune. Having customised them with seatbelts, rain and extra impact protection, and launched them in Brighton in July 2006 as a pilot scheme before an assault on London. The tuctucs' use of low-emission compressed natural gas also pleased Brighton's many green thinkers.

After the initial plaudits, Dominic soon had to deal with grief of the worst kind: taxi drivers' grief. Resenting the competition, and already paying stiff annual fees for the use of the station forecourt, Brighton cabbies treated the tuctucs with disdain, refusing to pick up passengers should one have broken down. Even bus drivers were known to have cut up the occasional tuctuc in traffic.

Since then the fuss has died down, and Dominic is looking to relaunch in spring 2007 with a new fleet, upgraded and more robust than the three-seaters now in operation. Current decorative themes – Circuit board, Friesian cow, Swiss cheese – will also be worked on.

Next stop – London!

Blanch House

Blanch House Hotel, 17 Atlingworth Street, BN2 1PL (01273 603504/www.blanchhouse. co.uk). **Lunch served** 12.30-2pm Tue-Sun. **Dinner served** 7-10pm Tue-Sat. **Set lunch** £13 2 courses, £16 3 courses. **Set dinner** £30 3 courses. **Tasting menu** £50 5 courses. **Credit** AmEx, MC, V.

As simple as its *Play School* letter b-in-a-house logo, the stark white basement interior of this boutique hotel (*see p74*) restaurant reflects the brevity of its menu, and simple set lunches and dinners policy. Selections are equally straightforward and well conceived: on our visit, five starters included a rolled halibut with sage and lemon, and rabbit with wild mushrooms and foie gras terrine; among the five mains on offer were a Duke of Berkshire pork belly with roasted apples and calvados jus, and chargrilled swordfish on a haricot bean broth with fennel purée and shellfish bisque. Equal delicacy is applied to the desserts, such as chocolate fondant with Cointreau mascarpone or the tarte au citron with grapefruit sorbet. All in all, a class act.

Café Belge

64 King's Road, BN1 1NA (01273 733290/ www.cafebelge.co.uk/html/brighton). **Lunch served** 11am-3pm Mon-Fri; 11am-4pm Sat, Sun. **Dinner served** 6-11pm daily. **Main courses** £7.95-£19.95. **Set lunch** £11.75 2 courses, £15.38 3 courses. **Credit** AmEx, MC, V (over £15).

Café Belge is more than just your standard Belgian beer bar. One of a mini Sussex chain of Flemish family heritage, this Brighton seafront branch opened its expansive doors in the summer of 2006, allowing locals the chance to try such delights as mussels prepared in 50 different ways, wild boar-and-beer sausages, Belgian beer stew and, of course, more than a hundred varieties of beer. As well as 14 fruit, 11 dark and 12 Trappist types, Café Belge boasts two dozen unusual beer cocktails (£7) including the Belgian Monk (Bacardi, coconut beer and Coke) and Black Forest (cherry and chocolate beer). Alternatively, splash out on the Tin Tin (£32.50), which blends champagne and raspberry beer to potent effect. There are seats outside in summer.

La Capannina

15 Madeira Place, BN2 1TN (01273 680839). **Lunch served** noon-2.30pm Mon-Sat. **Dinner served** 6-11pm Mon-Thur, Sun; 6-11.30pm Fri, Sat. **Meals served** noon-11pm daily (summer). **Main courses** £6.95-£16.95. **Set lunch** £8.95 2 courses. **Credit** AmEx, MC, V.

Hands down the best Italian in town. La Capannina is a cosy, family-run place set over two floors, both with a wooden, rustic feel. It is, however, the food – and the prices – that keep the regulars (its lively clientele includes a fair share of Kemp Town drag queens) coming back for more. Slight Sardinian touches pepper the extensive and

varied menu: the spicy sausage in the fusilli alla sarda or the roast piglet with rosemary, one of the chalked-up specials on the day of review. Otherwise there are 20 antipasti to choose from, four soups, including the stellar traditional chickpea option (there's also a humungous own-made fish stew at £14.50 and worth every lira) and 20 stone-baked pizzas. Of the 20 pastas, you can't go far wrong with the linguini with lobster and scallops (£10.50). The £8.95 lunch menu is such a bargain you'll come back the next day. House wines are available at £3.25 and £6.30 a glass, £10.20 a bottle. If you're celebrating, a bottle of Barolo (£29.95), perhaps. Desserts are imaginative, and include a couple of Sicilian provenance.

Esca

69-71 Preston Street, BN1 2HG (01273 326823/www.escabrighton.com). **Open** noon-2am Thur-Sat; noon-midnight Mon-Wed, Sun. **Meals served** noon-8pm daily. **Main courses** £4.95-£6.95. **Credit** AmEx, MC, V.

Preston Street, lined with cheap global eateries and takeaways, is the unlikely setting for this recently opened, quality lounge bar, restaurant and DJ club. Designed with taste by Amanda Blanch of Blanch House (*see p74* and *left*), the three-level maroon Esca accommodates families just up from the nearby beach with its great under-a-fiver pizzas and omelettes (although, sadly, no desserts as yet), hungover couples with snack lunches, Becks Vier on draught and a large TV screen, and night-owls with a bar and (generally house) DJ until 2am from Thursday to Saturday. The food is not an add-on – dishes come immaculately presented with a side salad drizzled in tasty, mustardy dressing. Throw in a dozen cocktails at standard prices, including a Fatboy Gin of Beefeater and raspberry purée, and you have a damn fine operation running from morning until well past bedtime.

Great Eastern

103 Trafalgar Street, BN1 4ER (01273 685681). **Open** noon-midnight Mon-Sat; noon-11pm Sun. **Meals served** noon-5pm daily; 6-10pm Mon, Wed. **Main courses** £3.45-£5.75. **Credit** MC, V (over £7.50).

Trafalgar Street, buttressing the eternally bohemian North Laine from what will be the New England Quarter around the train station, can lay claim to being Brighton's finest thoroughfare. Lined with wacky shops, the new ocontemporary art gallery (*see p80*) and quality bars and pubs, it is the domain of the tattooed and the pierced, the spiky and the unshaven. Of all their haunts, this lived-in tatty pub is by far the most congenial. A row of scuffed wooden tables and teetering shelves of books fill a cramped, low-ceilinged interior, the long bar counter buzzing with chat and willing eye contact. Popular themed nights held here include midweek S&M; otherwise the best day to visit is on a Sunday, to partake of the outstanding vegetarian roasts.

Hand in Hand

33 Upper St James' Street, BN2 1JN (01273 699595). **Open** noon-11pm Sun-Thur; noon-12pm Fri, Sat. **Credit** AmEx, Mc, V.
Neither a throbbing gay den of iniquity nor an indie student haunt, this small, traditional boozer deep in Kemp Town attracts an older, discerning clientele thanks to its outstanding range of ales, prominently advertised on the wall outside. The most appropriate choice here would be the ale made by nearby Kemptown Breweries, although you can also find varieties such as Ye Olde Trout, Stinger and Fursty Ferret. Lager drinkers will be delighted to find Hacker Pschorr, Munich's finest brew. The decor is equally and fittingly eclectic: old school ties, historic newspaper cuttings and weird pseudo-erotic shapes on the ceiling.

Momma Cherri's Big House

2-3 Little East Street, BN1 1HT (01273 325305/www.mommacherri.co.uk). **Lunch served** noon-2pm Tue-Fri; noon-3pm Sat. **Dinner served** 5-10pm Mon; 5-11pm Tue-Thur; 5pm-midnight Fri, Sat. **Meals served** 11am-8pm Sun. **Main courses** £8-£15. **Set lunch** £10 2 courses. **Set dinner** £15 2 courses. **Credit** AmEx, MC, V.
Success couldn't have happened to a nicer chef. Philadelphia-born Charita Jones, a one-time foster carer, backing singer and drama teacher, opened her cramped eaterie in 2001, providing kicking soul food at knockdown prices – at a loss. In stepped Gordon Ramsay, who made MCSFS a subject of his *Kitchen Nightmares*. He praised the food wholeheartedly ('the Ramsay plate returned to the kitchen empty') but came down heavily on Charita's business sense. In came the £10 Soul In A Bowl dinners, swifter service and TV viewers by the truckload. Within months the team had moved into a much larger property a few doors down, in Brighton's most central square. Logistics and location aside, the song remains the same: the black sounds of Memphis, Chicago and Detroit (gospel on Sundays) accompany authentic meat, fish or vegetable jambalaya, heavy enough to sink a Mississippi paddle steamer. Starters involve buffalo wings, baby back ribs in barbecue sauce and garlic prawns; desserts include pecan pie, ice-cream sundae or peach or blueberry cobbler. Finish three courses and you won't need to eat for a week.There are hearty breakfasts and brunches too, a menu for children (who are celebrated rather than merely accommodated), and Dixie, Lone Star, Cave Creek and Mexican beers. It's best to book in advance for weekends, as this joint is invariably jumping.

Pintxo People

95 Western Road, BN1 2LB (01273 732323/www.pintxopeople.co.uk). Café/Bar **Open** 8am-midnight Mon-Fri; 9am-11pm Sat; 9am-5pm Sun. *Restaurant* **Lunch served** noon-4pm Fri-Sun. **Dinner served** 6pm-midnight Tue-Thur; 6pm-1am Fri, Sat.

EYEING UP BRIGHTON

London has its big wheel, Blackpool has its famous tower – and Brighton? Brighton will have its i360, scheduled to open in summer 2008 and referred to by all as the **Brighton Eye**. The tower will be 600 feet high, with a glass and steel pod that will transport up to 125 visitors 456 feet up, allowing them a panoramic view spanning 25 miles on a clear day. Masterminding the project are David Marks and Julia Barfield, the husband-and-wife architectural team behind its London counterpart.

The observation mast is expected to attract half a million visitors a year and generate £10 million worth of tourist revenue for local businesses.

Secondly, and perhaps most importantly, it will solve once and for all the thorny, long-term problem of what to do with the site of Brighton's ruined West Pier.

Before construction begins, the wreckage of the collapsed pier will be cleared. (The end section is slated for renovation and development, and will be integrated into the overall complex). A heritage centre will also be set up.

Locals doubt whether such an ambitious scheme can be completed within just 18 months. But what is certain is that once the i360 is up, it will change the skyline and tourist value of Brighton forever.

Brighton Pier: gaudy and gloriously tacky.

Tapas £1-£7. **Main courses** £3-£14. **Set dinner** (for 10+ people) £28 3 courses, £35 5 courses & coffee. **Credit** AmEx, MC, V.

Winner of *Class* magazine's new bar of the year 2006-07, this much-talked-about shiny new tapas bar on the main shopping street leading out of the city centre lives up to its good reputation. Done out with a long zinc bar counter, with meat and cheese goodies under glass and a sturdy tap of Cruzcampo, Pintxo People provides superior tapas – cured meats, Galician tetillo cheese with quince, squid with paprika – at reasonable prices. Although not as ornate as the Basque tapas (pintxos) you'll find in Bilbao or San Sebastián, each creation is well presented, the bite-sized versions going for a mere £1 each. An array of colourful Spanish products line the back wall if you'd like to take anything home with you. Where PP also scores impressively is with drinks: fresh fruit smoothies (£5.50) until 5.30pm, fruit coffees (£3), La Asturiana cider (£2.50/£7.50), a range of reserve sherries chosen to complement particular pintxos and cocktails (£5.50) concocted with premium tequila – Tres Agaves of San Francisco, for example. Jugs of sangria (£11) change ingredients according to season. The upstairs space is open only in the evenings.

Red Roaster

1D St James' Street, BN1 2HS (01273 686668). **Open** 7am-7pm Mon-Fri; 8am-7pm Sat; 9am-6.30pm Sun. **Lunch served** 11am-5pm daily. **Main courses** £2.50-£4. **No credit cards.**

The red awning of Brighton's finest independent coffeehouse stands at the entrance to Kemp Town, its roomy interior abuzz with caffeine-fuelled conversation from morning to evening. Eighteen types of coffee, loaded or decaffeinated, are available from the sometimes slow-moving serving desk, from a humble £1.20 espresso to iced caffè mocha and various ice-cream and chocolate varieties. Teas (fruit, yogi and gunpowder), smoothies and steamers (milk with amaretto, hazelnut or sweet caramel) are also popular. Lunch is served from 11am to 5pm, comprising baguettes (free-range organic ham, feta and sun-dried tomato for example), sandwiches (such as the house houmous and grated carrot combination), ciabattas and salads, all under a fiver. The coffees are for sale, as are the photographs by Joe de Kats adorning the high-ceilinged space.

Riddle & Finns

12B Meeting House Lane, BN1 1HB (01273 323008/www.riddleandfinns.co.uk). **Open** noon-11pm Mon-Thur, Sun; noon-1.30am Fri, Sat. **Meals served** noon-10pm Mon-Thur, Sun; noon-11pm Fri, Sat. **Main courses** £10-£30. **Credit** AmEx, MC, V.

Wow, what have we here? The finest establishment to open in town in 2006, sister to the seaside Due South, R&F is an ambitious and accomplished champagne and oyster bar. Tucked in an alleyway halfway down North Street (follow the enticing smell), R&F greets the visitor with outdoor seating and a window on to Pat Timpson and his kitchen team in action. Inside the neat, white-tiled interior, a friendly waitress soon presents you with an amuse-gueule of bread with assorted spreads. Choosing from the extensive menu of a score of starters (monkfish cheek scampi, Scottish rope-grown mussels steamed with local cider, garlic, parsley and cream), and mains (house seafood stew, smoked haddock on mustard mash with a soft poached egg) can be tricky – let your waitress talk you through it. Oysters, of course, abound, hot or cold, rock or native, with spinach and Pernod, with fresh horseradish and vodka, for about £2 each plus 20p per topping. All the seafood is fresh – much is sourced locally, landed that day near Hove lagoon – and all is immaculately presented on a mound of ice. Of the 14 wines (ten whites), you will be encouraged to try the refreshing Chapel Down from Tenterden in Kent. Alternatively, choose from a dozen champagnes (RC Lemaire £7 a glass) or £8.50 cocktails to round proceedings off nicely.

Brighton

Chichester & Around

Live it up on the South Downs.

The south-west corner of West Sussex is green and pleasant England at its best. The rolling hills of the South Downs dominate the landscape, complemented by miles of sheltered coastline and characterful towns and villages. Much of the charm of this part of the country lies in its relative lack of development and relaxed pace of life. Even the county's administrative centre, the historic city of Chichester (which, notably, is far from the largest settlement in West Sussex), exudes a peacefully quaint market-town charm. The area is also a walker's paradise, with over 2,500 miles of public footpaths traversing countryside dotted with wildflowers and butterflies. West Sussex is one of the most heavily wooded counties in England and more than half of it, including Chichester Harbour, the Sussex Downs and the High Weald, is designated an Area of Outstanding Natural Beauty. The expanse of coast means those preferring more watery pursuits aren't left out either. Both Chichester Harbour and the charming village of Bosham are excellent for sailing, while further south the sea at Selsey is popular with divers – here you can explore jagged limestone outcrops, a submerged Roman road and a World War II landing craft along with a host of marine life.

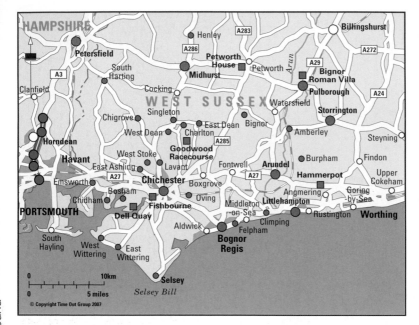

Chichester

In many ways, Chichester is the archetypal English market town (even if it is a city), but it comes with one crucial difference: as the mournful cry of seagulls will remind you, the water is not far away. It was founded in AD 70 by the Romans, who laid out the main street plan and built the original city walls, which were subsequently rebuilt in flint in medieval times. The main streets of the city – called, with unimpeachable logic, North, South, East and West Streets – slice it neatly into four areas. The cathedral dominates the south-west sector, while the finest of the Georgian buildings are in the south-east, in the streets known as the Pallants. The cathedral is still the centre of the city. Visible from miles away and immortalised by Turner in his painting of the Chichester Canal (*see p96* **Romans & Romantics**), it's a striking structure, best known for its spire and Marc Chagall stained-glass window. There are concerts here regularly; visit www.chichester cathedral.org.uk or call 01243 782595 for details. The other main attraction is the

Accommodation	★★★★★
Food & drink	★★★★★
Nightlife	★★★★★
Shopping	★★★★★
Culture	★★★★★
Sights	★★★★★
Scenery	★★★★★

Pallant House Gallery (9 North Pallant, 01243 774557, www.pallant.org.uk), hosting an outstanding collection of 20th-century British art that takes in works by Henry Moore, Peter Blake, Bridget Riley, Lucian Freud and Barbara Hepworth. Contemporary art shows here have also proved that the gallery has its finger firmly on the pulse. On Thursday nights admission is half-price and there's a free guided tour at 6pm.

South & west from Chichester

The sweet village of Bosham (pronounced 'Bozzum'), two miles west of Chichester, extends right down to the water's edge. The road here is only passable at low tide; many of the houses have a high stoop at the front door, evidence of past floods. Bosham's history as a fishing port dates back to Roman times (the Emperor Vespasian allegedly had a residence here; and Fishbourne Roman Palace is a few miles east, *see p96*); today, traces of this history can be found in the exquisitely simple Saxon church, which includes stones from the original Roman basilica along with a truly beautiful arched chapel in the crypt, lit only by a shaft of natural light from a small window. A stone coffin discovered in the church in the 19th century contained a child's body, thought to be a daughter of Canute. This, legend dictates, is the spot where he tried to turn back the tide, although some say it was at Hamwich, near Southampton. From Bosham, you can walk around the coast to Bosham Hoe, where a short ferry ride has, for centuries, saved travellers a 13-mile walk around the coast to the pretty village of West Itchenor. South of here are the twin villages of East and West Wittering. While pleasant in their own rights, the latter is still most famous as the long-time home of Rolling Stone Keith Richards (and, thus, the site of the infamous 1967 drugs bust, and its accompanying Mars Bar-related apocrypha). Its beach has also become a top destination at all states of the tide for windsurfers (X-train, West Wittering Windsurfing Club, 01243 513077, www.2xs.co.uk). The villages north and west of Bosham, meanwhile, are notable mainly for the pubs and pub-restaurants that dot them. Emsworth, a larger than expected town just over the border in Hampshire, boasts a pretty little waterfront; stop by on Sunday mornings to watch the locals race their remote-controlled boats across the calm, wide waters.

North & east from Chichester

As the flat coastal plain rises gently into the South Downs, a handful of attractions reveal themselves. But the main draw is the countryside. The 100-mile South Downs Way, the oldest long-distance footpath in Britain, passes through the area as it runs from Winchester to Seven Sisters near Dover. Most of the ancient trading route is also a bridleway, and as such is accessible to horse and mountain-bike riders. The 30-mile section that passes through West Sussex from South Harting to south of Storrington might be a bit much for a weekend, but there are plenty of shorter walks that give a taste of its sweeping views and enchanted woodlands. Bisecting the footpath as it crosses the county are several skinny roads, which spool out in all directions from Chichester and connect it to other major towns in the area: on the south coast, Bognor Regis and Littlehampton, with Felpham in between; to the north, Petersfield and the agreeable little market town of Midhurst. In between are numerous villages scattered with pub-restaurants and other attractions. Singleton houses the Weald & Downland Open Air Museum (01243 811348, www.wealddown.co.uk), a highly unusual collection of 40 historic buildings that have been rescued, rebuilt and restored to offer a fascinating historical journey through the region's architecture over the past 500 years. Among the structures are a Tudor farmstead, a 17th-century water mill and some Victorian labourers' cottages. Nearby are the West Dean Gardens (01243 818210, www.west dean.org.uk/site/gardens), inspirational for those of a horticultural bent. The kitchen garden includes Victorian greenhouses with fig and peach trees and grape vines; there's also a 300-foot pergola, 35 acres of ornamental grounds with walks around an arboretum, a licensed restaurant and a very upmarket gift shop. Summer events include a garden show and outdoor theatre. Further north, Pulborough is home to Parham House (01903 742021, information 01903

Bosham: a fishing port since Roman times.

744888, www.parhaminsussex.co.uk), a rare example of mid 20th-century restoration ideas in a large Elizabethan manor, highlighted by a fine panelled Long Gallery and Great Hall and set in 11 acres of gardens.

However, the biggest draw remains Goodwood House (01243 755048, recorded information 01243 755040, www.goodwood.co.uk, closed Nov-Feb), a beautifully restored Regency mansion in the heart of the countryside. The house is still home to the Earl and Countess of March, but is also open to the public; exhibits include paintings by Canaletto, Stubbs and Van Dyck, as well as Napoleon Bonaparte's campaign chair. Surrounding the house is an immense estate, containing everything from a sculpture garden (01243 538449, www.sculpture.org.uk, closed Dec-Feb) to a racetrack.

Arundel & Amberley

Seen from across the river, Arundel, with its castle and church at the top of the hill and the water at the bottom, looks more like a stage set than a real town. It's easy to understand why tourists in search of Olde Englande are so drawn to it. Still, despite the prevalence of coach parties and weekenders, it has a pleasing sense of being very much at ease with itself, its tiny streets lined with antiques shops, tearooms and homely places selling country jams. It's hard to imagine that as late as the 1920s it was still a working port, with big ships coming up the river. The imposing Arundel Castle (01903 882173, www.arundelcastle.org, closed Nov-Mar) was built in the 11th century by Roger de Montgomery but massively remodelled in the 18th and 19th centuries. Now the seat of the Dukes of Norfolk and Earls of Arundel, it's well worth exploring (though the cost of admission is high) for its fine collections of paintings (by Van Dyck, Gainsborough and Reynolds, among others), tapestries and furniture, and the gorgeous Fitzalan Chapel, otherwise only viewable through the wrought iron gates in the parish church. The Catholic Arundel Cathedral (01903 882297, www.arundel cathedral.org) opposite was built in 1873. It's Joseph Hansom's take on French Gothic. Its exterior is best viewed from a distance, but if you do decide to get close up, there's a fine rose window over the west door and, inside, the shrine of St Philip Howard, who converted to Catholicism after his father was beheaded by Elizabeth I for his part in Mary Queen of Scots' intrigues. The other notable attraction is the Arundel Wildfowl & Wetlands Trust (01903 883355, www. wwt.org.uk), which extends over 60 acres of parkland and lakes and is visited by thousands of migratory birds. It's lovely for a wander. From Arundel, it's only a short drive around to Amberley, also accessible via the river courtesy of Arun Cruises (Arundel Boat Yard or the Town Quay, 01903 882609). The village is home to Amberley Working Museum (01798 831370, www.amberleymuseum.co.uk), a fascinating spot that traces the working heritage of the region with numerous craftsmen demonstrating everything from blacksmithery to clay pipe manufacture.

Bailiffscourt Hotel & Health Spa

WHERE TO STAY

There's a huge range of accommodation in Chichester and, especially, the towns and villages surrounding it: a few ineffably posh country retreats are supplemented by mid-range hotels and affordable B&B accommodation. No matter the grade, however, prices throughout the area soar during the Festival of Speed and Glorious Goodwood; book months ahead or avoid them entirely. Several pubs listed in the Where to Eat & Drink section on *p95* also offer B&B accommodation. The better bets include the Fox Goes Free (*see p97*) and the White Horse Inn (*see p97*) at Chilgrove. On the edge of Midhurst, meanwhile, sits York House (Easebourne Street, 01730 814090, www.yorkhouserooms.co.uk), a handsome B&B that differs from the norm in several ways. For one thing, each of the two suites is in a small cottage adjacent to the main house and is split over two floors (bed upstairs, lounge at street level); for another, decor is crisp and style-mag modern, with power showers and skinny-screen TVs. Also in Midhurst is the Spread Eagle (South Street, 01730 816911, www.hshotels.co.uk), a historic hotel with old-English decor and on-site spa.

Amberley Castle

Amberley, West Sussex BN18 9LT (01798 831992/www.amberleycastle.co.uk). **Lunch served** noon-2pm, **dinner served** 7-9pm daily. **Set meal** £43 2 courses, £50 3 courses incl coffee. **Set lunch** (Mon-Sat) £20 2 courses, £25 3 courses. (Sun) £30 3 courses incl coffee. **Rates** £155-£335 double/twin; £285-£375 suite. **Credit** AmEx, DC, MC, V.
Amberley Castle has been around for some 900 years but first raised the portcullis to paying guests less than two decades ago. The accommodation is in 19 suites – each with a whirlpool bath – situated in numerous buildings behind 60-foot curtain walls. The hotel isn't shy about playing up its history, and why should it be? Built as a hunting lodge in 1103 by a certain Bishop Ralph Luffa, it was fortified in the 14th century before falling to Cromwell in the 1640s. Martin and Joy Cummings bought the property in 1988; since then, it's been run as an exclusive hotel, picking up various awards and being admitted into the prestigious Relais & Châteaux group. The rooms are all decorated individually but are uniformly plush and opulent. The grounds include a treehouse by the main gates, a tennis court, an 18-hole putting green and strolling peacocks; to add to the effect, the portcullis is still ceremonially raised and lowered each day. The restaurant, now in the hands of chef Jim Dugan (formerly at 36 on the Quay, and Lindsay House), serves a Modern European menu at lunch and dinner daily; if you land a reservation, be sure to dress for the occasion (no jeans and trainers).

TOURIST INFORMATION

Arundel
61 High Street, Arundel, West Sussex BN18 9AJ (01903 882268/ www.sussexbythesea.com).
Chichester
29A South Street, Chichester, West Sussex PO19 1AH (01243 775888/ www.chichester.gov.uk).

Bailiffscourt Hotel & Health Spa

Climping Street, Climping, nr Littlehampton, West Sussex BN17 5RW (01903 723511/ www.hshotels.co.uk). **Lunch served** noon-1.45pm, **dinner served** 7-9.30pm daily. **Set lunch** £11.50 2 courses, £16.50 3 courses. **Set dinner** £44.50 3 courses incl coffee. **Rates** half board £240-£350 double; £345-£575 suite. **Credit** AmEx, MC, V.
Bailiffscourt is one of the more extraordinary hotel properties in Sussex, a palimpsest of old English architectural styles in a delightfully secluded spot near the coast. In 1927, inspired by a small Norman chapel (still standing) on his land, Walter Guinness (son of the 1st Earl Iveagh of Kenwood, part of the brewing clan, and later assassinated in Cairo by the Stern Gang during World War II) asked the antiquarian Amyas Phillips to construct a medieval manor house to go with it. Crucially, Phillips used as many original pieces as possible, salvaged from around the country. Hence the 15th-century oak front door from the church at South Wanborough. Of a similar date is the complete gatehouse transported from Loxwood, reconstructed next to a 17th-century half-timbered house from Old Basing. Thoroughly well-appointed rooms are available in both, as well as in the stone-built main house, and also in a modern purpose-built block that lacks character but is more convenient (no steep narrow stairs, low beams or fun four-posters). A hotel since 1948, it is now run by Historic Sussex Hotels as a welcoming and laid-back high-end establishment with a decent restaurant (dining available in the candlelit courtyard in summer), a handsome new health spa (with indoor and outdoor pools, hot tub, steam room, sauna and well-equipped gym) and wide views over the marshes. And it's all just a five-minute walk from the pebbly beach and some great windsurfing.

West Stoke House

Downs Road, West Stoke, Chichester, West Sussex PO18 9BN (01243 575226/www.west stokehouse.co.uk). **Lunch served** 12.30-2.30pm Wed-Sun. **Dinner served** 7.30-9pm Wed-Sat. **Set lunch** (Wed-Sat) £17.50 2 courses. (Sun) £27.50 3 courses. **Set dinner** £35 3 courses. **Rates** £150-£175 double. **Credit** AmEx, DC, MC, V.
This elegant country retreat calls itself a 'restaurant with rooms', which is a little too modest given the careful attention to detail and service on offer.

Chichester & Around

A beautifully converted mansion house set in picture-perfect grounds, West Stoke House combines historic charm with contemporary comfort to great effect. There are five large double rooms to choose from, decked out in soothing neutrals, with crisp, white linen, flat-screen TVs and chic furnishings. Fantastic breakfasts add much to the relaxed appeal and the restaurant (Wed-Sun; also open to non-residents) offers adventurous Modern British cooking at lunch and dinner, meaning there's very little (if any) reason to set foot outside the grounds. Dishes include the likes of roasted loin of venison, pan-fried black bream or confit belly of Sussex pork; Sunday lunches are indulgently good. A brisk stroll through the five acres of gardens afterwards will help you work off the calories.

WHERE TO EAT & DRINK

Arundel and Chichester both have a decent spread of pubs and restaurants, but the best food is to be had out in the country. You can eat pretty well at several of the traditional country pubs in the area. The Crown & Anchor at Dell Quay, near Bosham (Dell Quay Road, 01243 781712), is the perfect place for a pint or a meal watching the comings and goings of the little boats and the sun setting over Chichester Harbour. Real ale aficionados should seek out the Black Horse at Amberley (High Street, 01798 831700), handy for the South Downs Way and walks along the banks of the River Arun.

Also recommended are the Old House at Home in Chidham (Cots Lane, 01243 572477), Donnington's Blacksmiths Arms (Selsey Road, 01243 783999), the 16th-century Woodmans Arms in Hammerpot

(01903 871240), where the landlord can provide a map of a local walk, or the Spotted Cow (1 High Street, 01903 783919) in Angmering, a former meeting place for smugglers, with a boules pitch and an obscure wheel game mounted on the ceiling. The Gribble Inn (Gribble Lane, 01243 786893, www.thegribble.co.uk), east of Chichester in Oving, brews its own ales, including Fursty Ferret, Plucking Pheasant and Pig's Ear, while the Star & Garter (01243 811318) in East Dean has a reputation for excellent food. More restrained are the Horse and Groom in East Ashling (01243 575339, www.thehorseandgroomchichester.com) and the historic Partridge Inn in Singleton (Singleton Lane, 01243 811251, www.thepartridgeinn.co.uk). This 16th-century pub serves up hearty pub grub. In addition to the establishments reviewed below, West Stoke House (*see p93*) merits special mention for its excellent evening menu, while Amberley Castle (*see p93*) also offers high-class dining and both Bailiffscourt (*see p93*) and the Spread Eagle (*see p93*) have well-regarded restaurants on site.

Duke of Cumberland

Henley Village, West Sussex GU27 3HQ (01428 652280). **Lunch served** noon-2.30pm daily. **Dinner served** 7-9.30pm Tue-Sat. **Main courses** £8.50-£15.95. **Credit** MC, V.
This wonderfully isolated pub is now well known for its fresh fish and pints of prawns, but the menu is also more ambitious. Cauliflower and tuna choux pastry buns and pan-fried salmon with cabbage parcels are the kind of thing that might feature. The garden menu (bar snacks) has

Duke of Cumberland

ROMANS & ROMANTICS

Chichester & Around

West Sussex is justly famous for champagne events such as Glorious Goodwood and the polo at Cowdray Park. So it comes as little surprise that the area has long been familiar with the high life. **Fishbourne Roman Palace** (Salthill Road, Fishbourne, PO19 3QS, 01243 785859) is the largest Roman residence excavated in Britain, and was probably once the finest accommodation north of the Alps. Rediscovered in 1960 by Professor Barry Cunliffe (recently dubbed Sir), it was constructed in the 1st century AD for King Tiberius Claudius Togidubnus and had about a hundred rooms. The foundations of around a quarter of them can still be seen, partly protected in the newly refurbished north wing. Here are at least 20 different mosaics, including the famous *Cupid on a Dolphin*.

Splendid Roman flooring can also be seen a few miles north-east at **Bignor Roman Villa** (Pulborough, RH20 1PH, 01798 869259), set in beautiful open farmland. The finest mosaics here depict Ganymede, cup-bearer to the Gods, in characteristic Phrygian bonnet, a portrait of Venus or maybe the lady of the house, and a snake-haired Head of Medusa in the changing room of the bathhouse.

Discovered in 1811, opened to the public in 1815 and still housed in antique thatched buildings, the excavations may well have been visited in the following few decades by some of the eclectic group of artists gathered under the patronage of the 3rd Lord Egremont at **Petworth House** (West Sussex GU28 0AE, 01798 342207). JMW Turner was a regular guest, and 19 of his paintings can be seen in their original setting. Along with scores of Old Masters, it adds up to one of the best examples of Regency taste in art, architecture and landscape. The Turners include several views of the Thames near Windsor, the celebrated *Egremont Sea Piece* and view of the new Chichester Canal. Most Romantic of all is *The Lake, Petworth: Sunset, Fighting Bucks* (1828), showing the 'Capability' Brown lake and park with an impressive fallow deer herd (the largest in England). The Countess of Egremont was a patron of William Blake, whose incredible illustration to Milton's *Paradise Lost* 'Satan Calling up His Legions' hangs here, along with characters from Spenser's *Faerie Queene* and *A Vision of the Last Judgement* (1808). For the previous eight years, Blake lived at Felpham, on the coast, having visions of angel ladders and being inspired by the fresh air and wide views to write his epic poem *Milton*, incidentally penning in his *Preface to Milton* (1804) lyrics now more famous as the hymn *Jerusalem*. He described Felpham as the 'sweetest spot on earth' and 'more spiritual than London' and his cottage can still be seen in the town. Eventually, though, the visionary poet tired of his chief patron William Hayley's 'polite disapprobation' and insulted a drunken soldier sent to look after the garden. Tried for High Treason in the church of **Greyfriars** (Priory Park, call Chichester Museum, 01243 784683), he was acquitted and soon after returned to London.

a choice of five caesar salads and seven varieties of ploughman's, including own-made pork and egg pie, and the garden itself is a miniature wonderland of ponds and paths. Interesting puddings might be Drambuie and oatmeal bavarois, or strawberry, elderflower and champagne terrine. From an eclectic wine list, English wines such as the local Nyetimber are likely to be available. With a roaring fire in winter and innumerable ales poured direct from their barrels, this is a lovely pub in which to idle away an afternoon with a pint.

Fox Goes Free

Charlton, West Sussex PO18 0HU (01243 811461/www.thefoxgoesfree.com). **Lunch served** noon-2.30pm, **dinner served** 6.30-10pm Mon-Fri. **Meals served** noon-10pm Sat, Sun. **Main courses** £8-£17.95. **Rates** £80 double. **Credit** AmEx, MC, V.

This 300-year-old country inn in the village of Charlton takes its name from William III's stopovers while on hunting trips to the Goodwood estate. These days, though, the low, dark-timbered nooks and large breezy garden play host to families and friends kicking back for a few pints and some hearty pub grub. A definite cut above, the menu here features dishes such as roast partridge with cabbage and bacon, and grilled cod with garlic butter and prawns rather than the scampi in a basket staples you might otherwise associate with country-boozer dining. Sundays are especially popular (with both locals and visitors) for the huge traditional roast dinners. There are always a few options for veggies (risotto, for example) and a good choice of beers and wine. Lovely views across the Downs from the apple tree-filled garden are another plus. Upstairs are five B&B rooms.

George & Dragon

Burpham, West Sussex BN18 9RR (01903 883131). **Lunch served** noon-2pm daily. **Dinner served** 7-9pm Mon-Sat. **Main courses** £10.95-£19.95. **Credit** AmEx, MC, V.

A winding Downland road from Arundel heads to this sweet little village (pronounced 'burfam'), complete with a rose-clad lychgate before the 12th-century flint church (where Mervyn Peake is buried in the churchyard). Just up the lane beyond the pub is a cricket pitch occupying a large Anglo-Saxon hillfort with wonderful views that once guarded the Arun Valley. The pub itself is pretty ancient, with an 18th-century smugglers' spinning jenny set in the ceiling, a simple way to settle arguments over the spoils that came upriver. The place is now narrowly more restaurant than pub, with an elegant dining area offering a menu full of Modern European fare (such as game terrine with celeriac remoulade or freshly baked tartlet of crab and tiger prawn with a sweet chilli dressing). Main courses might be whole sea bass, slow-cooked pork belly with root vegetable and plum sauce, confit of duck leg, or fillet steak with portobello mushrooms. An excellent variety of thick-cut sandwiches are also available at the bar.

St Martin's Organic Tearooms

3 St Martin's Street, Chichester, West Sussex PO19 1NP (01243 786715/www.organictea rooms.co.uk). **Meals served** 10am-6pm Mon-Sat. **Main courses** £5-£10. **No credit cards**.

Add a health-conscious dimension to your weekend away with lunch at this wholesome tearoom. Housed in an old terraced house sympathetically renovated in the 1970s, St Martin's is a charming labyrinth of nooks and crannies, as quiet and restful as the day is long. On offer are carefully prepared organic, mostly vegetarian dishes (fish sometimes features), including soups, salads, quiches and risottos. A selection of tempting cakes and desserts (apple crumble, chocolate sponge, scones, banana and walnut loaf) adds a vaguely sinful touch and there's a lovely garden for alfresco summer eating. An infectiously peaceful vibe throughout makes this a fine place to while away an hour or two.

36 on the Quay

47 South Street, Emsworth, Hampshire PO10 7EG (01243 375592/www.36onthequay.co.uk). **Lunch served** noon-1.45pm Tue-Fri. **Dinner served** 7-9.45pm Tue-Sat. **Set lunch** £18.95 2 courses, £23.95 3 courses. **Set meal** £45 3 courses, £65 10-course tasting menu. **Rates** £95 double; £130 £155 suite. **Credit** AmEx, DC, MC, V.

Fantastically located in a 17th-century quayside building, 36 on the Quay has a reputation for outstanding Modern British food. The setting is a pretty and pastel-coloured dining room with a large bay window that makes the most of the views. There's an emphasis on fish dishes (roasted brill with a mussel, onion and parsley chowder or sea bass fillet on a warm potato niçoise salad, for example), although there's plenty to tempt meat fans too. Desserts are worth saving space for, as is the British cheese plate. Alternatively, the sensational ten-course evening tasting menu (available by request at lunchtime) is surprisingly uncomplicated and beautifully balanced. Accommodation includes a room with a view over the water, three smaller B&B rooms and a small cottage.

White Horse Inn

1 High Street, Chilgrove, West Sussex PO18 9HX (01243 535219/www.whitehorse chilgrove.co.uk). **Lunch served** noon-2pm Tue-Sun. **Dinner served** 7-10pm Tue-Sat. **Main courses** £14.95-£20. **Rates** £95-£150 double. **Credit** MC, V.

Dining at this pub-restaurant-B&B is always an occasion. Organic fare and fresh meat and fish are the specialities: starters might include Selsey crab and avocado or black pudding mousse with bubble and squeak; mains span hearty organic steaks, seared tuna and an array of seasonal specials. There are also comfortable B&B rooms available (handy if the extensive wine cellar proves a little too tempting) and a very attractive garden with views on to open countryside.

Isle of Wight

A real treasure island.

The cost of the ferry crossing from Portsmouth to the Isle of Wight might seem pricey (given that it's only 3.9 miles across the sea), but once you arrive you'll agree that it's worth every penny. Wightlink Ferries (0870 582 7744, www.wightlink.co.uk) has a 24-hour shuttle service and a five-day return costs £48 for a car and up to four passengers, although special offer rates are often available online.

It's worth it because the roads, particularly outside the holidays, are quiet, and because the views, journeys, walks, landscapes and outdoor activities to be enjoyed here on land and water are as exhilarating as anything you'd get on the mainland, without spending five frustrating hours in the car to get to them. It's worth it because there aren't hundreds of dubious 'attractions' to annoy adults and disappoint children once you do get there. And it's worth it because it feels like stepping back in time to a genteel vision of Britain that's a welcome respite from urban grunge, traffic jams and MP3 players on buses.

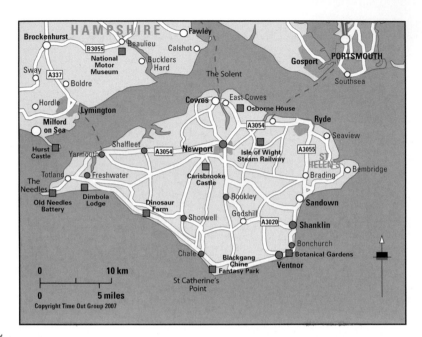

Copyright Time Out Group 2007

Accommodation	★★★☆☆
Food & drink	★★★☆☆
Nightlife	★☆☆☆☆
Shopping	★☆☆☆☆
Culture	★★☆☆☆
Sights	★★☆☆☆
Scenery	★★★☆☆

This is not to say that the Isle of Wight has become stuck forever in a rose-tinted version of England's past; changes, mostly for the better, have been trickling through the island's crevices during the past couple of years. Hotels have been upgraded and refurbished and excellent restaurants have opened that, combined with the natural beauties that abound here – the crumbling chalk cliffs, the downs, the creeks, the groynes and the landslips – create the perfect British getaway. From Tennyson Down, named in honour of the poet who lived nearby and described the air as being 'worth sixpence a pint', the Isle of Wight lies before you like a child's fantasy island. To the north-west, the River Yar flows out to the Solent past the castle guarding Yarmouth harbour at the far western tip of the island, the jagged chalk line of the Needles, jutting from the sea, ends with a red and white lighthouse; to the south is the great crumbling sweep of Compton Bay, while further south the sheer cliffs of Blackgang Chine fall dramatically (and literally) into the Channel.

Little England

Often described as recreating the whole of southern England in miniature, the island's 147 square miles contain rolling farmland, marshy estuaries, castles, cliffs, vineyards, beaches, steam trains and antique tube trains, Roman villas, dinosaur fossils, red squirrels and a whole clutch of manor houses. During the 1800s, visitors poured in from all over Europe to enjoy the water, the sea air and the balmy climate. Tennyson made his home, Farringford, at Freshwater (it is now a hotel) and the poet Swinburne was born (and buried) in Bonchurch, which is also where Dickens wrote *David Copperfield*; and the Russian writer Turgenev conceived his most famous novel, *Fathers and Sons*, while visiting Ventnor for the bathing. Meanwhile, at Dimbola Lodge, Tennyson's neighbour, the Victorian photographer Julia Margaret Cameron was taking pictures of whoever she could persuade to sit still long enough and developing the results in the coal shed. Charles I was held in the hilltop Norman Carisbroke Castle (near Newport, 01983 522107, www.english-heritage. org.uk) before being taken back to London to be executed. And, of course, Queen Victoria spent summers with her family at Osborne House (York Avenue, East Cowes, 01983 200022, www.english-heritage.org.uk), built in the style of an Italian villa and beautifully maintained since her death in 1901.

Today, the most popular areas for tourists are the East Wight resorts of Shanklin and Sandown, where daytrippers from the mainland swarm along the tat-filled promenade. The rest of the island is blissfully free of visitors, however, even at the height of summer. For unrivalled peace and quiet, visit in the winter when most of the attractions are closed, and the footpaths stretch out empty for miles and miles along spectacular coastline, particularly around the south-west of the island. But get here soon; this most beautiful part of the island is sadly disappearing into the sea, not inch by inch, but acre by acre. Every winter more cliffs collapse like a soufflé on to the beaches below, leaving fences and steps suspended precariously in mid-air.

The free pocket guide to the island (available on ferries and at tourist offices) is crammed with 'attractions', but unless it's raining stair rods and blowing a gale, give them a miss and explore the cliff paths, downs, woods, creeks and beaches instead. This is the best way to discover the Isle of Wight, a paradise for walkers, cyclists and horse riders. It boasts more footpaths per square mile than anywhere else in Britain – all meticulously signposted and maintained. The 77-mile coastal path around the island might be a bit much for a weekend, but to get a flavour of it take the train to Shanklin. Here you can join the path as it climbs up from the sea, before descending again through the mysterious ferny depths of the Landslip (so-called because much of it fell into the sea in 1810) to the pretty beach at Bonchurch. From there you can walk around Ventnor and – if you still have the energy – on to Steephill Cove and the Botanical Gardens and its Museum of Smuggling History, housed in the underground vaults (01983 855397, www.botanic.co.uk). Another lovely walk is along the north-west coast from Shalfleet to Yarmouth.

For beach fans, Sandown, Shanklin and Ryde offer all the traditional delights of miniature golf, amusement arcades and fish and chips. If that is your idea of hell, head for Compton Bay, a beautiful sweep of sand beneath collapsing cliffs, without a kiss-me-quick hat in sight. Here, surfers brave the waves, fossil hunters admire the casts of dinosaurs' footprints at low tide, kitesurfers leap and soar across the sea and paragliders hurl themselves off the cliffs.

Osborne House: if it was good enough for Queen Victoria…

Totland Bay, with good sand, clean water and views across the Solent to Hurst Castle, is a lovely place to watch the sun go down. It's also where you'll find the Needles Old Battery (01983 754772, www.nationaltrust.org.uk) Victorian fort, which also has spectacular views and was the site of secret rocket-testing in the 1950s and '60s. It may be the lack of people but there's still a mysterious, conspiratorial air about the place... you half expect to see a suspicious-looking foreigner being trailed by five meddling teenagers with a dog along the winding chalk paths. At high tide the beach all but disappears and the bay becomes a surfers' playground. Meanwhile, sailors weigh anchor in the natural harbours of Yarmouth, Cowes and Bembridge.

Many attractions are closed between the end of October and Easter, so phone ahead to check what's open when planning a visit. There are many seasonal events, including Britain's biggest walking festival in May, an international kite festival in July, a cycling festival in September and White Air, a festival of extreme sports, at the end of October. For information on cycling and walking, call Rights of Way (01983 823741, www.iwight.com) or get a map from a Tourist Information Centre (see below). For boat fans there is the Yarmouth Old Gaffers Classic Boat Festival during the May bank holiday weekend, the Round the Island Yacht Race in June and, of course, Cowes Week in August. Those looking for a quiet weekend might want to avoid this particular time as the place gets rammed. Also worth noting is the Isle of Wight Music Festival, which takes place in Newport in June (www.isleofwightfestival.com), and the increasingly popular Bestival (www.bestival.net), which, in 2007, is held from 7 to 9 September.

WHERE TO STAY

If you're looking for something outside the ordinary, how about a vintage Airstream caravan on a farm? Vintage Vacations (07802 758113, www.vintagevacations.com) has four of them, each sleeping four people and all boasting authentic, lovingly restored fixtures and fittings beefed up with mod cons such as CD players, toasters, air-con, heating and linen. Sited on a working rural farm, they have to be the ultimate in caravan chic, and are less expensive than you might think. The North Court (01983 740415, www.northcourt.info), meanwhile, offers another enticing rural option, this time near the tiny village of Shorwell, some five miles from the sea. A beautiful 17th-century manor house set in 14 acres of garden (including a grass tennis court), this was the former home of the deputy governor of the island and offers rare value for money: a panelled suite, including a sitting room with an 18th-century decorative plaster ceiling and an Adam period carved fireplace, can be had here for just £80 a night. The number of inns that also do good quality B&B are too numerous to mention, but the Crab & Lobster Inn (01983 872244, www.crabandlobster inn.co.uk) in Bembridge stands out for its sea views and food (see p106). Lugley's in Newport (see p106) also offers rooms for £75-£95 double.

George Hotel

Quay Street, Yarmouth, PO41 0PE (01983 760331/www.thegeorge.co.uk). **Rates** £180-£255 double. **Credit** AmEx, MC, V.
The bland exterior of this 17th-century townhouse – once home to the island's governor Sir Robert Holmes – hides what is undoubtedly one of the island's best hotels. Quiet luxury exudes from every wood-panelled inch, offering all the comforts of a five-star hotel, with the warmth and intimacy of a guesthouse. The 17 rooms are small, but this only adds to the feeling of cosiness, and the two balcony rooms, with large private terraces that lead directly to a delightful garden running down to the sea, are stunning. When the weather is good, breakfast is served in the garden (which looks out over the harbour and pier). When it's bad, a roaring fire makes the bar a fine place to have an aperitif before heading for dinner at the brasserie (the restaurant was closed for refurbishment as this guide went to press; see p106). If you're tempted out of this luxurious cocoon, there's an equally charming 13th-century town to be explored; wander down tiny lanes that end at the water's edge, while away time in tearooms and craft galleries, and walk to the end of the wooden pier to get a lovely view of the town and hotel (take a bottle of wine and some glasses, and really make the most of it).

Grange

9 Eastcliff Road, Shanklin, PO37 6AA (01983 867644/www.thegrangebythesea.com). **Rates** £80-£96 double. **Credit** MC, V.
Converted from flats into 17 nicely appointed modern rooms in 2005, the Grange is something of a curiosity in terms of accommodation offered.

(see p106)

TOURIST INFORMATION

Ryde
Isle of Wight Tourism, Westridge Centre, Brading Road, Ryde, PO33 1QS (01983 813818/www.island breaks.co.uk).
Ventnor
Coastal Path Visitors' Centre, Dudley Road, Ventnor, PO38 1EJ (01983 857220/www.coastalwight.gov.uk).

Outwardly, the late Georgian building seems like any other seaside hotel: extensive gardens lead to a gate through which it's a short stroll to the beach, the sitting room is welcoming and the dining room is pretty, with French windows leading to a flagstone terrace. But take a wander round the gardens and you're quite likely to chance upon a group practising tai chi or qigong, or honing their massage, dance or crime fiction writing skills. (The Grange offers short courses and weekly or weekend packages in a wide array of activities.) You don't have to take part in these; you can just book B&B and enjoy the laid-back ambience of the place (it's an honesty bar, sauna and friendly dog kind of place), but that might defeat the purpose of this relaxing escape from the day to day.

Priory Bay Hotel

Hambrough Hotel

Hambrough Road, Ventnor, PO38 1SQ (01983 856333/www.thehambrough.com). **Rates** £109-£169 double. **Credit** MC, V.

The seven-room Hambrough Hotel introduces the concept of boutique hotels to island life. Flat-screen TVs, DVD players, espresso machines, minibars and free Wi-Fi feature in all of the rooms, which – as you'd expect – have stylish contemporary fittings in neutral tones. There are splashes of colour in the bathroom tiling and soft furnishings, giving the place a dash of brightness, while cool greys hint at the vaguely art deco chic of the hotel's exterior. Bathrooms are gorgeous too, with underfloor heating and plenty of space. If you're lucky enough to be able to book one of the two luxury rooms (booking well in advance is advisable), it's quite possible that between the comforts of the room and the elegance of the seaview balconies you'll never make it down to the Ocean bar and restaurant (*see p106*); however, that would be a shame, because the Hambrough's attention to detail continues in the public spaces. The staff are uncommonly enthusiastic about their work; the barista was engaging several customers in a debate about the merits of different grappas on our recent visit.

Priory Bay Hotel

Priory Drive, Seaview, PO34 5BU (01983 613146/www.priorybay.co.uk). **Rates** £120-£180 double; £305-£2,000 3-4 nights cottage (sleeps 4). **Credit** AmEx, MC, V.

Taking a stroll around the 70 acres of this country hotel (which delightfully mixes medieval architecture with Tudor, Georgian and even 20th-century additions), or checking out the summer-season oyster bar flanking the beautiful private beach, it's easy to imagine yourself as the lord of the manor: playing the odd six-hole round of golf, taking a dip in the pretty outdoor pool before breakfasting heartily on the terrace or in the garden and making sure the oiks from the nearby caravan park don't wander in by mistake… life at the Priory Bay is very good indeed and, happily, the 18 rooms live up to the expectations created by the beauty of the exterior. In the older part of the building the cosy rooms are exotic and sensuous, a feeling heightened by dark, rich furnishings and decor. The newer parts of the building by contrast are much brighter, with huge windows, Georgian patterns, chaises longues and bright colours creating a languid air of bonhomie and age-old charm. Anyone for tennis?

Royal Hotel

Belgrave Road, Ventnor, PO38 1JJ (01983 852186/www.royalhoteliow.co.uk). **Rates** £140-£200 double; £170-£220 suite; £195-£240 family room (sleeps 4). **Credit** AmEx, DC, MC, V.

This grand old dame of the island hotels lacks the intimacy of the Hambrough or the Old House, but that's no bad thing if what you look for in a hotel is friendly, efficient service and luxurious

WIGHT LINES

If pootling around the lovely lanes and seaside towns in a 21st-century motor doesn't impart enough of a sense of the Isle of Wight as an Enid Blytonesque 'little England', the island's rail 'network' certainly will. At a mere 8.5 miles the Island Line is not so much a network as a small-scale electric railway that runs down the eastern side of the island to connect Shanklin with the ferry terminal at Ryde Head Pier (passing through Smallbrook Junction, where in summer months you can connect to the Isle of Wight Steam Railway to Wootton).

Board one of the Island Line's trains and you'll be taken back in time some 70 years to 1938. That's the date when the six little trains were manufactured – and keen-eyed

Londoners will feel a strong sense of déjà vu on boarding one, for these are refurbished London Transport tube stock (each train is made up of just two carriages), modified, repainted with a rather incongruous pink and blue dinosaur motif, and brought to the island in 1990 to replace even-more-ancient tube stock (1923) that had been running since 1967.

So what exactly are these geriatric Londoners doing here? Answer: they fit. Not in an 'aren't they quaint/just right for the olde England vibe' kind of way, but quite literally: they're the only trains that will fit through the Ryde Esplanade Tunnel. This short stretch of the line was prone to flooding so the road-bed was raised, thus reducing the tunnel's headroom to ten inches below that required for standard-sized trains. Where normal trains couldn't go, London's tube trains pluckily ventured.

In truth the trains are starting to show their age, and modern-day rail requirements, such as push buttons and warning panels, spoil the effects somewhat, but for anyone who's travelled on the London Underground, it's a delightful moment of recognition when you step into the carriage; and if you've time on your hands, it's well worth waiting for 007 or 009 – these boast the original LT red livery and really will take you back in time.

From February 2007, the line became part of the South Western Franchise. For further information on train times and schedules, see the website www.island-line.co.uk.

anonymity. There are 55 classically decorated rooms, many with wonderful views of the sea or perfectly tended gardens, along with numerous indoor and outdoor bars, lounges and seating areas. Add to this an outdoor (unheated) pool and a traditional restaurant menu and you have a fantastic country-hotel feel, with all the benefits of a pretty, lively town on your doorstep.

Seaview Hotel

High Street, Seaview, PO34 5EX (01983 612711/www.seaviewhotel.co.uk). **Rates** £120-£199 double; £195-£240 family room (sleeps 6); £499 wkend 2-bed self-catering cottage; £600-£2,000/wk self-catering cottage (sleeps 10). **Lunch served** noon-2pm, **dinner served** 6.30-9pm daily. **Main courses** £16.50-£22. **Credit** AmEx, DC, MC, V.

The award-winning Seaview is a small hotel situated in the centre of a popular sailing village, a minute's walk from the beach. It's surprisingly large, with 16 bedrooms, two bars and two restaurants serving excellent, fresh local produce. The Seaview gets booked up for long stays in the summer and is geared towards families. The children's menu includes dishes so sophisticated that they often tempt adults: mussels in cream and garlic, Seaview hot crab ramekin, macaroni cheese or fish pie, followed by summer berry eton mess or warm apple soup, ginger ice-cream and oat biscuits. Who needs nuggets? Dogs are welcome too. If there's no room in the hotel, two self-catering houses (one a former bank that sleeps up to ten – though this will no longer be available from Jan 2008; the other a fisherman's cottage with space for a family of four) are available.

Wellington Hotel

Belgrave Road, Ventnor, PO38 1JH (01983 856600/www.thewellingtonhotel.net). **Rates** £90-£135 double. **Credit** AmEx, MC. V.

Perched almost at the highest point of vertiginous Ventnor, the recently refurbished Wellington Hotel has one of the best locations in this pretty southern, old-fashioned town. Walk into your contemporary, simply furnished room and your sightline is an uninterrupted view of the sea, step out on to the wrought iron balcony and you're perched over the hotel's spacious, decked breakfast terrace (a steep flight of steps leads from here to the beach and the Spyglass Inn, *see p107*) and below that the town's rooftops. The fantastic sea views (in almost every room) lend a light, airy feel to the smallish rooms, which compensates for the cramped corridors that lead to them. Fixtures and fittings are far from first rate, but the beds are comfy and the rooms blissfully quiet.

WHERE TO EAT & DRINK

Sleepy Isle of Wight is fast becoming a foodie's heaven; along with the fine establishments we list below, excellent food can be had at a growing number of

Wellington Hotel

the island's pubs. Newtown estuary pub the New Inn (01983 531314, www.thenew-inn.co.uk) was the Isle of Wight Dining Pub of the year for 2002, 2003, 2005 and 2007. It's a wonderfully authentic and atmospheric coaching inn from 1743 but offers a thoroughly modern menu, with a special board that's as appealing as any restaurant's. The Crown Inn (Walkers Lane, 01983 740293, www.foodplanet.co.uk/crowninn) in the impossibly pretty thatched village of Shorwell is equally popular, and deservedly so. Located in the chalk downs and some prime island walking country, the beamed two-room lounge or shady garden are great places to stop for a wide-ranging and adventurous menu of food and ales (including Flowers, Tanglefoot and John Smith). The Bonchurch Inn (01983 852611, www.bonchurch-inn.co.uk), nestled under the steep cliffs of the pretty village from which it takes its name and centred around a cobbled courtyard, is definitely worth a visit; a one-time stables, the space is filled with curios and the courtyard is a lovely place in which to enjoy a pint in the sunshine. The delightfully spacious and sofa-stuffed 11th-century Red Lion (01983 754925) in Freshwater, West Wight, is another must if you're in the area. The inn is so popular that we advise you to book ahead if you are planning to try the excellent menu, which spans an enticing range from the imaginative – field mushrooms stuffed with crab and stilton, and Welsh rarebit-topped haddock – to the more traditional, such as fish cakes and ribeye steak.

If you're passing through Newport, Lugley's (33 Lugley Street, 01983 822 994, www.isleofwight.com) is a reasonably priced brasserie with rooms, and a good place to stop for top ciabatta sandwiches (smoked mackerel and horseradish ciabatta, say, or houmous and sun-blushed tomatoes on flatbread), served with excellent salt and pepper fries. The dinner menu is less café-like, and booking is recommended in the evening.

Thanks to its size, Rookley's Chequer's Inn (Niton Road, Rookley, 01983 840314, www.chequersinn-iow.co.uk) allows the different worlds of families and shooting parties to sit comfortably together and enjoy the tap ales, and an extensive menu majoring on fish and roasts. Its position, in the heart of the island, makes it a convenient and pleasant place to stop off while walking.

The George Hotel's (*see p102*) much-loved restaurant was closed for refurbishment as this guide went to press, but is expected to reopen in summer 2007 as an extension of the hotel's existing brasserie.

Baywatch Beach Restaurant

The Duver, St Helens, PO33 1RP (01983 873259). **Open** *Mar-Oct* **Breakfast served** 10.30am-noon, **lunch served** noon-5pm, **dinner served** 5.45-9.45pm daily. **Main courses** £7.50-£25. **Credit** MC, V.

Looking like a slightly rickety wooden train carriage with huge picture windows offering views out to sea, the Baywatch may not be as highly specified as a Conran-style gaff, but lovely touches like condiments sitting in little wooden boats hint at something special. During the day it's little more than an upmarket café on the beach serving top quality café lunches like crab and gruyère tartlet, Shetland Island moules, a gourmet burger or a selection of simple seafood dishes: cod, haddock, scampi, shell-on prawns, whitebait and so on. But for the evening this gorgeously located place dons its tux to offer a full restaurant menu, including pan-fried garlic langoustines, whole sea bass or the ultimate seafood platter. The emphasis is on simply cooked seafood and it's a winning proposition.

Buddle Inn

St Catherine's Road, Niton, Ventnor, PO38 2NE (01983 730243). **Open** 11am-11pm Mon-Thur; 11am-midnight Fri, Sat; noon-10.30pm Sun. **Lunch served** noon-2.45pm, **dinner served** 6-9pm daily. **Main courses** £6.95-£13.95. **Credit** MC, V.

Built in the 16th century as a farmhouse, this quaint clifftop pub manages to retain a sense of cosy bonhomie thanks to a huge inglenook fireplace, ancient flagstones and beams, and a wealth of old photographs that give it a personal, home-spun feel. Close to St Catherine's lighthouse at the southern tip of the island, and offering great views across the Channel, the inn has been a popular haunt for both smugglers and customs men for the 150 years it has been in business. The food menu is largely pub grub served in decent portions and there are always good real ales on tap, including local brews Godnams and Duck's Folly.

Light bar lunches also served. An adjoining bar in a converted barn, the scene of tea dances in World War II, is now a family room, with a pool table and games. This inn is the perfect place to take a break and enjoy the stunning sea views from the garden.

Crab & Lobster Inn

32 Forelands Field Road, Bembridge PO35 5TR (01983 872244/www.crabandlobster inn.co.uk). **Lunch served** *Summer* noon-3pm, **dinner served** 6-9.30pm daily. *Winter* **lunch served** noon-3pm, **dinner served** 6-9pm daily. **Meals served** 11am-11pm Sat; noon-10.30pm Sun. **Main courses** £4-£22. **Rates** £80 double. **Credit** DC, MC, V.

The Isle of Wight Dining Pub of 2006 is always busy but it's rammed at Sunday lunch – one look at the food and it's easy to see why. A largely seafood-based menu features mouth-watering dishes such as a half lobster with chips and salad (at just £12.95), crab cakes with fries, and seafood tagliatelle. There's a decent smattering of meat and veggie dishes too. All these are served by welcoming staff in a pretty outdoor area on the low cliffs or in the pleasant dining room, which adjoins a couple of cosy bar areas. The beer selection is as good as you'd expect, and the whole experience is pretty unbeatable – a neighbouring diner on our recent visit loudly declared his meal to be 'definitely the best pub food I've ever had'.

Ocean Bar & Restaurant

Hambrough Hotel, Hambrough Road, Ventnor, PO38 1SQ (01983 856333/www.the hambrough.com). **Lunch served** noon-2.30pm, **dinner served** 7-10.30pm daily. **Set lunch** £14.95 3 courses. **Set dinner** £35 3 courses. **Rates** £109-£169 double. **Credit** MC, V.

The latest addition to the island's culinary map. Unsurprisingly, given executive chef Simon McKenzie's CV – the Lanesborough, Gordon Ramsay and Marco Pierre White all feature – the food here is all about fresh, quality produce simply cooked. This approach makes for a necessarily small menu, but you'll still be spoilt for choice with starters such as pan-fried scallops or foie gras and mains including roasted English partridge and island mallard. Portions are large enough to satisfy, but small enough to leave room for the great puddings: exotic concoctions include cherry granita or lime and basil sorbet. If your interest in the ingredients extends to observing how the recipes are created, ask to be seated at the chef's table, which lies within feel of the kitchen and offers a great view of the action. If you do, the chef can devise a special tasting menu for up to eight people.

Hearty grub and great sea views at the Spyglass Inn.

Pond Café

Bonchurch Village Road, Bonchurch, PO38 1RG (01983 855666/www.thepondcafe.com). **Lunch served** noon 2.30pm, **dinner served** 7-10.30pm daily. **Main courses** £10.50-£14.50. **Credit** MC, V.

This tiny restaurant in the pretty village of Bonchurch just north of Ventnor is related to the boutique Hambrough Hotel (*see p103*) – and is every bit as slick a venture. Opened in June 2003 by chef David Thomson, the cosy and light-filled space provides a great counterpoint to the brooding vertiginous setting of the village, and offers a creative, daily changing menu with an emphasis on seasonal food. An excellent-value prix fixe early evening menu includes a perfectly balanced pea and mint soup, and tangy calamares as starters, fusilli with dolcelatte and walnuts, and oxtail with olive mash for mains, while the chocolate nemesis with ice-cream and almond biscotti is every bit as good as it sounds. A lovely post-dinner walk through this atmospheric and fascinating village should be all you need after such a feast, and there's always the Bonchurch Inn (*see p105*) to warm up in afterwards.

Priory Bay

Priory Drive, Seaview, PO34 5BU (01983 613146/www.priorybay.co.uk). **Lunch served** 12.30-2.15pm, **dinner served** 7-9.15pm daily. **Set lunch** £15.50 2 courses, £18.50 3 courses. **Set dinner** £23 2 courses, £29.50 3 courses. **Credit** AmEx, DC, MC, V.

At 'the country house hotel by the sea', dinner is an elegant, refined affair: from the sumptuous seascape frescoes that decorate the gold and azure Island dining room to the excellent (and good value) food served within it. Starters such as White Island tomato soup and Priory game terrine are subtle and delicate but full of flavour, while mains such as line-caught local sea bass, fillet of turbot and chargrilled local asparagus risotto offer delicious alternatives to the excellent meat dishes; among them fillet of Brading lamb and Highland fillet of beef. Desserts are inventive takes on traditional puddings; a crème brûlée is delicately flavoured with lavender and served with baby poached pear, rhubarb and custard is wittily reworked as rhubarb soufflé with custard ice-cream. If you're looking for a less formal affair, the bar and terrace menu in the brasserie is reasonably priced and just as appealing as the Island Room's fare.

Spyglass Inn

The Esplanade, Ventnor, PO38 1JX (01983 855338/www.thespyglass.com). **Open** 10.30am-11pm Mon-Sat; 10.30am-10.30pm Sun. **Lunch served** noon-9.30pm Mon-Sat; noon-9pm Sun. **Main courses** £6.95-£9. **Rates** £70 double. **Credit** MC, V.

There are two good reasons to sample a beer or two from the extensive and impressive range on offer at the Spyglass; one is the brilliant beachside location and the other is the surreal mass of seafaring objects and memorabilia that festoons every inch of the spacious quarry-tiled interior. A huge patio means you can enjoy wonderful sea views while partaking of reasonably priced traditional pub grub from an extensive menu. Dishes such as baked spuds, sausage and mash and seafood chowder may not win any food accolades, but if you're looking for a great spot in which to tuck into some hearty grub, this is the one. And you can walk off the huge portions with a rambling walk to the nearby Botanical Garden.

Isle of Wight

South Hams

Beautiful beaches and classy coastal towns.

The lush valleys and snaking rivers of the South Hams – frankly, the posh bit of Devon – are a magnet for golfers, water-sports enthusiasts and retirees, as well as a growing number of urban downshifters. To the west of Tor Bay and stretching from Dartmoor's rocky foot to the English Channel, the area's thriving market towns, spectacular coastline and chocolate-box scenery make it an ideal escape from the pace of city life. As a result, property prices have shot up in the past five years and continue to rise.

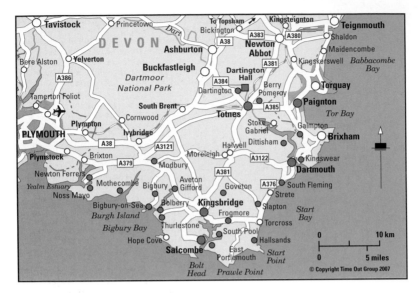

The attraction is obvious. Devon has some of the most stunning coast in the country. In summer it's all sparkling seas and sandy coves; in winter, rugged cliffs and roaring waves. Hedgerows, strewn with stunning wildflowers, frame every lane in the spring, while autumn sees glorious sunsets and balmy afternoons. Green lanes are a distinctive feature – ancient packhorse and drovers' tracks comprise a network of hidden routes running between tall hedge banks. *Exploring Green Lanes in the South Hams*, by Valerie Belsey, describes 24 such circular routes in the area.

There are some fine beaches (many of which are great for swimming, snorkelling, surfing, windsurfing and kitesurfing), secluded coves and wonderful coastal paths. This is also good sailing country, particularly around the Yealm estuary, Salcombe and Dartmouth.

Totnes, Kingsbridge and Dartmouth are the area's significant towns. All serve the local population year round and are by no means merely tourist destinations; Kingsbridge has little in the way of tourist attractions, although there are some interesting shops and a farmers' market. Many of the area's pretty inland villages lie along its rivers – the Dart, Erme, Yealm and Avon. To the west of the area around the Yealm estuary are some of the most picturesque villages imaginable. Noss Mayo and Newton Ferrers are havens for yachtie types and admirers of picture-postcard scenery. The villages enter into a little friendly rivalry as to which one is superior; the truth is that each has its

pros and cons. Noss Mayo is on the South West Coast Path and you can take a wonderful stroll through the village and wood that run along the river out to the sea. Here the path takes you along the cliffs and the Eddystone lighthouse in the far distance. You can take a circular walk from the National Trust car park at Worswell, with a lunch stop at the refurbished Ship Inn (see p119).

At low tide you can cross the Voss, the path between the two villages; at high tide you will need to take the longer walk or short drive through the lanes. As well as some delightful cottages, Newton Ferrers has a few small food shops and a good pub. The Dolphin Inn (1 Riverside Road East, 01752 872007, www.thedolphininndevon.co.uk) serves decent pub grub and a good range of real ales. Perch with a beer in the garden at the front, overlooking the river.

In Noss Mayo, the sweet Swan Inn (Pillory Hill, 01752 872392) offers outdoor seating, overlooking the public quay with fabulous views.

The River Erme reaches the sea at Mothecombe and the vast expanse of sand at low tide is a favourite with walkers and horse riders. There is a car park (this is privately owned by the estate; charges apply from Easter until the end of September) with a rather steep hill down to the beach, but the walk is well worth it. The beach is overlooked by the Flete Estate (01752 830253, www.flete.co.uk), the location for the film adaptation of Jane Austen's *Sense and Sensibility*.

South Hams

Accommodation	★★☆☆☆
Food & drink	★★★☆☆
Nightlife	☆☆☆☆☆
Shopping	★★★☆☆
Culture	★★☆☆☆
Sights	★☆☆☆☆
Scenery	★★★★★

Further around the coast are the wonderful beaches of Bigbury and Bantham, on either side of the Avon estuary; both are favoured spots for surfers along this stretch of coast. There are also growing numbers of kitesurfers, who make interesting viewing from the beach, café or pub.

You can undertake the eight-mile walk along both banks of the river via the 15th-century bridge at Aveton Gifford. Parking is available at both beaches and there is a good beach café at Bigbury, run by Venus (see p112). Just off the coast is Burgh Island with its splendid 1920s hotel (see p117), accessible at low tide by foot, or on a bizarre sea tractor. The hotel grounds are off-limits to daytrippers, but it is possible to book a table for lunch or dinner. Alternatively, you could settle for a pint and a baguette in the 14th-century smugglers' pub, the Pilchard Inn, and enjoy the views.

Further down the coast, Hope Cove is a pretty crab- and lobster-fishing village offering bracing walks and a welcome watering hole in the form of the Hope & Anchor. Just beyond, Bolt Tail juts into the sea, offering a fabulous view back to Bigbury Bay. This is the start of a breathtaking five-mile walk, across Bolberry Down, where the coastal path winds its way to Bolt Head, the rocky promontory that guards the mouth of the estuary. Heading east, you reach Salcombe, one of the most southerly towns in England. In the summer, it's heaving with second-homeowners, expensive yachts and the odd celebrity, earning it the sobriquet 'England's St Tropez' – much to the chagrin of the locals, who complain that the prices of property and eating out have spiralled out of control in recent years. In the winter, Salcombe is something of a ghost town, with many shops and restaurants closed until at least the school half-term in February. Having said all that, the place has good reason to be popular. Its position overlooking the water, the white sandy beaches, quaint fishermen's cottages, stylish nautical shops and choice of pubs and restaurants are all strong enticements.

Near Bolt Head, in the village of Sharpitor, is the clifftop Overbeck's Museum & Garden (01548 842893, www.nationaltrust.org.uk), an imposing Edwardian house owned until 1937 by the eccentric scientist Otto Overbeck. The upper floors are given over to a youth hostel (01548 842856, www.yha.org.uk), but downstairs you'll find a fascinating display of taxidermy, shipbuilding exhibits and a number of the scientist's bizarre inventions – look out for the Rejuvenator, a machine intended to extend human life expectancy. The terraced, subtropical gardens cover six acres and boast incredible views towards Salcombe.

From Salcombe's Ferry Steps, regular boats (Salcombe Ferry Company, 01548 842364) will take you to the scenic village of East Portlemouth, from where you can walk along the craggy cliffs to Gara Rock and Prawle Point. Look out for seals around Mattiscombe Beach, a secluded, sandy cove with plenty of rock pools to explore. Otherwise, there is little besides rugged coastline until you round the bend of Start Point, where the treacherous waters are littered with shipwrecks. There's a bracing walk downhill from the car park to Start Point lighthouse (01803 770606, tours available in summer).

From here you can take the coast path to 'new' Hallsands, a rather desolate hamlet at the end of a shingle beach, which replaced the original village after a local (and man-made) disaster. Controversial dredging along the beach at the turn of the 19th century undermined the natural shingle breakwater, and a heavy storm in 1917 destroyed the once-thriving fishing village. All that remain are some crumbling ruins clinging to the cliffs. Beyond Hallsands, you'll pass the hamlet of Beesands before arriving at Torcross, where you can get a latte, ice-cream or something a little more substantial at the

TOURIST INFORMATION

Dartmouth
The Engine House, Mayor's Avenue, Dartmouth, Devon TQ6 9YY (01803 834224/www.discoverdartmouth.com).
Kingsbridge
The Quay, Kingsbridge, Devon TQ7 1HS (01548 853195/ www.kingsbridgeinfo.co.uk).
Modbury
5 Modbury Court, Modbury, Devon PL21 0QR (01548 830159/ www.modburydevon.co.uk).
Salcombe
Council Hall, Market Street, Salcombe, Devon TQ8 8DE (01548 843927/www.salcombe information.co.uk).
Totnes
The Town Mill, Coronation Road, Totnes, Devon TQ9 5DF (01803 863168/www.totnesinformation.co.uk).
www.discoverdevon.com
www.south-hams.co.uk

beachside Seabreeze (01548 580697, www. seabreezebreaks.com), or head for the Start Bay Inn for its renowned fish and chips.

Heading up the coast towards Dartmouth you will pass Slapton Sands. This dramatic three-mile stretch of shingle beach is where Allied troops practised manoeuvres for the D-Day landings. In 1944, during a surprise German attack, 946 men lost their lives. Spot the Sherman tank in the car park – recovered from the water, it serves as a memorial. On the other side of the road is Slapton Ley Nature Reserve – the West Country's largest natural freshwater lake and home to some of the rarest birds in Britain. Just inland from the beach is the quaint little village of Slapton, which has a friendly pub, the Tower Inn (01548 580216, www.thetowerinn.com, *see p120*), offering good food, board games and a cosy fire. Outside is a large and attractive beer garden, overlooking the eponymous tower. Further along the coast road, as Start Bay opens up ahead, the scenery is so awesome that traffic slows as drivers take in the view. About three miles south of Dartmouth along the scenic coast road is the village of Stoke Fleming, where there are breathtaking cliff walks. Just beyond is the beautiful, golden shingle beach – with a pine forest backdrop – known as Blackpool Sands; it's clean, dog-free year round and has good facilities. Various water sports are available here: ask in the shop for details of tuition and equipment hire.

In addition, the Venus beachfront café dispenses everything from ice-creams and lattes to organic sandwiches and salads.

The South Hams' western coastline ends around Dartmouth. The steep drive into the town reveals the picturesque estuary and the pretty village of Kingswear across the water. In summer, Dartmouth's narrow streets – lined with cafés and boutiques, galleries and yachting emporia – are packed, and there is no denying the parking chaos. The Regatta (since 1839) takes place in late August (always including the last Friday in the month) and sees the town reach gridlock. Conversely, much of Dartmouth shuts down in January, when major redecoration is undertaken. It can be pleasantly quiet out of season, but, obviously, places to eat and stay are rather more limited.

Dartmouth has a long and interesting history: it was the departure point for the second crusade in 1147, the Pilgrim Fathers had their leaking boats repaired here en route to America (faulty work necessitated another stop at Plymouth), and during World War II, US warships set off for the Normandy beaches from here.

Dartmouth Castle (01803 833588, www.english-heritage.co.uk), completed in 1403, was the first in Britain to be purpose-built for artillery warfare. Perched on the cliffs near the mouth of the estuary, it is best reached in the summer by ferry from Dartmouth's South Embankment.

In the centre of town, the 'boat float', an attractive harbour for small craft, is overlooked by the Royal Castle Hotel (*see p118*). Beyond the boat float is the Promenade, which stretches the length of the waterfront along the Embankment and is a great place to take in some sea air or eat fish and chips – just beware of the greedy seagulls. There is also a wide choice of more sophisticated eateries and some superior pubs. Should you feel the need to get out of town – and you probably will in high season – there are some fabulous beaches and villages nearby. A ferry trip up the River Dart to Totnes is a lovely way to pass an afternoon. Riverlink (01803 834488,

www.riverlink.co.uk) provides cruises up and down the Dart between Totnes and Dartmouth most days during the season, taking about one and a quarter hours each way; a possible outing – even in poor weather – as you can remain under cover. The times vary according to the tides. A light-hearted commentary provides a bit of background and sights to look out for include the contemporary – Sharpham vineyard and creamery – as well as more ancient ones, such as Walter Raleigh's house. Spotting herons and cormorants is a bonus. For a shorter trip, just across the River Dart, lies Kingswear: a sweet Balamory-esque village, with pastel-painted cottages tightly packed on the hillside. On a headland to the east is the National Trust-owned Coleton Fishacre (01803 752466, www.nationaltrust.org.uk), an Arts and Crafts-style house with an art deco

Burgh Island Hotel

interior, built in the 1920s for Rupert D'Oyly Carte, son of impresario Richard. The grounds are a gardener's delight, incorporating woodland and rare rainforest species and a myriad of paths leading out to the cliff edge.

Dittisham (pronounced 'Ditsum' by locals) is a delightful yachting village on the banks of the Dart with a couple of friendly pubs and a riverside café. There are some wonderful walks along the river. For a fabulous place to stay try the Fingals Hotel (see p118).

If you want to leave the car behind, there is a small Dartmouth to Dittisham ferry running March to October. Once in Dittisham, you can ring the bell outside the Ferry Inn and summon a ferry across to the magical woodland Greenway Gardens (Galmpton, Churston Ferrers, 01803 842382, www.nationaltrust.org.uk), the former home of Agatha Christie. While the house is owned and occupied by her daughter and closed to the public, the National Trust is responsible for the garden (visitors by car must pre-book a parking space). There are plans to open the house to the public in 2008.

About 12 miles from Dartmouth, via the A3122 and A381, is Totnes, a bustling, ancient market town that has become a bit of a New Age centre. Herbalists, healers and alternative therapists have set up shop here (with names such as Inspirations, Crystals, Stoned – and the Conker Shoe Company), as well as artists in every discipline. There is a lively market every Friday and Saturday, where you can pick up anything from second-hand furniture and vintage clothes to fresh fish and handmade breads. There is also a monthly farmers' market in the Civic Hall, selling a wide range of local produce. Numerous buskers, hair-braiders and artists enliven the market area and the main strip, Fore Street. On Tuesdays during the summer months there is also an Elizabethan market, when locals in period garb sell handmade and second-hand goods and clothing for charity.

The history of the town stretches back to Saxon times when a fortified settlement was built to protect the upper reaches of the River Dart from Viking invasion. During the 16th century, Totnes was among the 20 richest towns in England, due largely to the Dartmoor tin and cloth trades. Fore Street runs up the steep hill from the Dart to the castle at the top of the town. It contains at least 60 examples of 16th-century buildings, so it's worth looking above shop-window level. Don't miss the Brutus stone (set into the pavement outside No.51); legend claims it's the stepping stone used by the founding king of Britain to reach the shore in 1170 BC.

South Hams

Amid the wide range of shops, selling everything from organic vegetables to incense, is the fine period building housing the Elizabethan Museum (70 Fore Street, 01803 863821, www.devonmuseums.net). It contains displays charting the town's history and a room dedicated to its best-known former residents, including Charles Babbage (1791-1871), inventor of the early precursor to the computer.

It's worth stopping off at the beautiful 15th-century red sandstone church of St Mary. Behind the church is the colonnaded Guildhall (01803 862147, www.totnestowncouncil.gov.uk), built around 1533 on the site of the former 11th-century priory. The council chamber, former magistrates' court and town gaol are all open to the public.

During the Civil War, both sides used the town as a base, and you can still see the table where Oliver Cromwell planned his local campaigns in 1646.

Totnes has some great eateries and food shops, including the fabulous Ticklemore Cheese Shop (1 Ticklemore Street, 01803 865926). If you are planning a picnic, make a beeline for award-winning Effings (50 Fore

TAKE ACTION

Messing about in boats is the primary source of entertainment around here, though walking and cycling are fabulous too.

BOATING

Devon Sailing
11 Smith Street, Dartmouth TQ6 9QR (01803 833399/www.devonsailing.com).

Dittisham Sailing School & Boat Hire
Anchorstone Café, Manor Street, Dittisham, Dartmouth TQ6 0EX (01803 722365).

Salcombe Powerboat School
Bolberry House, Bolberry, Salcombe TQ7 3DY (01548 842727/ www.salcombepowerboats.co.uk).

CANOEING

Canoe Adventures
1 Church Court, Harberton, Totnes TQ9 7UG (01803 865301/ www.canoeadventures.co.uk).

HORSE RIDING

Sorley Riding School
Loddiswell Road, Kingsbridge TQ7 4EH (01803 762750/www.sorleyridingschool.co.uk).

SURFING

Discovery Surf School
4 Belle Vue Rise, Hooe, Plymouth PL9 9QD (www.discoverysurf.com).

WATER SPORTS

Lushwind
07849 758987/www.lushwind.co.uk.

On Blackpool Sands
01803 770606/ www.blackpoolsands.co.uk.

Seabreeze Sports
Torcross, Kingsbridge TQ7 2TQ (01548 580697/www.seabreezebreaks.com).

Dartmouth

Street, 01803 863435), a foodie's paradise stocked with wonderful cheeses, charcuterie, breads and takeaway dishes prepared by the on-site chef. There are also a few tables at the back of the shop where you can enjoy a light lunch or a coffee and croissant.

Totnes Castle (01803 864406, www. english-heritage.org.uk, open Apr-Oct) sits perched on top of its grassy knoll giving uninterrupted 360-degree views over the town and surrounding countryside. Built shortly after the Norman conquest, it was one of the first stone forts to be constructed in Devon and it is an excellent example of a motte-and-bailey design. During the summer months the castle is a venue for special events; local theatre companies perform here, and there are medieval pageants, archery displays and court jesters.

At the bottom of town lies the area known as the Plains and over the bridge is Bridgetown. A short walk from here, Steamer Quay, with its riverside café and wooden playship, is the departure point for riverboat cruises to Dartmouth (Riverlink, 01803 834488, www.riverlink.co.uk). If you'd rather travel up towards Dartmoor, South Devon Railway steam trains (0845 345 1427, www.southdevonrailway.org, closed Nov-Mar) depart from the beautifully preserved station a short walk from the Totnes main-line station (follow the handy brown signs). The picturesque journey (it lasts about an hour and a half) along the river takes you to Buckfastleigh on the edge of Dartmoor.

Dartington Hall (01803 847100, www. dartingtonhall.com), just outside Totnes, is a world-renowned arts education centre and valuable cultural resource for Totnes and the South west. The medieval hall is magnificent – built in the late 1300s by the Earl of Huntingdon, it was saved from dereliction in 1925 when it was purchased by Dorothy and Leonard Elmhirst. The Elmhirsts turned the hall into a progressive school with creative, anti-authoritarian values (it closed in 1987). The Dartington Hall Trust now runs the estate – which is home to a number of organisations, including Dartington College of Arts – and promotes education and the arts. There is a year-round programme of cultural events, concerts, open-air theatre and film screenings and workshops. For details of what's on, including the Barn Cinema, which largely shows arthouse and foreign films, visit www.dartingtonarts.org.uk (box office 01803 847070). There is also a good pub at the hall, the White Hart (01803 847111, www.dartingtonhall.com), based in what would have originally been the kitchens of the 14th-century building. The menu relies on specified local producers, rather than an airy 'locally sourced and organic where possible', and the results are very good. The public is free to wander around the beautiful grounds and admire the ancient trees, plants and topiary and discover the number of sculptures hidden around the gardens. Also on the estate is the former headmaster's home, High Cross House, a fine example of 1930s architecture. It is now a gallery showcasing the Elmhirsts' own art collection. On the edge of the estate, a walk down the drive will lead you to the Dartington Cider Press Centre at Shinners Bridge (01803 847500, www.dartingtonciderpress.co.uk), where Dartington glass can be viewed and bought as well as work by local artists, clothing and jewellery. There are also a couple of cafés and gift, book and toy shops.

On the Paignton side of Totnes is the village of Berry Pomeroy, which also has a magnificent ruined castle (01803 866618, www.english-heritage.org.uk, open Apr-Oct) reputed to be the most haunted place in Britain; the wooded site certainly feels a bit eerie. The outer walls still stand and encircle the remains of a residence started by the Duke of Somerset but never completed. Excellent audio tours are available for a small charge and there is a café offering refreshments and surprisingly good Sunday lunches.

WHERE TO STAY

The wonderful Lamper Head (Cornworthy, Totnes, TQ9 7HF, 01803 722220, www.lamperhead.com), designed and constructed by architect Roderick James, opened in 2006. The stylish oak-framed coastal retreat (between Totnes and Dartmouth) sleeps 11 and houses an art collection, Italian furniture, a state of the art sound system, as well as extras including yoga sessions, massages and a chef for hire.

With lovely sea views, and overlooking the River Dart, Nonsuch House (Church Hill, Kingswear, 01803 752829, www.nonsuch-house.co.uk) is a great B&B run by Kit and Penny Noble. Kit also cooks up a storm in the kitchen.

Buckland-Tout-Saints Hotel & Restaurant

Goveton, nr Kingsbridge, Devon TQ7 2DS (01548 853055/www.tout-saints.co.uk). **Lunch served** noon-1.45pm, **dinner served** 7-8.45pm daily. **Set lunch** £12.95 2 courses; (Sun) £19.95 3 courses. **Set dinner** £30 3 courses. **Rates** £135-£185 double; £245 suite. **Credit** AmEx, MC, V.

Arriving at this 300 year-old country-house hotel is like stepping into the best kind of period drama. Off the beaten track, just a few miles from Kingsbridge, the hotel was sensitively refurbished in 2006 and several new bedrooms added. The panelled public rooms are sensational, enjoying views of the rolling parkland, which includes a croquet lawn and dovecote. In addition to the ten

Riverside relaxation at Dart Marina's Wildfire Bar and Bistro.

traditionally furnished original rooms, the six new rooms feature more contemporary decor. All rooms are en suite and individually styled. Golfing breaks are a speciality and midweek dinner, bed and breakfast mini-breaks can be enjoyed at favourable rates. Dogs are welcome in the grounds, but not the house. The award-winning restaurant is highly regarded locally and open to non-residents, who need to book in advance. Expect French-influenced cooking with dishes such as smoked salmon roulade stuffed with prawns, rocket salad and horseradish dressing or roast local rump of lamb served with dauphinoise potatoes and red wine sauce.

Burgh Island Hotel

Bigbury-on-Sea, Devon TQ7 4BG (01548 810514/www.burghisland.com). **Set lunch** £38 3 courses. **Set dinner** £55 3 courses. **Rates** DB&B £320-£340 double; £380-£500 suite. **Credit** MC, V.

Reached by sea tractor, over the sand on foot or by hotel-run taxi, depending on time and tide, this island is a one-off. The splendid hotel started life as a high-society hideaway in the late 1920s and '30s, for the likes of Noel Coward and Agatha Christie. Edward VIII even brought Wallis Simpson here. Since then, the hotel has had its ups and downs, but it has now been carefully restored to all its art deco glory, complete with many orig-inal pieces of furniture and classic bathrooms equipped with thoroughly modern REN toiletries. Rooms, named after famous visitors such as Amy Johnson, are decorated with appropriate memorabilia. It's a glamorous and grown-up place, not quite of this century. Televisions are out and cocktails are most definitely in, with dances held in the ballroom and guests encouraged to dress up. The Irish chef, having spent time in Australia, puts some fantastic fusion dishes on the menu – roast cod steak, lobster, nameko mushroom, spring onion, green-tea noodle, dashi broth, for example. Well respected for his fish cookery, he produces consistently good and imaginative food, often sourced locally. In fact, if you take a dip in the magical mermaid pool, you may even swim past your supper, as the lobster pots are positioned there to ensure a fresh catch. The island's ancient pub, the Pilchard Inn, has one bar reserved for residents of the hotel and serves great beer and food cooked in the hotel kitchen.

Browns Hotel & Bar

27-29 Victoria Road, Dartmouth, Devon TQ6 9RT (01803 832572/www. brownshoteldartmouth.co.uk). **Tapas served** 6.30-9pm Tue-Sat. **Tapas** £2.50-£9. **Rates** £85-£170 double. **Credit** AmEx, MC, V.

This stylish townhouse hotel in the centre of Dartmouth offers 'a modern take on an Edwardian house party', according to the guest book. There are ten individual (cosy, not huge) rooms decorated in earthy tones, many with attractive wooden beds, animal prints and textured finishes. Downstairs in the lively bar you can relax on the squashy sofas with a coffee or enjoy a selection of tapas and a glass of wine. Tapas are also served as sharing plates in the adjoining dining room and include some excellent use of authentic ingredients such as chorizo, pimientos de padron, queso manchego and membrillo, with a Spanish-led wine list to match. Breakfasts, complete with own-made sausages, are super.

Dart Marina

Sandquay Road, Dartmouth, Devon TQ6 9PH (01803 832580/www.dartmarina.com). **Lunch served** noon-2pm, **dinner served** 6.30-9pm daily. **Main courses** £15-£19. **Set lunch** £19.95 3 courses. **Set dinner** (non-residents) £28.95 2 courses, £35.95 3 courses; (pre-booked, residents only) £25 3 courses. **Rates** £195-£275. *Apartment* £225-£315. **Credit** MC, V.

Overlooking the estuary, this waterside hotel is frequented by both yachties and landlubbers. The new health spa with indoor pool, therapy rooms (offering Elemis treatments) and a fitness suite, is a particular draw, as are the 12 brand new luxury self-catering apartments that are perfect for short breaks. The stylish rooms are complemented with bathroom treats, fluffy robes, a laundry service, and some have superb views too. You hardly need to leave the complex as top-notch Modern British food can be enjoyed at the fancy River

Restaurant (where breakfast is served) or the more relaxed Wildfire Bar and Bistro. The nearby Floating Bridge pub is handy for casual meals and sandwiches. The town centre is a short walk away. Picnics can be arranged for boat trips up the River Dart.

Fingals

Coombe, Dittisham, Devon TQ6 0JA (01803 722398/www.fingals.co.uk). **Dinner served** 7.30-9.30pm Tue-Sat. **Set dinner** £30 4 courses. **Rates** £80-£160 double. **Credit** AmEx, MC, V.

Halfway between Totnes and Dartmouth, Fingals is a family-run, relaxed place to stay. The carefully restored and extended 17th-century farmhouse is set in delightful gardens, with quirky sculptures and the charms of croquet and lawn tennis on offer. There's also a heated conservatory pool, sauna, jacuzzi and visiting masseuse. Rooms are predominantly of the English country mould, but in the best possible taste. Families may want to opt for the stunning, self-catering barn, while the two-floor 'folly', a tiny old mill house with a four-poster bed and an upstairs balcony overlooking the stream, offers privacy for couples. There are roaring fires and antique carpets in the sitting room, books and sofas in the library, and dinner can either be taken dinner party style in the panelled dining room, with convivial host Richard Johnston and the other guests, or at your own table in the adjoining room. Closed January and February.

New Angel Rooms

51 Victoria Road, Dartmouth, Devon TQ6 9RT (01803 839425/www.thenewangel.co.uk). **Rates** £120-£140 double; £150 suite. **Credit** MC, V.

The six rooms in this converted Victorian house close to the centre of town are named after celebrity chef John Burton Race's children. All the rooms are en suite and individual in style with quirky artwork decorating the walls. To set the mood, a complimentary half bottle of champagne awaits you, with a wide variety of speciality teas and other goodies. The rooms are well appointed with swanky bathrooms and stylish modern decor. Breakfast, cooked by the New Angel chef, is taken downstairs. Parking can be arranged. Getaway packages include a course at the New Angel cookery school (learning how to prepare seasonal local produce), accommodation, and dinner at the fabulous New Angel restaurant (*see p120*).

Royal Seven Stars Hotel

The Plains, Totnes, Devon TQ9 5DD (01803 862125/www.royalsevenstars.co.uk). **Lunch served** noon-2.30pm, **dinner served** 6-9.30pm daily. **Main courses** £7.50-£15.95. **Rates** £99-£130 double. **Credit** MC, V.

This privately owned hotel at the centre of Totnes has recently been refurbished to a high standard and now boasts 16 attractive individually styled rooms. All rooms are en suite, some with jacuzzi. A former coaching inn, and sister hotel to the Royal Castle in Dartmouth, the hotel has accommodated Daniel Defoe no less, as well as various royals attending Dartmouth Naval College.

Royal Castle Hotel

11 The Quay, Dartmouth, Devon TQ6 9PS (01803 833033/www.royalcastle.co.uk). **Lunch served** noon-2.30pm, **dinner served** 6-10pm daily. **Main courses** £10-£20. **Rates** £125-£199 double. **Credit** AmEx, MC, V.

This hotel in the centre of Dartmouth has plenty of charm. The rooms at the front of the building have wonderful views over the boat float (an attractive harbour for small craft), Royal Avenue gardens, the estuary and the sea beyond. Built up around an Elizabethan courtyard, with lots of Tudor fireplaces, priests' holes and nooks and crannies to add to the atmosphere, it has been restored sensitively. The rooms are all individual – with none of the bulk-bought fixtures and fittings of large hotel chains – and many boast brass or

One word: book. It pays to be prepared at the New Angel.

four-poster beds and spa baths. The communal areas of the hotel are all comfortably furnished and there is a choice of bars, from the traditional pub-style Galleon, to the trendy, if rather stark, Harbour Bar. The recently revamped restaurant on the first floor offers great views as well as locally sourced, organic food. Special mini-break deals are available, including dinner, B&B or three nights for two in low season.

Thurlestone Hotel

Thurlestone, nr Kingsbridge, Devon TQ7 3NN (01548 560382/www.thurlestone.co.uk). **Lunch served** 12.30-1.45pm Sun. **Dinner served** 7.30-9pm daily. **Main courses** (lunch) £9.25-£14.50. **Set dinner** £35 4 courses. **Rates** £174-£238 double; £184-£252 family room; £224-£350 suite. **Credit** AmEx, MC, V. This large and well-regarded four-star hotel in the quaint seaside village of Thurlestone is still family owned after more than 100 years, and has the traditional high standards of service that come with such length of experience, and excellent facilities. Most rooms have palatial, glass-fronted balconies with views out to sea, while 'village view' rooms come in a tad cheaper. The interior of the hotel is very comfortable and entertainments include a heated outdoor pool with fabulous views, indoor pool and gym, plus a hair and beauty salon (using Decléor products). If golf is your thing, the hotel offers concessions on fees at both Bigbury and Dartmouth courses, and the Thurlestone links course is only five minutes away. In fine weather, lunch and drinks can be taken on the attractive terrace commanding expansive views of the bay. The restaurant makes good use of Devon produce and fresh fish. Simpler dining can be had at the adjoining Village Inn or Rock Pool Bistro.

WHERE TO EAT & DRINK

Diners have plenty of choice in upmarket Salcombe. In addition to the places listed below, also recommended by locals is Dusters (50 Fore Street, Salcombe, 01548 842634), an unpretentious, light and uncluttered bistro that has jazz on Sundays; booking is advisable.

Totnes also has some great eateries – over 40 at the last count. As well as the listed restaurants, locals recommend Fat Lemons Café (1 Ticklemore Court, Ticklemore Street, 01803 866888), with its pretty courtyard, delicious cakes and meze menu as well as wholesome vegetarian main courses served in an informal, unhurried setting. Just a few minutes from the centre of town, the Steam Packet Inn (St Peter's Quay, 01803 863880, www.steampacketinn.co.uk) is also an extremely pleasant place to sit out and have a coffee, glass of something or light meal.

The delightful gastropub, the Ship Inn (Noss Mayo, 01752 872387, www. nossmayo.com), is conveniently placed

along the circular walk from Worswell (*see p110*), and serves local and regional beers, and a daily menu focused on seasonal produce. Expect starters such as Morecambe Bay prawns on a buttered crumpet, mains like steak and ale pie with creamy mash. Simple ploughman's and sandwiches also feature. In the winter, log fires and newspapers are laid on, in summer you can eat out on the terrace.

There are a number of other notable pubs in the area, many overlooking the water and providing excellent food. In Tuckenhay, the Maltsters Arms (01803 732350, www.tuckenhay.com) offers several cosy rooms inside, jazz some evenings and a quayside barbecue as well as a daily changing menu. Just up the road, the Watermans Arms, with its outdoor tables, is another popular choice. In Dartmouth, the Windjammer (Victoria Road, 01803 832228), a family-run freehouse featured in the CAMRA Good Beer Guide, is a great place for a quiet pint and offers a seasonal menu. The atmospheric Cherub (13 Higher Street, 01803 832571, www.the-cherub. co.uk), dating from 1380, is Dartmouth's oldest building, and also CAMRA-recommended. Jan and Freddie's Brasserie (10 Fairfax Place, Dartmouth, 01803 832491, www.janandfreddiesbrasserie. co.uk; closed Sun) is rightly popular – try Devon mussels followed by Blackawton beef – as is the Dolphin pub (5 Market Square, 01803 833835), where a superb Sunday lunch is served. Over the water in Kingswear, the Ship Inn (High Street, 01803 752348) offers scrumpy and the last of the evening sun.

Alf Resco

Lower Street, Dartmouth, Devon TQ6 9JB (01803 835880/www.cafealfresco.co.uk). **Meals served** 7am-2pm Wed-Sun. **Dinner served** *Summer* 6.30-9.30pm daily. **Suppers** £10-£25. **Rates** £75-£85 double. *Self-catering apartment* £350/wk. **No credit cards**. Alf Fresco is a proper Dartmouth institution. The front courtyard is a splendid place for watching the world go by, while the interior has the intimacy of a bustling ship's cabin. Music is an important feature and weekends see local musicians strumming their stuff, often with a flamenco or jazz flavour. In the summer, managers Pete and Kate serve up weekend 'rustic suppers', which could feature anything from authentic Mexican dishes to an evening of sea shanties and locally caught seafood. The house salads and meze/charcuterie plates are also very popular. It's a Wi-Fi hotspot too, so you can check your mail over a hearty full English. They'll even provide the laptop if you don't have your own. If you can't bear to leave, there are two rooms with sea views available upstairs.

New Angel

2 South Embankment, Dartmouth, Devon TQ6 9BH (01803 839425/www.thenewangel.co.uk). **Breakfast served** 8.30-11am, **lunch served** noon-2.30pm Tue-Sun. **Dinner served** 6.30-10pm Tue-Sat. **Main courses** £19-£25. **Credit** AmEx, MC, V.

You'll have to book well in advance (often weeks) to eat at award-winning chef John Burton-Race's fantastic New Angel. This is an elegant, contemporary space with an urban-chic rather than beachside feel – though the sea is smack bang in front of you. Pricing is ambitious but justifiable, with top-class food and service. A starter of Diptford duck egg salad, with organic bacon, cos lettuce and parmesan/caesar dressing is a sublime mix of flavours and textures. New Angel lobster salad, tarragon mayonnaise, tomato dice and vinaigrette is another wildly successful dish. Note that the New Angel is closed for the whole of January.

Oyster Shack

Milburn Orchard Farm, Stakes Hill, Bigbury, Devon TQ7 4BE (01548 810876/www.oystershack.co.uk). **Meals served** *Summer* 9am-9pm daily. *Winter* 9am-9pm Tue-Sun. **Main courses** £8.95-£15.25. **Credit** MC, V.

The Oyster Shack – 'that seafood place' – is renowned. Always absolutely packed, booking is essential whatever day you choose to visit. The setting's part of the fun, with outdoor tables and a general air of busy, garlicky joyousness, but the main draw has to be the ultra-fresh seafood: own-farmed mussels and oysters, pan-fried sardines, potted shrimp, shell-on prawns and whatever the catch of the day is. If you don't fancy simple oysters au naturel or cracked crab, main courses are imaginative. Roast gurnard with white chilli beans and parma ham is a typical example. Note that the restaurant can be accessed from the tidal road at low tide from Aveton Gifford; it is signposted from the A379 travelling in the direction of Kingsbridge.

A new Oyster Shack opened in Salcombe in December 2006 (Hannaford's Landing, 10-13 Island Street, Salcombe, 01548 843596).

Pig Finca

The Old Bakery, The Promenade, Kingsbridge, Devon TQ7 1JD (01548 855777/www.pigfinca.com). **Meals served** 10am-3pm, 6-9.30pm Tue-Sun. **Main courses** £6.50-£12.95. **Credit** MC, V.

Opposite the quay and set back from the street, two doors down from the Ship, this little place has a slightly secretive hidden away feel. There's a lively Spanish vibe, with bright pink walls, young staff and cool music. Courtyard tables back and front, and dining upstairs or down, allow you to seek peace and quiet, sun or shade, whatever your preference. The wide-ranging day and evening menu (plus specials) is based around fine local organic ingredients as well as imported delicacies from the likes of Spanish food specialist Brindisa.

Breakfast might comprise morcilla (Spanish black pudding) or organic chorizo with free-range eggs; lunch perhaps Pig Finca meze platters, either vegetarian – including delights such as own-made houmous and artichoke hearts – or mixed, with boquerones, white fin tuna and other goodies. The evening menu gets a bit more elaborate with the likes of aromatic (organic) lamb tagine or roasted red peppers stuffed with pine nuts, garlic and herbs. A well-chosen and reasonably priced wine list includes treats that fit the menu, such as Manzanilla sherry or cava.

Rumour Wine Bar

30 High Street, Totnes, Devon TQ9 5RY (01803 864682/www.rumourtotnes.com). **Lunch served** noon-3pm Mon-Sat. **Dinner served** 6-10pm daily. **Main courses** £8.95-£15. **Credit** AmEx, MC, V.

Kick off an evening at this popular café-cum-wine-bar by sampling one of its decent range of beers (Erdinger, Leffe and Abbot ale are all on the menu) or wines by the bottle or glass. Your whetted appetite will not be disappointed by the well-priced menu and its imaginative, seasonal dishes. Try crab and celeriac cakes with lemon salsa or pan-fried john dory with buttered samphire, roast new potatoes and creamy leek sauce. Alternatively, legendary 'build your own' pizzas are handmade on the premises. It is essential to book for dinner.

Tower Inn

Church Road, Slapton, Devon TQ7 2PN (01548 580140/www.thetowerinn.com). **Meals served** *Summer* noon-2pm, 7-9pm daily. *Winter* noon-2pm, 7-9pm Tue-Sat. **Main courses** £9.95-£18.50. **Rates** B&B from £60. **Credit** MC, V.

This 14th-century inn, tucked away in the teensy village of Slapton, is appreciated by locals for its well-kept beers (St Austell, Adnams Best, Tanglefoot) and fine food. The cooking relies on local ingredients put together simply but creatively. At lunchtime, expect dishes such as trio of local sausages with mustard mash, while the evenings might see Thai fish cakes or cod on a purée of butter beans. On warm days, take lunch in the charming walled garden; when the weather turns, head indoors and snuggle up by the fire in the low-ceilinged bar. The B&B side offers three en suite doubles.

Waterside Bistro

10 Symons Passage, The Plains, Totnes, Devon TQ9 5YS (01803 864069). **Meals served** noon-3pm, 6-9.30pm daily. **Main courses** £9.95-£14.95. **Credit** MC, V.

A deservedly popular bistro serving up wine, coffee, cream teas and an imaginative lunch and dinner menu. Fresh fish features extensively, and you'll find dishes such as pan-fried tiger prawns with coriander, chilli and garlic really hit the spot.

There is a well-priced, wide-ranging wine list, featuring local Sharpham Dart Valley Reserve, among other more distant producers. Dessert wines are served by the glass to accompany lovely puds such as sharpham brie and grape chutney with french bread. Service is charming, even at the busiest times. Weather permitting, sit out back by the river and soak up the laid-back Devon vibe.

Willow

87 High Street, Totnes, Devon TQ9 5PB (01803 862605). **Meals served** 10am-5pm Mon, Tue, Thur; 9am-5pm, 7-9.30pm Wed, Fri, Sat. **Main courses** £7.20-£8.50. **No credit cards.**

Willow is a popular vegetarian café with high standards regarding food origins. The menu is global in feel with dishes such as caribbean casserole or fennel and melon risotto. Source is often specified, as are the ingredients' vegan/organic/gluten-free status. Light meals or more substantial dishes such as 'spicy frijoles': beans, pepper salsa, sour cream and cheddar cheese, wrapped in organic flour tortilla are available. There's a pretty courtyard at the back, helpful staff and a back room with a pile of toys for kids. The self-service counter offers freshly prepared salads, wheat-free quiches and caffeine-free alternatives to tea and coffee (as well as full-strength, fair-trade versions of the latter). There's a curry night on Wednesdays and music sessions on Friday nights. These are always pretty busy, so it's worth booking in advance if you can. Willow is also a mobile-free zone.

Wills

2-3 The Plains, Totnes, Devon TQ9 5DR (01803 865192/www.willsrestaurant.co.uk). **Meals served** 9am-4pm Mon; 9am-4pm, 7-9.30pm Tue-Fri; 9am-3pm, 7-9.30pm Sat; 9am-3pm Sun. **Main courses** £10.95-£19.95. **Credit** AmEx, MC, V.

Local boy explorer William Wills has his statue just opposite, and was also born in this Regency townhouse. These days locals flock to the house for quite a different reason. The restaurant offers a cooked to order Modern British-style menu, with plenty of imagination. On the ground floor there is a café for morning coffee, afternoon teas and light lunches. Like many Devon eateries, local free-range products are used where possible – in fact the stated aim at Wills is to purchase 80% of products locally and this is evident in the menu. Delicious starters might include sharpham brie, date and fig salad with toasted almonds or scallop and mushroom ravioli. Mains are also good: Avonwick lamb chops and salad potatoes with damson sauce; monkfish with braised lentils. Desserts like chocolate fondant or rice pudding finish things off nicely. Afternoon tea is also served.

Winking Prawn

Main Road, North Sands, Salcombe, Devon TQ8 8JW (01548 842326/www. winkingprawn.com). **Meals served** *Easter-Oct* 10.30am-9.30pm daily. *Nov-Easter* Sat, Sun, hours vary. Phone for details. **Main courses** £9.75-£19.95. **Credit** AmEx, DC, MC, V.

A friendly and relaxed café, and the only eaterie at North Sands, this place is reminiscent of beachfront cafés in more exotic locations. Sit outside in the garden on sunny days and soak up the view – and the rays – or head indoors to the creamy wooden tables when the evenings get chilly. The lunch menu incorporates baguettes, simple fish dishes, fruits de mer and excellent skin-on fries. In the evening more sophisticated options such as monkfish wrapped in smoky bacon on spinach mash appear on the menu. Meat and limited vegetarian options are also available, plus great nursery style puds. Winking Prawn is deservedly popular and booking is essential in the evening (but not necessary at lunch).

Old-fashioned charm awaits at the Royal Castle Hotel.

South Hams

Falmouth & the Roseland Peninsula

Cornish tasties.

The surf lessons, beach party and stag do image of holidays in Cornwall may dominate the headlines, but the area around Falmouth and the Roseland Peninsula is like another world – and a dreamy one at that. The merging of two river estuaries has created endless watery escapes, be they silent wooded creeks or secluded beaches with surprisingly clear waters. Add to this charming villages, excellent restaurants and a lively arts town, and you have a great mix for a weekend away, whatever the time of year. Famously favoured by surrealist artists (Lee Miller, Roland Penrose, Max Ernst, Man Ray et al) in the 1930s, the glamorous yachting set in the 1950s and '60s, and a string of A-listers including Pierce Brosnan, the Prince of Wales, Kate Winslet, Claudia Schiffer and Kofi Annan in recent years, the sheer beauty of this waterside haven could not ask for a more impressive string of endorsements.

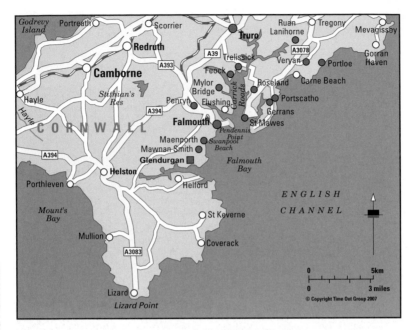

Dominated by the Carrick Roads, a large flooded river valley (or ria) that divides the area into two very distinct and different parts, the Fal Estuary presides over an intoxicating merge of landscapes and histories. Protected from the relentless Atlantic swell by the vast granite bulk of the Lizard Peninsula to the south and west, the rolling green hills that dip gently into the calm sea are a far cry from the rugged cliffs and pounding surf of Cornwall's north coast. Created after the last Ice Age, when meltwater caused the sea level to rise dramatically, the Carrick Roads is a large natural harbour (the world's third largest, after Rio de Janeiro and Sydney). Today, the vestiges of a long and prosperous maritime history (made rich by the Packet Ship trade, the docks and the pilchard boom), live on through the countless ships and sails that dot the horizon of this sailing paradise, while the rich crop of quality restaurants, pubs and hotels marks the proliferation of a burgeoning upmarket tourist trade.

All around the estuary there are lush, tranquil wooded creeks to explore. The Roseland Peninsula is quiet and sparsely populated – even in the busy summer months, it somehow seems to escape the hordes of holidaymakers that take over the north coast, remaining instead a haven for urban refugees and yachties. Tucked below the high open fields that form the peninsula's broad back, narrow lanes weave through dense woodland and skirt around idyllic creeks penetrating miles inland, either totally as nature left them or watched over by whitewashed granite cottages perched on the water's edge. On the peninsula's eastern flank, beautiful stretches of beach sit, often empty, looking out over sheltered bays and calm, translucent blue seas.

A short ferry ride across the mouth of the estuary to Falmouth presents a stark contrast. A bustling town put on the map by its historic docks, colourful maritime history (recognised by the National Maritime Museum here) and highly acclaimed art college (now University College Falmouth), pretty Falmouth combines its continuing working heritage with the kind of bohemian charm you find in St Ives and a moderate yachtie vibe. The

TOURIST INFORMATION

Falmouth
28 Killigrew Street, Falmouth, Cornwall TR11 3PN (01326 312300/www.go-cornwall.com).
St Mawes
Roseland Visitor Centre, Millennium Rooms, The Square, St Mawes, Cornwall TR2 5AG (01326 270440/www.acornishriver.co.uk).
www.falriverlinks.co.uk
www.swcp.org.uk
www.walkcornwall.com

Accommodation	★★★★☆
Food & drink	★★★☆☆
Nightlife	★☆☆☆☆
Shopping	★☆☆☆☆
Culture	★☆☆☆☆
Sights	★☆☆☆☆
Scenery	★★★★★

Enjoy boutiques and beaches in upmarket St Mawes.

town has also seen a boom in its creative industries in the last five years, something that's also stamped its mark on the place.

The mild year-round climate brought on by the Gulf Stream (it's not uncommon to see daffodils in November) also makes this a perfect habitat for subtropical plants, many of which can't be found anywhere else in the UK. Lush testament to the zeal of the Victorian plant hunters who brought back specimens from all over the world, the area's plentiful gardens contain plants from the Himalayas, Japan, China, Indonesia, Bermuda and the Andes, to name a few. Even outside these magnificent gardens, dracaena palms and bright blue agapanthus punctuate many a household flowerbed or suburban avenue.

At high tide, the river is navigable all the way to Truro, with regular passenger ferries making the trip every day (Easter-end Oct, call 01326 313234 for details).

St Mawes

Running 15 long miles from the A39 between Truro and St Austell, the A3078's sharp bends wind for miles across the spine of the Roseland, sweeping across open fields framed with pretty Cornish

Smuggler's Cottage

St Mawes has two town beaches: both are thin strips of sand revealed at low tide, with sheltered clear bathing water and sunny south-facing aspects. A short walk along the narrow road up to the headland leads to St Mawes Castle. Like its larger sister across the water, Pendennis Castle (*photo p123*), St Mawes Castle was built between 1539 and 1543 to defend against attacks from the French and Spanish that never came. When the castle was finally threatened with some serious action in the Civil War, its occupants quickly surrendered it to Parliamentarian forces, hence preserving its immaculate state (it is one of the finest, most complete examples of Henry VIII's chain of south-coast forts).

St Mawes Castle has the same clover-leaf design as Pendennis, but the three semicircular bastions that surround the four-storey central tower make it the more architecturally distinguished of the two. This castle also enjoys the benefits of its remote location; where Pendennis Point (below the castle on the Falmouth side) sees ice-cream vans, daytrippers and canoodling teenagers crowding the car park day and night, St Mawes enjoys nothing but pure, exposed rocks and fresh panoramic seascapes.

Back in town, there's a limited selection of shops and art galleries to browse, although Falmouth is by far the better option for a full day's shopping. In St Mawes, your best option is Onda (also owned by the Polizzis), up the 'ope' (narrow alleyway) by the Victory Inn (Victory Steps, Victory Hill, 01326 270456). This boutique contains a stylish selection of clothes and accessories by both renowned and local designers. Just down the road, Chalmers & Short (1 The Quay, 01326 270998) is an upmarket deli offering divine food and drink in a stylish café-wine bar setting. It's a great spot to enjoy a coffee and pain au chocolat while perusing the papers or simply gazing out over the harbour.

hedges and dipping down through wooded valleys as panoramic vistas of the sea flit by from time to time. Attractive as it may be, a couple of return trips to Truro or Falmouth along this road are certainly enough to make you swear to take the boat or King Harry ferry next time (it shortens the journey by at least 40 minutes). The only vehicular crossing of the Fal, King Harry (01872 862312, www.kingharry-info.co.uk; £6.50 return with car, 20p per foot passenger) is one of only five remaining chain ferries in the country. Crossing a narrow section of the Fal flanked on either side by thick woods, the five-minute ferry crossing may be short, but it's spectacular.

At the end of the A3078, stunning St Mawes has been a swanky holiday destination since Edwardian times. Neat whitewashed cottages and smart townhouses cling to the hillside above the small, sheltered harbour, with the dramatic shapes of dark Monterey pine trees framing the skyline on the brow of the hill behind. Across the clear, sheltered mouth of the Percuil River, the views of St Anthony lighthouse – again framed by Monterey pines – have graced the covers of many a glossy holiday magazine citing comparisons with the South of France. The Riviera-style gloss of this exclusive retreat was given further polish in 1999 by the renovation of the Hotel Tresanton by celebrated interior designer Olga Polizzi.

To the lighthouse

The striking St Anthony Head Lighthouse (c/o Trinity House, 01255 245011, www.trinityhouse.co.uk) was built in 1834, although a coal beacon burned at this crucial location for hundreds of years beforehand. Playing a critical part in guiding ships to safety both in the Carrick Roads and on the perilous Manicles Reef to the south, this lighthouse was also the set for the 1980s television series *Fraggle Rock*. The many defensive batteries around this point demonstrate its strategic importance throughout World War I and II. These days, it's a delightful spot to potter around and take in the sweeping coastal views to either side of this narrow finger of land, with benches conveniently placed at peaceful points along the path.

In the summer (1 Apr-30 Oct), take the St Mawes to Place ferry (07791 283884, daily every 30 mins, from 10am-4.30pm) across the Percuil River, then follow the pretty coast path around to the lighthouse. Alternatively, the journey takes around 20 minutes from St Mawes by road.

Just above the lighthouse, the South West Coast Path skirts along the top of the cliffs towards the old pilchard port of Portscatho, commanding great views over the broad sweep of Gerrans Bay all the way. Pilchards, which dominated the Cornish fishing industry in the 19th century and brought relative wealth to these tiny coastal communities, were not just used for food and trade; their oil also fuelled local lamps. Along the coast path just past Portscatho is Porthcurnick Beach, a sheltered and delightfully undeveloped sweep of sand; a mile or so further is the larger stretch of the lovely Pendower Beach, which extends a couple of miles, backed by dunes and low cliffs.

Around the Roseland Peninsula

There are plenty of beautiful spots to explore just a stone's throw from St Mawes. If you take the coastal path around from the castle and head inland/north up the shore, the views west across the Carrick Roads towards Mylor, Feock and Trelissick are superb. Wind slightly

St Mawes Castle

eastwards up St Just Creek to reach St-Just-in-Roseland Church, set in steep subtropical gardens on the side of the creek, with its sandbar and moored yachts. The granite church was consecrated in 1261, but evidence suggests there was building here as far back as 500. It is a breathtaking spot: 'to many people the most beautiful on earth', as John Betjeman gushed.

Further north, the Carrick Roads split into the River Fal and the Truro River, the latter being the wider and deeper of the two (navigable all the way to Truro at high tide). At Tolverne, 500 yards' walk from King Harry ferry, is Smuggler's Cottage (01872 580309, open Easter-Oct), a beautiful thatched cottage in an attractive location on a small grassy promontory, backed by woods. These days the picturesque spot is a regular stop for the boat trips chugging up the river to Truro – thanks in no small part to the cottage's excellent cream teas – but 60 years ago it played an important part in World War II, when it was requisitioned by the Admiralty in the build-up to the D-Day landings.

The River Fal, with its muddy floodplains of tufty grass, meanders through woods and fields (a bird lovers' paradise) up to the tranquil village of Ruan Lanihorne. This area grew rich on the pilchard boom and naval patronage in the 19th century, although it's hard to imagine it as anything other than the beautiful, sleepy backwater it is today. Near here, the King's Head (Ruan Lanihorne, 01872 501263, www.kingsheadruan.co.uk) is a popular gastropub that comes with plenty of glowing local recommendations.

It's worth taking the time to pay a brief visit to Veryan, a pretty village made famous for its curious thatched and crucifix-topped roundhouses, built in the 19th century by a local minister for his five daughters. Constructed without any corners, these houses apparently ensured that the devil would have nowhere to hide. There are also a couple of good local craft shops and galleries in the village.

A few miles on, follow the signs for Portloe and take the narrow lane down to this pristine fishing village, with its whitewashed and pastel-painted granite cottages tightly packed around a steep rocky inlet and harbour. Although the local fishermen still sell the day's catch on the small pebbly beach here, the smart four-wheel drives and Mercedes parked up the hill tell a very different story of the village's full- and part-time inhabitants. The coastal path heading westwards from here gives yet more stunning coastal views back towards the Roseland and nearby Gul Rock; poking dramatically out of the sea, this is a nesting ground for an array of seabirds.

Falmouth Harbour

Falmouth

The ferry crossing between St Mawes and Falmouth takes around 25 minutes. St Mawes Ferry Company (01872 862312) runs a daily service all year round.

Thriving, bustling Falmouth has many more accommodation, eating and drinking options than the peninsula opposite. It may not have the miles of glorious, unspoilt countryside, but is a convenient base if you want more than to simply hole up and chill out in luxury for the weekend. Its buzzing arts scene, which has grown up around the highly acclaimed University College Falmouth, pushes the boundaries further than Cornwall's mainstream watercolour-seascapes genre and lends the town a more cosmopolitan, progressive edge. The annual Falmouth Festival of Literature and Arts (www.falmouthfestival.co.uk, every Sept) includes an impressive programme of talks, workshops and performances from some of the UK's finest writers (the 2006 Festival featured the likes of John Hegley, Philip Marsden, William Dalrymple and Mark Lynas), as well as exhibitions from a varied mixture of local painters, artists, printmakers, sculptors, photographers, furniture makers and other craftsmen. In November, the annual Cornwall Film Festival (www.cornwall-film-festival.co.uk) gets bigger every year, and is also well worth checking out.

It may still has some way to go, but Falmouth is witnessing the beginnings of a budding café culture, which, mixed up with the countless traditional purveyors of cream teas, fish and chips, pasties and souvenirs, gives the place a colourful yet slightly confused personality.

To the south of Pendennis Point, a string of sandy beaches – interspersed with classic rock-pooling territory at low tide – face out over calm blue waters, often dotted with the white sails of yachts or large tankers taking shelter in the bay. Backed by a number of hotels (including the grand, imposing Falmouth Hotel, which was the town's first purpose-built tourist accommodation when it opened in 1865), Falmouth's beaches may lack the rugged natural beauty of the Roseland, but are a pleasant counterpoint to the busy town. The water is surprisingly clear (Gyllyngvase Beach boasts a European Blue Flag), and the light in the bay can be superb.

Until the 17th century, Falmouth was no more than a fishing village; Penryn was the main town, with Pendennis Castle proudly protecting the mouth of the river. Established as the chief base for the Packet Ships in 1689, which took the first international mail to the Continent and the colonies, Falmouth developed quickly. Its massive natural harbour – the first or last stop before heading out or back across the Atlantic, and a safe haven to ride out bad weather – ensured the town's fortunes.

Carrick Roads is the last remaining oyster fishery in Europe that is still dredged under sail and oar, with over 15 traditional working boats on duty between October and March. The beginning of the season is celebrated every October with the Falmouth Oyster Festival (01872 224367, 01326 312300, www.falmouthoyster festival.co.uk). Three days of lavish culinary celebrations are held in the impressive Events Square outside the National Maritime Museum, including cookery shows by celebrity chefs, local craft and produce markets, Falmouth Working Boat races and champagne- and oyster-tasting aplenty.

The aforementioned museum is housed in a stunning teaked wooden building (Discovery Quay, 01326 313388, www.nmmc.co.uk) and features a huge collection of small boats suspended from the ceiling in the main hall, as well as hands-on interactive displays, audio-visuals, talks and special exhibitions, covering all aspects of maritime life, from boat design to fascinating tales of survival at sea. One highlight is the natural underwater viewing location (one of only three in the world, apparently); another is the 360° views over the harbour and town from the top of the 95-foot tower, or the

stylish glass-fronted café on the first floor (which also serves an imaginative and tasty menu). Outside, a path leads around the quay to give more great views over the harbour and a close-up of the exclusive yachts moored outside. During the summer months, Events Square and Discovery Quay feel a little like the waterfront area of Barcelona.

Framing the square, the Shed (6-7 Tidemill House, Discovery Quay, 01326 318502) is a kooky tapas bar, café and restaurant, with kitsch decor, that comes highly recommended by Falmouth's trendier locals. Next door, the Quay Deli (3 Tidemill House, Discovery Quay 01326 210808) stocks a great variety of local cheeses, chutneys, meats and other delicacies, including dainty miniature pasties. On the southern flank of the square, Becky Biddle's (Maritime House, Discovery House, 01326 212233) is a stylish interiors shop selling a range of interesting products from both local and international designers. It's definitely worth stopping here for a browse, and you can grab an excellent coffee here too.

Heading into town from Discovery Quay, the road narrows into charming Arwenack Street, with its pretty pastel-coloured Georgian façades and a number of funky shops, cafés and restaurants. At the

Set sail at the National Maritime Museum.

Tap Room

dog-leg corner by the attractive granite Church of King Charles the Martyr (whose palm-framed square tower overlooking the harbour features on many a postcard), Arwenack becomes Church Street. Along this cobbled street – again flanked by handsome Georgian façades – is the Poly (01326 212300, www.thepoly.org), a buzzing hub of creativity comprising three exhibition spaces and an art house cinema, with regular theatre, dance and live music performances from around the world. There's also a new café-bar in the pipeline for the latter part of 2007. A little further along, the impressive art deco façade of the St George's Arcade marks the location of Falmouth's first custom-built cinema, opened in 1912. These days it's a hotchpotch arcade of second-hand and curiosity shops.

At the far end of town, after the inevitable chain stores, mobile phone shops and estate agents, is the charismatic old High Street. Here you can delve through the galleries, antiques and second-hand shops, grab a coffee and catch some folky, roots, soul, funk and jazz rhythms at Jam (32 High Street, 01326 219123, 01326 11722, www.jamrecords.co.uk), or head for the Old Brewery Yard a little further up, where a couple of great cafés sit alongside a regular outdoor second-hand book fair. Cinnamon Girl (01326 211457, www.cinnamongirl.co.uk) is a friendly organic café with great own-made food, wireless internet, and outside tables and chairs that form a perfect suntrap in the beautiful cobbled yard – even in early spring and late autumn. Opposite, the

Tap Room (01326 319888) is a chic continental-style bar serving great coffees, cakes and tapas during the day, and a good selection of wines, beers and cocktails until late at night. Near the top of the High Street stands the old town hall, originally a Congregational chapel presented to the town by Martin Lister Killigrew in 1725. It was also used as the Court House and, as such, was the scene of a famous trial in 1884 when two sailors were acquitted on a charge of cannibalism, having eaten the cabin boy while adrift in the Atlantic after their ship sank. Slightly less grisly, the friendly Star & Garter pub (52 High Street, 01326 318313) opposite has fantastic views over the harbour and a long-running and extremely popular jazz night on Mondays.

On the Moor, an attractive large continental-style square that serves as both market place and bus terminal, is another testament to the town's solid artistic identity, the award-winning Falmouth Art Gallery (Municipal Buildings, 01326 313863, www.falmouthartgallery.com, open 10am-5pm Mon-Sat, free entry). This is far beyond your average twee town gallery. Containing original works by major 19th- and 20th-century artists – including Alfred Mannings, HS Tuke, JM Waterhouse and Henry Moore – it also features upbeat and unusual contemporary art exhibitions. It's very family-friendly, with automata, a papier mâché show and children's workshops.

Leading sharply up off the Moor are the 111 steps of Jacob's Ladder, which ascend the large hill that sits above the town. The steps have no real biblical association as they were installed by Jacob Hamblen, a builder, tallow chandler and property owner, to facilitate access between his business (at the bottom) and some of his property (at the top). Once you get your breath back, follow the road around the brow of the hill for a fabulous panorama over the town's roofs, palm trees, church tower, docks, castle and out across the bay. The Seaview (Wodehouse Terrace, 01326 311359) pub is a good place to take it in with a quiet pint.

Pendennis Castle (01326 316594, open 10am-4pm daily) was built at the same time (1543) as its twin, St Mawes, around a mile across the estuary. A crucial defensive garrison from Tudor times to World War II, Pendennis is somewhat larger than St Mawes, having been extended by Elizabeth I at the end of the 16th century. During the Civil War, the young Prince Charles (who later became Charles II) hid here before escaping to the Continent – only just avoiding a siege of the castle by Parliamentarian forces. Visitors can explore the castle's fascinating history at the Discovery Centre, which also contains interactive displays and an exhibit on Tudor battles. In the summer, battle re-enactments take place on the gun deck, and a number of open-air concerts and plays are held on the lawn (see www.cornwall culture.co.uk for performance listings).

Just below the castle, a road runs all around the point, taking in the mighty docks on the way. After the introduction of the electric telegraph, Falmouth became one of the few places that ships could call in to get their cargo delivery orders. In 1860 the foundation of Falmouth Docks created a focus for maritime-related industries, and an extensive ship repair and maintenance industry developed. An observation platform on the Pendennis Road provides fascinating viewing. Beneath the road that leads around the point, a number of narrow paths weave between the rocks, trees and remains of defensive batteries. At low tide, you can clamber across the rocks and search the rockpools. At high tide, stroll around the well-kept path and gardens parallel to the road, ending up at the town's three sandy beaches.

The Helford River

No visit to Falmouth is complete without a boat trip up the enchanting Helford River, a few miles south of the town. Home to many a millionaire and rock star, the stunning landscape of gentle hills, dense woods, sandy beaches, clear waters, yachts and chocolate-box villages makes it an obvious choice for an idyllic retreat.

Two excellent National Trust Gardens, Trebah and Glendurgan, overlook the river

from the north bank (01872 322917, www.nationaltrust.org.uk, call or see websites for opening times). Trebah is a dramatic ravine garden tumbling down to a sheltered beach. Containing all manner of subtropical and native plants, it's said to be one of the top 80 gardens in the world. Glendurgan is also impressive, and has a recently restored laurel maze that is great fun for kids.

At Helford Passage, the Ferry Boat Inn (01326 250625, www.staustellbrewery. co.uk) sits right on the water's edge, and is a great spot for a beer and pub grub in the sunshine. Across the water on the south bank, Helford Village, with its granite thatched cottages (mostly converted into luxurious second homes), is twee but makes for a pleasant amble, rounded off by a pint in the Shipwright's Arms (Helford Village, 01326 231235) – which also has a prime waterside location, and terraced gardens stretching down to just above water level. Boat trips depart from Falmouth's Prince of Wales Pier (for timetable information, 01872 862312, www.falriverlinks.co.uk).

WHERE TO STAY

Sitting proudly on the beautiful and affluent north bank of the Helford River, a short drive from nearby Falmouth, the Budock Vean (Helford Passage, Mawnan Smith, Falmouth, 01326 252100, www.budock vean.co.uk) is a lavish four-star boasting its own golf course, tennis courts, pool and spa, and extensive gardens leading down to a private foreshore on the river, complete with private sun lounge. It's all about luxury here, although the emphasis is less on innovative interior design and more on the traditional values of an exclusive hotel. Highlights include multi-course dinners at the award-winning restaurant and sumptuous teas. Try the riverside Budock Vean Cream Tea – scones with clotted cream, jam and cakes – or, at £27.50 for two, the Celebration Tea, which also includes sandwiches and champagne.

Driftwood Hotel

Rosevine, nr Portscatho, Cornwall TR2 5EW (01872 580644/www.driftwoodhotel.co.uk). **Dinner served** 7-9.30pm daily. **Set dinner** £39 3 courses. **Rates** £190-£220 double. **Credit** AmEx, MC, V.

This enchanting privately owned beach house is set in seven acres of gardens leading down to the sea. Catering to families (there's a small separate games room for children) and groups of young people as well as couples, the Driftwood is all about carefully considered comfort. The hotel aims to give guests the best possible experience during their stay, whether they want to lay low and relax with magazines and board games or get out there and make the most of the magical Cornish coastline. Design is stylish and crisp but informal, with lots of driftwood (believe it or not), natural fabrics and stone. The award-winning restaurant, which features the best locally sourced produce cooked in imaginative pan-European and fusion styles, is another big pull, as are after-dinner drinks watching the moon on the water from the fantastic decking area. The restored weather-boarded cabin down in the gardens, with two bedrooms and a living room, is definitely worth booking if you possibly can.

Greenbank Hotel

Harbourside, Falmouth, Cornwall TR11 2SR (01326 312440/www.greenbank-hotel.com). **Lunch served** 12.30-2pm, **dinner served** 7-9.30pm daily. **Lunch main courses** £6-£8. **Set dinner** £20 1 course, £29.50 3 courses. **Rates** £105-195 double; £210-£260 suite. **Credit** AmEx, DC, MC, V.

Dating from 1640, the Greenbank is the oldest hotel in Falmouth and has an impressive history to go with it, boasting both Florence Nightingale and Kenneth '*Wind in the Willows*' Grahame as former guests. Aside from the display cases in the lobby, which proudly highlight this point, history is evident all around you at the Greenbank, with high ceilings, sweeping staircases and a traditional edge to the decor. However, moving with the times, the hotel has recently refurbished all of its bedrooms, bringing them tastefully up to date. No floral bedspreads here – simple lines and muted palettes bring a sense of sophistication and style to proceedings. Situated on the Falmouth harbour front with unrivalled views of Flushing and its own 16th-century private quay to boot, the hotel is, unsurprisingly, popular with the yachting crowd,

but is also a great base for anyone looking for something a bit special within a stone's throw of Falmouth town centre. If you are feeling decadent and your wallet can handle it, why not book the luxury Sheldrake Suite, complete with telescope, opulent four-poster bed and private balcony?

Hotel Tresanton

Lower Castle Road, St Mawes, Cornwall TR2 5DR (01326 270055/www.tresanton.com). **Rates** £130-£295 double; £200-£315 suite; £300-£435 family. **Credit** AmEx, MC, V.

Arguably one of the UK's best country hotels, renowned interior designer Olga Polizzi's Hotel Tresanton has become synonymous with waterside chic, and has played host to a stellar cast of international celebrities since it opened in 1999. Nevertheless, it still has a friendly, intimate and homely atmosphere that will make mere mortals feel welcome. Originally created in the 1940s as a yachtsmen's club, the hotel became a popular and well-known haunt for yachties and tourists in the 1950s and '60s. Polizzi bought the place in 1997 and spent two years and a cool £2 million renovating and restoring it, adding personal touches to every room (guests even have wellies provided for them).

A cluster of houses built into the hillside on different levels, 27 out of the Tresanton's 29 rooms look out over the sea and the St Anthony lighthouse on the headland beyond. Nautical patterns influence the design of some rooms, while others blend natural hues of cream and beige with dark wood and richly coloured fabrics. Original works of art adorn the hallways and lounge areas, with pieces by Terry Frost, Barbara Hepworth and acclaimed St Mawes sculptor Julian Dyson in the collection. Tresanton is truly a hotel for all seasons: spend a day aboard the *Pinuccia* (a 48ft

Hotel Tresanton: chic and unique

St Michael's Hotel & Spa

classic racing yacht built to represent Italy in the 1938 World Cup), followed by dinner on the terrace in summer; or make the most of the yoga, bridge and treatment weekend packages in the winter (Sarah Key, a physiotherapist who treats the royal family, hosts special programmes in November and March). A great selection of books, magazines and DVDs (there's also a private cinema here) is available all year round.

Lugger Hotel

Portloe, Cornwall TR2 5RD (01872 501322/ www.luggerhotel.com). **Rates** £160-£280 double. **Credit** AmEx, MC, V.

Elegantly simple and tastefully contemporary, the Lugger Hotel is ideal for anyone looking for a peaceful retreat with an added touch of luxury. Nestled into the cliffs above the tiny fishing village of Portloe, the 17th-century inn and fishermen's cottages that now collectively form the 21-room Lugger have been given a stylish 21st-century facelift. The spacious interiors, decorated in cream and chocolate with sumptuous leather sofas, serve to enhance rather than sacrifice the hotel's historic charm. There are picturesque views across the harbour to enjoy over dinner, and for post-prandial lingering there's a stoked log fire to sit by in winter and a terrace in summer. Understated sophistication is the order of the day here – perfect for urbanites seeking sanctuary from city life.

Nare Hotel

Carne Beach, Veryan-in-Roseland, Cornwall, TR2 5PF (01872 501111/www.thenare.com). Quarterdeck restaurant **Lunch served** 12.30-2.30pm, **dinner served** 7.15-9.30pm daily. **Set meals** £25 3 courses. *Main dining room* **Lunch served** 12.30-2pm Sun only.

Dinner served 7.15-9.30pm daily. **Tea served** 10am-5pm daily. **Set meals** £41 5 courses. **Rates** £230-£410 double; £388-£614 suite. **Credit** AmEx, MC, V.

Standing proud above Carne Beach on Gerrans Bay, the Nare is an elegant, traditional affair. First opened in 1925, the extended 40-room hotel still retains much of its original character, with winding corridors, roaring log fires and rooms bursting with antiques. Each of the individually decorated bedrooms adds to the sense of old world charm, from the comfortable countryside-view rooms to the luxurious sea-view suites, with carriage clocks, floral fabrics and high-backed armchairs throughout. As the highest rated four-star hotel in Cornwall, the Nare has justly won a slew of awards for its facilities, service and general atmosphere. From the indoor and outdoor pools, subtropical gardens leading down to the beach, sauna, gym, beauty salon and billiards room, to fine dining looking out over a breathtaking panorama, it has everything you would expect of a premium country hotel. It's the finishing touches that really make it special, though; a decanter of complimentary sherry in each room, fresh milk and hot-water bottles provided just before bedtime in the winter, cream tea served daily, and a lovingly selected 500-strong wine list to work your way through with dinner. Winter also sees a number of special activities put on to keep guests entertained, from wine- and cheese-tastings to theatre trips and special Christmas and New Year packages.

St Mawes Hotel

The Sea Front, St Mawes, Cornwall TR2 5DW (01326 270266/www.stmaweshotel.co.uk). **Lunch served** noon-2.30pm, **dinner served** 6-9pm daily. **Main courses** £5.75-£16.95. **Rates** £70-£120 double. **Credit** MC, V.

This friendly establishment on the waterfront in the centre of town has five simple but attractively decorated rooms. Warm yellows, natural wood and superb sea views create a relaxed mood and prices are incredibly reasonable for this well-heeled town. The brasserie and bar downstairs are extremely popular, so be warned that this may not be the most peaceful of retreats in the busy summer months.

St Michael's Hotel & Spa

Gyllyngvase Beach, Falmouth, Cornwall TR11 4NB (01326 312707/www.stmichaelshotel.co.uk). **Lunch served** noon-2pm, **dinner served** 6.30-9pm daily. **Main courses** £9-£14.95. **Rates** £84-£222 double. **Credit** AmEx, MC, V.
Less prominent than the imposing Falmouth Beach Hotel, St Michael's has the advantage of being situated right opposite Gyllyngvase Beach and ten minutes' walk from town. Set back from the main road by four acres of award-winning subtropical gardens (including a children's play area and special outdoor massage pagoda), St Michael's has a host of extra features to add to its allure – including a lovely indoor pool, sauna, jacuzzi, steam rooms, gym and sundeck. The fresh, nautical-inspired interior is original without being too gimmicky (where else would you find a boat for a reception desk and beach hut toilets?), and the comfortable rooms are all excellently equipped, clearly benefiting from the £2-million investment that has gone into the hotel in the last three years. The choice on the menu in the Flying Fish restaurant is impressive – as are the number of scenic lounges and outdoor terraces where you can enjoy a sunset drink.

WHERE TO EAT & DRINK

Perched on a hill just above the old High Street, the Boathouse (Trevethan Hill, Falmouth, 01326 315425), with unbeatable views over the river to Flushing, is a great place for food or drink. Enjoy the (sail) covered decking area outside, location of many a barbecue in the summer months. In winter, it's a case of appreciating the log fire and supping from a range of locally brewed Skinner's ales.

The Cove (Maenporth Beach, 01326 251136) is an understated venue set well back from a beautiful view that can only be glimpsed at a distance. Friendly, informal service combines with a varied menu.

Hunkydory's (46 Arwenack Street, Falmouth, 01326 212997) pleasingly curved bar offers the option of sitting in either the cosy wooden-beamed front room or the brighter steamship-style back room with its big booths. There's a stellar array of seafood, with crab, squid, mussels and king prawns all present, and chorizo, chillies, ginger, lime and pumpkin seeds among the supporting flavours.

Pandora Inn (Restronguet Creek, Mylor, 01326 372678) is a beautiful thatched 13th-century building housing one of the best-known pubs in the area. A warren of interconnected rooms, vaulted with low beams, dark wooden panels, benches and fireside tables, the pub has two floors, with the restaurant upstairs serving the same food in a more upmarket setting. Enjoy a drink on the jetty as the sun goes down, whether you fancy splashing out on food or not.

The long-established Seafood Bar (Lower Quay Street, Falmouth, 01326 315129) remains hugely popular with locals. The emphasis is on fantastic fresh local seafood cooked to simple perfection.

The spectacular location of the Three Mackerel (Swanpool, Falmouth, 01326 311886) – perched on the edge of a cliff with a lovely wooden deck overlooking clear blue waters – means people would probably come here whatever was served. The fact that the menu is an alluring mix of modern British and fusion cuisines, blending local meat and fish with Mediterranean and oriental influences to great effect, only adds to the appeal. There's an early evening terrace menu at weekends.

Blue South

35-37 Arwenack Street, Falmouth, Cornwall TR11 3JG (01326 212122/www.blue-bar. co.uk). **Meals served** noon-10pm Mon-Thur, Sun; noon-12pm Fri, Sat. **Main courses** £8-£12.50. **Credit** AmEx, MC, V.
Sister bar to the original beachside/surf hangout at Porthtowan on the north coast, Blue South brings the laid-back surfy vibe to town without the sandy flip flops. It's a friendly place, with a number of sofas, Wi-Fi, good coffees and an all-day menu of Mediterranean and oriental dishes (as well as the famous 'Blue Burger') day and night. After dark, things liven up somewhat as Blue is a popular drinking joint for Falmouth's art students and young professionals, who flock to the place for the great cocktails and beautiful people.

Hotel Tresanton

Lower Castle Road, St Mawes, Cornwall TR2 5DR (01326 270055/www.tresanton.com). **Lunch served** 12.30-2.30pm, **tea served** 3.30-5.30pm, **dinner served** 7-9.30pm daily. **Set lunch** £28 3 courses. **Set dinner** £39 3 courses. **Credit** AmEx, MC, V.
Dinner at the Tresanton exudes effortless quality – and so it should for its elevated prices. Here it feels like excellence comes naturally; choose exquisite fresh fish dishes, classic meat selections or imaginative vegetarian fare from a daily changing menu that emphasises fresh local produce. Summer sees cocktails and dinner on the terrace, complete with spectacular views over the St Anthony lighthouse and Fal Estuary, while

Three Mackerel

Enjoying an unbeatable location right, the Sticky Prawn has achieved great things since father-and-son team Paul and Ben Lightfoot took the place over three years ago. Housed inside an old fishermen's resting rooms, the place has an earthy charm – the heavy stone walls, wooden beams and cosy booths giving it an almost Beefeater-meets-galleon feel. The food, however, is simply excellent: tender sea bass steamed in light and fragrant ginger, soy and sesame or baked fillets of turbot with a tangy menallack chilli cheddar crust and smoked tomato butter. The wine list is a personal passion for Paul, and there are 11 excellent house wines available by the glass, as well as an impressive list from around the world that covers all bases. Catch a water taxi back to Falmouth afterwards to complete the experience.

Two Ten 200

30 Arwenack Street, Falmouth, Cornwall TR11 3JB (01326 210200/www.twoten200.co.uk). **Lunch served** *Summer* 11.30am-2.30pm Wed-Sat. **Dinner served** 6.30-9.30pm Tue-Sat. **Main courses** £12-£17. **Credit** MC, V.
You might not notice Two Ten 200 as it's tucked away in a basement off bustling Arwenack Street, but the loss would be all yours, as this newcomer is one of the best restaurants in town. Decked out in dark woods and creams with splashes of red, this is a sophisticated space. The attention to detail also extends to the menu, which offers delicious starters (scallops with butternut croutons and white wine, garlic and cream sauce), innovative main courses (the fillet of pork en croute with prunes, apricots and pine nuts seasoned with orange zest and spinach comes highly recommended) and fantastic desserts (the Two Ten Three includes one of each of the most popular desserts, including mango and raspberry pavlova, apricot and white chocolate bread and butter pudding, and rich chocolate pudding). With super-friendly, knowledgeable service to boot, this is a welcome addition to Falmouth's booming restaurant scene.

Victory Inn

Victory Hill, St Mawes, Cornwall TR2 5PQ (01326 270324/www.victory-inn.co.uk). **Lunch served** noon-2.30pm, **dinner served** 6.30-9.30pm daily. **Main courses** £6.95-£11.95. **Rates** £50-£100 double. **Credit** MC, V.
Formerly a fishermen's haunt, the Victory sees more chinos and blazers these days than it does yellow wellies and overalls. Its beamed interior retains an intimate old world vibe, while the restaurant upstairs – serving the same food – is fresh, airy and modern. Serving up a number of real ales and lagers, as well as an innovative pub menu that includes lots of fresh seafood (using as much local and organic produce as possible), this is a great place to while away those carefree holiday hours, be that a winter afternoon in front of a roaring log fire or a summery lunch on the outside table peeking out over the harbour.

winter is a cosy candlelit affair in the dining room. Non-residents on a budget can also stop by for light lunches and cream teas on the terrace, which is especially popular in the summer months.

Lugger

Portloe, Cornwall TR2 5RD (01872 501322/ www.luggerhotel.com). **Lunch served** noon-2pm, **dinner served** 7-9.30pm daily. **Set lunch** £20.50 3 courses. **Set dinner** £37.50 3 courses. **Credit** AmEx, MC, V.
A rich history (one landlord was hanged for smuggling in the 1890s), spectacular view and delectable menu should put this former 17th-century inn right up there on any visitor's dining wish list. With echoes of Soho about its decor and presentation, it's sure to impress even the staunchest of city lovers while the daily changing four-course menu of locally sourced produce (you can even watch the fishermen landing their daily catches on the rocky beach below) could convert them to harbourfront living permanently. Choices include a tian of Portloe crab, pan-fried Newlyn halibut with a pistachio and herb crust or venison with a brussels sprout purée (there's always a good choice for vegetarians too). Another option is to come for a summer lunch, when the tables on the beautiful cliff terrace really come into their own.

Sticky Prawn

Flushing Quay, Flushing, Falmouth, Cornwall TR11 5TY (01326 373734/www.thesticky prawn.co.uk). **Lunch served** noon-2.30pm daily. **Dinner served** 6.30-9pm Mon-Sat. **Main courses** £14.95-£30. **Credit** MC, V.

Isles of Scilly

Quiet beaches and a turbulent ocean.

The recent BBC documentary *An Island Parish* may have done the Isles of Scilly a disservice. Small, they are. Quiet, they definitely are. And if you're after nightlife more exciting than a pint or two of fine Ales of Scilly beer with the locals, there are other chapters to turn to. But the tranquillity, beauty and beguiling idiosyncrasies of the Scillies extend far beyond the kind of High Anglican eccentricity the Beeb seemed fixated on showing. In short, the Isles of Scilly are extraordinary. Not everyone will agree with us, but that's fine – with all due respect to the many Scillonians dependent on the tourist trade, the fewer the merrier.

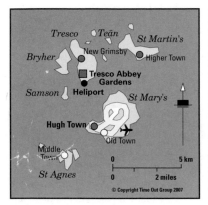

The archipelago, 28 miles out into the Atlantic from Cornwall's Land's End, is unmistakably English but feels magically 'other' as well. No wonder the Scillies are recognised in legend as the remains of the Lost Land of Lyonesse, to which King Arthur's men retreated after their leader's last fatal battle. Basking in the warmth of the Gulf Stream, the five inhabited islands – St Mary's and the 'off-islands' St Martin's, St Agnes, Tresco and Bryher – have been settled for at least 4,000 years, but are also surrounded by hundreds of unoccupied islets, rock formations, outcrops and ledges. Hardly surprising, then, that the surrounding waters are the watery graveyard of some 700 ships. When an Atlantic gale comes roaring in, it can be magnificently fierce.

It's not all treacherous seas and crashing foam. Within the ring of larger islands run channels that are positively Mediterranean in their brightness and hue. Once part of the Cornish mainland, and now home to a population of fewer than 3,000 (the vast majority of them on St Mary's), the granite-bedded Scillies sit in clear and shallow waters, fringed by genuinely golden, even, white-sand beaches and heather-covered headlands. They regularly take the lion's share of British summertime sun (their name comes from the Latin Sillinae insulae or 'Sun Isles') and the temperate climate nurtures a fecundity of wild flowers and subtropical vegetation (*see p142* **Good natured**). However, the sea temperature remains bracing even in August: perhaps part of the reason why the tourist-infestation that assails much of Cornwall during the summer seems to largely pass the Scillies by.

Today, carefully managed tourism dominates the economy, alongside fishing, low-impact farming, flower cultivation and small-scale family businesses – a far cry from the shipwreck-looting and smuggling that the inhabitants relied on in previous centuries. There is an abiding sense of the continuity of life here, evident in numerous prehistoric burial chambers, standing stones and settlements, as well as Roman and early Christian sites. And it's compounded by the fact that, except on St Mary's, there are practically no cars.

But, by any definition, these are small islands. Even St Mary's can muster no more than nine miles of country lanes, so it's very easy to get about entirely on foot. And when you've had enough of any one island, regular local boats connect each to its neighbours. This creates a fundamentally different pace of life. There are no theme parks or nightclubs – you come to the Scillies because you want to do very little in quantifiable terms (walk, read, chat and think productively about nothing much at all). Sure, there's good food, water sports (fabulous diving, especially) and atmospheric pubs, but the islands' main appeal are their beauty, stunning views and glorious isolation.

There's bad news too, though. 'Carefully managed tourism' means a holiday here will never come cheap – strikingly so in these days of bargain-basement flights and late hotel deals. There is only a relatively select range of accommodation options, especially on the off-islands, which keeps occupancy and hence prices comparatively high. All of the islands have general store provision, but again lack of competition on the off-islands allows the cost of imports to push up prices.

But perhaps now is the time to take such costs on the chin. If a train and a boat (*see p144* **Travelling tales**) can get you somewhere this lovely, this remote, this soothing, maybe green tourism doesn't have to be a tautology.

St Mary's

Although it's only two and a half miles across at its widest point, St Mary's is the largest of the Isles. This, together with its full road system, makes it closest in feel to the mainland. Its centre, Hugh Town, is bustling if you've already spent time on the other islands, laid-back if you've come from elsewhere. On a narrow isthmus on the island's south-western side, the town is flanked to the south by Porthcressa Beach, a pretty, sheltered bay, and to the north by the less appealing Town Beach where the

Accommodation	★★★★☆
Food & drink	★★★☆☆
Nightlife	☆☆☆☆☆
Shopping	☆☆☆☆☆
Culture	☆☆☆☆☆
Sights	★☆☆☆☆
Scenery	★★★★★

Isles of Scilly

Penzance ferry and inter-island passenger boats come and go. If you want to see the islanders' boating prowess first hand, the pilot gig races are a cheery spectacle (*see p140* **Getting the gig**); if you'd rather hone your own skills, there's always the Sailing Centre (01720 422060).

The Isles of Scilly Museum (Church Street, Hugh Town, 01720 422337, www.iosmuseum.org, closed Sun) provides archaeological, cultural and historical background in an appealingly old-fashioned style. There's no escaping the thread of disaster and loss, primarily from shipwrecks, but alongside the cases of flotsam and jetsam you'll find a Scilly shrew's nest in a discarded can, Iron Age axeheads and a Napoleonic dagger stick. Downstairs are stuffed birds and fish, including 6lb 2oz of broad-nosed eel.

Named after the fortifications built here in the 18th century, Garrison Hill rises up on the promontory west of Hugh Town, offering brilliant views. The dominant structure is the 16th-century, eight-pointed Star Castle, built as a defence against the Spanish Armada, but now a hotel (*see p145*).

In the other direction, Telegraph Road leads from Hugh Town towards the island's interior, passing Carreg Dhu (pronounced 'Crake Dew', meaning Black Rocks; 01720 422404), a volunteer-run community garden whose one and a half acres are quiet and fabulously overgrown with subtropical plants, shrubs and trees; a sign invites visitors to pick up tools and gloves left handy and get stuck into some weeding. It's open all year round, but call if visiting off-season. Here also begins a pleasant trail around the island's dozen galleries, open studios and craft shops, making a comfortable circuit south to the Old Town (a leaflet map of the route is widely available). A little further on is the Longstone Heritage Centre (01720 423770, closed mid Nov-early Mar), a local history museum covering environmentally themed topics such as the Torrey Canyon oil tanker disaster. A café, gift shop and very friendly cat are also on the premises, and there's internet access.

Heading east from Porthcressa Beach, a path loops south round jagged Peninnis Head, passing some intriguing geological formations such as the 'Kettle and Pans' close to the lighthouse. Beyond is the sheltered Old Town Bay whose straggling settlement was, until the 17th century, the island's main port.

East of Old Town, near the airport, the small bay at Porth Hellick is overlooked by a monument to Rear Admiral Sir Cloudesley Shovell, who steered his fleet into the rocks off the island during a storm in 1707, losing 2,000 men. Shovell's body was washed ashore the following day, and he

TOURIST INFORMATION

St Mary's
St Mary's Tourism, Hugh Town, St Mary's, Isles of Scilly TR21 0LL (01720 422536/www.simplyscilly.co.uk).
www.scillyonline.co.uk
www.tresco.co.uk
www.bryher-ios.co.uk

was later buried at Westminster Abbey. A mile to the north, Pelistry Bay is one of the most secluded and picturesque beaches on St Mary's. At low tide a sand bar enables you to cross to the idyllic Toll's Island; on no account attempt to swim across at high tide, since the sand bar causes vicious rip tides. Still near the airport, Camel Rock has over the last few years hosted a popular music festival for the August bank holiday. Local and mainland bands join forces against a spectacular marine backdrop.

A little to the north are the quieter pleasures of St Mary's Riding Centre (01720 423855). Alternatively, head north-west round the coast and you'll come to the most impressive prehistoric remains on the archipelago. Halangy Down has stone huts, a burial chamber and a standing stone that is thought to date to 2,000 BC.

Tresco

For some, a visit to the Scillies' privately run and closely managed island estate is altogether too cosseted, from the toy-town jollity of the tractor ride between the heliport and your chosen accommodation to the paucity of dining options (a hotel restaurant, a pub, a café) to transport only by hired golf cart or bicycle. Others will find in this a delicious simplicity.

The island's unassailable selling point is the renowned subtropical Abbey Gardens (01720 424105, www.tresco.co.uk/the_abbey_garden, gardens open daily, full facilities mid Feb-early Nov, £8.50). There's no denying the unique atmosphere of this singular experiment in horticulture, with fabulously exotic golden pheasants strutting about and each section screened off from the others to provide new vistas at every turn. It's relatively simple to lose your fellow visitors as well, even if a cruise-ship load of them sails up. When Augustus Smith arrived in 1834 to take on the lease of the islands (bringing much-needed educational and agricultural reforms), Tresco was exposed to fierce winds and far from sympathetic to the kind of vegetation now growing. To overcome this, Smith built tall windbreaks around the remains of the 12th-century Benedictine priory to shelter sloping terraces. Systematically laid out and developed by generations of the family (who still lease Tresco from the Duchy of

Isles of Scilly

GETTING THE GIG

Pilot gig racing is the main sport in the islands, with races taking place on Wednesday (women) and Friday (men) evenings in summer from Samson to the quay at Hugh Town.

The pilot gig is 32 feet of rowing boat, crewed by six oarsmen and a cox. The gigs originally conveyed expert pilots from the islands to seagoing ships: and some of those gigs, built over a century ago, are still racing today.

You can cheer on your island's crew from one of the passenger boats that follow every race (costing around £6 round-trip).

Cornwall), the gardens have over 20,000 plants from 80 countries, including succulents, palms, cacti and eucalyptus. Italianate landscaping adds perspective, enhanced by sculptures, arbours and ornamentation. Shakespeare productions and concerts are staged here in summer. There's an on-site visitors' centre and the £8.50 admission price includes access to Valhalla, a rather disappointing collection of salvaged ships' figureheads. The Garden Café is open to all-comers.

Tresco isn't only about the gardens, though. At two miles by one, it's the largest off-island, and the only isle apart from St Mary's with helicopter service (*see p144* **Travelling tales**). It has a varied topography, from exquisite, barely populated beaches (Appletree and Pentle Bays) lining the eastern and western shores, peaceful lakes (the Abbey and Great Pools) to secluded woodland and the heathered headland. Here you'll find two defensive fortifications: the 1651 Cromwell's Castle and, above it, the earlier King Charles's Castle look across the strait to Bryher and Hangman's Island, where 500 Royalists are said to have been executed in one day during the Civil War.

Most settlement on Tresco runs across the island between Old and New Grimsby. New Grimsby houses Gallery Tresco (01720 424925, www.tresco.co.uk/gallery), a single room of local art and a handful of souvenirs, which is located right in front of the sleepy little jetty and beached fishing boats. Many of the attractive stone cottages are now expensive timeshares, but a little back from the waterfront the New Inn (*see p145*) is the island's social heart. Its bar, crafted from wreck-reclaimed timber, is the site of the biannual Real Ale Festival in May and September, both popular months for birdwatchers eager to spot rare migratory birds. On the far side of the island, at Old Grimsby, lies the Island Hotel (*see p145*).

Bryher

Each isle has its passionate supporters, but among the most fervent are those who back Bryher, including author Michael Morpurgo; the 1989 film *When the Whales Came*, based on his novel, was both set and filmed here. Even within Scilly, Bryher feels like a place apart. Just across from Tresco (until quite recently the two were connected and can still be reached on foot at very low tide), it takes its name from the Celtic for 'place of hills'; to the north are Shipman Head Down and Watch Hill; in the south Samson Hill.

It's a beautifully wild island, generally undeveloped and looking out on stunning rock fortresses such as Scilly Rock, Castle Bryher and Maiden Bower (Gweal Hill offers the best sunset vantage in the Scillies, while Samson Hill does the same for the whole archipelago). Also on the western shore, Hell Bay delivers all the name suggests when a storm's up. A little further south, the Hell Bay Hotel (*see p143*) is one of the most dramatically positioned in England. Nearby, artist Richard Pearce (01720 423665, www.rpearce.net) has a similarly startling outlook from an Atlantic studio barely the size of a rowing boat (it is, in fact, a converted gig shed). Affable and bearded, the 'young Jim Pearce' is usually to be found here hard at work.

The considerably more sheltered east shore has fine beaches, such as Green Bay, and a friendly boat hire operation run by long-time islanders, the Bennetts (01720 422411). A circumambulation of Bryher takes little more than an hour but is wonderfully invigorating.

St Martin's

Growing flowers is the main industry here, which accounts for the colourful fields, but the island has attracted a number of sensitive entrepreneurial operations, from the organic smallholding and café at Little Arthur Farm (*see p143* Where to stay, eat & drink) to the impeccable St Martin's Bakery (Higher Town, 01720 423444, www.st martinsbakery.co.uk), which runs dedicated baking holidays. Judging by the homity pie and upside-down pineapple cake we tried, there are some serious skills ready to be passed on. A converted barn just up from the bakery's outdoor tables houses both its owners and their gallery, while Glencoe Cottage Shop supplies any requirements for bucket, spade or tourist tat.

You'll find stunning beaches and jaw-dropping views, in particular from St Martin's Head on the north-east coast. The island is sparsely inhabited and virtually pollution-free, making its waters among the best in the Scillies for scuba-diving. St Martin's Diving Services (Higher Town, St Martin's,

01720 422848, www.scillydiving.com) provides equipment and tuition for all levels.

St Martin's main quay lies on Par Beach, a slice of pure white sand lapped by translucent waters. Just inland are Higher Town, at the top of the hill, and along the bay St Martin's Vineyard & Winery (01720 423418, www.stmartinsvineyard.co.uk), where you can stock up on souvenir wine after a tour (Apr-Sept, closed Sat, Sun).

On the southern coast, Lawrence's Bay is long, sandy and perfect for collecting shells or just chilling out. Further west is Lower Town, from where you can enjoy terrific views across to the uninhabited islands of Teän and St Helen's, or suck down a pint at the Seven Stones (*see p142*). On the north coast Great Bay and Little Bay are secluded spots, the former frequently appearing on lists of the best British beaches. Climb across the boulders from the latter at low tide to wild White (pronounced 'Wit') Island to explore Underland Girt, a huge underground cave.

St Agnes

Craggy St Agnes is set apart from the cluster of Bryher, Tresco and St Martin's, and is the most south-westerly community in the British Isles. The simple lifestyle is fully embraced here: bird- and butterfly-watching are about as energetic as it gets.

Boats land and leave from Porth Conger, on the north-west of the island, under the watchful eye of the Turk's Head (*see p143*). There you'll also find St Agnes's most attractive beach, Covean. When the tide is right you can walk across the sand bar from here to the tiny island of Gugh (pronounced 'Goo'), where there are rocky outcrops, a Bronze Age burial chamber and a standing stone – or rather a crazily leaning stone.

Inland, St Agnes is dominated by the squat, white form of the Old Lighthouse, which dates from 1680, making it one of the oldest in England. Near to Periglis Cove on the western side of the island, outlined in large pebbles, is Troy Town Maze, said to have been laid out by the lighthouse keeper's bored son in 1729. Although since copied elsewhere in the Scillies, it was a layout unique in Britain.

The wild heathland of the wonderfully named Wingletang Down takes up much of the south of St Agnes, edged on its western side by impressive coastal scenery and on its eastern side by Beady Pool. This inlet takes its name from a haul of beads from a wrecked 17th-century Venetian trader that was washed up on the shores. Above the cove, two enormous boulders indented with a three-foot-deep basin form the Giant's Punchbowl, the most extraordinary rock formation on Scilly.

GOOD NATURED

It's not hard to see why the Isles of Scilly should be a sanctuary for seals, puffins, shearwaters and many migratory birds (see www.scillybirding.co.uk for details). The often clement weather brought by the Gulf Stream helps, as does the islands' seclusion from mainland predators such as foxes, badgers and snakes. Both the lesser white-toothed shrew (imperiously known in Latin as *Crocidura suaveoleus*) and the dwarf pansy are known nowhere but here. Marine life is as impressive, with kelp forests and jewel anemones, the resident grey seals, and passing porpoises and dolphins. No wonder Scilly was designated an Area of Outstanding Natural Beauty in 1975.

With so much wildlife on the islands there's no need to make special arrangements: ringed plovers will scuttle about your feet as you pick through anchor cables at Hugh Town, a rock pipit might feign injury to distract you from her nest as you take the Bryher coastal path. But Hugh Town's Quay Visitors' Centre (Harbourside Waiting Room, the Quay, 01720 422988, www.ios-wildlifetrust.org.uk), run by the Isles of Scilly Wildlife Trust, is a great place to start. Resident naturalist Will Wagstaff guides excellent walks (Mar-Oct, £9 not including boat fare), usually starting at 9.45am and lasting all day. The itinerary is posted by the quay, or phone 01720 422212 (www.islandwildlifetours.co.uk) for details. Will also runs slideshows at the church hall each Saturday (doors open 7.45pm, £4).

Many people take the opportunity of visiting the puffins on Annet island bird sanctuary (Apr-July) or take an evening trip in warmer months to search out Manx shearwaters, which feed their young at night to avoid the predations of black-backed gulls. You can also spend three hours snorkelling with grey seals off the Eastern Isles – organised by Island Sea Safaris (01720 422732, www.scillyonline.co.uk/seasafaris.html) for £37, sessions are carefully controlled to avoid upsetting the seals (no splashing, no touching, no chasing). The experience is absolutely magical.

The uninhabited islands

Samson, the largest uninhabited island, was populated until the 1850s, when poverty and the threat of eviction by Augustus Smith forced the islanders to resettle. A beautiful beach lies at the foot of North Hill, while significant prehistoric remains dot the slopes above. At low tide look out for the Samson Flats, the remains of ancient field systems that show up in the sands between Samson and Tresco.

No trip to the Scillies would be complete without a boat trip heading west to the extraordinary Bishop Rock Lighthouse, perched on a rock base little wider than its own circumference. Now automated, it was a miracle of construction (after several late Victorian attempts) and saved countless lives.

Teän, just off St Martin's, has large, crescent-shaped sandy beaches, while, behind it, St Helen's has the ruins of a church that are well worth exploring. On the other side of St Martin's, the milder Eastern Isles have fantastic beaches on Great Arthur and Great Ganilly. They are also home to puffins and grey seals, but the best place to spot these captivating creatures is the storm-harried Western Rocks beyond St Agnes, which bear the brunt of the Atlantic storms and have seen many shipwrecks.

WHERE TO STAY, EAT & DRINK

Due to the small supply of accommodation, it is essential to book in advance – and many places won't book for less than a week in peak season. This explains a certain pragmatism about even the most deluxe accommodation in Scilly: everything is set up to please posh granny as much as surf-teen, and beardie birder as much as strung-out family. Off-season (Nov-Feb), many businesses close, although there is growing interest in Christmas tourism.

There are a number of decent, English Tourism Council-rated B&Bs on St Mary's, among them the Grade II-listed Garrison House (01720 422972, www.garrisonhouse.co.uk), perched on the hill up to the Star Castle. On St Agnes, few options exist apart from self-catering cottages and camping, but Covean Cottage (01720 422620) is a lovely B&B. Polreath Guesthouse & Tearoom on St Martin's (Higher Town, 01720 422046, www.polreath.com, closed Sun) provides two en suite bedrooms, both with sea views, in a pretty 19th-century farmhouse. Own-made cakes and light lunches such as mackerel pâté or roasted vegetable and cheese tartlet are served in the little garden or conservatory, perhaps with a pot of green tea. There's alternative accommodation too: a sustainable eco-cabin at Little Arthur Farm (01720 422457), complete with wind turbine, solar panels and a wormery for 'waste'.

Apart from St Mary's, which has a relatively wide range of places to eat and drink, dining options on Scilly are restricted to the hotels, pubs and small cafés. Recommendations on St Mary's include the fab little licensed café and tea gardens at Carn Vean (Pelistry) and Hugh Town's Mermaid Inn (01720 422701), an atmospheric local with fine real ales and a sleepy dog stretched across the doorway. Food is served in the upstairs restaurant and, in 2006, a handsome new café-bar was added downstairs, serving wine, Guinness and light meals from a bar made out of a white gig.

The Vine Café (01720 423168) on Bryher is a relaxed and welcoming little place for a snack or a cake, with a fixed-price, two-course meal available in the evenings (bring your own wine). Bryher also has a great pub: the Fraggle Rock (01720 422222). Situated in a little granite house with a beer garden out front, it serves lunch and evening meals, including a renowned fish and chips, and pours a good pint of Sharp's Doom Bar. The first floor has sea views, internet access and incongruously bright stripped pine decor.

Looking down the steady slope to Par Beach on St Martin's, Little Arthur Farm Café (01720 422457) offers excellent salads and rolls filled with own-grown organic ingredients, soups such as nettle and onion, freshly caught shellfish and lovely cakes in a sweet black and white trellised conservatory. During the tourist season, it runs an excellent fish and chips night, as well as a 'bistro' night. At Lower Town, climb '111 steps to the best pub view', as the sign puts it. Pints of St Austell Tribute and Ales of Scilly Fair Weather will keep you enjoy the fine outside terrace at the Seven Stones (01720 423560).

On St Agnes a fine spot to enjoy a beer and local pasties is the garden of the Turk's Head (01720 422434), which looks back towards St Mary's. It serves its own Turk's Head ale and is the most south-westerly pub in the British Isles.

There's a good restaurant at each of the hotels below; non-residents should book.

Hell Bay Hotel

Bryher, Isles of Scilly TR23 0PR (01720 422947/www.hellbay.co.uk). **Lunch served** noon-3pm, **dinner served** 6.30-9pm daily. **Main courses** (lunch) £9.50-£17. **Set dinner** £35 3 courses. **Rates** D,B&B £260-£550 double suite. **Credit** MC, V.

In an unbeatable position on the edge of the Atlantic, Hell Bay Hotel is a pioneer of contemporary if not quite cutting-edge style in the Scillies. The relaxed, spacious suites, in soothing shades of blue and green, have a clean, New England feel (exposed A-frame beams) with a nautical slant (jaunty portholes in the doors). Most suites open on to private balconies or patios and have a sea view; all are equipped with VCRs and internet access. Small details are carefully attended to (an umbrella tucked behind the door, water and fresh milk in the fridge, a personal cafetière) encouraging you to overlook less appealing aspects (the gauche profusion of branded goods in the foyer). There's impressive modern art in the expansive bar area, as well as sculptures dotted about the place. The food seems a little unsure of itself – Hell Bay prawn cocktail sits beside caramelised scallops with leeks and orange butter sauce – but it can be eaten in the restaurant, bar or heated patio overlooking the Great Pool. Hell Bay makes a good stab at appealing to retirees, slop-around families and couples; facilities include a heated outdoor pool, golf and a little gym, sauna and spa bath. Opening for Christmas over the last couple of years, Hell Bay usually closes for a month after New Year.

Island Hotel

Old Grimsby, Tresco, Isles of Scilly TR24 0PU (01720 422883/www.tresco.co.uk). **Lunch served** noon-2.30pm, **dinner served** 7-9pm daily. **Main courses** (lunch) £6.50-£18. **Set dinner** £38 3 courses. **Rates** DB&B £246-£500 double; £332-£600 suite. **Credit** MC, V.

The front lawn of the Island Hotel sweeps down to the sheltered sands of Raven's Porth on one side,

TRAVELLING TALES

Scillonian transport is very much part of the island experience, but it can add complications if you're only on a short break. There are no scheduled services to or from the islands on a Sunday, and adverse weather can have a major bearing on departure times – sometimes even changing on the morning you're due to leave. Most hotels and B&Bs make sure you know about any alterations, but do check and be certain to take out travel insurance. And pack the remedies if you aren't a good sailor.

Most visitors will head to Penzance, then pick up the *Scillonian III* for St Mary's. The ferry (Isles of Scilly Travel, 0845 710 5555, www.ios-travel.co.uk, adult return £70-£92) makes pretty stately progress – the journey takes the best part of three hours – but it's a real pleasure to sit up on deck in the breeze on a sunny day. Isles of Scilly Travel also operate flights to St Mary. They aren't cheap, but are often the most convenient option. You can get a twin-prop Skybus from Southampton, Bristol, Exeter, Newquay or Land's End (adult return £100-£298).

The helicopter (01736 363871, www.islesofscillyhelicopter.com, adult return £75-£152) also departs from Penzance. Heading to either Tresco or St Mary's, the red and blue livery Sikorsky S61 takes less than half an hour, zooming out beyond cliffs, flying low enough for you to see the chopper's shadow through large, hip-height side windows.

When you're on the islands, transport remains an adventure, with a variety of open boats bouncing between islands, usually captained by some sardonic seadog. From St Mary's Quay, the St Mary's Boatmen's Association (01720 423999, www.scillyboating.co.uk) runs a daily connecting service to the off-islands – enquire at the tourist office, or look at the quayside blackboards for times.

Boat services also run regular half-day excursions out to Bishop Rock and the Western Rocks. Trips can be combined with sightseeing: chugging to St Martin's from Hugh Town you might opt to see the grey seals around the Eastern Isles; the round-trip will cost about £9. There are also more exotic options, such as voyages in a high-speed RIB – 'rigid inflatable boat'.

while the other side gives wonderful views of rocky islands and a single line of surf breaking at the reef – although you'll need to fork out for the upper luxury suite, Menavaur, to get the best out it. This pleasantly weathered, 'colonial-style' hotel has a five-star location and a peculiar layout that provides most rooms with some kind of sea view. The reception, bar and restaurant have all been given an airy revamp, in places an excessively colourful one in purple, violet and mauve. The rooms are generously proportioned, if a little dated in decor – but are being steadily refreshed. In the restaurant, there's a combination of traditional British and more modern, oriental accents, with a healthy representation of locally caught seafood; salads and sandwiches are served on the bar's large decked terrace overlooking the sea. You can work off the meals on the tennis court, in the heated outdoor swimming pool (May-Sept). More leisurely pursuits include croquet, pool or fussball. From 2007 the hotel is hosting yoga breaks, led by an experienced Iyengar instructor. The premises are closed over Christmas (usually Nov-Jan).

New Inn

New Grimsby, Tresco, Isles of Scilly TR24 0QQ (01720 422844/www.tresco.co.uk). **Lunch served** noon-2.30pm, **dinner served** 7-9pm daily. **Main courses** £7.95-£16. **Rates** £140-£210 double. **Credit** MC, V.

Tresco's only pub is the 'cheaper' option for accommodation on the island. In the jumble of different knocked-through buildings, the rooms have been brightened and lightened, with a cool blue and white colour scheme, but the place remains cuddly and old-fashioned enough for traditionalists. Things are much livelier in the cosy bar, which is panelled with shipwreck-salvaged wood. Sunny days seem to draw the entire population of the island to its shady outdoor terrace, also attended by cheekily well-fed sparrows and chaffinches. There's a fine selection of ales (for our visit Skinner's Tresco Tipple, Abbott and Don Juan's – a special for the New Inn itself) and wines, as well as food such as garlic tiger prawns, and chorizo and crayfish linguine. An additional conservatory-style space serves ice-cream and pastries, while more full-blooded, traditional meals are served in the hotel restaurant. A couple of rooms back right on to the heated outdoor pool (May-Sept), with a little patio space in front of each, and there's an unruly boules court in the charmingly clumsy three-step garden across the lane. If full board sounds daunting, the New Inn now allows slender metropolitan appetites to opt for a B&B rate instead.

St Martin's on the Isle Hotel

Lower Town, St Martin's, Isles of Scilly TR25 0QW (01720 422090/www.stmartinshotel. co.uk). **Open** Apr-Oct. **Lunch served** *Bar* phone for details. **Dinner served** *Restaurant* 7-9pm daily. **Set dinner** £42.50 3 courses. **Rates** DB&B £260-£300 double; £320-£340 family room; £370-£410 suite. **Credit** MC, V.

The only hotel on St Martin's is a rather angular building, something like an expanded rectory built of stern grey stone (it's meant to look like a cluster of cottages). It opened in 1989 and rather looks like it. The hotel overlooks gardens with incongruous Caribbean rush umbrellas (offset by a perky Union Flag) and, beyond them, the quay and beautiful sandy beach. Many of the rooms have enviable sea views, but are otherwise rather lacking in character. The decor in the residents' lounge could do with a refresh, although the relatively sleek new ground-floor bistro-bar suggests things might be moving – albeit slowly and with deference towards the hotel's loyal core clientele. Several large rooms with extra beds are geared towards families, and the kids will be excited by the swimming pool – steamily tucked away indoors, a definite rarity on Scilly. The main restaurant is on the first floor and has one prized table perched right in the angled window looking over the channel to Teän. The menu is pretty serious stuff – how about carpaccio of wild Bodmin venison with baby turnips, mange tout and local blackberries? Facilities include a tennis court, beneath Higher Town the other side of the island.

Star Castle Hotel

The Garrison, St Mary's, Isles of Scilly TR21 0JA (01720 422317/www.star-castle.co.uk). **Lunch served** noon-2pm, **dinner served** 6.30-8.30pm daily. **Main courses** (lunch) £7-£10. **Set dinner** £24.50 3 courses, £29.50 4 courses. **Rates** DB&B £130-£282 double; £204-£310 suite. **Credit** AmEx, MC, V.

This star-shaped granite Elizabethan castle is wonderfully atmospheric – try to get a room in the main hotel rather than one of the bungalows out back that make up the bulk of accommodation. Despite steady refurbishments, the prevailing style within the castle remains traditional; stay on the first floor to be in a point of the star, in the smaller rooms of the second floor for even better views. The bungalows were World War II barracks, but a recent revamp has left them modern and spacious, with deep red and solid wood fittings. The patios of rooms on the western side look over the cliffpath to the ocean, those to the east on to a lawn and green fields. There are two on-site restaurants – one is in the original, stone-walled officers' mess room in the castle; the other, only open in summer, is a bright conservatory with rather lovely vines growing inside. The former typically serves hearty fare (pan-fried pheasant breast with herbs and balsamic vinegar on winter leaves, perhaps); the conservatory tends to focus more on fish dishes. Both are tailored to the palate of an ageing clientele, with signs of a more modern sensibility. Facilities include an aggressively chlorinated pool within a strange greenhouse-type affair, grass tennis courts and a dark little subterranean dungeon bar that draws in locals as well as hotel residents. The Star Castle closes for a fortnight over Christmas.

Padstow & Rock

Eat your heart out at the ocean's edge.

An unparalleled weekend destination for mouth-watering cuisine and gobsmacking coastal scenery; this is a place where you can indulge in the tastes of a region that's been planted firmly in the UK's foodie spotlight. Sip award-winning wines while watching wild Atlantic rollers wallop the rugged sea cliffs, or tuck in to sumptuous fresh seafood and watch the sun set over the ocean. There's plenty of adrenalin action to be found on the sweeping sandy beaches and surf breaks, or you can meander through the wooded valley and verdant tapestry that follow the banks of the sheltered estuary inland.

Discover craggy bays and tortuous inlets – these natural features that once stalled development around the Camel estuary are now attractions in themselves. Where farming, fishing and mining were once the stalwarts of Cornish industry, it is now tourism that keeps the economy thriving. But thanks to the prime-quality local produce, talented chefs and the Rick Stein phenomenon, farming and fishing still feed the colossal wave of gastronomic tourism that the area has attracted (*see p156* **Foodie revolution**). In addition to its culinary repertoire, the fishing village of Padstow oozes Cornish charm of yesteryear, with a warren of cobbled streets that lead to the hubbub of the harbourside.

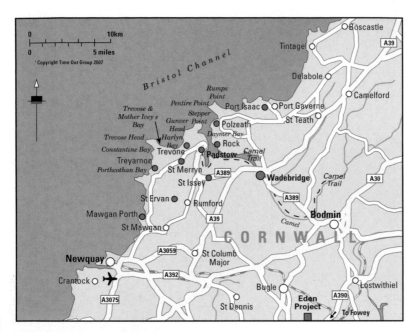

The approach to Padstow along the A389 is immediately soothing as you wind through low hills and sloping fields, past farm shops and a sprinkling of homesteads offering fresh eggs and organic produce. Once you've passed St Issey and St Petroc's, the road plunges and takes a looping detour, exposing a swipe of yellow sand that lines the blazing blue of the Camel estuary. Then before you know it you've arrived at the harbour: an animated marine shambles of crabbers, netters, yachts and pleasure cruisers. Surrounding the harbour, slate-hung, red-brick and grey-stone cottages accommodate pasty shops, boutiques, chippies, pubs and a smattering of classy restaurants. Evidence suggests that Padstow has been used as a port since the 16th century, though the demise of shipping here is down to the Doom Bar – shallow sandbanks at the mouth of the estuary on which many ships have foundered. The narrow winding streets create a picture-postcard setting ill-equipped to deal with peak-season traffic;

this is a destination to ditch the car and explore on foot or by bike. For details of riding along the Camel Trail, crossing the county in the footsteps of the Pilgrims along the Saints Way or even setting sail and feeling the wind in your hair, *see p154* **Sea the Action**.

History at the harbourside

If you can't attend the May day event of 'Obby 'Oss (*see p150* **Cultural highlights**), you can learn all about it in the Padstow Museum (Market Strand, 01841 532752, www.padstowmuseum.co.uk). This volunteer-staffed museum is a little worse for wear, and opening times vary, but it's a good spot to delve into Padstow's history. The Cinedrome (Lanadwell Street, 01841 532344, www.wtwcinemas.co.uk), which opened in 1919 as a music hall and theatre, also has a deceptively tired-looking exterior. Walking through the doors feels like stepping back in time, but in fact the cinema shows recent releases on an enlarged screen, with Dolby digital sound systems and luxury seats.

Another spot to uncover some of the area's past is St Petroc's church. This was dedicated to a monk by the name of St Petroc, who gave the town its name ('Petrock's Stow'). The church's most eye-catching features include a font with 12 apostles carved from Catacleuse stone and a medieval bench showing a fox preaching to a congregation of geese.

Accommodation	★★★★☆
Food & drink	★★★★☆
Nightlife	★★★★★
Shopping	★★★☆☆
Culture	★★☆☆☆
Sights	☆☆☆☆☆
Scenery	★★★★★

Linking the town to the church is the beginning of the Saints Way, a 30-mile ancient walking trail across the peninsula that links Padstow to Fowey on the south coast. The dark slate parish church houses the tombs of the Prideaux family, whose manor, Prideaux Place (01841 532411, www.prideauxplace.co.uk), sits imperiously in its own deer park above the harbour. The building dates from 1592 and is stuffed full of porcelain, antique glass, memorabilia and portraits by John Opie. There are other more unusual details too, including an art nouveau light switch, an ingenious early hi-fi system and a glorious 16th-century ceiling in the Great Chamber.

The stupendous, sweeping, golden beaches of North Cornwall.

Back in town visit the fascinating National Lobster Hatchery (South Quay, 01841 533877, www.nationallobster hatchery.co.uk) where you'll learn that lobsters taste with their feet, that they have three stomachs and can live to be about a hundred. If you want an overview of the town's location, head up past the lower beach landing point for the ferry, and follow the Chapel Stile field to the war memorial.

Retail therapy

Cornwall's not short of an artist or two, and if you fancy snooping around a few creative corners, Padstow is a pretty good place to do it. At the expense of more practical retail outlets for local residents, tourism has made way for plenty of galleries where you can select your own seascape to take home. For contemporary pieces have a browse in the Padstow Contemporary Art Gallery (Parnell Court, 01841 532242,

Padstow & Rock

CULTURAL HIGHLIGHTS

Arguably one of the UK's most vibrant May Day festivals is Padstow's 'Obby 'Oss, which celebrates the rite of spring. Two 'Oss'es – monstrous effigies made out of hoop-work, tarpaulin and sprays of horsehair – are paraded through the streets to the accompaniment of song, accordions and drums. The pulsing rhythms go on until midnight, marking the continuation of a tradition going back around 900 years and the resilience of the community.

But the famous 'Obby 'Oss isn't the only occasion that brings the area to life with music and festivities. In summer, traditional brass bands provide spectacular evening entertainment on Padstow's quayside, and neighbouring Wadebridge rocks its socks off at Cornwall's Folk Festival every August Bank Holiday (www.cornwallfolkfestival.com). Embrace the scenery that captured the creative talents of the late poet laureate Sir John Betjeman, and catch an atmospheric recital of his poetry as the sun sets on the grassy knoll of Brae Hill overlooking Daymer Bay (www.johnbetjeman.com).

www.padstowgallery.com), and the Blue Wing Gallery (Hornabrook Place, 01841 533999, www.blue-wing.co.uk) – in the latter you will also find a range of designer jewellery. For local landscapes to hang on your wall visit the Whistlefish Gallery (South Quay, 01209 202441, www.the whistlefish.com), or the olde village shop setting of the Drawing Room (Trevone, 01841 520409), where you can have a cuppa and find ocean-inspired paintings by resident Ian Reynolds. If you want to come face to face with a local artist behind colourful landscapes and furniture art, Grace Pattinson invites you into her tucked-away Car Space Studio (2 Fentonluna Lane, 01841 533546, www.lease-of-life.myeweb.net).

There's plenty of White Stuff, Fat Face, Crew Clothing and surf labels to be found, but if you fancy a bit of retail therapy beyond the sailing and surf-brand heaven, Padstow can offer some unusual finds. Let your purse strings loose among a heady mix of boutiques, antiques, craft shops and contemporary jewellery outlets. Visit the Padstow Mussel Co for a collection of gifts inspired by Cornwall (Market Square, 01841 533111, www.thepadstowmussel co.co.uk), or for wooden crafts and unique teak-root furniture try Dukeswood (Duke Street, 01841 533442, www.dukeswood. net). So you don't literally shop till you drop, fuel up with fresh coffee at one of a smattering of stylish cafés, an award-winning hot steak pasty from Chough's by the quayside (The Strand, 01841 532835, www.thechoughbakery.co.uk), a sticky treat from Stein's Pâtisserie (Middle Street, 01841 532700, www.rickstein. com), or a lip-smacking Roskilly's Cornish ice-cream. If it's a longer-lasting taste of Cornwall you want to take away with you, stock up on delicious local treats from the Padstow Farm Shop on the outskirts of the village (01841 533570, www.padstowfarm foods.biz) or Stein's Deli on the quayside (www.rickstein.com).

A beach for all seasons

The town is the epitome of a fishing village-turned-chic, but what you're really here for is its backdrop of stupendous scenery and golden beaches. Heading out west the estuary is lined with sweeping dune-backed sands, which stop short of the climb up to the imposing headland of Stepper Point. From here the coast path continues along blustery clifftops until it reaches the Edwardian holiday suburb of Trevone and Harlyn Bay – a popular surfing beach sheltered by Trevose Head and Cataclews Point. Trevone marks the start of 'the seven bays', a string of sandy coves that lace the cliffs together all the way to Porthcothan.

Beyond Trevose Head, Booby's Bay has the skeletal remnants of a German World War I ship preserved in the sand, while Polventor – or Mother Ivey's Bay – gets its name from a farmer's widow who claimed the rights to all the shipwreck pickings along this part of the coast. Big breakers come bulldozing into Constantine Bay, making it a surfers' favourite, but beginners and bathers should be aware of the hazardous rip tides. It is named after the chapel of St Constantine, which is now standing in ruins on Trevose Golf Course. A stone's throw to the south of Constantine, Treyarnon Bay is another good spot for surfing, although caravans, an open-air tide pool and ample car parking make it a crowded family spot in peak season.

Continue down the coast and there are endless scenic beaches and coves, each with their own characteristics and appeal. The sandy funnel of Porthcothan boasts dramatic cliffs, caves and blowholes, and at Bedruthan Steps, a steep ascent leads down to one of the wildest beaches of the West Country.

To the north of Padstow, across the Camel estuary, lie the twin resorts of Rock and Polzeath. It's a short ride on the Black Tor ferry (£3 return, on demand year round during daylight hours, no Sunday service during winter; see www.padstowlive.com for details), during which you can catch a panoramic view of the Camel Valley countryside, the mouth of the estuary and the horizon beyond the striking headlands of Stepper and Pentire Points. Slightly less accessible than the Padstow side, this is swimming, surfing, waterskiing and sailing country par excellence. But with its long stretches of fine white sands rinsed by the waters of the Camel estuary, Rock seems a little inappropriately named.

On approach to the Victorian-style houses and well-manicured driveways housing shiny 4WD chariots, it's not difficult to understand why Rock has been dubbed Kensington-on-Sea. This really is a destination for second-homers, and it's the monied west Londoners that flock here and bring it alive every summer. It's hard to put a finger on any distinctive features of a community, and the absence of any central amenities is indicated by the hordes of Rockites to-ing and fro-ing on the ferry to Padstow. It's an appealing location if you want to be removed from the bustle of Padstow, but with the advantage of late-running water-taxis in summer, there is no need to miss out on the town's gastronomic superiority at dinner.

While Rock fails to embody any trace of an authentic Cornish locale, the sweeping dunes and landscape on its doorstep do the exact opposite. In fact, the jaw-dropping scenery serves up some

of the best that Cornwall beholds – rolling greens contrasting with golden sands, topped off with the zillion hues of blue that streak the ocean and sky. The sweeping sands and dunes of Daymer Bay, beloved of kids, sun-worshippers and windsurfers, are backed by St Enodoc Golf Course – possibly one of the UK's most beautiful spots if you are inclined to spoil a good walk with the swing of a club.

The perfectly rounded grassy knoll of Brae Hill makes a great place for a picnic with a view over the rippled expanse of sand, and is also a divine spot to catch a recital of John Betjeman's poetry on a summer's evening. For now you have stepped into Betjeman country. The late poet laureate spent many holidays in this area, based in the hamlet of Trebetherick and exploring the edge of Polzeath and its surrounds by bicycle. Now he lies buried in the 13th-century church of St Enodoc (once known as 'Sinking Neddy' as it was all but buried in sand), whose wonky steeple rises up from amid the grass-bound dunes.

Rock's reputation as an upmarket summer haven has spilled over to Polzeath, where couples, more mature escapees and families mingle in the sandy bay. And while Rock is for sailing, Polzeath is for surfing. Home to yet another alluring beach and gentle surf that's perfect for beginners when the right conditions prevail, beyond the breakers of Polzeath loom the two National Trust headlands of Pentire and Rumps Points. The latter is home to the remains of an Iron Age fort, and a walk out to the promontories on a blustery day promises to blow the cobwebs away and leave you feeling inspired and exhilarated.

WHERE TO STAY

There's no shortage of accommodation to choose from, but as peak season sees the whole area bursting at the seams, make sure you book in advance. The tourist board has a full list of what's on offer, but here are a few that offer one thing Padstow and Rock do incredibly well: something a little bit special.

Those looking for something dramatic should try and book one of the two twin rooms at Mother Ivey Cottage (Trevose Head, 01841 520329) – a converted pilchard cellar with sea views of the Atlantic, which lies just yards away. Alternatively, for high-end luxury and a hefty dose of glamour head to Fowey and the splendid Pencalenick House (020 7747 6858, www.pencalenick house.com), which sleeps 16 people and comes complete with staff (all food and drink is included) and a private yacht.

Due to open in Trebetherick (above Daymer Bay, at the mouth of the Camel estuary) in summer 2007, the St Moritz

Hotel (www.stmoritzhotel.co.uk) will be the first five-star, purpose-built, luxury hotel in Cornwall for over 30 years. The £13.5 million hotel will comprise 48 bedrooms, including 16 suites and 32 doubles, and will feature a Cowshed spa, fully fitted gym, restaurant and outdoor dining deck, as well as a games room and a leisure suite.

Old Custom House

South Quay, Padstow, Cornwall PL28 8BL (01841 532359/www.smallandfriendly.co.uk). **Rates** £85-£180 double. **Credit** AmEx, DC, MC, V.

Standing right on the quayside, the Old Custom House is a listed building that has been refurbished to provide an intimate and stylish hotel. Most of the rooms boast harbour views, so you can wake up to the early-morning light rising over the estuary. The superior rooms are elegant and spacious, emphasising the seaside location with sand-coloured furniture and framed drawings of shells. For that extra touch of luxury, you can indulge in the hotel's spa and pampering packages at its Lavender Room beauty suite. The only downfall to being bang-smack in the middle of town is being perched right above the pub.

Prideaux Place

Padstow, Cornwall PL28 8RP (c/o Unique Homestays, 01637 881942/www.elizabethan. uniquehomestays.com). **Rates** £400 pp/pn. **Credit** DC, MC, V.

Camel Valley's vineyards produce more than just great photo opportunities.

When you're William the Conqueror's 24th grandson, and Jane Austen is your great, great, great aunt, you might be afforded the opportunity to live within the fairytale turrets of an 81-room Elizabethan Gothic mansion overlooking Padstow. And then to finance the upkeep of the 3,500 acres of grounds it comes with. But even if you don't boast such a pedigree, you can still nab the opportunity to spend a night in regal grandeur. If you don't mind splashing out for a special occasion, you can stay at the Prideaux-Brune's castle – in a wonderfully romantic turret suite for two. As well as the lavish, historical setting (which has seen the makings of many period films), what you get for your money is a champagne reception, estuary and ocean views, a super-king-size bed and a marble-clad bathroom with a hydromassage bath (and underwater lights), plus a shower that's like standing under Niagara Falls. Have breakfast served in bed, and indulge in a candlelit banquet in the grand Elizabethan dining room.

St Edmund's House

St Edmund's Lane, Padstow, Cornwall PL28 8BY (01841 532700/www.rickstein.com). **Rates** £260 double. **Credit** MC, V.

There are some stylish rooms above the Seafood Restaurant and at St Petroc's, as well as at the new Prospect House due to open in July 2007, but the best accommodation in the Stein empire is at St Edmund's House. Think a Hamptons style beach house, with six minimalist yet luxurious rooms overlooking private gardens and the Camel estuary. Each bears the name of a local bay, etched into its driftwood door sign, and rooms boast four-poster beds, en suite marble bathrooms, oak flooring and an ambience of seaside luxury; those on the ground floor also have a private deck area. Sink into the bath with the twinkling estuary in view or recline by the bay windows and you won't want to leave the comfort of your self-contained romantic retreat; but you're forced out for breakfast, which is served in the Seafood Restaurant.

St Enodoc

Rock, Cornwall PL27 6LA (01208 863394/ www.enodoc-hotel.co.uk). **Open** Mar-Nov. **Rates** £125-£230 double; £185-£385 suite; £150-£325 family suite. **Credit** AmEx, DC, MC, V.

This family-friendly hotel is a breath of fresh air, and a bastion of taste and decorum. St Enodoc's is impeccably chic without being frosty. From the airy reception and adjoining lounge with slate floors and original art, you climb up stairs and landings carpeted in candy stripes to equally bright rooms. (There are 16 in total, a quarter of which are family sized.) The grounds are pleasantly landscaped and the sheltered outdoor pool, heated from May to September, with wooden steamer chairs dotted around it, is a delight. Baths are big, showers torrent forth, handbasins are double-sized and fluffy bathrobes and decent toiletries are provided. The split-level restaurant has wooden floors, efficient staff and a smart menu of Cornish seafood (pan-fried skate or sea bass, for example)

SEA THE ACTION

Padstow and Rock's stunning scenery and beaches are more than good to look at. Get active.

TWO-WHEELED ADVENTURE

Trundle along the newly extended Camel Trail between Padstow, Wadebridge and the edge of Bodmin Moor. This two-tier adventure follows the level route of a disused railway from the glistening banks of the Camel estuary and through the wooded thickets of the Camel Valley (www.cycle cornwall.com). Bikes can be hired at Padstow Cycle Hire (South Quay, 01841 533533, www.padstowcyclehire.com), and there are pubs and tea shops en route for refuelling.

BEST FOOT FORWARD

Whether you've got a couple of hours or a couple of days to spare, Padstow and its surrounds boast some stunning coastal and countryside walks. Explore the Camel Trail on foot or follow in pilgrims' footsteps along the ancient 30-mile Saints Way from Padstow to Fowey. Trace the coastline to Gunver Head or all the way to Trevone, and encounter secret coves at the foot of the cliffs, staggering coastal views, blowholes and collapsed sea caves. Get blown away on the trail from Polzeath to the remnants of an Iron Age castle at Rumps Point, or step foot in John Betjeman country as you explore the golden expanse of Daymer Bay, the rolling dunes and climb the grassy knoll of Brae Hill. Wherever you choose to wander, pack a pair of binoculars and keep a look out for hawks, buzzards, seals and dolphins. (Route maps available from Padstow Tourist Information Centre; *see p149*).

CATCH YOUR SUPPER

Take a closer look at one of Cornwall's most important historic industries and catch your own supper when you hop aboard with the fishermen. At Padstow harbour you'll find plenty of fishing boats willing to take you onboard, and Padstow Angling Centre (01841 532762) offers deep-sea and mackerel fishing trips.

WET & WILD

Explore the Camel estuary in a sailing dinghy or powerboat with the Camel School of Seamanship (The Pontoon, Rock, 01208 862881, www.camel sailing.co.uk), or try Sailing at Rock for tuition onboard traditional Drascombe Luggers and Cornish Shrimpers (The Pontoon, Rock, 01208 841246). You can paddle along the tranquil waterways in a kayak with New Horizons (01208 262800, 07917 076794, www.ncdc.gov.uk), but if you want a bit more welly-on-the-water, the Camel Ski School offers waterskiing and wakeboarding (The Pontoon, Rock, 01208 862727, www.camel skischool.com), and there are high-speed boat trips departing from Padstow harbour (details from the Tourist Information Centre).

TEE OFF

Tee off on one of the finest links golf courses in the South-west. St Enodoc Golf Club in Rock (01208 863216, www.st-enodoc.co.uk) incorporates two beautifully sited courses on the edge of the estuary, one of which allows unrestricted access for visiting players. Also, enjoying a spectacular position over Constantine Bay is Trevose Golf Club (01841 520208, www.trevose-gc.co.uk), which has extensive country club facilities.

SURF'S UP

Surfboard hire and lessons are touted in almost every wave-licked sandy cove. Padstow's Harlyn Surf School (01841 533076, www.harlynsurf.co. uk) can combine tuition with bed and full board. On the other side of the estuary, Surf's Up! (Polzeath Beach, 01208 862003, www.surfsupsurf school.com) offers short or full-day surfing lessons, plus wetsuit and board hire, as does the Animal Surf School (Polzeath Beach, 0870 242 2856, www.animalsurfacademy. co.uk). You can hire all equipment from Anne's Cottage Surf Shop (Polzeath Beach, 01208 863317).

and locally produced meat, vegetables and cheese. Outside, the terrace looks over the gardens and pool to the Camel estuary. A little gate in the garden sets you on the footpath for the golf course, the beach, dunes and St Enodoc church, saving you the ghastly road down to the beach – it's crammed with 4X4s and has little or no pavement.

Tregea Hotel

16-18 High Street, Padstow, Cornwall PL28 8BB (0871 871 2686/www.tregea.co.uk). **Rates** £120 double. **Credit** AmEx, DC, MC, V. Behind the door of an ivy-fronted cottage at the top of the town, the Tregea (which literally translates as 'the house on the hill') is set back from the bustle of Padstow's harbour front. Having retained much of its 17th-century charm and character, it has been refurbished with a lick of contemporary style. Relax in the sumptuous sofas by the fireside, take the weight off over a tipple at the licensed bar, and retire to one of eight individual rooms oozing with Cornish coastal character. Local artwork, a sprinkling of shells, whitewashed and wicker furniture, and hues of blues and beiges enhance the beachy feel of the interior. There's limited parking – which is a luxury in Padstow – and the hotel extends into four additional rooms of the adjoining Ruskin House (www.ruskinhouse.com). Where Tregea does 'English country cottage with a twist', Ruskin House is more 'New England-style'. Whichever you choose to stay in, you can expect friendly service with a personal touch.

Treverbyn House

Station Road, Padstow, Cornwall PL28 8DA (01841 532855/www.treverbynhouse.com). **Rates** £30-£50 double. **Credit** DC, MC, V. A reasonably priced B&B in a grand Edwardian shell overlooking the Camel estuary. For a romantic weekend, hide out in the stylish decadence of the Turret Room, or choose a room with a cosy open fire for a winter retreat. A light smattering of chintz keeps the interior in keeping with its period, but the rooms are bright, airy and comfortable. A delicious breakfast with organic own-made preserves is served in your room, so you can relax happily in your worst nightwear and stare out at the estuary views. The most luxurious of a family of accommodation, Tregea is sister to the Treann (Dennis Road, 01841 533855, www.treverbynhouse.com/treann.html) and Pendeen House (Dennis Road, 01841 532724, www.pendeenhousepadstow.co.uk).

WHERE TO EAT & DRINK

Fresh local produce, a handful of masterchefs and more top-notch eateries than you can poke your knife and fork at. If you like food, you can't go wrong in and around Padstow. In addition to the best of a good bunch that are reviewed below, there are cafés, restaurants, pasty shops and plenty of pubs to be discovered from Porthcothan to Port Isaac. *See also p156* **Foodie revolution**.

Ebb

1A The Strand, Padstow, Cornwall PL28 8BS (01841 532565). **Dinner served** *Easter-late Oct* 7-9.30pm Mon, Wed-Sun. **Main courses** £13.50-£17.50. **Credit** MC, V. From an unassuming back alley location, the Ebb offers a smart and intimate dining experience. Attention to detail starts with good bread and olive oil, sparkling table settings, and just-so service in a modern room (beige, nicely lit, slightly disconcerting Schiele-esque art). The food and mood are similarly contemporary, with an emphasis on local and organic produce. A short menu combines fish favourites with Asian and Mediterranean borrowings, the latter a little more successfully in our experience. A tian of crab with guacamole and spiced cherry tomatoes makes a notable starter, followed by the likes of monkfish and shrimps in a fragrant five-spice sauce, or a more traditional herb-crusted cod. There's a varied dessert list, but if you've never tasted baby figs, this is the place to sample them in a delicious rum syrup with vanilla ice-cream.

Estuary

16-18 High Street, Padstow, Cornwall PL28 8RY (01841 532400/www.theestuaryrestaurant. com). **Dinner served** 6.30-9.30pm Tue-Sun. **Set dinner** £19.95 3 courses. **Credit** MC, V. Away from the hustle and bustle of the harbourside, the Estuary is an intimate 20-cover dining room housed in a 17th-century Cornish cottage. And while the venue makes much of its period charm, it has also dressed up in smart, contemporary style to combine fine dining with a friendly, unpretentious vibe. Simple dishes are neatly served, and uncluttered; classic flavours let the tasty, locally sourced ingredients do the talking. Try the crab bisque or excellent trio of Cornish fish; both showcase the succulent seafood that Padstow is famous for. Unlike so many other restaurants in the village, the menu isn't too biased towards fish and traditional dishes such as the lamb shank are beautifully cooked. A pleasant dining experience with a very reasonable price tag, but in a place like Padstow the Estuary isn't destined to be the talk of the town.

L'Estuaire

Pavilion Building, Rock Road, Rock, Wadebridge, Cornwall PL27 6JS (01208 862622). **Lunch served** 12.30-2pm, **dinner served** 7-9pm Wed-Sun. **Main courses** £15-£24.50. **Set lunch** £22 3 courses. **Set dinner** £42 tasting menu. **Credit** AmEx, MC, V. Formerly the Michelin-starred Black Pig – one of Cornwall's most applauded restaurants – L'Estuaire now serves fine French cuisine created from local produce. So defiantly français is the theme that the menu comes first in French before English translations. Hues of beige hint at understated sophistication, but character-wise L'Estuaire falls short to the point of dullness. That said, with a chef that has worked with the likes of Raymond Blanc, the food pulls off the continental style with success. Confit duck ravioli is rich and tasty with a delicate consommé, while oysters come gently doused in red wine and parsley jus. Mains include fillet of turbot with citrus fruit, fennel and star anise, and honeyed pork with snails and cider sauce.

Harbour Inn

Strand Street, Padstow, Cornwall PL28 8BL (01841 533148). **Open** noon-10pm daily. **Lunch served** noon-2pm, **dinner served** 6-9pm daily. **Main courses** £6-£9. **Credit** MC, V.
Tucked just behind the quay, this is a refreshingly local spot for a Cornish ale or a stiff gin and tonic. Under the low ceilings fat leather sofas beg you to get comfortable by the log fire, while the wooden floorboards and boating paraphernalia give the place a nautical ambience. If you find yourself hankering for unfussy pub grub at a reasonable price tag, check out the handwritten menus.

London Inn

Lanadwell Street, Padstow, Cornwall PL28 8AN (01841 532554). **Lunch served** noon-2pm, **dinner served** 6.30-9pm daily. **Main courses** £6.95-£7.95. **Set lunch** (Sun) £6.50 1 course, £8.50 2 courses, £10.50 3 courses. **Credit** AmEx, MC, V.
Originally three fishermen's cottages nestling in the inner streets behind the quay, this is a proper local boozer right off the foodie trail. It's a fine place to sup a traditional Cornish ale, just don't expect a trendy wine list or plump sofas to sit on. There is, however, plenty of local character as well as lots of local characters to spin you a yarn or two. A traditional inn packed with nautical apparatus and good vibes.

Margot's Bistro

11 Duke Street, Padstow, Cornwall PL28 8AB (01841 533441/www.margots.co.uk). **Lunch served** noon-2pm Tue-Sat. **Dinner served** 7-9pm Tue-Sat. **Main courses** (lunch) £10.95-£16.95; (dinner) £14.50-£16.95. **Set dinner** £21.50 2 courses, £25.95 3 courses, £32 tasting menu. **Credit** AmEx, MC, V.

FOODIE REVOLUTION

Since piscatorial magnate Rick Stein put Padstow in the culinary spotlight, this petite harbourside village has risen to fame as the foodie capital of the region. From its beginnings at the flagship Seafood Restaurant, 'Padstein' was born as the celebrity chef's signature was smattered across three restaurants, a fish and chip shop, a deli (South Quay, 01841 533466 ext 432), pâtisserie (01841 533901), gift shop (8 Middle Street, 01841 532221), accommodation (*see p152*) and a famous seafood school (01841 533466, www.rickstein.com).

For visitors, the Rick Stein 'theme park' can get a tad infuriating, as you have to look hard to avoid his stamp on everything from your T-shirt to your wine bottle. But under his tutelage, Padstow shed its ragged fishing jersey for a natty white dinner jacket to become one of the most popular dining destinations in the region.

Since his empire has turned heads towards the area's perfect marriage of top-quality local produce and stunning scenery, Stein is no longer the only name in town with a strictly 'source local' manifesto and a smart dining room to boot. To his credit he was the catalyst that showcased the calibre of Cornish produce to the foodie world, and that in turn has given rise to a whole host of delectable restaurants where you can experience a taste of the West Country. Your taste buds will be assaulted by seasonal flavours and mouth-watering ingredients plucked straight from the surrounding ocean and countryside. His food lives up to its reputation, but Stein's is just one slice of this gastronomic haven waiting to be explored.

Margot's may not have the celebrity status of a Rick Stein's, but it's almost as difficult to get a table. Even out of season it is often fully booked. Happily, there's only one sitting per night, which, when you do get a table, makes it a very relaxed affair (a little slow even, particularly if you haven't released the throttle and hit Cornish gear yet). Small and quirky, it has a blue and sand-coloured interior, an intimate atmosphere, and chatty staff. Food comes in sizeable portions and is sourced daily from local suppliers: mackerel fillets with truffle oil, plump and juicy scallops, succulent Cornish lamb with rosemary jus, and wild sea bass on herby mash all feature.

Mariners Rock

Slipway, Rock, Cornwall PL27 6LD (01208 863679/www.marinersrock.com). Summer **Lunch served** 12.30-3.30pm, **dinner served** 6.30-9.30pm daily. *Winter* **Lunch served** 12.30-3.30pm, **dinner served** 6.30-9.30pm Mon, Thur-Sun. **Main courses** £10-£16. **Credit** MC, V.

If you want to mix with the sailing crowd, there's nowhere better to catch them than in this swanky bar and restaurant overlooking the yacht club and the mouth of the estuary. And if you're not there to talk boating, you can focus on the stunning views over the water to Padstow, or sink into a leather sofa by the roaring log fire on a cooler winter's eve.

No. 6

Middle Street, Padstow, Cornwall PL28 8AP (01841 532093/www.number6inpadstow. co.uk). **Dinner served** *Summer* 5.30-10pm daily. *Winter* 6.30-10pm Tue-Sat. **Main courses** £16.50-£26. **Set dinner** £38 2 courses, £45 3 courses, £60 tasting menu. **Credit** AmEx, MC, V.

Keeping Stein's Seafood Restaurant well and truly on its toes, No. 6 was launched by a team headed up by one of Gordon Ramsay's protégés. Bedecked in a swanky, contemporary style with black and white checked floors, funky crockery and suited waiters, the restaurant is as well dressed as the food. Sweet chilli and spiced avocado accompany perfectly seared carpaccio of tuna, Launceston lamb is made daringly complex courtesy of sweetbreads, liver and kidneys, and monkfish comes with oxtail cottage pie. Everything comes beautifully presented and bursting with innovative flavour. A sorbet palette cleanser, for example, comes with popping candy, and vanilla, lemongrass and white chocolate mousse is filled with fresh mango purée and served with pickled ginger ice-cream. Well worth the detour from Stein-land.

Oyster Catcher

Polzeath, Wadebridge, Cornwall PL27 6TG (01208 862371/www.smallandfriendly.co.uk). **Open/meals served** *Summer* 11am-midnight daily. *Winter* noon-11pm daily. **Main courses** £9. **Credit** AmEx, MC, V.

This is a pleasant pint-stop with a view over the beach – especially welcome if you've done a bit of legwork over to Padstow, St Enodoc and Daymer Bay. There's a fabulous patio for surf-spotting on sunny days and snug sofas for blustery afternoons. And if you fancy stopping over after one too many, upstairs there are self-catering apartments for hire.

Pescadou Restaurant

South Quay, Padstow, Cornwall PL28 8BL (01841 532359/www.pescadou.co.uk). **Lunch served** noon-2pm, **dinner served** 7-9pm daily. **Main courses** £6.95-£17.95. **Credit** AmEx, MC, V.

As the name suggests, this is a place for fish-lovers. A mix of classic and contemporary in both design and cuisine, Pescadou tailors its menu around the best of what is caught on its doorstep (it has a prime harbourside position). And even if it's not plucked from the ocean outside, pickings such as the succulent Fal river rope-grown mussels won't be sourced from too far away. While the selection attempts to cater outside of its seafood speciality, options such as roasted butternut squash, aubergine and plum tart seem bland next to succulent roasted cod fillet with a cornish yarg and pesto crust, or the grilled half-shell scallops dressed with sweet chilli, lime and coriander.

R Bar

6 North Quay, Padstow, Cornwall PL28 8AG, (01841 532218/www.rojanos.co.uk/r-bar). **Open** noon-11.30pm. Closed in winter. **Main courses** tapas at £1.75 each (lunch); £8.95-£13.95 (dinner). **Credit** MC, V.

Just as the restaurants of the town have had a makeover, so the bars are updating their style and joining the ranks of the hip upcountry hangouts. With swanky red stools and leather sofas set against a funky wood interior, this vibrant new bar at the edge of the harbour is spot on for coffee, cocktails, wine and tapas.

Ripley's

St Merryn, Padstow, Cornwall PL28 8NQ (01841 520179). **Open** *Mar-Nov* **Dinner served** 7-9.30pm Tue-Sat. **Main courses** £15.50-£20. **Set menu** £20 3 courses. **Credit** MC, V.

Set up by a former head chef from Rick Stein's Seafood Restaurant, Ripley's bears all the marks of a top-quality establishment, but has ditched the frills in favour of a bistro-style menu. And still the food is so good (sourced from local farmers and Cornish producers where possible) that it has earned a Michelin star. Housed in a beautiful white-washed cottage, with tasteful and understated decor (wooden beams, stylish furniture), Ripley's offers a relaxed dining environment. The small menu of local seafood and meat changes daily; vegetarians should order in advance. Tuck into flawless dishes such as pheasant and chestnut terrine, grilled mackerel topped with a subtle hazelnut

Pride of place.
Regal grandeur
comes as stand
at Prideaux Plac

dressing, or show-stealing john dory with chicory and grapefruit. The food is great, the prices are reasonable, so it goes without saying you need to book in advance. If you can't get a table, head for the chef's Ripley & Pope Delicatessen across the road where you can stock up on ingredients to create your own culinary masterpieces (01841 521407).

Shipwrights Inn

North Quay, Padstow, Cornwall PL25 8AF (01841 532451). **Open/meals served** noon-9pm daily. **Main courses** £9-£12. **Credit** AmEx, MC, V.

Sat right beside the ferry departure slip, this popular bar can be heaving in the summer, but it's a great spot to sit outside and watch quayside life. Recently decked out, both upstairs and downstairs show off harbour views and a contemporary nautical theme with a rustic edge.

Rick Stein's Café

10 Middle Street, Padstow, Cornwall PL28 8AP (01841 532700/www.rickstein.com). **Breakfast served** 8am-10am, **lunch served** noon-3pm, **dinner served** 6pm-10pm daily (7.30-9pm Nov-late-Feb). **Main courses** £9.50-£16.95. **Credit** MC, V.

With none of the pretension yet oodles of style, this is the sort of place you can be just as happy slurping coffee behind a newspaper, as dressed up for Sunday lunch. A nautical theme befits its location; stripy cushions, watercolours adorning wood-panelled walls, and a courtyard for sunny afternoons. The seafood, even in its simplest form, is fantastic, with firm favourites such as salt and pepper prawns, Thai fish cakes and devilled mackerel regularly featuring on a seasonal menu that changes daily. Among the classic fish dishes you'll find the gamey flavours of baked guinea fowl and smoked sausage and a hearty chickpea, parsley and cod stew. Although it's the most relaxed and affordable under the Stein banner, this place definitely delivers.

St Petroc's Bistro

4 New Street, Padstow, Cornwall PL28 8EA (01841 532700/www.rickstein.com). **Lunch served** noon-2.30pm daily. **Dinner served** *Summer* 6.30-10pm daily. *Winter* 7-9.30pm daily. **Main courses** £12.50-£18.95. **Credit** MC, V.

The fifth oldest building in Padstow, St Petroc's has blended its more traditional character with a contemporary Stein twist. A more simple bistro menu bears all the quality of the man himself, but his signature piscatorial theme is diluted by a range of meat, game and vegetarian dishes. The menu changes daily according to what's in, what's left and what's been caught, and although it makes light reading it caters for all tastes – and comes with an affordable price tag. The ribeye steak with a béarnaise sauce is a simple favourite cooked to perfection (although on our visit the cut was Scottish,

and not Cornish-reared), and again, the roast cod says everything about the superb quality of local fish that Rick Stein has been raving about for years.

Seafood Restaurant

Riverside, Padstow, Cornwall PL28 8BY (01841 532700/www.rickstein.com). **Lunch served** noon-2.30pm, **dinner served** 7-10pm daily. **Main courses** £17.50-£44. **Set dinner** £65 7 courses. **Credit**, MC, V.

The jewel in the crown of the Stein empire, his flagship establishment is the place to head if you're out to impress and there's no limit to your budget. The seafood is beyond reproach, the stuff of pilgrimage: a vast, impeccably sourced variety, from its simple Padstow lobster and oysters sourced from the Helford, Ireland and France, to the innovative combinations of monkfish vindaloo, mackerel stuffed with ginger and chilli masala, and sea bass with vanilla vinaigrette. Cod and chips was as good as could be imagined. Hake with bay leaves, onion and garlic was flat-out superb. But outside its specialism the restaurant falls down when judged against others of this (hefty) price band. And although the ambience oozes with a sleek and contemporary style, £8.50 is a lot to pay for a dessert, however good.

Stein's Fish & Chips

South Quay, Padstow, Cornwall PL28 8RL (01841 532700/www.rickstein.com). **Lunch served** *Summer* noon-2.30pm, **dinner served** 5-9pm Mon-Sat; noon-6pm Sun. *Winter* times vary. **Main courses** £6-£11.45. **Credit** MC, V.

The impressive choice of fish varieties on offer here blows your average fish and chip shop out of the water. But despite boasting a menu that changes according to the day's catch, as well as some excellent shellfish, service here can be sluggish. And don't expect a plate or cutlery, even if you choose to eat in. At least the beer comes in a glass, and the pebbled counters, shell-framed mirrors and clean interior create a comfortable beachy atmosphere – although it's all too easily drowned by the hordes of families clamouring to sample a taste of the Stein reputation. Ultimately, it's the food that matters, and the quality of the fish is flawless. Expect generous portions of plump, juicy fillets encased in a perfect golden batter (or grilled if you prefer), served with steaming hot, crispy-shelled chips and a slice of fresh lemon. It's worth the wait.

Stein's Pâtisserie

Lanadwell Street, Padstow, Cornwall PL28 8AN (01841 533901/www.rickstein.com). **Open** *Summer* 9am-5pm Mon-Sat; 10am-4pm Sun. *Winter* 10am-4pm Mon-Sat; 10am-3pm Sun. **Credit** (minimum £10) MC, V.

Handcrafted cakes, pastries, truffles and gigantic meringues will have you salivating at the window display, and before you know it you will be sucked into this tardis of delectable sticky treats.

Mendips

The hills are alive…

Rising up from the marshy lowlands of the Somerset Levels in the south and stretching up to the River Avon and Chew Valley Lake – with Bath beyond – in the north, the Mendip Hills are one of the most beautiful corners of England. This is karst country: the Mendips may have more than their fair share of sheep-nibbled rolling green fields, bounded by dry stone walls and old villages, but really they're famous for cave-riddled hills, dramatic escarpments, dry gorges and sinks. From Glastonbury's ancient holy sites to the miniature cathedral city of Wells, the Mendips are about bracing walks, village pubs with locally brewed beer straight out of a barrel, happy dogs, dramatic panoramas and bluebell-carpeted forests.

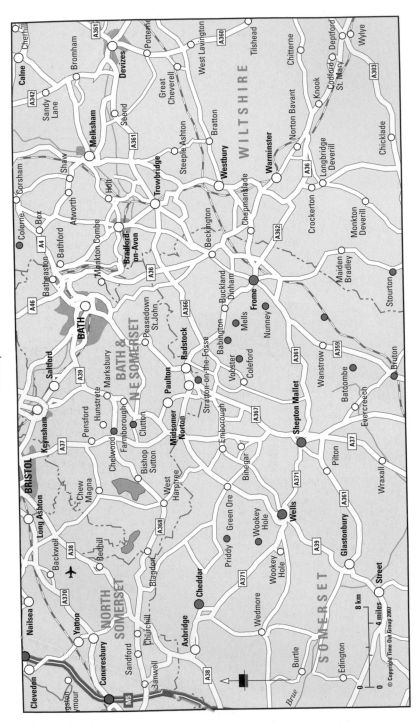

Mendips

In north-east Somerset, rising up gently between stately Bath and sanctified Glastonbury, the Mendip hills are an exceptionally lovely part of the world. Estate agents jump at the chance to compare this area to the Cotswolds, but the atmosphere is very different. More laid-back and welcoming, less precious and considerably less clogged with coach parties, the Mendips have a particular congeniality. Here you'll find bridle paths and ponies, astounding scrumpy and plenty of wide open spaces. Indeed, the hills are green and pleasant in the way Blake might have been picturing when he penned *Jerusalem*.

To the south of the range lies Wells, the smallest cathedral city in England. Its cathedral is possibly the most beautiful in Britain, the niches in its west front occupied by 300 medieval figure sculptures. Kings, bishops, angels and apostles survey a greensward close that keeps the proper little city at a respectable distance. Inside, the nave's unique 'scissor arches' look as if they might have been designed yesterday. In fact, they've been holding up the tower for almost 700 years. Stop to consult the ingenious clock invented by Brother Lightfoot in the 14th century, and watch the valiant knights joust while the sun, moon and stars revolve on the stroke of every quarter. Elsewhere in the city, it's worth leaving time to see the swans ring a bell to demand their supper in the moat of the Bishop's Palace; strolling through the city's ancient market place is another timeless pleasure.

Going underground

When the Middle Ages begin to pall, head a couple of miles west to Wookey Hole, where HG Wells taught at the local school. The caves here (www.wookey.co.uk) are a tourist magnet; run by circus supremo Gerry Cottle, they boast old-fashioned fairground attractions, a museum and a paper mill, which still produces fine handmade vellum. Wookey Hole has been drawing in illustrious visitors for centuries. Daniel Defoe wasn't impressed; Alexander Pope had the stalactites shot down for his grotto at Twickenham; Coleridge, who was probably on something, was put in mind of Xanadu.

The site is dramatic enough to hold its own against the not exactly psychedelic sound-and-light effects that have been installed, and you can escape the queues and crowds by visiting out of season.

Natural wonders abound on the south-facing flanks of the Mendips, reaching their commercialised apotheosis in Cheddar. Just beyond Wookey is the much smaller and less cheesy Ebbor Gorge, a wooded National Nature Reserve surrounding a craggy limestone gulch – home to the lesser horseshoe bat. Several well-signposted walks are recommended, none likely to be terribly busy at any time of year, offering stunning views over the vale of Glastonbury. Further up the same road, Priddy is an old agricultural village on the tops, laced about by wonderful drystone walls. A couple of unreconstructed local boozers sit near an expansive green in the middle.

If you think that's as escapist as it gets, try heading towards the eastern end of the region. Here, winding roads run between high hedges and earthen banks, through hidden valleys and across fast-flowing fords. It's one of those secret Catholic enclaves of the countryside that have preserved a different pace of life. By way of examples, seek out the neo-Gothic glory of Downside Abbey and the Benedictines near Stratton-on-the-Fosse; check out the moated ruin of a Frenchified 14th-century castle in sleepy Nunney; or amble into the gorgeous old village of Mells. A medieval street leads up to a churchyard where Siegfried Sassoon, Ronald Knox and Violet Bonham Carter are buried. The church itself contains memorials by Eric Gill, Edwin Lutyens and Edward Burne-Jones, as well as an unusual equine sculpture by Sir Alfred Munnings commemorating Edward Horner, who was killed in World War I. One of his ancestors was probably (not) Little Jack Horner, who sat in a corner

Accommodation	★★★★☆
Food & drink	★★★☆☆
Nightlife	☆☆☆☆☆
Shopping	☆☆☆☆☆
Culture	★☆☆☆☆
Sights	★★★☆☆
Scenery	★★★★☆

TOURIST INFORMATION

Cheddar
The Gorge, Cheddar, Somerset BS27 3QE (01934 744071/ www.somerset.gov.uk).
Frome
Round Tower, 2 Bridge Street, Frome, Somerset BA11 1BB (01373 467271/ www.somerset.gov.uk).
Glastonbury
9 High Street, Glastonbury, Somerset BA6 9DP (01458 832954/ www.glastonburytic.co.uk).
Shepton Mallet
70 High Street, Shepton Mallet, Somerset BA4 5AS (01749 345258/ www.sheptonmallet.org).

pulling a plum (the deeds to the Manor of Mells at the Dissolution, supposedly) out of a pie with his thumb. In Mells there are plenty of thumbs in pies, as well as games, terrier races, market stalls and much jollity on the village's annual Daffodil Day in early April. Nursery rhymes crop up again for no apparent reason a short way to the north in Kilmersdon, where Jack and Jill took their ill-fated jaunt up the hill.

Frome is the major market town in the east, once busy enough making cloth to be described by William Cobbett in the early 19th century as 'a sort of little Manchester'. It may come as some surprise that this part of the country has never been a stranger to heavy industry. Quarries, mines and breweries are still responsible for some of its character, though ever less of its workforce, in towns like Shepton Mallet, Midsomer Norton and Radstock.

Evidence of the Mendips' very earliest communities can be found on a quiet spur of a hill near the village of Wellow. Constructed some 5,000 years ago, Stoney Littleton Long Barrow is a remarkable chambered tomb. Unusually, you're allowed to clamber inside the four-foot entrance, decorated with an ammonite, and ponder upon the lives led by the occupants of this impressive burial site. Children (and grown-ups) may get slightly spooked. If that's not

your thing, head over to the highly rated Wellow Trekking Centre (01225 834376) for a spot of wholesome pony hacking, carriage hire or kiddie quad biking.

Further south, some ten miles east of Shepton Mallet across the valley of the Frome, Stourhead (01747 841152, www.nationaltrust.org.uk) is a Palladian mansion with one of the most beautiful landscaped gardens in all England. Designed by the banker Henry Hoare in the 18th century, it has a fine array of follies surrounding the lake, including a grotto, a Tuscan Temple of Flora, an obelisk, a pantheon and a Temple of Apollo. The most dramatic of them all can be found a couple of miles' walk west through the woods: King Alfred's Tower, a 160-foot triangular brick structure, was erected in 1772 to commemorate a nearby Saxon victory more than 900 years earlier. It gives tremendous views towards the mellow contours of the Mendips.

WHERE TO STAY

There are a number of wonderful options in the Mendips area, and many of the establishments featured in the Where to Eat & Drink section (*see p167*) have rooms too, notably the Old Priory (*see p170*), the White Hart Inn (*see p171*) and the Talbot (*see p170*).

Ston Easton Park
18th-century
Palladian mansion
complete with rive

Cheddar

Babington House

*Babington, nr Frome, Somerset BA11 3RW
(01373 812266/www.babingtonhouse.co.uk).*
Rates £270-£365 double (non-members);
£230-£320 double (members). **Credit** AmEx,
DC, MC, V.

Babington started life as the louche country get-away of private drinking club Soho House, but has quickly evolved into one of Britain's best hotels. The 18th-century manor house oozes charm and relaxed hospitality, providing an idyllic getaway for the young families and sybaritic professionals who flock here. Stroll on the sloping lakeside lawns, play on the tennis courts or swim a length or two in your pool of choice (there's one in the barn, and a wonderful open-air affair by the river-bank). Or simply lie back and be pummelled and smeared with Cowshed beauty products. Couples could be equally happy never straying from their rooms, equipped with huge beds and baths, superb showers and funky furniture and fittings – including flat-screen TVs with DVD players. In the attic, room six has a hot tub on its balcony, with lovely views over the lake. Babington is equally good for families, with rooms in the Stable Block equipped with everything from XBoxes to microwaves and milk. There's also 'The Little House'; essentially, a drop-in crèche for over-ones. A few judicious rules (kids are barred from the pool at certain hours, and some of the public rooms) ensure that it never feels overrun. Meals are served room service, or in the main house. Breakfasts are particularly splendid – you can sit on the terrace with sweeping views of the lawns and pond, ducks quacking at your feet, and consume giant portions of fruit, bacon, muffins and kippers. But staff are generally relaxed about when (and what) you eat, and how you spend your days.

Charlton House

*Charlton Road, Shepton Mallet, nr Bath,
Somerset BA4 4PR (01749 342008/www.
charltonhouse.com).* **Rates** £180-£375 double;
£465 suite. **Credit** AmEx, DC, MC, V.

Bought in 1996 by Roger and Monty Saul, founders of the Mulberry fashion label, this 17th-century manor-house hotel cum indulgent sanc-tuary is deservedly famous for its restaurant and state-of-the-art spa. Bijou in scale and beautifully designed, Monty's Spa features an indoor and outdoor ozone-treated hydrotherapy pool, a laco-nium, sauna and steam room. Two of the guest bedrooms – Hayloft and Chesterblade – are also kitted out to enable couples to enjoy simultaneous treatments. Each of the 25 bedrooms and suites has its own distinct identity, but all feature rich hues, sumptuous fabrics (Mulberry, naturally) and gorgeous antiques. It's got a traditional country house feel, without being remotely stuffy or old-fashioned. Romantics will be swept off their feet by the secret garden room; other cham-bers feature grand four-poster beds, private court-yards and spectacular bathrooms (check out Ostler's unique copper bath). Really, the whole place is perfect for lovers' trysts. A sumptuous three-course dinner in the acclaimed restaurant (*see p167*) is an unmissable part of the whole experience.

George Inn

*High Street, Norton St Philip, nr Bath,
Somerset BA2 7LH (01373 834224/www.
thegeorgeinn-nsp.co.uk).* **Rates** £80-£110
double. **Open** *Bar* 11am-2.30pm, 5.30-11pm
Mon-Sat; noon-2.30pm, 7-10.30pm Sun. **Lunch
served** noon-2pm, **dinner served** 7-9pm
daily. **Main courses** £10-£16. **Credit** AmEx,
MC, V.

Dating back to 1322, the George is a magnificent Grade I-listed, stone-built coaching inn with a rich history; Samuel Pepys, en route to nearby Bath, once dined here for the princely sum of ten shillings. At one time the inn had at least 20 rooms, but it now has eight – three with handmade repro four-posters and the rest doubles, all with charmingly uneven wooden floors, furniture in keeping with the antiquity of the place and surprisingly decent bathrooms. Downstairs, you can sip a contemplative pint in the flagstone-floored bar, warmed in winter by a roaring log fire. In summer, the pub's back garden, overlooking the pretty village church and cricket pitch, is a delightful place to while away an afternoon.

Hunstrete House Hotel

Chelwood, nr Bath, Somerset BS39 4NS (01761 490490/www.hunstretehouse.co.uk). **Rates** £180-£215 double; £260-£285 suite. **Credit** AmEx, DC, MC, V.
Turn off a narrow, winding lane on the western edge of the Mendip hills, head down an imposing tree-lined avenue, and at the end of it you'll find this pretty Georgian country-house hotel. In the capable hands of manager Mark Dridge and chef Matt Lord, it's everything you would hope it would be – assuming you want lashings of old English charm, polite manners and fine dining. The hotel is surrounded by 71 acres of woodlands and gardens, with a deer park, swimming pool, architectural follies and a walled Victorian garden. There are 25 serene en suite bedrooms, each named after a local bird. Decorated in tasteful, traditional fashion, some with swagged four-poster beds, they offer various but equally lovely views over the deer park, paddocks and croquet lawn. Spa sessions (massage, reiki, private yoga) can be arranged in advance, and sporting types will love the easy access to everything from tennis and riding to clay pigeon shooting. Special rates are available for those wishing to partake of dinner, bed and breakfast – the restaurant is extremely smart (*see p170*).

Lucknam Park

Colerne, Chippenham, Wiltshire SN14 8AZ (01225 742777/www.lucknampark.co.uk). **Rates** £245-£450 double; £535-£895 suite. **Credit** AmEx, DC, MC, V.
A private country home until 1987, Lucknam Park is, quite simply, stunning. Entry to the estate is via an impressive mile-long avenue, lined with beech and lime trees that were planted in 1827. The original, central part of the house was built in around 1700, the bowed wings added at a later stage. The 13 suites and 29 bedrooms are spread throughout the main house and the pretty courtyard behind, offering calm and understated luxury. Most splendid of all are the grand master suites, both of which feature imposing four-poster beds, large seating areas and a writing desk (you'll feel like a character from a Jane Austen novel). While the Michelin-starred restaurant wasn't entirely faultless, on the whole the seasonal food met our very high expectations, and the waiters were a treat. A word of advice: save room for the cheeseboard, which was among the best we've ever seen. Breakfast, too, was sublime. The attached equestrian centre isn't cheap (around £70 per hour for a hack) but is well regarded, and you'd be hard pressed to find a prettier area in which to ride. Other facilities include floodlit tennis courts and an indoor pool, plus a spa (closed for a six-month refurb from September 2007), jacuzzi and sauna.

Spread Eagle

Stourton, Stourhead, nr Warminster, Wiltshire BA12 6QE (01747 840587/ www.spreadeagleinn.com). **Rates** £110 double. **Lunch served** noon-3pm, **dinner served** 7-9pm daily. **Main courses** £7-£14.50. **Credit** MC, V.
The Spread Eagle boasts an unrivalled setting, amid the verdant, landscaped grounds of the National Trust-owned Stourhead House. Although it's mobbed by visitors on summer days, once the hordes have gone home you're likely to have the place almost to yourself. The bar serves up hearty, traditional meals starring locally sourced ingredients – the menu might include estate venison casserole with juniper, red wine, rosemary and shallot dumplings, or lamb shank served with pickled red cabbage, bramley apple, sultanas and redcurrant sauce. Locally brewed beers, real ales and a short but thoughfully chosen wine list provide the perfect accompaniment. Walk it all off with a stroll in the gardens, before retreating to one of the five sweetly old-fashioned bedrooms, all of which have private bathrooms.

Ston Easton Park

Ston Easton, nr Bath, Somerset BA3 4DF (01761 241631/www.stoneaston.co.uk). **Rates** £240-£420 double; £755 cottage. **Credit** AmEx, DC, MC, V.
A stately, austere-looking 18th-century Palladian mansion, Ston Easton Park is now run as a comfortable and surprisingly warm and friendly hotel. The Grade I-listed house's interior is packed with period features, including some extraordinary plasterwork and an original Edwardian kitchen, complete with copper pans, for an authentic 'below stairs' dining experience. Upstairs, the Cedar Tree restaurant (*see p167*) has garnered a reputation for reliable, locally sourced cuisine, often featuring herbs and vegetables from the Victorian kitchen garden. In summer, guests can order a picnic, borrow a rug and find a quiet corner of the grounds – often joined by the ever-hopeful resident spaniel, Sweep.
The master bedroom has a great view over the park to the east, while most of the rooms are beautifully proportioned, with large bathrooms and new handmade beds. Down by the river, the fully serviced Gardener's Cottage is a dinky little hideaway close to the extensive kitchen garden and greenhouses; it sleeps six.

Swan

*Sadler Street, Wells, Somerset BA5 2RX
(01749 836300/www.swanhotelwells.co.uk).*
Rates £134-£170 double. **Credit** AmEx, DC,
MC, V.

You couldn't get a much more central location
than this – and a garden between the ancient
buildings across the road gives this small, 15th-
century hotel a picture-perfect view of Wells
Cathedral. The beautifully decorated main building has some 35 bedrooms; the remaining 15 are
found in the adjacent Coach House. Put a request
in if you fancy kipping in one of the antique four
posters. Downstairs is the bar, and an oak-panelled restaurant; in summer, you can sample the
award-winning fare in the lovely walled garden.
Enquire about dinner, bed and breakfast deals
when you make your booking.

Wookey Hole Inn

*Wookey Hole Road, Wookey Hole, nr Wells,
Somerset BA5 1BP (01749 676677/www.
wookeyholeinn.com).* **Open** *Bar* noon-3pm,
6-11.30pm Mon-Sat. **Lunch served** noon-
12.30pm daily. **Dinner served** 7-9.30pm
Mon-Sat. **Main courses** £12.25-£18.50.
Rates £90-£100 double. **Credit** AmEx,
MC, V.

Its half-timbered exterior may look conventional enough, but this pub with rooms has some
endearingly eccentric touches inside. Colourful,
informal and laid-back, with wicker chairs in the
dining area, games of Jenga and backgammon
dotted around the bar area and kooky sculptures
in the garden, the Wookey Hole Inn has been popular with weekenders from Bristol and London
for some time. There are five airy, quirkily decorated rooms; the best is room two with its view
of the churchyard and garden, but all have
decent Japanese-style handmade beds, a
widescreen TV and either a shower or bath en
suite. Booking ahead is essential, and only continental breakfasts are served. For lunch and
supper, the restaurant rustles up freshly prepared wholesome recipes at fairly reasonable
prices. The bar offers a wide selection of Belgian
beers and real ales, and is sometimes patronised
by the resident spaniel, Ben.

WHERE TO EAT & DRINK

Blostin's

*29 Waterloo Road, Shepton Mallet, Somerset
BA4 5HH (01749 343648/www.blostins.co.uk).*
Dinner served 7-9.30pm Tue-Sat. **Set
dinner** £15.95 2 courses, £17.95 3 courses.
Credit MC, V.

Right on the road, but quiet, clean and bright
inside, this long-standing local restaurant has
earned itself a loyal following. It serves largely
traditional dinner combinations such as venison
with red cabbage and game sauce, and honey-
roasted pork loin with apples and cider brandy
sauce. There's also a small but perfectly formed
vegetarian menu, offering simple but satisfying

fare (grilled goat's cheese with toasted muffin to
start, perhaps, followed by roasted fennel and
tomatoes with couscous and broad beans). The
capably handled menu is backed up by a serious,
nicely balanced wine list. It may not have the
most sophisticated of ambiences or daring of
menus, but this place has a steady, seemingly
unchanging charm of its own.

Boxer's

*1 St Thomas Street, Wells, Somerset BA5 2UU
(01749 672317/www.thefountaininn.co.uk).*
Open *Bar* noon-2.30pm, 6-11pm Mon-Sat;
noon-2.30pm, 7-10.30pm Sun. **Lunch served**
noon-2pm daily. **Dinner served** 6-9.30pm
Mon-Sat; 7-9.30pm Sun. **Main courses** £10.25-
£17.50. **Credit** AmEx, MC, V.

Occupying a first-floor room in the old Fountain
Inn, Boxer's has a warm, convivial atmosphere,
even at the busiest of times. The light, woody
room soon fills up with a hungry crowd, eagerly
tucking into retro starters (deep-fried brie, moz-
zarella-topped stuffed mushrooms), followed by
slow-roasted lamb shank, seared salmon or chargrilled steak. Free-range beef, lamb and pork are
supplied by a local producer from nearby Priddy
– the specially made beef, Butcombe beer and
thyme sausages are a treat. The menu is backed
up by some excellent Spanish wines, and the
atmosphere is cheerful and easygoing. At lunch
offerings include the likes of chicken liver pâté on
toast, generously filled sandwiches, ploughman's
platters and big salads.

Cedar Tree Restaurant

*Ston Easton, nr Bath, Somerset BA3 4DF
(01761 241631/www.stoneaston.co.uk).*
Lunch served noon-2pm, **dinner served**
7-9.30pm daily. **Set lunch** £17.50 2 courses,
£22.50 3 courses. **Set dinner** £44.50 3 courses.
Credit AmEx, DC, MC, V.

A small, oak-panelled dining room provides an
elegant setting for fine dining at the country-
house hotel, Ston Easton Park (*see p166*). Fresh,
local ingredients play a starring role on the ambitious, eclectic menu, which ranges from hearty
British classics such as trio of lamb with tomato
and thyme jus to more delicate vegetarian and
fish options (grilled sea bass with coriander couscous, poached asparagus, coconut and lime
broth, for example). Thankfully, help is at hand
for diners who can't choose between the very
tempting puddings on offer – the assiette of
desserts delivers a sample of each.

Charlton House Restaurant

*Charlton Road, Shepton Mallet, nr Bath,
Somerset BA4 4PR (01749 342008/www.
charltonhouse.com).* **Lunch served** 12.30-
2pm, **dinner served** 7.30-9.30pm daily.
Set lunch £22 2 courses, £27 3 courses.
Set dinner £52.50 3 courses. **Credit** AmEx,
DC, MC, V.

Owned by Roger Saul, founder of fashion brand Mulberry, the Restaurant at Charlton House has been one of the most sophisticated, not to mention expensive, operations in the area for some time. Well-kept back lawns slope down from a young apple orchard to the conservatory dining room where guests can sample Saul's organic, seasonal produce as prepared by talented new head chef Elisha Carter. Carter's style is 'British seasonal, with French foundations and a little West Indian flair' and he caters to piscivores and carnivores particularly well. Fillet of plaice wrapped in venison ham is as delicious as it is unusual, while the more conventional west country pork with turnips, compote of apricots and cider sauce is a succulent delight. With a

Wells Cathedral: the most beautiful in all England.

legendary wine list and richly sweet desserts (including fig tart with tobacco ice-cream and mandarin cheesecake with orange curd), this is a restaurant that practically guarantees a meal that's memorable for all the right reasons – although at a price. For a real treat, book into one of the luxuriously appointed suites and bedrooms upstairs (*see p165*).

City Arms

69 High Street, Wells, Somerset BA5 2AG (01749 673916/www.thecityarmsatwells. co.uk). **Open** *Bar* 9am-11pm Mon-Wed; 9am-midnight Thur-Sat; 11am-11pm Sun. **Meals served** noon-9.30pm Mon-Wed; noon-9pm Thur-Sun. **Main courses** £6.25-£16.95. **Credit** AmEx, MC, V.

This 400-year-old converted jail makes for a surprisingly pretty pub, with few references to its less than salubrious past. The buildings form a horseshoe around the small central courtyard, and there's a jasmine-scented terrace up top for summer dining. Inside, the flagstone floors have been worn smooth – and best watch your head as you pass through doorways. The seasonal menu might include sausages with garlic mash, onion gravy and peas (which proved perfect fare for a wintry day), while the equally good steak and Tanglefoot Ale pie was topped with perfect puff pastry. We also appreciated the bowls of chunky cheddar cubes, red onions and crackers, strict 'No Alcopops' bar policy and fine array of real ales.

Garrick's Head

8 St John's Place, Bath, Somerset BA1 1ET (01225 318368). **Open** *Bar* noon-11pm Mon-Thur; noon-12.30am Fri, Sat; noon-10.30pm Sun. **Lunch served** noon-3pm daily. **Dinner served** 6-10.30pm Mon-Sat. **Main courses** £9-£15. **Credit** AmEx, MC, V.

New landlords Amanda and Charlie Digney reopened this gastropub-cum-restaurant in 2006. Just as they did at the King William, also in Bath, the Digneys have put together a winning combination of seasonal fare and cheerful decor. The gutsy British menu favours slow cooking (pea and ham soup, slow-roasted pork belly and the like), while the alfresco dining area is a favourite with people-watchers. The pub is handily situated next door to the Theatre Royal – one of the oldest surviving theatres in the country.

Goodfellows

5 Sadler Street, Wells, Somerset BA5 2RR (01749 673866/www.goodfellowswells.co.uk). **Lunch served** noon-2pm Tue-Sat. **Dinner served** 7-9.30pm Thur-Sat. **Main courses** £7.50-£24. **Set lunch** £12.50 2 courses, £15 3 courses. **Set dinner** £33 3 courses. **Credit** AmEx, MC, V.

Adam Fellows packs a great deal into this diminutive, two-floored space. The small seafood restaurant opens with a pâtisserie, wet fish counter, deli and just a handful of tables on the ground floor. Pop in for freshly baked croissants and orange juice in the morning, or peruse the offerings fresh off the boats that ply the Devonshire and Cornish coasts. You'll need to make your way down the corkscrew stairs to find Fellows' light and airy open-plan kitchen, where just a few tables wrap around the counter. The menu reflects the day's catch and sings with modern, Mediterranean flavours.

Mendips

Griffin

25 Milk Street, Frome, Somerset BA11 3DB (01373 467766). **Open** 5-11pm Mon-Fri; 5pm-1am Sat; noon-3pm, 6-11pm Sun. **No credit cards.**
Owned by the adjoining Milk Street Brewery, the Griffin is a gem of a place. A small bar in a small room that's decidedly shabby-chic and welcoming, it's tricky to find but well worth the effort. This is one of the more happening pubs in Frome, with a variety of poetry and music events in the upstairs room and displays of interesting artwork on the walls. Landlord Andrew Savin refuses to sell lager – instead, you can quaff beers from the microbrewery next door, or try one of the many guest ales.

Hunstrete House Restaurant

Chelwood, nr Bath, Somerset BS39 4N5 (01761 490490/www.hunstretehouse.co.uk). **Lunch served** noon-2pm, **dinner served** 7-9.30pm daily. **Set meals** £37.75 2 courses, £47.75 3 courses. **Credit** AmEx, DC, MC, V.
Following pre-dinner drinks in front of a roaring log fire, or a dusk inspection of the pretty gardens, guests are ushered into the small classical dining room, which looks out on to the Italianate courtyard – itself popular with alfresco diners in warmer months – for an evening of understated elegance. Chef Matt Lord works to a seasonal menu with French influences, with many of the ingredients sourced from local producers or grown in the hotel's walled Victorian gardens. Dishes might include a tortellini of wild mushrooms, seared hand-dived scallops or a terrine of duck and foie gras, with fillet of beef and braised ox cheek or tarragon-stuffed saddle of rabbit to follow. Simply stunning.

Moody Goose at the Old Priory

17-19 Church Square, Midsomer Norton, Bath, Somerset BA3 2HX (0176 141 6784/www.moodygoose.co.uk). **Lunch served** noon-1.30pm, **dinner served** 7-9.30pm Mon-Sat. **Main courses** £18.50-£21. **Set lunch** £19.50 3 courses. **Set dinner** £25 3 courses. **Credit** AmEx, MC, V.
After ten years in nearby Bath, the owners of the popular Moody Goose fell in love with a medieval priory in the centre of Midsomer Norton, and so moved their restaurant here in 2005. The Old Priory dates back to 1152, making it one of the oldest houses in Somerset, and retains its original 14th-century fireplaces, an intact 15th-century well in the courtyard, and a secret tunnel that runs from underneath the kitchen floor to the 15th-century Catholic church. Upstairs, there are seven beautifully decorated bedrooms. Stephen Shore's small and much-acclaimed restaurant was awarded a Michelin star once again in 2006, and continues to provide Modern British cuisine with a classical French twist (fillet of brill with sweet potato fondant and caviar butter sauce, for example) in a very romantic setting.

Old Spot

12 Sadler Street, Wells, Somerset BA5 2SE (01749 689099). **Lunch served** 12.30-2.30pm Wed-Sun. **Dinner served** 7-10.30pm Tue-Sat. **Set lunch** £17.50 2 courses. **Set dinner** £26.50 3 courses. **Credit** AmEx, MC, V.
Chef Ian Bates worked under Simon Hopkinson (author of the much-acclaimed *Roast Chicken and Other Stories*) for four years, and it shows. The menu changes weekly and is kept short: no more than five or six dishes per course, each gutsy, bold and impossible to choose between. The British dishes nod towards Mediterranean flavours and prices are kept reasonably low, while the decor is masculine and simple: enormous glass windows that conceal nothing from passers-by in the street, wood panelling and leather sofas. Ask for one of the tables to the rear of the restaurant – they look out over Cathedral Square.

Ring O Bells

Widcombe Parade, Bath, Somerset BA2 4JT (01225 448870/www.ringobellsbath.com). **Lunch served** noon-2.30 daily. **Dinner served** 6-9.30pm Mon-Sat. **Main courses** £9.80-£11.50. **Credit** MC, V.
There's been an alehouse here since 1827 – though things have evolved considerably since the early days. It's now a stylish, family-run gastropub that concentrates on good quality, locally sourced food. It has a loyal following and is generally considered to be the best of its kind in Bath. The ever-changing French-British menu might include salmon gravadlax with blinis and a horseradish and beetroot salad, duck rillette with pickled onions and warm bread, daily fish specials or sirloin steak with oven-dried tomato and red onion butter. The beer is also locally sourced, coming from Frome's Milk Street Brewery.

Seymour Arms

Witham Friary, Frome, Somerset BA11 5HF (01749 850742). **Open** *Bar* 11am-2.30pm, 6-11pm Mon-Sat; noon-3pm, 7-10.30pm Sun. **No credit cards.**
Built around 1866-67 as part of the Duke of Somerset's estate, the Seymour Arms seems to have remained unchanged for decades. Indeed, it's the kind of place you have to travel a long way to find these days. Surviving almost entirely on loyal local custom, it offers bar billiards, pale green fixed benches round the wall of one of its two large rooms, and not much else. Beers are served through a glass partition – and really, what more do you need? There's a delightful and quiet little garden beside the railway embankment too. The pub doesn't do food – only sweets, snacks and tobacco.

Talbot

High Street, Mells, Frome, Somerset BA11 3PN (01373 812254/www.talbotinn.com). **Open** *Bar* noon-2pm Sat, Sun; 6.30-10.30pm daily. **Lunch served** noon-2pm, **dinner served** 6.45-9pm daily. **Main courses** £15-£20. **Rates** £95-£145 double. **Credit** MC, V.

At the heart of the gloriously pretty, honey-coloured village of Mells, the Talbot has won a fine reputation for its food. Locals flock here for the seafood, fresh from the fishing boats at Brixham. Specials of the day might include whole lemon sole grilled with fresh herbs, or a poached skate wing finished with nut-brown butter, capers, prawns and lemon. The main evening menu offers plenty of good, solid meaty options (steaks, whole-some pies, pot-roasted lamb, Gressingham duck), while lunchtime brings some simpler options – hearty ploughman's, soups and local ham with free-range egg and chips. Round the back there's a sunny garden with a petanque pitch beneath old stone walls. You can also stay here – several of the well-proportioned rooms look out towards the old manor house.

Three Horseshoes Inn

Batcombe, Shepton Mallet, Somerset BA4 6HE (01749 850359/www.3horseshoesbatcombe. co.uk). **Open** *Bar* noon-3pm, 6.30-11pm daily. **Lunch served** noon-2pm daily. **Dinner served** 7-9pm Mon-Sat. **Main courses** £9.75-£18.75. **Credit** MC, V.

This 17th-century coaching inn sits by the church in the lovely village of Batcombe. Inside is a snug, low-ceilinged bar, where regulars sagely sip real ales and sample the guest cider; outside there's a patio, large garden and children's play area. Food prices are on the steep side, but you're paying for the quality of the organic, seasonal ingredients as well as the accomplished cooking. Mains might include sautéed free-range guinea fowl, Cornish haddock on celeriac mash, sirloin of west country beef with chips, or own-made chicken kiev with parma ham.

Truffles

95 High Street, Bruton, Somerset BA10 0AR (01749 812255/www.trufflesbruton.co.uk). **Lunch served** noon-2pm Thur-Sun. **Dinner served** 7-9.30pm Tue-Sat. **Set lunch** £16.95 3 courses. (Sun) £18.95 3 courses. **Set dinner** £29.95 3 courses. **Credit** MC, V.

Truffles is a diminutive, rose-clad place with pansies in the window boxes and headroom best described as cosy. Booking is essential: starched linen tablecloths and a superb monthly changing menu keep this award-winning place topping the list for culinary finesse in this solid old town. Dishes are unpretentious and immaculately presented: pan-fried lemon sole with sautéed potatoes, purple sprouting broccoli and tartare sauce, or fillet of rare-breed Devonshire Red beef served with chunky chips, seasonal vegetables and red wine jus, for example. Suppliers are listed at the bottom of the menu, so you know the provenance of what's on your plate. To finish, tuck into a rhubarb trifle, baked vanilla cheesecake or sip a relaxing glass of Somerset cider brandy.

Tucker's Grave

Faulkland, Radstock, Somerset BA3 5XF (01373 834230). **Open** *Bar* noon-3pm, 6-11pm Mon-Sat; noon-3pm, 7-10.30pm Sun. **No credit cards.**

On the main road between Faulkland and Norton St Philip, this country local is the real deal. The mid 18th-century stone-built cottage is on the site of a local suicide from that period, but it's far from gloomy. Step inside the pub and you'll be handed real ale direct from the barrel (there being no bar as such) or a pint of proper Thatchers cider, then given a chance to enjoy the two completely unspoiled little rooms, one with a real fire, and the company of the locals. Come the winter months, the owner has been known to get out the chestnut-roasting pan, providing impromptu bar snacks all round.

Vobster Inn

Lower Vobster, nr Radstock, Somerset BA3 5RJ (01373 812920/www.vobsterinn.co.uk). **Lunch served** noon-2pm daily. **Dinner served** 7-9pm Mon-Thur; 7-9.30pm Fri, Sat. **Main courses** £9-£17.50. **Credit** AmEx, MC, V.

Located in the village of Lower Vobster, this friendly pub's simple way with seafood has won it national accolades – and if lobster is ever on the menu, you can rest assured that, funny spellings aside, it will be deliciously and expertly cooked. Starters might include seared scallops or goat's cheese salad, followed by mains of grilled plaice with citrus butter and brown shrimps, smoked haddock and crab risotto, or six-hour braised beef, accompanied by wild garlic risotto and buttered vegetables. Still, it's hard to resist the legendary fish and chips. Likewise the indulgent desserts: bread and butter pudding with clotted cream or lemon posset with red berries, for example. Despite its foodie credentials, the Vobster is also a drinkers' pub, with proper real ales like Buxton's and Marley's Ghost, plus a fairly extensive wine list.

White Hart Inn

Ford, nr Chippenham, Wiltshire SN14 8RP (01249 782213/www.roomattheinn.info). **Meals served** noon-9.30pm Mon-Sat; noon-9pm Sun. **Main courses** £7.95-£19. **Credit** DC, MC, V.

Set over a peaceful trout stream in the lovely Wyvern Valley, this 16th-century coaching inn is as likely to be full of shooting parties in tweed and khaki as it is families on tour. Sunny days can be spent lounging on the large terrace; when the weather's less than perfect, the warren of rooms inside are toasty warm, thanks to roaring fires. Food takes in smart modern pub fare, with one eye firmly on its city-slicker clientele: the square white plates clash with the decor, but the food is simple and freshly made, and the service charming. There are also 11 simple bedrooms upstairs for sleepovers.

Bristol

No longer a slave to its past.

England's sixth largest city once had a reputation as a hard-working merchant city with plenty of time for industry and commerce, but little time for the trappings of tourism and leisure. Since the 18th century, Bristol has lived in the shadow of her elegant little sister upriver: Bath, though smaller and culturally less diverse, has always been the tourist honeypot in this area, leaving Bristol's many charms to go largely unnoticed – even by its own residents. In the last few years, though, Bristol has been redressing the balance and asserting itself as an ideal weekend break destination. Thanks to its proximity to both coast and countryside, with swathes of green spaces, mountain bike trails and other adventure activities on its doorstep, the city combines a contemporary urban vibe with a healthy glow that comes from play in the great outdoors. Its fascinating past is brought to life by a number of engrossing historical sites and museums, while ever-more stylish restaurants, cafés and boutiques provide welcome distraction between photo opportunities.

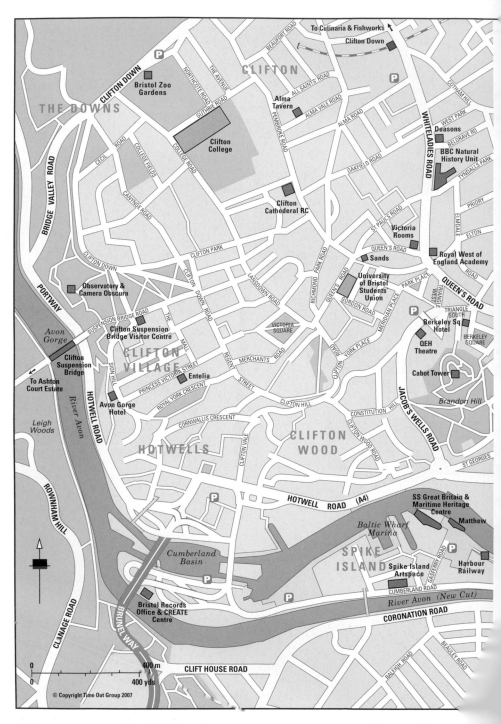

Bristol

To Culinaria & Fishworks
Clifton Down
Clifton Down

CLIFTON DOWN
P

BEAUFORT ROAD

CLIFTON
THE AVENUE
ALL SAINTS ROAD
NORTHCOTE ROAD
P

Bristol Zoo
Gardens

THE DOWNS

CECIL ROAD
COLLEGE FIELDS
GUTHRIE ROAD
Clifton
College
COLLEGE ROAD

Alma
Tavern

PEMBROKE ROAD
ALMA VALE ROAD
ALMA ROAD

WEST PARK
COTHAM HILL
BELGRAVE RD
Deasons
WHITELADIES ROAD
BBC Natural
History Unit
PRIORY
TYNDALLS PARK
ELMDALE
ELTON

CANTOCK ROAD

OAKFIELD ROAD

BRIDGE VALLEY ROAD

Clifton
Cathedral RC

ST PAUL'S ROAD
Victoria
Rooms
Royal West of
England Academy

CLIFTON PARK
CLIFTON DOWN
CLIFTON DOWN ROAD

Sands

QUEEN'S ROAD
PARK PLACE
TRIANGLE SOUTH
QUEEN'S ROAD

PORTWAY

Observatory &
Camera Obscura

LANSDOWN ROAD
RICHMOND PARK ROAD
QUEENS ROAD
GORDON ROAD
University
of Bristol
Students'
Union
MERIDIAN PLACE
TRIANGLE WEST
P
BERKELEY
SQUARE
Berkeley Sq
Hotel

Avon
Gorge

SUSPENSION BRIDGE ROAD

Clifton Suspension
Bridge Visitor Centre

THE MALL

VICTORIA
SQUARE
CLIFTON

QEH
Theatre
Cabot Tower

CLIFTON
VILLAGE
SION HILL
PRINCESS VICTORIA STREET
Entelia

REGENT STREET
MERCHANTS ROAD
YORK PLACE

JACOB'S WELLS ROAD

Brandon Hill

Clifton
Suspension
Bridge

To Ashton
Court Estate

River Avon

HOTWELL ROAD

ROYAL YORK CRESCENT
Avon Gorge
Hotel

CORNWALLIS CRESCENT

CLIFTON HILL

CONSTITUTION HILL

CLIFTON
WOOD

CLIFTON WOOD ROAD

ST GEORGES

Leigh
Woods

HOTWELLS

CLIFTON VALE

ROWNHAM HILL

HOTWELL ROAD (A4)

SS Great Britain &
Maritime Heritage
Centre
Matthew

Baltic Wharf
Marina

Cumberland
Basin

P

SPIKE
ISLAND
Spike Island
Artspace

GASFERRY ROAD
P
Harbour
Railway

CLINAGE ROAD

BRUNEL WAY

P

Bristol Records
Office & CREATE
Centre

CUMBERLAND ROAD

River Avon (New Cut)

CORONATION ROAD

RALEIGH ROAD
BEAULEY ROAD

0   400 m
0   400 yds

CLIFT HOUSE ROAD

© Copyright Time Out Group 2007

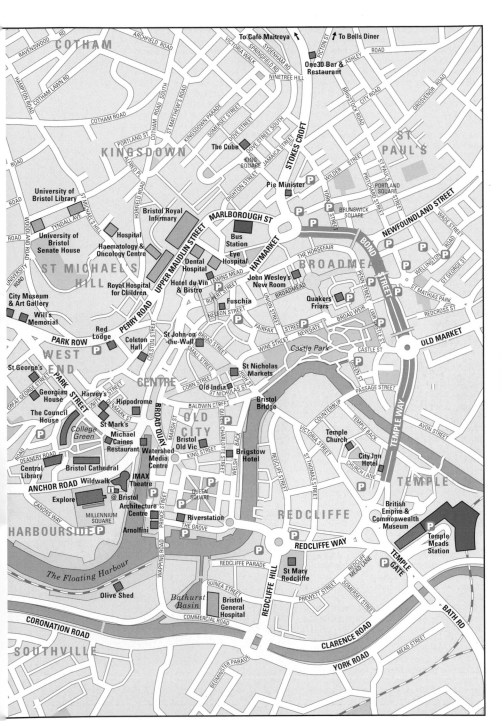

Bristol

In autumn 2002 the former engine shed at Temple Meads station became the clumsily named but thoughtfully compiled British Empire & Commonwealth Museum (Station Approach, Temple Meads, 0117 925 4980, www.empiremuseum.co.uk). Tracing the history of the Empire and Commonwealth from the early explorers to today's multiracial communities, it offers an international perspective on the motives, achievements, exploitation and impact of British imperialism. The museum handles this controversial subject with a laudable degree of imagination, using interactive displays, artefacts sourced from other major museum collections and some fascinating early photos, films and oral history exhibits to bring the subject to life.

In summer, make the most of Bristol's wide open spaces and outdoor festivals and, after dark, head for the city's critically acclaimed music, clubbing and theatre venues. Culturally, ethnically and economically diverse, this is a city where the maritime and industrial achievements of the past provide a context for present-day artistic and cultural success. Here too, ambitious self-promotion is tempered by a laid-back, easy-living attitude.

Clifton

With its grand crescents and elegant Georgian architecture, this desirable residential suburb was developed during the late 18th and early 19th centuries. Clifton didn't become part of the city until 1835 and has managed to retain its exclusive (not to say snobbish) character to this day, looking down on the rest of Bristol from its imperious perch to the north-west. Royal York Crescent stretches in a wide arc for a quarter of a mile, making it the longest Georgian crescent in the UK. At the heart of the district, picturesque Clifton Village is an amalgam of bijou boutiques, traditional shops, cafés, restaurants and pastel-coloured terraces – perfect for Saturday-afternoon pottering.

Close by is Brunel's Suspension Bridge, which spans the chasm of the Avon Gorge. Despite the best efforts of quarry companies and road-builders, the gorge retains much of its wild, romantic scenery and the bridge is truly majestic. It measures 702 feet across and spans the gorge 245 feet above the river. The best views are either from the large terrace of the Avon Gorge Hotel to the south, or from the edge of Clifton and Durdham Downs to the north. Stretching for 400 acres east from the Avon Gorge, the Downs provide a vast, grassy, breezy playground for scores of dog-walkers, Sunday footballers, joggers and kite-flyers. Award-winning Bristol Zoo Gardens (0117 974 7399, www.bristolzoo.org.uk) is nearby.

On the other side of the bridge, Ashton Court and Leigh Woods offer further opportunity for walks. Both are criss-crossed with mountain bike trails – marked and unmarked – which have been variously named as Picnic, Ho Chi Minh and Porn by locals, and parts of which make up the yellow and red Timberland Trails.

In summer, the main events on Bristol's calendar are the Ashton Court Festival (www.ashtoncourtfestival.com), Bristol Balloon Fiesta (www.bristolfiesta.co.uk) and the International Kite and Air Creations Festival (www.kite-festival.org).

Harbourside

A stroll and ferry trip around Bristol's harbourside is a great way to get a feel for the city's maritime past. First, make your way along the river to the Arnolfini (Narrow Quay, 0117 917 2300, www.arnolfini.org.uk), a leading arts centre with a bar, gallery, cinema and shop that reopened in autumn 2005 following an extensive redevelopment programme.

SS *Great Britain*

Bristol

Outside is a pensive-looking statue of the Genoese explorer John Cabot, who set out from Bristol in 1497 and discovered Newfoundland. Cross the narrow swing bridge to the red and white hulk of what was once the Bristol Industrial Museum and follow the tracks of the old steam railway along the docks, past new designer apartment complexes, to the SS *Great Britain* (Great Western Dockyard, Gas Ferry Road, 0117 926 0680, www.ssgreat britain.org). Designed by Isambard Kingdom Brunel, she was the first ocean-going ship to be constructed of iron and driven by a propeller (rather than paddles). Despite the ignominy of sitting high and dry in a dock, she still exudes an air of former grandeur. Moored next to the SS *Great Britain* is the touchingly small and fragile-looking *Matthew* (0117 927 6868, www.matthew. co.uk), a life-size working replica of the boat sailed by John Cabot to Newfoundland, built in 1997 to commemorate the 500-year anniversary of his Atlantic crossing. There are hour-long harbour cruises (£8.50) on the *Matthew*, as well as four-hour trips to Portishead (£65) that take you under the Clifton Suspension Bridge.

Unaccompanied adults may find the super-abundance of levers, buttons, screens and pulleys at Explore@tBristol (Anchor Road, Harbourside, 0845 345 1235, www.at-bristol.org.uk) somewhat overwhelming, but for families this place is a rainy day godsend. In-yer-face corporate sponsorship detracts from the appeal of some exhibits, but there's serious science here among all the gadgetry. Across the piazza is Wildwalk@tBristol, an impressive exhibition devoted to the natural world. Interactive screens and film footage are complemented by live exhibits – fish, insects, spiders, reptiles and two walk-through botanical habitats – to create an informative, thought-provoking attraction. An IMAX cinema is housed in the same building. Afterwards, take a stroll among the water features, skateboarders and statues in Millennium Square.

When you've finished, catch a ferry with the Bristol Ferry Boat Company (0117 927 3416, www.bristolferryboat. co.uk) to one of the charming harbourside pubs: Cottage Inn (Baltic Wharf, Cumberland Road, Hotwells, 0117 921 5256); the Mardyke (Hotwell Road, 0117 907 7499); or the Ostrich (Lower Guinea Street, 0117 927 3774).

WHERE TO STAY

Despite its size, Bristol still suffers from a dearth of good, stylish accommodation options. The chains are represented in abundance – the Marriott Royal (College Green, 0117 925 5100, www.marriott

Accommodation	★★☆☆☆
Food & drink	★★★☆☆
Nightlife	★★★★★
Shopping	★★★☆☆
Culture	★★★★☆
Sights	★★★☆☆
Scenery	★★★☆☆

hotels.com) is the most luxurious option, while the Premier Travel Inn (Llandoger Trow, King Street, 0870 990 6424) is cheap and central. However, there are few independent ventures offering rooms and services beyond the ordinary. Boutique-style guesthouses and B&Bs are also conspicuous by their absence.

Belgrave

25 Upper Belgrave Road, Clifton, BS8 2XL (0117 946 6006/www.bristolbedandbreakfast. com). **Rates** £60-£65 double. **Credit** MC, V.
Bristol born and bred owners Mike and Kay Taylor run a tight yet jovial ship at the Belgrave, which has stunning vistas across Bristol at the back and views over the Clifton and Durdham Downs to the front. With only four rooms, there's a homely, friendly atmosphere at this B&B, which is housed in a stately property dating from 1860. The period interior has been largely retained, bar the fresh touch of contemporary neutral colours and modern shower rooms. Downstairs, a large twin bedroom opens out to a patio garden where breakfast can be taken in summer. Prepared on the Aga to your liking, breakfast can also be brought to your room so that you can linger over it in your dressing gown.

Berkeley Square Hotel

15 Berkeley Square, BS8 1HB (0117 925 4000/ www.cliftonhotels.com). **Rates** £95-£145 double. **Credit** AmEx, MC, V.
With an enviable position on an imposing Georgian square in Clifton, the flagship of this Bristol hotel mini chain enjoys fine views over the city from its upper floors. There is an appealing, open-plan reception area and lounge, and although the eccentric fittings look as though they originated from a West End prop cupboard – stuffed peacock, leopard-print cushions, chaises longues and customised projection of swaying trees – the overall effect is bright and good-humoured. Adjoining is the more restrained Square restaurant, which is open to the public until 9pm but reserved for hotel guests and members later in the evening. The same applies to the hotel's basement bar. The executive suites are smallish, considering the price, but have a contemporary vibe, with clean lines, bright colours, CD and DVD players and minibars – the complimentary decanter of sherry is a nice touch. Other hotels in the group may be cheaper, but the Berkeley is the best.

Bristol

Clifton Arcade

City Inn Hotel

*Temple Way, BS1 6BF (0117 925 1001/
www.cityinn.com).* **Rates** £65-£129 double.
Credit AmEx, DC, MC, V.
Close to Temple Meads station but backing on to
the leafier surrounds of Temple Gardens, this
sleek hotel is very much a corporate hangout in
the week. However, its attention to detail and
guest-focused ethos make it a good option for
weekend leisure visitors too. The contemporary
rooms avoid the anonymity of the larger chains
thanks to bright decor, large windows and excellent facilities: air-conditioning, 24-hour room
service, CD/DVD player, satellite TV and broadband internet access are standard, with free Wi-
Fi in the public areas. Rooms are also, thankfully,
well soundproofed against noise from the busy
main road. Classy Modern British cuisine is
served in the City Café.

Hotel du Vin & Bistro

*The Sugar House, Narrow Lewins Mead, BS1
2NU (0117 925 5577/www.hotelduvin.com).*
Rates £140-£155 double/twin; £195-£320
suite. **Credit** AmEx, DC, MC, V.
This place is a welcome change from the city's
usual identikit accommodation. A sheltered courtyard leads from the busy, concrete lined main
road into a haven of sensitive restoration, thoughtful styling and good taste. Converted from an
18th-century sugar warehouse, the Hotel du Vin
features exposed brickwork, wooden floors and

metal joists – all providing a soft industrial-chic
setting for spacious bedrooms and loft suites in
chocolate brown, beige and cream, with Egyptian
linen bedclothes, stand-alone baths and enormous
walk-in showers. On the ground floor, the comfortable lounge bar has a gentlemen's club vibe,
with carefully distressed leather sofas, low lights
and its own cigar humidor. Beyond is a formal dining room where excellent French and Modern
British bistro-style cuisine is accompanied by an
exemplary wine list. Regular tastings and wine
masterclasses are held throughout the year.

Mercure Brigstow Hotel

*Welsh Back, BS1 4SP (0117 929 1030/
www.mercure.com).* **Rates** £95-£169 double;
£175-£250 suite. **Credit** AmEx, DC, MC, V.
The harbourside Brigstow is both practical and
good-looking (although the decor in the rooms
could do with bringing up to date in line with the
public spaces), and is perfectly situated for the
centre of town and the docks. It has 116 rooms –
you'll pay around £10 extra for a river view – kitted out in a subtle palette of beige, red and green,
with air-conditioning, internet access and a plasma
TV screen in the bathroom. Shiny wooden floors
and overhanging mezzanine balconies impart a
hint of cruise-ship styling to the large, sleek reception area and open-plan Ellipse bar and restaurant
on the ground floor. Other facilities include a business centre, conference rooms and 24-hour room
service. Weekend B&B is good value.

WHERE TO EAT & DRINK

Bristol benefits from some award-winning restaurants, as well as decent mid-range options and a scattering of very special neighbourhood eateries. The more appealing bars and pubs tend to be outside the city centre, although there are some notable exceptions, such as the unmissable Mr Wolf's (35 St Stephen's Street, 0117 927 3221), a noodle, cocktail and music bar where the inimitable friendly atmosphere ensures a loyal local following. Another good bet for music while you eat is the Tantric Jazz Café (39-41 St Nicholas Street, 0117 940 2304, www.tantric-jazz.co.uk), a mellow venue serving Lebanese food to a jazz soundtrack.

On Bristol's dockside, a converted red-brick Victorian wine warehouse shelters the much-loved Watershed media centre and cinema (1 Canons Road, 0117 927 5100, www.watershed.co.uk), which has an airy bar-cum-café. Nearby is the River (1 Canons Road, 0117 930 0498, www.theriverbristol.com), a popular, spacious bar that serves cocktails for the boozers and a sausage-and-mash menu for the gorgers.

On the other side of the harbour, just off Queen's Square, is the Mud Dock Café (40 The Grove, 0117 934 9734, www.mud-dock.com). It bizarrely but successfully combines a mountain bike shop with an atmospheric bistro, and now even provides bike lock-ups and showers for pedalling customers. Also here is the

TOURIST INFORMATION

The Foyer, Wilds Walk, Harbourside, BS1 5DB (0906 711 2191/ www.visitbristol.co.uk).

Severnshed (The Grove, 0117 925 1212, www.severnshed.co.uk), a spacious former boat shed designed by Isambard Kingdom Brunel. Its waterside terrace is perfect for summer lunches, while inside a sleek mobile bar separates the formal dining room from the funky drinking area.

Another good spot in the centre is the summer-only Spyglass Barbecue & Grill (Welsh Back, 0117 927 2800, www.spyglassbristol.co.uk), located on a converted barge. And don't miss the food stalls at St Nicholas Markets (Corn Street, 0117 922 4017) for an affordable global range of lunchtime snacks.

Heading up towards Clifton, there are noodles at Budokan (31 Colston Street, 0117 914 1488, www.budokan.co.uk) and Wagamama (63 Queen's Road, 0117 922 1188, www.wagamama.com). Good coffee, light bites and dozens of work-shy students can be found at the Boston Tea Party (75 Park Street, 0117 929 8601) – a good place for a rest midway through the steep walk up Park Street. If you're in need of more substantial fare, stop off at the Gourmet Burger Kitchen (74 Park Street, 0117 316 9162, www.gbkinfo.com) for superior burgers and milkshakes. Just around the corner, the Woods (1 Park

Arnolfini

Bristol

Street Avenue, 0117 925 0890) is a chilled-out bar with Moroccan-style seating upstairs and an outdoor terrace in summer.

In Clifton Village, the Mall (The Mall, 0117 974 5318) is just the place to relax after a yomp across the Downs; kick back into the comfortably worn seating to enjoy a coffee, a pint or some decent bar food. Nearby is Bar Chocolat (19 The Mall, 0117 974 7000, www.bar-chocolat.com), a café devoted entirely to the sweet stuff: artful piles of sweets, cake and biscuits, plus mugs of wickedly decadent hot chocolate. Also worth a visit is the tiny, funky Amoeba (10 Kings Road, off Boyces Avenue, 0117 946 6461), where you can buy designer furniture and artwork as well as drinks.

There are dozens of bars and restaurants lining the Whiteladies strip; many become unbearably crowded at the weekends, but offer a good time during the week. Try Bar Humbug (89 Whiteladies Road, 0117 904 0061, www.barhumbug.co.uk) for top-quality cocktails and a relaxed atmosphere, or the Picture House Bar (44 Whiteladies Road, 0117 973 9302), where part of a long-derelict cinema has been transformed into an opulent cocktail venue. Across the road, the best pizza in town can be had at Planet Pizza (see p185), while nearby Papa Deli (84 Alma Road, 0117 973 6569,

BRIGHT LIGHTS

In Clifton, the **Dojo Bar** (12-16 Park Row, 0117 925 1177) is an intimate and ever-popular little party den, thanks to a music policy that incorporates everything from soul to funk and hip hop. The outside area is a lovely spot on a summer's evening too. Just down nearby Park Street, the **Elbow Room** (No.64, 0117 930 0242, www.theelbowroom.co.uk) combines full-size pool tables with a small and sweaty dancefloor; Sunday is reggae night.

Still further down the hill, **Bar Three** (9 Park Street, 0117 930 4561, www.barthree.com) is an ambitious, glammed-up bar, club and restaurant empire, with original wood panelling and a cocktail-sipping, dressed-to-kill clientele.

Nearby is the subterranean **Tube** (Unity Street, 0117 930 4429, www.tubebar.co.uk), owned by Massive Attack and run by BlowPop. An eclectic array of nights (including the odd hip hop karaoke session) attracts a trendy, friendly crowd.

The **Queenshilling** (9 Frogmore Street, 0117 926 4342, www. queenshilling.com), the city's most popular gay club. Drinks promotions and high jinks abound, whether it's the midweek karaoke try-out or Friday night's chart and dance music extravaganza.

The Bristol **Academy** (Frogmore Street, 0117 927 9227, www.bristol-academy.co.uk) is Bristol's largest live music venue, hosting nationally touring rock, indie and dance acts that haven't quite graduated to the arena circuit. It also features big-name DJs and funky breakbeats from local supremos **BlowPop** (www.blowpop.co.uk), regularly including the likes of Mr Scruff.

BlowPop nights also take place monthly at **Thekla Social** (The Grove, East Mud Dock, 0117 929 3301), a nightclub and live music venue on a boat in the Bristol Docks, recently taken over by the owners of the Social Bars in London.

In the city centre, the intimate **Native** (15 Small Street, 0117 930 4217, www.nativebristol.com) has been steadily drawing the crowds ever since it opened in 2005, with residents that include Boca45, Dave Smeaton and Neil Kitsell (Rainy But Funky), and the Leisure Allstars.

www.papadeli.co.uk) is top for foodie treats, including gooey chocolate brownies with juicy cherries. Just off Whiteladies on Cotham Hill, Not Just Cake (1B Pitville Place, Cotham Hill, 0117 973 2007, www.notjustcake.com) is a funky pink and white coffee and cupcake shop. Opposite, the Deco Lounge (50 Cotham Hill, 0117 373 2688) serves decent bar food, coffees and drinks until late.

North of the centre, the Hare on the Hill (41 Thomas Street North, Kingsdown, 0117 908 1982) serves delicious local Bath Ales and simple food to a mix of regulars. Beyond, Gloucester Road is the bohemian alternative to the brashness of Whiteladies Road, with a range of hip, appealing restaurants, bars and cafés. Head to the Tinto Lounge (344 Gloucester Road, 0117 942 0526) for all-day, post-hangover lounging with newspapers, board games and restorative brekkies, or the Prince of Wales (5 Gloucester Road, 0117 924 5552) for good real ales, a friendly mixed clientele and excellent organic pub grub.

Heading back towards the city centre and down Cheltenham Road, the Pipe & Slippers (118 Cheltenham Road, 0117 942 7711, www.thepipeandslippers.com), serves European and local beers as well as pies from Pie Minister (*see p184*), and the Bristolian organic café (2 Picton Street, no phone) are classic Montpellier hangouts. On Sunday nights, there's music and thalis for £5 at the One Stop Thali Café (12 York Road, 0117 942 6687, www.onestopthali.co.uk), a vegetarian and vegan temple to Asian street food with a kitsch pink interior.

The City Café at the City Inn (*see p178*) and the restaurant at Hotel du Vin (*see p178*) are also worth remembering.

Albion Public House & Dining Rooms

Boyces Avenue, Clifton Village, BS8 4AA (0117 973 3522/www.thealbionclifton.co.uk). **Open** 5-11pm Mon; noon-11pm Tue-Thur; noon-midnight Fri, Sat; noon-11pm Sun. **Brunch served** noon-2.30pm Sat, Sun. **Lunch served** noon-2.30pm Tue-Fri; noon-all gone Sun. **Dinner served** 7-10pm Tue-Sat. **Barbecue served** from 6.30pm Sun. **Main courses** £6-£18.50. **Credit** MC, V.
Tucked away at the bottom of tiny Boyces Avenue, opposite the Clifton Arcade, the Albion is unfailingly popular with Cliftonites. The heavy wooden tables outside are bustling in summer, while indoors the homely atmosphere and open fire invite cosy conversation and comfort eating in winter. The concise à la carte menu, based on West Country seasonal produce, is a corker. A typical starter might be local squash soup with chestnuts and sage or Cornish scallops with parsnip purée, while main courses such as rare roast mallard with red cabbage, butternut purée and fondant potato or baked hake with white wine, mushrooms and parsley mash are superb. If you've still got room after the generous portions, it'll be hard to choose between the sticky toffee pudding with clotted cream or the caramelised Cox's tarte tatin with caramel ice-cream for two. The wine list is predominantly Old World, while the service is friendly and attentive. Sunday lunch is also a laudable affair.

La Barrique

225 Gloucester Road, BS7 8NR (0117 944 5500/www.bistrolabarrique.co.uk). **Meals served** 11am-10pm daily. **Main courses** £9.50-£13.95. **Credit** MC, V.
This neighbourhood bistro serving French-style tapas or 'petits plats' has been a hit ever since it opened in early 2006, drawing Cliftonites – who would never otherwise be seen dead on Gloucester Road – to the area. Typical petits plats served up by renowned local chef Michel Lemoine, its owner, might include caramelised red onion, goat's cheese and sweet potato tatin, navarin of lamb with Mediterranean vegetables, bean cassoulet and wild mushroom risotto. The extensive wine list numbers 53 bottles in total; impressively, 47 are available by the glass. Friendly, knowledgeable waiting staff are happy to advise on your choice. Booking is recommended.

Bell's Diner

1-3 York Road, BS6 5QB (0117 924 0357/www.bellsdiner.com). **Lunch served** noon-2pm Tue-Fri. **Dinner served** 7-10pm Mon-Sat. **Main courses** £13-£19.50. **Tasting menu** £45 7 courses Mon-Thur (max 6 people). **Credit** AmEx, MC, V.
This long-running restaurant remains at the forefront of Bristol's dining scene. Housed in a converted grocer's shop, it makes good use of the quirky space. There's a small reception at the entrance, with a crackling log fire in winter, and two dining rooms: one rustic and atmospheric, the other modern and sleek. The menu of contemporary British food, with Mediterranean influences, changes daily. Among the starters on our visit were a quail jelly consommé with tea-smoked quail breast, pea shoots and pea nuts, and a beef carpaccio with beetroot sorbet and horseradish cream. Braised pork comes with savoy cabbage, juniper jus and truffle macaroni cheese, while sea trout is served with asparagus, broad beans, peas and liquorice sabayon. The wine list includes good-value regional bottles, and there are surprising versions of favourite desserts for those with waistbands to spare.

Bordeaux Quay

Bordeaux Quay, V-Shed, Canons Way, BS1 5UH (0117 943 1200/www.bordeauxquay.co.uk). **Open** *Deli* 8am-10pm Mon-Sat; 8am-4pm Sun. *Bar* 11am-11pm Mon-Sat; 11am-4pm Sun. *Brasserie* 10am-10pm Mon-Sat; 8am-

4pm Sun. *Restaurant* 12.30-10pm Mon-Sat.
Main courses £8.50-£18.50. **Credit** MC, V.
With a prime location overlooking Bristol's harbourside, Bordeaux Quay is a groundbreaking project that combines a downstairs deli and brasserie with an exclusive first-floor restaurant, in a building designed to produce zero waste – rainwater is collected to use to flush the toilets, there are solar panels on the roof and staff uniforms are fashioned from organic hemp. So far, so right on. Unfortunately, the one thing that can let it down is not the serene atmosphere nor the locally sourced ingredients, but the kitchen. While a starter of chicken liver parfait with red onion marmalade in the upstairs restaurant was rich and satisfying, a main of red mullet with spaghetti, fennel, chilli, lemon and parsley arrived cold. The day was saved, however, by a sinfully indulgent treacle tart, guaranteed to play havoc with blood sugar levels while wowing the taste buds. The house Bordeaux is a robust red among a neat selection of regional wines that are also available by the glass.

Café Maitreya

89 St Mark's Road, BS5 6HY (0117 951 0100/ www.cafemaitreya.co.uk). **Dinner served** 6.45-9.45pm Tue-Sat. **Set dinner** £16.95 2 courses, £20.95 3 courses. **Credit** MC, V.
Consistently rated as the UK's top gourmet vegetarian restaurant by the Vegetarian Society, Café Maitreya's food is 100% vegetarian and strives to use only organic, environmentally friendly and fair-trade ingredients. The result is fresh, tasty and highly accomplished. Maitreya's lavender-coloured frontage occupies a corner site on busy St Mark's Road, welcoming customers into a light, open-plan dining room. A sophisticated evening menu might include a wild mushroom cocotte of blewitts and paris pinks cooked in rich red wine and paprika sauce, with a pumpkin seed and rosemary crust. This can be followed by a cockle-warming roast butternut squash, pistachio and smoked cheddar tartlet, with crispy pink fir apple potatoes, baby leeks and green tomato chutney. A range of organic wines provides the perfect accompaniment.

Culinaria

1 Chandos Road, Redland, BS6 6PG (0117 973 7999/www.culinariabristol.co.uk). **Lunch served** noon-2pm Fri, Sat. **Dinner served** 6.30-9.30pm Wed-Sat. **Main courses** £11.50-£15.50. **Credit** MC, V.
This small, sassy neighbourhood bistro run by Stephen and Judy Markwick is Redland's most inviting restaurant – walk by of a lunchtime or an evening and you'll spy a tempting plate of steaming home-made pasties in the window. The modest dining room is decorated in a clean, subtle palette of cream and blue, with wooden floors and room for 30 diners, while the rest of the space is devoted to a counter of luscious dinner-party food to go. The pared-down menu offers French,

Find industrial ch at this former sug warehouse – Hot du Vin & Bistro.

British and Mediterranean dishes that are low on fuss but high on flavour. Fusion cooking is cast aside in favour of classics cooked with integrity and aplomb: provençal fish soup, pheasant rissoles, scallops with artichokes, leg of venison, cassoulet and the like are followed by utterly delicious desserts such as rice pudding, Tunisian orange cake and St Emilion au chocolat. There's a small courtyard for alfresco drinking.

Deason's

43 Whiteladies Road, BS8 2LS (0117 973 6230/www.deasons.co.uk). *Restaurant* **Lunch served** noon-2.30pm Tue-Fri, Sun. **Dinner served** 7-10pm Tue-Thur; 7-10.30pm Fri, Sat. **Main courses** £14.50-£19.50. **Set Sunday lunch** £15 2 courses, £20 3 courses. *Café* **Food served** 10.30am-6pm Tue-Sat; noon-3pm Sun. **Main courses** £3.75-£13. **Credit** AmEx, DC, MC, V.
One of Bristol's most accomplished restaurants. Faultless French service and arresting flower arrangements can't dispel the slightly stilted atmosphere, but the unfussy interior allows the

Bristol

food to take centre stage. Jason Deason's extensive travels and culinary finesse are both in evidence throughout the contemporary menu of British and fusion dishes. Choose from the main menu: a juniper and bay leaf smoked kangaroo loin with warm mixed game scotch egg and jerusalem artichoke purée, perhaps, followed by slow-roasted local free-range pork with black pudding stuffing, served with braised leek and butterbean cassoulet. Or go for the lighter terrace menu and opt for a simple, fresh, grilled market fish with a side order of chunky chips with sea salt and cider vinegar, followed by pumpkin pie with maple and pecan ice-cream. The French and international wine list is supported by a selection of Emilio Lustau sherries.

FishWorks

128 Whiteladies Road, Clifton, BS8 2RS (0117 974 4433/www.fishworks.co.uk/bristol). **Lunch served** noon-2.30pm, **dinner served** 6-10.30pm Tue-Sat. **Main courses** £7.50-£25. **Credit** AmEx, MC, V.
FishWorks serves what is arguably the freshest fish and seafood in town, shipped in daily from around the British coast to ensure a specials board full of variety. Alongside the specials are 'classic' dishes that exemplify a simple and respectful attitude to fish cooking. Try the vat of steamed South Devon mussels, dripping with wine and parsley, or a grilled swordfish with Moroccan spices and tomato salad. A deep-blue colour scheme, hint of nautical paraphernalia and buzzy atmosphere provide the perfect setting. You can buy some piscine goodies to take home from the fishmonger's counter, or learn culinary tips at FishWorks' acclaimed cookery school.

Goldbrick House

Goldbrick House, 69 Park Street, BS1 5PB (0117 945 1950/www.goldbrickhouse.co.uk). **Open** *Café* 9am-11pm Mon-Sat; 9am-6pm Sun. *Restaurant* noon-3pm, 6-11pm Mon-Fri; 11am-11pm Sat; 11am-6pm Sun. **Main courses** *Café* £3.95-£9.95. *Restaurant* £13-£19.50. **Credit** AmEx, DC, MC, V.
The recently opened Goldbrick House on Park Street is an undeniably chic and welcoming spot, with its plush interior of heavy wallpaper, mottled gold ceilings and grand chandeliers softened by leather and suede furniture to lounge in. With a champagne and cocktail bar downstairs and a restaurant upstairs, it caters equally well for diners who want an informal meal with friends, and those who want to make more of the occasion. The bar has a concise menu of generous and delicious breakfasts, brunches, pastas, salads and bruschette, alongside specials such as venison hotpot. For puds, try an almond, peach and ginger crumble or an indulgent chocolate tart – all hovering around the £6 mark. Upstairs prices soar nearer £18 for mains, including the likes of guinea fowl, lamb wellington and catch of the day.

Greens' Dining Room

25 Zetland Road, BS6 7AH (0117 924 6437/ www.greensdiningroom.com). **Lunch served** 12.30-2.30pm Tue-Sun. **Dinner served** 6.30-10.30pm Tue-Sat. **Main courses** (lunch) £6-£10. **Set dinner** £25 3 courses. **Credit** MC, V.
One of the most relaxed restaurants in Bristol, Greens' Dining Room, hidden away on Zetland Road in Redland, opened in autumn 2006 and is quietly making a name for itself. The set menu takes its influences from England, France, Spain and Italy, and includes such starters as a lip-smacking beetroot soup with horseradish and a delicate smoked duck breast with celeriac remoulade. Tenderloin of pork with lentils and green sauce was sublime, as was hake with chickpeas, chorizo and aïoli. The more adventurous might opt for pigeon chartreuse with turnips and juniper. A chocolate and almond pithivier or lemon and goat's cheese tart will push waistlines to the limit. The wine list is evenly divided between the Old and New Worlds, with the odd Greek wine making an appearance; half of the wines are available by the glass or carafe. Spot on.

Old India

The Old Stock Exchange, 34 St Nicholas Street, BS1 1TL (0117 922 1136/www.oldindia.co.uk). **Lunch served** noon-2pm, **dinner served** 6-11.30pm Mon-Sat. **Main courses** £6.50-£14. **Set lunch** (Mon-Thur) £6.95 2 courses, £8 3 courses, incl soft drink. **Pre-theatre dinner** (6-7pm) £12 2 courses incl tea/coffee. **Credit** AmEx, MC, V.
Housed in Bristol's Grade II-listed former Stock Exchange and making full use of the building's innate grandeur, this Indian restaurant is a real eye-opener. The beautiful mahogany-panelled dining room and colonial club atmosphere provide a conducive setting in which to try high-class, modern Indian cooking, modelled on the cuisine of Moghul princes. Traditional dishes are given an avant-garde makeover to create delicious contemporary flavours. Chicken tikka masala was superb – a rich tomato sauce with tender chicken chunks, served with fluffy pilau rice and a fruity peshwari naan. Other sumptuous main courses include an aromatic rogan josh with meltingly moist lamb, and international wines or Indian beers provide the perfect liquid accompaniment. Take a look at the original Victorian tiled bathrooms before you leave.

Olive Shed

Princes Wharf, BS1 4RN (0117 929 1960/ www.therealolivecompany.co.uk). **Lunch served** noon-3pm Tue-Sun. **Dinner served** 6-10pm Tue-Sat. **Main courses** £7.50-£14. **Credit** MC, V.
The menu at this delightful restaurant and deli is dominated by vegetarian and seafood dishes made from seasonal organic ingredients. A plate of mixed tapas is an excellent way to sample the

goodies on show on the ground floor – Spanish tortilla, fresh anchovies and, of course, the company's superlative olives. A starter of salt cod brandade, garlic croute and sauce vierge or beetroot and orange salad with a warm pickled walnut and tarragon dressing can be followed by a casserole of monkfish, palourds, corn and borlotti beans served with wild rice, or roast skate wing with spinach, nutmeg and beurre noisette. To round things off, try the roast figs with maple syrup and vanilla ice-cream. Poised on the edge of Bristol Docks, the Olive Shed comes into its own in the summer, when you can sit outside to enjoy the Mediterranean tapas and organic wine while the sun sets on an industrial-lite backdrop.

One30 Bar & Restaurant

130 Cheltenham Road, BS6 5RW (0117 944 2442/www.one30.co.uk). **Brunch/lunch served** 11am-3pm daily. **Dinner served** 6pm-midnight Mon-Sat. **Main courses** £8.50-£14.50. **Tapas** £2.50-£6.50. **Credit** MC, V.
This is a fantastic gastrobar. Exposed brick walls, shiny wooden floors and inviting leather sofas create a familiar but unpretentious setting for Friday evening drinks, Sunday afternoon lounging or informal dining on any day of the week. Hang about in the bar area for accomplished signature cocktails, including the One30 – rum infused with vanilla and fig – and a cutting-edge tapas menu that includes unmissable fried goat's cheese with preserved lemons and marjoram. The restaurant offers serious bistro food, cooked with real flair. If you can tear yourself away from the irresistible tapas, then start with the open ravioli of pot-roast rabbit, garlic and rosemary. Main dishes might include roast pork loin with apples, morcilla, fondant potato, thyme and cider or hearty winter warmers such as ribeye steak with fat chips and béarnaise sauce. Great stuff.

Pie Minister

24 Stokes Croft, BS1 3PR (0117 942 9500/ www.pieminister.co.uk). **Meals served** 9.30am-7pm Mon-Wed; 11am-7pm Thur-Sat; 11am-4pm Sun. **Main courses** £2.95-£4.95. **Credit** (over £5) AmEx, MC, V.
With some pleasant café-style seating out front and a vast pie-producing kitchen out back, Pie Minister has already become a Bristol institution. Pies are made by hand using top-notch ingredients, including free-range meat and local seasonal vegetables. Among the favourites are humble pie (British beef, shallots, real ale and rosemary) and

CLASS ACTS

Artistically inclined Bristol has more than its fair share of excellent theatres. The Edwardian Bristol **Hippodrome** (St Augustine's Parade, 0870 607 7500, www.getlive.co.uk/bristol) is one of the largest provincial stages in the country, and plays host to a steady stream of West End musicals, celebrity-festooned pantomimes and other crowd-pleasers. Cary Grant was a call-boy here before making his fortune in Hollywood.

However, it's the Bristol Old Vic at the **Theatre Royal** (King Street, 0117 987 7877, www.bristol-old-vic.co.uk, closed mid July-end Aug) that's the jewel in the city's theatre crown, and considered the foremost production company in the South-west. Also at the Theatre Royal are the New Vic, which stages in-house work and touring productions, and the excellent Basement Theatre, a forum for new writers.

The Old Vic does not, however, hold the monopoly on quality theatre or imaginative use of space. The **Tobacco Factory** (Raleigh Road, Southville, 0117 902 0344, www.tobaccofactory.com), a studio theatre housed in a former warehouse, is the scene of some of the city's most innovative productions, including the award-winning 'Shakespeare at the Tobacco Factory' series.

Less well known, the **QEH** (Jacob's Wells Road, 0117 930 3082) is housed in an ultra-modern building, with a three-sided 220-seater auditorium. It offers a nicely judged selection of fringe drama, dance shows and improv work.

Zero waste, maximum taste at Bordeaux Quay.

the Spanish-themed matador (beef, chorizo, olives, tomatoes, sherry and butter beans). Pie Minister's deserved success means its pies are also available in selected pubs around town, and they go down very well with a decent pint of beer.

Planet Pizza

83 Whiteladies Road, BS8 2NT (0117 907 7112/www.planetpizza.co.uk). **Open** 11am-11pm daily. **Main courses** £6.95-£12.95. **Credit** MC, V.

If you want pizza, then there's only one place to go in Bristol: Planet Pizza. With 14 pizzas to choose from, going by such names as capricorn (goat's cheese, caramelised onions and rocket), saturn (smoked bacon, wiltshire ham and mushrooms) and alpha centauri (artichoke hearts, bell peppers and olives), you'll be seeing stars by the time it comes to finally making a decision. There are mouth-watering salads on the side and a good selection of bottled beers and draught beers to round things off. Planet Pizza has another branch on Gloucester Road too.

Riverstation

The Grove, BS1 4RB (0117 914 4434/ www.riverstation.co.uk). Bar & Kitchen **Meals served** noon-10pm Mon-Sat; noon-9pm Sun. **Main courses** £2.50-£9.50. *Restaurant* **Lunch served** noon-2.30pm Mon-Fri; 10.30am-2.30pm Sat; noon-3pm Sun. **Dinner served** 6-10.30pm Mon-Thur; 6-10.30pm Fri; 6-11pm Sat; 6-9pm Sun. **Pre-theatre dinner served** 6-7.15pm. **Main courses** £12.50-£18. **Set lunch** £12 2 courses, £14.50 3 courses. *Sun* £15.50 2 courses, £18.75 3 courses. **Pre-theatre menu** Mon-Fri, Sun. £9 (main course incl glass of beer/wine). **Credit** MC, V.

The converted former HQ of the river police is an architectural fusion of stone, hardwoods and acres of glass. It's also one of Bristol's most stylish restaurants. On the ground floor (deck one), a deli, bar and outside terrace provide the perfect pit stop for light lunches, while upstairs a second deck opens out into a 120-seater restaurant. The Modern European food is as uplifting as the surroundings. Squid is given a Spanish flavour, slow-cooked with red wine, rosemary, chorizo and broad beans, while roast cod with spinach, puy lentils and salsa verde continues the theme. A warm ginger pudding with clotted cream and butterscotch sauce is just one of many irresistible desserts. The global wine list has been thoughtfully put together to complete this class act.

Sands

95 Queen's Road, Clifton, BS8 1LW (0117 973 9734/www.sandsrestaurant.co.uk). **Lunch served** noon-2.30pm, **dinner served** 6-11pm daily. **Main courses** £8.95-£13.95. **Set meze** £15.95-£17.50 2 courses (minimum 2). **Credit** AmEx, MC, V.

At the entrance to this spacious, low-lit basement venue, scattered cushions provide a suitably laid-back setting in which to sample a shisha or a sweet Arabic coffee. Beyond, creamy, plaster walls and tucked-away alcoves are softly illuminated by lanterns. This place is atmospheric enough to whisk you away from the humdrum of Queen's Road, but mercifully steers well clear of any tired *Arabian Nights* theming. The indecisive can plump for the special Lebanese meze (£17.50), which delivers a vast quantity of irresistible flavours. Start with sultry, smoky baba ganoush, silky houmous, kibbeh and fattoush, served with wonderfully light pitta breads. Follow this with a mixed grill of tender chicken served with grilled onions, tomatoes and green peppers, or the melt-in-the-mouth lamb shank with herbed rice. Service is smiling and efficient, the ambience romantic and unhurried.

Bristol

Malmesbury & Tetbury

Rub shoulders with the toffs in 4x4 country.

Unless you have a strong interest in hunting, the royal family or polo, you'll be forgiven for professing a lack of knowledge on where Malmesbury and Tetbury actually are, let alone what they're about. The towns and surrounding chunk of land that make up northern Wiltshire and the southern reaches of Gloucestershire – on the doorstep of the Cotswolds – throw up few obvious picture-postcard images, and definitely can't be said to be victims of overexposure.

Scenically, the area is a fairly undramatic landscape of gently undulating farmland, broken by spindly hedges and scattered stands of trees. Socially, it's conservative (and Conservative) central, and home to several royal estates, including Prince Charles's Highgrove and Princess Anne's Gatcombe Park, with Badminton Park (home of the famous horse trials) also in the area. This land of pheasants, tweedy types and muddy 4x4s can be something of an eye-opener to outsiders who think that the stereotypical English toff is a dying breed; a visit to any of the pubs around here should make it apparent that this isn't the case.

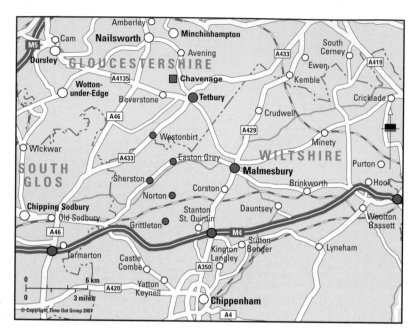

Aside from social observation, antiques hunting and garden visits, there is relatively little to do or see in Malmesbury, Tetbury or the surrounding villages. Yet it's this lack of landmark sites that's part of the attraction of a weekend break here. With several outstanding hotels – two of which (Calcot Manor and Whatley Manor) have fabulous spas – and some excellent restaurants, the area offers the perfect excuse for a few days of pure indulgence. If you get excited by locally grown and caught produce and classical British cuisine then you're in for a treat, with wild game and traditional puddings to be found on most restaurant menus.

Malmesbury

In 1998, Malmesbury had a spotlight cast in its direction by the international media when two Tamworth pigs – who became known as the Tamworth Two – escaped from the town's abattoir. After going on a nine-day countryside rampage the courageous pair were eventually tracked down, but the event, and subsequent BBC TV drama, *The Legend of the Tamworth Two*, highlighted just how much of an English rural cliché Malmesbury – with its quiet streets, village pubs, local eccentrics and surrounding villages – is to outsiders.

One also has to wonder whether the Tamworth Two were the most exciting thing to have happened in the town since 1703, when Hannah Twynnoy became the last

person in England to be eaten by a tiger (it had escaped from a local menagerie; today, she is remembered by a grave in Malmesbury churchyard). This is a town where nothing really happens – slowly. As a guilt-free destination for the perennially lazy, Malmesbury, and its surrounding countryside, is an ancient, cobbled dream of excellent food, antiques, walks and idle, boozy contemplation.

Yet the Tamworth Two aside, Malmesbury has managed to rack up some other claims to fame in its 1,300-odd years. Philosopher Thomas Hobbes was born in these parts, proving that boozy contemplation brings its own rewards, and it was home to 12th-century chronicler William of Malmesbury.

The town is also the site of Malmesbury Abbey (01666 826666, www.malmesbury abbey.com), a work of intense beauty that was once three times its still-impressive size. That such a commanding church was built here is no surprise. Because of its superb natural defences – the hilltop town is surrounded by rivers on three sides – Malmesbury has been occupied since earliest recorded times. In 880, King Alfred was impressed enough to name Malmesbury a borough, making it the oldest in England. The abbey was founded by Aldhelm in 676, though the basic structure you see today dates from the 12th century. Some of its earliest notable features are the south porch, containing a wonderful Norman arch, while later additions included an immense spire, taller than that of Salisbury Cathedral, which collapsed during a storm in the early 16th century. In 1010, Brother Eilmer attempted to fly from the tower with a pair of artificial wings, breaking both his legs in the process; the crippled monk subsequently became something of a symbol for the town.

On Henry VIII's Dissolution of the Monasteries in 1539, the abbey became a parish church, but then suffered centuries of neglect (by the 18th century it was being used as a barn and animal shed). It wasn't until the 20th century, when significant restoration work was undertaken, that the situation began to be reversed. In the north aisle is the (empty) tomb of King Athelstan, while the south face still bears pockmarks from cannon and gunshot from the Civil War, when the town was heavily fought over.

Alongside the abbey are the lovely five-acre Abbey House Gardens (Market Cross, 01666 822212, www.abbeyhousegardens.co.uk, closed 22 Oct-20 Mar), Malmesbury's pride and joy. Ian and Barbara Pollard (famous for being the 'naked gardeners') bought 16th-century Abbey House over a decade ago and started to develop its gardens to reflect the long history of the site. Within them you'll find a Saxon arch, a Celtic cross garden, a herb garden, an ornamental pond and 130 varieties of apple cordon and 2,000 of rose. Guided tours of the garden can be pre-booked.

The famous Market Cross that stands next to the gardens was built in the late 15th century – the carved octagonal structure is one of the best-preserved structures of its kind in England, and still serves its purpose – a farmers' market takes place here on the second and fourth Saturday of every month (9am-1pm).

Accommodation	★★★★★
Food & drink	★★★☆☆
Nightlife	★★★★★
Shopping	★★★★★
Culture	★★★★★
Sights	★★★★★
Scenery	★★★★★

And that's about the extent of Malmesbury's permanent attractions. The tourist office (*see p193*) can supply an interesting town guide and a booklet detailing a must-do river walk that snakes around the foot of the old town, plus information on annual events, such as the carnival that take place here in the last two weeks of August, and the WOMAD festival, held here for the first time in July 2007.

Tetbury

Just five miles north-west of Malmesbury lies Tetbury. The animosity between the two towns in Saxon times was considerable (Malmesbury was in Wessex, Tetbury in Mercia). These days, that rivalry is more concerned with which town has better hotels, finer restaurants and more interesting shops.

On one count Tetbury certainly wins: antiques shops. There are so many (with a huge concentration on Long Street, also the home of the Police Museum at No.63) that, as one resident confided, 'you can't even find anywhere that sells underwear any more'. Tetbury's other main feature is the sheltered Market House in the town centre; built on stilts in 1655, it still serves as the town's meeting point, and hosts a

Malmesbury & Tetbury

Chavenage House

market on Wednesdays. The Georgian Gothic church of St Mary the Virgin is also worth a look – it's said to boast the fourth highest church spire in England.

A monastery was built at Tetbury in 681, and during the Middle Ages the town grew in importance, becoming famed for one of the country's best wool and yarn markets. The Industrial Revolution bypassed the town, leaving it economically impoverished but architecturally preserved, and gently pottering along its ancient streets (such as Gumstool Hill, site of the annual Woolsack Races on spring bank holiday Monday – the main event in the town's calendar) remains the number one leisure activity today.

For an unusually personal country-house experience, head to Elizabethan Chavenage House (01666 502329, www.chavenage. com, closed Oct-Apr) just outside Tetbury, where owner David Lowsley-Williams is often on hand to show guests around. The handsome house, built over a medieval original, and virtually unchanged for 400 years, has its own ghost. During the Civil War, its Parliamentarian owner, Nathaniel Stephens, was cursed by his own daughter for (reluctantly) acquiescing in the execution of Charles I. He died shortly afterwards, and legend has it that the headless king arrived in a hearse to carry his body away – a phenomenon repeated after the death of every patriarch in the line.

Another popular local spot is Trull House Gardens (01285 841255, www.trullhouse. co.uk, closed Nov-Easter), an intimate, eight-acre garden set in rolling countryside between Tetbury and Cirencester. Charming feature include a large lily pond, terraced gardens, a sunken garden leading to a summer house and a wilderness area that is alive with bulbs in spring and grasses and wild flowers in summer. Tea and own-made cakes can be taken outside.

The only attraction of national importance in the area (apart from Prince Charles's nearby private Highgrove estate) is the superlative Westonbirt National Arboretum (01666 880220, www.forestry.gov.uk/ westonbirt), located a few miles south-west of Tetbury. Westonbirt is world-famed for its stunning collection of over 17,000 specimens, including many rare species, and the National Maple Collection, spread over 600 acres of Grade I-listed landscape interlaced with 18 miles of marked trails. Started by Robert Holford in the 1830s, and run by the Forestry Commission since 1956, the arboretum now pulls in around 350,000 visitors annually and offers year-round interest. Spring sees the spectacular flowering of camellias, magnolias and rhododendrons, and huge swathes of bluebells carpeting the woods; in summer grassland flowers come into their own, and the handkerchief and umbrella trees are in blossom. The blaze of autumn colour (at its best in the last two weeks of October), particularly from the Japanese maples, makes a trip to New England redundant. And, even in winter, willows, witch hazels and bright-stemmed dogwoods provide colour. Dogs are welcome at Westonbirt, although there are designated 'dog-free' areas. Of the many annual events held here, highlights include the summer open-air classical concerts with fireworks as part of the Festival of Wood, and the

All-year round colour at Westonbirt National Arboretum.

Calcot Manor Hotel

Enchanted Wood illuminated trail, held over 12 nights in December. For further information, including details of free guided walks, call 01666 880220.

WHERE TO STAY

The upmarket Calcot Manor is just one of the reasons to head for this area. The Priory Inn gastropub (*see p193*), with 14 rooms, is another decent option. Also worth considering is Tetbury's Snooty Fox (Market Place, 01666 502436, www.snooty-fox. co.uk), a traditional coaching inn – it's centrally located and very welcoming.

Calcot Manor Hotel

Junction of A46 & A4135, 3 miles from Tetbury, Gloucestershire GL8 8YJ (01666 890391/www.calcotmanor.co.uk). **Rates** £205-£245 double; £245 suite. **Credit** AmEx, MC, V.
The Calcot Manor estate goes way back. It consists of an early 14th-century farmhouse and a 16th-century manor house, set within a flower-filled courtyard of ancient barns and 17th-century stables. The place was converted into a hotel in the 1980s; the Barn, a new venue for conferences, is the latest restoration project. The hotel has a fresh and contemporary vibe, and is regularly voted one of the UK's friendliest, most stylish and most enjoyable places to stay. Its secret lies in its inclusiveness. The complex is justly famed for its family-friendliness, but by keeping the family facilities largely separate from the main building, the hotel never feels overwhelmed by children.

One of Calcot's major draws is its impressive spa. Opened in 2003, it offers a broad spectrum of treatments (Guinot facials, Thalgo body wraps, alternative therapies) and features indoor and outdoor pools, a hammam massage table, dry flotation bed, sauna, steam room, exercise studio and, best of all, an outdoor hot tub facing a log fire. (Children are only allowed in the spa from 3.45-5.15pm daily, plus 8.45-10.15am at weekends.) Further outdoor facilities include tennis courts and a footpath/cycle track (bikes can be borrowed) that winds its way through the estate's impressive 220 acres of grounds.

Only nine of the 34 bedrooms (all en suite) are within the main house; these have deliberately been given a more traditional look than those located in various buildings around the grounds, and are orientated towards couples. All are individually decorated in muted colours, with sleek bathrooms and facilities that include CD systems and swish TVs. Calcot offers two eating options, the informal Gumstool Inn and the posher Conservatory (where younger children are 'discouraged'); *see p193*.

Close Hotel

Long Street, Tetbury, Gloucestershire GL8 8AQ (01666 502272/www.theclose-hotel.com). **Rates** £100-£180 double. **Credit** AmEx, DC, MC, V.
In contrast to the contemporary country-house appeal of the Rectory (*see p192*), the charms of the 15-room Close Hotel are very much old school. Set within a splendid 16th-century townhouse in the centre of Tetbury, this is a place of swagged curtains, rich, multi-hued decor, oil paintings in gilded frames, dark wood and antique furniture. Yet the hotel is smart and unstuffy, and a recent refurbishment has modernised the vibe somewhat. All of the bedrooms have hand-painted bathrooms, antique dressing tables and all mod

cons; the best three have four-poster beds and views over the walled gardens. Attractions include a notable restaurant (*see p193*), a stylish bar area and very friendly staff.

Old Bell

Abbey Row, Malmesbury, Wiltshire SN16 0BW (01666 822344/www.oldbellhotel.com). **Rates** £125-£200 double. **Credit** AmEx, MC, V.
Within spitting distance of Malmesbury Abbey, and claiming to be England's oldest purpose-built hotel (dating back to 1220, when it was built to entertain important guests to the abbey), the 31-room Old Bell exudes a cosy, old-style charm. The building was extensively refurbished by new owners at the start of the decade, and now offers four different grades of accommodation, with half the rooms located in the main house, and the other half in the adjoining Coach House. Rooms (all en suite) are individually decorated in a trad – but elegant – way, with modern touches such as Sky TV, DVD players and broadband internet access. It's worth paying more for one of the superior rooms if you want views of the abbey. The Grade-I listed status prevents the hotel from having exercise or spa facilities, but staff are happy to arrange access to a nearby gym; massages (from £28.50) are available on-site in the treatment room. There's a good restaurant (*see p194*) and the relaxed lounges are ideal for a cream tea in front of the log fire in winter.

Rectory Hotel

Crudwell, Malmesbury, Wiltshire SN16 9EP (01666 577194/www.therectoryhotel.com). **Rates** £105-£175 double. **Credit** MC, V.
The latest addition to the area's accommodation options is also one of the best. Jonathan Barry and Julian Muggridge bought this elegant Georgian manor house in 2005, with the objective of creating a classic country hotel with a contemporary twist. That the project was a labour of love as much as a business undertaking is immediately evident; the reception/drawing room is beautifully decorated with a harmonious and individual mix of antiques, candles, photographs and sculptures. Softly spoken staff are welcoming but unintrusive.

Upstairs, the 12 bedrooms, each named after a district of Gloucestershire, are all of a good size. Each one is different, but they feature beds with hand-sprung mattresses, fine Egyptian linens, antique furniture, well-equipped bathrooms (complete with bathrobes and handmade products), and views over the three-acre gardens. There is one designated room for those with kids in tow – but note that the atmosphere here is more orientated towards couples.

Additional draws are the charming bar area (complete with a Bill Amberg leather bar, sash windows and a log fire), beautiful Victorian walled gardens, a croquet lawn, a heated outdoor swimming pool (open during the summer), and a superb Modern British restaurant (*see p194*). An excellent choice for a weekend of calm indulgence.

Whatley Manor Hotel

Easton Grey, Wiltshire SN16 0RB (01666 822888/www.whatleymanor.com). **Rates** £280-£850 double. **Credit** AmEx, MC, V.
Swiss owner Christian Landholt's objective is to create an air of exclusivity here. Guests approach the Grade II-listed property via a long driveway lined with lime trees and Cotswold stone walls until they reach a grand oak doorway that opens automatically, revealing a beautifully kept courtyard behind. Converted at vast expense in 2004, Whatley is the 'rarefied bubble of low-key luxury, peace and total privacy' that its brochure asserts, and children under 12 aren't accommodated. The staff are extremely attentive, efficient and good-natured (although perhaps a little subservient for some), and this is the sort of place where, even when all 23 rooms (eight suites and 15 doubles) are occupied, guests have little contact with each other. So if you want buzz, look elsewhere, but if you want to escape and your pockets are deep, this is the place for you.

Quality is apparent in everything, from the silk rugs, limestone floors, handmade French wallpaper and Italian furniture in the lounge areas to the

Kick back and enjoy the country-house charm of the Rectory Hotel.

Floris bathroom products, extremely comfortable beds and Bang & Olufsen TVs in the bedrooms. Gourmets are catered for by the hotel's two restaurants, Le Mazot and the Dining Room (see p194). The latest addition, completed in 2006, is a luxury 40-seater cinema, used mainly for private screenings and presentations.

Another draw is the Aquarius Spa (use of which is included in the room prices). The centrepiece is one of the biggest and best hydrotherapy pools in the country (although we found the water a little cold). As well as a wide range of professional treatments (by La Prairie, at extra cost), the spa includes four thermal cabins, a wave dream sensory room, a camomile steam grotto, showers infused with mint and other scents, a gym and a 'VIP suite', where couples can indulge in a tailored package of pampering for two.

Surrounding the house are 12 acres of stunning formal gardens (made up of 26 different areas that include a rose garden and a herbaceous garden, and feature specially commissioned sculptures). These lead down to woodland and a wildflower meadow bordering a tributary of the Avon. Created by Wisley-trained Barry Holman, and inspired by the original 1920s plan, the gardens are remarkably mature considering there was nothing but grass here a few years ago. They have a tranquillity and sense of privacy that is only disturbed by the occasional helicopter landing on the lawn.

WHERE TO EAT & DRINK

Among the best drinking pubs in the area are the Vine Tree in Norton (see p195), the Neeld Arms in Grittleton (01249 782470, www.neeldarms.co.uk), just north of the M4, and the Wheatsheaf Inn in Crudwell (01666 577739, www.wheatsheaf crudwell.co.uk), which also has a good range of food. Tetbury's Priory Inn (London Road, 01666 502251, www.theprioryinn. co.uk) uses locally sourced ingredients to create fabulous dishes such as pan-grilled Madgett's Farm duck breast or Cockleford smoked trout fillet. The area's eateries also offer ample opportunity to indulge in wild game.

Close Hotel

Long Street, Tetbury, Gloucestershire GL8 8AQ (01666 502272/www.theclose-hotel.com). **Lunch served** noon-2pm, **dinner served** 7-9.30pm daily. **Main courses** £11-£14. **Set lunch** £9.90 3 courses. **Set dinner** £29.50 3 courses. **Cream tea** £4.95, 2-6pm daily. **Credit** AmEx, DC, MC, V.

Historically known for its exclusivity, the Garden restaurant at the Close has eased up somewhat in recent years. That said, it's still an opulent space in which to enjoy some fine English cooking, with grand fireplaces, huge gilded mirrors, draped curtains and parquet flooring. The wisteria clad stone exterior is also a delight to behold. Dishes feature

TOURIST INFORMATION

Malmesbury
Town Hall, Market Lane, Malmesbury, Wiltshire SN16 9BZ (01666 823748/ www.malmesbury.gov.uk).
Tetbury
33 Church Street, Tetbury, Gloucestershire GL8 8JG (01666 503552/www.tetbury.org).

high-quality, often local ingredients. Typical starters (the 'opening act') might be cream of watercress soup or sauté of black pudding; mains (the 'second scene') are the likes of venison with game pie, saddle of wild rabbit with roast vegetables, or braised lamb shank with potato and thyme purée. Desserts (the 'finale') don't let the side down, with bread and butter pudding, hazelnut soufflé with warm chocolate sauce, or a good choice of mainly English cheeses.

A bar and terrace menu offers lighter meals such as Cornish crab and smoked haddock fish cakes or Gloucester Old Spot sausages and mash. This is also the place to visit if you're in the mood for a traditional Cotswold cream tea.

Conservatory & Gumstool Inn at Calcot Manor

Nr Tetbury, Gloucestershire GL8 8YJ (01666 890391/www.calcotmanor.co.uk). **Lunch served** noon-2pm daily. **Dinner served** 7-9.30pm Mon-Sat; 7-9pm Sun. *Conservatory* **Main courses** £13-£16. *Gumstool Inn* **Main courses** £10-£16. **Both Credit** AmEx, DC, MC, V.

Calcot Manor's fine dining restaurant has lovely countryside views and plenty of natural light, but the atmosphere can be rather lacklustre. There's a rather corporate feel, with generic 'modern' decor and cheesy music, and staff who are polite but distant. The draw is chef-director Michael Croft's well-executed, modish dishes. Starters include scallops with puy lentils and bacon, and a rich pumpkin and truffle ravioli, while mains feature the likes of seared wild sea bass, organic Highgrove beef and roast rack of venison. A lack of vegetarian dishes reflects the area's conservative tastes, although daily specials plump up the options. Save room for dessert, if the choices such as kirsch cherry and almond clafoutis or iced pineapple parfait take your fancy.

A cheaper option is the neighbouring, pub-like Gumstool Inn. It shares a kitchen with the Conservatory, but the menu is more eclectic and the atmosphere cosier and more casual. Mains might include smoked haddock fish cakes with lemon and dill butter and half a roast pheasant with bacon and bread sauce. Inviting lighter dishes such as plum tomato and caramelised red onion tart with taleggio and rocket are also available. A pleasant outside terrace accommodates diners on warmer days.

Malmesbury & Tetbury

Dining Room & Le Mazot at Whatley Manor

Easton Grey, Wiltshire SN16 0RB (01666 822888/www.whatleymanor.com). Dining Room **Dinner served** 7-10pm Wed-Sun. **Set dinner** £60 3 courses. *Le Mazot* **Lunch served** noon-2pm, **dinner served** 7-10pm daily. **Main courses** £14.50-£19.50. **Set lunch** £21.50 3 courses. **Credit** AmEx, MC, V.

Head chef Martin Burge oversees the two restaurants at Whatley, and has a Michelin star to his name. The talented chef earned his culinary spurs working for (among others) Raymond Blanc and John Burton Race.

The haute cuisine Dining Room has knowledgeable waiting staff, ready to explain the elements of each dish. Jerusalem artichoke cream with roast salsify, caramelised baby onions and mushroom hazelnut emulsion, or loin of wild hare roasted with its own sausage, served with pumpkin purée and braised red cabbage, are typical starters. Mains might be steamed fillet of dover sole on braised salsify and fennel, topped with truffle foam, or loin of Balmoral Estate venison pan-fried and dressed with époisse, served with potato gratin and a chocolate-gel and port reduction. The seven-course tasting menu is a good way to sample Burge's creative talent to the full.

Le Mazot is a more informal brasserie, but nevertheless the dishes remain anything but simple – perhaps duck breast roasted with honey and served with celeriac purée and reduced Madeira sauce, or butternut squash ravioli on braised salsify with green beans, pine nuts and parmesan shavings. Jazz nights are sometimes held here, and the place is popular with well-turned out locals.

The only discordant note in both restaurants is the surroundings. The Dining Room comprises three anonymous and rather old-fashioned little rooms, while Le Mazot is housed within an oddly incongruous mock Swiss chalet.

Old Bell

Abbey Row, Malmesbury, Wiltshire SN16 0AG (01666 822344/www.oldbellhotel.com). **Lunch served** 12.15-2pm daily. **Dinner served** 7-9pm Mon-Thur, Sun; 7-9.30pm Fri, Sat. **Main courses** £19.50-£40. **Cream tea** £5.75, 3-6pm daily. **Credit** AmEx, MC, V.

Talented executive chef Tom Rains is still running the show at the Old Bell's restaurant, with his contemporary interpretations of traditional dishes and precise execution – meals are as much about presentation as flavours here. Among his signature dishes are poached scallops, Dublin Bay prawns, saffron and aromatic vegetables; fillet of Scottish beef, rösti potato, broad beans, morels and truffle jus; and breasts of squab pigeon with foie gras, red cabbage, fondant potato and thyme jus. If you can stretch to it, go for the seven-course taster menu that includes some of these dishes. For dessert, you won't better his classic bread and butter pudding, the house special. The traditionally decorated yet comfortable dining room is presided over with great charm and efficiency by restaurant manager Saverio Buchicchio, who is happy to talk you through the extensive wine list. In the summer, customers can dine outside on the peaceful terrace. For light meals or traditional cream teas, make yourself at home in one of the Old Bell's two snug lounges.

Rattlebone Inn

Church Street, Sherston, Wiltshire SN16 0LR (01666 840871). **Lunch served** noon-2.30pm Mon-Sat; noon-3pm Sun. **Dinner served** 6-9pm Mon-Sat. **Main courses** £7-£15. **Credit** MC, V.

One of two pubs in the lovely village of Sherston (the other being the Carpenter's Arms), the 16th-century Rattlebone achieved a certain notoriety in early 2002 for being the place where Prince Harry was reportedly caught under-age drinking (Highgrove is just up the road). It's a Young's pub, so the beer's quality can be taken as read, and the food in the restaurant area is ambitious, fresh and wide-ranging, covering everything from sandwiches and hearty ploughman's platters to free-range bangers and mash or wild boar. Grab a table close to the log fire in colder months, or enjoy a pint over a leisurely game of boules in one of the two garden areas in the summer. (The pub's annual boules tournament is held on the second Saturday in July.) Active minds will appreciate the many games on offer, and the place hosts acoustic music events monthly.

Rectory Hotel Restaurant

Rectory Hotel, Crudwell, Malmesbury, Wiltshire SN16 9EP (01666 577194/www.therectory hotel.co.uk). **Lunch served** noon-2pm, **dinner served** 7-10pm daily. **Main courses** £13-£18.25. **Credit** MC, V.

With simple but atmospheric decor – bare floorboards, wood-panelled walls and smartly arranged square wooden tables that look out on to the garden – and a quiet, relaxed vibe, the Rectory Hotel's restaurant is the perfect setting in which to enjoy Peter Fairclough's celebration of British cuisine. (In the summer, meals can also be enjoyed in the formal Victorian garden.) His dishes achieve a balance between sophisticated and hearty, and his interest in the ideals of the Slow Food Movement is immediately evident. The menu highlights local produce and seasonal ingredients – including a good selection of wild game. Starters might include cullen skink (a Scottish soup of smoked haddock, potatoes and onions), pheasant ravioli with parsnip purée and a lentil jus, or a salad of goat's cheese with pea shoots and a pear and walnut dressing.

Mains are equally tempting: roast loin of venison with bubble 'n' squeak and blackberry infused jus, say, or pan-fried loin of Gloucestershire Old Spot pork with potato gratin and herb-infused butter beans. Desserts – summer berry trifle or bramley apple and blackberry nutty crumble with rum and raisin ice-cream, for example – are resolutely British. The cheese board includes cornish yarg, chambertin, stilton and cotswold organic brie. The wine list is more than a match for the menu, and has a good range of dessert wines.

Smoking Dog

62 High Street, Malmesbury, Wiltshire SN16 9AT (01666 825823/www.sabrain.co.uk). **Lunch served** noon-3pm, **dinner served** 6.30-9.30pm daily. **Main courses** £7.95-£14. **Credit** MC, V.

This popular 17th-century Cotswold stone pub at the lower end of Malmesbury's short High Street offers an above-average selection of snacks (ciabattas, burgers, sausages and mash, and so on) as well as more ambitious dishes. The good range of beers includes several real ales (Archers Best, Brains' the Rev James and two guest ales) and, if you're visiting in May, check if you're in time for the annual sausage and ale festival – the ideal marriage of meat and mead. A beer garden at the back offers lovely views over the picturesque town. The Smoking Dog proudly displays a Wing Wheel – the rare metal plaques were, apparently, the 17th-century equivalent of a Michelin (or *Time Out*) guide window sticker.

Trouble House

Cirencester Road, Tetbury, Gloucestershire GL8 8SG (01666 502206/www.troublehouse. co.uk). **Lunch served** noon-2pm Tue-Sat; noon-2pm Sun. **Dinner served** 7-9.30pm Tue-Sat. **Main courses** £15.95-£18.00. **Credit** AmEx, DC, MC, V.

Michael and Sarah Bedford's rustic gastropub has held a Michelin star since 2004, and deservedly so – yet the place remains a down-to-earth establishment. Inside the heavily wood-panelled space, the emphasis is on the quality of ingredients, with produce coming from local suppliers where possible. Grilled sardines with sweet pepper piperade, and baked st marcelin cheese with roast tomatoes and mixed leaves are typical starters, while mains continue the Modern British bent with dishes such as rabbit and tarragon pie, roast Cornish cod with smoked haddock chowder, and roast guinea fowl with wild mushroom and truffle risotto. Desserts are similarly tempting, and there's an excellent selection of cheese, as well as a good wine list and Wadworth ales. There are many old-wives' tales concerning the 18th-century building's curious name, although the owners concede that the most likely origin is its location, near a plot of land known as the Troubles – so-called because it was regularly flooded. Between 1959 and 1964 the place was served by a railway line – the Trouble House Halt – built specifically to serve the pub.

Vine Tree

Foxley Road, Norton, nr Malmesbury, Wiltshire SN16 0JP (01666 837654). **Lunch served** noon-2pm Mon-Fri; noon-2.30pm Sat, Sun. **Dinner served** 7-9.30pm Mon-Fri; 7-9.45pm Sat. **Main courses** £11-£16.95. **Credit** AmEx, MC, V.

An excellent option for lunch, as long as you're prepared to get here early – the small 18th-century mill house draws a broad age range of locals and thus fills up quickly at weekends, despite its remote location. All come for the high-standard, freshly prepared pub grub, and the welcoming, relaxed atmosphere. There's normally a choice of roasts for Sunday lunch (on our visit, sirloin of local beef with Yorkshire pudding, loin of Gloucestershire Old Spot with apple sauce and crackling, or free-range chicken breast) – at £10.95 including all the trimmings. There are plenty of other options on offer, from the likes of seafood paella to roast butternut squash filled with ratatouille, plus smaller dishes such as hefty ciabatta sandwiches or a selection of charcuterie. Draught Butcombe or Tinners Cornish bitter make a good accompaniment. Puddings – sticky toffee pudding, pear and almond frangipane tart, and locally made ice-cream – are a real treat here.

Whatley Manor Hotel

South-west Cotswolds

Picture-perfect villages with countryside to match.

This beguiling slice of Gloucestershire, the last hurrah of the Cotswolds before the hills sweep down to the Severn Valley to the west and Wiltshire to the south, is, in the main, refreshingly tourist-free. Perhaps that's why so many celebs have chosen to make it their home (there are rumoured to be more stars per square metre in the Cirencester branch of Waitrose than in the one in Notting Hill).

The relative scarcity of visitors doesn't mean, however, that there's nothing to do. On the contrary, this is England at its stereotypical best: voluptuous, hedgerow-streaked countryside, inviting hearty country walks and a proliferation of excellent pubs (mainly of the 'gastro' variety). The only downside is that you'll probably need to dig deep into your pocket when it comes to accommodation and eating out. But it is worth it – there are a couple of standout hotels in the area.

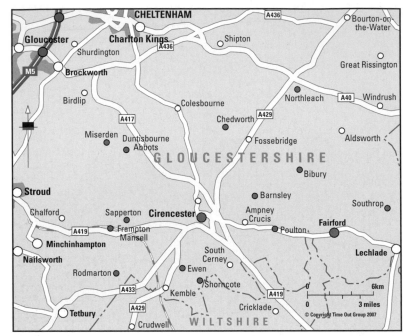

For a glimpse, though, of chocolate-box, tourist-rich Cotswolds, the gorgeous village of Bibury, ten miles north-east of Cirencester, is worth a visit (particularly if you're here out of season, when you may have the place more or less to yourself). William Morris's claim that this is 'the most beautiful village in England' crops up so frequently in literature about the place that you start to wonder whether its inclusion is some kind of legal requirement. That said, you can see what Morris was on about. Across the bridge from the Swan Hotel (*see p199*) are the two paying attractions of the village – Bibury Trout Farm (01285 740215, www.biburytrout farm.co.uk), where kids can have fun making the water boil with fish at feeding time; and Arlington Mill (01285 740368, www.bibury.com/arlington-mill), a museum, tearoom and shop. Near here you'll find

Arlington Row, a perfect example of typical Cotswold cottages, now owned by the National Trust. When Henry Ford visited in the 1920s he liked them so much he tried to take them back to America with him, but was stopped. The walk from here along the river to Coln St Aldwyns is particularly recommended.

Bibury may get all the visitors, but there are perfect honey-hued Cotswold villages to be discovered all over this area – take any minor road and you'll stumble across a clutch of them in a matter of minutes.

Anyone with an interest in Roman history should take in both Cirencester (Roman Corinium) and the Roman villa at Chedworth, to the north. Corinium was one of Roman Britain's most important settlements, and its heritage is brought to life in the town's enjoyable Corinium Museum (01285 655611, www.ciren cester.co.uk/coriniummuseum); the remains of Corinium's amphitheatre can still be seen on the western edge of the modern town. Near to Chedworth are

TOURIST INFORMATION

Cirencester
Cirencester Tourist Office, Cornhall Market Place, Cirencester, Gloucs GL7 2NW (01285 654180).
Cotswolds
Cotswold Tourism Office, Cotswold District Council, Trinity Road, Cirencester, Gloucestershire GL7 1PX (01285 623006).
www.cirencester.gov.uk/tourism
www.cotswolds.com

Accommodation	★★★★★
Food & drink	★★★★☆
Nightlife	★★★★★
Shopping	★★★☆☆
Culture	★★★★★
Sights	★★★★★
Scenery	★★★★☆

the excavated remains of one of the largest Roman villas to be found in Britain (01242 890256, www.nationaltrust. org.uk). The site, which was originally excavated in 1864, includes more than a mile of walls, mosaics, two bathhouses and hypocausts (the Romans' version of central heating).

Garden-lovers are well served in this part of the country. In addition to the charming Cerney House Gardens (Cerney House, North Cerney, 01285 831205, www.cerney gardens.com), there is the impressive Misarden Park Gardens at Miserden, between Cirencester and Cheltenham (01285 821303, www.gardens-guide.com, closed Oct-Mar), where the 17th-century, 12-acre gardens overlook the Golden Valley. The site contains a walled garden, an arboretum, a yew walk and topiary, including some designed by Edward Lutyens.

Spreading out around Shorncote, more than 140 lakes over an area of 40 square miles make up the Cotswold Water Park (Keynes Country Park, Spratsgate Lane, Shorncote, 01285 861459, www.water park.org). On the main sports lakes visitors can indulge in sailing, canoeing, waterskiing, windsurfing and jetskiing, and hire watercraft or stick to land-based activities such as cycling and horse riding. Elsewhere nature has the upper hand, with two country parks (one with a children's beach) offering fine walking (including guided wildlife walks) and birdwatching.

A programme of children's activities is run in the school holidays. To quote David Bellamy: 'It's a blooming marvellous place!'

Cirencester has some reasonable shops and frequent markets, but if you crave a more metropolitan buzz and the chance to splash some serious cash, head to elegant Cheltenham, which offers by far the best shopping in the area. There are a couple of decent museums too.

WHERE TO STAY

For the area's two best hotels, Barnsley House and Cowley Manor, *see p202*. If you're on a budget, then the owners of the former also run the Village Pub in Barnsley (*see p205*), which has six pleasing rooms above it (01285 740421, www.thevillage pub.co.uk). Another excellent gastropub, the Wild Duck in Ewen (*see p205*) also offers good rooms. Of the area's B&Bs, a good bet is the Old Rectory in Rodmarton (01285 841246, www.rodmarton.com, from £60 double), parts of which date from the 16th century.

In Bibury, the Bibury Court Hotel (01285 740337, www.biburycourt.com, £150-£195 double) has a decent restaurant and is set in six acres of lovely gardens.

No.12

12 Park Street, Cirencester, Gloucestershire GL7 2BW (01285 640232/www.no12 cirencester.co.uk). **Rates** £80 double. **Credit** AmEx, MC, V.

Boutique hotels might be relatively commonplace these days, but boutique B&Bs are far more unusual. However, the best place to stay in Cirencester is just such an establishment – within a Grade II-listed Georgian townhouse in the centre of town you'll find four large, immaculately groomed bedrooms with extra long beds (maybe a French bateau lit or antique leather sleigh bed), feather pillows and sleek, contemporary bathrooms (equipped with Molton Brown toiletries and bathrobes). Friendly service and a good breakfast included in the price are further attractions.

Swan Hotel

Bibury, Gloucestershire GL7 5NW (01285 740695/www.cotswold-inns-hotels.co.uk). **Rates** £145-£265 double. **Credit** AmEx, DC, MC, V.

The Swan is superbly located alongside the River Coln and right next to Bibury's beautiful old bridge. The building dates from the 16th century – the coal shed was used to hold local prisoners before they were transported to larger jails in the area. Its 20 bedrooms are floral-heavy but perfectly comfortable and all have great bathrooms – five with jacuzzis. The hotel bottles its own spring water, which you'll also find in the starched-to-the-hilt restaurant, and has a spa offering a full range of treatments (best booked in advance).

Cerney House Gardens

WHERE TO EAT & DRINK

There can't be a greater concentration of gastropubs anywhere else in the country than in this little corner of Gloucestershire. There's certainly no lack of high-quality cooking and prices reflect this. Though it's fine to have just a drink in these places, it does mean that it's getting increasingly difficult to find a pub that does simple, cheapish bar grub in these parts.

If you want to cook your own food, there are plenty of farm shops in the area. One of the best is the Butts Farm Shop (which featured on Rick Stein's *Food Heroes* TV show), near South Cerney, just south of Cirencester (01285 862224, www.thebutts farmshop.com). Cirencester's Abbey Home Farm (01283 640441, www.theorganic farmshop.co.uk) stocks organic meats and eggs, as well as fruit and veg.

Messin' about in boats, at Cotswold Water Park.

Allium

1 London Street, Market Place, Fairford, Gloucestershire GL7 4AH (01285 712200/ www.allium.uk.net). **Lunch served** noon-2pm Wed-Sat; noon-3pm Sun. **Dinner served** 7-10pm Wed-Sat. **Set lunch** £16 2 courses, £19.50 3 courses. **Set dinner** £28.50 2 courses, £32.50 3 courses; £45 10-course tasting menu. **Credit** MC, V.

Modern restaurants (that aren't in pubs) are rare indeed in this part of the world – Allium is one of this uncommon breed. Its stark white interior, proactive service and discreet local art mark it out as an ambitious operation, and the food largely lives up to its billing. The lunch menu changes daily, the evening selection seasonally, and both make full use of the wealth of excellent local suppliers to produce dishes such as cerney goat's cheese 'button' with gem lettuce, fresh peas, lemon and Kelmscott Park bacon, followed by steamed turbot with fresh borlotti beans, marjoram, chicory and orange, and cherry clafoutis with marzipan ice-cream and caramelised almonds.

Barnsley House

Barnsley, nr Cirencester, Gloucestershire GL7 5EE (01285 740000/www.barnsley house.com). **Lunch served** noon-2.30pm, **dinner served** 7-9.30pm daily. **Set lunch** £19.50 2 courses, £25.50 3 courses. **Set dinner** £39.50 3 courses, £46 4 courses. **Credit** AmEx, MC, V.

Barnsley House (*see p202*) is a wonderfully stylish and intimate hotel, with chefs that make good use of its extensive kitchen gardens. Breakfast means warm pastries and muffins, endless quantities of super-fresh orange juice and coffee, and a top-notch fry-up. The restaurant is smallish, light and classically plain and the daily changing menu reads temptingly, with four or five choices at each course. Dishes are of the bistro ilk and include the likes of grilled herring with warm potato salad, own-made bresaola with feta, walnuts and herbs, lamb with pea and celery risotto, and tenderloin of pork with runner beans, roasted cherry tomato and sage gravy. You can certainly eat well here, though some of the dishes are not as well executed as they could be (watery risotto, overly salty feta). A little more attention to detail is needed for the restaurant to match the hotel's quality and verve.

Bell at Sapperton

Sapperton, Gloucestershire GL7 6LE (01285 760298/www.foodatthebell.co.uk). **Lunch served** noon-2pm daily. **Dinner served** 7-9.30pm Mon-Sat; 7-9pm Sun. Closed Mon during winter (except bank hols). **Main courses** £9.50-£16. **Credit** MC, V.

For some years now, the Bell has enjoyed a deserved reputation for its food. Outside, the pub is a typical Cotswold stone hostelry; inside, pine furniture and contemporary prints decorate a series of interlinking rooms, and tables are well spaced. The menu makes good use of local ingredients, and might include hearty fare like shank of Cotswold lamb with a garden mint and pea risotto, and pan-fried calf's liver with smoked bacon and onion gravy.

The lunchtime ploughman's is a particular treat, featuring four fine local cheeses (cerney ash pyramid, cotswold blue brie, smarts double gloucester and hills farm camembert).

South-west Cotswolds

COWLEY MANOR AND BARNSLEY HOUSE

Within the last five years two outstanding hotels have opened in this corner of Gloucestershire, blasting out the chintz and bringing in metropolitan chic in terms of design, comfort, service and food. While both Cowley Manor and Barnsley House are clearly part of the same movement that has revolutionised the hotel trade in Britain, they offer somewhat different experiences for the visitor and display interesting contrasts.

Jessica Sainsbury and her husband Peter Frankopan opened Cowley Manor in 2002, having transformed the place (latterly used as a residential home) with the help of a dedicated roster of designers and architects. The tone is stylish but unfussy – the staff uniform is a variation on jeans and T-shirts – but absolutely professional.

The neo-classical 19th-century manor house is stately on a manageable scale, and affords fine views over the attractively landscaped grounds, focused on a picture-perfect lake. The 30 rooms are individual in size and layout but all are decorated with strong, appealing splashes of colour and striking pieces of furniture. Each also offers the same state-of-the-art facilities, such as Loewe TVs with DVD players and quality music systems. Bathrooms are tranquil havens in neutral shades, with deep baths and huge showers, lashings of luscious lotions and potions, plenty of white towels and robes, and underfloor heating.

The public rooms are grand but groovy (the papier-mâché animal heads in the spacious bar can't fail to raise a smile). The billiard room is an intimate, chocolate leather-panelled refuge, while the carved floor to ceiling wood panelling in the dining room and 12 dramatic dangling light fittings infuse the dining room with glamour. The food here is classy bistro fare (though sadly not at bistro prices), and the wine list is a tempting and well-chosen one, with some interesting bottles on offer (particularly from the USA).

The modernist c.side spa offers a range of desirable indulgences in its treatment rooms, plus a gym, sauna, steam room and two pools (indoor and outdoor).

Tim Haigh and Rupert Pendered opened Barnsley House a year after Cowley Manor. The house was built in 1697 by Brereton Bouchier, squire of Barnsley, and ultimately came into possession of the Verey family. In the 1950s, celebrated gardener Rosemary Verey began redesigning the garden, transforming it into its present layout – an object example of a classic small-scale English country-house garden (complete with kitchen garden).

The ten bedrooms (eight more are due to have been added by the time this guide is published) are the height of contemporary luxury, decorated in subtle tones and equipped with Bose sound systems, plasma-screen and LCD TVs (including one in the bathroom), huge beds with Egyptian cotton sheets, and artworks individually chosen for each room. Although the mini-bars contain only water, fresh orange juice and champagne, a welcome touch is that these are complimentary. The fabulous spare-no-expense bathrooms have free-standing baths and are stocked with desirable smellies.

The owners have, thankfully, chosen to keep many of the house's original features in place; exposed beams and original staircases remind the visitor that this is a 17th-century building at heart. This mix of old and new continues throughout the hotel – so much so that the modern public spaces can come as a shock: this is especially true of the tiny bar on the ground floor. With its black and red decor (including red leather seats), it's no exaggeration to say that it wouldn't look out of place in a swanky New York hotel. Other public areas include a modern reading room and a clean-lined dining room where decent poshed-up bistro dishes are served.

As we went to press, a spa and pool were due to open, bringing Barnsley House's facilities more into line with those offered at Cowley Manor.

So, if you want to blow a wad of cash on a few days of luxury, should you choose Barnsley or Cowley? It all comes down to the atmosphere you want. Both hotels offer very similar standards of luxury, design, service and facilities (Cowley is definitely more appropriate if you have kids). Most of the differences between the two are down to the buildings they occupy – Barnsley House is a lot older and smaller in scale than Cowley. If you want buzz and big spaces, go for Cowley Manor; if you favour intimacy and privacy, then Barnsley House is probably the place for you.

BARNSLEY HOUSE

Barnsley, Gloucestershire GL7 5EE (01285 740000/www.barnsleyhouse.com). **Rates** £275-£475. **Credit** MC, V.

COWLEY MANOR

Cowley, nr Cheltenham, Gloucestershire GL53 9NL (01242 870900/www.cowleymanor.com). **Rates** £245-£470. **Credit** AmEx, DC, MC, V.

Cowley Manor

The luxury is piled as high as the pillows at No.12.

Cowley Manor

Cowley, Gloucestershire GL53 9NL (01242 870900/www.cowleymanor.com). **Lunch served** noon-2.30pm daily. **Dinner served** 7-10.30pm daily. **Main courses** £16.50-£19. **Credit** AmEx, DC, MC, V.

Ultra-cool Cowley Manor (*see p202*) offers an enticing combination of modern design and facilities within an imposing Victorian neo-classical mansion. Its lofty-ceilinged dining room, clad in elaborately carved wood panelling, is an elegant and glamorous space, but far from overbearing – service is attentive but thoroughly relaxed. The dinner menu offers an eclectic selection of bistro dishes, which are cooked with aplomb (though heftily priced). Starters include Scottish scallops, seared and served on cauliflower purée with zippy pepper pesto and Cornish crab with crème fraîche, peppers, lemon and shallot oil. Mains are also good: a classic fillet steak and chips with béarnaise, say, or breast of Gressingham duck with glass noodles, pak choi, carrots, leeks and plum sauce. The fresh-tasting desserts, such as elderflower and champagne jelly with summer berries, are worth saving room for.

Falcon Inn

London Road, Poulton, Gloucestershire GL7 5HN (01285 850844/www.thefalconpoulton.co.uk). **Open** Tue-Sun; no dinner on Sun. **Lunch served** noon-2pm, **dinner served** 7-9pm daily. **Main courses** £8-£16. **Set lunch** (Sun) £15 2 courses, £20 3 courses. **Credit** MC, V.

Simple wooden furniture and aubergine and sage tones give the Falcon a distinctive, contemporary feel. The pub-restaurant's (there's a comfortable bar area too) lunch menu changes daily and its dinner menu monthly, with most ingredients sourced from local suppliers. Specials might be spiced corn soup with chillies and crème fraîche,

own-made burger and chips, or escalope of free-range chicken with saffron rice and pizzaiola sauce. In terms of drinks, wines are fairly priced (house bottles start at £11.50) and there are usually two cask ales available (one of which is Hook Norton Best).

Jesse's Bistro

The Stableyard, Blackjack Street, Cirencester, Gloucestershire GL7 2AA (01285 641497/www.jessesbistro.co.uk). **Lunch served** noon-2.30pm daily. **Dinner served** 7-9.30pm Wed-Sat. **Main courses** £9.50-£18.50. **Credit** MC, V.

Cirencester has a decent range of ethnic eateries but the best spot to dine is unassuming Jesse's Bistro, tucked down an alleyway off Blackjack Street in the centre of town. The focus within the atmospheric stone-floored restaurant is the wood-fired oven, where most of the cooking is done. Try, perhaps, the hearty lamb shank with sherry and lentil stew and redcurrant sauce, or a simple sirloin steak with garlic and herb butter. Prices may be more restaurant than bistro, but the quality is similarly high. All the excellent meat is supplied by neighbouring Jesse Smith Butcher's, and Jesse's empire also includes a cheese shop and fish slab (you'll find five or so fish dishes on the menu – and there's always a good veggie option too). The wine list is tempting as well, with more than 20 available by the glass.

Seven Tuns

Queen's Street, Chedworth, Gloucestershire GL54 4AE (01285 720242). **Lunch served** noon-2.30pm Mon-Fri; noon-3pm Sun. **Dinner served** 6.30-9.30pm Mon-Sat; 6.30-9pm Sun. **Main courses** £7-£15. Set menus available on request. **Credit** MC, V.

You're spoilt for choice at this large, friendly 17th-century pub in the lovely (though confusingly laid out) village of Chedworth. The small bar area, with log fire, wooden booths and tables, has an interesting bar menu (filled baguettes, baked potatoes, ploughman's, house salad of warm chicken, bacon and avocado). Out back is a modern restaurant (where you can sample the likes of tomato, basil and brie brochette, and seafood chowder), and there's another, more up-to-date bar too. In summer, the revolving South African barbecue in the garden comes into its own. You'll always find some good cask ales on tap.

Swan

Southrop, Gloucestershire GL7 3NU (01367 850205/www.theswanatsouthrop.co.uk). **Lunch served** noon-2.30pm Mon-Sat; noon-3pm Sun. **Dinner served** 7-9.30pm Mon-Sat; 7-9pm Sun. **Main courses** £9.50-£18. **Set meal** £12.50 2 courses; £16.50 3 courses. **Credit** MC, V.

Yet another classy village pub-restaurant, the Swan is a characterful, low-ceilinged, modern art-specked hostelry offering first-rate pan-European fare at London restaurant prices. Main courses from the evening menu might be fillet of pork wrapped in prosciutto with mashed potato, button onions, currants, capers and parsley, or squid ink risotto with grilled squid and gremolata. Best value is the prix fixe lunch menu, which offers the likes of butternut squash and oregano soup, grilled lambs' kidneys with deep-fried polenta, red onion gravy and parsley, and pistachio parfait.

Village Pub

High Street, Barnsley, Gloucestershire GL7 5EF (01285 740421/www.thevillagepub.co.uk). **Lunch served** noon-2.30pm Mon-Fri; noon-3pm Sat, Sun. **Dinner served** 7-9.30pm Mon-Thur, Sun; 7-10pm Fri, Sat. **Main courses** £9.50-£15.50. **Rates** £90-£125 double. **Credit** MC, V.

From pre-dinner beers to postprandial chocolates and coffee, the Village Pub really delivers. Diners have a choice of five rooms, each decorated in a different style; subtle paint effects, wood panelling and flagstones are a common theme. The menu – now presided over by Piero Boi (previously head chef at Sartoria in London) – makes a virtue of simplicity in flavour and presentation, but there's still plenty of scope for imagination: witness, for instance, the earthy flavours of john dory with braised octopus, chickpeas, tomato and oregano, and lambs' sweetbreads with broad beans and wild mushroom risotto cake. And when in Gloucestershire… you have to try the twice-baked double gloucester soufflé.

Wild Duck Inn

Drakes Island, Ewen, Gloucestershire GL7 6BY (01285 770310/www.thewildduckinn.co.uk). **Lunch served** noon-2pm, **dinner served** 6.45-10pm Mon-Fri. **Meals served** noon-10pm Sat; noon-9.30pm Sun. **Main courses** £8-£20. **Rates** £110-£165 double; £165 suite. **Credit** AmEx, MC, V.

Dark red walls, low beams and irreverently encased and beheaded wildlife upon the walls give the busy 16th-century Wild Duck a groovy charm. Diners spill through a series of interconnecting rooms with ample nooks and crannies, and there's a lovely tree-shaded garden (complete with giant chess set) out back. Prices aren't low, but neither is the quality of the likes of chargrilled ribeye steak with tiger prawns, roast garlic butter, chips and salad, or pan-fried sea bass fillet with dauphinoise potatoes, asparagus and hollandaise sauce.

Bibury

STROUD AND THE FIVE VALLEYS

The south-west tip of the Cotswolds is one of the most interesting, beguilingly beautiful yet least touristy areas in the region. Five wonderfully intimate wooded valleys meet at the town of Stroud, which has been a centre of industrial, artistic and spiritual activity for centuries.

Despite its stunning setting, Stroud is as far from an anodyne Cotswold town as you can imagine. It's a gritty working town and quite downmarket in parts, yet it is also a centre for green politics and alternative thinking (in the past non-denominational religions of every hue flourished here), and has long attracted artists and craftspeople. Since 2002 Stroud has proudly trumpeted its status as a 'Fairtrade town', with many of its shops and businesses using and selling fairly traded goods. Organic food can also be found in abundance, and the weekly Saturday Farmers' Market (01453 758060, www.madein stroud.co.uk) showcases 50 or so stalls offering a fabulous range of foodstuffs – including Old Spot pork (from pigs fed on apples) and double gloucester cheese – all produced within 30 miles of the town. It's worth timing your visit to take in the annual Stroud Fringe music and arts festival (www.stroudfringe. co.uk), which features more than 150 acts.

The area around Stroud is heavily populated, yet the narrow wooded valleys easily absorb the villages, giving a feeling of man in harmony with, rather than battling against, nature. Despite the bucolic setting, the valleys around the town have long been associated with industry; the roots of the cloth industry in the area are traceable back to the 14th century. From the early 17th century until the first half of the 20th century, textile production boomed around Stroud (the British army's famous redcoats were made here – and,

Rococo Garden

Woodchester Mansion

rumour has it, the bluecoats of the French too), and it is the mill buildings that still litter the area, and the canals built to serve them, that provide much of the unique man-made character of the five valleys.

One of these valleys, the Slad Valley, was home to the young Laurie Lee, and his portrayal of his childhood here, *Cider With Rosie*, provides a marvellously evocative yet unromantic testament of what life was like in the area in the early 20th century. Lee is buried in the churchyard of Slad Church.

Here's a couple of gems for trivia fans: Edwin Budding, a Stroudie, invented the lawnmower in 1830 after seeing the way that cloth was shaved in the area's mills – his original model can be seen in the Stroud Museum in the Park (01453 763394, www.stroud.gov.uk/museum); and the last ever fatal duel to be fought in Britain took place in Stroud in 1807 – the grave of the unfortunate loser (his opponent turned and shot him before the count had been completed), Lieutenant Delmont, can be found in the churchyard of St Laurence.

Of the paying attractions in the immediate area, the best is the stunning, unfinished Victorian Gothic Woodchester Mansion (01453 861541, www.wood chestermansion.org.uk), south of Stroud, and, to the north of the town, the unique Rococo Garden in the gorgeous village of Painswick (01452 813204, www.rococogarden.co.uk).

Woodstock to Burford

West Oxfordshire's loveliest market towns.

The triangle of countryside between Oxford, Chipping Norton and Cirencester is one of the prettiest, most photogenic parts of England. This hasn't always been the case, but the Cotswolds are now universally regarded as being 'terribly nice' – not to mention a bit posh. The two main tourist centres, Burford and Woodstock, are attractive representations of a certain kind of English rural idyll; outside the market towns, tiny, honey-coloured, thatched villages cluster round crumbling churches and imposing stately piles. Throughout the area, upmarket shops sell expensive bric-a-brac to well-heeled weekend breakers, and an air of quiet contentment prevails.

Wealth first came to the area with the Romans, who introduced a long-woolled breed of sheep, the Cotswold Lion, to these parts. Cotswold wool soon gained an international reputation, and the money it brought in paid for the churches and grand houses that still dominate the area. In the Middle Ages, grazing herds took precedence over human residents, occupying great tracts of land; in some cases, people were even evacuated from villages to give the sheep more room.

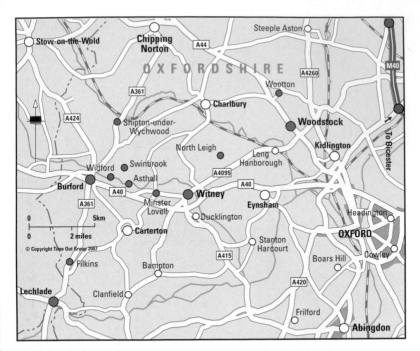

These days the Cotswolds' main money-spinner is tourism, which has resulted in some steep prices and a slew of themed attractions. Yet the real draw – the rich countryside, dotted with ruins and historical houses – is free. Quiet roads and leafy footpaths run between most of the small villages and are perfect for leisurely rambles, with pretty country pubs en route to ease the effort. Pick up a Burford Trail leaflet from the Tourist Office (see p210) for some ideas. The Thames Path (www.thames-path.co.uk) also passes this way; the river becomes navigable at Lechlade, with plenty of tour boats around to prove it.

TOURIST INFORMATION

Burford
The Brewery, Sheep Street, Burford, Oxfordshire OX18 4LP (01993 823558).
Witney
26 Market Square, Witney, Oxfordshire OX28 6BB (01993 775802).
Woodstock
The Oxfordshire Museum, Park Street, Woodstock, Oxfordshire OX20 4SN (01993 813276).
www.oxfordshirecotswolds.org
www.wakeuptowoodstock.com

The historic market town of Woodstock lies eight miles north of Oxford, perfectly placed for those wishing to visit the twin monuments to extravagance, Blenheim Palace (0870 060 2080, www.blenheim palace.com) and Bicester Village. The former is the country seat of the Duke of Marlborough and birthplace of Sir Winston Churchill; the luxury and splendour of Sir John Vanbrugh's design is breathtaking, and its sheer size will stop first-time visitors in their tracks. The same could be said of Bicester Village (50 Pingle Drive, 01869 323200, www.bicester-village.co. uk), a massive outdoor shopping mall that sells name brands at large discounts. The crowds at both are daunting; visit early.

Woodstock itself is best known for two trades – glove-making and decorative steel work. You can find out more about the area's heritage at the wide-ranging Oxfordshire Museum (Park Street, 01993 811456, www.oxfordshire.gov.uk), but you won't see many signs of artisan life in the streets, which are filled with cars bringing custom to the classy pubs and restaurants. Among the visitors are Oxonians (often embarrassed student-parent pairings) on evenings out of town; like all of the places featured in this chapter, Woodstock makes an excellent base for those who don't want to stay in Oxford itself.

Garden lovers should take a detour north to Rousham House (01869 347110, www.

rousham.org), near Steeple Aston. The imposing – if rather gloomy – Jacobean mansion was remodelled in Tudor Gothic style by William Kent, a predecessor of 'Capability' Brown, in the 18th century. But the real highlight here is his outstanding garden, inspired by Italian landscape painting. Rousham is determinedly and delightfully uncommercialised, with no shop or tearoom; you're encouraged to bring a picnic and wander the grounds.

From Woodstock to Burford

As you head west from Woodstock to Burford, stop for a stroll around the village of Minster Lovell. Quiet and remarkably unspoiled, it boasts a gorgeous 15th-century church and the romantic ruins of Minster Lovell Hall. Dating from the 1440s, the hall and its restored medieval dovecote make an imposing sight on the banks of the River Windrush, and the thatched cottages are some of the prettiest around. It's worth taking further detours to visit Swinbrook, where Nancy Mitford is buried, picturesque Asthall and the Roman ruins at North Leigh, which include some wonderful mosaics now kept under shelter.

Also between Woodstock and Burford is Witney. Despite being one of the largest towns in the Cotswolds, it offers fewer tourist attractions than its neighbours. Famous for manufacturing blankets, its sights include the first medieval marketplace in England, attractive almshouses and the magnificent St Mary's church. For more local history, drop by the charming Cogges Manor Farm Museum (Church Lane, 01993 772602, www.west oxon.gov.uk), which aims to recreate rural Victorian Oxfordshire with costumed guides and a 20-acre working farm, complete with traditional breeds of livestock. In the activities room, children can try on Victorian clothes and play with replica toys.

The elegant, historic coaching town of Burford is the jewel of the Cotswolds, and makes a delightful, if pricey, base from which to explore the surrounding countryside (leaflets suggesting local walks can be found at the tourist office). The broad High Street comprises a welter of pretty buildings clinging to the slope leading down to the River Windrush. Smart shopping opportunities abound; it's smattered with middle-England gift and antiques shops, as well as England's oldest pharmacy, an excellent delicatessen and a few beauty salons for those vital post-walk pedicures. For much of the year, the town is chock-full of traffic; visit in early spring or winter to get the best out of it.

Among the attractions is Burford Garden Company (Shilton Road, 01993 823117, www.burford.co.uk), a mammoth garden

centre that is a huge draw all year round. Cotswold Wildlife Park (01993 823006, www.cotswoldwildlifepark.co.uk) has stunning gardens, set out around a listed Victorian manor house. Spacious paddocks house big cats, zebras, red pandas and monkeys, with separate buildings for reptiles, bats and insects. A 'wolf wood', home to four beautiful but bored-looking Canadian timber wolves, opened in 2006; the penguin pool, mini railway and adventure playground are always a hit with youngsters. There's a decent café, but outdoor facilities are good so bring a picnic and enjoy the extensive grounds.

Burford also has one or two less commercial claims to fame. Nell Gwynn visited a number of times, and the fruit of her liaisons with Charles II, Charles Beauclerk, was made Earl of Burford. In May 1649, at the end of the Civil War, Cromwell and his men imprisoned 340 Levellers in Burford's Norman church; carvings made by the incarcerated soldiers and bullet holes from the ringleaders' executions can still be seen. Insights into Burford's history can be found in the Tolsey Museum (126 High Street, 01993 823196). If you want to explore the area on two wheels, hire bicycles at Burford Bike Hire (Woollands, Barns Lane, 01993 823326).

Around Burford

To the north of Burford, there are paintings and fragments of Roman mosaics in the tiny church at Widford. The petite village of Shipton-under-Wychwood also boasts a pretty church, with some Pre-Raphaelite archangels and a stained-glass window designed by the William Morris Company.

To see how the Cotswolds earned their crust before the tourist invasion, visit Cotswold Woollen Weavers (01367 860491, www.naturalbest.co.uk) in Filkins. At this working mill and museum, you can watch fleece being woven into fabric, then purchase a wide range of clothes, rugs and cushions from its shop.

Near Lechlade, and about eight miles south of Burford, is Kelmscott Manor (01367 252486, www.kelmscottmanor. co.uk, closed Oct-Mar), the country home of William Morris, writer, socialist and innovator in the Arts and Crafts movement. Co-leasing the Tudor farmhouse with Pre-Raphaelite painter Dante Gabriel Rossetti, Morris lived here from the summer of 1871

MORRIS MAJORS

'Have nothing in your house that you do not know to be useful or believe to be beautiful.' The tenets of the Arts and Crafts movement were that artisans should be regarded as artists, that furniture and decorative art should be hand-crafted rather than industrially manufactured, and that it should be affordable. What would William Morris (*see p211*) make of his designs – and those of his peers, Burne-Jones and Rossetti – being reproduced on a myriad of gift items in 'heritage' shops?

For the most part, however, his philosophy holds true in the Cotswolds. No flat-pack catalogues here; this is *Horse & Hound* country. There are rows of impossibly lovely cottages, with curtains proudly drawn open to reveal traditional, tasteful interiors. Most modern residences just can't pull off the classic country-home look, but a traditional decorative flourish or two can often transform sometimes-bland contemporary interiors; even with space and wallet restrictions, you can bypass Cath Kidston for a real piece of country chic, picked up from one of the many dealers that abound in these parts. Visit www.cotswolds-antiques-art.com for local information on traders and exhibitions.

Burford's High Street is a particularly rich treasure trove of antiques shops. Here you'll find English and continental furniture (plus porcelain and more) at Jonathan Fyson (Nos.50-52, 01993 823204) and David Pickup (No.115, 01993 822555). Antiques at the George (No.104, 01993 823319) offers two floors of glass-cased goodies for browsing, and don't miss Bygones (No.29, 01993 823588), a tiny, lovely shop where shabby-chic retro kitchenware is arrayed alongside more antiquarian pieces. Woodstock's Market Place offers similarly rich pickings: Antiques of Woodstock (No.18, 01993 811818) specialises in oak furniture, John Howard (No.6, 01993 811332) in 18th- and 19th-century British pottery. Woodstock Arts & Antiques (No.14, 01993 810077) has interesting porcelain, glass, clocks and paintings. On Market Street, the focus at Lapina (No.17, 01993 813618) is on 'gems from the east', such as lacquerware and oriental furnishings. More museum than shop, and packed full of colourful and curious items, Maybury (16B Angel Yard, off Market Street, 01993 813902) stocks responsibly sourced goods from the Far East: religious figures, handmade screens, exquisite tiles made from shells (by-products of the food and pearl industry), plus antique ceremonial garments and jewellery.

For really ambitious home makeovers, it's worth visiting the Cotswold Reclamation Company in nearby Little Rissington (01451 820292, www.cotswoldreclamation. com) to check out its huge range of reclaimed building materials, from Victorian floorboards and fireplaces to cast-iron radiators and garden statuary.

until his death in 1896; he lies buried in Kelmscott Village churchyard. Built in 1570, the house is large but not ostentatious, and is now primarily a showcase for the work of Morris – tapestries, fabrics and wallpapers, plus examples of his printing, painting and writing – and his wife Janey, who helped to revive traditional embroidery techniques.

WHERE TO STAY

Accommodation is also offered at the Angel at Burford, the King's Head and the Lamb in Shipton-under-Wychwood (*see p214* Where to Eat & Drink). In Southrop, there's the charming Old Post Office (01367 850231, www.theoldepostoffice. org), a 14th-century cottage, and in the pretty conservation area of Shipton-under-Wychwood, Court Farm (01993 831515, www.courtfarmbb.com) is a traditional farmhouse B&B.

Bay Tree Hotel

Sheep Street, Burford, Oxfordshire OX18 4LW (01993 822791/www.cotswold-inns-hotels. co.uk). **Rates** £165-£175 double; £240-£250 suite. **Credit** AmEx, DC, MC, V.
Sprawling over three ancient buildings, which between them offer 14 rooms and seven suites of differing character, the accommodation here boasts heritage colour schemes, tasteful antiques and first-rate facilities. Some rooms face the charming garden, while others overlook picturesque Sheep Street. Period features such as leaded windows, flagstone floors and cosy fireplaces combine harmoniously with flat-screen TVs and top-notch bathrooms, so character isn't sacrificed to modern comforts. A pleasantly laid-back bar and excellent restaurant (*see p214*) are further draws. Ambience aside, what impresses most here is the exemplary service; nothing is too much trouble for the lovely, welcoming staff.

Bear

Park Street, Woodstock, Oxfordshire OX20 ISZ (0870 400 8202/www.bearhotelwoodstock. co.uk). **Rates** £184-£230 double; £284-£350 suite. **Credit** AmEx, DC, MC, V.
Owned by the Macdonald Hotels chain, Woodstock's largest hotel comprises an impressive 13th-century coaching inn and an adjoining glove factory, converted into guest rooms and conference facilities in the 1960s. Happily, the corporate aspects don't really detract from the main building's grandeur and appeal – there are still plenty of winding corridors, creaky wooden floors, oak beams and fireplaces for atmosphere, and a snug little bar for quiet drinks. Richard Burton and Elizabeth Taylor once famously holed up here and, rather spookily, the ghosts of a young girl and her baby son are said to haunt two of the rooms in the main building (we're not revealing which).

Burford House Hotel

99 High Street, Burford, Oxfordshire OX18 4QA (01993 823151/www.burfordhouse.co.uk). **Rates** £125-£155 double; £235 2-bed suite. **Credit** AmEx, MC, V.
At this informal and intimate townhouse hotel, staff strike a perfect balance between providing top-quality service and making guests feel at home. Eight well-sized and beautifully decorated bedrooms occupy the 17th-century listed building, all with their own bathrooms (one has a decadent tub for two). Communal areas include a courtyard garden and two inviting sitting rooms (with an interestingly stocked honesty bar) shared with the sweet resident cat. Breakfast, lunch and afternoon tea are served (residents only Sun, Mon) with plenty of scrumptious own-baked goodies; the quality is evident and produce is locally sourced where possible. You'll need to make your own arrangements for dinner, but staff are happy to help out with recommendations and reservations.

Feathers Hotel

16-20 Market Street, Woodstock, Oxfordshire OX20 1SX (01993 812291/www.feathers. co.uk). **Rates** £135-£185 double; £200-£275 suite. **Credit** AmEx, DC, MC, V.
Made up of seven interconnected 17th-century houses, and named by a stuffed bird-collecting former hotelier, Feathers is a snug maze of corridors and elegantly furnished bedrooms, the best of which is equipped with its own private steam room. Despite a certain air of faded glory, it remains Woodstock's most prominent hotel; service is smoothly professional but never lofty. The garden is pleasant on balmy afternoons; in winter, the wood-panelled lounge with huge fireplace is perfect for relaxed drinks. There's also a beauty salon, Preen (treatments must be pre-booked), and a fine-dining restaurant (*see p215*) and less formal bistro on site.

King's Arms Hotel

19 Market Street, Woodstock, Oxfordshire OX20 1SU (01993 813636/www.kings-hotel-woodstock.co.uk). **Rates** £140-£150 double. **Credit** AmEx, MC, V.
A comfortable, contemporary hotel, just across the road from the traditional, flowery Feathers (*see above*), the King's Arms offers a very different experience. The listed Georgian building has been painstakingly renovated to retain its character, but is carefully balanced with neutral tones and modern furnishings; the only dark furniture you'll find here are the leather chairs in the restaurant, a converted billiards room. The 15 (14 doubles and one twin) bedrooms – all named after kings – are simply, stylishly and individually appointed, with Wi-Fi and good en suites. There's decent bistro fare (with appealing vegetarian options) in the restaurant, while the bar is popular with Woodstock's youth – so expect a bit of noise on your way up to bed.

Lamb Inn & Restaurant

*Sheep Street, Burford, Oxfordshire OX18 4LR
(01993 823155/www.lambinn-burford.co.uk).*
Rates £145-£255 double. **Credit** MC, V.
A few doors down from the Bay Tree (*see p213*),
the Lamb makes an equally appealing period
place to stay; the 15 well-equipped rooms are full
of warmth and character, with nice personal
touches such as proper leaf tea-making facilities
and own-made flapjacks awaiting as you flop into
your room, laden with bags. Many of the rooms
overlook a sheltered courtyard, where guests can
lunch in summer. There are intimate bars and
lounge areas in which to settle by the fire with a
drink; a well-regarded restaurant (*see p215*)
rounds off this pleasantly laid-back operation.

WHERE TO EAT & DRINK

Attractive country pubs and restaurants
abound, but this is moneyed land; while
standards are high, so are prices, and
tastes tend to the conservative. Don't
be surprised to see guests sporting black
tie in your hotel dining room.

On Burford High Street, the Golden
Pheasant (01993 823223, www.golden
pheasant-burford.co.uk) and the Bull Hotel
(No.105, 01993 822220, www.oldbull
hotel.com) both serve decent bar meals.
Off the main drag, the tankard-bedecked
Royal Oak (26 Witney Street, 01993
823278) is popular for its pies. The Plough
in Clanfield (01367 810222, www.the
ploughclanfield.co.uk) is a truly impressive
Elizabethan manor house hotel, famed
for its game and seafood restaurant.
Woodstock has the well-regarded Chinese
restaurant Chef Imperial (22 High Street,
01993 813591), Brothertons Brasserie (1
High Street, 01993 811114, closed Tue),
and Hampers deli and café (31-33 Oxford
Street, 01993 811535) for light bites.

Angel at Burford

*14 Witney Street, Burford, Oxfordshire OX18
4SN (01993 822714/www.theangelatburford.
co.uk).* **Lunch served** noon-2pm Tue-Sat;
12.30-3.30pm Sun. **Dinner served** 7-9.30pm
Tue-Sat. **Main courses** £10.50-£18.50. **Rates**
£75-£110 double. **Credit** MC, V.
This 16th-century coaching inn has an appealing
bricks-and-beams interior for winter dining and a
narrow garden for when the weather's on form.
Order at the bar (seating is limited if you're just in
for an Adnams) and you'll be taken to one of the
various dining areas. Smoked haddock rarebit or
fish cakes might be on the lunch menu; at dinner,
when booking is essential, you'll find heartier fare
such as venison steak, pan-fried calf's liver or
seafood risotto; it's all well presented and compe-
tently cooked, if a touch pricey. Top marks for
desserts, especially the orange crème caramel with
Grand Marnier syrup. Three en suite rooms are
available if you've overindulged in pint or plate.

Bay Tree Hotel

*Sheep Street, Burford, Oxfordshire OX18
4LW (01993 822791/www.cotswold-inns-
hotels.co.uk).* **Lunch served** noon-2pm daily.
Dinner served 7-9pm Mon-Fri, Sun; 7-9.30pm
Sat. **Set lunch** £12.95 2 courses, £15.95 3
courses. **Set dinner** £24.95 2 courses, £27.95
3 courses. **Credit** AmEx, DC, MC, V.
The airy dining room overlooks verdant gardens
at this excellent hotel, and the food lives up to the
setting. While the menu doesn't stray far from the
traditional, ingredients are first class, dishes arrive
attractively but unfussily presented and portions
are generous. Artichoke and split pea soup and
roasted loin of Gloucestershire Old Spot were
appetisingly colourful and flavoursome, butternut
squash and wild mushroom risotto was autumn-
on-a-plate perfection, and a child's meal of Cotswold
sausages with creamy, herby mash was polished
off at record speed by the small boy in our party.
Service is discreetly attentive and obliging.

Just another
pretty street in
photogenic
Woodstock.

Feathers Hotel

16-20 Market Street, Woodstock, Oxfordshire OX20 1SX (01993 812291/www.feathers. co.uk). **Lunch served** 12.30-2pm, **dinner served** 7-9pm daily. **Set lunch** £19 2 courses, £24.50 3 courses. **Set dinner** £37.50 2 courses, £46 3 courses. **Credit** AmEx, DC, MC, V.

The Feathers offers an intimate fine dining experience in its antique, oak-panelled dining room. Head chef Simon Garbutt (Babington House) has produced a modern-leaning European menu: salad of anjou pigeon to start, perhaps, followed by braised haunch of venison with roasted root vegetables – winning winter comfort food, beautifully cooked and presented. The lunchtime 'market menu' is a gourmet steal at £19, offering hearty fare such as rump of lamb or roast mackerel. Postprandial coffee and petits fours can be taken in the study, where the soothing sounds of a crackling fire are interrupted by occasional whistles – and surreal comments – from Johann, resident parrot, in the corridor outside. A minor complaint: a pre-ordered vegetarian meal unimaginatively featured the same ingredients in both starter and main course.

Fleece

11 Church Green, Witney, Oxfordshire OX28 4AZ (01993 892270/www.peachpubs.com). **Lunch served** noon-2.30pm Mon-Sat; noon-3pm Sun. **Dinner served** 6.30-10pm Mon-Sat; 6.30-9.30pm Sun. **Main courses** £9-£16. **Credit** AmEx, MC, V.

An unexpectedly modern Cotswolds find, the Fleece wouldn't look out of place in Islington thanks to its contemporary (and somewhat chain-like) decor of light wood and leather banquettes. That's no bad thing, and it's certainly a popular spot with Witney's twenty- and thirtysomethings. The front bar can get rather crowded; head for the quieter back restaurant or dine outdoors if the sun's out. Load up a deli board from a vegetarian-friendly antipasti and cheese selection, or choose from the fish and charcuterie. For bigger appetites, there's also a choice of four stone-baked pizzas plus steak, stuffed sea bass, fish cakes and chicken escalope. Portions are generous, prices reasonable and the staff are young and friendly.

King's Head

Chapel Hill, Wootton, Oxfordshire OX20 1DX (01993 811340/www.kings-head.co.uk). **Lunch served** noon-2pm daily. **Dinner served** 7-8.30pm Mon-Fri; 7-9pm Sat. **Main courses** £9.95-£16.95. **Rates** £75-£100 double. **Credit** MC, V.

The intimate restaurant at this atmospheric 17th-century pub is a big hit with local (and loaded) foodies. A fat wallet is called for, but the Modern European menu is expertly prepared and presented, if unnecessarily over-embellished with phrases such as 'finished with a fresh parsley crust'. Ignore the irritating verbal flourishes and just tuck in – the food is very good. Sample roast rack of lamb with ratatouille, or Orkney fillet steak served with

potato rösti and wild mushrooms. Daily specials feature fresh fish; steamed pink sea bream with a saffron fondue, or roast monkfish, perhaps. Book for dinner. The pub also offers accommodation, including a self-contained converted barn.

Lamb Inn

High Street, Shipton-under-Wychwood, Oxfordshire OX7 6DQ (01993 830465). **Lunch served** noon-2.30pm, **dinner served** 6.30-9.30pm Mon-Sat. **Meals served** noon-3.30pm Sun. **Main courses** £11-£22. **Set lunch** (Sun) £12 2 courses. **Credit** MC, V.

You'll still find locals supping Abbot Ale in this picturesque Cotswold-stone inn, but a management change in 2006 saw the focus shift to food and wine. The dining area lost a table to make space for a welcoming lounging space, equipped with a comfy, cushion-laden sofa; a fine spot for a cappuccino or glass of shiraz. The menu has also successfully moved from old-fashioned pub grub standards to gastro favourites like slow-cooked belly of pork, Gressingham duck and aged Hereford steak. Sunday lunch is a bargain at £12 for two courses.

Lamb Inn & Restaurant

Sheep Street, Burford, Oxfordshire OX18 4LR (01993 823155/www.lambinn-burford.co.uk). **Lunch served** noon-2.30pm Mon-Fri; noon-3pm Sat, Sun. **Dinner served** 7-9.30pm Mon-Sat; 7-9pm Sun. **Main courses** £8.50-£14. **Set lunch** (Sun) £27.50 3 courses. **Set dinner** £32.50 3 courses. **Credit** MC, V.

The Lamb's restaurant is reached via a distinctive stone-flagged corridor leading from the cosy pub, where you may also dine. While formal, it isn't fusty – fellow diners during our lunchtime visit included guffawing American businessmen demolishing huge steaks, and a family group with children messing up the pristine table linen. The menu is uncomplicated, hearty, seasonal and drawn from local produce where possible: from the fresh fish board, pan-fried gilthead bream with baby leeks was wonderful, while cauliflower risotto was rich and creamy (though featured overly fatty pancetta). A very grown-up jam roly-poly and custard rounded off the meal with satisfied sighs.

Red Lion

South Side, Steeple Aston, Oxfordshire OX25 4RY (01869 340225). **Lunch served** noon-2.30pm Mon-Sat; noon-4pm Sun. **Dinner served** 6-9pm Mon-Sat. **Main courses** £7-£15. **Set lunch** (Sun) £12.95 2 courses, £15.95 3 courses. **Credit** MC, V.

A small, attractive country pub boasting a paved garden, low-ceilinged bar (complete with resident spaniel), separate lounge with squashy leather sofas, and wood-beamed conservatory dining room (children are permitted). Food is fairly traditional, but the ham off the bone is absolutely top-rate; game pie goes down a treat with a pint of Old Hookey. It's a popular local, so book at weekends.

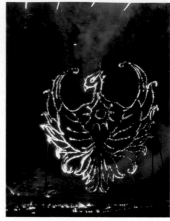

Brecon Beacons

Ballooning, boating, boarding and, of course, books.

The Black Mountains that make up the eastern half of the Brecon Beacons National Park present an ethereal rural landscape. Bleakly beautiful, this region's rugged hills and deep valleys have captivated countless artists, writers and craftsmen since the early 1900s. Many of them were inspired enough to make the area their permanent home, and the social enclaves that have formed here over the years (particularly in the 1970s) give it a creative, bohemian feel.

With a section of the Offa's Dyke Path running south from Hay Bluff along the ridge above the Olchon Valley and Vale of Ewyas until it meets the River Monnow, the Black Mountains (not to be confused with the Black Mountain in the western Brecon Beacons) straddle England and Wales: Powys is to the west; Herefordshire to the east. Life on the borders has been simply and honestly captured by Bruce Chatwin in *On the Black Hill*. First published in 1982, this tale of the inseparable Jones twins, Benjamin and Lewis, is set on the Vision, a farm resting in the Vale of Ewyas. The colourful characters that pepper the late author's celebrated novel can still be happened upon today, from the sheep farmer in the pub worrying about how much his yearlings will fetch at market to the hippies communing with nature, living in yurts down some dingly dell.

Brecon Beacons

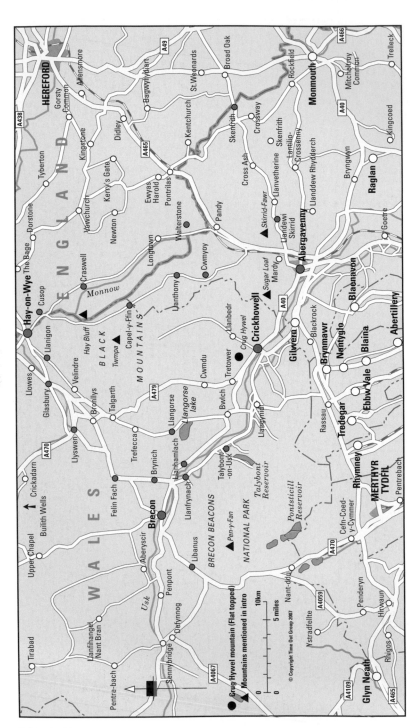

Accommodation	★★★☆☆
Food & drink	★★★☆☆
Nightlife	★☆☆☆☆
Shopping	★★☆☆☆
Culture	★★☆☆☆
Sights	★☆☆☆☆
Scenery	★★★★★

You'll find plenty of opportunity for cerebral activities here. Get lost among the miles of dusty bookshelves in Hay-on-Wye's specialist bookshops (the town is, purportedly, the world's largest second-hand book centre and, fittingly for its unconventional nature, has recently been twinned with Timbuktu) or simply wander beside streams, through woods or on the hills with your head in the clouds.

There's plenty of diversion for outdoor types too. Whether you're into walking, horse riding, mountain biking or boarding, climbing, canoeing, white-water rafting or even sailing, you'll find no end of high-energy pursuits.

Spring and summer are obviously the busiest times. Although there's no guarantee of good weather – this is Wales after all – the area's riverbanks make prime spots for lazing between cool swims on hot days and the countryside is as green as can be. But do come off-season to experience the true spirit of the Black Mountains. In late autumn the emerald fronds of bracken turn russet-gold, setting the mountain escarpments on fire. During winter the dark silhouettes of frost-bitten ridges glimpsed through the branches of naked trees are a dramatic sight.

All booked up

Hay-on-Wye – rarely referred to locally by its Welsh name Y Gelli Gandryll – surrounds a crumbling castle, which is often eerily illuminated by green and purple lights at night. Behind its tumbledown walls lives the town's self-proclaimed king, Richard Booth. This is an eccentric town, to say the least. Bookworm Booth first launched his second-hand tome trade here in 1961 and declared Hay an independent state on 1 April 1977.

Hay is now a second-hand book empire, with 39 shops lining its narrow streets. The grandes dames are Richard Booth's Bookshop (44 Lion Street, 01497 820322, www.richardbooth.demon.co.uk), with over 400,000 titles, and the Hay Cinema Bookshop (Castle Street, 01497 820071, www.haycinemabookshop.co.uk), covering everything from travel to religion to economics. Meanwhile, Boz Books (13A Castle Street, 01497 821277, www.bozbooks.co.uk) sells only works by Charles Dickens (aka Boz) and other 19th-century authors, while Rose's Books (14 Broad Street, 01497 820013, www.rosesbooks.com) specialises in rare and out-of-print children's and illustrated books. Pick up the 'Hay-on-Wye Town of Books' leaflet from the Tourist Information Centre (see p218) for easy navigation. May heralds the prestigious Hay Literary Festival, when the literati, from young wordsmiths to wrinkly intellectuals, revel in ten days of full-on bibliophilia (see p228 **Way on high**).

Still, it's not all about books. The Haymakers (St Johns Place, 01497 820556, www.haymakers.co.uk) sells works by a co-operative of local artists and craftsmen, while a not-to-be-missed shop is the Great English Outdoors (Mortimer House, Castle Street, 01497 821205, www.greatenglish.co.uk). Run by leather-worker Athene English, it stocks a covetable range of traditional Welsh blankets, wallets and cases made from 214-year-old reindeer hide and an array of quirky antique finds. A few steps away, you'll find Charlie Hicks Greengrocer (22 Castle Street, 01497 822742, www.charliehicks.com). Owned and run by Charlie Hicks, co-presenter of BBC Radio 4's Veg Talk, all produce is seasonal and is sourced from small growers.

TOURIST INFORMATION

Abergavenny
Monmouth Road, Abergavenny, Monmouthshire NP7 5HL (01873 857588/www.abergavenny.co.uk).
Brecon
Cattle Market Car Park, Brecon, Powys LD3 9DA (01874 622485/ www.visitbreconbeacons.com).
Crickhowell
Beaufort Chambers, Beaufort Street, Crickhowell, Powys NP8 1AA (01873 812105).
Hay-on-Wye
Craft Centre, Oxford Road, Hay-on-Wye, Herefordshire HE3 5EA (01497 820144/www.hay-on-wye.co.uk/craftcentre).
Knighton
Offa's Dyke Centre, West Street, Knighton, Powys LD7 1EN (01547 528753/www.offasdyke. demon.co.uk).
Libanus
Brecon Beacons Mountain Centre, Libanus, Powys LD3 8ER (01874 623366/www.breconbeacons.org).
www.brecon-beacons.net
www.gomidwales.co.uk
www.hay-on-wye.co.uk
www.tourism.powys.gov.uk
www.visitwyevalley.com

Brecon Beacons

'he views from Hay Bluff are worth the trek.

In warm weather, there's nothing better than packing a picnic – stock up with supplies of organic cider and freshly made goodies from Hay Wholefoods & Delicatessen (41 Lion Street, 01497 820708) – and following the path north from Hay Bridge along the Wye until you reach the Warren. Here you'll find meadows, a pebbly beach and a popular swimming spot. For canoeists, the Warren marks the final stretch of the three- to four-hour paddle downriver from Glasbury to Hay.

As the nights draw in, the spectacle that is Hay on Fire (01497 820453, www.hay onfire.co.uk) gives the town something to look forward to – it returned in October 2006 after a decade's absence. Dance and percussion, lantern-making and other family workshops are nicely timed to coincide with the autumn half-term holidays, and culminate in a procession and fireworks show, featuring a dragon, torchlight, samba bands, fire sculptures, and fireworks down by the River Wye.

Hay Bluff to Llanthony Priory

Rising above Hay-on-Wye is Hay Bluff. You can pick up the Offa's Dyke Path from the bottom of the Hay school car park and follow it through Cusop Dingle and all the way to the summit of Hay Bluff.

Alternatively, drive to the stone circle car park on Hay Common and make your ascent from there. The relatively effortless climb to the top is, on a clear day, rewarded with magnificent views of the Wye Valley.

Directly south-east of the Bluff rises the promontory of Twmpa, or Lord Hereford's Knob. Between the two mountains the Gospel Pass, a single-track road, cuts into the Vale of Ewyas. It passes through Capel-y-Ffin, a tiny hamlet with a white chapel, where the sculptor Eric Gill and a bunch of artist friends lived during the 1920s, and down on to Llanthony Priory. There are riding stables at both Capel-y-Ffin and Llanthony.

Half of the priory (founded in 1107 by William de Lacy, brother of the Lord of Ewyas; www.castlewales.com/ llantho.html) still clings to the adjoining house; the remainder stands in ruins. Columns of old walls and great arches thrust skywards, backdropped by misty hills. From here there is a magical walk up and over the ridge above the priory (Offa's Dyke Path again) and into the Olchon Valley below.

South of Llanthony is Cwmyoy (Vale of the Yoke). Here, built on a land slip, the higgledy-piggledy medieval church of St Martin has masterful stone lettering on its headstones, both inside and out. An engraving dated 1682 hangs on a wall near the altar and reads: 'Thomas Price he take his nap in our common mother lap waiting to heare the bridegroome say awake my dear and come away.' Look out also for the 13th-century crucifix.

Brecon to Abergavenny

The market town of Brecon (Aberhonddu) has all the hustle and bustle of Hay, but without the charm. However, it's a convenient base if you're planning to explore both the Central Brecon Beacons and the Black Mountains in the same trip. Brecon Cathedral (01874 623857, www.breconcathedral.org.uk) and Castle, parts of which date back to Norman times, perch on the hill. The River Usk flows through Brecon and pleasant strolls can be had along the Promenade, a stretch of water north of the centre.

Meanwhile, the Brecon and Monmouthshire Canal starts south of the centre. At the Canal Basin you'll find Brecon Theatre (Canal Wharf, 01874 611622, www.theatrbrycheiniog.co.uk), a lively regional performing arts venue. Brecon comes alive on the second Saturday of the month, when the Brecknockshire Farmers' Market is held in the covered Market Hall (High Street, 01874 610008, 10am-2pm, www. brecknockfarmersmarkets.org.uk). The main event in summer is the Brecon Jazz Festival (01874 625511, www.brecon jazz.co.uk), which attracts big names as well as new talent.

The Black Mountains

Llangorse Lake

Just west of Brecon is Libanus and the Brecon Beacons Mountain Centre (01874 623366, www.breconbeacons.org). Here you can pick up a wide range of maps, leaflets, walking books and other information. There's also a tearoom and plenty of walks to choose from should you decide to make it your starting point for a day. The most popular hike in the Central Brecon Beacons is the ascent of Pen-y-Fan (pronounced 'Pen-ur-Van'), the highest mountain in south Wales at 2,907 feet. The traditional five-mile route starts from the Storey Arms on the A470 and should only be attempted in fine weather. A more adventurous alternative would be to start from Llanfrynach village and make your way up the 10.5-mile route that approaches the summit of Pen-y-Fan via the lower peak of Fan-y-Big – a name Dylan Thomas would have surely approved of.

Heading south-east out of Brecon on the A40 towards Crickhowell and Abergavenny, you'll see a sign for Llangorse on your left and then a bit further along again, a sign to Talybont-on-Usk on your right. The waters of Llangorse Lake, the largest natural lake in south Wales, offer sailing and canoeing, while the village also acts as a hub for climbing and horse riding. At Talybont-on-Usk, have a waterside drink at the Star Inn (01874 676635), famed for its variety of real ales, before walking out to the Blaen-y-Glyn waterfalls at the head of the Talybont-on-Usk Valley above the reservoir. You can also pick up the Taff Trail here, a 55-mile cycle route that links Brecon with the Welsh capital, Cardiff, passing along disused tram lines and railroads on its course.

At Crickhowell the pretty 16th-century bridge over the Usk here has 12 arches on one side and 13 on the other, with walks along the river and past the salmon pits.

In town, fill your knapsack with snacks from the baker and grocers on the High Street for the fairly gentle five-mile circular walk around Crug Hywel, its flat top earning it the nickname of Table Mountain. At the 1,481-foot summit you'll find an Iron Age fort that affords impressive views of the Usk Valley and the Central Brecon Beacons. The Crickhowell Adventure shop (1 High Street, 01873 810020) is a good source of local info.

The market town of Abergavenny acts as the bottom left-hand corner of the triangle formed with Hay-on-Wye and Brecon, the Black Mountains lying within its bounds. Other than during the successful Abergavenny Food Festival (www.abergavennyfoodfestival.com), there's no real reason to linger except, perhaps, for a wander round the Norman castle (Castle Street, 01873 854282). Here, in 1175, the vengeful William de Braose slaughtered a score of local Welshmen after inviting them for a Christmas feast at his table. It's nearly as bloody a task to find a decent watering or dining hole in town, but if you're parched try the Hen and Chickens (01873 853613), a traditional pub on Flannel Street serving real ales. The Angel Hotel (*see p226*) is the other saving grace.

Abergavenny's main appeal is the surrounding peaks of the Sugar Loaf, Blorenge and Skirrid Fawr mountains. The annual Three Peaks Trial, held on the last Saturday of March (www.cardiffoutdoor group.org.uk), is an 18-mile endurance test that attempts each in succession. If you're not feeling quite so extreme, take your pick and tackle just one. The 3.5-mile circuit of Skirrid Fawr (Holy Mountain) starts near the foodies' favourite, the Walnut Tree Inn – a factor that may aid your decision-making.

WHERE TO STAY

There's no shortage of friendly, family-run B&Bs in the Black Mountains and Brecon Beacons (tourist offices can supply you with lists of local ones), just beware the chintz. When it comes to hotels, especially those with a dash of style, choices are more limited. Plan well ahead for the Hay Literary Festival, which runs from late May to early June, and the Brecon Jazz Festival in August, as accommodation can get booked up as much as a year in advance.

For the best self-catering accommodation in the Beacons, the Courtyard Wing at Penpont, a Grade I-listed country house and estate with walled gardens, a Green Man maze and private fishing, sleeps up to 17 people in six single, twin and double rooms (01874 636202, www.penpont. com). It is situated five miles west of Brecon, directly off the A40 between

ACTION STATIONS

BOATING

Beacon Park Boats
Llanfoist Wharf, Abergavenny, Monmouthshire NP7 9NG (01873 858277/www.beaconpark boats.com).

Brecon Boats
The Travellers Rest Inn, Talybont-on-Usk, Brecon, Powys LD3 7YP (01874 676401).

Cambrian Cruisers
Ty Newydd, Pencelli, Brecon, Powys LD3 7LJ (01874 665315/www.cambriancruisers.co.uk).

Castle Narrowboats
Church Road Wharf, Gilwern, Abergavenny, Monmouthshire NP7 0EP (01873 830001/ www.castlenarrowboats.co.uk).

Dragonfly Cruises
Canal Road, Brecon, Powys LD3 7HL (07831 685222/www.dragonfly-cruises.co.uk).

Red Line Boats
Gotyre Wharf, Llanover, Abergavenny, Monmouthshire NP7 9EW (01873 880516/ www.redlineboats.co.uk).

CANOEING & KAYAKING

Paddles & Peddles
15 Castle Street, Hay-on-Wye, Herefordshire HR3 5DF (01497 820604/www.canoehire.co.uk).

Wye Valley Canoe Centre
The Boathouse, Glasbury-on-Wye, Herefordshire HR3 5NP (01497 847213/ www.wyevalleycanoes.co.uk).

CYCLE HIRE

Bikes and Hikes
1 Warle Cottage, Llanddew, Brecon, Powys LD3 9TF (01874 610071/www.bikesandhikes.co.uk).

Bi-Ped Cycles
10 Ship Street, Brecon, Powys LD3 9AF (01874 622296/www.bipedcycles.co.uk).

Pedalaway
Trereece Barn, Llangarron, Ross-on-Wye, Herefordshire HR9 6NH (01989 770357/ www.pedalaway.com).

GLIDING, HANG-GLIDING & PARAGLIDING

Black Mountains Gliding Club
The Airfield, Talgarth, Brecon, Powys LD3 0EJ (01874 711463/www.talgarthgc. co.uk).

Paraventure Sports
Garn Llech Farmhouse, Upper Llanover, Abergavenny, Monmouthshire NP7 9ER (01873 881127/www.paraventure.co.uk).

HORSE RIDING

Black Mountains Holidays
Cantref Riding Centre & Adventure Farm, Upper Cantref Farm, Cantref, Brecon, Powys LD3 8LR (01874 665223/ www.cantref.com).

Ellesmere Riding Centre
Llangorse, Brecon, Powys LD3 7UN (01874 658252/www.trail-riding.co.uk).

Free Rein
The Coach House, Clyro Court, Clyro, Herefordshire HR3 5LE (01497 821356/ www.free-rein.co.uk).

Golden Castle Riding Stables
Llangattock, Crickhowell, Powys NP8 1PY (01873 812649/www.golden-castle.co.uk).

Brecon and Llandovery. For bed and breakfast in Brecon itself try Cantre Selyf (5 Lion Street, 01874 622904, www.cantreselyf.co.uk), which dates from the 17th century, with mainly 18th-century interiors. Owner Helen Roberts is famed for her breakfasts and serves up a choice of full English, smoked salmon and scrambled eggs, vegetarian cheese-and-leek sausages, omelette of your choice or french toast, yoghurt and fruit.

Grange Trekking
The Grange, Capel-y-Ffin, Abergavenny, Monmouthshire NP7 7NP (01873 890215/ www.grangetrekking.co.uk).

Llanthony Riding & Trekking
Court Farm, Llanthony, Abergavenny, Monmouthshire NP7 7NN (01873 890359/ www.llanthony.co.uk).

Tregoyd Mountain Riders
Tregoyd, Three Cocks, Brecon, Powys LD3 0SP (01497 847351/www.tregoydriding.co.uk).

Trevelog Trekking
Llanthony, Abergavenny, Monmouthshire NP7 7NW (01873 890216/www.pony-trekking.net).

HOT-AIR BALLOON FLIGHTS

Bailey Balloons
From LLanarth Village Hall, between Abergavenny and Raglan, Monmouthshire NP15 2AU (01275 375 300/www.baileyballoons.co.uk).

Flying Colours
44 Ham Green, Bristol, BS20 0HA (01873 840045/www.baileyballoons.co.uk).

MULTI-ACTIVITY CENTRES

Black Mountain Activities
Three Cocks, Brecon, Powys LD3 0SD (01497 847897/www.blackmountain.co.uk).

Mountain & Water
2 Upper Cwm Nant Gam, Llanelly Hill, nr Abergavenny, Monmouthshire NP7 0RF (01873 831825/www.mountainandwater.co.uk).

Sky Trek
Llangorse Rope & Riding Centre, Llangorse, Brecon, Powys LD3 7UH (01874 658272/ www.activityuk.com).

Kilvert's Hotel (*see p227*) in Hay-on-Wye has 11 rooms as well as a decent restaurant. Also in Hay, just across the bridge from the town centre, Dawn Farnworth enthusiastically welcomes guests aboard her tightly run ship at Start (01497 821391, www.the-start.net). This convivial B&B has an enviable riverside location and the three en suite rooms (one with bath) are immaculate. A large terrace looks out over the garden, stomping ground of the hens that will be laying your breakfast eggs.

Two miles from here in Llanigon, the Old Post Office (01497 820008, www.oldpost-office.co.uk) is a relaxed vegetarian B&B with understated decor and no pretences. It's worth paying the £10 extra per person per night for the attic room, which has views across to the Begwns in the west and the Black Mountains in the east. The owners also run Oxford Cottage in Hay-on-Wye (Oxford Road, 01497 820008, www.oxfordcottage.co.uk, £22 per person per night). It sleeps up to six people and you'll find all the ingredients you need to cook your own breakfast in the fridge.

The fabulous Pwll-y-Faedda near Erwood (01982 560202, www.pwllyfaedda.co.uk) is a rather special place to stay. The 1920s fishing lodge is situated on the banks of the River Wye, with private fishing and surrounding walks. The lodge can sleep up to 12 and all bedrooms, except the Blue twin room, look over the Wye. Look out for Pwll-y-Faedda's new series of special gourmet evenings in 2007.

Bell at Skenfrith
Monmouthshire NP7 8UH (01600 750235/ www.skenfrith.co.uk). **Rates** £105-£185 double. **Credit** (over £10) AmEx, MC, V.
A winding drive from either Monmouth or Abergavenny, through the hills of the Welsh Marches down to the Monnow Valley, takes you to one of the most stylish hotels in mid Wales, the Bell at Skenfrith. Accommodation here is simple but luxurious, with plenty of attention to detail. There are Welsh blankets on the beds, freshly ground coffee and a thermos of milk, Cath Collins toiletries, a jar of handmade biscuits and a bottle of 25-year-old whiskey in each room. Two of them – Tups Indispensable and Whickham's Fancy – even have four-poster beds. In the attic, the Barret's Bane and Coch-a-bonn-ddu suites are perfect for families, while well-behaved dogs are welcome at the hotel by prior arrangement. Dinner in the restaurant is a real treat (*see p228*).

Drawing Room
Between Cwmbach & Builth Wells, Powys LD2 3RT (01982 552493/www.the-drawing-room.co.uk). **Rates** £210-£230 double (incl dinner). **Credit** MC, V.

Fine dining and a luxurious stay await you at the Bell at Skenfrith.

Although the Drawing Room is a bit out on a limb for the Brecon Beacons, the journey to Cwmbach near Builth Wells is certainly worthwhile. For a start, this restaurant with rooms is conveniently located for forays into the remote, untouched Elan Valley – though, sadly, there are no walks directly from the B&B. Secondly, the rooms are impeccable. And thirdly, the food is superb (*see p229*). Converted from an early 18th-century wool packing house turned Georgian residence, the Drawing Room has three bijou rooms that go by the names of Phoebe, Oliver and Otis, each one individually done out in Laura Ashley and Fired Earth decor. Piles of cushions and fluffy towels, delicious Penhaligon's toiletries and DVD players in each room are all part of the creature comforts, as is the offering of fresh coffee delivered to your room in the morning and hot chocolate before you go to bed. The shelves of the downstairs drawing room are suitably stuffed with food and cookery books, while the small library of DVDs should suffice if you've forgotten to bring your favourite flick.

Peterstone Court Country House Hotel & Bistro

Llanhamlach, Brecon, Powys LD3 7YB (01874 665387/www.peterstone-court.com). **Lunch served** noon-2pm, **dinner served** 7-9.30pm daily. **Main courses** £12.50-£16.50. **Set lunch** (Sun) £14.50 2 courses, £18.50 3 courses. **Rates** £90-£170 double. **Credit** AmEx, MC, V. Peterstone Court, situated back off the Brecon Road between Brecon and Crickhowell, is well located for many of the area's main attractions. It's a great place to stay for those wanting to mountain bike the Taff Loop or walk along the River Usk and Brecon Canal. Owned by Jess and

Glyn Bridgeman and Sean Gerrard, who have turned the nearby Nantyffin Cider Mill Inn (*see p229*) into an award-winning restaurant, this Georgian manor house hotel successfully combines the luxury of traditional furnishings and decor with contemporary comforts such as DVDs and flat-screen TVs in the bedrooms and modern art hanging in the stairwells. The hotel's breakfast room and terrace have views of the Central Brecon Beacons, there's a heated outdoor pool and tepees in the garden during summer. There is a subterranean gym for hotel guests – though it in no way competes with the natural playground outside – while the treatment rooms and relaxation cave are a welcome place of retreat when the weather turns nasty.

WHERE TO EAT & DRINK

The Brecons has an incredible number of eating and drinking options, from simple cafés, to snug pubs, to world-class restaurants. Abergavenny's Angel Hotel (15 Cross Street, 01873 857121, www.angelhotelabergavenny.com) is as good a place as any to start your culinary tour. This former Georgian coaching inn was bought and restored by Caradog Hotels around five years ago and chef/director Mark Turton offers well-planned menus at low prices. Starters of whole tiger prawns sautéed with olive oil, garlic, flat parsley and white wine come dramatically presented. Main courses, meanwhile, might include a generous plateful of the local staple, roast leg of Welsh lamb, complete with mint sauce and al dente veg. Puddings of dark chocolate mousse cake with Grand Marnier ice-cream are hugely tempting. The wine list is short, well chosen and priced to sell.

Another good option is the Barn at Brynich (01874 623480, www.brynich. co.uk), an old farm that has been renovated to a high standard. The restaurant, which takes up the whole of the central barn, has a dramatic feel: beams, a stone fireplace and whitewash mixed with local red mud create a rich, roseate glow. Outside, a children's play area makes it a godsend to families. Meals are rudimentary, using organic and local produce wherever possible. A starter of terrine of ham hock and parsley with pear chutney and warm melba toast is typical Barn fare. The excellent Welsh Black steak and Breconshire ale pie with mushrooms is a winner, while other 'Barn Favourites' include a trio of local sausages with mash and onion gravy. Vegetarians are not left out either, with mixed pepper tartlets with goat's cheese and tomato marmalade among the options. The wine list here is short and predominantly New World.

In Hay-on-Wye, the Blue Boar (Castle Street, 01497 820884) is a proper local institution and makes a snug spot for cosy chats around the open fire. Go for reliable choices such as the steak and chips or Welsh rarebit. It's good for a pint or a glass of wine at any time, and stays open late during the Hay Literary Festival. Also in Hay is Kilvert's Hotel (The Bullring, 01497 821042, www.kilverts.co.uk), which has a roomy bar and decent pub food. Popular at any time, the place comes into its own during the festival and in summer when you can sit by the pond with a poetry book in one hand and a pint in the other. Kilvert's also has a decent restaurant.

The Bull's Head (Craswell, 01981 510616) is located on the eastern side of the Black Hill. The pub is exalted for its generous menu (using locally reared and grown meat and vegetables) and its ales brewed at the Wye Valley Brewery. The traditional Welsh faggots with stilton mash or Craswell's 'crassie' pie with beef, bacon and Butty Bach ale gravy are prime examples. If there's one thing the Bull's Head is famous for, however, it's the enormous 'huffer' sandwiches: try the Atkins dieter's nemesis, the chips and cheddar huffer. Be sure to wash it down with a Dorothy Goodbody stout or a Golden Valley perry.

Café (39 High Street, 01874 611191) is the best place in Brecon for an own-made cake or pudding with a fair trade/organic frothy cappuccino or hot chocolate. Refuel at lunchtime with hearty basics like cheese toasties, lasagne, or chilli with a jacket potato. Also worth a look here is Richard and Louise Gudsell's restaurant Tipple 'n' Tiffin (Theatr Brycheiniog, Canal Wharf, 01874 611866), located on the ground-floor corner of the theatre that overlooks Brecon's tiny canal basin. All dishes are somewhere between a starter and main course in size, and designed to be shared. Penclawdd cockles served with crispy bacon, salad and salsa vie for attention with game sausages on root mash with caramelised shallot and claret gravy. Appealing dishes are slow-roasted lamb with peppers and onions on potato and leek bake or a substantial chorizo, feta, sun-blush tomato and olive salad.

For sweet-toothed indulgence head for Shepherds Ice Cream Parlour & Coffee Shop (9 High Town, 01497 821898, www.shepherdsicecream.co.uk), an Edwardian-style ice-cream parlour on the main high street. The delicious sheep's milk ice-cream is rich enough to eliminate the need for cream, butter or eggs. That means you can lick away at such flavours as damson, hazelnut or ginger without doing too much damage to your waistline. Try the fresh fruit sorbets – especially the one-lick-and-you-can't-stop mango and chilli flavour – and the ice-cream cakes too. A branch has recently opened in Hereford (22 Widemarsh Street, 01432 266444).

Shepherds Ice Cream Parlour & Coffee Shop

Bell at Skenfrith

Monmouthshire NP7 8UH (01600 750235/ www.skenfrith.co.uk). **Lunch served** noon-2.30pm daily. **Dinner served** 7-9.30pm Mon-Sat; 7-9pm Sun. **Main courses** £14.50-£18.50. **Set Sunday lunch** £21.50 3 courses. **Credit** AmEx, MC, V.

Make sure that you work up a hunger with a romp across the Welsh Marches or along the Monnow Valley before visiting the Bell at Skenfrith as you will want to finish every morsel on your plate. A blackboard in the restaurant lists the restaurant's food suppliers – organic salads and herbs from the Skenfrith kitchen garden, beef, venison and lamb from the Welsh venison centre, and free-range duck from Madgett's Farm near Chepstow. All of these local ingredients and more are incorporated into a generous menu of seven starters, main and desserts, including pan-seared scallops with braised pak choi, chorizo and herb dressing, fillet of Brecon beef with garlic and mushroom mashed potato, wilted spinach and red wine jus, and dark chocolate bavarois with Grand Marnier soaked cherries and chocolate tuille biscuits. The

WAY ON HIGH

For a small, rural town Hay-on-Wye boasts one hell of a visitors' book. And where else in the world might you happen upon the likes of Goldie Hawn, Salman Rushdie, Al Gore, PJ Harvey, Louis de Bernières, David Lodge, Joseph Heller, Maya Angelou, Zadie Smith, Arthur Miller, Bill Clinton (the list continues on, and on, and on...) in a place with a population of a mere 1,300?

Every year around 80,000 (and rising) visitors descend on this tome town to listen to artists, politicians, comedians, playwrights, novelists, critics and academics discuss ideas and read from their work.

Launched in 1988 by Peter Florence with the proceeds of a poker game between young graduates, the **Hay Festival** has gone from being a weekend-long pub-garden event to a ten-day frenzy of scholarly gymnastics in a dedicated site just outside town. And there's plenty of music and partying thrown in too.

Despite the floods of national and international pilgrims to Hay Festival, the events – of which there is an archive of over 30,000 – are still on the whole an intimate experience. Many of the venues are around the size of a small marquee and filled with a hungry intellectual audience, whose passion for great words penned and read by favourite authors is palpable. Meanwhile, there's plenty for kids to get their ears and eyeballs into with the likes of *Lemony Snickett* and Jacqueline Wilson drawing excitable crowds of youngsters.

Sadly, though, the festival has been a victim of new technology. Since ticket sales went online, you're far less likely to be able to stroll up to the box office on the day of an event and get your audience with, say, John Updike or Edna O'Brien. As with accommodation, festival-goers' mantra must now be: 'Book ahead, book ahead, book ahead.'

Still, if you can't get tickets for the main festival, you'll be pleased to learn the Hay Festival season in London takes place in October, December sees the Hay Festival Weekender back in Wales and there are now international events taking place in Spain (Segovia Festival) and Colombia (Cartagena Festival).

HAY FESTIVAL

Information 0870 787 2848/box office 0870 990 1299, www.hayfestival.com.

Brecon Beacons

mind-blowing wine list includes everything from a 1997 Monnow Valley Seyval Blanc right up to a 1986 Château Mouton Rothschild Pouillac from the Bordeaux wine region. Closed Mon from Nov-Mar.

Drawing Room

Between Cwmbach & Builth Wells, Powys LD2 3RT (01982 552493/www.the-drawing-room.co.uk). **Dinner served** 7-9pm Tue-Sat. **Set dinner** £32 2 courses, £40 3 courses. **Credit** MC, V.

The Drawing Room is a three-bedroom boutique B&B, where dinner is also part of the deal. Fortunately, the cosy restaurant is also open to non-residents – just be sure to book. On arrival drinks and canapés, such as a parmesan basket with cream cheese and own-cured smoked salmon, are served in the drawing room while you choose from the carefully selected three-course menu. Proprietors Melanie and Colin Dawson, who previously owned the successful Toll House gastropub 30 miles down the road, describe their culinary style as traditional French with a modern twist made with the freshest seasonal food. This translates to such starters as a carpaccio of local venison with organic leaves, a fillet of Welsh beef with butternut squash and smoked lardons for mains or a trio of wild-flower honey, caramel and white chocolate with ginger ice-creams for dessert. The concise wine list leans towards France.

Felin Fach Griffin

Felin Fach, nr Brecon, Powys LD3 0UB (01874 620111/www.eatdrinksleep.ltd.uk). **Lunch served** 12.30-2.30pm Tue-Sun. **Dinner served** 6.30-9.30pm daily. **Main courses** £15.60-£17.90. **Credit** MC, V.

An award-winning and atmospheric gastropub. A sprawling interior with subdued lighting and well-chosen background music sets the scene for the excellent food to follow. Starters include terrine of chicken confit and foie gras with sauce gribiche, or dressed Portland crab with watercress, apple and melba toast. Main courses such as Cornish cod with boulangère potatoes, beurre noisette and summer truffle or corn-fed chicken breast with garden peas, pancetta and wild mushroom sauce are typical. Unusual desserts like apricots in elderflower syrup with raspberry sorbet are light and appealing – just as you'd expect of this local star.

Gliffaes Country House Hotel

Crickhowell, Powys NP8 1RH (01874 730371/ www.gliffaes.com). **Lunch served** noon-2.30pm, **dinner served** 7.30-9.15pm daily. **Main courses** £12-£17. **Set dinner** £26 2 courses, £32 3 courses. **Credit** MC, V.

The menu at this relaxed country-house hotel focuses on classics with a modern twist. A supporter of the Slow Food Movement, Gliffaes has a policy of sourcing at least two thirds of its fresh produce from within 25 miles of the hotel, while the fish is delivered fresh overnight from Cornwall

and is bought from sustainable stock. All food is seasonal and so dishes may change daily. Among the options you might find an enticing warm salad of wood pigeon, figs, fennel, balsamic and wine jus or a duck liver parfait with own-made brioche and caramelised red onion for starters. Mains, meanwhile, include pork tenderloin with melt in the mouth fondant potatoes, lentil and bacon, cider and thyme sauce. For vegetarians, the perl las risotto with roast chicory and smoked cherry tomato won't disappoint. The wine list includes house wines at £12.50.

Nantyffin Cider Mill Inn

Brecon Road, Crickhowell, Powys NP8 1SG (01873 810775/www.cidermill.co.uk). **Lunch served** noon-2.30pm Tue-Sun. **Dinner served** 6.30-9.30pm Tue-Sat. **Main courses** £10.95-£16.95. **Set lunch** (Tue-Fri) £12.95 2 courses, £16.95 3 courses. **Credit** AmEx, MC, V.

Chef Sean Gerrard has built up something of a local dining empire with his business partners Glyn and Jessica Bridgeman. The group also owns the neighbouring Manor Hotel (Brecon Road, Crickhowell, 01873 810212, www.manorhotel.co.uk) and the wonderfully located Peterstone Court (*see p226*) as well as this flagship inn. Nantyffin Cider Mill's vivid pink-washed frontage is unmissable from its bold roadside position. The menu has an equally confident character, with lots of Mediterranean influences enhanced by outside tables in summer. You'll find starters such as baked Welsh goat's cheese tartlet and substantial mains like confit of lamb with creamed herb mash and rosemary and garlic sauce or fresh fish from the blackboard. All three restaurants serve organic duck, chicken and lamb from their own farm in Llangynidr.

White Swan

Llanfrynach, Powys LD3 7BZ (01874 665276/www.the-white-swan.com). **Lunch served** noon-2pm Tue-Sat; noon-2.30pm Sun. **Dinner served** 7-9.30pm Tue-Sat; 7-9pm Sun. **Main courses** £8.95-£16.95. **Credit** MC, V.

It takes some finding, but this gastropub certainly provides a fine setting. The dining room facing the village church looks great – all ancient wood and stone surfaces – but is only open during the evening. Lunch is served in the bar overlooking the terrace. Meat and veg are local and there's an excellent selection of fish delivered every other day from Swansea, which is a main feature on the daily specials blackboard. Starters include cannelloni filled with chicken, leek, smoked bacon and tintern, and baked portobello mushrooms stuffed with goat's cheese, basil, garlic and pine nuts. For the adventurous, mains might be a haunch of Brecon venison with a braised offal faggot, sage mash and pepper cassis jus or a cannon of Welsh mountain lamb wrapped in leek, apple and rosemary with chive mash. The short but sweet wine list features good-value New World bottles among Old World stars.

Brecon Beacons

Ludlow

Take it slow in Shropshire's gastro capital.

It may be its location, just far enough from a major motorway to dissuade casual travellers. It may be its history, rich and tangible but not defined by one headline-grabbing event. It may simply be fashion, Shropshire never having been favoured by the TV travel shows and their printed counterparts. Whatever the reason, Ludlow benefits immeasurably from its relative obscurity. It's popular, sure, especially in summer. But it's not yet too popular: the crowds that descend on the town are manageable, and the locals have yet to tire of them.

Walking through its cosy centre, Ludlow's past is as plain as day. There are no fewer than 500 listed buildings here, an astonishing figure in a town that has a population of under 10,000 people, and the majority remain in wonderful shape. Some are grand and imposing, chief among them the castle and the church. Others are quieter and less forthcoming, sturdily straightforward residential properties tucked away off the main market square.

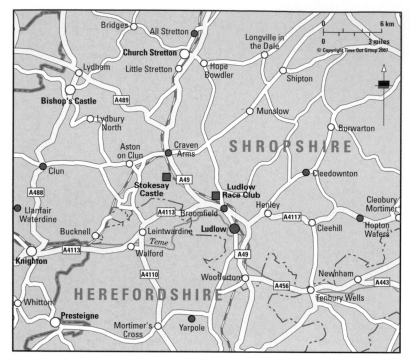

However, Ludlow also has a thriving present; this is no mere chocolate-box town. By remaining a largely old-fashioned place, Ludlow has pre-empted current consumer trends for independent producers, proving that what goes around always comes around eventually. Chain stores are almost entirely absent from its centre, which instead holds two independent bookshops, specialist stores selling cheese, chocolate and beer, and no fewer than four small butchers. There is a tangible sense of community at every turn, and the pace of life is so unhurried that Ludlow has officially been recognised by the international Slow Movement as Britain's first official 'Slow City' (www.cittaslow.org.uk).

What threatened to kill Ludlow has only made it stronger. In the early 1990s, Tesco announced it was opening a superstore in town. Some locals were concerned: could local shops survive the corporate onslaught? Determined to keep the town alive, they played to their strengths; in 1994, they organised the town's first annual Food Festival, a three-day showcase for local producers. A slew of outstanding restaurants sprung up here soon after, inspired by the abundance of excellent local produce, and the town gradually assumed a reputation as a real foodie

haven. Tesco eventually came, but the town not only survived but thrived. These days, Ludlow is a happy marriage of something old and something new, and a role model for towns in 21st-century Britain.

Built to last

Ludlow Castle (Castle Square, 01584 873355, www.ludlowcastle.com), built in the 11th century to protect England from attacks by the Welsh, is one of England's most romantic ruins. The roof has long since gone, but the castle's proud limestone walls remain, turning various shades of pink and purple in the evening sun. The castle is both architecturally significant, combining Norman, medieval and Tudor styles, and historically important. It was once the home of Roger Mortimer, who toppled Edward II in 1326 and put Ludlow on the political map, and later played an important part in the Wars of the Roses. Prince Arthur died here on his honeymoon with Catherine of Aragon, allowing Henry VIII to become king.

Dating back to 1199 but modified at various points since, St Laurence's Church remains a magnificent building, so much so that the combination of Norman and early English architecture is often assumed to be a cathedral. The church's tower dominates

Accommodation	★★★☆☆
Food & drink	★★★★★
Nightlife	★☆☆☆☆
Shopping	★★★☆☆
Culture	★☆☆☆☆
Sights	★★☆☆☆
Scenery	★★★★☆

the skyline; if you climb the 200 steps to the top, you'll be afforded the best views in Ludlow. The ashes of writer AE Housman are buried just outside the church. Listen for the carillon, which chimes a different tune each day of the week at 8am, noon, 4pm and 8pm.

While both church and castle are worth a visit, Ludlow truly rewards the wanderer. The centre of the town is small and very walkable, lined with roughly 500 listed buildings of various shapes, sizes, grades and ages. Pick up a copy of the Ludlow Town Trail leaflet, available for £1.50 from a variety of spots around town. The fold-out map provides a little context for the history that's visible on every corner.

Shopping in Ludlow

The great beauty of Ludlow is that it's far from a staid museum: it remains a thriving market town with a strong sense of local community. Regular street markets are held on Monday, Wednesday, Friday and Saturday in Castle Square, which also hosts an antique and flea market (first and third Sundays of the month), a books and crafts market (second Sunday of the month), a local produce market (second Thursday of the month) and a handful of other more sporadic events.

Away from the market, Ludlow's twin shopping fortes are food and antiques. Despite a population of less than 10,000, the town supports no fewer than four butchers: Carters (6 King Street, 01584 874665), DW Walls (14 High Street, 01584 872060), AH Griffiths (11 Bull Ring, 01584 872141) and Andrew Francis (1 Market Street, 01584 872008). Put your newly purchased meat into a sandwich using bread from the famous SC Price & Son (7 Castle Street, 01584 872815), R Walton (7-8 Market Street, 01584 872088) or Richard C Swift (5 Parkway, off Corve Street, 01584 874767).

Other shops offer a range of specialities. Chocoholics should head for the Chocolate Gourmet (16 Castle Square, 01584 879332, www.chocolategourmet.co.uk), while cheese connoisseurs swear by Mousetrap Cheese (6 Church Street, 01584 879556). The Deli on the Square (4 Church Street, 01584 877353, www.delionthesquare.co.uk) offers a range

of epicurean delights; the Farmers' Produce Market (1 Mill Street, 01584 873532) and the Fruit Basket (2-3 Church Street, 01584 874838) are both great for fruit and veg; and the Marches Little Beer Shoppe (2 Old Street, 01584 878999) sells rare local and imported beers. For more on local food, see www.localtoludlow.org.

Antiques shops are ten a penny in Ludlow, especially on Corve Street. For old furniture, porcelain and glass, Corve Street Antiques (141A Corve Street, 01584 879100) is good value; at the other end of the price scale, G&D Ginger (5 Corve Street, 01584 876939) specialises in high-quality, antique oak and country furniture. Somewhere in the middle lies the Ludlow Period House Shop (141 Corve Street, 01584 877276, www.periodhouseshops. com), which sells an enticing range of curios and accessories (including many reproductions). But the most striking shop is Dinham House (Dinham Road, below the castle, 01584 878100, www.clear viewstoves.com). The largest Georgian house in Ludlow, it was once occupied by Lucien Bonaparte, Napoleon's brother, who lived here for six months in 1811. These days, it's a showroom for wood-burning stoves by Clearview and handcrafted furniture, but it manages to retain a grand period feel.

Get outside

One of the nicest little strolls in the area is accessible from the very centre of Ludlow. From the castle, walk downhill towards Dinham Bridge; but instead of crossing the bridge, follow the road around to the right. You'll soon come to the lovely Linney Riverside Park, where you can rent a rowing boat in season and take to the idyllic River Teme that runs around the town.

Alternatively, head downhill from the castle past Dinham House, and then cross over Dinham Bridge. If you're only in the mood for a short amble (20 minutes or so), turn left along the river. The path soon rises and takes you on to Whitcliffe Common, which yields fine views of Ludlow, before leading downhill again to Ludford Bridge Road. Turn left and cross over the bridge, and you're back in town. For something more ambitious, turn right instead of left after the bridge and follow the path along the edge of the hill. The Mortimer Trail, a 30-mile walk, takes in Mortimer Forest (prime wildlife-watching territory) and ends in the village of Kington.

Guided walks help put Ludlow into perspective. Run by the Ludlow Historical Research Group, walks start by the cannon at the castle entrance at 2.30pm every Saturday and Sunday from Easter to late September (daily during Ludlow Festival),

Ludlow

and cost £2 for adults or £1 for kids. For details, phone 01584 874205. For more information on walks in the Ludlow area, visit the Tourist Information Centre (*see* p235). And for cycling holidays, contact Wheely Wonderful (01568 770755, www.wheelywonderfulcycling.co.uk).

Beyond Ludlow

The rolling countryside surrounding Ludlow – windswept hills, lush valleys, gurgling streams – is an attraction in its own right, but it also contains a couple of bona fide tourist attractions. Chief among them is Stokesay Castle (between Ludlow and Craven Arms on the A49, 01588 672544, www.english-heritage.org.uk), widely considered to be England's finest 13th-century manor house. Technically, it's not a castle at all, but it resembles one: back in 1291, Edward I granted its owner a 'licence to crenellate' the tower for defence purposes. It's notable for its grand hall, the ornate, panelled living room, and a tower that affords fine views.

Up in Craven Arms, the Shropshire Hills Discovery Centre (School Road, Craven Arms, 01588 676000, www.shropshire. gov.uk/discover.nsf) traces the evolution of the Shropshire landscape. The museum, devoted to the study of nature, ecology and archaeology, is notable for its amazing grass roof and an exhibition on the Shropshire mammoth, and also offers visitors several guided walks. Also in Craven Arms is the Land of Lost Content (aka the National Museum of British Popular Culture; The Market Hall, Market Street, Craven Arms, 01588 676176, www.lolc.org.uk), an agreeably disparate collection of ephemera from years gone by.

Other towns and villages are also worth a detour. Hidden in a green valley, the nearby village of Clun was immortalised by AE Housman for being 'the quietest under the sun' – a description that still applies today. Bishop's Castle, a village north-west of Clun, is famous for its beer: real ale drinkers sup in droves at its independent, pub-based breweries. Church Stretton, 30 minutes north of Ludlow along the A49,

has a dramatic backdrop: the town and its surrounding communities and countryside have been dubbed Little Switzerland on account of the hilly terrain.

An hour's drive north-east of Ludlow, Ironbridge is famous as the 'birthplace of the Industrial Revolution'. Ten museums are strewn along the densely forested, mineral-rich Severn Gorge, where, in 1709, ironmaster Abraham Darby first used coke as a fuel for smelting iron. His experiments revolutionised transport, engineering and construction. Today, you can walk across the eponymous Iron Bridge, built in 1777, learn about the role of iron in industrialisation at the Museum of Iron or stroll through a replica Victorian town. For details of all the museums, call 01952 884391 or see www.ironbridge.org.uk.

Festive fun

The Ludlow Food Festival (01584 873957, www.foodfestival.co.uk), the town's most famous event, attracts foodies from across Britain. Held every September, it features events such as the Ludlow Sausage Trail (eat your way around the town's butchers), the Real Ale Trail (drink your way around its pubs) and the Festival Loaf (say goodbye to your fancy new low-carb diet). The grounds of Ludlow Castle become the setting for an all-day picnic. The Slow Food Movement (01584 879599, www.slowfoodludlow.org. uk), big in these parts, is also out in full, albeit laid-back, force.

Other events include the Ludlow Medieval Christmas Fayre (www.ludlowcraftevents. co.uk), a craft show held near the end of November, and the Ludlow Festival (late June-early July, 01584 872150, www. ludlowfestival.co.uk), which features an array of cultural performances. Located a couple of miles north of town on the A49, Ludlow Racecourse (Bromfield, Ludlow, 01584 856221, www.ludlow-racecourse. co.uk) hosts roughly 15 National Hunt races a year. And year-round, the Assembly Rooms (1 Mill Street, Ludlow, 01584 878141, www.ludlowassemblyrooms.co. uk) is Ludlow's cultural centre, screening films and staging music and plays.

One of England's most romantic ruins: 11th-century Ludlow Castle.

WHERE TO STAY

In addition to the hotels, B&Bs and inns detailed below, a few other options are worthy of recommendation. The Waterdine (*see p239*) boasts three quaintly decorated rooms above its excellent restaurant, housed in a 16th-century pub by the river on the Welsh border. There are also rooms above Church Inn (*see p238*) and De Grey's in Ludlow (*see p239*) and the Crown at Hopton (*see p238*) just outside it.

Birches Mill

Clun, Craven Arms, Shropshire SY7 8NL (01588 640409/www.birchesmill.co.uk). **Rates** £76-£84 double; £285-£438 2-bed cottage; £359-£556 4-bed cottage. **Credit** MC, V.
Boasting a secluded, postcard-perfect setting in a lush valley amid the Shropshire hills, this stone mill house (closed Nov-Feb) is one of the area's most appealing places to stay. The oldest parts of the house date from 1640, but the history isn't overwhelming; the beautiful old furniture is complemented by tasteful hints of modernity, including a wonderfully cosy living room. The complex of buildings also includes five self-catering cottages (open year-round) with their own wood-burning stoves. Be sure to pick up a jar or two of the moreish, own-made jams and chutneys before you leave.

Bromley Court

Lower Broad Street, Ludlow, Shropshire SY8 1PQ (01584 876996/www.ludlowhotels.com). **Rates** £95-£120 double. **Credit** AmEx, MC, V.
Comprising three 17th-century cottages, tucked away on a quiet street within a stone's throw or two from the Buttercross, Bromley Court aims for a kind of old-fashioned English cutesiness. Each cottage has low-beamed ceilings, creaky stairs and sloping floors, with antique beds, patchwork quilts and William Morris fabrics adding to the cosiness. The cottages all open on to a shared garden. The operation is now run by the folks behind the Bull pub a short walk away on Corve Street; if you're after a cooked breakfast in the morning, they'll happily provide one.

Clive Bar & Restaurant with Rooms

Bromfield, Ludlow, Shropshire SY8 2JR (01584 856565/www.theclive.co.uk). **Rates** £75-£97.50 double; £110-£170 family. **Credit** AmEx, MC, V.
Located right by the side of the A49, a five-minute drive north-west of Ludlow, the Clive is a slicker-than-average restaurant with rooms. The rustic element of the various old buildings – stone exteriors, wooden beams inside – have been tidily combined with a more modern design sensibility, reflected in the halogen lights and stylish, grey-tiled bathrooms. Everything is in very good condition, and the rooms are far more spacious than is the norm around these parts. For the restaurant, *see p238*.

Dinham Hall

By the Castle, Ludlow, Shropshire SY8 1EJ (01584 876464/www.dinhamhall.co.uk). **Rates** £140-£190 double; £240 suite. **Credit** AmEx, DC, MC, V.
This elegant Georgian pile dates back to 1792, but it's served as a hotel only since the early 1980s, having spent the better part of two centuries as a private residence and, latterly, a boarding house for boys at the local grammar school. Happily, the rooms have been redecorated since the brats left, in a fashion that's both handsome and highly sympathetic. Each of the 13 rooms, some of which overlook the castle or the river, is done out in a slightly different style; as a group, they're very much variations on the same crisp, plush theme. Downstairs, the public rooms are country-house posh; a new atrium holds an eating area that's more casual than the main restaurant (*see p239*).

Feathers

The Bull Ring, Ludlow, Shropshire SY8 1AA (01584 875261/www.feathersatludlow.co.uk). **Rates** £105-£185 double. **Credit** AmEx, DC, MC, V.
Possibly the most famous building in Ludlow, the crooked yet characterful Feathers looms down over the Bull Ring from the top of Corve Street; you can almost hear its 500-year-old timber frame creaking on windy days. The hotel looks small from the outside, but it actually comes with 40 rooms, spreadeagled across a network of corridors that extend over the adjacent shops. The decoration in the rooms is in tune with the building's heritage: rich, heavy and a bit ragged around the edges. A similarly opulent restaurant offers three-course dinners nightly; the adjoining bar, redecorated in eyebrow-raisingly modern style in early 2007, is rather less formal.

Jinlye Guest House

Castle Hill, All Stretton, Church Stretton, Shropshire SY6 6JP (01694 723243/ www.jinlye.co.uk). **Rates** £76-£84 double; £250-£335/wk self-catering. **Credit** (over £100) MC, V.
The address says 'Church Stretton', but this quaint old house is actually situated a fair distance above it, on the edge of Long Mynd and the sprawling Shropshire countryside. Long Mynd actually means 'long mountain', and the mountain does indeed stretch for seven miles. Enticing in summer and dramatic in winter, the location could scarcely be bettered, offering amazing views and terrific walking opportunities on every corner. The stone guesthouse, built as a crofter's cottage in the 18th century, does a fine job at living up to its location. All six rooms are individually decorated in handsome antique furniture with occasionally opulent touches; try Wild Moor, which comes with a characterful 17th-century bed complete with intricately carved headboard. From here, it's roughly 30 minutes by car to Ludlow.

FOOD FEST

Over the last decade, while a number of restaurants in the town have gone about turning fabulous local produce into a succession of Michelin stars, Ludlow's reputation as a foodie capital has grown. This part of Shropshire has remained an agricultural area, and the idea of good, locally produced food seems embedded in the fabric of the place. The small producers remain, cultivating their business from an array of small shops in the middle of town. But, as of 2007, they now have a little more competition.

Located a few minutes from the middle of town in Bromfield, the **Ludlow Food Centre** (01584 856239, www.ludlowfoodcentre.co. uk) has been three years and nearly £3 million in the making. Set up by the Earl of Plymouth Estates, on whose land it sits, and housed in a purpose-built complex next to the Clive (*see p235 and p238*), the centre is devoted to local food in general and food produced by farmers on the estates in particular.

In total, the centre will draw at least 80 per cent of its produce from the counties of Shropshire, Herefordshire, Worcestershire and Powys. Even the furniture that lines the main building is made nearby, created by Powys-based designer David Colwell using sycamore from the estates.

The focal point of the hugely innovative enterprise is a large food hall lined with eight glass-fronted workshops, where visitors can watch artisans working with foodstuffs brought in from the farms and elsewhere. The dairy will use milk from the estates to make cheese and ice-cream, for example, while a kitchen will take estate-farmed meat from the on-site butcher and create pies and other edible goodies. A café will be serving dishes created from these and other ingredients, and there are even classes planned. Says managing director Sandy Boyd, who set up the hugely successful farm shops at Chatsworth in Derbyshire before heading west to Ludlow, 'We want to make it accessible to as many people as we possibly can.'

Some small independents have expressed concern that the centre will adversely affect business. Boyd, however, hopes that the centre will complement the existing food shops.

Boyd aims to attract 250,000 customers a year – a sizeable number in a town with a population of under 10,000 and limited tourist infrastructure. But given Ludlow's engaged relationship with food, only a fool would bet against him.

Mr Underhill's

Dinham Weir, Ludlow, Shropshire SY8 1EH (01584 874431/www.mr-underhills.co.uk). **Rates** £135-£175 double; £195-£260 suite. **Credit** MC, V.
Tucked away behind the castle, this collection of buildings sits spectacularly on the banks of the swimmer-friendly River Teme, the weir causing the water to rush right around the operation's justly famed eaterie (*see p239*). To make the most of the space in the main house, hosts Judy and Chris Bradley engaged the services of a designer who usually works with the interiors of motor cruisers. The results are stylish and cultured, with specially made blonde wood furnishings and crisp white linens offering a lovely backdrop to the river views. The Shed is a capacious recent addition to the property, as is the two-storey, two-bed suite in the Miller's House across the road. Ten minutes away lies the Old School, a self-contained lodging house that opened in May 2007.

Moor Hall

Cleedownton, nr Ludlow, Shropshire SY8 3EG (01584 823209/www.moorhall.co.uk). **Rates** £50-£56 double. **No credit cards.**
This Georgian country pile, four miles from Ludlow, is the stuff of period romantic fiction. The view from every ivy-framed window resembles a landscape painting. And the public rooms – two sitting rooms, a dining room and a library bar – are pure *Country Life*, with ticking grandfather clocks, velvet curtains and paintings of nautical scenes. The bedrooms are comfortable but plain, but the real romance is in curling up with a book by the fire or walking by the lake or gardens. No children under ten.

Mulberry House

10 Corve Street, Ludlow, Shropshire SY8 1DA (01584 876765/www.tencorvestreet.co.uk). **Rates** £45-£90 double. **Credit** MC, V.
Located right in the heart of Ludlow, this discreet Georgian B&B is marked only by a small sign next to the front door. Inside, owners Anna and Robert Reed have decorated the sturdy property in an elegant style. Rooms are painted in eye-catching Georgian shades (Chinese blue, crimson, orchard green), with beds covered in plain white linen. Antique furniture and *toile de Jouy* fabrics add to the period feel. Breakfast is cooked with food acquired from the local butchers and bakers just up the road. No children.

Overton Grange

Old Hereford Road, Ludlow, Shropshire SY8 4AD (01584 873500/www.overtongrange hotel.com). **Rates** £130-£240 double. **Credit** MC, V.
Once fusty and traditional, this stately Edwardian house was recently subjected to a long-overdue makeover, eradicating the chintz and china dolls in favour of a plainer, more 21st-century look:

TOURIST INFORMATION
Ludlow
Castle Street, Ludlow SY8 1AS
(01584 875053/www.ludlow.org.uk).

white bedding offset by rich plums and silvery greys; tactile suedes, satins and velvets; and occasional retro touches. The rest of the house, from the oak-panelled breakfast room to the plush library, retains a pleasingly old world feel. The restaurant here has a good reputation.

WHERE TO EAT & DRINK

Between the market stalls, the specialist food shops and the restaurants, Ludlow's reputation as an unrivalled foodie destination is wholly justified. The town's highlights are detailed in full, but there are a number of other options worth further investigation. The Courtyard Café Restaurant (2 Quality Square, 01584 878080, www.thecourtyard-ludlow.co.uk) offers simple, stylish cooking (risottos, steaks, tarts and the like) in a pleasingly secluded location in the centre of town.

Good food is not limited to Ludlow. Outside the town there's a handful of pubs serve food that's a cut above the norm. Among them are the Crown Country Inn (Munslow, nr Craven Arms, 01584 841205, www.crowncountryinn.co.uk) and the more modern Roebuck Inn (Brimfield, nr Ludlow, 01584 711230, www.theroebuckinn.co.uk).

In addition to the watering holes listed below, both Ye Olde Bull Ring Tavern (The Bull Ring, 01584 872311) and the Wheatsheaf Inn (Lower Broad Street, 01584 872980, www.wheatsheaf-ludlow.co.uk) are decent spots in which to enjoy a pint or two. But drinkers should also consider a detour to the delightful town of Bishop's Castle, which boasts not one but two pubs with breweries: the Three Tuns (Salop Street, Bishop's Castle, 01588 638797) and the Six Bells (Church Street, Bishop's Castle, 01588 630144).

Unicorn Inn (66 Corve Street, 01584 873555, www.unicorninnludlow.co.uk) is a ten-minute walk from the centre of Ludlow, and this 17th-century pub was once considered to serve the best pub grub around. Sadly, it changed hands and since then things have slipped. We hope it can get its stride back.

Le Bécasse

17 Corve Street, Ludlow, Shropshire SY8 1DA (01584 872325). **Lunch served** 12.15-1.45pm Wed-Sat. **Dinner served** 7.30-9.30pm Tue-Sat. **Set lunch** £25 3 courses. **Set dinner** £42.50 3 courses. **Credit** MC, V.

Ludlow

Overton Grange

Originally opened as the Oaks in the 1990s by Ken Adams (now of the Waterdine, *see p239*), this unassuming Ludlow restaurant was taken over several years ago and became considerably more assuming. It was renamed Hibiscus by French chef Claude Bosi, who achieved a great level of renown (and two Michelin stars) for his sophisticated, adventurous cooking. Now, it's all change once more. In early 2007, Bosi decided to head to London and sold his restaurant to Alan Murchison, the chef at L'Ortolan in Reading. The handover and name-change were due to happen as the guide went to press, but this definitely looks like one to watch.

Bell Inn

Green Lane, Yarpole, Herefordshire HR6 0BD (01568 780359/www.thebellinnyarpole.co.uk). **Lunch served** noon-3pm, **dinner served** 6.30-11pm Tue-Sun. **Main courses** £13.50-£14.50. **Set lunch** (Sun) £11.50 2 courses, £14.95 3 courses. **Credit** MC, V.

Claude Bosi may have sold Hibiscus in Ludlow and followed the yellow brick road to London, but he's retained his interest in this tidy little pub in the nearby village of Yarpole. Bosi and wife Claire own the Bell, which is managed by Claude's brother Cedric. Mark Jones's menu applies a number of appealing twists – some of them quite substantial – to traditional English cuisine, ending up with a menu that's two-thirds gastropub and one-third French restaurant. From the list of starters, we enjoyed a twice-baked cheddar soufflé with tarragon mousseline; for mains, the pork belly was decent, but the steak and ale pie was a real knockout. Pleasingly, there's also a list of more straightforward food on the blackboards: soups, baguettes, even a ploughman's lunch. Local ales wash it all down nicely.

Church Inn

The Buttercross, Ludlow, Shropshire SY8 1AW (01584 872174/www.thechurchinn.com). **Lunch served** noon-2.30pm Mon-Fri; noon-3pm Sat; noon-3.30pm Sun. **Dinner served**

6.30-9pm Mon-Sat; 6.30-8.30pm Sun. **Main courses** £7.95-£10.45. **Rates** £60-£80 double. **Credit** MC, V.

Ludlow's best pub is also its most pleasingly old-fashioned. Set in the shadow of St Laurence's Church, it offers more ales than most livers can handle (including many local brews, all kept in beautiful nick) and an agreeably straightforward menu of pub food classics. While the Church definitely draws its share of visitors, it's a local pub above all else, albeit one in which interlopers are welcomed with cheery saloon-room banter. Keep an eye out for the fabulous nutcracker, permanently attached to the far side of the bar. A very easy place in which to lose track of an evening.

Clive Bar & Restaurant with Rooms

Bromfield, Shropshire SY8 2JR (01584 856565/www.theclive.co.uk). Restaurant **Meals served** 11am-11pm daily. **Main courses** £6.95-£15.95. *Bar* **Meals served** 11am-11pm daily. **Main courses** £7.95-£12.95. **Credit** AmEx, MC, V.

This large building provides wayfarers with 15 rooms (*see p235*), but the dining room is also popular with locals: on the damp February Thursday we visited, the two restaurant rooms were fully booked. The venue was redecorated in early 2007 to a crisp modern finish; you could pretty much say the same about the menu, which features over ten starters and twelve mains served all day. The ingredients are sourced locally where possible; we especially enjoyed the Wenlock Edge Farm ham, a kind of English prosciutto served with fig and melon. For mains, the braised and roasted rabbit was a little dry, but the seafood and fennel casserole was more engaging. Chocolate mousse with green tea ice-cream makes a pleasing end to the meal.

Crown at Hopton

Hopton Wafers, Cleobury Mortimer, Worcestershire DY14 0NB (01299 270372/www.crownathopton.co.uk). **Lunch served** noon-2.30pm Mon-Sat; noon-6pm Sun.

Dinner served 6.30-9.30pm daily. **Main courses** *Restaurant* £12.95-£22.95; *Bar* £6-£15. **Rates** £95-£115 double. **Credit** MC, V.
This ivy-covered, 16th-century coaching inn, a 20-minute drive from Ludlow, is a real sight for travellers' sore eyes whatever time they arrive. During sunny days, visitors can enjoy its marvellous setting in the heart of Shropshire's rolling countryside. And at night, its glowing, firelit windows are a truly cheerful prospect. There are 18 agreeable bedrooms upstairs, but the Crown is perhaps best approached as a countryside inn, particularly notable for its superior pub grub alongside its ranges of ales, wines and whiskies in the homely original building and newer extension.

De Grey's

5-6 Broad Street, Ludlow, Shropshire SY8 1BG (01584 872764/www.degreys.co.uk). **Meals served** 9am-5pm Mon-Thur; 9am-5.30pm Fri, Sat; 11am-5pm Sun. **Main courses** £4.85-£11.95. **Set Sunday lunch** 12.30-2pm; £13.95 2 courses, £17.50 3 courses. **Breakfast** £6.10-£7.35. **Credit** MC, V.
Beamed ceilings, copper pots and aproned waitresses provide a pleasingly old-fashioned ambience at Ludlow's famous tearoom, which boasts a history dating back to 1570. It's bustling almost every day: afternoon tea is the operation's raison d'être, but it also dishes up early breakfasts and is a hugely popular spot for lunch. The menu includes tempting own-made soups, fresh sandwiches, jacket potatoes and more substantial dishes (roasted confit of duck leg, for example); the medley of cakes, buns and pastries will break through the resolve of even the most determined dieters – though unfortunately, more recently, we have also received reports of stale cake and surly service. A shop at the front offers takeaway treats; there are also nine bedrooms.

Dinham Hall

By the castle, Ludlow, Shropshire SY8 1EJ (01584 876464/www.dinhamhall.co.uk). **Lunch served** 12.30-1.45pm, **tea served** 3-5.30pm, **dinner served** 7-8.45pm daily. **Main courses** (lunch) £14.50-£16.50. **Set dinner** £38.50 5 courses. **Credit** AmEx, DC, MC, V.
The restaurant at Dinham Hall offers an appealing complement to the hotel in which it's housed (*see p235*). Staff are keen to stress that the ingredients are sourced from local suppliers, which in itself means that the menu changes regularly as the seasons wind through the year. The nightly set menu generally offers a choice of four options for each course. A typical meal might begin with smoked pigeon breast served with fennel and coriander, moving on to loin of Gloucester Old Spot set on wilted savoy cabbage and glazed silverskins, and ending with warm sticky toffee pudding. Sadly, we've also had reports of unremarkable lunch served on bare cheap wooden tables in a back breakfast room without much outlook.

Koo

127 Old Street, Ludlow, Shropshire SY8 1NU (01584 878462/www.koo-ook.co.uk). **Dinner served** 7-10pm Thur-Sat. **Set dinner** £22.95 4 courses. **Credit** AmEx, MC, V.
Koo might strike an unexpected note in this most quintessentially English of towns, but it's by no means an inharmonious one. Tucked away at the bottom of Old Street, a five-minute stroll down the hill from the town centre, turquoise-tinted Koo is the town's sole Japanese restaurant, offering a steady selection of food in a room that's as colourful as it is cosy. The four-course menu offers a few choices, but ordinarily begins with a selection of sushi. Other courses might include tsukune (glazed chicken and sweet potato cakes) and buta yuanyaki (a marinated pork dish).

Mr Underhill's

Dinham Weir, Ludlow, Shropshire SY8 1EH (01584 874431/www.mr-underhills.co.uk). **Dinner served** 7.30-11.30pm Wed-Sun. **Set dinner** £45 7 courses. **Credit** MC, V.
The hotel side of this operation is very good (*see p236*). The Michelin-starred restaurant, though, is nothing short of exceptional. While Judy Bradley oversees proceedings in the comfortable dining room (long and thin, the tables at the end overlooking the river), husband Chris takes charge in the kitchen, compiling a daily changing, seven-course tasting menu with considerable elan. Highlights during our visit included a blissful foie gras custard layered with sweetcorn cream and a sesame glaze; a perfectly balanced medley of slow-roasted fillet of beef, ox cheek pie and roasted vegetables; and, for dessert, a wonderfully playful Highland parfait. The wine list is strong enough to keep pace with the meals at what is arguably the best restaurant in this most food-oriented of towns.

Waterdine

Llanfair Waterdine, nr Knighton, Shropshire LD7 1TU (01547 528214/www.waterdine. com). **Lunch served** noon-1pm Tue-Sun. **Dinner served** 7-9pm Tue-Sat. **Set lunch** £23.50 2 courses, £30 3 courses. **Set dinner** £30 3 courses. **Credit** MC, V. Bookings only.
In the mid 1990s, chef Ken Adams garnered an excellent reputation at the Oaks restaurant in Ludlow. After selling up to Claude Bosi, Adams and wife Isabel moved out to this storied old pub, constructed in the 16th century as a drovers' inn, and set about converting it into a restaurant with rooms. The three cosy bedrooms are pleasant and countrified, but it's the cooking that's the real draw: uncomplicated yet cultured, and achieved with a real lightness of touch. The menu changes daily, with many of the vegetables grown by Isabel in the grounds of the pub. We enjoyed melt-in-the-mouth veal sweetbreads with a gentle apple and hazelnut sauce; perfectly pitched venison accompanied by celeriac remoulade; a hearty yet not overwhelming rack of lamb; and a treacle and walnut tart with freshly made kumquat ice-cream.

Ludlow

Orford to Southwold

A peaceful (and fast disappearing) patch of English coastline.

The Suffolk coast was declared an Area of Outstanding Natural Beauty back in 1970 and, from the soft sands of Southwold to the misty quayside at Orford, the award is richly deserved. Blots on the landscape are few and far between, but even the imposing dome of Sizewell nuclear power station somehow fits in with the bleak but beautiful surroundings. Compared to most of southern Britain, the area is largely undeveloped. The vibe is more peace and quiet than Penny Falls, and nature is the big force – nowhere is this more apparent than in the crumbling cliffs and ruined buildings of Dunwich which, as Paul Theroux said, 'is famous for no longer existing'.

The area's brooding, atmospheric side is probably least noticeable during the height of the summer, when crowds frolic on Southwold's sand, and music lovers attend the Proms season at Snape Maltings. But if you ever happen to be in, say, Orford, on a biting winter's day, walking in the shadow of the commanding castle keep, past the fuliginous fug of the blackened smokehouse as the mist rolls slowly and silently in from the River Alde, you'll know you're somewhere pretty special.

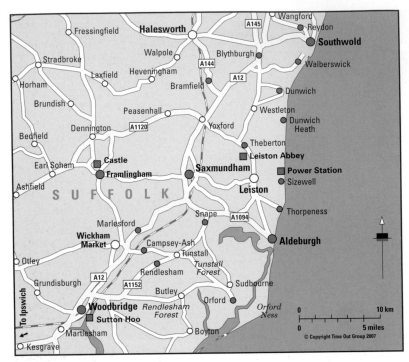

Woodbridge to Orford

There's plenty to explore along the Suffolk coast. Woodbridge, a few miles north-east of Ipswich, may be inland now, but this lively one-time shipbuilding port makes an agreeable introduction to the area. Stretching back up a hill from the River Deben, you'll find a scattering of minor sights (Woodbridge Tide Mill, the Suffolk Horse Museum, Woodbridge Museum), plus antiques shops, pubs and restaurants. St Mary's Parish Church is home to the heaviest bells in Suffolk as well as the Deben Millennium Frieze – a 20-foot embroidered depiction of Woodbridge history over the past 2,000 years. Near Woodbridge, the 12th-century Framlingham Castle (Framlingham, 01728 724189, www.english-heritage.org.uk) has its walls but no keep. It also has 13 towers linked together by a walkway and overlooking an impressive moat.

On the opposite bank of the river from the town is the site of the most celebrated archaeological find made in Britain, Sutton Hoo (01394 389700, www.nationaltrust. org.uk). Sometimes referred to as 'page one of the history of England', the fabulous treasure-stuffed ship of a seventh-century East Anglian king was discovered nearly 70 years ago by a local archaeologist,

having lain undisturbed for some 1,300 years. Reality gives way to replica these days, as most of the treasure is now in the British Museum, but some pieces are on display in the exhibition centre.

Between Woodbridge and the coast, the wind-whipped Rendlesham and Tunstall forests provide a barrier that only adds to the invigorating feeling of isolation in little Orford. Overlooked by the wonderfully intact keep of 12th-century Orford Castle (01394 450472, www.english-heritage. org.uk), which was built by Plantaganet King Henry II and offers stunning views from the battlements, the place offers walking, eating and drinking opportunities, and the chance to contemplate the immense expanse of Orford Ness (access information/ferry crossing 01394 450057, www.nationaltrust.org.uk), the largest vegetated shingle spit in Europe and a unique habitat for plants and birds. In

Accommodation	★★★☆☆
Food & drink	★★★★☆
Nightlife	☆☆☆☆☆
Shopping	★★☆☆☆
Culture	★★★☆☆
Sights	★★★★★
Scenery	★★★★☆

the 12th century, the then-nascent shingle spit provided a sheltered harbour for Orford. Unfortunately, it wouldn't stop growing (it grows about 50 feet every year) and it now all but cuts the village off from the sea. Boat trips run from the quay. Pick up picnic supplies from Richardson's Smokehouse (Bakers Lane, 01394 450103) or the shop attached to the Butley-Orford Oysterage (Market Hill, 01394 450277, www.butleyorfordoysterage.co.uk, *see p250*), and take a quick look at the Norman church of St Bartholomew – Benjamin Britten's *Noye's Fludde* (Noah's Flood) received its first performance here.

Aldeburgh to Dunwich

The next major settlement on the coast heading north is Aldeburgh, synonomous with Benjamin Britten and his creative and personal partner Peter Pears. The couple lived in the Red House in Aldeburgh from 1957 until their deaths in 1976 (Britten) and 1986 (Pears). Today, the house, where Britten wrote many of his finest works including the *War Requiem*, is open to the public. But perhaps the best way to capture the essence of Britten's relationship with Aldeburgh is to listen to the opera that established him as one of the country's leading composers. *Peter Grimes* is a wonderfully tortured vision of the corruption of innocence, but it also gives a real insight into man's relationship with the sea. As Britten himself said, he wanted 'to express

my awareness of the perpetual struggle of men and women whose livelihood depends on the sea'. Maggi Hambling's giant scallop sculpture on Aldeburgh Beach is dedicated to Britten.

Not many of Aldeburgh's residents now depend on the sea for their livelihood, though, with summer tourists swelling the coffers of this classy if slightly austere town. A stroll down the wide high street, which runs parallel to the water, will show that there's plenty of wealthy weekenders around. Palmer & Burnett (No.46, 01728 454698) is a lovely interiors shop selling funky gifts and homeware, and there are a couple of excellent delis: 152 – at No.152 (01728 454594, www.152 aldeburgh.co.uk) – and the Aldeburgh Food Hall at No.183 (01728 454535).

Constant erosion of the coastline means that Aldeburgh's current seafront is something of a jumble – it was never meant to face the waves. The oldest building in town is here – the 16th-century moot hall – as is a shiny modern lifeboat station and a popular boating pond. If you don't fancy eating at any of the town's excellent restaurants, then you could join the High Street queues at the excellent Aldeburgh Fish & Chip Shop (No.226, 01728 452250) or the Golden Galleon (*see p250*) and then take your booty on to the pebbly beach.

Heading back on to the A12 to Southwold, tiny Saxmundham seems to have more ironmongers than anything else, but is also home to the lovely Bell Hotel (*see p247*),

Aldeburgh Beach

Find Benjamin Britten's memorial, and a few whose lives still depend on the sea – on Aldeburgh Beach.

with rooms and food as well as Adnams ales. If you take the B1122 towards Southwold, you'll drive through the little village of Theberton (two miles north of Leiston). Its church, St Peter's, is worth a visit: it has a lovely round tower and thatched roof, and the entrance porch holds the remains of a Zeppelin airship that crashed nearby in 1917.

Thorpeness, a couple of miles north of Aldeburgh, is a surreal little place. With rows of black-boarded and half-timbered houses, it has the air of a Tudor theme village. The entire settlement was dreamed up as a fashionable resort by GS Ogilvie when he bought the Sizewell Estate in 1910. Go for a row on the Meare, dug by hand by navvies, and sprinkled with 20 islands named after characters in *Peter Pan* in honour of Ogilvie's friend JM Barrie. Ogilvie also created a well and used a windmill to pump water to a tank on top of an 87-foot tower, which he disguised as an overgrown house, known as the 'House in the Clouds'. This extraordinary folly is inhabited, so, unfortunately, cannot be visited, unlike the windmill (01394 384948, www.suffolkcoastandheaths.org). The Dolphin Inn (Peace Place, 01728 454941), which has rooms and a sizeable restaurant area, is good for refreshments.

A little further up the coast is the area's most controversial presence: Sizewell twin nuclear power stations. Apart from the legion of pylons striding across the coastal flats, the power stations are a low-key presence. The huge white dome of Sizewell B, the UK's only pressurised water reactor, is the most distinctive feature along this coast. There's a moderately popular beach by the power station for the truly blithe.

A few miles further north, Dunwich Heath (01728 648505, www.nationaltrust.org.uk) is a wonderful expanse of National Trust-owned land made all the more tempting by a slice of cake and a cup of tea in the tearooms, located in a row of old coastguard's cottages. The views from up here on the heath are spectacular, although Sizewell is the real landmark on the horizon. If you have the energy, head down the footpath to the beach and it's an hour's tough march along the shingle to Dunwich, although be warned: it's two steps forward, one step back.

It seems hard to imagine that tiny Dunwich was once a thriving port (*see p246* **Life on the edge**). Little evidence of its former glory now remains beyond the sparse ruins of Greyfriars Abbey and the salvaged remains of All Saints church and leper chapel in the churchyard of St James's. Don't miss the wonderful Dunwich Museum (St James Street, 01728 648796, open Mar-Oct), which tells the story of this strange place and,

together with a few cottages, a good pub (the Ship) and a seaside café, is all that remains of the town.

Southwold & around

The northern extent of this area is marked by Southwold. Like Aldeburgh down the coast, the invasion of the SHOs (second-home owners) has proved a mixed blessing for this handsome Georgian town. While the influx has proved profitable for the town and its independent shops and hotels (if you want a weekend room at the Swan or Crown, you need to think about booking months, not days, in advance), the summer traffic, both human and motorised, can be oppressive and locals are being priced out of the property market. Some put the SHO percentage as high as 60 per cent these days. Fortunately, though, nothing can dampen the spirits of the place and it is a truly magical spot to spend a few days, summer or winter.

There are two branches of stylish boutique Collen & Clare (25 Market Place, 01502 724823 and 33 High Street, 01502 724854, www.collenandclare.co.uk), where shoppers will find a good range of clothing, lingerie and accessories from the likes of Johnny Loves Rosie and Pringle.

The sandy and constantly improving beach now looks more South of France than Suffolk and beats Aldeburgh's shingle beach hands down, Hambling shell or no Hambling shell, and the range of eating and drinking options on the High Street is superb. For that you have to thank the town's most dominant force, Adnams, which owns the Swan, the Crown and several of the town's pubs, and also runs one of the finest booze shops in Suffolk.

The pier, which houses a wonderfully retro amusement arcade, is another plus with a curious water clock to amuse the kids. If the weather's bad, even better – a bracing stroll to the end of the pier, with the waves of the North Sea crashing beneath, is enough to clear your head after a few pints of Broadside the night

---

TOURIST INFORMATION

Aldeburgh
152 High Street, Aldeburgh, Suffolk IP15 5AQ (01728 453637/www.suffolk coastal.gov.uk).
Southwold
69 High Street, Southwold, Suffolk IP18 6DS (01502 724729/www. visit-southwold.co.uk).
Woodbridge
Station Buildings, Station Road, Woodbridge, Suffolk IP12 4AJ (01394 382240/www.suffolkcoastal.gov.uk).

before. Look back inland and you'll spot another of Southwold's most famous landmarks, the 100-foot-high lighthouse (01255 245011, www.trinityhouse.co.uk). For a small fee, you can climb the spiral staircase to the very top and survey the area it protects – although its role is now pretty redundant and rumour has it that the lights will go out in the not too distant future. Ah well, it'll make some SHO a lovely one-up, one-down.

During the summer, Southwold is a cultured hangout, with Jill Freud's theatre company taking up residence, plus endless circuses, fêtes and 'medieval fayres'. Another must is the 20-minute walk along the seafront or cross-country to the little rowing boat ferry over the River Blyth to Walberswick. The area along the Southwold side of the river is lined with attractive old fishermen's huts, and many sell their catch from here. One of the best is the Sole Bay Fish Company (01502 724241), which sells fish and shellfish.

With just ten yards from sea to plate, it doesn't get much fresher than this.

After a crab sandwich, hop on the ferry over to Walberswick, a picture perfect village that was once home to painter Philip Wilson Steer and now hides a selection of media luvvies. In addition to the excellent Bell Inn, the village also boasts a curious church-within-a-church. In the Middle Ages Walberswick was a sizeable port, and the original, 15th-century St Andrew's was to be a mighty church to reflect the status of the town. But the port's fortunes declined before the church was finished and much of it was dismantled to build the far smaller church that lies within the older building's ruins.

The blue riband event in Walberswick is the British Open Crabbing Championship, held every August on the banks of the River Blyth. The basic idea is simple – over a 90-minute period, and armed only with a single line and bait of your choice, the person landing the single heaviest crab wins.

LIFE ON THE EDGE

Apart from the lengthy queues outside Flora Tearooms, there's nothing to indicate that Dunwich was ever anything other than the sleepy village it is today – a single high street is all that remains of what was once East Anglia's second largest town outside Norwich.

In 1086, the Domesday Book recorded that Dunwich was home to 3,000 people, and by the 13th century it had 18 churches and boasted 80 trading ships, compared to Ipswich's 30. Up to 5,000 people lived within its walls, trading with the Baltics, Iceland, France and the Low Countries. Monasteries, hospitals, palaces and even a mint reflected the town's role as a busy trading port and one of England's major shipbuilding centres. But then the very thing that had made the town rich ripped its heart out, burying its success under mountains of sand and shingle.

The beginning of the end was in 1286, when a large storm swept much of the town into the sea and the Dunwich River was partly silted up. The end of the end came on the night of 19 January 1328, when an equally fierce storm swept some 400 houses and three churches into the sea. A quarter of the town had been lost and the remainder slipped into the sea during the next two to three hundred years.

For a glimpse of Dunwich's past, head out of the village towards Sizewell and walk along the cliff top. If you peer through the undergrowth, you can still spot the remains of the last gravestone in the graveyard of the now-submerged All Saints clinging desperately to the cliff edge. The rest of his fellow internees now lie quarter of a mile out to sea and it's said, on stormy nights, after a couple of pints of Broadside, you can hear the church bells tolling beneath the icy waves.

Southwold's beach huts

A fee of £1 is payable to enter, and all equipment (buckets, bait and line) is available on site for a small charge. Last year saw Rosie East walk away with first prize, beating off 700 competitors with a nipper weighing 5oz. For something a little more thrilling take a trip on the 12-seat *Coastal Voyager* (07887 525082), a high-speed rigid inflatable that zips along the coast on the 30-minute Sea Blast voyage.

Inland from Walberswick lies Blythburgh, a tiny village unfortunately bisected by the A12. The huge, light-suffused Holy Trinity church here is known as the 'Cathedral of the Marshes'. Its hammer-beam roof is decorated with 12 glorious painted angels, which probably escaped decapitation by iconoclastic puritans in the 17th century thanks to their naccessibility. Carvings of the seven deadly sins adorn the pew ends. Climb up the spiral stairs to the right of the exit to peek inside the impressive priests' room.

WHERE TO STAY

Demand for accommodation far outstrips supply on this part of the Suffolk coast, so book as far in advance as possible. If you're struggling to find a room, Saxmundham's Bell Hotel (31 High Street, 01728 602331), which dates back to the 17th century, has ten modest, reasonably priced rooms and is well located for Aldeburgh's overspill during the festival at Snape Maltings. Further up the coast, the Randolph in Reydon (Wangford Road, 01502 723603, www.therandolph.co.uk) has ten rooms and is within walking

distance of Southwold's many attractions a mile away. The classily made-over Victorian pub serves Adnams beer and is named after the brewer's friend Sir Randolph Churchill. Food is standard gastro fare.

Southwold's Acton Lodge (18 South Green, 01502 723217, www.visit-southwold.com/acton) is a popular B&B on the edge of handsome South Green with views of the sea or marshes towards Walberswick and Dunwich. Breakfasts are particularly notable.

In Woodbridge, the Crown Hotel (Quay Street, The Thoroughfare, 01394 384242, www.oldenglishinns.co.uk) is centrally located and offers 21 well-furnished rooms as well as a cosy bar and restaurant.

Right on the beach at Orford Ness is a Landmark Trust Martello Tower (www. landmarktrust.org.uk) where you can spend a weekend watching the waves crashing beneath your window.

In Aldeburgh, there are a couple of B&Bs that are worth a look, including Ocean House (25 Crag Path, 01728 452094), which has wonderful sea views and the solid and traditional Wentworth Hotel (Wentworth Road, 01728 452312, www.wentworth-aldeburgh.com), which has 30 rooms, a terrace, restaurant and bar.

Bell Inn

Ferry Road, Walberswick, Suffolk IP18 6TN (01502 723109/www.blythweb.co.uk/bellinn). **Rates** £75-£100 double; £100-£140 family room. **Credit** MC, V.

Walberswick's charms are no secret and the place can feel more like Hampstead than East Anglia,

Snape Maltings

but there's no denying the delight of the 600-year-old Bell Inn, situated towards the ferry crossing to Southwold. Atmospheric and rambling, with brick exterior and beamed interior, the Bell is all log fires and flagged floors, with six simple rooms, sea views and above-average pub grub. There's a family room for those who want to avoid the hurly-burly of the popular bar. Unsurprisingly, there's a two-night minimum stay at weekends.

Crown & Castle

Orford, Woodbridge, Suffolk IP12 2LJ (01394 450205/www.crownandcastle.co.uk). **Rates** £320-£420 double; £450 family (prices cover obligatory 2-night stay). **Credit** MC, V.
It's a long old drag to Orford from the Ipswich-Lowestoft main road, but in the case of the Crown there is light aplenty at the end of the B1084. This is a place where relaxation is a given, far from the madding crowds of Aldeburgh and Southwold, but enjoying the same stunning stretch of heritage coastline. In fact, in terms of sights, Orford offers rich pickings aplenty for such a petite place, with a handsome Norman castle and the eerie 12-mile Orford Ness shingle spit on your doorstep for rousing the appetite. Talking of appetites, food is right at the heart of the Crown's success – which comes as no surprise when you discover the place is run by food writer Ruth Watson and husband David – and local produce naturally features heavily, from Suffolk pheasant to Snape asparagus, plus a few choice local brews on offer. The relaxed vibe continues upstairs with bedrooms kitted out in cool, light paints and fabrics, with big comfy beds and power showers in the bathrooms. All in all, the perfect spot for a weekend's intense R&R.

Crown Hotel

90 High Street, Southwold, Suffolk IP18 6DP (01502 722275/www.adnams.co.uk). **Rates** £136-£166 double; £176-£206 suite; £156-£186 family room. **Credit** MC, V.
The Crown, which started life as a humble posting inn called the Nag's Head, is a pub, wine bar, restaurant and small hotel in one. Now owned and restored in pastel hues by Adnams, it's a smaller, cheaper and less classy sibling to the Swan (*see below*). There are 14 simply decorated but fully equipped rooms, some with exposed beams. Watch out for rooms at the back overlooking the car park, which can be noisy. Food is a strong point here although the bookings system leaves something to be desired. There is one small restaurant that takes reservations, but the Crown's USP is its more casual (but still fairly pricey) bar-restaurant, which operates on a first-come first-served basis. Fine on a Wednesday in winter, but on summer Saturdays the list often closes as early as 8pm, with the 30 people on the list confined to the cute but claustrophobic 'Back Bar' for the long wait. Fortunately, the gastro fare is almost worth the delay. Midweek break offers include meals in the restaurant (phone for details).

Laurel House

23 Lee Road, Aldeburgh, Suffolk, IP15 5EY (01728 452775/www.laurel-house.net). **Rates** £75. **No credit cards**.
Chintz-free Laurel House, a few minutes' walk from the seafront (or a minute's pedal if you borrow one of the house bikes) is a beautifully restored Victorian townhouse B&B owned by Cristina di Paola and Damian Risdon. The two bedrooms (one double, one twin), both with private bathroom, are laid out along simple, uncluttered lines, and an equally uncluttered breakfast awaits downstairs in the morning – fresh fruit salad, cereals, own-made bread and the like – to get you ready to face the elements. If the elements get the better of you, never fear: Cristina is also a qualified massage therapist (£38 per hour).

Old Rectory

Station Road, Campsea Ashe, Suffolk IP13 0PU (01728 746524/www.theoldrectorysuffolk. com). **Rates** £95-£120 double. **Credit** MC, V.
This elegant Georgian house, situated in the tiny inland village of Campsea Ashe near Woodbridge, has just eight rooms but plenty of character. Decor is tasteful: polished wood, pale furnishings, rugs, cushions and bright white linen. The excellent no-choice dinner (three courses for £28, served Monday through Friday) is particularly recommended. Breakfast the following morning is also good with a focus on fresh local produce (sausages and eggs come from nearby farms).

Swan Hotel

Market Place, Southwold, Suffolk IP18 6EG (01502 722186/www.adnams.co.uk). **Rates** £156-£186 double; £216-£246 suite. **Credit** MC, V.
A more expensive alternative to the Crown (*see above*), the self-assured Swan has long been the hub of Southwold social life, and deservedly so. There are 26 bedrooms in the main hotel and a further 17 garden rooms, all decorated in an understated version of country-house style. Bathrooms, though small, are modern and well equipped. Service remains great and the sea views (if you get a front bedroom) are superb. Continental breakfast is available in your room, or you can opt for the superior full English version served in the well-appointed dining room overlooking Southwold's market place. The food is a cut above, and the bar makes a less frenetic alternative to the Crown (*see above*) if you fancy a lighter bite. Therapist Tanya Bradbury also offers a fantastic range of Dr Hauschka facials, massages and other relaxing treatments. A class act.

WHERE TO EAT & DRINK

The best pubs in Southwold are those that allow alfresco spillover during fine weather. The best of the bunch is the wonderfully atmospheric Lord Nelson, between Market Hill and the sea. In summer, you can take your pint of Adnams to the seafront or sit in the walled patio out the back. In winter, the fire is lit and the atmosphere is intimate verging on crowded. The Red Lion has a prime spot looking down across Southwold's fancy South Green. Drinkers can sit at tables out front or laze on the grass with a pint of Broadside. Other options include the family-friendly, more foodie-oriented Sole Bay Inn, bang opposite the lighthouse, or the Lighthouse restaurant (77 High Street, 01728 453377), which offers reasonably priced food, with dishes such as crayfish and dolcelatte salad. Further inland, in Bramfield, the Queen's Head (the Street, 01986 784214, www.queensheadbram field.co.uk) has a great garden with plenty of seating and serves quality gastro food.

In Woodbridge, the Old Bell & Steelyard on New Street (No.103, 01394 382933) serves up a decent pint and steak and ale pie. The King's Head on Market Hill (No.17, 01394 387750) offers pub grub in either the bar or the dining room and serves a lovely pint of Suffolk cider.

In Snape, pubs that are worth a visit include the Crown Inn (Bridge Road, 01728 688324), which is good for food, and the Golden Key (Priory Road, 01728 688510). In Aldeburgh, one of the best hostelries is the tiny, friendly, locals-packed White Hart on the High Street. And don't miss out on a trip to the superb and well-positioned Bell Inn (see p249) in pretty Walberswick.

In addition to the restaurants and cafés given detailed reviews below, the Crown & Castle's (see p247) Trinity Bistro is worth a visit. It uses lots of local produce and serves adventurous dishes such as Orford-caught skate with brown shrimps, sautéed cucumber and nut-brown butter or roast Suffolk guinea fowl with butternut squash and saffron risotto.

In Aldeburgh, 152 (152 High Street, 01728 454594, www.152aldeburgh.co.uk) offers a contemporary fish-focused menu, while in Southwold, quirkily decorated Mark's Fish Shop (32 High Street, 01502 723585) does its bit for more traditional culinary tastes. Alternatively, head for Woodbridge and the Galley (21 Market Hill, 01394 380055, www.galley.uk.com) for modern dishes with a twist (chargrilled loin of pork coated with North African spices and own-made plum ketchup, for example) and great service.

Butley-Orford Oysterage

Market Hill, Orford, Suffolk IP12 2LH (01394 450277/www.butleyorfordoysterage.co.uk). **Lunch served** noon-2.15pm daily. **Dinner served** *Apr, May, Sept, Oct* 6.30-9pm Wed-Fri; 6-9pm Sat. *June-Sept* 6.30-9pm Mon-Fri, Sun; 6-9pm Sat. *Nov-Mar* 6.30-9pm Fri; 6-9pm Sat. **Main courses** £7-£14.50. **Credit** MC, V.

The fantastic Oysterage is not just a restaurant but also a shop, smoking house and HQ of a tiny fleet of fishing boats. From the freshest of local catches comes skate, sole, herring or sprats, and, of course, oysters from the creek, all of which make their way to the tables in the tiny, stripped-down dining room with the minimum of fuss or intervention. Most dishes from the blackboard menu – such as smoked trout with horseradish sauce or smoked mackerel with mustard sauce – are served simply, with bread and butter, new potatoes or a side salad.

Farmcafé

Main Road (A12), Marlesford, Suffolk IP13 0AG (01728 747717/www.farmcafe.co.uk). **Meals served** *Summer* 7am-5pm Mon-Sat; 8am-5pm Sun. *Winter* 7am-3pm Mon-Fri; 7am-4pm Sat; 8am-4pm Sun. **Main courses** £4.40-£8.40. **Credit** MC, V.

Many driving past this unprepossessing cream-coloured building set beside the A12 at Marlesford would not give it a second glance. Step inside, though, and you find a simple, compact space that leads on to a terrace protected against the elements, Parisian-style, by plastic walls and heaters, with chunky tables, modern art, stone floors and lots of touristy leaflets and local events posters. Breakfasts, lunches and cream teas are on offer and the focus is on local, organic produce. There's also a small organic farm shop attached.

Flora Tearooms

The Beach, Dunwich, Suffolk IP17 3DR (01728 648433). **Meals served** *Mar, Apr, Oct, Nov* 11am-3pm daily. *May-Sept* 11am-5pm daily. **Main courses** £5-£6.50. **Unlicensed**. **Corkage** no charge. **Credit** MC, V.

Drive through Dunwich village to the beach and you will reach the Flora Tearooms, a black, weatherboarded, shed-like building that looks straight on to the beach car park. On a warm summer's day the place is packed to the hilt with families queuing out of the door, all waiting for the magical fish and chips served inside. With its serried rows of plain tables inside and picnic sets outside, there is no denying that the Flora Tearooms is extremely basic. But it has been battering for day trippers and holidaymakers for years, touting a no-frills fish and chips menu of lemon sole, cod, haddock and plaice, with a few modern offerings like whole grilled brill or skate. If you're looking for a souvenir to take home, cast your eyes skywards – the walls and ceiling are draped with one of the most bizarre collections of tea towels this side of your grandmother's kitchen.

Golden Galleon

137 High Street, Aldeburgh, Suffolk IP15 5AR (01728 454685). **Lunch served** noon-2pm Mon-Fri; noon-2.30pm Sat. **Dinner served** 5-8pm Mon-Wed, Fri; 4.30-8pm Sat. **Meals served** noon-7pm Sun. **Main courses** £5.50-£7.50. **No credit cards**.

Excellent takeaways can be had here (and at sister chippie the Aldeburgh Fish & Chip Shop, *see p243*), but it's worth heading upstairs to the spick and span dining room. Here you can take your time over the splendid servings of fish, chips, mushy peas, bread and butter and cups of tea. All fabulous, and served with a smile. Our only complaint – the overly vinegary wally (gherkin).

Harbour Inn

Black Shore, Southwold, Suffolk IP18 6TA (01502 722381). **Lunch served** noon-2.30pm, **dinner served** 6-9pm daily. **Main courses** £8-£14. **Credit** MC, V.

After a long day crabbing or walking against the North Sea winds that whip along the beach, settle down with a pint of Adnams in this cosy harbourside pub with its atmospheric clutter-filled rooms. Fish and chips is the best choice here, and for traditionalists, Fridays means it comes wrapped in paper. For an indication of the awesome power of the sea, have a look on the wall outside – a marker shows the flood level during the storm of 1953.

Lighthouse

Find peace, and some fine dining, at the Crown & Castle.

77 High Street, Aldeburgh, Suffolk IP15 5AU (01728 453377/www.thelighthouse restaurant.co.uk). **Lunch served** noon-2pm Mon-Fri; noon-2.30pm Sat, Sun. **Dinner served** 6.30-10pm daily. **Main courses** £8.50-£15.75. **Credit** AmEx, MC, V.

Sara Fox and Peter Hill's culinary empire is the lynchpin of the town's impressive foodie scene.

Sara runs the acclaimed local cookery school (www.aldeburghcookeryschool.com), with day courses ranging from Men in the Kitchen to Shellfish, and the couple's daughter also owns the Munchies café further up the High Street (No.163, 01728 454566), serving tea, coffee and all-day snacks. The Lighthouse concentrates on daily-changing lunch, dinner and 'cinema' menus. Most of the food comes from the sea, and it is refreshingly unpretentious: potted Norfolk shrimps with toast and lemon or Lighthouse fish soup, followed by Lowestoft-caught skate wing with black butter and capers, new potatoes and vegetables, and boozy banana pancake to finish. Well, you're bound to have an appetite after all that sea air.

Ship Inn

St James Street, Dunwich, Suffolk IP17 3DT (01728 648219). **Lunch served** noon-3pm, **dinner served** 6-9pm Mon-Fri. **Meals served** noon-10pm Sat, Sun. **Main courses** £7.95-£12. **Rates** £50-£75 double; £75-£105 family. **Credit** MC, V.

If you fancy something a little more relaxed than the frying melee of the Flora Tearooms (*see p250*), then head for the Ship, a thoroughly laid-back pub on the village high street, which serves up excellent fish and chips, as well as other pub staples. But the real star here is the pub itself, with a characterful main room complete with lovely fire and very friendly staff, although if you have kids in tow you might end up in the fairly characterless dining room. The place also has a few simple bedrooms upstairs.

Bury St Edmunds
to Lavenham

Grand manor houses and classic country pubs
make up Suffolk's hidden charms.

Inland Suffolk may not top the list of many travellers' dream
destinations, but those who bother to make the trip are richly
rewarded. To be frank, the interior of the county is the part that most
holidaymakers drive through on the way to somewhere else. But while
it may not hold the obvious attractions of its neighbours – the Norfolk
Broads to the north, windswept coastal towns to the east, Constable
country to the south and Cambridge to the west – the lack of tourist
overcrowding makes its quiet charms and lovely scenery all the more
appealing to the discerning visitor.

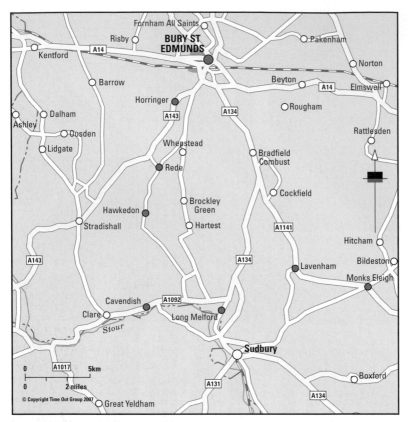

The county's very English, rolling landscape is characterised by narrow, twisting roads, isolated farms, small hamlets and patches of woodland, and you can go for hours without seeing a soul. There are signs of life – the occasional deer, a hare and plenty of pheasants – and the odd distant gunshot is a reminder that you're not entirely alone. It's perfect walking and cycling territory, especially for those not hugely enamoured of uphill slogs; even the laziest legs can cope with this landscape. You could compare it with the Cotswolds in some respects – but it's not as twee, and is more accessible from London and the south.

Chocolate-box villages

Rural tranquillity is the order of the day in Suffolk, and its villages are quiet, unassuming places. At the heart of many is a much-loved local pub; impressive 'wool churches', testament to the county's medieval wool-trade wealth, are common too. A few are just extraordinarily pretty,

with a handful of honeysuckle-clad cottages gathered round a sweet little village green. Away from Lavenham and Bury St Edmunds, A-roads naturally draw you towards Cavendish and Long Melford, if not for their rich pickings in antiques shops, then certainly for their good restaurants.

Leaving the beaten track brings surprises in the shape of thatched cottages in bright pinks and yellows. The multicoloured village of Hartest, for example, is set in as big a valley as you're likely to find in this part of the world; Hawkedon, on the other hand, feels like it's on top of

Accommodation	★★★☆☆
Food & drink	★★★☆☆
Nightlife	★☆☆☆☆
Shopping	★☆☆☆☆
Culture	★☆☆☆☆
Sights	★☆☆☆☆
Scenery	★★★☆☆

the world, but then its nearest neighbour is Rede – at 420 feet, it's the highest village in Suffolk.

These are places where history seems to ooze from soil and stone. Even the place names have a historical resonance: Latin, Saxon, Scandinavian and Norman French tongues inform the names of whole clusters of villages. The Romans left their mark in roads and numerous archaeological sites along the routes; the Saxon and, especially, Norman influences can be seen in ruined castles and churches. The Domesday Book recounts numerous manors and holdings in Suffolk, and there is no question that it was a hugely rich and powerful area for centuries, right up until the Industrial Revolution.

The wealth that was enjoyed here during the Middle Ages, when Suffolk was the centre of the woollen cloth-making trade, is manifest in churches such as those at Long Melford and Lavenham. The splendour of Elizabethan England is evident in such great manor houses as Melford Hall and Kentwell Hall, both at the northern edge of Long Melford and open to the public – though it's worth checking before your visit as opening days vary throughout the year. Melford Hall (01787 379228, www. nationaltrust.org.uk, closed Nov-Mar) is a red-brick turreted manor house where Queen Elizabeth I once dined in 1578, soon after it was completed. New points of interest include a tearoom and the Beatrix Potter Room, displaying watercolours and drawings by the famed author, who was a frequent visitor to the house (she was the cousin of the grandmother of the current owner). Melford Hall's neighbour, Kentwell Hall (01787 310207, www.kentwell.co.uk, opening times vary), is off the A134 between Bury St Edmunds and Sudbury, a bland but pleasant market town that's home to Thomas Gainsborough's House (46 Gainsborough Street, 01787 372958, www.gainsborough.org, open 10am-5pm Mon-Sat). Like Melford, Kentwell is another red-brick Tudor mansion, bought in 1971 and restored from a state of dilapidation by the Phillips family, who now use it as their home. It's widely known for its Tudor re-creations, but is worth visiting at other times too: kids will love the traditional farm, and the expansive gardens make for pleasant walks. With its moats, maze and camera obscura, it's sometimes

difficult to tell what's original and what's been introduced at the owner's whim, but who cares?

Bury St Edmunds

'A handsome little town of thriving and cleanly appearance.' This was how Dickens described Bury St Edmunds in *The Pickwick Papers*, and it's a succinct and accurate picture. In the early 19th century, Bury made its money from textiles. These days sugar and beer are the dominant industries (sometimes there's a noticeable whiff in the air), but the town still resembles a Victorian burgher – solid, upright and intolerant of decadence and disorder. On market days it's busy with hawkers and shoppers from all around, bustling through the pedestrianised grid of streets around Cornhill and the Butter Market. Prior to 1871, when the market was disbanded due to complaints of 'rowdyism', Bury's market used to stretch as far as Angel Hill, the gentle slope that runs parallel to the Abbey Gardens. The modern market is the largest of its kind in East Anglia, and takes place on Wednesdays and Saturdays. But when trading stops and the stalls have been dismantled, the streets are swept until they gleam, and an air of civic pride pervades.

It's a very welcoming town, with a helpful Tourist Information Centre (*see p254*) and a sedate, intelligent take on its past, which extends to the obvious efforts to preserve monuments and stop modernity from encroaching in too brash and inappropriate a manner. Let's hope things don't change too much with the opening of a new £100-million shopping development on the site of the former cattle market, which is due to be completed some time in 2009.

Bury grew up around the Benedictine Abbey of Edmund – medieval England's patron saint – and was from the seventh century onwards a place of pilgrimage. Its motto is 'Shrine of a king, cradle of the law', a reference to the oath sworn in 1214 by the barons of England in the abbey to force King John to accept the demands later enshrined in Magna Carta. Following the Dissolution of the Monasteries in 1539, much of the abbey disappeared, but its ruins can be seen in the well-groomed Abbey Gardens.

Also worth a mention is the annual Bury Festival. Held over two weeks in May (www.buryfestival.co.uk), it features art, music, dance, theatre, walks and more.

We're only here for the beer

Next to the abbey stands Suffolk's only cathedral, St Edmundsbury (01284 754933, www.stedscathedral.co.uk). Work commenced in 1510 and is only now reaching completion. The original building didn't include a tower because the adjacent abbey had several, but in 2005 work was finished on the 150-foot neo-Gothic lantern tower; the east cloisters, new Chapel of the Apostles and a crypt chapel were nearing completion as this guide went to press. On 12 November 2004 the cathedral became the place of pilgrimage for thousands of musicians and listeners attending the funeral of the DJ John Peel. He is buried in the nearby village of Great Finborough, where he lived and from where he broadcast many of his programmes.

The Abbey Gardens and cathedral are overlooked on one side by the ivy-festooned Angel Hotel, where Charles Dickens stayed, and at the far end by the Athenaeum assembly rooms, where he gave public readings. A little further along the road, directly opposite the end of Churchgate Street, is the Norman Tower. Built between 1120 and 1148, it is the most complete surviving building of the original abbey complex.

The highly informative Greene King Visitor Centre (Westgate Street, 01284 714297) provides an amusing reminder that Bury's monastic past wasn't all piety and servitude; the monks played a vital part in the town's beer-brewing heritage. Find out about the 700-year history of Greene King at the museum, and take a guided tour of the working brewhouse, which ends with a sampling in the tap room. Directly across the road is the Theatre Royal (01284 755127, www.theatreroyal.org), one of the oldest surviving theatres in Britain. Owned by the National Trust, this Grade I-listed building, built in 1819, is due to reopen in September 2007 following a massive £5.1-million restoration project. Subsequently, visitors will be able to appreciate its elegant Georgian interior with improved facilities.

Bang in the town centre is Moyse's Hall Museum (Cornhill, 01284 706183). Moyse's Hall dates from 1180 and claims to be the oldest surviving residential house in England. The truth about its origins are shrouded in mystery, but it has been a museum of archaeology and local history since 1899, and has an eclectic exhibition comprising local discoveries and donations. These include man traps, mummified cats and relics from the notorious Red Barn murder, for which William Corder was convicted and hanged in 1828.

Also worth a browse is the sweet Bury St Edmunds Art Gallery (Cornhill, 01284 762081, www.burystedmundsartgallery. org), just around the corner from Moyse's Hall on the Market Cross and housed in Robert Adam's only public building in the area. In addition to its regularly changing exhibitions, the museum has a small shop

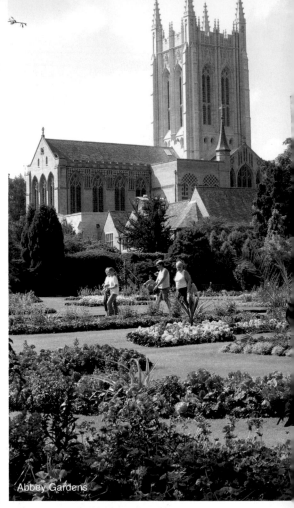

Abbey Gardens

with lovely one-off pieces (jewellery, textiles, glass, ceramics and prints) by local artists who have exhibited here.

A short drive from the town, Ickworth House (Ickworth, Horringer, 01284 735270, www.nationaltrust.org.uk) is a totally outlandish property whose construction was begun in 1795 by Frederick Augustus Hervey, fourth Earl of Bristol, to house his collection of fine art. The building was not completed before his death. The government took it over in 1956 in lieu of death duties and then gave it to the National Trust. Set in 'Capability' Brown parkland with a deer enclosure and a Georgian summerhouse, the main building houses paintings by Titian, Gainsborough and Velázquez, among others. The east wing is now a luxury hotel (see p258). The house and its Italianate garden are open from March to October; the park is open all year round.

Lovely Lavenham

The much-photographed medieval town of Lavenham is the jewel in Suffolk's crown. First awarded a market charter in 1257, for four centuries it grew rich on the wool trade. In the 15th century, Lavenham enjoyed a disproportionate share of the export market, and by the time of the tax assessment of 1523-26 it was listed as the 14th richest town in England, above more highly populated cities such as York and Lincoln. Wars in Europe in the first half of the 16th century saw a rapid decline in trade, and when the Industrial Revolution of the 18th century took cloth-making away to the hill towns of the north, Lavenham was left architecturally frozen in time. Many of its timbered buildings and halls date from the 14th and 15th centuries, when its wealthiest merchants were at their most confident and flamboyant.

The church, while lacking some of the charisma of the smaller village churches nearby, is a magnificent, imposing structure that rises up in black and grey flint and stone against the fields behind.

As with many local wool churches, a browse inside soon yields clues to the identity of the town's wealthiest merchants, who were undoubtedly hoping to secure themselves a place in heaven through investment in God. Lavenham's most noteworthy include John de Vere, Earl of Oxford, and Thomas Spryng III. De Vere's emblems, the star and the boar, are visible not only in the wooden carvings of the porch he paid for, but in the stonework of the church tower and along the roof. Spryng was responsible for the magnificent wooden screen that creates a private family chapel inside the church.

As visitors meander through the town, home to over 300 listed buildings, wondering at its remarkably untouched beams and crooked angles, only a very observant few will notice that telegraph lines have been hidden underground to preserve its character. The Tourist Information Centre on Lady Street (*see p254*) provides informative maps and pamphlets, or an Exploring Lavenham audio tour is available from Lavenham Pharmacy (3 High Street, 01787 247284, closed Sun

The medieval market town of Lavenham: the jewel in Suffolk's crown.

Jan-mid Mar). Head to the Market Place to look around the early 16th-century, timber-framed Guildhall of Corpus Christi (01787 247646, www.nationaltrust.org.uk), celebrated by architects as one of the finest medieval buildings in England. It houses exhibitions on local history and the woollen cloth trade, and has a walled garden with an interesting collection of dye plants; there are demonstrations of spinning and weaving on the loom most Thursdays. The neighbouring Little Hall (01787 247179, www.littlehall.org.uk, closed Nov-Mar) is a delightfully timbered building with lovely gardens, and offers further insight into the impact of wool money.

WHERE TO STAY

If you can afford the rates, look no further than the Ickworth Hotel & Restaurant (Horringer, Bury St Edmunds, 01284 735350, www.luxuryfamilyhotels.com), located in the east wing of a National Trust property and set in 1,800 acres of National Trust parkland. Vast rooms are ornately furnished with a mix of stately home grandeur and contemporary largesse, staff are helpful and friendly, and there are few family-friendly establishments that manage to cater to the different needs of children and adults quite as well as Ickworth. The self-catering apartments in the Dower House offer even more flexibility.

For romantic weekends à deux, try the highly acclaimed Great House (Market Place, Lavenham, 01787 247431, www.greathouse.co.uk). It's a restaurant (see p259) with rooms above – so if over-indulgence should get the better of you, you can simply stagger upstairs and sleep it off. Rooms are quirky but unmistakably luxurious, with sweet sloping ceilings and exposed beams in the attic room, and a majestic four-poster in room one; all five have en suite bathrooms.

The Bildeston Crown (High Street, Bildeston, 01449 740510), a timber-framed pub, is a perfect combination of the traditional and modern. All ten bedrooms have flat-screen TVs. One has a four-poster bed; others are funkier. Food varies from posh sarnies and fish and chips to dishes such as rabbit with tarragon gnocchi and capers or veal with truffle risotto.

For a straightforward B&B, try Folly House (Folly Lane, Whepstead, 01284 735207), which has two rooms – including a family room with a cot. There's a nice downstairs lounge for guests and lovely views over the surrounding countryside, but the pièce de résistance has to be the indoor heated pool (open Easter-Oct). In summer, there's a barbecue in the garden.

The Black Lion (see p260) and the Angel Hotel (see p261) also have rooms.

Swan at Lavenham

Lavenham Priory

*Water Street, Lavenham, Suffolk CO10 9RW
(01787 247404/www.lavenhampriory.co.uk).*
Rates £98-£128 double; £138-£160 suite.
Credit MC, V.
A stay at this award-winning historic house is definitely conducive to romance – if you're seeking to impress your beloved, you can't go wrong here. It's a Grade I-listed, timber-framed merchant's house with six splendid rooms, owned and run by Gilli and Tim Pitt. The whole place has been lovingly restored to its Elizabethan period look, with carefully sourced furniture and impressive attention to detail. Each room offers a different bed or bath experience – four-posters, slipper, claw-foot – nothing kinky you understand, just exquisite and bespoke. There's the Great Chamber, with its Napoleonic Polonaise bed and en suite slipper bath; the Painted Chamber, so-called because of the extant late medieval paintings on the walls and beams; and the Gallery Chamber, with its locally made cherrywood sleigh bed. The Priory Suite has its own staircase down to a private living room, where the floor has a small window revealing the underground stream below.

Thoughtful touches we particularly liked include sliding panels that allow fresh air to blow in through the original timber-framed windows, and the fact that tea- and coffee-making facilities in each room include herbal teas and a cafetière. At breakfast, guests can squeeze their own juice while they await the arrival of their full English, which comes with handmade Musk's Newmarket sausages. For further relaxation there's the lovely 13th-century Great Hall, as well as a cosy guests' sitting room. Need we go on? Perhaps just to add that you should book well ahead and beware of the 10.30am checkout.

Swan at Lavenham

*High Street, Lavenham, Suffolk CO10 9QA
(01787 247477/www.theswanatlavenham.
co.uk).* **Rates** £120-£160 double; £190-£230 suite. **Credit** AmEx, DC, MC, V.
There's no shortage of antique charm and character at the Swan, which is housed in a deceptively large and labyrinthine complex of half-timbered, 14th-century buildings. Its imposing Wool Hall, vast galleried dining room, oak panelling and chunky beams mean that you're always aware of its heritage. But this is matched by whitewashed walls, roman blinds and contemporary furniture that make the place swish and comfortable without being showy or stuffy. In the Old Bar, the walls of signatures and medals provide a neat homage to the American soldiers and pilots who were based near Lavenham during World War II. The Garden Bar is lighter, opening out on to the hotel's small and peaceful private garden.

Upstairs, low overhead beams mean you have to keep your head down in the corridors, but you can safely straighten up once ensconced in your room. The 'feature' rooms and suites are gorgeous, some with original medieval wall paintings and four-poster beds, but even the small rooms pack plenty of character. Notes: traffic noise can encroach, so ask for a quiet room if you're a light sleeper, and breakfast, served in the beautiful Gallery Restaurant, isn't always as it should be – the kitchen had run out of porridge, and the (good) pâtisserie wasn't compensation enough.

WHERE TO EAT & DRINK

Beer aficionados will do well in Bury – after all, it is the home of Greene King. Worth visiting for a swift half is one of Britain's smallest pubs, the Grade II-listed Nutshell (The Traverse, 01284 764867). For some light refreshment with more elbow room, try the Grid (34 Abbeygate Street, 01284 706004), where tapas-style snacks are served at outdoor tables in summer.

There are some fine independent eateries around these parts too. In Lavenham, the Great House (*see p258*) has been owned and run by Martine and Régis Crépy since 1985. (They're also behind the Maison Bleue in Bury St Edmunds, *see p261*). The main dining room is wonderfully atmospheric, with a huge fireplace and original beams. The food is full-on French fare, while the wine list leans the same way, with prices starting at a very reasonable £2.10 for a glass of house wine.

The Beehive (The Street, Horringer, Bury St Edmunds, 01284 735260) is a cosy, low-ceilinged gastropub with a well-balanced, daily changing menu. For a lighter meal, tuck into the cheese plate, accompanied by one of the wines from the well-chosen list. Over in Rede, the Plough (The Green, 01284 789208) is a traditional English pub with an extensive blackboard menu (fresh fish, grills, vegetarian options and light snacks); the choice of wines by the glass and well-kept ales deserve a mention too.

Angel Hotel

*Market Place, Lavenham, Suffolk CO10 9QZ
(01787 247388/www.theangelhotel-lavenham.
co.uk).* **Lunch served** noon-2.15pm, **dinner served** 6.45-9.15pm daily. **Main courses** £8.95-£16. **Rates** B&B (Mon-Sun, Fri) £80 double. DB&B (Fri & Sat or Sat & Sun nights) £245 double 2 nights. **Credit** AmEx, MC, V.
Conveniently located at the corner of the village marketplace, the Angel was first licensed back in 1420 and has seen the supping of many a pint. The bright, airy restaurant has windows along two walls, making it a lovely spot from which to watch the world by day, and a softly lit place to dine, drink and soak up the atmosphere in the evening. The room is a happily modern mix of pub and restaurant, with overhead beams, an open fire and a 1930s oak bar at its hub. There's a traditional touch to the food too: we tucked into an excellent lamb casserole with haricot beans and gleamingly fresh veg, plus a superior steak and ale pie with

Angel Hotel

diet-busting potato dauphinois. There are also fish dishes, vegetarian options and a couple of salads (the lunch menu features more salads, as well as lighter fare). The wine list includes a good range by the glass, and decent prices to boot. It's popular, so do reserve a table.

Black Lion

Church Walk, The Green, Long Melford, Suffolk CO10 9DN (01787 312356/ www.blacklionhotel.net). Wine bar **Lunch served** noon-2pm, **dinner served** 7-9.30pm daily. *Restaurant* **Dinner served** 7-9.30pm daily. **Main courses** £10.95-£19. **Set lunch** (Sun) £18.95 3 courses. **Rates** £120-£195 double; £135-£195 suite. **Credit** AmEx, MC, V.
You might want to skip the formal restaurant at the Black Lion and make a beeline for the relaxed bar area. The speciality here is satisfying, solid English fare (hare terrine with watercress salad and damson chutney, roast pheasant with bubble and squeak, rabbit casserole with Suffolk black bacon), with traditional old favourites such as haddock and chips, and sausage and mash. Award-winning head chef Annette Beasant uses plenty of local and seasonal produce in her cooking and is clearly very talented – all of the dishes we tried hit the mark. In warmer weather you can relax out on the pleasant terrace and gaze across at Melford Hall.

Crown

The Green, Hartest, Suffolk IP29 4DH (01284 830250). **Lunch served** noon-2.30pm, **dinner served** 6-9pm Mon-Fri.

Meals served 11am-9pm Sat; noon-8.30pm Sun. **Main courses** £5-£15. **Credit** AmEx, MC, V.
This Greene King pub is right on the village green of a beautiful Suffolk village. All the signs indicate it must once have been an authentic local country boozer, but over the years it's been transformed into a far more family-friendly proposition. Outside, a climbing frame and slide should keep the children amused while you enjoy a pint in the garden. Food is above the pre-prepared standard: choose from a huge range of dishes, from pies and steaks to fish and daily specials. But if you're looking for a quiet drink, best wait until the evening.

George

The Green, Cavendish, Suffolk CO10 8BA (01787 280248). **Lunch served** noon-2.30pm Tue-Sat; noon-3pm Sun. **Dinner served** 6.30-9.30pm Tue-Fri; 7-10pm Sat. **Main courses** (Sat dinner only) £10.95-£22.95. **Set meal** (Mon-Sat) £9.95 1 course, £12.95 2 courses, £15.95 3 courses. **Rates** £75-£95 double. **Credit** AmEx, MC, V.
Overlooking Cavendish's peaceful village green, this yellow-painted inn is idyllically located. Inside, medieval features – authentically worm-eaten beams, timbered walls hiding daub and wattle, and an old stone fireplace – are artfully blended with contemporary modern art, antique shop finds and tasteful, neutral colours. In the daytime, the lighter lunchtime menu might include halloumi and aubergine salad or a giant portion of fish of the day accompanied by chunky chips; in the evenings, it all becomes a bit smarter. The focus, says the owner, is 'good,

Set lunch (Tue-Fri) £15 2 courses.
Set dinner (Tue-Thur) £15 2 courses.
Credit AmEx, MC, V.
Take no heed of the old-fashioned decor, and concentrate on the menu instead. It too can seem as if it was devised in the 1970s (mushroom stroganoff, anyone?), but there are some interesting twists, and of several meals here, we've only seen a couple of less-than-stellar results. For starters, sesame prawn toasties with soy dip are ethereally light, while mains range from calf's liver with bacon (cooked to perfection) to scampi tempura with chips (a tad greasy, but featuring top-quality fish). Save room for dessert and you won't be disappointed: crème brûlée with sour cherries is a boozy delight. The wine list has some pricey options, but also plenty of affordable surprises, including a stunning Colchagua Valley merlot from Chile. Even with plenty of local competition, this place stands out from the crowd.

Swan

*The Street, Monks Eleigh, Suffolk IP7 7AU
(01449 741391/www.monkseleigh.com).* **Open** noon-3pm, 7-11pm Wed-Sun. **Lunch served** noon-2pm, **dinner served** 7-9.30pm Wed-Sun. **Main courses** £9-£15. **Credit** MC, V.
From the outside, the Swan is a textbook 16th-century English country pub. Inside, however, it's another story. The pub's interior has been modernised on an open plan, and the polished wood floor and contemporary lighting are definitely more restaurant than hostelry. But it's still a fine place for a drink, with excellently kept Adnams ales on tap. Chef Nigel Ramsbottom – who previously worked at the famed Walnut Tree in Abergavenny – cultivates a network of small producers to supply his strictly seasonal menus. Starters might include smoked whole king prawns with lemon mayonnaise or lightly curried parsnip soup, while mains could be whole roast sea bass with ginger coriander butter or roast pork loin. This is straightforward cooking that makes the most of the chef's skill, technique and perfect timing, and prices are reasonable too.

Tickled Pink Tearooms

*17 High Street, Lavenham, Suffolk CO10 9PT
(01787 248438).* **Meals served** 10.30am-5pm daily. **Main courses** £3-£5.95.
No credit cards.
A delightfully olde-worlde atmosphere and friendly service attract a steady stream of tourists and locals to these spotless tearooms. The two-storey, 16th-century premises are on the small side, though there are also a few tables outside. Food choices cover the basics: choose from a selection of sarnies, salads, soups and spuds. This place's real forte, though, is own-made cakes – chocolate, carrot and St Clements (oranges and lemons, of course). If all that sightseeing has taken its toll, go the whole hog and enjoy a full cream tea. There's even rumoured to be a ghost on site, though there was no sign of him when we last visited.

wholesome British food with a twist'. It may have all the accoutrements of a smart country restaurant, but you can just call in for a relaxed pint if you'd rather.

Maison Bleue

30-31 Churchgate Street, Bury St Edmunds, Suffolk IP33 1RG (01284 760623/www.maison bleue.co.uk). **Lunch served** noon-2.30pm Tue-Fri; noon-2pm Sat. **Dinner served** 7-9.30pm Tue-Thur; 6.30-10pm Fri, Sat. **Main courses** £9.95-£27.95. **Set lunch** £13.95 2 courses, £15.95 3 courses. **Set dinner** £23.95 3 courses. **Credit** AmEx, MC, V.
Something of a local institution, thanks to its efficient and well-informed French staff, excellent reputation for fresh fish, and chic but unpretentious interior. Although Maison Bleue bills itself as a seafood restaurant – oysters, prawns, scallops, tuna, monkfish and more are all present and correct – the meat dishes are no slouch, and there's also a vegetarian option. Everything we tried was excellent, even from the great-value set lunch menu (if you're on a budget the wine list will please too, with house white and red coming in at a tenner). Puddings tip a nod to British classics as well as French. Cooking, presentation, service: all exude a well-founded confidence. *See also p258 Great House.*

Scutchers of Long Melford

Westgate Street, Long Melford, Suffolk CO10 9DP (01787 310200/www.scutchers.com). **Lunch served** noon-2pm, **dinner served** 7-9.30pm Tue-Sat. **Main courses** £15-£20.

North Norfolk coast

Wild coastal scenery that doesn't fall flat.

It was Noel Coward in *Private Lives* who labelled (some might say libelled) Norfolk as 'very flat'. In doing so he was dismissing an area that, at 2,067 square miles, is England's fifth-largest county and ranges from the (OK, less than mountainous) Fens in the west to the watery thoroughfares of the Broads in the east, and includes scores of unspoilt villages and myriad acres of untrampled countryside.

Some of the wildest, most exhilarating scenery is to be found on the north Norfolk coast, much of which has been designated an Area of Outstanding Natural Beauty.

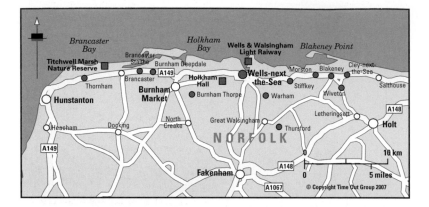

The stretch of salt marshes, creeks and windswept sandy beaches is renowned for its bird life, and draws spotters and walkers from across the UK and beyond. There's plenty here for the lover of history too. From the Middle Ages until the Industrial Revolution (which largely bypassed it), Norfolk was one of the country's most prosperous and populous counties. Evidence can be found in the wealth of ecclesiastical architecture that remains: almost all of the county's many little villages boast a church that's worth a second look.

Even if all you're after is a cosy retreat from urban life, the Norfolk coast has few equals. The area's isolation has meant that its hostelries have had to strive hard for custom. In the past decade the quality of both food and drink has soared – whether it be beer brewed from Norfolk barley (try Woodforde's prize-winning ales), Cromer crab with samphire freshly picked from the salt marshes, Brancaster mussels or locally smoked North Sea herring. In winter there's a wealth of game, with hare, pheasant and venison (perhaps from the Queen's herd at Sandringham) making frequent appearances. For a selection of the best places to find Norfolk-grown food, see p270 **Consuming passions**).

It is the sea, however, that remains one of the biggest draws to the area. The trick when visiting the coast is to know your tides. At low tide, the 'beaches' on the Wash (Snettisham, Heacham) are mere mud flats; from Hunstanton to Wells, you'll get vast expanses of sand and need binoculars to see any waves; yet at points east of Weybourne (including the resorts of Sheringham and Cromer), low tide is prime time, when, as well as pebbles, you'll get a couple of hundred yards of castle-builder's sand before the sea.

At high tide, the Wash becomes quenched, Wells Beach dramatically reduces in size (sirens sound to warn bathers against being cut off on the dunes), while crabbing boats flood into the harbour to unload their snapping cargo. At high tide, too, the sand at Weybourne, Sheringham and Cromer is completely covered and only pebbles remain on view, though in winter you might enjoy an absolutely spectacular windswept walk, scored to the crashing of waves against the sea defences.

Links to the local tide tables can be found at http://new.edp24.co.uk and www.lynnnews.co.uk. Times of high tides are also published on Fridays and Tuesdays, on page two of the *Lynn News*, and from Monday to Saturday on page two of the *Eastern Daily Press* – both newspapers (costing 50p and 45p respectively) are sold at most local shops and newsagents.

It's certainly worth ordering a copy of Friday's *Eastern Daily Press* (known locally as the *EDP*) if you plan to stay for a weekend. This publication outsells all the national dailies in Norfolk and is full of quirky nuggets about life in the county. Friday's issue contains a weekly events guide, an excellent compendium of village fêtes, country and western dances, gigs, pantos, attractions and exhibitions taking place throughout Norfolk. Friday's issue also contains the property section – worth noting should you be smitten with life here.

Below we've described the highlights to be found on the most beautiful section of the north Norfolk coast. The winding A149 between Thornham and Cley (little more than a lane in places, and slow-going in the August high season) goes through several attractive villages, though you'll find yet more enticements just off it – from picturesque fishermen's cottages and hidden-away harbours on the seaward side, to quiet hamlets and rolling countryside inland. Yes, including hills.

Thornham to Burnham Market

Head east along the A149 from the bucket-and-spade bustle of Hunstanton and you soon reach a wilder stretch of coastline. Thornham is a typical village of this area, hugging the main road. Small cottages of clunch, reddish-brown carstone and knapped flint can be seen on the High Street (the A149), but if you take the little road north, down Station Lane (which becomes Staithe Lane), you'll cross the Peddars Way and Norfolk Coastal Path. This ancient route can be followed west for a two-and-a-half-mile hike along the salt marshes (with the sea visible in the distance) to the little village of Holme-next-the-Sea, but you can also pick up the coastal path at many villages east of here.

Continuing along the A149, you next encounter the village of Titchwell, home of the Titchwell Marsh Nature Reserve (01485 210779, www.rspb.org.uk), a wetland reserve run by the Royal Society for the Protection of Birds. On the lagoons and foreshore, winter visitors include dunlins and bar-tailed godwits, Brent geese, teals and widgeon, while avocets, sedge warblers and marsh harriers can be spotted in summer. The RSPB runs a visitor's centre, shop (stocking birdwatching paraphernalia) and a café; there's a charge for parking.

Beach-lovers should continue along the A149 to Brancaster. Turn north down Broad Lane until you reach a car park (charge payable). The beach – a huge expanse of sand past a hotel, beach kiosk and golf course – is one of Norfolk's best, and even in summer you don't have to walk far to have the place virtually to yourself. The currents, however, can be treacherous.

Brancaster is famous for its mussels, and during the season (when there's an 'r' in the month), bags of tender little bivalves are sold from fishermen's cottages in Brancaster Staithe. Small boats litter the silted-up inlets of the harbour; only at high tide can they make their way out to sea. The coastal path runs along the harbour, and you can walk across the marshes a mile to Burnham Deepdale, where there's an interesting new daytime-only eaterie on a parade of shops off the A149 – the Deepdale Café (01485 211055, www.deepdalecafe.co.uk), with great-value food ranging from enticing sandwiches to roast Sunday lunches and specials such

Sheringham

Wells Beach

as fig, parmesan and red onion frittata, or a selection of tapas. From Deepdale, it's worth making a detour a couple of miles inland (by car) to Burnham Market.

In the 13th century, the River Burn was navigable by seagoing boats as far as Burnham Thorpe, now almost three miles inland. Silting of the river led to a decrease in the commercial importance of the clutch of villages known as the Burnhams, but in the past 20 years there's been a curious and profound transformation in the fortunes of the largest of these villages, Burnham Market, a handsome old place with a long, tree-lined green at its centre. Perhaps encouraged by the success of the area's first gastropub, the Hoste Arms (*see p272*), affluent newcomers – many from London and the home counties – started buying up Burnham's beautiful old houses for use as second homes. The consequences have been mixed for the area. Here, more than anywhere else in the county, locals have been priced out of the market and the Norfolk accent is rarely heard. Yet the newcomers' money has allowed some of the county's most interesting shops to flourish. High-quality food is a highlight. Gather the ingredients for a picnic at the first-class deli Humble Pie (Market Place, 01328 738581), the traditional baker's W Groom (Market Place, 01328 738289) and Satchells Wines (North Street, 01328 738272). Gurneys Fish Shop (Market Place, 01328 738967) is great for smoked fish, while non-food treats include two bookshops – Brazen Head (Market Place, 01328 730700) for second-hand books and

White House (Market Place, 01328 730270) for new books and maps – plus various clothes, antiques and gift shops.

Burnham Market to Wells

Burnham Thorpe, a mile and a half inland from Burnham Market, is a tiny village most notable for being the birthplace of Horatio Nelson. Nelson held a farewell party at the pub (now called the Lord Nelson, *see p275*) before returning to sea in 1793.

From here, it's best to head for the B1155 to rejoin the coast road, which you reach just west of Holkham. The land for miles around this area is owned by the Coke family, the Earls of Leicester. Holkham Hall, their stately pile (rebuilt in the Palladian style during the 18th century), is open on selected days in summer (01328 710227, www.holkham.co.uk), though the gardens stay open longer. Holkham also has a beach, a pleasant sandy inlet reached on foot from the car park (pay and display) through pine woods. It's best to visit near high tide.

Less than two miles east of Holkham is the little town of Wells-next-the-Sea, which manages to cram in a beach resort, fishing port, picturesque shopping street and leafy green within its small circumference. The 'Burnham Market effect' has only recently had an impact here, so although there's fine dining at the Crown Hotel (*see p274* Where to Eat & Drink) and Italianate foodstuffs at the Wells Deli by the quay (15 The Quay, 01328 711171, www.wellsdeli.co.uk), there are also old-fashioned independentshops – a butcher's, a baker's, a fishmonger's and a hardware store – along the Staithe, a narrow high street that runs uphill from the quay. Crab fishing from the quay is a popular pastime; buy the wherewithal (line, bait, bucket and net cost less than £5) from ML Walsingham & Son (78 Staithe Street, 01328 710438), about 100 yards up from the quay (this shop also hires out bicycles). While on the quay, take a look at the Albatross (07979 087228), a large sailing vessel built in Holland in 1899. Below decks you'll find a cosy (if rough round the edges) bar where savoury and sweet Dutch pancakes are served. On-board accommodation is available too.

The sandy beach is a mile away from the town (there's a pay-and-display car park near the beach). Come at high tide or you'll have a long walk to the water. The other main local attraction is off the A149 just to the east of town. The Wells & Walsingham Light Railway (01328 711630, www.north norfolk.co.uk/walsinghamrail) operates a narrow-gauge steam locomotive to the beautiful village of Little Walsingham (30 minutes). Walsingham has been an important place of Christian pilgrimage for nigh-on 1,000 years; devout members of the Catholic and Orthodox churches are still drawn to the (rebuilt) shrine of Our Lady of Walsingham. Half-timbered medieval buildings are plentiful along the narrow streets, and there are enough tearooms, gift shops (religious souvenirs

a speciality) and pubs to fill an afternoon before you catch the train back to Wells. With the 2006 opening of the Walsingham Farms Shop (see p270 **Consuming passions**), you can stock up on first-class local food here too; the same partnership also runs a great new fish and chip restaurant, the Norfolk Riddle (2 Wells Road, Walsingham, 01328 821903). There's Norfolk apple juice, cider and beer on the drinks menu and fabulous bread and butter pud for afters.

To walk off your meal, head for the ruins and peaceful gardens of Walsingham Abbey; they're particularly popular in February for snowdrop walks (details from Walsingham Tourist Information Office, see p264).

Wells to Cley

The coast road gets narrower east of Wells as it goes through the little villages of Stiffkey (pronounced 'Stukey' by locals) and Morston. Look out for seasonal produce sold from roadside cottages: mussels, oysters, honeycomb and samphire. Stiffkey's pub, the Red Lion (44 Wells Road, Stiffkey, Wells-next-the-Sea, 01328 830552, www.stiffkey.com) is worth a look-in for its beers (Woodforde's Wherry, straight from the barrel), its food (featuring local ingredients), and its views across to the River Stiffkey. Pub-lovers should also make a little detour inland to the west of Stiffkey to pay homage to the Three

Burnham Market

Take a tip from the Blakeney Point seals, and just relax.

Horseshoes at Warham (69 Bridge Street, Warham All Saints, Norfolk NR23 1NL, 01328 710547), which has a classic old interior as well as well-kept ales, decent food (pies a speciality), and accommodation.

Trips to view the seals at Blakeney Point are run from Morston quay (contact Bean's Boats, 01263 740038, www.beansboat trips.co.uk; or Temple's Seal Trips, 01263 740791, www.sealtrips.co.uk), though we'd recommend continuing on to the idyllic coastal village of Blakeney, which is peacefully sited well off the main road. The sea proper can be seen in the distance, but the creeks leading to the quay fill at high tide and motor boats (run by Bean's, *see p269*) carry passengers out to the spit of land where a sizeable colony of seals can be viewed at surprisingly close quarters. Trips cost £7.50 (£4 under-14s). Hardy souls can take the two-and-a-half-mile hike from Blakeney along the coastal path and back inland to Cley.

Just to the east of the pay-and-display car park at Blakeney quay, there's a large duck pond that's home to many colourful species of wildfowl. Across the road are the vaulted cellars of the 14th-century Guildhall (admission free), which, in the 19th century, were used as a mortuary for drowned mariners.

Blakeney's two narrow streets down to the quay contain a handful of shops, pubs and restaurants, including a deli and a fishmonger's. However, if you're after local delicacies to take home, continue along the A149 to Cley-next-the-Sea, home of the Cley Smokehouse and Picnic Fayre (*see p270* **Consuming passions**). Cley can also

be used as a base for hikes. The energetic should take the lane east of the village down to the shingle beach (about half a mile; there's a paying car park) and from there it's possible to trek to Blakeney Point (four miles there and back). Keep a seaward eye out for seals along the way. A more leisurely stroll starts from Church Lane (off the A149 by Picnic Fayre) and runs past Cley's impressive church. This was built in the 13th century, when the village was a prosperous port; don't miss the stunning south porch, with its traceried battlements and fan-vaulted roof. Continue for half a mile along the serene Glaven valley to Wiveton and the welcoming Bell pub (Blakeney Road, Wiveton, 01263 740101, www.wivetonbell.co.uk), where John and Lucy Olsen give pub food a Danish tweak, and serve Adnams and Woodforde's ales.

WHERE TO STAY

Many of the pubs featured in Where to Eat & Drink (*see p274*) also have rooms.

The Lifeboat Inn (Ship Lane, Thornham, 01485 512236, www.lifeboatinn.co.uk) is a pleasantly ramshackle old pub with rooms, serving a crowd-pleasing bar menu (bowls of mussels, fish and chips) alongside real ales; dogs, kids, muddy boots – all are welcome.

George Hotel

High Street, Cley-next-the-Sea, Norfolk NR25 7RN (01263 740652/www.thegeorgehotelcley. com). **Lunch served** noon-2.15pm Mon-Fri; noon-2.30pm Sat, Sun. **Dinner served** 6.30-

CONSUMING PASSIONS

It's not often that Norfolk finds itself at the forefront of a national movement, but blessed as it is with a wealth of indigenous produce, the county is now one of Britain's most enticing places in which to indulge in a spot of food tourism. Visiting one of the several specialist food and drink shops near to the coast, or better still wending your way to the door of the producer, is a rewarding way of exploring the area.

What you can purchase will be determined by your accommodation and travelling plans, of course. Keeping a bag of mussels in the boot of your car for a few days is not feasible. But seafood isn't precluded to those staying at hotels; head for the Cley Smokehouse to find a variety of marine life preserved by the age-old process of smoking – much of it suitable for picnic food or for taking back home on the final day of your stay. This modest-sized shop is famous for turning North Sea herring into buckling, kippers, bloaters and red herring; it also smokes eel, cod's roe, trout and haddock, and sells fresh-dressed crab, fish pâtés and potted brown shrimps. While in Cley, you can buy everything else you might need for an outdoor feast at Picnic Fayre – from local cheeses such as binham blue to specialist breads, cakes and the shop's own range of jams and chutneys.

During the summer, rippling vistas of golden-hued barley can be seen throughout Norfolk. Some of this crop helps feed the county's burgeoning microbrewery sector. You'll find more than 40 locally brewed beers – from nine breweries including Woodforde's of Woodbastwick and the Humpty Dumpty Brewery of Reedham – at the Real Ale Shop, based in a farm just off the B1105, two miles inland from Wells. Alternatively, if cider is your tipple, visit Whin Hill Cider's shop, bar and cider-works, sited in an 18th-century barn in Wells' main car park, just west of the Ark Royal pub. Here you can sample the firm's apple juice, cider and perry – either by the glass or in bottled form.

One of Norfolk's latest foodie hotspots is the medieval village of Little Walsingham. In 2006, several neighbouring farms got together to form a partnership dedicated to promoting the produce they had grown or reared. The Walsingham Farms Shop was duly opened in July 2006 in a converted barn. It's an astoundingly well-stocked place, featuring not only the raw materials (quails' eggs, honey, fruit, vegetables and various cuts of meat – with posters detailing the history of each farm), but a counter full of choice pies, quiches and even ready-meals, cooked using these ingredients. In addition, the shop stocks top produce from all over Norfolk: Narborough smoked trout, flour milled at Letheringsett Water Mill, apple juice from the Royal Fruit Farm at Sandringham, smoked norfolk dapple cheese, dairy goods (milk, ice-cream, yoghurt) from Pointens of Stody, and dozens of other local foodstuffs. In one of the out-buildings to the main shop, the Chocolate Deli makes and sells a tempting range of chocolates, including a selection incorporating Walsingham honey.

The current Earl of Leicester has done much to promote Norfolk produce, culminating in the opening of the Marsh Larder of Holkham, situated in the grounds of his stately home, Holkham Hall. Here you can buy venison and game from the Holkham Estate, as well as various locally sourced comestibles such as Mrs Temple's warham cheese with mustard seed, and tomato ketchup and pickles from Channel's Norfolk Preserves. There's also a small café on the site, and a kitchenware and wine shop run by Adnams Brewery.

Finally, if you're keen on meeting Norfolk's food producers in situ, try to get a copy of the Local Products Directory (last published 2005) available from the Tourist Information Centre. The Directory, which can also be downloaded at www.norfolkcoast aonb.org.uk, is an invaluable source for all hunters and gatherers.

CHOCOLATE DELI
Guild Street, Little Walsingham, Norfolk NR22 6BU (01328 820100/www.thechocolatedeli.co.uk).

CLEY SMOKEHOUSE
High Street, Cley-next-the-Sea, Norfolk NR25 7RF (01263 740282/www.cleysmokehouse.com).

MARSH LARDER OF HOLKHAM
Ancient House, Main Road, Holkham, Wells-next-the-Sea, Norfolk NR23 1AD (01328 711285).

PICNIC FAYRE
The Old Forge, Cley, Norfolk NR25 7AP (01263 740587/www.picnic-fayre.co.uk).

REAL ALE SHOP
Branthill Farm, Fakenham Dry Road (B1105), Wells-next-the-Sea, Norfolk NR23 1SB (01328 710810/www.therealaleshop.co.uk).

WALSINGHAM FARMS SHOP
Guild Street, Walsingham, Norfolk NR22 6BU (01328 821877/www.walsinghamfarmsshop.co.uk).

WHIN HILL CIDER
The Stables, Stearman's Yard, off Freeman Street, Wells-next-the-Sea, Norfolk NR23 1BW (01328 711033/0776 957 1423/www.whinhillcider.co.uk).

North Norfolk coast

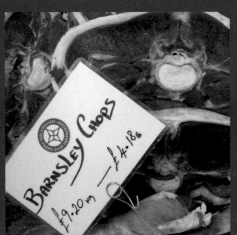

Titchwell Manor

9pm daily. **Main courses** £7.95-£14.95.
Rates £50-£110 double; £75-£130 suite; £90-
£120 apartment. **Credit** MC, V.

If the crowds in neighbouring Holkham and Wells prove too much (and too London) to bear, head to peculiar little Cley (no newsagent or grocers, but an organic store, smokehouse, lovely bookshop and two galleries says it all), and the enjoyable calm of the George, a pretty country inn that appeals on all fronts. As the rooms were being refurbished during our recent visit it's hard to say what they'll end up like, but if their previous look was anything to judge by – clean, simple furnishings, comfortable beds and individual touches in each room – we're expecting good things. Another hopeful indicator is the understated, modern restaurant with its helpful, genial staff. It serves up a decent range of dishes that span sandwiches through to à la carte, all simply cooked and reasonably priced. Try the rump steak and onion ciabatta, Morston mussels, Blakeney oysters or a Cley Smokehouse platter of salmon and prawns. And all that's before you get to the vast selection of meat and veggie dishes. If you overdo it, a post-lunch meander down the road will bring you to Blakeney Point, where stunning walks along windswept dykes and equally windswept beaches can last anything from 30 minutes to the rest of the day… a decision probably determined by whether you succumb to the excellent selection of own-made puds on offer.

Hoste Arms

The Green, Burnham Market, Norfolk PE31 8HD (01328 738777/www.hostearms.co.uk). **Lunch served** noon-2pm, **dinner served** 7-9pm daily. **Main courses** £8.95-£16.50. **Rates** £122-£188 double; £158-£193 suite. **Credit** MC, V.

Paul and Jeanne Whittome bought this yellow-painted 17th-century inn on Burnham Market green in 1989, and paved the way for the village's subsequent gentrification and reputation as a holiday hotspot. Formerly a coaching inn, livestock auction house and assizes, it's now a pub, restaurant and hotel rolled into one appealing package. The conservatory with its deep leather armchairs is ideal for afternoon tea or pre-dinner cocktails, while the convivial pub area offers an open fire and real ales. Work by local artists – ornithological paintings by Bruce Pearson and coastline photos by Harry Cory-Wright – are scattered about, and there's also a small art gallery. The food served in the wood-panelled dining room is a draw, from the lavish breakfast (the porridge with honey is recommended) to the extensive dinner menu. Local ingredients (Brancaster mussels, Burnham Creek oysters, Holkham Estate venison) and homely dishes (steak and kidney pudding, burger and chips) mix with more international flavours (swordfish sashimi, pad thai chicken) – plus a 300-bin wine list.

Jeanne is responsible for the exuberant (some might say eccentric) decor: the country-house-style decor of the bedrooms makes much use of boldly patterned fabrics and draped beds (including some four-posters), while the Zulu Wing reflects her South African heritage with its dark leather furniture, assegais, masks and native artworks. There's also an annex, the Railway Inn, a five-minute walk away, which has smaller bedrooms with en suite shower only and no phone. Families and larger groups keen to self-cater might be interested in the separate holiday cottage, which sleeps eight. Facilities for kids could be better (cots are available, but there are no nappy-changing facilities) and the Hoste's literature stresses that 'well-behaved' children are welcome (kids under 14 pay £25 per night).

Morston Hall

*The Street, Morston, Norfolk NR25 7AA
(01263 741041/www.morstonhall.com).* **Rates**
£250-£280 double. **Credit** AmEx, DC, MC, V.
From the flagstone-floored porch to the airy conservatory overlooking the spacious garden, this
award-winning country house hotel is a bastion of
traditional comfort. You get the feeling Agatha
Christie would feel right at home among the flowery curtains and cosy armchairs (just right for curling up with a good book), although it's not
overbearingly old-fashioned. Each of the rooms
comes with a bath and shower, toiletries, bathrobes
and CD and VCR players. The large flint building
is grand enough to provide a sense of occasion but
small enough to feel welcoming – just seven rooms
and space for 40 in the dining room – though six
new suites, housed in a separate building at the
rear of the garden, are due to open in August 2007.
The hotel's restaurant is excellent (*see p275*).

Rose & Crown

*Old Church Road, Snettisham, Norfolk PE31
7LX (01485 541382/www.roseandcrown
snettisham.co.uk).* **Meals served** noon-2pm
Mon-Fri; noon-2.30pm Sat, Sun. **Dinner served**
6.30-9pm Mon-Fri; 6.30-9.30pm Sat, Sun. **Main
courses** £8.25-£14.25. **Rates** £85-£95 double.
Credit MC, V.
Within easy striking distance of the coast and the
royal family's winter gaff at Sandringham, the
Rose & Crown is a curious mixture of old and new.

easy-going charm
good local food
at the popular
Victoria.

It combines the functions of village pub, smartish
restaurant and well-appointed little hotel. The
location, on the edge of the large village of
Snettisham – near the church and opposite the
cricket pitch – is serene. Three snug bars (low ceilings, pamment floors, Woodforde's ales, loqua-
cious locals) are at the centre of the pub, the oldest
part of which dates back to the 14th century. Food,
from an ample and enticing menu, can be eaten in
a variety of locations: at bar tables, in a modern
and vividly coloured restaurant room, in the capacious garden room, or outside at picnic tables. The
choice of dishes changes regularly but might
include Brancaster mussels in Sandringham cider,
thyme and crème fraîche, or butternut squash and
mascarpone risotto, followed by the likes of
steamed sea bass with warm basil potato salad
and roast red pepper paste, or a dish of four
flavourful meatballs in an intensely savoury tomato and oregano sauce with al dente spaghetti.
　The Rose & Crown's 16 bedrooms also vary in
style – from richly coloured oak-beamed spaces to
contemporary, pastel-hued rooms in the new extension (completed 2005); two ground-floor rooms
have full disabled access. Power showers, Molton
Brown toiletries, bottled mineral water and Wi-Fi,
all included in the price, add a note of luxury.
Hairdryers and TVs are provided, as are coffee-
and tea-making facilities (Thermoses containing
fresh milk are a nice touch). There's ample choice
for breakfast, including a vegetarian assembly, a
whole kipper (with poached egg and spinach) as
well as a hefty full English. Inside, a new residents'
lounge is due to be completed in 2007.

Titchwell Manor

*Titchwell, Norfolk PE31 8BB (01485 210221/
www.titchwellmanor.com).* **Rates** £180-£220.
Credit AmEx, MC, V.
There's a very welcoming vibe at Titchwell Manor,
and staff are happy to help. There are lovely leather
sofas to collapse in after a walk on the beach (or for
a pre-dinner drink) and there's space to wander in
the grounds. The place is undergoing a gradual
refurbishment, meaning that some rooms are currently much nicer than others (though all are spick
and span) – when you book ask for one of the new
rooms. Those at the front have sea views while a
new extension at the back looks over the fields.
There are TVs and a selection of books in the bedrooms, but no video or DVD players (and it does
rain in Norfolk...). There are two dining rooms – the
same menu is served in both, but families are
encouraged to eat in the less formal room. The food
is good, and local produce (Norfolk lamb, Holkham
venison, mussels and oysters from Brancaster) is
used where possible. The hotel is family-friendly,
but not to the detriment of other guests, and some
rooms are set aside for those with pets.

Victoria

*Park Road, Holkham, Norfolk NR23 1RG
(01328 711008/www.victoriaatholkham.co.uk).*
Lunch served noon-2.30pm; **dinner served**

7-9.30pm daily. **Main courses** £12-£17.
Rates £120-£160 double; £120-£220 lodge.
Credit MC, V.

The proximity to Holkham Beach is reason alone to stay here, but the easygoing charm of this small hotel and restaurant on the edge of the Holkham Estate also counts for a lot. The place is decorated in a low-key but stylish way, with furniture from Rajasthan mixing with modern TVs and gleaming bathrooms; there's a big fire in the lounge area, together with squashy, lived-in sofas and a bar. Staff are friendly and eager to help, rather than slick. As far as the rooms themselves are concerned, no two are the same; options include attic suites or two-bedroom 'lodges' (effectively, small houses) elsewhere on the estate – it's worth checking exactly what size and shape of room you're getting. Meals are served in the ground-floor dining room (and in the bar – substantial sandwiches, soup, excellent fish and chips). Both menus make use of local produce – often very local, such as Holkham steaks or burgers made from estate venison, as well as mussels from Thornham or crabs from Cromer. Prices here, for rooms and in the restaurant, are a little steep given the deluxe-pub nature of the enterprise, but that doesn't deter the Victoria's many fans – the place is regularly fully booked.

WHERE TO EAT & DRINK

Bear in mind that the hotels we have listed above also have noteworthy restaurants, most notably Morston Hall (see p275).

Also worth a visit are the Crown (The Buttlands, Wells-next-the-Sea, 01328 710209, www.thecrownhotelwells.co.uk), which has an imaginative global menu, and the White Horse (Main Road, Brancaster Staithe, 01485 210262, www.whitehorsebrancaster.co.uk). Here you'll find a sunny terrace, complete with great views of the Norfolk Coastal Path, and an impressive menu based around seasonal shellfish and other local produce.

Cookie's Crab Shop
The Green, Salthouse, Holt, Norfolk NR25 7AJ (01263 740352/www.salthouse.org.uk).
Meals served 9am-6pm Mon-Thur, Sun; 9am-8pm Fri, Sat. **Main courses** £4.80-£9.50.
No credit cards.

At Cookie's Crab Shop royal salads, crammed with mouth-watering seafood, overflow from quaint tearoom plates that look like they've seen good service during the café's 50-year history. You'll find no frills here: dining is at cramped tables in a garden shed, or outside in a pagoda or under parasols. Alternatively, you can take your food on to a small piece of green near the road and picnic while gazing across at the salt marshes. Soft drinks, including Norfolk apple juice, are sold, or you can bring your own alcohol. The menu is limited to a couple of soups (including smoky kipper and tomato), takeaway sandwiches and a wide

choice of seafood salads. The aforementioned royal salads include a wealth of ingredients – smoked mackerel, anchovies, crayfish tails, prawns, own-made coleslaw – as well as the star attraction (crab, smoked salmon, smoked eel, lobster). Round things off with one of the tremendous sticky toffee puddings. Staff are remarkably patient given the weekend crowds.

Fishes
Market Place, Burnham Market, Norfolk PE31 8HE (01328 738588/www.fishesrestaurant. co.uk). **Lunch served** noon-2pm Tue-Sun.
Dinner served 7-9.30pm Tue-Sat. **Set lunch** £19 2 courses, £22 3 courses. **Set dinner** £32 2 courses, £37 3 courses. **Credit** MC, V.

This family-run restaurant next to the Hoste Arms prides itself on its use of local and sustainably caught fish and shellfish. The menu (updated twice a day) is a treat, mixing deeply comforting dishes (smoked haddock with poached egg and savoy cabbage; Scarborough cod with chips) with more exotic fare (oven-roast butterfish kebab with chilli sauce; seven-spiced blue fin tuna) – all top quality. The puds – passion fruit panna cotta, say, or own-made ice-cream and sorbet – are equally good. Bay windows overlook the green, and slatted wooden blinds, rattan chairs and light pine tables provide a calm, contemporary feel. Upstairs are two new guest rooms (both en suite doubles). Scandinavian in feel, they're decorated with Lloyd Loom furniture and soothing colours; good-value B&B and dinner deals are available midweek.

Jolly Sailors
Main Road (A149), Brancaster Staithe, Norfolk PE31 8BJ (01485 210314/www.jolly sailors.co.uk). **Meals served** noon-9pm daily.
Main courses £9-£19. **Credit** MC, V.

During the summer, you're in danger of encountering morris dancers in the attractive gardens of this popular old pub, but it's in the colder months that the Jolly Sailors really comes into its own. Walkers and yachting folk stop by to warm up near the fire in the bonhomous main bar, perhaps ordering a pint of Old Les (brewed on-site) to aid the thawing process. As well as the no-nonsense bar (tiled floor, wooden benches) there's a couple of capacious dining rooms. Food might include mussels from the beds across the road.

King's Arms
Westgate Street, Blakeney, Norfolk NR25 7NQ (01263 740341). **Meals served** noon-9.30pm Mon-Sat; noon-9pm Sun. **Main courses** £6.95-£14.95. **Rates** £65 double; £75 apartment.
Credit MC, V.

Little has been changed to attract the area's newer, urbane residents at this gorgeously cosy old place. Norfolk accents resound throughout the three tiny low-ceilinged rooms, especially after the consumption of a few pints of Theakston Best, Marston's Pedigree or Old Speckled Hen. Yet newcomers are welcomed, and the pub is especially popular with walkers fresh from the salt marshes. Slow-roasted brisket of beef or local mussels might be on the bar menu; a bizarre collection of *Black and White Minstrel Show* posters is on the walls; and there's accommodation upstairs, a real fire in the grate, and a family room out back.

Lord Nelson

Walsingham Road, Burnham Thorpe, Norfolk PE31 8HL (01328 738241/www.nelsonslocal. co.uk). **Lunch served** noon-2pm Mon-Fri; noon-2.30pm Sat, Sun. **Dinner served** 7-9pm Mon-Sat. **Main courses** £9-£17.95. **Credit** MC, V.
Nelson memorabilia adorns this whitewashed classic boozer in Nelson's home village. Built in 1637, its high-backed wooden settles, stone-flagged floor, brick fireplace and comfortable snugs create the ideal setting to enjoy a pint of Nelson's Revenge – served straight from the cask and delivered to your table by friendly staff – or a tot of Nelson's Blood spiced brandy. Food is of higher quality (and price) than your average pub grub: you could tuck into own-made leek and potato soup, followed by succulent braised lamb shank or red mullet with smoked paprika and pesto sauce, and a very superior bread and butter pudding. There's also a large sunny garden.

Morston Hall

The Street, Morston, Norfolk NR25 7AA (01263 741041/www.morstonhall.com). **Lunch served** 12.30-1pm Sun. **Dinner served** 7.30-8pm daily. **Set lunch** £32 3 courses. **Set dinner** £46 4 courses. **Credit** AmEx, DC, MC, V.
This is a fine place to stay (*see p273*), but it's the hotel's gastronomic credentials that are the real draw; the place has been booked almost solid since chef Galton Blackiston (who runs the hotel with his wife Tracy) appeared on the *Great British Menu*

TV series in 2006. Rates might seem pricey, but a night here includes a four-course dinner and breakfast (non-guests can book dinner too), though you have to pay extra for wine. The dinner menu is fixed – no choices – so warn them in advance of any dietary requirements. For a Michelin-starred chef, Galton is disarmingly keen to get feedback on the food, which focuses on local produce cooked simply but exquisitely. The rich creaminess of lightly seared foie gras, atop toasted brioche, is offset by a rhubarby jus; pearly white, herb-crusted cod comes with tomato fondue and a lemony beurre blanc. This might be followed by pink-tinged fillet of roast (locally reared) beef. To finish, there's a pudding (tarte tatin with butterscotch ice-cream on our visit) or an array of British cheeses, plus petits fours and coffee. Thankfully, it's only a short stagger upstairs to bed.

White Horse Hotel

4 High Street, Blakeney, Norfolk NR25 7AL (01263 740574/www.blakeneywhitehorse.co.uk). **Lunch served** *Bar* noon-2pm, **dinner served** 6-9pm daily. *Restaurant* **Dinner served** 7-9pm Tue-Sat. **Main courses** £10-£17. **Rates** £70-£130 double; £80-£120 family. **Credit** MC, V.
A rabbit warren of a place, the White Horse is a friendly and unpretentious spot for a drink, a meal or an overnight stay. You can eat in the bar or airy conservatory or (at dinner only) in the yellow-walled restaurant in the former stables. The menu – a definite notch above pub grub – is big on fish and shellfish, with an emphasis on local produce (Norfolk lamb, Morston mussels, prawns from the Cley Smokehouse, pâté made from local game). Upstairs are nine bedrooms (all recently refurbished), simply decorated in cream and blue, with striped blinds and large beds. Get the Harbour room, if you can: it's the biggest, and has the best seafront views. There's also a family room on the ground floor, separate from the rest of the building.

No frills, but the freshest of seafood at Cookie's Crab Shop.

Manchester

Northern soul.

The last decade has seen as furious a programme of regeneration and rebuilding in Manchester as it has experienced since the cotton mills and their attendant slums sprang up in the 19th century, when it was catchily dubbed Cottonopolis. Driven largely by the 1996 IRA bomb and the staging of the Commonwealth Games in 2002, recent projects have left areas of the centre unrecognisable to anyone who last saw them ten years earlier. Some of this flurry of development may have come at a cost, as much of the character of the old city is now subsumed under pricey new accommodation. But the city long associated with innovation remains as vibrant as ever, and the compact, human-sized centre now has a plethora of new attractions to appease the 21st-century cityphile.

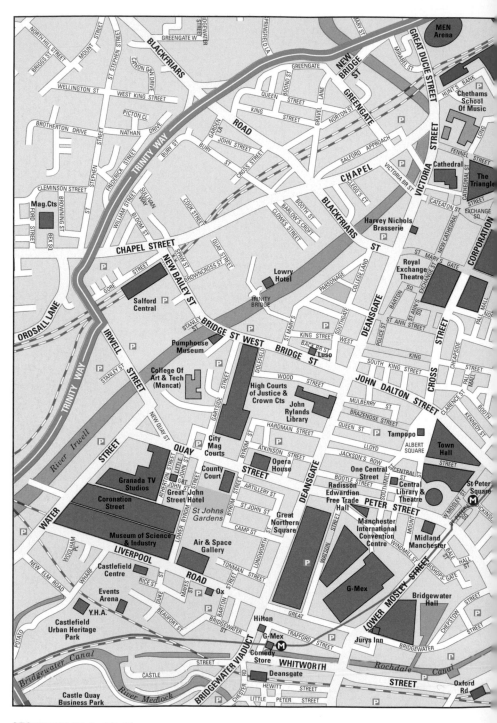

Manchester

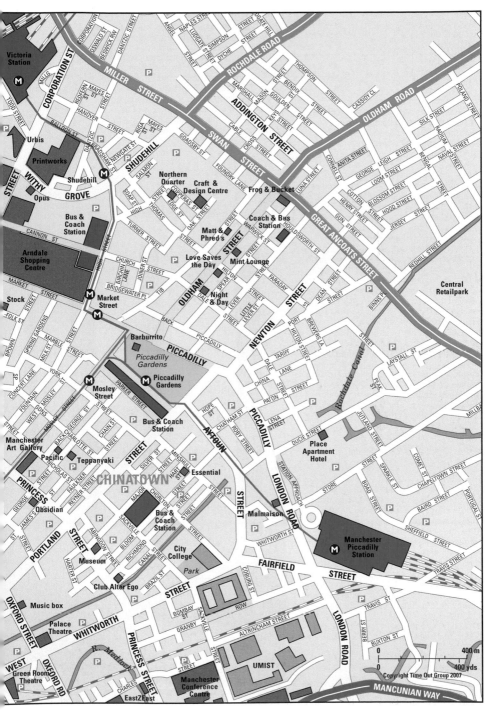

Victoria
Station

CORPORATION ST

MILLER STREET

SWAN STREET

ROCHDALE ROAD

OLDHAM ROAD

ADDINGTON STREET

GREAT ANCOATS STREET

Urbis

Printworks

Opus

Shudehill

SHUDEHILL

GROVE

WITHY

Northern
Quarter

Craft &
Design Centre

Frog & Bucket

Bus &
Coach
Station

Arndale
Shopping
Centre

CANNON ST

Matt &
Phred's

Coach & Bus
Station

Central
Retailpark

Stock

Market
Street

Love Saves
the Day

Mint Lounge

OLDHAM STREET

Night
& Day

NEWTON STREET

Barburrito

PICCADILLY

Piccadilly
Gardens

Rochdale Canal

Mosley
Street

Piccadilly
Gardens

Bus & Coach
Station

Manchester
Art Gallery

Pacific

Teppanyaki

Essential

Place
Apartment
Hotel

CHINATOWN

PRINCESS STREET

Obsidian

Bus &
Coach
Station

Malmaison

Manchester
Piccadilly
Station

PORTLAND STREET

Museum

City
College

Park

LONDON ROAD

FAIRFIELD STREET

Club Alter Ego

STREET

Music box

Palace
Theatre

WHITWORTH

OXFORD STREET

WEST

OXFORD RD

Green Room
Theatre

PRINCESS STREET

R. Medlock

EastZEast

UMIST

Manchester
Conference
Centre

0   400 m
0   400 yds

Copyright Time Out Group 2007

MANCUNIAN WAY

Manchester

Accommodation	★★★★☆
Food & drink	★★★★★
Nightlife	★★★★☆
Shopping	★★★★★
Culture	★★★☆☆
Sights	★★☆☆☆
Scenery	★☆☆☆☆

Old favourites such as the Manchester Art Gallery and Manchester Museum have had major refits, while entirely new attractions such as the stunning Urbis museum, Sportcity and Salford's Lowry arts centre and Imperial War Museum North (*see p286*) have arrived, housed in impressively modern premises. Meanwhile, urban landscape projects such as Cathedral Gardens and Exchange Square have added some much-needed breathing space.

The city's once-neglected Northern Quarter – a hinterland of adult shops and empty warehouses not too long ago – is now home to vast numbers of vintage boutiques, independent record shops and hip bars and eateries. The gay scene has bounced back too, after a few years of its venues featuring unwillingly on the hellish hen-party trail.

The city can also boast record-breaking numbers of annual festivals, celebrating its thriving food and music scenes. And for those into historical treasures and heritage attractions, the grand merchants' houses and half-timbered pubs are still very much present and correct and part of the allure – it's just that they're now set against a far more cosmopolitan backdrop. For more on the very best that Manchester has to offer, check out our website www.timeout.com/manchester.

Shopping

The last decade has seen Manchester ascend from high street mediocrity to a retail playground worth at least twice Philip Green's personal pension fund. While many cities have bulldozed their heritage to make way for bland new malls and chain stores, Manchester has cleverly made room for both – resulting in a tale of two retail cities that manage to happily co-exist; independent boutiques and small-scale collectibles shops are within strolling distance of top-flight department stores and high street chains.

The city's department stores include House of Fraser – still rather confusingly referred to as 'Kendals', which was its previous incarnation (Deansgate, 0161 832 3414, www.houseoffraser.co.uk). It offers six floors of retail therapy, with a good cosmetics department and menswear section in the basement.

Selfridges (Exchange Square, 0870 837 7377, www.selfridges.com) is worth a visit for the basement food hall alone – but its funky fashions shouldn't be missed either. Harvey Nichols (Exchange Square, 0161 828 8888, www.harveynichols.com) is undoubtedly expensive, but still worth a look if you're into flashy labels.

Designer shops aren't in short supply in Manchester, and the first port of call for the fashion pack should be King Street. Among the stellar line-up are Vivienne Westwood (47 Spring Gardens, King Street, 0161 835 2121, www.hervia. com), Armani Collezioni (Atlas Chambers, King Street, 0161 819 5757, www. emporioarmani.co.uk), Emporio Armani (84-86 King Street, 0161 839 8789, www.emporioarmani.co.uk) and DKNY (76-80 King Street, 0161 819 1048, www.dkny.com).

Impressive cocktails as well as views on Cloud 23 at the Hilton.

A more eclectic shopping experience can be found in the Northern Quarter. Oi Polloi (70 Tib Street, 0161 831 7870, www.oipolloi.com) sells clothes sourced from New York, with lots of hip menswear labels, while the nearby Rags to Bitches (60 Tib Street, 0161 835 9265, www.rags-to-bitches.co.uk) is an upmarket vintage boutique offering one-offs and customised pieces. The legendary Afflecks Palace (52 Church Street, 0161 834 2039, www.afflecks-palace.co.uk) is a four-storey wonderland of gothic and vintage clothes, kitsch posters, rock T-shirts, skate gear and jewellery, while Manchester Craft & Design Centre (17 Oak Street, 0161 832 4274, www.craftanddesign.com) is a calm cloister of exciting city-made sculptures, jewellery and ceramics.

Manchester and music are inseparable, and there are plenty of great record shops in town. Try Piccadilly Records (53 Oldham Street, 0161 839 8008) for an unsurpassed mix of new and rare vinyl, Beatin' Rhythm (42 Tib Street, 0161 834 7783, www.beatinrhythm.com) for 1960s soul, blues, country and rock 'n' roll, or Fat City (20 Oldham Street, 0161 237 1181, www.fatcity.co.uk) for hip hop beats and independent releases.

If the high street's calling, though, there are few shopping areas in Britain that can beat the combined forces of the Arndale, with its fancy new extension, and Market Street. The plethora of popular chain stores pull in the crowds every weekend. Those after upmarket brands on a budget, meanwhile, should take a trip over to Salford for the 25 to 75 per cent discounts offered at the Lowry Outlet Mall (The Quays, Salford Quays, 0161 848 1850, www.lowrydesigneroutlet.com).

WHERE TO STAY

In addition to the hotels given detailed reviews below, the Ox gastropub (see p289) has nine en suite bedrooms, and is within easy walking distance of the city centre. Although breakfast isn't available, there are plenty of places nearby where you can grab a bite to eat.

Great John Street Hotel

Great John Street, M3 4FD (0161 831 3211/ www.eclectic-hotel-collection.com). **Rates** £235-£450 suite. **Credit** AmEx, DC, MC, V.

Great John Street, an Eclectic Collection hotel, pulls out all the stops to deliver a truly luxurious boutique experience, making it one of the most stylish options in town. Housed in an old Victorian school by the *Coronation Street* set, the hotel offers duplex suites only, each uniquely designed. Hand-carved furniture, roll-top baths and super-sexy fabrics and fittings lend the place a modern-vintage feel that's more New York than Manchester. High-speed internet access and CD players are provided in all rooms, and the absence of a restaurant and guest parking is made up for by a butler's tray for breakfast, a chi-chi ground-floor bar and a rooftop hot tub.

Hilton

303 Deansgate, M3 4LQ (0161 870 1600/ www.hilton.co.uk/manchester). **Rates** £109-£179 double; £350-£1,100 suite. **Credit** AmEx, DC, MC, V.
There may be a set of swanky apartments above, but for 23 impressive floors the city's new Beetham Tower belongs to the Hilton, as the unmissable branding proclaims. Rooms are kitted out with all the latest technology (ergonomic work stations, laptop access, high-speed internet) and have floor-to-ceiling windows. Cloud 23 bar, at the top, is straight out of *Lost in Translation*; the ground-floor Podium restaurant-bar doesn't have the impressive views, but does do great food. And for those looking for some healthy indulgence, there are three spa treatment rooms.

Jurys Inn

56 Great Bridgewater Street, M1 5LE (0161 953 8888/www.bookajurysinn.com). **Rates** £89-£145 double; £109-£165 double (incl breakfast). **Credit** AmEx, DC, MC, V.
Handily situated for Bridgewater Hall, Manchester Central (aka G-Mex) and the Deansgate Locks, this purpose-built outpost of the Jurys chain offers fairly priced, good-standard accommodation. The bedrooms and communal areas have been refurbished according to the inoffensive, generically modern brand spec. Unique to this Jurys is the Inntro bar, with plasma-screen sport action. Ask for a room at the front to watch the Hallé musicians coming and going from the back door of Bridgewater Hall.

Lowry Hotel

50 Dearmans Place, Chapel Wharf, M3 5LH (0161 827 4000/www.thelowryhotel.com). **Rates** £285-£315 double; £735-£1,845 suite. **Credit** AmEx, DC, MC, V.
The hotel of choice for visiting actors, politicians and Premiership footballers, the Lowry is the city's original five-star hideaway. The address may officially be Salford, but the hotel is located right on the city centre's edge, on the banks of the murky River Irwell. Everything in this Rocco Forte hotel is exactly as it should be – huge, achingly hip rooms (165 of them) with super-sized

NIGHTLIFE

The creativity and diversity that made Manchester the clubbing and independent music capital of Europe remain evident today, 20 years after the acid house revolution. With the Northern Quarter radiating creative vibrancy, new musicians making their mark and genre-bending club promoters running riot, the variety, quality and energy of the after-dark scene is on trademark roof-raising, trainer-wrecking form.

Manchester does, however, have its share of identikit chain bars. If you're looking for a good central bet, **One Central Street** (1 Central Street, 0161 211 9000, www. onecentralstreet.co.uk) is a beautifully designed, atmospheric basement bar and club with a big sound system, fabulous cocktails and diverse music policy. But for a wider selection of quirky independent bars, head to the Northern Quarter. **Matt and Phred's Jazz Club** (64 Tib Street, 0161 831 7002, www.mattandphreds.com) is Manchester's only live jazz music club, with legendarily good pizza and cocktails, while **Night & Day** (26 Oldham Street, 0161 236 4597, www.nightnday.org) is the place to catch tomorrow's big act, or cult faves hanging out and – if you're lucky – playing intimate sets. The Northern Quarter's favourite nightclub is former burlesque bar **Mint Lounge** (46-50 Oldham Street, 0161 228 1495, www.mintlounge. com), hosting an array of house, hip hop (Fat City hip hop session Friends & Family has landed a

regular residency), reggae, mix 'n' mash and live music events that have made it one of the city's most exciting venues. But you'll need to venture further north of the centre into Ancoats for the biggest club in town, **Sankey's** (Beehive Mill, Radium Street, Ancoats, 0161 236 5444, www.sankeys.info), which had a rapid but extensive refit in 2006. The club's eclectic, forward-thinking music policy attracts superstar DJs, with the infamous electro- and techno-based Friday night Tribal Sessions still going strong.

Across town, the scene is less vintage Adidas, more hairdressers, handbags and honeydew martinis. Drinking on Deansgate and Deansgate Locks, a stretch of railway arch conversions along the Rochdale Canal, is a self-consciously glamorous affair, with evenings normally starting in one of myriad cocktail bars and leading on to dressy dance clubs like **Emporia** (2B Whitworth Street West, 0161 236 8833, www.emporia.co.uk). Proceed only with designer labels present, correct and on display.

Over in the Gay Village, **Essential** (Bloom Street, 0161 236 0077, www.essentialmanchester.com), the city's gay superclub, is still going strong after over a decade in business. For a less predictable night in the Village, head to **Club Alter Ego** (105-107 Princess Street, 0161 237 1749, www.clubalterego. co.uk), home of evergreen innovative indie shindig Poptastic. For esoteric beats in the south of the city, check

Matt & Phred's Jazz Club

out **Music Box** (65 Oxford Street, 0161 236 9971, www.themusicbox. info), host to Mr Scruff's legendary – and legendarily diverse – Keep it Unreal nights. The basement club **South** (4a South King Street, 0161 831 7756) is excellent: Fridays mean stomping northern soul, and on Saturdays the Boon Army faithful pile in for indie, dance and disco.

If clubbing isn't your bag, check out Manchester's healthy comedy circuit. The stand-up scene revolves around three central locations: the flagship **Comedy Store** (Arches 3-4 Deansgate Locks, Whitworth Street West, 0161 839 9595, www.thecomedystore.co.uk); old favourite the **Frog & Bucket** (102 Oldham Street, 0161 236 9805, www.frogandbucket.com); and newcomer **Opus** (The Printworks, Units 21-23, Withy Grove, 0161 834 2414, www.opusmanchester.com). Comedy City, a night launched in September 2006 at the City of Manchester Stadium, may soon be joining this holy triangle. For the latest reviews and listings, check out www.timeout.com/manchester.

beds, original modern art, discreet service, high-speed internet access, marble en suite bathrooms and clued-up staff; many rooms also have riverside views. There's a swanky spa with a full range of treatments and a gym, and the serene River Restaurant, run by champion chef Eyck Zimmer, is a further draw. It's also well placed for forays to Selfridges, Harvey Nichols and the MEN Arena.

Malmaison

Piccadilly, M1 1LZ (0161 278 1000/www.malmaison-manchester.com). **Rates** £150 double; £210-£395 suite. **Credit** AmEx, DC, MC, V.
A favourite with visiting bands and celebs, the Mal is a first choice for those who like to think of themselves as stylish sorts. The old Joshua Hoyle textile mill recently received a £1.8-million facelift, introducing a dark-toned red, brown and black colour scheme to many of the suites, now located in a new extension. Comfy beds, power showers, CD players and internet access feature in all the rooms, while suites are also equipped with LCD TVs and Bose Lifestyle systems. The star of the new line-up is the seriously sexy Moulin Rouge room; the freestanding bath in the lounge takes around 30 minutes to fill, such is its depth. A gym, the Petit Spa and an opulent brasserie round things off nicely. Well placed for the Gay Village and Piccadilly station.

Midland Manchester

Peter Street, M60 2DS (0161 236 3333/ www.qhotels.co.uk). **Rates** £185-£215 double; £250-£500 suite. **Credit** AmEx, DC, MC, V.
This grand old dame of Manchester hotels opened in 1905. She's had her fair share of high-profile visitors over the decades (among them Winston Churchill and Princess Anne), and goes down in history as the place where Charles Stewart Rolls and Frederick Henry Royce met. After a few years in the wilderness, the Midland is back on glamorous form after a massive £15-million makeover by new owners Q Hotels. The feel is stately modern classic throughout, from the sleek, marble-floored reception to the richly furnished rooms. The recently opened Colony restaurant has an impressive Modern European menu, with special pre-theatre deals, while the basement health spa is suitably decadent.

Place Apartment Hotel

Ducie Street, Piccadilly, M1 2TP (0161 778 7500/www.theplacehotel.com). **Open** *Bar* 9pm-3am Fri, Sat. *Cocktail Lounge* noon-3am Mon-Sat. **Lunch served** noon-2pm, **dinner served** 5-10pm Mon-Sat. **Rates** £145 double; £226 deluxe apartment; £350 penthouse. **Credit** AmEx (hotel only), DC (hotel only), MC, V.
Individually designed loft-style apartments in a converted Grade II-listed warehouse give the Place its distinctive edge – and make a night here feel as if you're staying in a friend's pad (albeit a friend

with far too much money). All apartments have shiny new kitchens, separate bedrooms, Sky TV, DVDs and CD players. Deluxe apartments have even higher levels of luxury, exposed brick walls and great views of the city. The bathrooms are suitably sumptuous, and a continental breakfast can be delivered to your apartment on request. The Cotton House restaurant (0161 237 5052), which has a champagne cocktail lounge, has gained a reputation as one of the best, and most atmospheric, places to eat in this part of the city. Best to book a table in advance.

Radisson Edwardian

Free Trade Hall, Peter Street, M2 5GP (0161 835 9929/www.radissonedwardian.com). **Rates** £241 double; £375-£1,500 suite. **Credit** AmEx, DC, JCB, MC, V.
Some may say that turning the Free Trade Hall – a building with almost biblical significance to the city – into a hotel is criminal, but the Radisson made real efforts to do so sympathetically when it converted the building in 2004. The Italianate façade has been retained, along with many of the building's original features. A new extension houses 263 deluxe bedrooms, each with a king-size bed, lots of sleek technology, Wi-Fi internet access and a marble bathroom. Suites are named after stars who have performed or spoken at the hall, with Dylan and Fitzgerald making penthouse appearances (the hall was where Dylan famously received his 'Judas!' heckle, after he strummed an electric guitar), and Gladstone and Dickens patronising the meeting rooms. A luxurious health spa features a swimming pool, saunas and Elemis treatments. Well placed for theatreland.

WHERE TO EAT & DRINK

Only those who haven't visited Manchester for the past decade can have failed to notice the culinary shift that has occurred in the land of black pudding and Boddies in recent times. This shift has resulted in an explosion not only in the number of restaurants in the city, but also in the quality and range of cuisines on offer, with plenty of globe-spanning styles. The Food & Drink Festival (0161 228 0006, www.foodanddrinkfestival.com), held in October, is now one of the area's liveliest annual events. Manchester's renowned bar scene continues to be as exciting and eclectic as ever; few major cities can boast as many unreconstituted old ale houses sitting next to sleek new cocktail joints and grill bars – it's this diversity that makes a pub crawl around town so rewarding.

The Northern Quarter's range of bars and eateries continues to reflect the healthy economy in this former wasteland. Bluu (Smithfield Market, off Thomas Street, 0161 839 7195, www.bluu.co.uk) is a cool perma-popular restaurant-bar in the trendiest part of the NQ that successfully mixes the traditional (fish finger butties) with the more contemporary (halloumi cheese and roasted aubergine butties) on its bar menu. Dry Bar (28-30 Oldham Street, 0161 236 9840), once owned by Factory Records, was the first style bar in the city and a must-visit for any 'Madchester' or Haçienda veterans. And for a decent range of beers and eclectic DJs, try Cord (8 Dorsey Street, off Tib Street, 0161 832 9494,www.cordbar.com), with its intimate booths and homely feel. It can feel terrifyingly cramped at weekends; for a calmer visit, stop by in the daytime for a pickled egg or gourmet pie.

In Castlefield, the Choice Bar & Restaurant (Castle Quay, Castlefield, 0161 833 3400, www.choicebarandrestaurant.co.uk) has won several awards since launching in 2001; its menu should suit those with a taste for refined British flavours and an eye for outstanding presentation. Dukes 92 (18-25 Castle Street, Castlefield, 0161 839 8646, www.dukes92.com) is as popular as ever, its canalside patio being one of the best outdoor spots from which to enjoy a summer pint and chunky gourmet sandwich or cheese plate. The Hilton's Cloud 23 (23rd floor, Hilton, 303 Deansgate, 0161 870 1688), in the flash (and initially controversial) new Beetham Tower, affords fabulous views of the city from its sleek surrounds. Not one for vertigo sufferers.

The Gay Village is still in rude health, with a clutch of shiny bars to tempt you over to the wild side of Canal Street. Queer (4 Canal Street, 0161 228 1360, www. queer-manchester.com) serves food to a chilled soundtrack during the day; come nightfall, resident DJs make it a favoured spot in which to warm up before moving on to Essential (*see p282*). Just up the street is Manto (46 Canal Street, 0161 236 2667, www.mantobar.com), the place that once provided a catalyst for change in the city by showcasing the vibrancy of the gay scene behind a glass frontage for the first time. Now more institution than rebellious innovator, it's nevertheless still a big draw.

If you're after a more traditional drinking experience, Manchester certainly won't disappoint. The Briton's Protection (50 Great Bridgewater Street, Castlefield, 0161 236 5895) is a fabulous, dark, tiled and wood-panelled gem. Its whisky menu has to be the most complete this side of the Trossachs. The Knott Bar (374 Deansgate, 0161 839 9229) proves that real ale isn't the preserve of the CAMRA set. You can't miss Peveril of the Peak (127 Great Bridgewater Street, 0161 236 6364): the emerald-green tiled exterior of the Grade II-listed building makes it one of the most distinctive pubs in Manchester. Mr

Thomas's Chop House (52 Cross Street, 0161 832 2245, www.tomschophouse. com) is a genuine Victorian boozer with a wonderful carved and tiled interior; the food is good too.

Barburrito

1 Piccadilly Gardens, M1 1RG (0161 228 6479/ www.barburrito.co.uk). **Open** 11am-9pm Mon-Sat; noon-6pm Sun. **Main courses** £2.75-£4.75. **No credit cards.**
It seems amazing that Barburrito, 'the UK's first burrito bar', opened as recently as it did (in 2006). The compile-your-own burrito format has caught on so quickly that the only downside is the queue that this place can generate. We're reliably informed that the menu goes beyond the slow-braised pork flavoured with bay leaves and orange (£3.10/£4.50), but we haven't got past it yet.

EastZEast

Nr Ibis Hotel, Princess Street, M1 7DG (0161 244 5353/www.eastzeast.com). **Open** 5pm-midnight Mon-Thur, Sun; 5pm-1am Fri, Sat. **Main courses** £5.95-£11.95. **Credit** AmEx, MC, V.
Although you might be tempted by the curry mile's bright lights, be warned: it's rare to find good food among the endless gaudiness. Punjabi specialist EastZEast is, however, an altogether classier option. The family behind this hotel/restaurant previously worked in Bradford for over 50 years, and all of this experience shows in the superb service and delicious karahi dishes.

Greens

43 Lapwing Lane, West Didsbury, M20 2NT (0161 434 4259). **Lunch served** noon-2pm Tue-Fri; 12.30-3.30pm Sun. **Dinner served** 5.30-10.30pm daily. **Main courses** £10.95. **Set dinner** (5.30-7pm Mon-Fri, Sun) £12.95 2 courses. **Credit** MC, V.
After a visit to Greens, it's more or less compulsory for carnivores to exclaim 'I loved it, and I'm not even vegetarian'. The two-course set menu (available in the early evening on weekdays and Sundays) is fab, but if you're out on a Saturday night, we'd recommend the cheshire goat's cheese and pine nut salad with rocket, spinach and watercress, followed by potato hash and artichokes, sun-blush tomatoes, kalamata olives and dill. Oh, and save a little room for the white chocolate cheesecake with dark chocolate sauce.

Harvey Nichols Brasserie

2nd Floor, Exchange Square, M1 1AD (0161 828 8898/www.harveynichols.com). **Meals served** 10am-6pm Mon; 10am-10.30pm Tue-Sat; 10am-5pm Sun. **Main courses** £10.50-£15. **Credit** AmEx, DC, MC, V.
Often busier than the store itself, this funky, minimalist venture offers some of the best Modern British cooking in town, with the likes of chilled

gazpacho, classic sole meunière and roasted chicken ballotine featuring on the well-balanced menu. Service is efficient – so it's a good choice if you don't want to hang around too much between courses. The wine list is top-notch.

Isinglass

46 Flixton Road, Urmston, M41 5AB (0161 749 8400/www.isinglassrestaurant.co.uk). **Open** 11.30am-10.30pm Tue-Fri; 11am-10.30pm Sat, Sun. **Main courses** £9.75-£15.95. **Set lunch** (Sun) £13.95 2 courses, £16.95 3 courses. **Credit** AmEx, DC, MC, V.
Suburban Urmston is the unlikely home of Isinglass, one of Manchester's most impressive restaurants. Opened by Julie Bagnoli and Lisa

Walker, this idiosyncratic establishment takes the oft-empty promise of only using local ingredients – and shows what can be achieved when experts hold themselves to it. Most impressive of all, the evident quality comes at very affordable prices.

Love Saves the Day

345 Deansgate, M3 4LG (0161 834 2266/ www.lovesavestheday.com). **Open** 8am-7pm Mon, Tue; 8am-8pm Wed; 8am-9pm Thur, Fri; 10am-6pm Sat; 10am-4pm Sun. **Main courses** £7-£8.50. **Set dinner** (6-9pm Thur) £12 2 courses, £15 3 courses. **Credit** MC, V.
Foodie hearts were broken when the Oldham Street LSTD closed – but lifted when the Deansgate outpost of this neighbourhood deli reopened.

SIGHTSEEING

IMPERIAL WAR MUSEUM NORTH

The Quays, Trafford Wharf, Trafford Park, M17 1TZ (0161 836 4000/www.iwm.org.uk). **Open** Mar-Oct 10am-6pm daily. Nov-Feb 10am-5pm daily. **Admission** free.
The brain-boggling design of the Imperial War Museum North was based on a concept by renowned architect Daniel Libeskind. Inside, the floors and doors gently slope and disorientate the unwary visitor. More a museum of peace than a museum of war, it works hard – and mainly succeeds – at being an entertaining and educational multimedia-led venue.

JOHN RYLANDS LIBRARY

150 Deansgate, M3 3EH (0161 306 0555/www. library.manchester.ac.uk). **Open** 10am-5pm Mon, Wed-Sat; noon-5pm Tue, Sun. **Admission** free.
Despite giving the impression of near-medieval antiquity, this glorious building is in fact just over a century old, and now has an entire new entrance wing. First opened in 1900, among its astonishing treasures are the world's oldest surviving fragment of the New Testament and a manuscript collection that spans five millennia and encompasses over 50 languages. The guided tours are highly recommended.

LOWRY

Pier 8, Salford Quays, M50 3AZ (0870 787 5780/ www.thelowry.com). **Open** 11am-5pm Mon-Fri, Sun; 10am-5pm Sat. **Admission** free (call or see website for show and event prices).
The Lowry marked a tipping point for the previously isolated Salford Quays development area when it opened in spring 2000. The landmark waterside building houses an extensive collection of LS Lowry's art, as well as an excellent and ever-changing programme of painting, sculpture and photographic work. It has also hosted more award-winning theatre productions than any other regional venue.

MANCHESTER ART GALLERY

Mosley Street, M2 3JL (0161 235 8888/ www.manchestergalleries.org). **Open** 10am-5pm Tue-Sun. **Admission** free.
This three-storey gallery is home to some stunning Pre-Raphaelite art. The building itself had a £35-million extension and refit in 2002, letting in more light, opening a new wing and installing a lively, interactive children's gallery. The shop has a great selection of specialist art books.

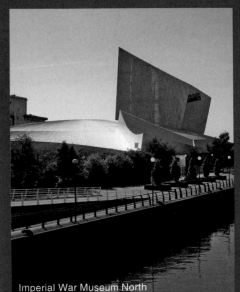
Imperial War Museum North

Passers-by are often seized by the smell of fresh coffee, or by sudden cravings for fresh pasta or a sit-down with soup at the window tables. Simple, splendid platters are priced at £7, while the special bistro menu in operation on Thursday evenings could include anything from jerk chicken to a no-nonsense steak, watercress and brie salad. The Sunday brunch is hangover-defyingly good.

Luso

63 Bridge Street, M3 3BQ (0161 839 5550/ www.lusorestaurant.co.uk). **Meals served** noon-10.30pm Mon-Sat; noon-10pm Sun. **Pesticos served** 12-5.30pm daily. **Main courses** £9.95-£21.50. **Pesticos** £2.95-£6.50. **Credit** AmEx, MC, V.

Arguably Manchester's most popular opening of 2006, Jane and Carlos Cortes's Luso has brought inventive Portuguese food to the city centre. Luso's menu ventures in the footsteps of Portuguese travellers and, as such, features vindaloo and tempura dishes. Despite this laudable experimentation, favourites like the house-salted salt cod still feature. (For the uninitiated, 'pesticos' are small, more-ish, tapas-like dishes.)

Northern Quarter Restaurant & Bar

108 High Street, M4 1HQ (0161 832 7115/ www.tnq.co.uk). **Open** noon-10.30pm Tue-Sat; noon-7pm Sun. **Main courses** £10.25-£19.50.

MANCHESTER MUSEUM

The University of Manchester, Oxford Road, M13 9PL (0161 275 2634/www.museum.man.ac.uk). **Open** 10am-5pm Tue-Sat; 11am-4pm Mon, Sun. **Admission** free.
Formerly a rather dusty example of a museum in the old-school mould, this place received a refit and general sprucing up in 2003, allowing some much-needed daylight to reach its murky corners. Highlights include a notable collection of Egyptian mummies and a striking skeleton of a Tyrannosaurus, posed in full hunting mode.

MUSEUM OF SCIENCE & INDUSTRY IN MANCHESTER

Liverpool Road, Castlefield, M3 4FP (0161 832 2244/www.msim.org.uk). **Open** 10am-5pm daily. **Admission** free.
A family-friendly playground of vintage technology, set amid the converted remains of Liverpool Road's 1830s railway station. Highlights include a walkthrough replica of the Victorian sewer system (more interesting than it sounds), a huge Power Hall of thrusting, steaming turbines, and the equally impressive Air and Space Hall, featuring a pantheon of airborne greats.

URBIS

Cathedral Gardens, M4 3BG (0161 605 8200/ www.urbis.org.uk). **Open** 10am-6pm Mon-Wed, Sat; 10am-8pm Thur-Sat. **Admission** free.
You can't fail to notice this huge, glass-clad ski-slope of a building. The transparent wedge is home to Urbis – the museum of the modern city. It had a shaky start but, thanks to a new curator, things are on the up. Through exhibitions covering street art, graphic design and club culture, cities as far apart as São Paulo and Tokyo are dissected.

Urbis

Manchester

Set meals (noon-7pm Tue-Sat) £9.95 2 courses. **Set lunch** (noon-7pm Sun) £11.95 2 courses. **Credit** MC, V.
New head chef Jason Wass has piloted this handsome restaurant away from its former Middle Eastern style, towards a more classic Modern British/European proposition. Lovely dishes such as roasted garlic and cherry tomato risotto, oven-roasted wood pigeon and spiced monkfish with sweet potato mash have turned the place into a jewel on the Northern Quarter's High Street – an absolute must for any visiting foodies. The Sunday lunch menu is well worth a look.

Obsidian

18-24 Princess Street, M1 4LY (0161 238 4348/www.obsidianmanchester.co.uk). **Lunch served** noon-2.30pm, **dinner served** 6-10pm Mon-Sat. **Main courses** £11.50-£19.50. **Set lunch** (noon-5pm Sun) £12.95 3 courses. **Pre-theatre menu** (6-10pm Mon-Fri) £13.95 3 courses. **Bar food** (noon-10pm Mon-Fri) £2.50-£9.95. **Credit** AmEx, MC, V.
This restaurant and bar are located within the chic Arora International hotel, but Obsidian is just as popular with the Manc crowd as it is with expense-accounting visitors to the city. Head chef

MARKETING MANCHESTER

Everyone likes a bargain, but Manchester's markets are about more than six pairs of socks for a pound. The following markets all offer a compelling alternative to the high street, with unique goods and personal service. Also look out for the less regular markets that are held in the city centre throughout the year – in particular, St Ann's Square's fine food market and the German market at Christmas.

On the Northern Quarter side of the Arndale lies the permanent **Arndale Market** (49 High Street, 0161 832 3552, www.arndalemarket.co.uk, 8am-6pm Mon-Sat, 11am-5pm Sun). Formerly a grim repository of cheap tat, it's upped its game and now offers speciality teas, organic breads and arts and crafts. It's worth a look, if only to marvel at the sudden absence of fluorescent lingerie.

At the gateway to the Northern Quarter, the **Fashion Market** (Tib Street, 10am-5pm Sat) allows up-and-coming designers to showcase their collections. Quirky jewellery mingles with customised vintage pieces, one-off leather bags, prints and handmade silk cushions. And it's always possible you'll be buying from the next Matthew Williamson.

A more traditional, personal vibe prevails at the small but bustling **Longsight Market** (Dickenson Road, Longsight, 0161 225 9859, 9am-4.30pm Wed & Fri, 9am-5pm Sat), where you can acquire cheap and cheery fashions and fabrics, plus meats, veg and exotic spices. For a slice of bucolic heaven, check out **Manchester Farmers' Market** (Piccadilly Gardens, 10am-6pm 2nd & 4th Fri & Sat of month). If you want to know the name of the goat that produced the milk for your cheese, this is the place. Smallholders from across the North-west set up stalls offering organic meats, veg, cheese, cakes and wine. You can even find the not so native (but organic!) ostrich burgers.

If size is your priority, then **Bury Market** (Bury, 9am-4.30pm Mon-Fri, 9am-5pm Sat) should fit the bill. It's the biggest market in the North-west, and a mere 20-minute drive from Manchester city centre. The most fun happens on Wednesdays, Fridays and Saturdays, when everything from household goods to cheap clothes are rummaged through by eager bargain-hunters. For more on the city's markets, visit www.manchester.gov.uk/markets.

Adrian Bailey's cooking is adventurous, but never offputtingly so: aided by ingredients sourced from local suppliers, he lets the flavours do the work. You can't really go wrong with anything on the menu, but the whole Goosnargh duck cooked two ways and served with duck-fat roast potatoes, seasonal vegetables and cherry sauce is ridiculously good. The bar scene is pretty lively.

Ox

71 Liverpool Road, Castlefield, M3 4NQ (0161 839 7740/www.theox.co.uk). **Open** *Bar* 11am-2am Mon-Thur; 11am-midnight Fri, Sat. **Lunch served** noon-3pm, **dinner served** 5-9.30pm Mon-Sat. **Meals served** noon-7pm Sun. **Rates** £49.95-£69.95 double. **Credit** AmEx, MC, V.

It's well known that this award-winning gastropub is the place for *Coronation Street* spotting. What's less widely known is that it has nine comfortable rooms, each with its own funky style; the overall feel is retro-cool meets vintage chic. Food-wise, it steers a steady course through hearty, classic English fare – so starters might include rabbit and pheasant terrine with fruity chutney, or hearty Bury black pudding with caramelised roasted apples. There's commendable attention too; beer-battered hake and fat chips, for instance, arrive accompanied by pea and mint purée and own-made tomato ketchup.

Pacific

58-60 George Street, M1 4HF (0161 228 6668/ www.pacificrestaurant.co.uk). Chinese **Meals served** noon-midnight daily. **Main courses** £7.50-£70. **Dim sum** £2.50-£3.20. **Set menu** £19-£35.50 4 courses (minimum 2 people). *Thai* **Lunch served** noon-3pm, **dinner served** 6pm-midnight Mon-Sat. **Meals served** noon-10.30pm Sun. **Dim sum** £4.90. **Main courses** £8.90-£15.50. **Buffet** (noon-3pm) £6.50. **Set meal** £20-£38. **Credit** AmEx, MC, V.

Technically, this is one venue, but it has two separate sections – Chinese food downstairs and Thai up – that operate almost as two different restaurants, complete with separate opening hours. Both share a chic, modern look, but the Thai section offers the better food, with deep-fried fish in sweet tamarind sauce the house speciality.

Stock

The Stock Exchange, 4 Norfolk Street, M2 1DW (0161 839 6644/www.stockrestaurant. co.uk). **Meals served** noon-10pm Mon-Sat. **Main courses** £6.50-£19.25. **Set meal** (noon-2.30pm, 5.30-7pm Mon-Sat) £13.50 2 courses, £16.50 3 courses. **Credit** AmEx, MC, V.

Stock's name and imposing atmosphere survive from the Edwardian building's previous incarnation as Manchester's Stock Exchange, and the Italian menu has flavours that rival the venue's stature. The calf's liver and parmesan risotto is wonderful, and the Italian wines excellent.

Tampopo

16 Albert Square, M2 5PF (0161 819 1966/ www.tampopo.co.uk). **Meals served** noon-11pm Mon-Sat; noon-10pm Sun. **Main courses** £6.95-£8.95. **Set lunch** (noon-5pm) £6.95 2 courses. **Set dinner** £14.95-£16.95 3 courses. **Credit** AmEx, MC, V.

Despite its subterranean location, Tampopo has a pleasantly light and airy feel, and the shared long benches and tables give the restaurant a convivial buzz when the place is full. Rather than restricting itself to one country, Tampopo's menu incorporates tastes from Japan, Malaysia, Indonesia and other Eastern destinations to deliver a Most Wanted of the region's cooking. The tasty noodle dishes are renowned.

Teppanyaki

Connaught Building, 58-60 George Street, M1 4HF (0161 228 2219/www.teppanyaki-manchester.co.uk). **Open** noon-2pm, 6-11pm Mon-Fri; 6-11pm Sat. **Main courses** £12.95-£24.20. **Set lunch** £11 2 courses. **Set dinner** £24.20-£38.50 4 courses. **Pre-theatre dinner** £18.65 3 courses. **Credit** AmEx, DC, MC, V.

Teppanyaki is the Japanese style of cooking that uses an iron griddle – *teppan* translates as iron plate, *yaki* as grilled. Here, awesome chefs prepare the ingredients in the kitchen and then cook them in front of your eyes, so that you can see the skill and fresh ingredients that go into each dish. Tuck in to specialities like king prawns and jumbo scallops or ozuyaki beef. With excellent sushi and sashimi as a further draw, it's worth splashing out here.

Harrogate

Swanky spa town.

Yorkshire changes radically when you arrive in Harrogate. On the map it is only seven miles across the border into North Yorkshire, but it feels like another country. The rough industrial edges of South Yorkshire and the Pennines are smoothed out by a town that could fit ideologically into the Cotswolds. Where Leeds smells of new money, Harrogate's wealth feels old and settled. Any flat caps here are in the expensive tweed of the squirearchy.

The arrival is undeniably splendid. First, there's the giant green fringe of the Stray, 215 acres of formal common that hallucinates in spring with millions of crocuses and daffodils. Next up is the handsome stock of stone mansions and seductive shops that are dotted through the town's elegant heart. Yes, Harrogate soon announces itself as a spa town par excellence.

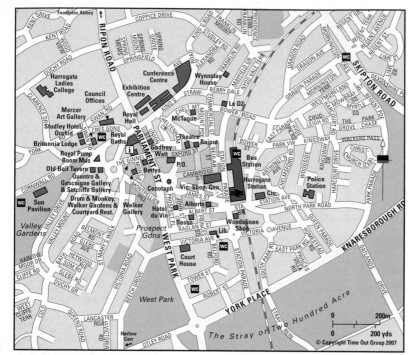

The Stray or Two Hundred Acre

0 ————— 200m
0 ————— 200 yds

© Copyright Time Out Group 2007

No town in the North-east can really compete with Harrogate for pleasure and indulgence. Don't head here looking for clubs packed with trendies or cafés full of intellectuals – come simply for a shameless, materialistic gorge. At its selective best Harrogate really delivers in the art, food, shopping and all-round consumption stakes. The town has emerged as a highly desirable destination and continues to sharpen up its act.

It's true that caricatures of the crusted *Country Life* set who came to define a highly conservative town can still be found – like endangered game, at their favourite watering holes – but Harrogate really has moved on. Indeed, the town has returned a Lib Dem MP since 1997.

Likewise, the well-starched traditional bars and restaurants of old Harrogate now sit comfortably alongside the smart modern aesthetics of newer venues. Restaurants such as Sasso and Quantro (*see p301*) define Harrogate's best new cooking, but a spot of light refreshment and pot of tea at the incomparable Bettys Café Tea Rooms (*see p300*) remains an unmissable experience.

Today, there are as many galleries dealing in contemporary art as there are Victorian Dales landscapes in Harrogate. And while the town's fusty old heavyweight hotels still look great on the outside, there are plenty of stylish B&Bs and quirky boutique numbers to choose from too.

The perfect Harrogate itinerary carefully mixes the best of both worlds; a touch of the old with a dash of the new. A natural starting point is the Royal Pump Room Museum (Crown Place, 01423 556188, www.harrogate.gov.uk/museums) for the story of the town and its 88 different mineral springs, that supposedly cured everything from gout to psoriasis. The sulphur spring beneath the Pump Room still works; drink a shot for free or take home a bottle for 99p. Everyone agrees the taste is vile, giving rise to crafty claims that it can only be dispelled by sucking on Farrah's Harrogate Toffee, still sold in its traditional blue and silver tins from Farrah's shop around the corner on Montpellier Parade (01423 883000, www.farrahs.com).

For the full spa experience, indulge yourself with a visit to the fabulously restored, mosaic-clad Turkish Baths (*see p302* **Soak up some history**), followed by a massage or facial at the adjoining Health Spa. Book yourself into the Treatment Rooms (8 Royal Parade, 01423 875678, www.beauty-thetreatmentrooms.co.uk) or Jennifer Parker (9 Cheltenham Crescent, 01423 701010) for more serious (and seriously relaxing) pampering.

Accommodation	★★★☆☆
Food & drink	★★★☆☆
Nightlife	★☆☆☆☆
Shopping	★★★☆☆
Culture	★☆☆☆☆
Sights	★★☆☆☆
Scenery	★★★☆☆

The revamped showcase gardens at Harlow Carr are another stellar attraction (*see p294* **Garden party**). Indeed, Harrogate is a town of parks and flowers, famous for its spring and autumn flower shows, glorious bedding displays and frequent Floral Town prizes. Even the most cynical sneerer at municipal flowerbeds would be softened by the timeless, gentle pleasure of the Elgar Walk through the Valley Gardens, supposedly the route taken by Sir Edward during his stay at the Majestic Hotel. Watch the model boats on Sunday mornings, or enjoy an ice-cream from the Magnesia Well Café (01423 525149) on the greensward beneath the bandstand, accompanied by a proper Yorkshire brass band.

Cultural Harrogate is marked by theatre, the conference centre concerts and the annual Harrogate International Festival (www.harrogate-festival.org.uk), a week-long festival of classical, jazz and world music held in July. It runs in tandem with the Harrogate Crime Writing Festival; participants have included PD James, Frederick Forsyth, Ian Rankin and Val McDermid. Harrogate, after all, is where Agatha Christie was famously found after a nationwide search when she mysteriously went missing for 11 days in 1926. She ended up at the Old Swan Hotel, known then as the Harrogate Hydropathic.

Two things that never go away here are art and antiques. The Mercer Art Gallery (Swan Road, 01423 556188, www.harrogate.gov.uk/museums), housed in the town's oldest spa building – the Promenade Rooms – belies its age with a challenging modern edge to many of its exhibitions. Elsewhere, the commercial scene features regular antiques fairs and a permanent showcase of polished work. With a couple of snooty exceptions, browsing is very much welcome. The Sutcliffe Galleries (5 Royal Parade, 01423 562976, www.sutcliffegalleries.co.uk) and Walker Gallery (6 Montpellier Gardens,

01423 567933, www.walkerfineart.co.uk) both deal in pricey, 19th-century paintings. If you're after a local angle, McTague of Harrogate (17-19 Cheltenham Mount, 01423 567086, www.mctague.co.uk) has a strong line in Yorkshire locations.

Contemporary work can be found in Rb Tribal Arts of Harrogate (1 Crown Place, 01423 520599), the Anstey Galleries (33 Swan Road, 01423 500102, www.ansteygalleries.co.uk), the Gascoigne Gallery (Royal Parade, 01423 525000) and Walker Contemporary Gallery (13 Montpellier Gardens, 01423 526366, www.walkerfineart.co.uk). Godfrey & Watt (7-8 Westminster Arcade, 01423 525300, www.godfreyandwatt.co.uk) sells paintings, Lucy Casson's tin sculptures, Guy Taplin's wooden decoys and a fine selection of glass, ceramics and modern jewellery.

Harrogate's hinterland boasts a wealth of impressive places to visit. It's a natural launch pad for outings to Nidderdale and the lovely Yorkshire Dales National Park; Fountains Abbey (*see p294* **Garden party**), with the adjoining deer park and ornamental lakes of Studley Royal, is a World Heritage Site; Harewood House is a royal stately home with a lake, a bird garden and a vast, landscaped chunk of Yorkshire; Ripley Castle is a popular destination with a pretty estate village.

At Knaresborough, ten minutes away by road or rail, you can hire wooden rowing boats on the River Nidd from Blenkhorns Boats (01423 862105), or walk along Nidd Gorge, a densely wooded valley with bridges, footpaths and boardwalks maintained by the Woodland Trust (www.wt-woods.org.uk/niddgorge). Another delightful short walk is among the almost secret rocks and lake of Plumpton Rocks, a privately owned estate at Spofforth, five miles east of Harrogate. Ten miles north-west, the National Trust site at Brimham Rocks (01423 780688, www.nationaltrust.org.uk) has more weird and wonderful rock formations to explore.

WHERE TO STAY

In Harrogate's 19th-century heyday as a fashionable spa, grand hotels sprouted up all over town, and doctors in top hats and frock coats would dash from one to another on their rounds. The birth of the NHS in the 1940s led to Harrogate's decline as a spa. Hotels closed or became nursing homes or apartments. Of the old relics, the Cairn, the Old Swan and the mighty Majestic remain, primarily serving the conference trade. The Crown, where Alan Bennett based a TV programme of gentle reminiscences on his childhood, called *Dinner at Noon*, is undergoing a total refurbishment. Early reports sound promising.

TOURIST INFORMATION

Royal Baths, Crescent Road, Harrogate, North Yorkshire HG1 2RR (01423 537300/www.enjoy harrogate.com).

Also worth a mention are the centrally located Britannia Lodge (01423 508482, www.britlodge.co.uk) and comfortable B&B Wynnstay House (01423 560476, www.wynnstayhouse.com). A few miles out of town, the General Tarleton (01423 340284, www.generaltarleton.co.uk) offers stylishly-appointed, comfortable rooms and has an excellent restaurant (*see p301*).

Boar's Head Hotel
Ripley Castle Estate, Ripley, North Yorkshire HG3 3AY (01423 771888/www.boarshead ripley.co.uk). **Rates** £125-£150 double. **Credit** AmEx, MC, V.
This upmarket pub-cum-hotel, part of the Ripley Castle estate, is situated four miles north of Harrogate. Set in a cobbled market square, it offers a decent restaurant (*see p300*), along with 25 ele-

GARDEN PARTY

There are two particularly spectacular trips worth making from Harrogate. The first is a visit to Fountains Abbey, Britain's largest monastic ruin; the second a gentle saunter and matchless afternoon tea at the gardens of the Royal Horticultural Society at Harlow Carr.

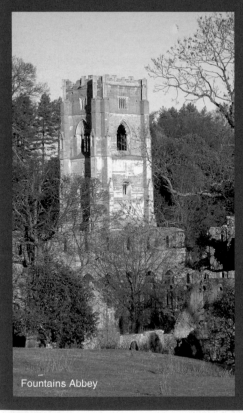

Fountains Abbey

Under dynamic curator Matthew Wilson, the gardens at Harlow Carr have been transformed from the pleasant retreat where Percy Thrower first launched TV gardening – in black and white – into a hot modern attraction. Spread across 68 acres of natural valley and sloping lawns just south of Harrogate, the gardens provide a rewarding afternoon for expert botanists and dilettantes alike.

'If it grows here, it will grow anywhere,' say gardeners, because high rainfall, heavy clay and acid soil with damaging frost pockets make Harlow Carr one of the most challenging horticultural sites in the country. Not that you'd know as you saunter the double herbaceous border, stroll the wildflower meadow rich in cowslips, primroses and snake's head fritillaries, or breathe in the aromas of the scented garden planted with jasmine, honeysuckle and wisteria.

Starriest of all, though, are the Gardens Through Time. The seven themed historical gardens span over 200 years and illustrate the changes in style and fashion, from the Regency period through Lutyens and Jekyll to the Festival of Britain, and ending with Diarmuid Gavin's 21st-century garden.

gant bedrooms, each decorated in its own individual style. There's also the benefit of a lovely castle, gardens and deer park on the doorstep.

Gallon House

47 Kirkgate, Knaresborough, North Yorkshire HG5 8BZ (01423 862102/www.gallon-house. co.uk). **Rates** £99 double. **No credit cards.**

The beautifully located Gallon House is just five miles outside of Harrogate, in neighbouring Knaresborough. This tiny hotel (just three bedrooms, all en suite) is perched on a clifftop overlooking the Nidd Gorge, Knaresborough Castle and a magnificent railway viaduct. Inside there are marble fireplaces, oak floors, plump sofas and splendid chandeliers in the public rooms, while the bedrooms boast a host of added extras. There

There's also an excellent plant centre, a bookshop, a seductive gift shop and a hugely popular branch of Bettys (*see p300*) – subject to inevitable queues, but worth the wait.

Thirteen miles north of Harrogate stand the majestic ruins of Fountains Abbey, a World Heritage Site and a richly rewarding day out.

Founded in 1152 by 13 Benedictine monks (later to become Cistercians) who were exiled from York to what was then a wild and inhospitable valley on the banks of the River Skell, Fountains Abbey grew into one of the most important and wealthy monasteries in England until the Dissolution of the Monasteries in 1539. Today, it is the most complete Cistercian abbey in Britain and one of our greatest treasures.

Enter via the Visitors' Centre, with its National Trust shop and café, and follow either of the two paths down to the abbey. It is undeniably stunning. The nave and great windows retain their original height, while the cellarium is a breathtaking vaulted cellar.

From the abbey, follow the footpath by the River Skell to the Studley Royal Water Garden, created in the 17th century by John Aislabie, the MP for Ripon who was disqualified

from public office after the disastrous South Sea Bubble affair.

Happily for us, he retreated to his beautiful Studley and constructed the gardens, with their temples, water features and woodland walks. Cross the stepping stones and take tea or ice-cream at the Studley Royal tearoom before the return walk to the car park.

Alternatively, by arriving at the Studley Royal entrance you can explore in reverse through the deer park, water gardens and woods before the show-stopping finale of the abbey itself.

There are daytime and evening activities throughout the year, from plays, concerts and musical theatre on summer evenings to floodlit carol services at Christmas, and winter walks to watch the deer being fed.

HARLOW CARR GARDENS

Crag Lane, Beckwithshaw, Harrogate, North Yorkshire HG3 1QB (01423 724666/www.rhs. org.uk/harlowcarr). **Open** Mar-Oct 9.30am-last entry 5pm daily (except Christmas Day). Nov-Feb 9.30am-last entry 4pm daily. **Price** £6; £2 children; free under-6s; £5 each groups (10+).

FOUNTAINS ABBEY & STUDLEY ROYAL WATER GARDEN

Ripon, nr Harrogate, North Yorkshire HG4 3DY (01765 608888/www.fountainsabbey.org.uk). **Open** times vary; call or check website for details. **Price** £7.50; £4 children; £20 family ticket.

The sleek, chic surrounds of the Hotel du Vin.

are quilted bedspreads, CD players, baskets of books, bathrobes and tea-making trays that include complimentary cordial and Black Sheep beer alongside the usual suspects. A basket of 12 things you might have forgotten – razor, toothbrush, tights and so on – is another thoughtful touch. The hotel's owner, Rick Hodgson, is a renowned Yorkshire chef, so a good breakfast should be assured. Dinner is available if you book it in advance.

Hotel du Vin

Prospect Place, Harrogate, North Yorkshire HG1 1LB (01423 856800/www.hotelduvin. com). **Rates** £120-£140 double; £145-£275 suite. **Lunch served** noon-2pm Mon-Sat; 12.30-2.30pm Sun. **Dinner served** 6.30-10pm Mon-Thur, Sun; 6.30-10.30pm Fri, Sat. **Main courses** £13.50-£17.50. **Set meals** £15.50 3 courses. **Credit** AmEx, DC, MC, V.
This boutique hotel – part of the Hotel du Vin chain – quietly announces itself with a small, discreet wall plaque on its exterior. Created from a row of Georgian terraces overlooking the Stray, this is a reliable, sophisticated and stylish place to stay. The decor throughout is modern, open-plan and consciously quirky: a purple billiard table, worn leather chairs, a realist mural painted on forbiddingly dark walls, distressed wood floors. A stainless-steel staircase leads up to 43 modish bedrooms, featuring the likes of Egyptian cotton sheets, plasma screens, DVD players, roll-top baths and power showers. Weekends are busy, with the excellent bar and bistro (dishes range from simple steaks to roast venison and seared tuna niçoise) attracting a fashionable local crowd.

Rudding Park

Follifoot, Harrogate, North Yorkshire HG3 1JH (01423 871350/www.ruddingpark.com). **Rates** £175-£195 double; £270-£330 suite. **Lunch served** noon-2.30pm, **dinner served** 7-9.30pm daily. **Main courses** £13.50-£19.50. **Credit** AmEx, DC, MC, V.
This large Regency house hotel, set in rolling parkland just outside Harrogate, is the centrepiece of the ever-expanding Rudding empire. (It also features an 18-hole golf course, another six-hole course under construction, self-catering lodges and camping and caravan sites). The hotel itself has a corporate, contemporary feel and bedrooms are fluffed up with mounds of pillows, crisp white sheets, smart toiletries and soft bathrobes. The superior Clocktower restaurant operates to high standards (*see p300*). The whole place is very opulent, very expense-account and very comfortable for a big splash weekend. If you'd prefer something a little more low key, the 50-acre holiday park is set away among the pine trees and offers self-catering lodges (for both weekly and weekend hire), a caravan site and camping. Facilities include a pub, shop, playground and outdoor heated swimming pool.

Studley Hotel

28 Swan Road, Harrogate, North Yorkshire HG1 2SE (01423 560425/www.studleyhotel. co.uk). **Rates** £99-£109 double; £150 suite. **Credit** AmEx, DC, MC, V.
At first glance, this solid, stone-walled establishment near the Valley Gardens looks like the quintessential Harrogate hotel of swirly carpets and Anaglypta walls. But the bedrooms have been revamped with pleasant contemporary furnishings in neutral colours, and the reception and corridors are set to follow suit. Added value comes courtesy of the basement Orchid restaurant, which serves superior oriental dishes (*see p301*). There's a swimming pool available at the nearby Swallow St George hotel.

Yorke Arms at Ramsgill

Ramsgill-in-Nidderdale, North Yorkshire HG3 5RL (01423 755243/www.yorke-arms.co.uk). **Rates** £300-£380 double. **Credit** AmEx, DC, MC, V.
Describing itself as a 'restaurant with rooms', the Yorke Arms at Ramsgill is one of the district's most luxurious accommodation options. It's a 20-mile drive up Nidderdale but this former shooting lodge on the village green is well worth the detour. Food – prepared by owner Frances Atkins – is stunning (*see p301*). Accommodation boasts beautifully furnished bedrooms with all the usual facilities, plus LCD TVs and lovely Dales views. The public rooms, meanwhile, have a soothing, country-house feel, with lots of polished oak, roaring fires and classic chintz.

WHERE TO EAT & DRINK

For a town as well groomed as Harrogate, eating and drinking can be disappointing, with too many chains and formulaic joints competing for the conference trade. Choose carefully from a handful of good central restaurants, or head out to one of three superior quality gastropubs in the countryside.

Along with the eateries mentioned below, the Courtyard Restaurant (01423 530708) in the antiques quarter is worth a visit for its inventive seasonal fare. Likewise, Harrogate stalwart the Drum & Monkey (01423 502650, www.drumand monkey.co.uk) is a fine choice: excellent seafood dishes with a fantastic, traditional vibe. Alberts (2 Albert Street, 01423 568446, www.albertsharrogate.co.uk) is a bright contemporary brasserie serving steaks, fish and chips, pasta dishes, salads and sandwiches.

Run by Perveen Khan and her three sons, Rajput (11 Cheltenham Parade, 01423 562113, www.rajput.co.uk) is a real find. It began serving up its mix of home-style and modern Indian dishes in 1992, and remains one of Harrogate's best Indian restaurants.

SHOP(UP)LIFTING

Harrogate

Fine art and antiques lovers should head for the Montpellier Quarter, which is positively stuffed with antiques shops. Install the children at **Pots 2 Go** for a pottery painting session (25 Montpellier Parade, 01423 524797) and explore.

For top-end 18th-century English furniture, Georgian silver or antique glass, browse **Armstrongs** (10-11 Montpellier Parade, 01423 506 8430), **Paul Wetherell** (30 Montpellier Parade, 01423 507 8100) or **Charles Lumb** (2 Montpellier Gardens, 01423 503776). More affordable are the stalls within the **Montpellier Mews Antique Market** (Montpellier Street, 01423 530484) and the **Ginnel Antiques Centre** (The Ginnel, off Parliament Street, 01423 567182).

Should you feel the chill, the Montpellier Quarter is also well stocked with quality woollies. Traditional Scottish cashmere specialist **Hawick Cashmere** (20 Montpellier Parade, 01423 502519) has sweaters in a gorgeous range of colours. **Billie and Gruff** (32 Montpellier Parade, 01423 817396) sells jeans and jewellery as well as cashmere, and there are more cosy knits in **Toast** (23 Montpellier Parade, 01423 507746).

More stylish clothes shopping can be found round the corner at **Morgan Clare's** (3 Montpellier Gardens, 01423 565709) or **Julie Fitzmaurice** (38 Parliament Street, 01423 562932), which stocks couture as well as Paul Costello and Original Blues. **Lynx** (20 West Park, 01423 523845) has a wide range of labels, including Viktor & Rolf, Ann Louise Roswald, John Smedley and more. **Lynx for men** (12 West Park, 01423 521486) is a few doors away.

The most amazing shop in Harrogate, however, is its most discreet. It never advertises and it never opens on Saturdays, so you'll have to extend your weekend for a visit. **Woods** (65-69 Station Parade, 01423 530111, www.woodsof harrogate.com) is a sumptuous linen shop on three floors, serviced by an old and beautifully maintained lift. The quality is incomparable, whether it's a pure linen dishcloth for £8.50 or an Egyptian cotton sheet at £259.

Food lovers will appreciate Harrogate more for its gourmet shopping than its handful of noteworthy restaurants. Start at **Weeton's** (23-24 West Park, 01423 507100), a gourmet supermarket with a fabulous array of organic and local vegetables, top-grade meat, cheeses and luscious pies and pastries. The shelves are stacked with superb Yorkshire produce, from Mackenzie's smoked salmon from the smokery on Blubberhouses Moor to jams from Rosebud Preserves, in the heart of the Yorkshire Dales.

Next stop **Bettys** (*see p300*), whose first tearoom opened in 1919. There are now six branches, including one at the Royal Horticultural Society Gardens at **Harlow Carr** (*see p294 Garden party*), but this is the flagship where the string quartet first struck up and where pinafores are still starched to imperial standards.

For all the history and tradition, there's nothing dated about its superb baking. The window displays a dozen different breads every day: wholegrain, Turkestan, parmesan and herb, sun-dried tomato, Yorkshire cobble. Inside are more temptations: crumpets, pikelets, fruit tarts, gingerbread, fruit loaf and Bettys' famous Fat Rascals – best served warm with butter. Exotic teas and coffees provide the perfect accompaniment: single estate Darjeeling or a wine-flavoured Yemeni Mocha, perhaps.

Bettys also has its own acclaimed cookery school (01423 814016, www.bettyscookeryschool.co.uk). It runs day courses on bread, pastry, chocolate and more, plus children's courses; prices average £145. Book well in advance.

The **Cheeseboard** (1 Commercial Street, 01423 508837) has a strong selection of domestic and European cheeses. Go local with a Supreme Wensleydale from Hawes, or one of Judy Bell's excellent blues from her farm near Thirsk – Yorkshire blue, Byland blue or a creamy buffalo blue from a Yorkshire water buffalo herd. For a short parade that packs in four terrific gourmet shops, head for Kings Road, beyond the Conference Centre. **Ramus Seafoods** (Nos.132-136, 01423 563271) offers a fine array of wet fish and seafood, from east coast crab to Canadian lobster. Ramus will put together a platter of any size to take back to your lodgings, brimming with lobster, oysters, shrimp and smoked salmon. **Regal Fruiterers** (No.144, 01423 509609) supplies both ordinary and exotic fruit and veg. Then there's **Arcimboldo's** (No.146, 01423

508760), a smart independent deli whose house cooks make delicious pies, pastries and takeaway dishes. Next door, **Thierry Dumouchel's** (No.146A, 01423 502534) has gorgeous baguettes and French pâtisserie, including fruit tarts and sublime almond croissants.

At the other end of town, but worth the trek, is one of the few specialist food bookshops outside London. **Allison Wagstaff's Cook Book Shop** (Spring Cottage, Cold Bath Place, 01423 536537) has a particularly comprehensive 'professional' section, and is also a good place for unusual kitchen gadgets and every kind of cookie cutter imaginable. If all those glossy cookbooks whet your appetite, head for a light lunch and more goodies to take home at Rupert Titchmarsh's Italian deli, **Tartufo** (49 Cold Bath Road, 01423 564270, www.tartufo.co.uk).

Harrogate

Montpellier

For drinking in Harrogate, the Old Bell Tavern (6 Royal Parade, 01423 507930, www.markettowntaverns.co.uk) serves eight real ales and Belgian and German beers. Housed in Farrah's old toffee shop opposite the Pump Room, it also has a serviceable upstairs restaurant.

There's usually a lively weekend scene at the Hotel du Vin (*see p297*).

Bettys Café Tea Rooms

1 Parliament Street, Harrogate, North Yorkshire HG1 2QU (01423 502746/ www.bettysandtaylors.co.uk). **Meals served** 9am-9pm daily. **Main courses** £7-£11. **Credit** MC, V.

This famous retreat is renowned for its exquisite morning coffees and afternoon teas, but caters equally well for proper meals. Tuck into old favourites such as Bettys caesar salad, club sandwiches or rösti served with bacon and raclette cheese. There's also a corrupting selection of cakes, organic ice-creams and pastries – the Yorkshire curd tart is a must. Children are welcomed with a Little Rascals menu, offering the likes of wensleydale cheese sandwiches, chicken goujons in breadcrumbs, milkshakes and ice-cream 'clown' cones. Early evening is the best time to beat the queues (no bookings are taken). Alcohol is served.

Boar's Head Hotel

Ripley Castle Estate, Ripley, North Yorkshire HG3 3AY (01423 771888/www.boarshead ripley.co.uk). Bistro **Lunch served** noon-2pm, **dinner served** 7-9pm daily. **Main courses** £10.95-£16. *Restaurant* **Lunch served** noon-2pm, **dinner served** 7-9pm daily. **Main courses** £30-£39.50. **Credit** AmEx, DC, MC, V.

A traditional coaching inn, the Boar's Head (*see p294*) is set in a picture-postcard estate village. Do the castle and gardens, then make your way here to lunch on hearty dishes like baked cod, pan-fried fillet of beef or goat's cheese and leek terrine. There's also a hotel dining room that offers a more sophisticated menu, including dishes such as ballotine of corn-fed chicken, noisette of lamb and pan-fried red mullet. Leave room for desserts along the rhubarb trifle lines.

Brio

Unit 1J Hornbeam Park Drive, Harrogate, North Yorkshire HG2 8RA (01423 870005/ www.brios.co.uk). **Meals served** noon-10pm Mon-Sat. **Main courses** £13-£18.50. **Credit** DC, MC, V.

Brio was one of the brightest lights in contemporary dining in Harrogate, until a devastating fire in 2005 razed it to the ground. The business then reopened on a trading estate on the edge of town, serving family-friendly pasta and pizza dishes and a fine selection of own-made deserts. It's

Bettys Café Tea Rooms

good, though not as modish as the original. In 2007, a brand new outpost opened on the prestigious Kings Road.

Clocktower

Rudding Park, Follifoot, Harrogate, North Yorkshire HG3 1JH (01423 871350/www. ruddingpark.com). **Lunch served** noon-2.30pm, **dinner served** 7-9.30pm daily. **Main courses** £13.50-£19.50. **Credit** AmEx, DC, MC, V.

The smart Clocktower restaurant is part of the ambitious Rudding Park estate (*see p297*). Talented head chef Stephanie Moon has created a distinctive menu – available in the bar, dining room, conservatory or garden – that's bursting with regional flavour: North York Moors partridge, organic beefburgers with wensleydale cheese, Nidderdale lamb shank, Scarborough woof (wolf fish) cake, local venison with Pontefract (liquorice) sauce. Even the bread and butter pudding comes with Yorkshire clotted cream.

Le D2

7 Bower Road, Harrogate, North Yorkshire HG1 1BB (01423 502700/www.led2.co.uk). **Lunch served** noon-2pm Tue-Sat. **Dinner served** 6pm-late Tue-Sat; 6-10pm Sun. **Main courses** £8.95-£16.95. **Set lunch** £7.95 2 courses, £10.95 3 courses. **Set dinner** £13.95 2 courses, £17.95 3 courses. **Credit** MC, V.
Run and owned by the two Ds, David and Dominique, this sparky little brasserie serves appealing modern fare. The set menus are very reasonably-priced; in the evening, your options might include classic french onion soup with gruyère croute or crispy duck salad to start, then grilled salmon with a crab, herb and mustard crust or braised beef daube to follow. Lemon walls and blue and white spotted tablecloths add a feisty finish to a sturdy stone terrace.

General Tarleton Inn

Boroughbridge Road, Ferrensby, North Yorkshire HG5 0PZ (01423 340284/ www.generaltarleton.co.uk). Bar Brasserie **Lunch served** noon-2pm, **dinner served** 6-9.15pm daily. **Main courses** £8.95-£17.50. *Restaurant* **Lunch served** noon-1.45pm Sun. **Dinner served** 6-9.15pm Mon-Sat. **Set dinner** £32.95 3 courses. **Set Sunday lunch** £22.95 3 courses. **Credit** AmEx, DC, MC, V.
Cosy up to the fire in the Tarleton's traditional bar or try the more formal dining room on for size. Both serve up excellent, high-quality dishes: roast rack of Yorkshire Dales lamb and duckling breast with seared foie gras might be found on the restaurant menu; potted pork, steak and ale pudding, and hog sausages feature in the bar (where you can also enjoy a pint of locally brewed Black Sheep ale). There's a kids' menu, but all ages will love the treacle tart or sticky toffee pud.

Oxford Street Brasserie

34 Oxford Street, Harrogate, North Yorkshire HG1 1PP (01423 505300). **Lunch served** noon-2.30pm Mon-Sat. **Dinner served** 5.30-9.30pm Tue-Sat. **Main courses** £10.95-£25. **Set lunch** £10 3 courses. **Credit** MC, V.
A buzzing, modern eaterie that opens for brunch through to dinner, serving such global brasserie dishes as goat's cheese soufflé, ham terrine, haddock rarebit and Thai mussels with coconut and lemongrass. Staff are solicitous and knowledgeable.

Orchid

Studley Hotel, 28 Swan Road, Harrogate, North Yorkshire HG1 2SE (01423 560425/ www.studleyhotel.co.uk). **Lunch served** noon-

2pm Mon-Fri, Sun. **Dinner served** 6.30-10pm daily. **Main courses** £9.25-£19.95. **Set meals** £26.95 4 courses. **Credit** AmEx, DC, MC, V.
Hotel dining rooms are often the kiss of death to fine dining, but not at the Studley Hotel. The menu fuses Malaysian, Thai and Chinese dishes to great effect, creating a brilliant oriental restaurant that's packed out every night with locals as well as residents. Try a Malaysian chicken satay with peanut sauce, followed by Thai seafood kapaow – a shellfish and vegetable stir fry with a wallop of bird's eye chilli. Finish off with mango pudding with cream, and a soothing jasmine tea. Book early for the Sunday buffet lunch.

Quantro

3 Royal Parade, Harrogate, North Yorkshire HG1 2SZ (01423 503034/www.quantro.co.uk). **Lunch served** noon-2pm Mon-Sat. **Dinner served** 6-10pm Mon-Fri; 6-10.30pm Sat. **Main courses** £11.60-£16.50. **Credit** AmEx, MC, V.
Light and airy Quantro offers a contemporary setting that suits its lively, inventive menu perfectly. Try delicious dishes such as wild rice spinach cakes with Thai curried vegetables or jasmine smoked duck breast with oyster mushroom risotto. Children under eight aren't admitted.

Sasso

8-10 Princes Square, Harrogate, North Yorkshire HG1 1LX (01423 508838). **Lunch served** noon-2pm Tue-Sat. **Dinner served** 6.30-10pm Mon-Thur; 6.30-10.30pm Fri, Sat. **Main courses** £8.90-£19.75. **Credit** MC, V.
A relaxed and unpretentious trattoria offering fantastic quality cooking. Stefano Lancelotti makes his own pasta, and the difference shows in his perfect cannelloni filled with parsley and ricotta, topped with gorgonzola and walnuts, or his fresh ravioli with lobster. He also does rabbit wrapped in speck with rosemary and garlic, lamb cutlets with a parmesan crust, then proper panna cotta, lemon tart with mixed berry sauce or limoncello sorbet for afters. The food is top value too – check out the £7.50 set lunch menu.

Yorke Arms at Ramsgill

Ramsgill-in-Nidderdale, North Yorkshire HG3 5RL (01423 755243/www.yorke-arms.co.uk). **Lunch served** noon-2pm daily. **Dinner served** 7-9pm Mon-Sat. **Main courses** £20-£24. **Credit** AmEx, DC, MC, V.
Drive out to Upper Nidderdale in prime Dales countryside, where Frances Atkins has transformed the lovely Yorke Arms into a destination hotel (*see p297*) and restaurant. She carefully sources local produce to present a tasting menu and confident carte of Modern British dishes that have earned her a Michelin star. Superior dishes might include saddle of venison or Nidderdale lamb pie. For dessert, look out for her beautifully matched assembly of lemon jelly with floating islands and honey madeleines.

SOAK UP SOME HISTORY

In the 18th and 19th centuries, visitors flocked to Harrogate to drink and bathe in the mineral springs, renowned for their supposed healing properties. The Promenade Rooms (now the Mercer Art Gallery), Pump Room and the Royal Bath Assembly Rooms were lavishly built for visitors 'taking the cure'.

When the Royal Baths opened in 1897, it was considered the most advanced hydrotherapy centre in the world. Here the affluent classes, even royalty, took electric-shock baths, Vichy massages and peat baths. Grand ladies held bath-chair races down Parliament Street, and so many ministers visited it was said they could have held a cabinet meeting. Harrogate was a medicinal spa equal to any in Europe.

Today, the Royal Baths is a ravishing location for a branch of JD Wetherspoon, Revolution bar and nightclub and the Tourist Information Bureau. But Harrogate Council has kept control of one notable gem: the Turkish Baths. It's one of only three Victorian Turkish Baths in England (the others are in Carlisle and Swindon, and neither are as complete as these). The Islamic arches, glazed brickwork, mosaics, painted ceilings and terrazzo floors have been restored at a cost of £1 million, and the rooms have been brought back to dazzling life.

Set aside two and a half hours for the full hammam experience. There are single-sex and mixed sessions throughout the day and evening (swimsuits are required for all sessions), while tours run on Wednesday mornings (before the heat is turned on).

There's a no-booking policy, so it's best to turn up early. Change in the oak and mahogany cubicles, shower, then enter the steam room where eucalyptus vapours clear the airways. The cold-water plunge pool is a bracing preparation for a series of interconnecting heat rooms that follow, all elaborately decorated in Moorish style.

Progress through the warm tepidarium, the hot calidarium and the even hotter laconium. Repeat the cycle as often as required, taking showers or plunges in between.

To round it all off, spend at least half an hour cooling down on the comfortable beds in the frigidarium (which is actually pleasantly warm). This is an essential part of the process in order to reacclimatise to the outside world.

A weekend session costs £16.50. The adjoining Health Spa (01423 556746) offers a whole range of treatments that must be booked in advance: have a facial (£38), full body massage (£40.25) and manicure (£18.35), or invest in a half-day pampering package (£75). It may not cure your lumbago, but you will stride out feeling clean, relaxed and exhilarated.

ROYAL BATHS

Parliament Street, Harrogate, North Yorkshire HG1 2WH (01423 556746/www.harrogate. gov.uk/turkishbaths). **Open** daily (except bank holidays). Timetable information for ladies', men's and mixed sessions is available on the website.

Harrogate

Helmsley & Harome

The moors the merrier.

A doughty, stone-built market town, Helmsley makes a jolly handsome base for a weekend in this wonderful corner of the North Yorkshire Moors. Harome (pronounced as in 'harum scarum') is a small outlying village made famous by the gastronomic expertise and top hospitality offered at the local Star Inn. Both are set in the pretty Hambledon and Cleveland Hills, less than an hour's drive from York or the coast at Whitby via the scenic route (a shortage of local taxis, along with the dearth of weekend public transport, means that you really can't do without a car here).

The main ways of filling time between enormous breakfasts, fish and chip lunches and formal dinners are village explorations, long country walks, scenic drives and pottering around historic buildings and gardens. Sporting pursuits range from hill hikes to hunting or shooting. (Gun rooms are a standard hotel facility in these parts.)

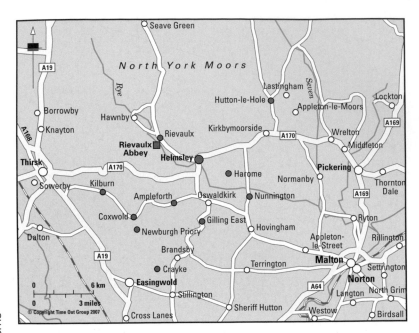

North York Moors

Seave Green

Borrowby
Knayton
Hawnby
Rye
Rievaulx
Rievaulx
Abbey
Helmsley
Thirsk
Sowerby
Kilburn
Ampleforth
Coxwold
Newburgh Priory
Dalton
Brandsby
Crayke

Lastingham
Hutton-le-Hole
Appleton-le-Moors
Lockton
Seven
Kirkbymoorside
Wrelton
Middleton
Harome
Normanby
Pickering
Oswaldkirk
Nunnington
Gilling East
Hovingham
Appleton-le-Street
Rillington
Terrington
Malton
Settrington
Easingwold
Stillington
Sheriff Hutton
Norton
Langton
North Grim
Westow
Cross Lanes
Birdsall

Thornton Dale

0   6 km
0   3 miles
© Copyright Time Out Group 2007

Helmsley itself is a small, solid little town
on the fast-flowing River Rye, with an
attractive market square surrounded
by well-kept stone buildings. These house
an array of hotels and hostelries, along
with some interesting independent shops.
Market day is Friday, but the shopping is
good all week, with a mix of art galleries,
bookshops, antiques and decent gift
shops, along with an improbably small
but appealing department store, Browns
(22 Market Place, 01439 770247).
Nor should you even think of leaving town
without making a purchase at Hunters
(13 Market Place, 01439 771876,
www.huntersofhelmsley.co.uk). This
legendary deli and grocer's on the square
peddles a vast amount of local edibles,
many of them pies.

Once you've done the shops, it's time
for the sights. Helmsley Castle (Castle
Gate, 01439 770442, www.english-
heritage.org.uk/helsmleycastle) comprises
an imposing 12th-century keep, a Tudor
ruin and a visitors' centre where excavated
artefacts are on display. Duncombe Park
(01439 770213, www.duncombepark.com),

the family home of Lord and Lady
Feversham, is a grand stately home dating
from 1713; its grounds are a rare and fine
example of relatively untouched garden
design from the period.

A stalwartly British weekend events
programme takes place in the summer
offering steam fairs, dog shows, band
music, falconry and antiques fairs. Also
worth a visit is Helmsley Walled Garden
(Cleveland Way, 01439 771427,
www.helmsleywalledgarden.co.uk, closed
Nov-Mar): once the kitchen garden for the
Duncombe Estate, it's now a calming and
charming spot containing unusual varieties
of Yorkshire apples and clematis.

Hard by Helmsley is one of Britain's
finest monastic sites, Rievaulx Abbey
(Rievaulx, 01439 798228, www.english-
heritage.org.uk/rievaulxabbey). The name,
pronounced 'reevo', means 'in the valley
of the Rye', and indeed the best approach
is along the Cleveland Way. Starting in
Helmsley, it's an easy three-mile walk
through the beautiful Rye Valley. The first
view of the ruined 13th-century abbey
is quite magnificent: a Gothic church
and cloister open to the sky, silhouetted
against the densely wooded hills. The site
is of immense significance both historically
and architecturally: the Cistercian monks
dominated not only the spiritual but also
the economic life of the area for centuries
(as detailed in the accompanying exhibition
'The Work of God and Man'). The ruins of
the refectory and outbuildings are almost

TOURIST INFORMATION

Helmsley
Helmsley Castle Visitor Centre,
Castlegate, Helmsley, North Yorkshire
YO62 5AB (01439 770173/
www.ryedale.gov.uk/tourism).

Helmsley & Harome

Accommodation	★★★☆☆
Food & drink	★★★☆☆
Nightlife	☆☆☆☆☆
Shopping	★★☆☆☆
Culture	☆☆☆☆☆
Sights	★★☆☆☆
Scenery	★★★★☆

as impressive as those of the abbey itself, as the mid-morning light dapples the grass through high arches and broken tracery.

On the hill above, Rievaulx Terrace and Temples (01439 798340/748283, www.nationaltrust.org.uk, closed Nov-mid Mar) were laid out in the 18th century to capitalise on the superb views of the ruins below. Neo-classical temples (one of which is as impressive inside as out) flank a wide expanse of lawn along the ridge. Still to the west of Helmsley, the rolling country south of the A170 is worth a look, continuing the theme of ecclesiastical ruins and historic homes. Here too is the partly be-thatched village of Harome – with a pond, a cricket obsession and the Corner Shop (01439 770082). Now run by the owners of the Star Inn (*see p309*), the shop's tempting wares include fine meats, wines, cheeses and own-made quiches and bread.

Just south of the village is Nunnington Hall (Nunnington, 01439 748283, www.nationaltrust.org.uk, closed Nov-mid Mar), a 17th-century manor house with a haunted maid's room. To the east is Ampleforth, with its famous Benedictine public school. Church services at Ampleforth Abbey are accompanied by a boys' choir of notable quality, ensconced in pews carved by the 'Mouseman' Robert Thompson (*see below*). Nearby Byland Abbey is another striking ecclesiastical ruin (with an excellent pub in the shadow of its shattered west end), while Newburgh Priory (01347 868435, closed July-Apr, call for days & times) is a Tudor mansion with some public access; Oliver Cromwell is among its former residents.

In the same village, Coxwold, is the former home of the innovative 18th-century novelist Laurence Sterne (he named the house Shandy Hall, after his landmark character, Tristram). Now a fascinating museum about his life (01347 868465, closed Nov-Easter), the house featured in Michael Winterbottom's 2005 film *A Cock and Bull Story*. The area from here towards Thirsk is known for its cabinet-making, and the next village, Kilburn, is home to the Mouseman Visitor Centre & Gallery (01347 869102, www.robert thompsons.co.uk/visitor-centre, closed

Taking it easy at one of Helmsley's watering holes.

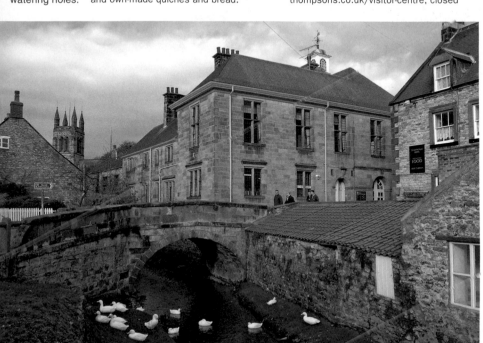

in Oct and Mon & Tue Nov-Dec). The
...tre displays works by Robert Thompson,
...e fine furniture maker known for his
odent trademark, and sells pieces made
by his descendants. You can also admire
his designs in the local church.

The massive Kilburn White Horse, carved
into the nearby hillside, is a curiosity
dating from an ambitious school project of
1857. Into the nearer reaches of the North
York Moors National Park – rather undersold
as 'the largest single expanse of heather
in the world' – there are rewarding drives
and bike rides up nearby deep-cut dales.
Farndale is particularly pretty – notably
the path from Low Mill to Church House.
Hutton-le-Hole is the archetypal moorland
village, with little becks and village greens,
where the enjoyable, open-air Ryedale
Folk Museum (01751 417367, www.
ryedalefolkmuseum.co.uk) comprises 17
fully accessorised old buildings, including
a remarkable Edwardian photographic
studio, and a witches' hovel. Check the
website for opening times.

WHERE TO STAY

In addition to the places below, several
of the venues in Where to Eat & Drink (see
p309) also offer attractive accommodation,
notably the Abbey Inn and Durham Ox.

Another option in Helmsley is the
Macdonald Black Swan Hotel (Market
Place, 0870 400 8112, www.macdonald
hotels.co.uk/blackswan), an old coaching
inn. It's part of a chain, but has a smart
and individual appearance.

No.54 (54 Bondgate, Helmsley, 01439
771533, www.no54.co.uk) looks just like
all the other flat-fronted stone houses in its
terrace, but its past as a veterinary surgery
has equipped it well for B&B-dom, with the
reception rooms transformed into a
breakfast room and lounge. The treatment
rooms, grouped around a pretty courtyard,
have become secluded, corridor-free
bedrooms. Worth mentioning as a curio,
though a little out of the area, is Crab
Manor in Asenby (Dishforth Road, 01845
577286, www.crabandlobster.co.uk), a
Georgian house whose rooms are each
modelled after a different luxury hotel.

Feversham Arms

*Helmsley, North Yorkshire YO62 5AG (01439
770766/www.fevershamarms.com).* **Rates**
£200-£235 double; £300-£365 suite (incl
breakfast, dinner). **Credit** AmEx, MC, V.
Round the corner from the Market Square, next to
the parish church, the Feversham Arms occupies
several mellow, bow-windowed townhouses.
Within, the atmosphere is smart, comfortable and
countrified, and owner Simon Rhatigan and his
staff provide a warm, unaffected welcome. Out

Corner Shop, Harome.

back, a landscaped terrace and patio surround the
swimming pool – perfect for basking in the sun.
The 21 rooms and suites are done out in an agreeable, traditional style, courtesy of the likes of
Designers Guild and Fired Earth, with plenty of
CDs and DVDs for the Bang & Olufsen systems.
The recently renovated attic rooms are especially
cosy, with their own wood-burning stoves.
Downstairs, the two bar/lounges have real fires
and well-stocked bookshelves, and are convivial
spots at any time of day. The restaurant is formal,
but not dauntingly so. You can get casual room-
service meals (the breakfasts are tremendous), but
dinner is meant to be an occasion, with most people dressing up a notch from the outdoor gear
that's the daytime norm. The food emphasises
quality over complexity: seafood fresh from
Whitby might rub shoulders with (local) English
vernacular – loin of rabbit with black pudding
stuffing – on a stylish Modern European menu.
The hotel has also garnered a reputation for its
special events: Christmas carol dinner concerts,
noteworthy after-supper speakers and the like.
Keep an eye out for the many special deals too.

Helmsley & Harome

Star Inn

*Harome, nr Helmsley, North Yorkshire
YO62 5JE (01439 770397/www.thestarat
harome.co.uk).* **Rates** £130-£230 double.
Credit MC, V.

For the best part of a decade, the Star Inn has kept
the small village of Harome firmly on the map for
gourmands and bon-viveurs hailing from far and
wide. And staying the night is really the only way
to properly appreciate the food and wine (*see
p311*) without enduring a winding car journey
home. Just across the road from the pub, Cross
House Lodge is a comfortable, stone-built place
with eight individually decorated double rooms.
Room five is the largest, complete with a medium-
sized snooker table and views over the surrounding farmland. Downstairs, a superb bumper
breakfast of locally produced smoked fish, ham
and eggs and other treats is served in the
Wheelhouse, a log cabin-type affair housing a
huge round table. Three larger suites are available ten minutes' walk through the village in
Black Eagle Cottage. The most recent addition to
the Star's firmament of accommodation is the
(self-catering or serviced) farmhouse in the village, the family home of former owners Andrew
and Jacquie Pern. Stock up on yet more food
(much of it local, some of it produced in the restaurant kitchen) from the Star Inn's Corner Shop
(next to the pub, *see p309*).

WHERE TO EAT & DRINK

First, note that most hotels will rustle up
decent packed lunches for days out, as
will Hunters (*see p306*) – also an excellent
source of picnic provisions. Secon.
in mind that the Feversham Arms he
(*see p308*) also operates as a fine-d
restaurant at dinner and offers a gastr
style menu at lunch (and hot drinks with
wensleydale and fruit cake at any time).
If you're visiting Hutton-le-Hole or pretty
Farndale, the Plough at Fadmoor (Main
Street, 01751 431515) is rated locally
for its food. For a novelty, drive east to
Pickering or Grosmont to pick up one of
the Pullman dining services (lunch £38,
dinner £45) on the scenic North Yorkshire
Moors Railway (01751 472508,
www.nymr.co.uk) – there's even a murder
mystery package (£57) available.

Surprisingly perhaps, beer-drinkers have
a slightly lean time of it in these parts.
The New Inn at Cropton (01751 417330,
www.croptonbrewery.com) is a proper local,
though, and brews nine of its own beers.
Brewery tours are offered year-round, and
by appointment out of season. Helmsley
doesn't have any truly unmissable pubs,
but we'd recommend the Feathers (Market
Place, 01439 770275), a rambling place
that's popular with the local youth and
gentry, for a decent glass of wine. Another
locals' local is the Royal Oak (Market
Place, no phone).

The old-school Crown (Market Place,
Helmsley, 01439 770297) is a family-
owned, 16th-century coaching house, with
a splendidly traditional line in high teas
(fish and chips, bread and butter, and
own-made cakes, buns, scones and pies).

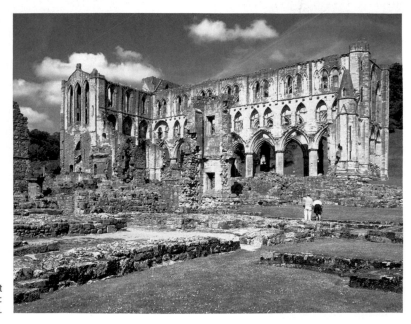

Helmsley's finest
monastic ruins:
Rievaulx Abbey.

Gourmands and bon-viveurs flock to the Star Inn at Harome.

The 17th-century Fairfax Arms (Main Street, Gilling East, 01439 788212, www.fairfaxarms.co.uk) pleases both locals and visitors. The former enjoy its good, unpretentious food and real ales (it's a freehouse), while the latter are also charmed by its pleasant accomodation and the duck-populated stream in the beer garden. The setting is idyllic too, close by the village's castle, church and miniature railway, which takes passengers on summer Sundays.

Conveniently parked at the start of the Cleveland Way, Ryeburn Tearooms (Cleveland Way, Helmsley, 01439 770331) is a local institution – and a National Ice Cream Champion. The 45 or so toothsome ice-creams and sorbets (made on the premises from cream from local herds) come in a seductive array of flavours, from tiramisu to bilberry yoghurt. Presentation ranges from the unadorned cone to the wastrel sundae. The cake menu is no less tempting, with eight or so sliceables flaunting themselves shamelessly in the display cabinet. If you prefer something plainer, there are toasties and teacakes, or just a good cup of coffee – though be warned, a chocolate will shimmy its way on to the saucer.

Abbey Inn

Byland Abbey, Coxwold, North Yorkshire YO61 4BD (01347 868204/www.bylandabbeyinn. co.uk). **Lunch served** noon-2pm Tue-Sat; noon-3pm Sun. **Dinner served** 6.30-9pm Mon-Sat. **Main courses** £9-£17.50. **Credit** MC, V.

Byland Abbey may be marked as a village on the map, but it seems to have only two buildings, both handsome and historic. The first comprises the ruins of a 12th-century Cistercian abbey. Facing it across a tiny country road stands the Abbey Inn, dating from the early 17th century. Broad, beautiful and liberally swathed in ivy, it affords superb views of the abbey from its front windows and outside tables. Inside, country kitchen tables mingle easily with tapestry-backed chairs and a multitude of rugs in a capacious interior that sits halfway between pub and restaurant. The feeling is one of an enterprise that's on top of its game, with tables full right through to closing time and professional but friendly staff. The menu is restaurant rather than gastropub, and fairly ambitious Modern British at that: hearty main courses of a cold winter evening might be braised local pheasant with juniper berries and haggis wrapped in smoked bacon, with whisky and thyme jus, or venison haunch with redcurrant glaze and onion compote. Flavourful starters could include fresh Whitby mackerel and confit potato terrine with griddled aubergine, anchovy and caper tapenade, or king scallops with lime and chilli dressing. The wine list is a considered one, with many by the glass; cask ales include Timothy Taylor Landlord.

Durham Ox

Westway, Crayke, North Yorkshire YO61 4TE (01347 821506/www.thedurhamox.com). **Lunch served** noon-2.30pm Mon-Sat; noon-3pm Sun. **Dinner served** 6-9.30pm Mon-Fri; 6-10pm Sat; 6-8.30pm Sun. **Main courses** £11.95-£15.95. **Rates** £80-£160 double. **Credit** AmEx, MC, V.

From the outside, the Durham Ox looks like an uncomplicated, weatherworn country pub. Inside, however, there are a few surprises: a thoroughly accomplished kitchen, open fires and charming accommodation to boot. A delicatessen counter to one side offers home-made condiments, olive jams and other epicurean delights, while an oak-panelled bar and cottage-style dining room provide the setting for freshly prepared meals made from the best possible seasonal ingredients – some local, others sourced direct from France. The menu changes regularly, but a typical sample might include home-cured salmon with pickled red cabbage for a starter, with Crayke-shot pheasant pot-roasted with bread sauce, or monkfish with vine cherry tomatoes to follow. After one of the fruity desserts, you may feel obliged to emulate the Grand Old Duke of York's men, who reputedly marched up and down the hill outside.

Star Inn

Harome, nr Helmsley, North Yorkshire YO62 5JE (01439 770397/www.thestaro harome.co.uk). **Lunch served** 11.30am-2pm, **dinner served** 6.30-9.30pm Tue-Sat. **Meals served** noon-6pm Sun. **Main courses** £14.50-£22.50. **Credit** MC, V.

The Michelin-starred dining room here has established itself as one of the leading lights on the area's culinary scene for a good few years now. Not as exorbitant in price as others in its class, the menu concentrates on bringing out the best in the local produce (fish from Whitby; meat, fruit and veg from the surrounding farms) with a little help from further afield when necessary and according to season. So for a selection of winter starters, locally grown Swiss chard might find itself teamed up with Lincolnshire poacher cheese and beer-battered onion fritters, or grilled black pudding with pan-fried foie gras, Pickering watercress, apple and vanilla chutney and a scrumpy reduction. Main courses could include roast pheasant from a local shoot or Duncombe Park fallow deer with juniper, creamed curly kale, braised 'candy' beetroot and York ham lardons. Our plate of Leckenby's reared lamb was an extraordinary medley of succulent morsels, concocted out of just about every imaginable part of the wee animal and accompanied by pearl barley and garden mint hollandaise. Starters of freshly steamed Shetland mussels in cider cream with wilted spinach were cooked absolutely au point, delivering a delicious bowl of sea-fresh soup smacking of apples in the wake of the shellfish. Interesting breads are freshly baked. Best of all, these treats are served up in a thoroughly congenial Yorkshire country pub by cheerful young staff.

Windermere & Ambleside

The rugged Lakeland that provided inspiration for
Wordsworth – and a certain Miss Potter.

Panoramic landscapes, postcard-perfect views and a plethora of
pubs and country houses epitomise the attraction of Windermere
and Ambleside. The spectacular scenery has inspired writers, poets
and artists for centuries. It also finds favour with tourists – around
12 million every year. And after the film release of *Miss Potter*, the
area will no doubt catch the fancy of yet more visitors.

Just off the M6, Windermere is the most commercialised of Cumbria's
lakes, but it's also surrounded by the most alluring undulating hills,
woodland and villages. The seasonal splendour isn't restricted to
summertime either. Visit in spring for the brilliant blooms of daffodils
immortalised by Wordsworth, in autumn for the burnished hues
of auburn leaves or in winter for bracing walks across the fells
and relative peace and quiet.

Dispensing with the stuffiness and reserve of yesteryear, many of Windermere and Ambleside's sumptuous country houses have been refurbished so you'll find a relaxed and welcoming atmosphere. At the sharp end of the accommodation scale, expect steamy jacuzzis, modern Cumbrian cooking with a Gaelic flourish, and cutting-edge technology in the rooms. Our favourite destinations for fabulous views and elegant indulgence include Gilpin Lodge and the Samling. The area's pub and café meals have also never tasted better, showcasing regional produce with adventure and flair.

Despite the summertime car-and-caravan hold-ups, and the crowds around ice-cream kiosks and trinket shops, this is an area that retains all the appeal of a rural idyll. Visit for a chintz-and-china afternoon tea by the lakefront, plan a strenuous hike across the fells, unwind in a luxurious hotel, or pack a picnic and take the kids on the steamer. And remember – just a ramble away from the populated lakeside you can be as lonely as a cloud, immersed in unspoilt Wordsworth territory.

Windermere & Bowness

Windermere is England's largest lake, about ten and a half miles long and two hundred feet deep. It's the Lake District's centre for water sports, but the days of powerboats zipping across the water came to an end with the enforcement of a ten-mile-an-hour speed limit. Lakes Leisure Windermere (015394 47183, www.lakes leisure.org.uk/windermere) has a range of water-sports classes, including canoeing and windsurfing. Take a deep breath before plunging in, though – even in summer, the water can be pretty chilly.

Windermere town, a mile inland from the lake, has virtually merged with its twin, Bowness-on-Windermere. Bowness, with its lakefront location and small bay, attracts the lion's share of visitors.

It was the arrival of the railway in the 1840s that transformed this remote, rural outpost into a tourist attraction, bringing people from the rapidly industrialising cities to enjoy fresh air and views. The Victorian heritage is still much in evidence today in the form of stone guesthouses and B&Bs, as well as some fine country houses. Many of these elegantly appointed buildings – former residences of wealthy industrialists and landed families – are now upmarket hotels: Langdale Chase, Gilpin Lodge and Miller Howe are a few notables that still retain a silver-service-and-bone-china kind of appeal. They also boast stunning views from lakeside lounges and conservatories that make ideal locations for afternoon tea. Such teas are a Lakeland speciality: if you book a day ahead, many

TOURIST INFORMATION

Ambleside
Central Buildings, Market Cross, Ambleside, Cumbria LA22 9BS (015394 32582/www.ambleside online.co.uk).
Bowness
Bowness Bay, Bowness-on-Windermere, Cumbria LA23 3HJ, (015394 42895/ www.lakelandgateway.info).
Windermere
Victoria Street, Windermere, Cumbria LA23 1AD (015394 46499/ www.lakelandgateway.info).

hotels will lay on a mid-afternoon feast, complete with Dundee cake, Darjeeling, finger sandwiches, scones, tray bakes and stacks of hot buttered toast. French pâtisserie doesn't get this far north, at least not for tea.

If you're not a seasoned walker, water-sports enthusiast or pampered guest, there's another way to enjoy the area: take a trip on an old-fashioned steamer. Windermere Lake Cruises offers steamer trips that reveal stunning fell views, secluded bays and wooded islands (015394 43360, www.windermere-lake cruises.co.uk). The southern end of the lake boasts some strikingly unspoiled scenery and is noticeably more peaceful than the north. Boats and steamers make regular stops at Bowness, Brockhole, Ambleside and Lakeside – all are great spots for pottering and ambling. Public transport is good – if walking or sitting on a steamer isn't for you, hop on a bus to nearby Coniston for the scenic route across the fells.

The Lake District Visitor Centre (015394 46601, www.lake-district.gov.uk) is the best place to check out what's going on. Get off the ferry at Brockhole and drop in. There's plenty for kids to do here: supervised outdoor workshops, treasure trails and entertaining talks. The centre's indoor exhibitions and café can also save the day when the heavens open with Lakeland rain. The centre is surrounded by 30 acres of gardens and grounds, including a wildflower meadow and kitchen garden.

Blackwell the Arts and Crafts House (Bowness-on-Windermere, 015394 46139, www.blackwell.org.uk), located just south of Bowness, has a dramatic hillside presence looking over Windermere. Built at the turn of the 19th century, its quirky design, clever use of natural light, and artistic flourishes are an ideal backdrop for its gallery. Run by the Lakeland Arts Trust, Blackwell has a wide range of exhibits, from 17th-century craftwork collections

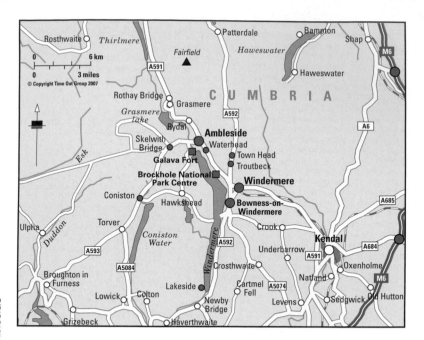

to contemporary art displays, and, of course, Arts and Crafts pieces. Pop into the café afterwards and linger over a glass of own-made lemonade and a scrumptious slice of tea bread.

On the main road from Bowness to Ambleside, the Windermere Steamboat Museum (015394 45565, www.steam boat.co.uk) is home to one of the world's finest collections of historical steam boats. It's an absolute gem; check out the Arthur Ransome exhibition and the boats used in the BBC's version of *Swallows and Amazons*. The museum is currently undergoing a £465,000 renovation, and is closed until further notice.

Ambleside

With its stone-and-slate buildings set against a backdrop of hills, Ambleside embodies the quintessentially English charm of a northern market town. Many visitors believe the rugged landscape and well-weathered town marketplace

Accommodation	★★★★☆
Food & drink	★★★★☆
Nightlife	★★★★★
Shopping	★★★★★
Culture	★★★★★
Sights	★★★★★
Scenery	★★★★★

are best appreciated off-season when the pace of life slows dramatically.

Between three scenic fells – Loughrigg, Fairfield and Wansfell – it has been a centre of local trade for centuries. Today, its main trade is tourism, while the surrounding area is big on sheep farming. Beatrix Potter's storytelling prowess may have spawned a whole industry of souvenir shops and guided tours in these parts, but she's also admired for breeding Herdwick sheep and keeping rural traditions alive. Tapping into the current wave of interest in her life generated by the film *Miss Potter*, local tourist groups have been quick to devise 'Potter trails', or themed walks and activities – find out more on www.visitmisspotter.com.

Also of interest is Waterhead (a stopping point for the Windermere ferry) with its elegant, orderly rows of Victorian guesthouses and hotels. The Romans set up base in Fort Galava, near present-day Waterhead, over 2,000 years ago. After they moved on to higher ground, the area was pretty much left alone until the development of the tourist industry in the 1850s saw steam boats chugging up and down the lake, off-loading fashionable, well-heeled visitors.

A refuelling stop and base for exploring the nearby hills and hamlets, Ambleside is also where walkers and climbers can pick up the latest waterproofs, sturdy boots and bobble hats.

Delis and trendy organic food shops have also made their mark, but the old-school cafés and shops are still holding their own. A Taste of Lakeland (1-3 Rydal Road, 015394 32319, www.atasteoflakeland. co.uk), lives up to its name, rounding up a fine selection of foods from the area's farms and cottage industries. Besides outstanding preserves, the shop stocks bottled beers from local breweries such as Barngates, Coniston, Dent and Tirril.

Fronting the main car park on Ambleside's Bridge Street in the oldest part of the town, and precariously balanced over a tiny bridge across Stock Beck, is Bridge House (closed Nov-Mar, 015394 32617, www.national trust.org.uk). Built in the 17th century, it's probably the most photographed building in the Lake District. While you're there, pop into Adrian Sankey's Workshop (Rydal Road, 015394 33039, www.glassmakers. co.uk) for a display of glass-blowing using traditional medieval techniques.

Walks

There is a wealth of scenic walks hugging the lake or meandering through woodland in the Windermere and Ambleside areas. Orrest Head is only a 20-minute walk from Windermere town centre and its crowds. The walk is more of a leisurely amble than a full-on challenge. You'll be rewarded with panoramic views of Windermere below and rolling fells south of the lake.

Troutbeck and Troutbeck Bridge, sited close to Windermere and Ambleside, are as famed for the low-level surrounding walks as for their stone-fronted 17th-century inns. The Queen's Head Hotel and the Mortal Man are both handily located on the walkers' circuit – a great spot to tank up with top-quality local beer. While you're in the area, drop in and visit Townend – a wealthy Yeoman's cottage, built in 1623 and preserved with its original carved oak panelling in pristine condition (closed Nov-Mar, 015394 32628, www.nationaltrust.org.uk).

For respite from summer crowds, a gentle walk from Stock Ghyll Lane, behind the Salutation Hotel, in the centre of Ambleside, leads to a myriad of waterfalls, the best known of which is 70-foot-high Stockgyll Force. Visit in spring and, yes, there will certainly be a host of golden daffodils.

For the more adventurous, there are steeper fells such as Wansfell and Loughrigg. As walkers know, it's a good idea to check the weather forecast before setting out, and to be prepared for fluctuating temperatures.

WHERE TO STAY

There's no shortage of excellent places to stay in and around Windermere and Ambleside. In addition to the venues listed below, the majestic former hunting lodge

osy country style and upmarket fort food at the nch Bowl Inn.

of Holbeck Ghyll (Holbeck Lane, 015394 32375, www.holbeckghyll.com) is a great luxury option. It has an on-site spa and offers excellent French and British cuisine. (Renée Zellweger stayed here while filming *Miss Potter*). Country houses Linthwaite House (Crook Road, 015394 88600, www.linthwaite.com) and Rothay Manor (Ambleside, 015394 33605, www.rothay manor.co.uk) are also good choices. Choose Linthwaite for its striking grounds and relaxed retreat feel; Rothay for croquet on the lawn, fantastic Sunday lunches and traditional styling. Grade II-listed Storrs Hall (Windermere, 015394 47111, www.elh.co.uk/hotels/storrshall) has fabulous views, excellent food and a glamorous feel. See also the Drunken Duck Inn (*see p320*) and the Queen's Head (*see p321*).

Gilpin Lodge

Gilpin Lodge, Crook Road, Windermere, Cumbria LA23 3NE (015394 88818/www. gilpinlodge.co.uk). **Rates** £95-£145 double; £115-£180 suite (B&B less £20 p/p). **Credit** AmEx, DC, MC, V.
Surrounded by fells and woodland, the family-run Gilpin Lodge offers friendly service and a seamless blend of tradition and modernity. Recently refurbished rooms and suites are spacious and elegantly appointed, each boasting a distinctive character. If homely chic is your style, opt for floral prints, comfy armchairs, fresh flowers and classic furnishings. For those with more urban tastes, there are sharper suites resplendent with mod cons, sleek bathrooms and private jacuzzis. In the main house, four well-spaced dining rooms also offer themed decor including a bright and airy garden room that opens out on to the terrace in summer. Breakfast feasts (champagne sorbet, specialist teas, full English, tempting veggie options) are magnificent.

Langdale Chase

Windermere, Cumbria LA23 1LW (015394 32201/www.langdalechase.co.uk). **Rates** £69-£99 double B&B (midweek only); £109-£139 double D,B&B (weekends only). **Credit** AmEx, MC, V.
Blessed with ringside views of the lake from its reception rooms and terraces, the Langdale Chase is a sprawling country house surrounded by six acres of landscaped gardens and woodland. It shuns new wave decor in favour of traditional grandeur – expect carved dark-wood fixtures, ornate fireplaces, a majestic oak staircase and a minstrels' gallery. Rooms are fairly standard in decor terms (the views are the main selling point) with lots of bold floral prints, pinks and blues. It's worth checking out the room above the boathouse, sited outside the main hotel – it's so close to the lake that you can hear water lap against the walls.

Lindeth Howe

Lindeth Drive, Longtail Hill, Windermere, Cumbria LA23 3JF (015394 45759/www. lindeth-howe.co.uk). **Rates** £150-£230 double B&B. **Lunch served** noon-2pm, **dinner served** 7-9pm daily. **Set lunch** (Mon-Sat) £10 2 courses, £15 3 courses; (Sun) £11.95 2 courses, £16.95 3 courses. **Set dinner** £36.50 5 courses. **Credit** AmEx, MC, V.
This impressive 36-bedroom country house is set on a hillside and enjoys panoramic views of the lake below. Its previous owner was Beatrix Potter, who bought it for her mother, and tasteful reminders of this connection anoint the welcoming lounges and comfortable rooms. Dining here is a smart affair – expect a five-course seasonal dinner menu with vegetarian options. Choices might include Cartmel smoked salmon, roast Cumbrian lamb with redcurrant and wine sauce, and black pudding with pear and vanilla purée. For rainy days, there's a sauna, sun beds and a swimming pool.

Miller Howe

Rayrigg Road, Windermere, Cumbria LA23 1EY (015394 42536/www.millerhowe.com). **Rates** £85-£145 double (incl dinner); £110-£180 suite (incl dinner). **Lunch served** 12.30-1.45pm, **afternoon tea served** 4-5.30pm, **dinner served** 6.45-8.45pm daily. **Set lunch** (Mon-Sat) £21.50 3 courses; (Sun) £25 4 courses. **Set dinner** £42.50 6 courses. **Credit** AmEx, MC, V.
One of the most famous country-house hotels, Miller Howe may have lost some of its sheen in recent years, but the flamboyant furnishings are still as popular as ever. There's no shortage of drapes, flounces and tassels, or cherubic figurines and porcelain collections to admire. Besides the split-level dining room, there are three elegant lounges, plus an appealing colonial-style conservatory and garden terrace offering magnificent views across the lake. Bedrooms are equally opulent; we're talking floral prints, cushions, chandeliers – the works. Cooking isn't quite as memorable as the decor and there's a dated formal French feel to much of the menu. The cook's a dab hand with British puddings, though (the sticky toffee pudding is scrumptious), and the cream teas and fruit cakes are exquisite. Soak up the rarefied atmosphere and start the day with a Buck's Fizz cooked breakfast.

Punch Bowl Inn

Crosthwaite, Lyth Valley, Cumbria LA8 8HR (015395 68237/www.the-punchbowl.co.uk). **Rates** £110-£280 double B&B. **Credit** AmEx, MC, V.
The recently refurbished Punch Bowl is sister venue to the renowned Drunken Duck Inn. And, much like its sibling, this nine-room hotel displays a penchant for tasteful country-style decor. There's a spacious pub and a restaurant with traditional stone fireplaces and weighty wooden

beams. The menu includes tempting delights such as steamed Scottish mussels, Herdwick lamb with wild mushrooms and braised leeks, and apple crème brûlée. Bedrooms are swish but not chintzy, with underfloor heating and power showers, flat-screen TVs and comfortable armchairs.

Samling
Ambleside Road, Windermere, Cumbria LA23 1LR (015394 31922/www.thesamling.com). **Rates** £200 B&B-£290 D,B&B double; £430 B&B-£520 D,B&B suite. **Credit** AmEx, MC, V.
A modern incarnation of a country-house hotel, the Samling's hilltop location offers splendid views of the lake below. There are distinctive suites set in rustic stone cottages as well as rooms in the main house. Each has its own appeal, be it a cosy fireplace, an attic setting, rainshower bath or private terrace. You'll find all the trappings of a top-end hotel (fantastic breakfasts, flat-screen TVs) along with the tranquillity you'd expect of a rural retreat.

Waterhead Hotel
Lake Road, Ambleside, Cumbria LA22 0ER (015394 32566/www.elh.co.uk/hotels/waterhead). **Rates** £49-£118. **Lunch served** 12.30-2.30pm, **dinner served** 7-9.30pm, **all day menu served** 11am-6pm daily. **Main courses** £13.25-£16.95. **Credit** AmEx, DC, MC, V.
A classy refurbishment here aims at a sophisticated Soho feel with the odd nod to the Lakeland locale. There is art everywhere and giant pebbles under glass in the bar area; even the towel rail looks like a work of art. Martin Campbell's photographs of local waterfalls adorn the doors of the 41 rooms. The almost aggressively lit restaurant, the Bay, has striking blue glass tableware and superb views of the lake. Fell-bred beef and lamb and Grizedale venison are on the menu (from £13 and upwards). Guests can use the leisure facilities and pool at the Low Wood Hotel down the road.

WHERE TO EAT & DRINK
Whether you're staving off hiking-induced starvation with a vast plate of cake or indulging in fine restaurant fare, the Lake District has much to offer the discerning foodie. Many of the area's hotels have made food a real focus and on recent visits we have been impressed by the clever use of local ingredients and classic British flavours. You'll encounter delicious seasonal dishes such as local wild duck, Herdwick lamb roasts, regional cheeses and fruit crumbles – all sitting alongside classic French sauces and hot soufflés.

Outside the hotels there is plenty to get your taste buds around. Try Jericho's (Birch Street, Windermere, 015394 42522, www.jerichos.co.uk) Modern European offerings or the retro delights on offer at Porthole Eating House (3 Ash Street,

Bowness-on-Windermere, 015394 42793, www.portholeeatinghouse.co.uk), which is set in a charming 17th-century cottage. In Ambleside, Lucy's on a Plate (Church Street, 015394 31191, www.lucysof ambleside.co.uk) serves up excellent meals throughout the day: imaginative breakfasts, tasty lunchtime focaccias and hearty mains (and the 'Up the Duff Pudding Club', first Wed each month £20, for dessert lovers, see website). Zeffirellis (Compton Road, 015394 33845, www.zeffirellis.co.uk), also in Ambleside, is a restaurant, jazz bar and cinema offering fresh, modern dishes with an Italian twist.

You'll find the local pubs are also excellent. In addition to those mentioned below, we recommend the Watermill Inn (Ings, nr Staveley, Kendal, 01539 821309, www.watermillinn.co.uk), located two miles east of Windermere. Here you'll find a wide range of regional brews, and hearty staples such as beef and ale pie made with Coniston Bluebird beer.

And for the kind of indulgence that only a long lakeside walk can truly justify, Ambleside's Apple Pie Eating House (Rydal Road, 015394 33679) is a must-visit. It bakes the best tray bakes for miles, and for a few pennies, you can bag a currant slice, a square of chewy Grasmere gingerbread and a deliciously syrupy flapjack. Its café serves great value meals too – hearty Cumberland sausage and cider pies, and ace cream teas.

Blackwell Tearoom
Bowness-on-Windermere, Cumbria LA23 3JT (015394 46139/www.blackwell.org.uk). **Meals served** 10am-5pm daily. **Daily main course special** £6.95. **Credit** AmEx, MC, V.
Built in the early 20th century, Blackwell Arts and Crafts House is acclaimed for its light and airy rooms, distinctive architecture and views across the lake. After exploring the gallery and museum, drop in at the bright and cheerful café for refreshments. Light lunches include popular British classics such as bubble and squeak, and potted shrimps, as well as European choices like gorgonzola and air-dried ham sandwiches and ciabattas. On sunny days you can kick back on one of the garden terraces overlooking the lake. A fine selection of tea breads, tray bakes and cakes makes this an ideal choice for afternoon tea.

Chesters Café by the River
Skelwith Bridge, nr Ambleside, Cumbria LA22 9NN (015394 32553/www.chesters-cafeby theriver.co.uk). **Open** 10am-5pm daily. **Lunch served** noon-3.30pm daily. **Main courses** £6.50-£10.95. **Credit** MC, V.
Handily located by the River Brathay, Chesters offers a modern take on rustic tradition. It's a spacious venue with a wood-burning stove, squashy

sofas and an informal vibe. In summer there's the added appeal of a riverside terrace for alfresco dining. Own-made cakes and sweet treats are a big draw – indulge in billowy meringues, chocolate sponges, treacle tarts and flapjacks. Mains are also hearty affairs with quality ingredients. Huge helpings of Cumberland sausage and mash come surrounded by a moat of meaty gravy and there's a tasty array of salads and pasta dishes. Take a postprandial amble over to the nearby interiors store to browse a stylish selection of home furnishings.

Drunken Duck Inn

Barngates, Ambleside, Cumbria LA22 0NG (015394 36347/www.drunkenduckinn.co.uk). Restaurant **Lunch served** noon-2.15pm, **dinner served** 6-9pm daily. **Main courses** £12.95-£24.95. *Bar* **Meals served** noon-4pm daily. **Food** £4.25-£7.95. **Rates** £95-£235 double. **Credit** AmEx, MC, V.

The Drunken Duck is one of the Lake District's finest treasures. Its seamless combination of award-winning own-brews, rustic pub decor and fine Modern British cooking attracts a healthy mix of seasoned walkers, nature-loving visitors and locals out for a few pints. Meals are a sight more pricey than the homely surroundings suggest. The Duck's big on using local suppliers and regional produce and you may well order a hot soufflé made with Kendal cheddar cheese, or locally reared roast lamb. Portions are hefty, so it's best to work up an appetite beforehand. Puds are just a touch aspirational – if you can, go for the steamed sponges and pies rather than overly fussy French-style creations. Breakfasts (residents only) are memorable – take your pick from the likes of softly set poached eggs, classic Cumberland sausage fry-ups and posh eggy bread. This spot is one of Cumbria's best-loved inns; it's no surprise that its 16 rooms are booked months in advance.

Gilpin Lodge

Gilpin Lodge, Crook Road, Windermere, Cumbria LA23 3NE (015394 88818/www.gilpinlodge.co.uk). **Lunch served** noon-2pm daily. **Tea served** 3.30-5.30pm Mon-Sat; 4-5.30pm Sun. **Dinner served** 5.45-9.15pm daily. **Lunch main courses** £4.25-£12.95. **Set breakfast** £16.50 3 courses. **Set lunch** (Sun) £20 2 courses, £25 3 courses, £28 3 courses. **Set dinner** £47 5 courses & canapés. **Credit** AmEx, DC, MC, V.

Experience some of the Lake District's finest cooking at this award-winning spot. Dishes are deliciously imaginative, combining vibrant British flavours with French cooking methods. Examples of this might include a full-flavoured lobster bisque, scented with hints of sweet vanilla or locally procured wild duck with tangy braised red cabbage. Ingredients are organic where possible and often locally sourced. Sunday lunch, afternoon tea and extravagant breakfasts are all catered for with finesse.

Glass House

Rydal Road, Ambleside, Cumbria LA22 9AN (015394 32137/www.theglasshouserestaurant. co.uk). **Lunch served** noon-5pm daily. **Supper served** 6.30-7.30pm Mon-Fri, Sun. **Dinner served** 6.30-9.30pm Mon-Fri, Sun; 6.30-10pm Sat. **Main courses** £6-£18.50. **Set supper** £12.50 2 courses, £15 3 courses. **Credit** MC, V.

Housed in a converted 15th-century mill, the Glass House's impressive glass frontage lends it a contemporary air that works well with its Modern European menu. At lunchtime, open sandwiches, chunky soups, grills and hearty hotpots cater to all tastes and appetites. There's also an early supper laid on for cinema-goers and early diners. A varied dinner menu ups the tone, with dishes such as risotto, steaks and seafood. The dessert menu reads like a dream – lemony meringues, own-made ices and big, bold trifles.

Langdale Chase

Windermere, Cumbria LA23 1LW (015394 32201/www.langdalechase.co.uk). Restaurant **Lunch served** noon-2pm; **tea served** 2.30-5.30pm, **dinner served** 7-9pm daily. **Set breakfast** £8.95 full English & continental. **Set lunch** £18.95 3 courses incl coffee. **Set dinner** £34 4 courses incl coffee. *Bar* **Food served** noon-10pm daily. **Credit** AmEx, MC, V.

The Langdale's restaurant menu offers a choice of indulgent Mediterranean-style dishes and Modern British innovations. Dishes are inventive and delicious: Morecambe Bay shrimps served with walnut bread or wild partridge with pancetta and thyme, for example. Service is faultless – friendly, professional and down-to-earth. It's worth saving space for one of the indulgent desserts. This is a popular destination for weddings and conferences.

Mortal Man

Troutbeck, Windermere, Cumbria LA23 1PL (015394 33193/www.themortalman.com). **Lunch served** noon-2pm, **dinner served** 7-9.30pm daily. **Main courses** *Restaurant* £11-£19.50. *Bar* £9-£14. **Rates** £45-£55 double B&B; £65-£75 double D,B&B. **Credit** AmEx, MC, V.

A favourite destination with ramblers and nature lovers, the Mortal Man has every reason to celebrate its famed longevity as a 300-year-old inn. Panoramic views of the Troutbeck Valley and its surrounding fells are a big attraction, as is the cosy warmth of the traditional pub, its log fires and excellent selection of local beers. After a change of ownership in early 2007, plans are afoot to give the 12-bedroom hotel an upmarket makeover.

Punch Bowl Inn

Crosthwaite, Lyth Valley, Cumbria LA8 8HR (015395 68237/www.the-punchbowl.co.uk). **Lunch served** noon-3pm, **dinner served** 6-9pm daily. **Main courses** £9.50-£24. **Credit** AmEx, MC, V.

Meals here are always memorable and well matched with a choice of wines and excellent local beers. Much of the produce is sourced locally and cooking is as much about regional flavours as it is about Modern European combinations. Culinary gems on offer here include hearty cottage pie, beef and beer stew studded with herby dumplings, organic trout from Hawkshead and a top-quality selection of local cheeses. Always known for excellent food, this place has the potential to become just as renowned as its sister venue the Drunken Duck Inn (*see p320*).

Queen's Head

Troutbeck, Townhead, Windermere, Cumbria LA23 1PW (015394 32174/www.queens headhotel.com). **Meals served** noon-9pm daily. **Main courses** £12.95-£16.25. **Set meal** £18.50 3 courses incl coffee. **Rates** £42.50-£105 double. **Credit** MC, V.

This sturdy 17th-century coaching inn is popular with hardy local walkers who gather by its fireside (even off-season) to sup excellent local beers (Coniston Brewing Company's Bluebird Bitter or Tirril Brewery's Old Faithful). It's also home to a Pandora's Box of quirky historical features. How an Elizabethan four-poster bed frame came to be embedded in the dark-wood bar is anyone's guess, but it does look at home. There's also an impressive, centuries-old oak-carved Mayor's chair, kept in the parlour on the first floor and still used on ceremonial occasions.

Panoramic and picture-postcard perfect landscapes.

The kitchen could take a few pointers from the simplicity of the inn's homely atmosphere. Among the new wave combos on offer, it's the hearty staples that really shine. Treats worth ordering include coarse country pâté served with pickled Troutbeck damsons, grilled turbot topped with shrimp butter, and roast chicken with vegetable casserole. The three-course set menu, pegged at £18.50, is good value and this is a cheery base (there are also rooms available) from which to explore nearby Windermere, the higher fells and Ambleside.

Samling

Ambleside Road, Windermere, Cumbria LA23 1LR (015394 31922/www.thesamling.com). **Lunch served** by appointment noon-2pm, **dinner served** by appointment 7-9.30pm daily. **Set lunch** £25 2 courses, £38 3 courses. **Set dinner** £55 4 courses, £67 9-course tasting menu. **Credit** AmEx, MC, V.

Samling is known for its modish menus and seasonal ingredients. A typical winter menu, for example, would feature some flavoursome renditions of game, roast chicken with crisp glistening skin, and succulent braised lamb. Even humble root veggies are given a stylish makeover at Samling – think velvety celeriac purée and caramelised swede slices as accompaniments. Dressed-up nursery puds such as frozen apple crumble are definitely worth the indulgence. Professional and friendly staff are quietly attentive and as much at ease chatting about local brews as they are discussing the fine dining menu.

Edinburgh

So many ways to amuse your bouche.

Edinburgh is the best, and it's official. Readers of a well-known broadsheet newspaper have voted it the UK's favourite city destination every year since 2000, and it's hardly difficult to see why. This is a World Heritage centre with nearly 1,000 years of history in its stones. It plays host to the biggest annual arts festival on the planet, puts on a huge New Year's Eve street party, and has one of the most acclaimed restaurant scenes in the British Isles outside London.

As the capital of Scotland for more than 500 years, and with a recently buoyant economy, the city has mouth *and* trousers: assurance, tradition and the money to make the wheels go round.

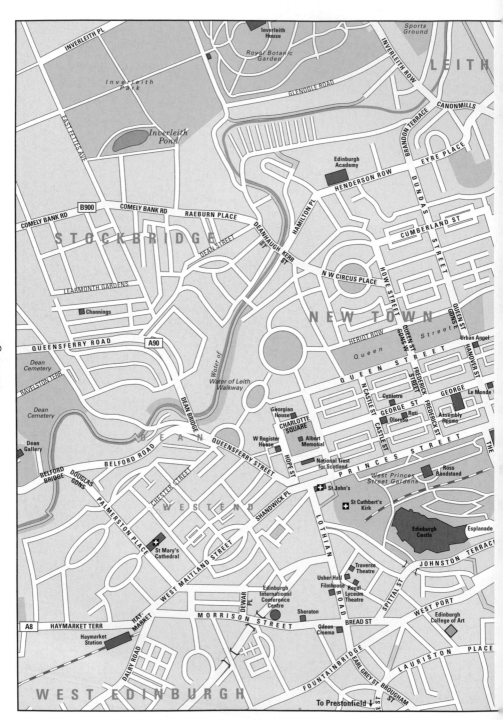

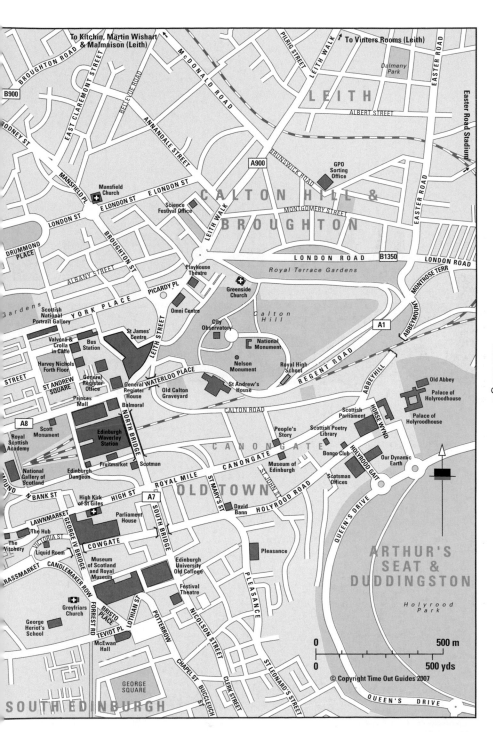

/CityBreaks

ABERDEEN | DUNDEE | EDINBURGH | GLASGOW | INVERNESS | STIRLING

Beauty & urban aren't words you'd normally associate with each other. Unless you've been to one of Scotland's six cities. Boutique hotels, exclusive bars and stylish shopping – they're all here. It's finding them amongst some of the UK's most innovative and original urban architecture that sets the Scottish CityBreak experience apart.

Come to Scotland and look up.
www.visitscotland.com/citybreaks

Accommodation	★★★★☆
Food & drink	★★★★☆
Nightlife	★★★☆☆
Shopping	★★★☆☆
Culture	★★★★★
Sights	★★★☆☆
Scenery	★★★★☆

Earlier history notwithstanding, Edinburgh's story really gets going with Malcolm III's establishment of a castle in the 11th century, consolidated by David I, who founded Holyrood Abbey in the 12th. Castle and abbey were a handy mile apart, providing an east–west axis around which the medieval Old Town developed. Today, that axis is known as the Royal Mile (*see p330*), encompassing the Lawnmarket, High Street and Canongate.

Then there are later associations with the Stewarts (James IV built the Palace of Holyroodhouse in the late 15th century), personalities from the 16th century like John Knox and Mary Queen of Scots, the brutal 17th-century 'killing times' with Covenanters striving for freedom of worship, the Enlightenment (virtually invented in Scotland, according to author Arthur Herman) and the creation of an elegant New Town from the late 18th century. As a summary this hardly scratches the surface, but it can all be investigated around the city today.

Edinburgh was the first-choice site for the re-establishment of a Scottish Parliament in 1999, and has also been a traditional centre for the courts, civil service, academics, bankers and actuaries. Put this all together and you get a certain demeanour: a traditional aversion to vulgarity, a lack of brashness, a bourgeois assurance. Edinburgh takes its pleasures in a particular manner...

While there may be an upsurge in style bars, streets with cheap pubs and clubs, student areas, and locales like Leith where new money mixes with an ingrained saltiness, the city is far better defined by the biggest event of its year, when visitor numbers hit a phenomenal peak. August is the month of 'the Festival', a handy catch-all term that encompasses the official International Festival as well as the Fringe, Film, Book, and Jazz and Blues Festivals, plus the Military Tattoo – all administratively separate. If you're looking for a quiet romantic weekend, pick another month. For unparalleled vibrancy, walk this way.

At the more wintry end of things, the Capital Christmas is a lively mix of family attractions and city centre funfair that runs throughout December, largely for locals. Edinburgh's Hogmanay, meanwhile, is a four-day extravaganza that builds up to a massive street party on 31 December and into the small hours of the new year, attracting visitors from all over the world. Its headline concert, aimed at a mainstream audience, has recently attracted names like Texas and KT Tunstall.

Year-round entertainments include dedicated comedy clubs, art house cinema and the National Galleries of Scotland, as well as a commendable collection of smaller, independent art galleries, regular classical concerts and a small core of contemporary music venues. These encompass everything from the occasional blockbuster gig (the Red Hot Chili Peppers or Live8 at Murrayfield, the national rugby stadium, for example) to more intimate indie music at venues like the Liquid Room (*see p335*), as well as clubs catering to fans of every dancefloor genre. Theatregoers also enjoy a variety of venues, staging everything from the classics to new experimental work. The city has plenty of expansive green spaces too, including the Royal Botanic Garden and Holyrood Park with the 823-foot volcanic peak Arthur's Seat at its centre. Then, of course, there are those excellent places to eat, bars with more varieties of whisky than you knew existed, a small but well-established gay scene, and much more besides.

Edinburgh

Arthur's Seat

TOURIST INFORMATION

Edinburgh & Lothians Tourist
Information Centre, 3 Princes Street
(above Princes Mall), New Town,
EH2 2QP (0131 473 3800/
www.edinburgh.org).
www.edinburghfestivals.co.uk
www.edinburgh-galleries.co.uk

WHERE TO STAY

In addition to the hotels given detailed
reviews below, good places to stay in
Edinburgh include the comfortable and
classy Malmaison (1 Tower Place, Leith,
0131 468 5000, www.malmaison-
edinburgh.com), the glamorous Witchery
(*see p334*) and the Sheraton Grand
(1 Festival Square, 0131 229 9131,
www.starwoodhotels.com/sheraton).

Balmoral

*1 Princes Street, EH2 2EQ (0131 556 2414/
www.thebalmoralhotel.com).* **Rates** £345-£510
double; £640-£1,575 suite. **Credit** AmEx, DC,
MC, V.

A kilted doorman welcomes you to 'Scotland's
most famous address' where the trappings are
everything you would expect from a five-star
hotel: marble floors, crystal chandeliers and attentive service that's rarely intrusive. The Balmoral
was substantially refurbished in 2003-04, and the
rooms now offer cool, earthy colours and geometric
shapes. Some have great views of the city centre,
while others overlook the hotel's Palm Court. Here,
afternoon tea is served in serene splendour and is
a local institution in its own right. There's a popular spa, and the excellent dining choices include
Hadrian's, a decent and informal brasserie, or the
Michelin-starred flagship restaurant Number One.
Under the control of chef Jeff Bland, the latter has
a Modern European style and is among the very
best places to dine in the city.

Channings

*12-16 South Learmonth Gardens, EH4 1EZ
(0131 274 7401/www.channings.co.uk).* **Rates**
£110-£195 double; £170-£285 suite. **Credit**
AmEx, DC, MC, V.

The Town House Company is a revered hotel business in Edinburgh, with some very individual
properties in the New Town and West End. All
have their own special features (from serious
restaurants to dedicated butlers), but the mix at
Channings is particularly attractive. The hotel is
contemporary and tasteful, and the excellent basement brasserie is run by the talented Hubert
Lamort. Five new top-floor suites were unveiled
in 2006, based around a Shackleton theme (polar
explorer Sir Ernest Shackleton once lived here).
These variously boast wet rooms, big monochrome art-photos of Shackleton's ship, the
Endurance, adjacent to baths that could house an
iceberg, splendid views over the north of the city
or the hotel's garden, and more. The establishment
even manages to feel secluded, despite being just
half a mile from Princes Street. Other Town House
hotels include the upmarket Howard (www.the-
howard.com) or the chic, boutique Bonham
(www.thebonham.com).

Le Monde

*16 George Street, EH2 2PF (0131 270 3900/
www.lemondehotel.co.uk).* **Rates** £145-£345
suite. **Credit** AmEx, DC, MC, V.

Part of a £12-million entertainment complex in a
former office building, Le Monde is one of a rash of
new contemporary hotels that arrived in the envi-
rons of George Street in 2006. Its name gives a clue

Luxe bathrooms
and swanky suite
ensure Channing
stands out from
the crowd.

Sheraton Grand

to its unique selling point: 17 of the 18 suites are decked out in the style of an actual world city, while Atlantis provides the theme for the final room. Each has a very different feel: Tokyo is serene, with beautiful framed kimonos on the wall and *Lost in Translation* on the DVD player; New York resembles a Manhattan loft; and Reykjavik has cool blue walls, volcanic rock and lampstands like blocks of ice. The fun continues in the bathrooms with plasma screens and waterproof remotes. If you want to 'travel', the hotel is happy for guests to move from room to room each night during their stay, subject to availability – all good escapism.

Prestonfield

Priestfield Road, EH16 5UT (0131 225 7800/ www.prestonfield.com). **Rates** £225-£275 double; £295-£350 suite. **Credit** AmEx, DC, MC, V.

Sister to the esteemed Witchery restaurant and suites, Prestonfield is owned by Edinburgh's star restaurateur James Thomson (who also owns the Tower, *see p333*). As you'd expect, the food here is excellent – the Rhubarb restaurant is very much a destination in its own right, with adventurous dishes such as seared turbot with langoustine crushed potatoes or breast of Loué chicken with creamed savoy cabbage among the many options. On the accommodation front, things are sumptuously luxurious; think opulent antique furniture and rich silk brocades. The mansion itself dates back to 1687, and although Prestonfield makes the most of its history there are plenty of high-tech 21st-century touches. Plasma-screen TVs, DVD players and expensive sound systems should keep you entertained, though the peacocks and Highland cows sauntering around the grounds do a good job of that too.

Scotsman

20 North Bridge, EH1 1YT (0131 556 5565/ www.thescotsmanhotel.co.uk). **Rates** £200-£500 double; £380-£2,000 suite. **Credit** AmEx, DC, MC, V.

Housed in the former offices of the *Scotsman* newspaper, this luxury hotel features rooms with thoughtful, contemporary design touches, DVD and CD players, internet access and widescreen televisions. There's a buzzing brasserie (North Bridge), which serves a Scottish breakfast so hearty you won't need to eat again till dinner, and a reverential fine dining room (Vermilion). To counteract some of the inevitable overindulgence, there's a health club with a stainless-steel swimming pool straight out of James Bond. The hotel also has its own private cinema, and a serene spa offering fantastic Cowshed treatments. Bang in the city centre, the Scotsman manages to pull off the trick of feeling like a real refuge from the bustle outside.

WHERE TO EAT & DRINK

Before you even contemplate the gourmet delights on offer in this fine city, we recommend you get stuck into some whisky (this is Scotland after all). There are some excellent venues in Edinburgh where discerning drinkers can sample the rarest of single malts. The Scotch Malt Whisky Society bottles whisky from individual casks, whose output only runs to a few hundred bottles. Membership is required but it's not overly expensive, and there is a choice of two members' rooms to sit and sip in (the Vaults, 87 Giles Street, Leith, 0131 554 3451, or 28 Queen Street, New Town, 0131 220 2044, www.smws.com) – decent food is available in both. The best

SIGHTSEEING

EDINBURGH CASTLE

Castlehill, EH1 2NG (0131 225 9846/
www.historic-scotland.gov.uk). **Open** *Winter*
9.30am-5pm daily. *Summer* 9.30am-6pm daily.
Admission £11; £9 concessions; £5.50 5-15s;
free under-5s. **Credit** AmEx, MC, V.
Everyone goes to Edinburgh Castle and you should
too. It has incomparable views from its battlements,
it houses the oldest surviving structure in the city
(the early 12th-century St Margaret's Chapel), it's
home to the Scottish crown jewels, and it sits on
a volcanic plug estimated to be around 350 million
years old. Some of its most interesting buildings
date from the 15th century (the great hall and a
particularly sturdy palace), but one of the most
affecting is the Scottish National War Memorial
(www.snwm.org). Once a simple barracks, it was
completely refurbished in the 1920s as a shrine
and hall of honour for the many service personnel
who died in World War I. (It now also commemorates
those from conflicts since 1918.) If you associate
castle tours with the boredom of school trips, you
could be pleasantly surprised.

National Museum of Scotland

NATIONAL MUSEUM OF SCOTLAND

Chambers Street, EH1 1JF (0131 247 4422/
www.nms.ac.uk). **Open** 10am-5pm daily.
Admission free. **Credit** (shop) MC, V.
Everything you ever wanted to know about Scotland,
from its geological origins and early inhabitants,
through the start of recorded history and all the way
to the impact of the Industrial Revolution, the British
Empire and beyond. Many of the artefacts are first
class, the narrative flow through the galleries is
considered and coherent, and it's all housed in an
award-winning building that opened at the end of
1998 (the Tower restaurant, *see p333*, is on the
top floor). Whether you're looking at a 4,000-year-
old torc from Dumfriesshire or Jacobite bits and
bobs from the 18th century, this museum confers
a real sense of Scotland through time. The modern
building adjoins the old Royal Museum, a Victorian
establishment originally intended as a showpiece
for industry, but now offering blockbuster exhibitions
as well as natural history, applied arts, science and
technology. A four-year redevelopment began in 2007,
so some areas will be closed during that time; the
National Museum of Scotland will be unaffected.

THE ROYAL MILE

Not so much a single venue as the thoroughfare
that forms the backbone of the Old Town. The Royal
Mile runs downhill from the castle in the west to
the late 15th-century Palace of Holyroodhouse in
the east. En route it takes in attractions like the
Camera Obscura; Gladstone's Land (a beautifully

preserved, 17th-century merchant's house); Lady
Stair's House (a museum dedicated to Scottish
writers Burns, Scott and Stevenson); St Giles,
the High Kirk of Edinburgh (a cathedral in pre-
Reformation times, with its 15th-century tower
intact); the Tron Kirk; the Scottish Storytelling
Centre (a 2006 addition) with John Knox's House
adjacent; the Museum of Childhood; the People's
Story (a social history museum housed in the late
16th-century Canongate Tollbooth); and more.
Right at the bottom, by the palace, you can also
find the ruins of Holyrood Abbey, the dramatic and
controversially expensive new Scottish Parliament
building (*photo right*), and the Queen's Gallery, with
its rolling exhibition of art from the royal collections.
Before the moneyed classes moved out to the
New Town, the Royal Mile and its surrounds *were*
Edinburgh – so it's definitely worth a walk, browsing
the various distractions as the mood takes you.

ROYAL YACHT BRITANNIA

Ocean Terminal, Ocean Drive, Leith, EH6 6JJ
(0131 555 5566/www.royalyachtbritannia.co.uk).
Open *Winter* 10am-3.30pm daily. *Summer* 9.30am-
4.30pm daily. **Admission** £9.50; £7.50 concessions;
£5.50 5-15s; £26.50 family (2+3); free under-5s.
Credit AmEx, MC, V.
Launched in 1953, the year of Elizabeth's
coronation, the *Britannia* was used by the royals
for state visits, holidays and diplomatic missions
until it was decommissioned at the end of 1997.
It arrived in Leith as a tourist attraction in 1998,
and proved so popular that it had chalked up two
million visitors by the end of 2005. The yacht is
berthed in the working Western Harbour, with
access via the top floor of the Ocean Terminal
shopping mall. Although the ship's exterior has an

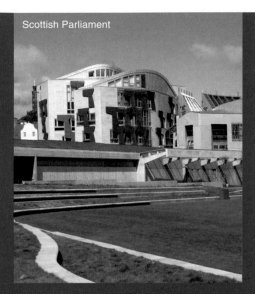

Scottish Parliament

art deco beauty, the interior is dated and suburban – the drawing room being the worst offender. However, you'll be following in the footsteps of Gandhi, Reagan and other luminaries of world politics who have been entertained in the state dining room. The old girl's deck also provides a great view of Edinburgh's waterfront, and the huge development effort happening in Leith, Newhaven and beyond. Before 1995, much of what you can see was derelict dockland – now it's all expensive apartments, offices and retail premises, with much more still to come.

SCOTTISH NATIONAL GALLERY OF MODERN ART

75 Belford Road, EH4 3DR (0131 624 6200/ www.nationalgalleries.org).**Open** 10am-5pm daily. **Admission** free. **Credit** (shop) MC, V.

About a mile from the west end of Princes Street, this gallery offers a real contrast to the city-centre bustle. Start with a peaceful stroll around the grounds, home to sculptures by the likes of Henry Moore, Barbara Hepworth and Rachel Whiteread, as well as a major environmental installation by Charles Jencks, called Landform. Inside the gracious 1820s building, two spacious floors house a permanent collection featuring big names like Magritte and Pollock, as well as temporary exhibitions. In recent years, artists featured have included local hero John Bellany, Cindy Sherman, Lucien Freud, Andy Warhol and Robert Mapplethorpe. Many Edinburghers treat this as a perfect Sunday afternoon's outing, and the basement café isn't bad either. Across the road at No.73, the Dean Gallery acts as an overspill space, but with a particular emphasis on the work of Sir Eduardo Paolozzi.

pubs for whisky include the Bow Bar (80 West Bow, 0131 226 7667), Kays (39 Jamaica Street, 0131 225 1858), the Canny Man's (239 Morningside Road, 0131 447 1484) and Bennet's (8 Leven Street, 0131 229 5143).

Edinburgh also has a good selection of café-bars where you can snack or drink, with the latest generation (2006) clustered around the George Street area. Amicus Apple (17 Frederick Street, 0131 226 6055) is the most amenable and enthusiastic, while the lounge spaces in new hotels like Tigerlily (125 George Street, 0131 225 5005, www.tigerlilyedinburgh. co.uk) or the Hudson (9-11 Hope Street, 0131 247 7000, www.thehudsonhotel. co.uk) are also popular. The enduring example of robust hipsterdom is the City Café (19 Blair Street, 0131 220 0125), while the Blue Moon is Edinburgh's homely gay café-bar (36 Broughton Street, 0131 556 2788) and the Regent its best gay-friendly cask ale pub (2 Montrose Terrace, Calton Hill, 0131 661 8198). Vegetarian bar and restaurant David Bann (56-58 St Mary's Street, 0131 556 5888, www.davidbann.com) is another fine choice for relaxed but stylish drinking and dining. Debate rages over the best café in Edinburgh, but Glass & Thompson (2 Dundas Street, 0131 557 0909) edges it thanks to its excellent food.

Neighbourhood bistros have been a big success story in the city in recent years. First Coast (97-101 Dalry Road, 0131 313 4404, www.first-coast.co.uk) and the New Bell (233 Causewayside, 0131 668 2868, www.thenewbell.com) are both deservedly popular. One area developing a seriously top-class foodie reputation, however, is Leith. Already home to Restaurant Martin Wishart (*see p333*), it welcomed both the Kitchin (*see p332*) and the Plumed Horse (50-54 Henderson Street, 0131 554 5556) in 2006, the latter under the charge of Tony Borthwick, who had a Michelin star from the restaurant's previous incarnation in south-west Scotland. Leith is also blessed with some great seafood venues, including Fisher's (1 Shore, 0131 554 5666) and Skippers (1A Dock Place, 0131 554 1018, www.skippers.co.uk).

Meanwhile, the pick of the city's Indian restaurants would include Roti (*see p333*), Suruchi (14A Nicolson Street, 0131 556 6583) and the vegetarian Kalpna (2-3 St Patrick Square, 0131 667 9890). Other Asian notables are Thai restaurant Dusit (49A Thistle Street, 0131 220 6846), excellent Chinese eaterie Kweilin (19-21 Dundas Street, 0131 557 1875, www.kweilin.co.uk) and Bonsai (46 West Richmond Street, 0131 668 3847, www.bonsaibarbistro.co.uk), a friendly little Japanese bistro.

Edinburgh

Asian aside, the most popular cuisine is Italian. Just behind the Sheraton Grand, Santini matches contemporary decor with high-quality fare (8 Conference Square, 0131 221 7788), but the most celebrated Italian name in these parts is Valvona & Crolla, a delicatessen dating to 1934. At the back of the shop (19 Elm Row, Leith Walk, 0131 556 6066, www.valvonacrolla. co.uk) is its Caffè Bar. There's nothing overelaborate here, just good food made from great ingredients, served during the day. Its big sister (offering dinner as well as daytime snacks) is the VinCaffè (11 Multrees Walk, off St Andrew's Square, 0131 557 0088).

Centotre

103 George Street, EH2 3ES (0131 225 1550/ www.centotre.com). **Meals served** 8am-10pm Mon-Thur; 8am-10.30pm Fri, Sat; 11am-5pm Sun. **Main courses** £8.95-£20. **Credit** AmEx, MC, V.

This buzzy all-day Italian eaterie is set in an imposing former bank, giving it a decidedly grand feel (all huge pillars and stately cornicing). Simplicity is central to the ethos here, with well-prepared, fuss-free dishes based on quality ingredients. Typical pasta dishes include casareccia with oak smoked salmon, parmigiano reggiano, cream and dill, or spaghettini with spinach, broccoli, olive oil, parsley and garlic. There are also dishes involving halibut, Borders lamb, or even Aberdeen Angus steak with rocket and chips. Pizza is a real forte, however; don't miss the salsiccia, with spicy Italian sausage, fior di latte and tomato. Desserts include classics like crema cotta, ice-creams that actually taste Italian, and a selection of very good cheeses. There are also some great Italian wines, and the grappa is an education.

Harvey Nichols Forth Floor

Harvey Nichols, 30-34 St Andrew's Square, EH2 2AD (0131 524 8350/www.harveynichols. com). **Meals served** *Brasserie* 10am-5.30pm Mon; 10am-10pm Tue-Sat; 11am-5pm Sun. **Main courses** £10-£15.50. **Set lunch** £14.50 2 courses, £17.50 3 courses. **Set dinner** £14.50 2 courses, £17.50 3 courses. *Restaurant* **Lunch served** noon-3pm Mon-Fri; noon-3.30pm Sat, Sun. **Dinner served** 6-10pm Tue-Sat. **Main courses** £15.50-£23. **Set lunch** £21 2 courses, £25 3 courses. *Both* **Credit** AmEx, DC, MC, V.

Now well established as one of Edinburgh's better places to eat, drink and snack, Forth Floor sits above three storeys of the city's most aspirational retail. Dries van Noten frocks aside, the views are tremendous – a brilliant urban skyline one way, the Firth of Forth the other, hence the punning name. During the day, it's a quick stop for shoppers, but at night there's a real buzz under the red, recessed lights. The restaurant has a more elaborate menu than the bar-brasserie,

and better sightlines – but it's effectively all one space, discreetly divided by a glass partition. Over in a far corner of the fourth floor you will also find a small cocktail bar. In the restaurant, three courses might offer foie gras terrine with herb salad and Sauternes jelly, roast lamb with minted pea purée, sweetbreads and asparagus, and pear, prune and armagnac tart. There are also special events (Valentine's Day dinners, jazz on Sundays, an Edinburgh International Festival Fireworks dinner with a great view of the pyrotechnics), so phone for details of what's on while you're in town.

Kitchin

78 Commercial Quay, Leith, EH6 6LX (0131 555 1755/www.thekitchin.com). **Lunch served** 12.30-2pm Tue-Sat. **Dinner served** 7-10pm Tue-Thur; 6.45-10.30pm Fri, Sat. **Main courses** £19-£24. **Set lunch** £15.50 2 courses, £19.50 3 courses. **Credit** AmEx, MC,V.

The Kitchin is one of the key establishments currently making Leith a centre of foodie excellence. It arrived in summer 2006 and is a husband and wife business, with Tom Kitchin in the kitchen and his partner Michaela in charge of front of house. Tom has quite a pedigree, having worked with big names in the foodie firmament like Pierre Koffman, Guy Savoy and Alain Ducasse. Housed in a converted warehouse, the entrance is through a light, contemporary conservatory, with the darker dining space at the back. Kitchin's food is all about freshness and seasonality, and although the menu sounds straightforward, the talent here is more than apparent. At dinner, scallops (hand-dived) come nicely balanced with ceps, rocket leaves and parmesan, while wild Scottish mallard is accompanied by perfectly prepared cabbage and parsnip. A gratin of figs, blackberries and other fruits with vanilla ice-cream would be a typical and delicious dessert. More than half the wine list is pitched at £25 or under.

Oloroso

33 Castle Street, EH2 3DN (0131 226 7614/ www.oloroso.co.uk). **Lunch served** noon-2.30pm, **dinner served** 7-10.30pm daily. **Main courses** £14.50-£27. **Set lunch** (Sun) £15 2 courses, £19.95 3 courses. **Credit** AmEx, MC, V.

Over the last six years, Oloroso has gone from new kid on the block to established destination bar-restaurant. It has a reputation for quality cooking and sharp, contemporary decor. The grills are particularly impressive, and the modish à la carte dinner menu offers creative three-course delights such as sweet potato and lime leaf soup, seared sea bass with butternut squash purée, and chocolate and prune terrine with cassis sorbet and candied ugli fruit. There's also a lengthy international wine list. Oloroso sits atop a city centre office building (lift to the third floor then stairs to the fourth), so it has excellent views and a roof terrace

Shapes

from which to enjoy the ephemeral Scottish summer. Irrespective of the weather, the bar is usually buzzing and many come simply to drink or snack, bypassing the more formal dining space.

Restaurant Martin Wishart

54 The Shore, Leith, EH6 6RA (0131 553 3557/www.martin-wishart.co.uk). **Lunch served** noon-2pm, **dinner served** 7-10pm Tue-Sat. **Set lunch** £22.50 3 courses. **Dinner** £50 3 courses. **Credit** AmEx, MC, V.

In the historic heart of Leith, Wishart's establishment has retained a Michelin star since 2001 – and the food is sublime. Subtle frothy pumpkin purée with vegetable shavings served in a small glass vase as an amuse bouche; intense jerusalem artichoke soup as a starter; a dainty bouillabaisse or fillet of veal with foie gras mousse to follow. Then for pudding, achingly good almond and pear tart with armagnac ice-cream. The sommelier is brilliant, the front-of-house staff approachable and efficient, and the kitchen crew could well be the best in the city. The premises got a makeover at the beginning of 2006, giving them a more contemporary look, so there's no resting on the laurels either. One of Scotland's best, it

has separate tasting (£60) and vegetarian menus (dishes such as emmental and parmesan soufflé, and herb risotto feature) too.

Roti

70 Rose Street, North Lane, EH2 3DX (0131 225 1233/www.roti.uk.com). **Lunch served** noon-2pm Tue-Fri. **Dinner served** 6-11pm Tue-Sat. **Main courses** £12-£16. **Set lunch** £15.95 2 courses, £19.95 3 courses. **Credit** AmEx, DC, MC, V.

For years, this undistinguished back lane near Princes Street was home to a much-loved restaurant called Martin's, which closed its doors in summer 2005. Tony Singh of Oloroso fame (*see p332*) did the carpe diem thing and swiftly moved in with a new spin on Indian cuisine: 'not an Indian restaurant but it does offer Indian food,' says its slogan. So you won't find kormas and bhunas here, but you will find dishes such as spiced, chargrilled king prawns, fenugreeked john dory with vegetable masala, Goan fish curry or seared halibut in coconut and vegetable stew. Desserts are elaborate, with a visual wow factor. The decor is understated with lots of subtle subcontinental touches, and Roti has been a big hit since its launch.

Tower

Museum of Scotland, Chambers Street, EH1 1JF (0131 225 3003/www.tower-restaurant. com). **Lunch served** noon-5pm, **dinner served** 5-11pm daily. **Main courses** £12-£29. **Set lunch** £9.95 2 courses. **Pre-theatre** (5-6.30pm) £12.50 2 courses. **Credit** AmEx, DC, MC, V.

Opened by local star restaurateur James Thomson in 1998, this stylish, contemporary restaurant above Scotland's premier museum is on everyone's list of best Edinburgh eateries (Thomson also runs the Witchery and the luxury hotel Prestonfield, *see p334 & p329*). Access is via the main museum entrance; once inside, you take a lift to the top floor, from which the Old Town views are incomparable. There are light lunch and pre-theatre menus, but à la carte offers excellent choices, including crustacea (Argyll oysters with shallot and pickled vegetable vinegar) and a chargrill list (fillet steak served with a tattie scone, tomato, mushroom and garlic butter, for example). Three courses at dinner, meanwhile, could bring halloumi with apple and cucumber tsatsiki to start; cod fillet with peas, onion and pancetta for a main dish and plum and almond tart with frozen yoghurt and honey crème anglaise to finish. There's also a good wine list and a terrace.

Shapes

Bankhead Avenue, Sighthill, EH11 4BY (0131 453 2666/www.shapesrestaurant.co.uk). **Lunch served** noon-3pm Mon-Sat. **Dinner served** 6.30-9.30pm Fri, Sat. **Main courses** £12.50-£28. **Credit** MC, V.

Shapes is now more than five years old, but remains one of the city's better kept restaurant secrets – its fantastically unfashionable location adds to the mystique. Effectively, it's the dining arm of an antique and reproduction furniture business on an industrial estate towards the city's western fringes. Lunch is open to all, but 'membership' is required for dinner on Fridays and Saturdays (this, however, simply requires you to add your name and address to the restaurant's database). From the outside, Shapes looks like a big green shed; on the inside the decor is a riot of fixtures and fittings that shouldn't work but somehow do. This establishment isn't just here for effect, though – the food is seriously good. Dishes such as grilled asparagus with poached egg and mustard hollandaise, monkfish with celeriac purée and minted white chocolate mousse with raspberries are all well conceived and delicious. Definitely worth the trip from the centre of Edinburgh.

urbanangel

121 Hanover Street, EH2 1DJ (0131 225 6215/www.urban-angel.co.uk). **Meals served** 10am-10pm Mon-Thur; 10am-11pm Fri, Sat; 10am-5pm Sun. **Main courses** £6.95-£11.50. **Credit** AmEx, MC, V.

This basement eaterie maintains high ethical standards, using organic, free range and fair trade ingredients. During the day it serves as a café and takeaway, offering brunch, sandwiches, salads and the like, but evening sees it morph into a proper restaurant with dinner and daily specials. Its tapas-size dishes (fresh anchovies, artichoke hearts, or a top-notch houmous) serve well as starters, while mains include the likes of crayfish risotto, salmon fillet or seriously good vegetarian options such as Mediterranean vegetable and mushroom tart with parmesan pastry. The puddings are homely, and this is a relaxed place to eat in the heart of the city.

Vintners Rooms

The Vaults, 87 Giles Street, Leith EH6 6BZ (0131 554 6767/www.thevintnersrooms.com). **Lunch served** noon-2pm Tue-Sat. **Dinner served** 7-10pm Tue-Sat. **Main courses** £19.50-£25. **Set lunch** £16 2 courses, £19.50 3 courses. **Credit** AmEx, MC, V.

At the corner of a Leith backstreet sits a former wine warehouse with a history dating to the late 16th century. Its first floor houses the Scotch Malt Whisky Society (*see p329*), while the ground floor has the entirely unrelated Vintners Rooms, a classy French-style fixture on the local scene for more than 20 years. It has gone in and out of fashion during that time, but lately there has been an upsurge in appreciative murmurs thanks to chef Patrice Ginestière and front of house maestro Silvio Praino (a familiar and friendly face for local foodies, having been patron at a couple of popular eateries over the last decade). Diners have the choice of the homely bar area or a small adjacent room with elaborate plasterwork – the latter tends to be fairly stark

during the day, but better at night. Dinner options include tuna tartare with courgette velouté, duck with blueberry and honey sauce, and excellent crêpe suzette. There's also an interesting and varied wine list, as you would expect in an old wine warehouse.

Witchery by the Castle

Castlehill, Royal Mile, EH1 2NF (0131 225 5613/www.thewitchery.com). **Lunch served** noon-4pm, **dinner served** 5.30-11.30pm daily. **Main courses** £15-£50. **Set meal** (noon-4pm, 5.30-6.30pm, 10.30-11.30pm) £12.95 2 courses. **Credit** AmEx, DC, MC, V.

One late 16th-century venue just yards from Edinburgh Castle's esplanade, two dining rooms and loads of ambience. James Thomson's Witchery, with its prime location, red leather, wood panelling and candlelit interior, has been the city's primary destination restaurant for years. He added the Secret Garden in 1989, which is even more fairytale than the adjacent original (they both work from the same kitchen), and the building even has seven gorgeous suites for sleepovers. A typical three-course dinner in either the Witchery or the Secret Garden could bring Anstruther crab mayonnaise to start, roast monkfish with ham hock to follow, and passion fruit and mascarpone trifle for pudding. The wine list is show-off huge, and if there's one criticism here it concerns expectation. For a romantic or atmospheric dinner the establishment is second to none, but the quality of cooking sometimes falls short of its stratospheric billing. If you don't want the full, premium-price experience, try lunch or the theatre supper.

Opal Lounge

NIGHTLIFE

Local licensing laws mean Edinburgh has a range of venues that stay open late. Café-bars like Rick's (55A Frederick Street, 0131 622 7800) or the long-established Basement (10A-12A Broughton Street, 0131 557 0097) keep going until 1am, as does the latest word in hip cocktail hangouts, Dragonfly (52 West Port, 0131 228 4543). Others, like the designery Opal Lounge (51A George Street, 0131 226 2275), the North African-accented Medina (45-47 Lothian Street, 0131 225 6313) or the East European-themed Pivo (2-6 Calton Road, 0131 557 2925) are open until 3am, as is the legendary live music pub Whistle Binkies (7 Niddry Street, 0131 557 5114). Nightclubs also generally keep going until 3am. The general areas of Lothian Road and the Cowgate attract a young, loud, up-for-it crowd, and are worth avoiding if you're after a restrained sort of night. Alternatively, try one of the below.

Bongo Club

37 Holyrood Road, EH8 8BA (0131 558 7604/ www.thebongoclub.co.uk). Open Café 1-7pm daily. Events 9pm-1am Mon-Thu; 11pm-3am Fri-Sat; 10pm-3am Sun. **Admission** free-£10. **No credit cards.**
For more than a decade, the Bongo has operated as a venue and multi-arts facility, running a student-like café and exhibition space during the day then hosting assorted clubs later on. You'll find dance classes, ceilidhs, live music and regular nights like Headspin (funk, disco, hip hop), the Messenger

Sound System (roots and dub reggae) and Give It Some (funk, soul and jazz). It's rough round the edges, but a blessed escape from chipmunk house.

Liquid Room

9C Victoria Street, EH1 2HE (0131 225 2564/ www.liquidroom.com). Open 10.30pm-3am. **Admission** £1-£15. **No credit cards.**
One of Edinburgh's top venues for music and big name guest DJs, this space also hosts regular club nights like the Snatch Social (Thursdays, a kind of cabaret-cum-club crossover with hip hop and funk) and Evol (Fridays, an indie night from the dawn of time). Then again, you might just catch someone like Darren Emerson. During August, the Liquid Room becomes a prime site for the T On The Fringe music festival, hosting the likes of Lambchop, the Fratellis and the Dandy Warhols.

Vegas

Various venues throughout Scotland (booking line 0131 220 3234/558 3824/www.vegasscotland. co.uk). Open 10pm-3am Sat. **Admission** £7-£10. **Credit** (advance booking only) AmEx, MC, V.
Vegas attracts a wide age range of clubbers, inviting attendees to dress up Rat Pack style (though the dress code is generally interpreted quite loosely) for a glamorous night out. The club features showgirls, jazz, funk and swing bands, Sinatra-style crooners and the occasional burlesque act. You can often catch it at Ego (14 Picardy Place, EH1 3JT, 0131 478 7434) but it has also ventured to Ocean Terminal shopping mall in Leith and the sculpture galleries of Edinburgh College of Art.

Edinburgh

Glasgow

Splash some cash in Scotland's shopping capital.

It's the biggest city in Scotland, it has the best nightlife, grand Victorian architecture, enough culture to keep art and museum junkies happy, some swish hotels and great restaurants, plus one more feather in its cap – outside the capital, Glasgow is now the UK's number one destination for shopping. However, it wasn't always thus.

Back in the late fifth century, the city was quite bucolic. The origin myth is necessarily vague but by the early sixth century a holy man called Ninian is said to have consecrated a burial ground on or near where Glasgow Cathedral stands today. Nothing much happened for almost a century until another holy man came along and founded a monastic community around the same site: the city's patron saint, Mungo. Given its raised position and proximity to a fordable stretch of the Clyde, the location made geographic sense.

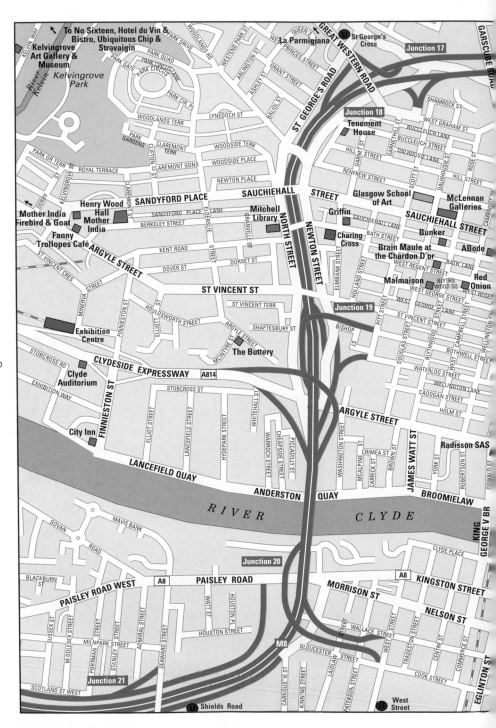

Glasgow

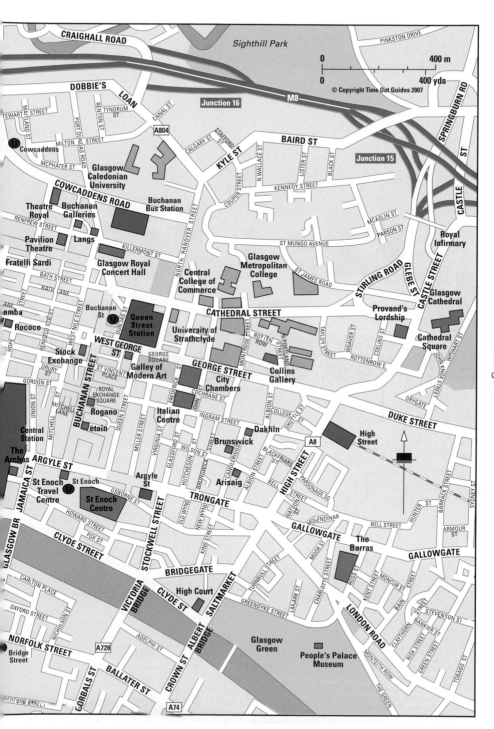

Glasgow

urban beauty

ABERDEEN | DUNDEE | EDINBURGH | GLASGOW | INVERNESS | STIRLING

Beauty & urban aren't words you'd normally associate with each other. Unless you've been to one of Scotland's six cities. Boutique hotels, exclusive bars and stylish shopping – they're all here. It's finding them amongst some of the UK's most innovative and original urban architecture that sets the Scottish CityBreak experience apart.

Come to Scotland and look up.
www.visitscotland.com/citybreaks

Live it. Visit Scotland.
visitscotland.com 0845 22 55 121
The No.1 booking and information service for Scotland.

Accommodation	★★★☆☆
Food & drink	★★★★☆
Nightlife	★★★★★
Shopping	★★★★★
Culture	★★★★☆
Sights	★★★★☆
Scenery	★★☆☆☆

There's harder evidence of Glasgow's growing status as a trading town from the 12th century onwards and it really started to hit the mercantilism big time in the 18th century, particularly with tobacco. This laid a commercial substructure for the city's massive expansion in the 19th century. The Industrial Revolution saw Glasgow and its satellites become a world centre for heavy industry and shipbuilding. The population exploded – nudging over 1.1 million by the 1930s – and in its heyday Glasgow was known as 'the second city of the Empire', but this status didn't last.

After World War II, the inexorable closures of engineering works and shipyards took their toll and by the 1970s the city's reputation was based around urban dereliction, endemic poverty, sectarianism, population decline and a tough street culture. In peripheral housing estates, deprivation has bitten deep and profoundly serious issues with drink, drugs and crime persist to this day. But the face that Glasgow presents to visitors has been completely reinvented in the last couple of decades.

The 'green hollow' (glas chu in Gaelic) was European City of Culture in 1990, then UK City of Architecture and Design in 1999. A wave of new hotels and restaurants has opened, as have important facilities such as the Burrell Collection (1983), the Scottish Exhibition and Conference Centre (1985), the Royal Concert Hall (1990), the Gallery of Modern Art (1996), the Clyde Auditorium (1997) and the Glasgow Science Centre (2001). There was more drum-beating in summer 2006 when Kelvingrove Art Gallery and Museum – Glasgow's cultural lodestone – reopened after a three-year restoration project (*see p348* **Sightseeing**).

The city also makes a fuss of famous son Charles Rennie Mackintosh: architect, designer and artist. In 1996, the beautiful House for an Art Lover opened in Bellahouston Park, inspired by a set of his drawings from 1901 (10 Dumbreck Road, 0141 353 4770, www.houseforanartlover. co.uk). Fans can also see a reconstruction of interiors from where he lived from 1906 to 1914 at the Mackintosh House in the Hunterian Art Gallery at 82 Hillhead Street (0141 3305431, www.hunterian.gla.ac.uk) as well as displays of his drawings, designs and watercolours. His biggest architectural work meanwhile, the Glasgow School of Art in Renfrew Street (No.167, 0141 3534500, www.gsa.ac.uk), does guided tours. The website of the Charles Rennie Mackintosh Society (www.crmsociety.com) is useful for finding out what's on offer and when you can go to see it.

For visitors who woould prefer to spend time shopping rather than looking at art nouveau, this town really is a retail mecca. Buchanan Galleries, at the north end of Buchanan Street (No.220, 0141 333 9898, www.buchanangalleries.co.uk) is the biggest mall in Scotland with all the household names. Princes Square, also on Buchanan Street, is smaller but more self-consciously upmarket, with the likes of Dower & Hall, Jo Malone and Calvin Klein (48 Buchanan Street, 0141 221 0324, www.princessquare.co.uk). Argyle Street, Buchanan Street and Sauchiehall Street themselves are stuffed with shops, the Argyle Arcade is the city's specialist jewellery mall, while Ingram Street boasts the Italian Centre mini-mall.

Walk along the riverside, heading west from the city centre, and you see more evidence of prosperity in plush apartments and commercial developments, complemented at Finnieston by the Clyde Arc (2006). The Arc crosses the river diagonally and locals have dubbed the £20-million structure 'the Squinty Bridge'. From 2007, a commercial seaplane service has even been given permission to start flying charters to the Highlands and Islands from this stretch of the Clyde (Loch Lomond Seaplanes, PO Box 26613, Helensburgh, 0870 242 1457, www.loch lomondseaplanes.com) – more testimony to Glasgow's hard-won status as a city destination of choice.

WHERE TO STAY

Glasgow is a city with an abundance of good places to stay. As well as the options that we've listed below, City Inn (Finnieston Quay, 0141 240 1002, www.cityinn.com), beside the 'Squinty Bridge', is another good possibility. It's part of a small chain of modern hotels and has a small gym and a Modern European-style restaurant. Langs (2 Port Dundas Place, 0141 333 1500, www.langshotels.co.uk), meanwhile, is both well located, it's next to the Royal Concert Hall, and well equipped, guests will find PlayStations, CD players and Wi-Fi waiting for them in their rooms.

> ## TOURIST INFORMATION
> 11 George Square, G2 1DY (0141 204 4480/www.seeglasgow.com).

ABode

ABode

*129 Bath Street, G2 2SY (0141 572 6000/
www.abodehotels.co.uk/glasgow).* **Rates**
£125-£170 double; £225 suite. **Credit**
AmEx, DC, MC, V.

Formerly known as the ArtHouse, a 2005 takeover
saw hotelier Andrew Brownsword and Michelin-
starred chef Michael Caines rebrand this establishment as part of their ABode mini-chain. The
neat, modern rooms would still be familiar to anyone who stayed here previously, but it's all change
in the basement, with a new café-bar and cocktail
bar, and on the ground floor where MC at ABode
(*see p347*) – a serious contender for the title of
Glasgow's best restaurant – is situated. A listed
building that dates back to 1911, this was once an
office for the Department of Education, and an air
of Edwardian dignity manages to shine through
the later design makeovers and beyond the aural
stylings of the chill-out CD in your room. ABode
has a good location too if you want central
Glasgow on your doorstep.

Brunswick

*106-108 Brunswick Street, Merchant City,
G1 1TF (0141 552 0001/www.brunswickhotel.
co.uk).* **Rates** £65-£95 double; £395 suite.
Credit AmEx, DC, MC, V.

An independent boutique hotel with only 18
rooms (all of which are different) the Brunswick
is a straightforward, uncluttered choice for
accommodation in Glasgow's Merchant City,
south east of George Square. Chic minimalism is
the design ethic, and the hotel also boasts a very
smart, split-level penthouse suite that might double as a Ligne Roset furniture store – which makes
the name of the Italian-slanted café-bar, Brutti Ma
Buoni ('ugly but good'), all the more amusing. The
Merchant City itself is stuffed full of bars and
restaurants so this establishment, with its keenly
priced rooms, makes an ideal stopover if you're
stepping out to the area's manifold delights.

Hotel du Vin & Bistro at One Devonshire Gardens

*1 Devonshire Gardens, G12 0UX (0141 339
2001/www.onedevonshiregardens.com).* **Rates**
£140-£305 double; £375-£925 suite. **Credit**
AmEx, MC, V.

Quick history: the property company MWB Group
bought all the Malmaison hotels in 2000 and then
added the commendable Hotel du Vin & Bistro
chain to its portfolio in 2004. A 2005 cash injec-
tion saw it aim for expansion (with more
Malmaisons and more Hotels du Vin to come) and
in 2006 it acquired one of the UK's most celebrated hotels, One Devonshire Gardens. Comprising
five conjoined Victorian townhouses set back
from the Great Western Road (around two-and-a-
half miles from Glasgow city centre), it was
rebranded as a Hotel du Vin deluxe. Each room or
suite still has a classic, individual design and modern facilities (Bose CD player, DVD player, Wi-Fi)
while dining now centres around a French-

flavoured bistro and grill. Whether the revamped
One Devonshire Gardens retains its status as 'easily the best in the city' will become clear throughout 2007 and beyond.

Malmaison

*278 West George Street, G2 4LL (0141 572
1000/www.malmaison.com).* **Rates** £150-£170
double; £200-£295 suite. **Credit** AmEx, DC,
MC, V.

Glasgow's Malmaison is housed in a converted
19th-century Greek Orthodox church to the west
of Glasgow's central city grid. The rooms all had
a makeover in 2005 so have a fresh, confident look
and the contemporary colour schemes typical of
this upmarket chain. If your budget can run to the
cost of a suite, then some of these are attractively
split-level. One is named after the 'Big Yin' – come-
dian and local hero Billy Connolly – and boasts a
stand-alone tartan bath. The approach to the bar
is fun (you enter from above, down a metal staircase), while the brasserie sits in the old church
crypt and aims for a 'Francophile-with-knobs-on'
appearance to complement the more modern, but
equally French, menu.

Radisson SAS

*301 Argyle Street, G2 8DL (0141 204 3333/
www.radisson.com).* **Rates** £149-£180 double;
£185-£390 suite. **Credit** AmEx, DC, MC, V.

The Radisson SAS is hardly low key. Big, bold
and audacious, it landed on Argyle Street at the
end of 2002 but is exactly the kind of establishment to appeal to Glasgow's self-image. The exterior is colourful and the rooms are all fairly swish
coming in three basic types: 'City', 'Modern' and
'Nordic', some with excellent views (there are also
larger 'Business' rooms and suites). No irritating
internet charges here, though – it's free whether
by wire or Wi-Fi. Other facilities include a reasonable gym, pool and sauna (all operated by the
LA Fitness chain), a couple of bars and two restaurants. One of these is Spanish-themed with decent
tapas; the other modern Mediterranean and a little more formal; dinner aside, guests rave about
the quality of the breakfasts. A hefty presence in
the heart of the city.

WHERE TO EAT & DRINK

Glaswegians love their modern café-bars,
old-school boozers, designer restaurants
and curry houses. But what they don't love
is a surplus of formality – excess bullshit in
other words. So an affable, big bloke from
Pakistan bringing a steaming dish of lamb
bhuna to the table is fine; a delicate young
woman from Thailand politely offering a
prawn wrapped in translucent pastry is
less popular (Glasgow has only a handful
of Thai restaurants but loads of Indian-style
ones). The city has also lacked fine-dining
restaurants considered chi-chi enough for
Michelin stars for several years now,

probably because the locals can't be bothered with the fuss that surrounds eating in them. This certainly doesn't mean an absence of seriously good restaurants, but even the very best tend to have a classlessness that their equivalents elsewhere might not. Aside from the selection listed below there are quite a few eateries that are worth a visit. The Buttery (652 Argyle Street, 0141 221 8188, www.eatbuttery.com) was closed for a spruce-up as this guide went to press but will continue to serve the imaginative, high-quality dishes that have won it acclaim when it reopens in summer 2007. Brian Maule at the Chardon d'Or (176 West Regent Street, 0141 248 3801, www. brianmaule.com) is another fine place to eat offering fantastic French-style cooking in modern surroundings.

For a Scottish bistro try Arisaig (140 St Vincent Street, 0141 204 5399, www. arisaigrestaurant.co.uk), while fish lovers will want to check out the buzzing city centre branch of Two Fat Ladies (118A Blythswood Street, 0141 847 0088, www.twofatladies.org), the homelier west end original (88 Dumbarton Road, 0141 339 1944, www.twofatladies.org) or the more formal Gamba (225A West George Street, 0141 572 0899, www.gamba. co.uk). The reputation of Rogano (11 Exchange Place, off Buchanan Street, 0141 248 4055, www.roganoglasgow. com) waxes and wanes but its authentic 1930s art deco interior is still unrivalled for seafood lovers and everyone else.

The pick of the Italians would still be the upmarket La Parmigiana (447 Great Western Road, 0141 334 0686, www. laparmigiana.co.uk) and Fratelli Sarti (133 Wellington Street, 0141 248 2228, www.fratellisarti.com). The latter is appealing, traditional and only one part of the burgeoning Fratelli Sarti empire (there's another restaurant round the corner at 121 Bath Street, and several more in the city centre). Glasgow's designer-ish Chinese

Rustic furniture, stained glass windows and fine food and drink at Café Gandolfi.

étain

restaurant is Dragon-i (311-313 Hope Street, 0141 332 7728), handy for the Theatre Royal, as is the scatter-cushion hippie chic and Mediterranean flavours of Café Hula along the street (321 Hope Street, 0141 353 1660, www.cafehula.co.uk).

And so to curry. Mother India's Café (1355 Argyle Street, 0141 339 9145, www.motherindia.co.uk) has long been acknowledged as one of the city's best. At the original premises (28 Westminster Terrace, 0141 221 1663, www.mother india.co.uk) it added a cellar dining space in 2006, but also has a tapas-style café nearby. The Wee Curry Shops (7 Buccleuch Street, 0141 353 0777; 29 Ashton Lane, 0141 357 5280, www.motherindia.co.uk) are owned by the same people and provide an informal, down-home experience. The Ashoka (108 Elderslie Street, 0141 221 1761, www.ashokakaraoke.com) heads the other direction in decor terms, its basement space a deep, rich red. The Shish Mahal has been a comfort to locals since 1964 (60-68 Park Road, 0141 334 7899, www.shishmahal.co.uk), but there is some evidence of Glaswegian curry moving into the 21st century of late with the south Indian food at Dakhin (see p347).

The best gastropubs include Stravaigin Café Bar (see p350), Bar Gandolfi (64 Albion Street, 0141 552 4462, www. cafegandolfi.com) with the more restaurant-like Café Gandolfi downstairs (0141 552 6813), and the Liquid Ship (171 Great Western Road, 0141 331 1901, www.stravaigin.com/liquid.htm). Honourable mentions also go to old Caledonian stager Babbity Bowster (16-18 Blackfriars Street, 0141 552 5055) and the roomy, laid-back Firebird (1321 Argyle Street, 0141 334 0594), which has arguably the best pizzas in the city.

For more of that eats-drinks crossover, Glasgow has a vast number of modern café-bars that transform into pre-club haunts or drinking dens as the evening

MC at ABode

progresses. There is a fair turnover among these venues as proprietors aim for 'the next big trend', but some of the more durable include the studenty Bar 10 (10 Mitchell Lane, 0141 572 1448), the music-venue-pub-café Bunker (193-199 Bath Street, 0141 229 1427, www.the bunkerbar.com), the exuberant Lite Bar at the Corinthian (191 Ingram Street, 0141 552 1101, www.g1group.co.uk) where the decor vaults right the way over the top, the rather more laid-back Goat (1287 Argyle Street, 0141 357 7373, www.the goat.co.uk) and the splendid Chinaski's

with its bourbon and cigar garden (239 North Street, 0141 221 0061).

Traditional pubs include the Horseshoe (17 Drury Street, 0141 229 5711), the legendary and antique Scotia (112 Stockwell Street, 0141 552 8681), or the Edwardian-era Griffin (266 Bath Street, 0141 331 5171). The Bon Accord (153 North Street, 0141 248 4427) has good real ales and whiskies, while the almost Neolithic decor of the Ben Nevis (1147 Argyle Street, 0141 576 5204, www. bennevisbar.com) provides another quality whisky-tippling environment.

Finally, the scrumptiously decorated Polo Lounge is the pick of Glasgow's gay bars (84 Wilson Street, 0141 553 1221, www.g1group.co.uk) and stays open every night to 3am.

Dakhin

89 Candleriggs, G1 1NP (0141 553 2585/ www.dakhin.com). **Lunch served** noon-2pm, **dinner served** 5-11pm Mon-Fri. **Meals served** 1-11pm Sat, Sun. **Main courses** £5.25-£17.50. **Set meal** £9.95. **Credit** AmEx, MC, V.

Glasgow has traditionally loved its robust Indian food, invariably washed down with gallons of lager. In recent years, however, some more mature Indian restaurants have sprung up, food-wise none more so than Dakhin. Housed in a large and fairly simple first-floor room (with open kitchen) in the Merchant City, it focuses on south Indian cuisine: stuffed dosas and uttapams (lentil and rice-flour pancakes) are the house speciality. No vindaloo pig-out here then, but you could have a simple clear spicy lentil soup to start (rasam), then monkfish in tamarind sauce as a main (meen moilee) – or just opt for a great big masala dosa (stuffed with spiced potato and vegetables). For a change, try the north Indian sister business that's located nearby (Dhabba, 44 Candleriggs, 0141 553 1249, www.thedhabba.com).

étain

Princes Square, Buchanan Street, G1 3JX (0141 225 5630/www.conran.com/www.zinc bar.co.uk). **Lunch served** noon-2.30pm Mon-Fri, Sun. **Dinner served** 6.30-9.30pm Mon-Thur, Sun; 6-9.30pm Fri, Sat. **Set meal** £26 2 courses, £32 3 courses. **Credit** AmEx, DC, MC, V.

Tucked away on the top floor of Princes Square shopping mall, this chic eaterie was formerly one of Sir Terence Conran's elite fine-dining restaurants. The new owner, the Zinc Bar & Grill group, also has other eateries across the UK. You gain access to étain via the mall, or by its own lift in Springfield Court (to the rear of the building). Decor is light, minimal and contemporary within an impressive, yet discreet space. Three typical French-flavoured dinner courses from chef Neil Clark could offer glazed Loch Fyne oysters with tarragon and parsley to start, Gressingham duck breast with haricot blanc casserole, and jerusalem artichoke lyonnaise as a main and rhubarb crumble tart for dessert. Sadly, they still stick that 'discretionary' 12.5% service charge on the bill (uncommon in Scotland). The more informal Glasgow outlet of Zinc Bar & Grill is adjacent on the same floor of Princes Square (0845 658 6868).

Fanny Trollope's Café

1066 Argyle Street, G3 8LY (0141 564 6464/www.fannytrollopes.co.uk). **Lunch served** (bookings only) noon-2pm Tue-Sat,

dinner served 6-10pm Tue-Sat. **Main courses** £7.95-£15.95. **Pre-theatre menu** £12.95 3 courses. **No credit cards.**

Fanny Trollope and her sister, Betty, fled Brazil in the 1920s, aiming for Portugal. They missed, and ended up in Glasgow. Fanny found a job in an Argyle Street café, while Betty eventually opened a bar on the Broomielaw (Sweaty Betty's). When it opened in 2003 – just along the road from where Fanny once worked – the choice of name was obvious. Food-wise it was an instant hit, gaining awards and many plaudits; then it had a 2005 relaunch. Run by Mo Abdulla (who cooks along with Gary Bayless), it offers three courses such as red wine poached pear with dunsyre blue cheese salad, followed by roast pork belly with smoked paprika and fennel, and rhubarb fool to finish. It's BYOB (great if you fancy a really good wine) and what it lacks in finesse, it makes up for with shedloads of character. Abdulla also runs a Scottish restaurant in the west of the city (Roastit Bubbly Jocks, 450 Dumbarton Road, 0141 339 3355), which is also well worth the taxi ride.

MC at ABode

ABode, 129 Bath Street, G2 2SY (0141 572 6000/www.abodehotels.co.uk/glasgow). **Lunch served** noon-2.30pm Mon-Sat. **Dinner served** 7-10pm Mon-Thur; 6.30-10pm Fri, Sat. **Main courses** £17.50 £22.95. **Set lunch** £13 2 courses, £17.50 3 courses. **Credit** AmEx, DC, MC, V.

The restaurant at the ABode hotel (*see p343*) came on the scene in 2005. The kitchen is technically the brainchild of the Michelin-starred Michael Caines (hence the MC in the name), who made his name at Gidleigh Park in Devon, but he has other interests and can't be everywhere at once. Fortunately, the chef who *is* here is the talented Martin Donnelly, and he's very good indeed. It's a contemporary room but with some original white ceramic tiling and a glass-sided wine pantry. Three courses might offer a sublime pumpkin and wild mushroom risotto with mascarpone and pumpkin oil, venison with red cabbage, potato fondant and celeriac purée, and a signature cranachan soufflé and raspberry sorbet. Great cooking, decent wines, and a real shot in the arm for the upper end of the local restaurant scene.

No. Sixteen

16 Byres Road, G11 5JY (0141 339 2544/ www.number16.co.uk). **Lunch served** noon-2.30pm Mon-Sat; 12.30-3pm Sun. **Dinner served** 5.30pm-last orders 9.30pm daily. **Pre-theatre** 5.30-6pm Mon-Fri, Sun. **Main courses** £12.50-£16.50. **Set lunch** £11.95 2 courses, £14.40 3 courses. **Credit** AmEx, MC, V.

No. Sixteen's slightly distressed, light grey frontage and driftwood-style window installation give it a look that could almost pass for a seaside bistro. Given that there are very few tables on its two floors, relaxation is not always guaranteed, however; fortunately, good cooking comes as

SIGHTSEEING

There's plenty to visit in the Glasgow area and, happily, the splendid Kelvingrove Art Gallery and Museum has now reopened after a major refurbishment.

CATHEDRAL PRECINCT

The prosperous merchants of 18th-century Glasgow and the industrialists of the 19th century preserved virtually nothing of the medieval town – almost the entire city is Victorian or later. Fortunately, there is one corner that gives some sense of a deeper history. Glasgow Cathedral (Castle Street, 0141 552 8198, www.glasgow cathedral.org.uk) was built largely between the 13th and 15th centuries, allegedly on a site that has now featured a religious building of some kind for more than 1,400 years. The adjacent cemetery (the Necropolis) is Victorian-Gothic but weathered enough to add to the sense of timelessness. Nearby is St Mungo's Museum of Religious Life and Art (2 Castle Street, 0141 553 2557, www.glasgowmuseums.com), which is a faux-medieval building but with some interesting artefacts and displays (including the UK's first permanent Zen garden), while the Provand's Lordship (3 Castle Street, 0141 552 8819, www.glasgowmuseums.com) is the city's oldest house (1471) and now serves as a museum of 15th-century life.

BURRELL COLLECTION

Pollok Country Park, 2060 Pollokshaws Road, G43 1AT (0141 287 2550/www.glasgowmuseums.com). **Open** 10am-5pm Mon-Thur, Sat; 11am-5pm Fri, Sun. **Admission** free. **Credit** *Shop* AmEx, MC, V.
This was regarded as the jewel in the crown of local attractions when it opened in 1983, and more than 20 years later it's still going strong. Sir William Burrell was a rich shipping owner with a penchant for collecting wonderful art from all over the world. He gave his rather tremendous collection to the City of Glasgow in 1944 but for years no decent home could be found for it (Sir William died in 1958). The grounds of Pollok Country Park became available in 1967, but it still took another 16 years to get the purpose-built gallery up and running. It now houses over 9,000 works ranging from medieval tapestries to paintings by Degas and Cézanne, oriental ceramics to sculptures by Epstein and Rodin. Set aside at least a day to do it justice.

GLASGOW CITY CHAMBERS

George Square, G2 1DU (0141 287 4018/ www.glasgow.gov.uk). **Open** 8am-5pm Mon-Fri. **Admission** free.
This is the home of local government and testament to Glasgow's old reputation as the 'second city of the Empire' – the sheer Italianate cockiness of the City Chambers is quite something to behold. Queen Victoria opened the building in

Burrell Collection

Provand's Lordship

1888. Architect William Young based the entrance on the Arch of Constantine in Rome, there's an amazing marble staircase and you really feel you should be bumping into Lucretia Borgia here rather than a councillor mulling over problems with non-domestic rates or management of local parks. There are free guided tours twice a day, Monday to Friday (10.30am and 2.30pm), except on weekends or public holidays.

GALLERY OF MODERN ART

Royal Exchange Square, G1 3AH (0141 229 1996/www.glasgowmuseums.com). **Open** *Gallery* 10am-5pm Mon-Wed, Sat; 10am-8pm Thur; 11am-5pm Fri, Sun. *Library* 5-8pm Mon, Tue; 10am-5pm Wed, Sat; 10am-8pm Thur; 11am-5pm Fri, Sun. **Admission** free. **Credit** *Shop* MC, V.
This is a very handy central location for one of the most popular modern art galleries in the UK. It's housed in a building, parts of which date to 1778 (a merchant's mansion), others to 1827 (the former Royal Exchange), although it didn't actually open as a gallery until 1996. The surrounding square is full of shops and cafés, many with outside tables, and on sunny summer weekends the whole area buzzes with people doing coffee, wine or lunch. As for the art, it has a definite local slant from established Scottish names like Peter Howson or Stephen Campbell to the likes of 1996 Turner Prize winner Douglas Gordon or 1997 nominee Christine Borland. But don't expect it

to be parochial, however. There's a changing programme of exhibitions and other examples of artworks from across the globe.

KELVINGROVE ART GALLERY & MUSEUM

Argyle Street, G3 8AG (0141 287 2699/www.glasgowmuseums.com). **Open** 10am-5pm Mon-Thur, Sat; 11am-5pm Fri, Sun. **Admission** free. **Credit** *Shop, Restaurant* MC, V.
It's impossible to underestimate how important the Kelvingrove Art Gallery and Museum has been to Glaswegian life over the last century. The elaborate red sandstone edifice opened in 1901 and came to house one of Europe's most important civic art collections spanning Scottish colourists (Fergusson, Peploe), Dutch masters (Rembrandt), Italian Renaissance painters (Botticelli), the Impressionists (Monet, Degas) and others. It also had an amazing collection of weapons and armour, a great natural history display and much more – all attracting visitor numbers by the end of the 20th century hovering around the one million a year mark. However, there simply wasn't space to display everything, so in 2003 it closed for a £28-million restoration. The gallery reopened in 2006 looking more spruce than ever. Whether gazing at Dalí's *Christ of St John on the Cross* or simply keeping the kids amused courtesy of the real Spitfire hanging over their heads in the main west gallery, this is the place to be.

Kelvingrove Art Gallery & Museum

standard from chef Grant Neil. The reputation of this place has been growing steadily for years under the steady ownership of Margaret and Ronald Campbell – even the most demanding critics have been fairly generous with their praise. Dishes include the likes of crispy confit duck leg with orange salad and beetroot emulsion, seared monkfish and scallops with aubergine, tomato, sauce vierge and herbs, and walnut and honey tart. The wine list is pretty good too.

Rococo

202 West George Street, G2 2NR (0141 221 5004/www.rococoglasgow.com). **Lunch served** noon-2.30pm, **dinner served** 6.30-9.30pm daily. **Set lunch** £19.50 3 courses. **Set dinner** £39.50 3 courses. **Pre-theatre menu served** 5-6.30pm/£19.50 3 courses. **Credit** AmEx, MC, V.

One of Glasgow's more self-consciously chic restaurants, Rococo is a classy operation – thanks in large part to its head chef, Mark Tamburrini. The basement premises are plush, modern and restrained, and there's a serious wine list with some heavyweight names from Bordeaux, elsewhere in France, and further afield. Dinner might start with pan-roasted Oban scallops with bok choi, shiitake and coconut broth, and be followed by roast fillet of char with mushroom and broad bean risotto, glazed asparagus and foie gras froth. Desserts are equally impressive: a winter berry millefeuille with Cointreau sabayon and lemon sorbet, for example. With good service to boot, Rococo is at the top of its game, and among the very best to be found in Glasgow.

Sisters

36 Kelvingrove Street, G3 7RZ (0141 564 1157/www.thesisters.co.uk). **Lunch served** noon-2.30pm Tue-Sat. **Dinner served** 7-8.30pm Tue-Thur; 6.30-9.15pm Fri, Sat. **Main courses** £14.95-£17.95. **Set lunch & pre-theatre menu** (served 5.30-7pm Tue-Thur; 5.30-6.30pm Fri, Sat) £16.95 3 courses. **Credit** MC, V.

A typical evening here will see tables of young women, smart couples and mixed groups (perhaps including the odd guy with ill-advised hair) all seated in the single long, stylish room where charcoal and black predominate, along with abstract art. The menu's ingredients have a Scottish slant (venison from Arisaig, smoked salmon from Ullapool, crab from Lewis), but dishes have a modern spin to them, so scallops on a risotto of Lewis crab is made with pink peppercorn and ginger butter; venison with mashed parsnip and vegetables is cooked with maple syrup; and rhubarb and apple crumble is served with delicious honeycomb ice-cream. This is the second business venture for owners the O'Donnell sisters – the original Sisters restaurant is in Jordanhill (1A Ashwood Gardens, 0141 434 1179), while the Kelvingrove incarnation opened in autumn 2005 and has been understandably popular ever since.

Stravaigin/Stravaigin Café-Bar

28 Gibson Street, G12 8NX (0141 334 2665/www.stravaigin.com). Café **Meals served** 11am-10.30pm daily. **Main courses** £7.95-£19.95. *Restaurant* **Meals served** noon-11pm Fri-Sun; 11am-11pm Mon-Thur. **Main courses** £12.65-£22.50. *Both* **Pre-theatre menu** (served 5-7pm Mon-Fri, Sun; 5-6.30pm Sat) £13.95 3 courses. *Both* **Credit** AmEx, DC, MC, V.

Stravaigin has been around since the mid 1990s, and when it opened in Gibson Street it fast became a Glasgow favourite. It's a basement with simple modern decor, red brick walls and an attempt at providing meals with a sustainable food philosophy of 'think global, eat local'. Rated by many to be among the city's top five restaurants, typical dishes include 'wild thing' terrine (pheasant, wood pigeon and mallard wrapped in serrano ham) and monkfish baked in vine leaves with grilled aubergine and garlic orzo, plus king prawn taramasalata. Gibson Street also has the ground-floor Stravaigin Café-Bar, a more informal space featuring seriously superior pub grub like mackerel with puy lentil salad, or Cuban black bean fritters on buttered greens. The millennium addition to the empire was Stravaigin 2 (8 Ruthven Lane, off Byres Road, 0141 334 7165), a converted townhouse with decorative greenery outside and a contemporary bistro interior. The global approach takes full effect here with more extravagant flavour combinations – it's also famed for its burgers: chicken, beef or ostrich.

Ubiquitous Chip

12 Ashton Lane, G12 8SJ (0141 334 5007/ www.ubiquitouschip.co.uk). Brasserie **Meals served** noon-11pm Mon-Sat; 12.30-11pm Sun. **Main courses** £6.15-£15.45. *Restaurant* **Lunch served** noon-2.30pm Mon-Sat; 12.30-3pm Sun. **Dinner served** 5.30-11pm Mon-Sat; 6.30-11pm Sun. **Set lunch** £22.80 2 courses, £28.65 3 courses, (Sun) £18.65 3 courses. **Set dinner** £34.85 2 courses, £39.85 3 courses. *Both* **Credit** AmEx, DC, MC, V.

The Chip has been around since 1971; and muralist and novelist Alasdair Gray's works aid the sense of entering in to something special. This is a complex of adjoining venues including an upstairs bistro, bars, a formal ground-floor dining room and – perhaps the most celebrated – a cobbled courtyard with tables. The courtyard is covered and has a water feature, and what the decorative plant life lacks in youth it makes up for in biomass. The cooking is adventurous: rabbit, pear and pistachio sausage with basil cabbage to start; ling on clapshot (mashed swede and potato) with chilli-roasted red pepper and crispy seaweed as a main; oatmeal ice-cream with fruit compote to finish. The fact that you're eating in a Glaswegian (even Scottish) culinary institution often forgives lapses from excellence, but this is one of the few places where you could imagine patrons gesturing at passers-by, mouthing the words, 'Come on inside, it's pure magic.'

Local, but never parochial: Glasgow's Gallery of Modern Art.

NIGHTLIFE

If it's nightlife you're after, you're in the right city. There are more gig venues, pre-club bars and clubs than anywhere else in Scotland. In fact, Glasgow definitely rates as a European-class destination for clubbing and music, let alone a UK one.

If you want to see a band, then Barrowlands is the classic choice (242 Gallowgate, 0141 552 4601, www.glasgow-barrowland.com). It's a former dance hall and everyone from Babyshambles to the Zutons have graced the stage. The Carling Academy (121 Eglinton Street, 0905 020 3999, www.glasgow-academy.co.uk) is a former cinema that fulfils a similar role with recent acts like Amy Winehouse, the Nine Inch Nails and the Fratellis. Meanwhile, the Scottish Exhibition and Conference Centre at Finnieston (SECC, 0141 248 3000, www.secc.co.uk) is a cavernous, riverside venue with a hall that can hold thousands, and also has the armadillo-like Clyde Auditorium adjacent for more polite,

sit-down moments. Another celebrated venue is King Tut's Wah Wah Hut (272A St Vincent Street, 0141 221 5279, www.kingtuts.co.uk).

As for clubs themselves, the most popular include the multimedia Arches (253 Argyle Street, 0870 240 7528, www.the arches.co.uk), which does theatre and live music as well as hosting regular big-name DJs; also the Tunnel (84 Mitchell Street, 0141 204 1000, www.tunnelglasgow. co.uk), another attraction for big-name DJs; and the Sub Club (22 Jamaica Street, 0141 248 4600, www.subclub.co.uk), a basement with history and attitude. The Centre for Contemporary Arts (350 Sauchiehall Street, 0141 352 4900, www.cca-glasgow.com) isn't a club as such but has interesting one-off nights, while the Ferry (25 Anderston Quay, 0141 553 0606, www.the-ferry.co.uk) is an actual ferry boat moored on the Clyde. Here you will find regular music gigs and it also hosts Vegas! (www.vegasscotland.co.uk) once a month.

Mid Argyll & Bute

Loch and loll.

One of the biggest draws for visiting Mid Argyll and Bute is the sense of being away from it all, a feeling of space and detachment in hills and sea lochs that seem wonderfully wild and remote – even though much of the area is within 50 miles of Glasgow as the crow flies.

Perhaps the fact that it isn't always easy to get here is what gives the area its sense of remoteness. From Portavadie on the west coast of Cowal you may be able to see the lights of Tarbert twinkling just four miles away across the southern reaches of Loch Fyne, and the small vehicle ferry takes all of 25 minutes to cross between the two, but if you miss the last sailing of the day you face a 90-mile round-the-houses drive to get from one to the other.

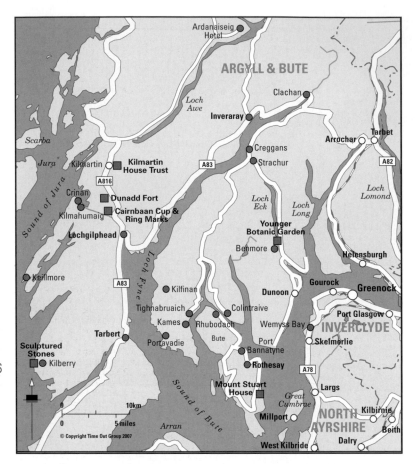

Ardanaiseig Hotel

ARGYLL & BUTE

Loch Awe

Clachan

INVERARAY

Creggans

Strachur

Tarbet

Arrochar

A82

Scarba

Jura

Kilmartin

Kilmartin House Trust

A83

Loch Lomond

A816

Crinan

Dunadd Fort

Loch Eck

Loch Long

Kilmahumaig

Cairnbaan Cup & Ring Marks

Younger Botanic Garden

Lochgilphead

Benmore

Helensburgh

Keillmore

A83

Kilfinan

Gourock

Greenock

Tighnabruaich

Colintraive

Dunoon

Port Glasgow

Kames

Rhubodach

Wemyss Bay

INVERCLYDE

Tarbert

Portavadie

Bute

Port

Skelmorlie

Sculptured Stones

Kilberry

Bannatyne

Rothesay

A78

Mount Stuart House

Largs

Great Cumbrae

NORTH AYRSHIRE

Kilbirnie

10km

Millport

Beith

0   5 miles

Arran

Sound of Bute

West Kilbride

Dalry

© Copyright Time Out Group 2007

This means you should pay due attention to ferry timetables when visiting the area, but it also opens up a perspective often forgotten in the age of personal motor transport. The sea lochs of Argyll may be viewed as an obstacle to the average Ford Focus driver, but once upon a time they were highways rather than barriers. Settled by people who came to be skilled in seafaring, they linked islands and peninsulas that hold profound historical significance for modern Scotland. This area has long had links with the north-east of Ireland, for example. Kilmartin Valley in particular (*see p388* **School of rock**), which is littered with prehistoric monuments, is also home to the hill fort of Dunadd where the Dark Age Irish settlers, the Scotti, anchored their kingdom. Later, they gave Scotland its modern name. At Kilmartin's southern end is evidence of a more recent history, however: the Crinan

Canal, a short cut from Loch Fyne to the western seaways for more than 200 years.

Immediately south is Knapdale, the hinterland off the main road down to Campbeltown. Either side of the remote Loch Sween on its west coast are reminders that this wasn't always such a backwater. The ruins of Castle Sween date from the 12th century, while the early 13th-century Keills Chapel, almost at the very end of nowhere on a small spit of land at the far side of the loch, has an incredible collection of Celtic cross slabs as well as the seventh-century cross that once stood outside.

North-east of Knapdale, via the small town of Lochgilphead, are the upper reaches of Loch Fyne. This loch has scenic qualities of its own, but 24 miles from Lochgilphead on the western shore, you'll find the area's traditional tourist destination: Inveraray. This is a planned town, commissioned by the third Duke of

Argyll and completed in the 1770s. The architectural style and whitewashed buildings give it a definite atmosphere, while it's also home to attractions like Inveraray Jail, a 19th-century courthouse and prison that is now an interactive museum (01499 302381, www.inverarayjail.co.uk). Then there's the 18th-century Inveraray Castle (01499 302203, www.inveraray-castle. com), a fairytale extravaganza, initially entertained by the second Duke of Argyll in 1720, actually started by the third Duke in 1746, and completed by the fifth Duke in 1789. The Armoury Hall is particularly impressive, and overall this is the confident work of a pro-Hanoverian family on home turf, in the years following the final defeat of Jacobitism.

Mid Argyll and Bute is an area pregnant with history and, despite its proximity to the big city, arriving here feels a little like stepping back in time. Most visitors will come via Glasgow and there are two main routes. The north-west option out of the city, the A82, is fairly urban for the first nine miles but then views of the Clyde open up and it doesn't take long to reach Loch Lomond, such a popular tourist area that it's almost a Scottish national icon. The road hugs the west bank of the loch as far as Tarbet (not to be confused with Tarbert), then the A83 goes through Arrochar and around the head of Loch Long before climbing steeply up Glen Croe to the wonderfully named viewpoint, Rest and Be Thankful. It also skirts an area of mountains known as the Arrochar Alps – these are particularly dramatic on top and the biggest, Beinn Ime, rises to 3,317 feet. From the Rest and Be Thankful it's all downhill through Glen Kinglas to the head of Loch Fyne – a fun drive.

Alternatively, if you leave Glasgow on the M8 westbound and follow the signs, you'll reach Gourock (26 miles, via the A8 and A770). Once you're properly out of the clutches of the city, the views along the south bank of the Clyde are expansive; going through Port Glasgow and Greenock you also get a fascinating glimpse of the area's industrial past.

At Gourock, you can catch the ferry to Dunoon on the Cowal Peninsula. Cowal is divided from the rest of the mainland by Loch Fyne on one side, the Firth of Clyde and Loch Long on the other, so almost feels like an island itself. Caledonian MacBrayne operates the 25-minute service (08705 650000, www.calmac.co.uk), which runs virtually every hour, with around a dozen sailings a day even in winter, but check the website for precise times and ticket details. Western Ferries operates a similar service from McInroy's Point around two miles west of Gourock on the A770 (01369 704452, www.western-ferries.co.uk), also to Dunoon.

On the other side of Cowal, Caledonian MacBrayne runs the short crossing from Portavadie (this is little more than a slipway) to far-flung Tarbert. This village, at the junction of Knapdale and the Mull of Kintyre, is in a truly beautiful setting and approaching it from seaward is a rare experience.

Cowal has long had a reputation for peace and quiet, although that takes a buffeting once a year when the Cowal Highland Gathering (01369 703206, www.cowalgathering.com) hits Dunoon towards the end of August. This is the world's biggest Highland games, dating from 1893. It lasts for three days and includes all the shinty, athletics, bagpiping and Highland dancing you would expect, but in addition takes on the atmosphere of an enormous village fête with events and stalls. Cowal is also home to the Botanic Garden at Benmore (01369 706261, www.rbge.org.uk), around seven miles north of Dunoon. This is an outpost of the Royal Botanic Garden in Edinburgh and was gifted to the nation in 1925 by HG Younger of the old Edinburgh brewing family. Its avenue of giant sierra redwoods, planted in 1863, is simply awesome and you could easily spend a day just wandering. It's typical Cowal with placid countryside and the smell of the outdoors. Unless you take up the activities offered via some local hotels (fishing, sailing, shooting) there isn't really much to do around here – and that's just how people like it.

South of the Cowal Peninsula, across two strips of water known as the Kyles of Bute, lies the Isle of Bute itself. It was once a prime holiday destination for the Glaswegian working classes, and the main town of Rothesay (population just over 7,000) still has that atmosphere of walks on the esplanade and candy floss. From the 1970s, of course, holiday habits changed, Glaswegians headed for the Spanish costas, and in recent decades the island has been searching for a new identity. All the same, Bute is home to one of the most amazing stately homes anywhere in the UK – the Victorian Gothic fantasy of Mount Stuart (*see p360* **Bring me the bed of Citizen Kane**). Caledonian MacBrayne operates the 35-minute service from Wemyss Bay (west of Glasgow via the M8, A8 and A78) to Rothesay, as well

Mid Argyll & Bute

Accommodation	★★★☆☆
Food & drink	★★★☆☆
Nightlife	☆☆☆☆☆
Shopping	☆☆☆☆☆
Culture	★★☆☆☆
Sights	★☆☆☆☆
Scenery	★★★★★

SCHOOL OF ROCK

Scotland is not short on history, yet nowhere else has quite the atmosphere or sense of immanence as Kilmartin. In a short stretch of countryside just north of Lochgilphead, you can find up to 150 prehistoric monuments, plus another couple of hundred from later periods. The sheer concentration of the past here really does give you pause. Fortunately, there is an excellent visitors' centre to help make sense of it all, and it also does good food (Kilmartin House Museum, 01546 510278, www. kilmartin.org; for its Glebe Cairn Restaurant, *see p393*).

One of the best places to start is the top of Dunadd, at Kilmartin's south end. It's an outcrop all of 177 feet high, so takes no time to climb, and gives all-round views of the valley – a spookily flat and enclosed space. Although people have probably been here since the last Ice Age, it's said that the Scotti from Ireland settled and created a kingdom – Dalriada – around the sixth century. Dunadd was their hill fort. Today, it's a much etiolated pile with little surviving to show what it would have been like at its peak, but the carving of a footprint on one of the summit rocks, used in coronation ceremonies for the Dalriadan kings, can still be seen.

From Dunadd, Kilmartin House is just four miles north, and parking spots by the main road en route – adjacent to standing stones and other features – are fairly obvious. All the same, the visitors' centre is the best place to pick up a comprehensive guide to the valley's beaten and unbeaten tracks. There are henges, barrows, chambered cairns and much more around here but, ultimately, it's all about people – wherever you're from, Kilmartin provides a sense of human endeavour through time: early settlement, prehistory, ancient links between what we now call Argyll and Antrim, early Christianity, Dark Ages kingdoms, the legacy of that Scotti name, plus a haunting sense of attention having shifted. For thousands of years, Kilmartin was an important centre. Now it's quiet, peripheral and you could easily pass through it in five minutes by car. Stop a while.

as the regular, five-minute crossing from Colintraive on Cowal to Rhubodach on Bute's north coast.

A weekend in this environment is the exact opposite of a shopping, clubbing, designer café-bar break. Instead the area is scenic and contemplative – ideal for lolling around – and there are some very good hotels and restaurants. Also, if you know where to look, you can find historical sites that trace human settlement in these parts from prehistory through to the infrastructural developments of the 19th century – quite a mix.

WHERE TO STAY

Mid Argyll and Bute is neither populous nor teeming with huge budget hotels – and that's precisely why people visit. All the things that make for dependable, if predictable, travelling in other parts of the UK simply ain't here. Because there is a limited number of decent places to stay, it's essential to book ahead, especially at the height of the summer season. As well as the places listed below, the Ardaneiseig Hotel at Loch Awe (*see p358 & p361*) has 16 rooms, many with a loch view.

An Lochan

Tighnabruaich, Argyll PA21 2BE (01700 811239/www.anlochan.co.uk). **Rates** £100-£190 double. **Credit** MC, V.
Way back in 1997 the McKie family took over the old Royal Hotel at Tighnabruaich and transformed it into a haven of good taste and elevated cooking (*see p392*). Despite this quality, the name still smacked of run-down old west of Scotland accommodation and coach parties, so in 2006 they bit the bullet and did a little rebranding, hence An Lochan (although the entrance vestibule still has the old name tiled into the floor). Tighnabruaich is strung out along the coast overlooking the Kyle of Bute and An Lochan commands open views. (There are a dozen serviced moorings directly outside the hotel so you can even arrive by boat.) The rooms are all nicely and individually done up, most looking out to the water, while public spaces have loads of contemporary landscapes and still lifes. Activities span fishing, sailing, walking and more – or you could just kick back in the informal public bar and have a few drams.

Creggans Inn

Strachur, Argyll PA27 8BX (01369 860279/ www.creggans-inn.co.uk). **Rates** £110-£130 double; £150-£170 suite. **Lunch served** noon-2.45pm, **dinner served** 6-8.45pm daily. **Main courses** £7.50-£15.50. **Set dinner** £32 4 courses. **Credit** MC, V.
This is a lochside establishment with history. Not only has there been an inn on the site for

TOURIST INFORMATION

Dunoon
7 Alexandra Parade, Dunoon, Argyll PA23 8AB (0870 720 0629).
Inveraray
Front Street, Inveraray, Argyll PA32 8UY (0870 720 0616).
Lochgilphead
Lochnell Street, Lochgilphead, Argyll PA31 8JL (0870 720 0618).
Isle of Bute
Victoria Street, Rothesay, Isle of Bute PA20 0AH (0870 720 0619/www.isle-of-bute.com).
Tarbert
Harbour Street, Tarbert, Argyll PA29 6UD (0870 720 0624).
www.visitscotland.com
www.visitscottishheartlands.com

around 400 years, but in 1957 Sir Fitzroy MacLean bought these very premises. This remarkable man was a diplomat, soldier, traveller and writer. One of his best-loved books is *Eastern Approaches*, an account of his career from 1937 to 1945, spanning travels in the USSR, service with the SAS in North Africa, and his role as Churchill's military representative to Tito in Yugoslavia. Sir Fitzroy died in 1996 and the Creggans first passed to his son Sir Charles, then in 2000 to Alex Robertson. The rooms are serviceable, some with great views of Loch Fyne, but, above all, this is just the place to sit in the bar, order up some good bar food (venison sausages with Arran mustard mash, perhaps), sip your pint, and read something by the man himself.

Crinan Hotel

Crinan by Lochgilphead, Argyll PA31 8SR (01546 830261/www.crinanhotel.com). **Lunch served** noon-3pm, **dinner served** 7-8.30pm daily. **Main courses** £9.95-£16.95. **Set dinner** £42.50 4 courses. **Rates** £130-£190 double; £230-£300 suite. **Credit** MC, V.
Glory be, they haven't retired yet. Your voluble host Nick Ryan and his artist wife Frances Macdonald have been running the Crinan Hotel for more than 35 years, and they're still on the ball. The hotel sits in the tiny eponymous hamlet at the western end of the Crinan Canal and looks north across the pocket-sized Loch Crinan to Duntrune Castle, north-west over the Sound of Jura. On the outside the hotel is a white, four-storey edifice that looks slightly out of place on the Argyll coast (the old original building has been much adapted), while decor in the bedrooms is more 1970s than modern boutique. But the personal touch of the proprietors (including artworks by Frances), the standard of cooking in the main restaurant (*see p394*) and the fabulous location make the Crinan Hotel a winner. There is also decent food in the bar where you can rub shoulders with passing fishermen.

Mid Argyll & Bute

George Hotel

Main Street East, Inveraray, Argyll PA32 8TT (01499 302111/www.thegeorgehotel.co. uk). **Meals served** noon-9pm daily. **Main courses** £5.95-£15.95. **Rates** £70 double; £90-£140 suite. **Credit** MC, V.

Bang in the middle of the third Duke of Argyll's planned town of Inveraray, the George dates to 1770 and as soon as you walk over the doorstep you imagine it could actually be 1770. (The Duke was a staunch Hanoverian, hence the hotel's name. It was hardly going to be called the Bonnie Prince Charlie.) Rooms have been done over in a style sympathetic to their Georgian origins, some with four-poster beds. You'll find friendly staff, an appealing bar with an open fire, wooden ceiling, flagstone floor and exposed stone walls, and there's a great choice of whiskies and decent food too (fish and shellfish from Loch Fyne). This is a commendable venue for sinking into a mindset from more than two centuries ago – and you can even find the splendid specialist whisky shop Loch Fyne Whiskies directly opposite (www.lfw.co.uk).

Kilberry Inn

Kilberry Road, Kilberry, nr Tarbert, Argyll PA29 6YD (01880 770223/www.kilberryinn. com). **Rates** £90 double. **Credit** MC, V.

The Kilberry Inn's owners used to run a great little seafood restaurant in Tarbert called the Anchorage, now sadly gone. Fortunately, in 2005 they decided to take over this celebrated inn and restaurant around 13 miles west along the B8024. The Kilberry has long been acknowledged as a great place to hide away and the updated menu (*see p394*) and decor really hit the spot. There's a

ARDANAISEIG

Originally built during the reign of William IV for Colonel James Archibald Campbell, Ardanaiseig sits on the north-west shore of Loch Awe in splendid isolation, around three miles up a single track road from the hamlet of Kilchrenan, which, in turn, is six miles from Taynuilt on the main A85. Or if you have been visiting Kilmartin (*see p388* **School of rock**) and are in an adventurous mood, head north and just after a mile you'll see the B840 to the hamlet of Ford. From there, it's around 15 miles up a road less travelled on the west side of Loch Awe to Kilchrenan, then on to the hotel (the views trade off against pot holes and logging trucks, so mind how you go).

Current owner Bennie Gray also has an antiques business in London, so Ardanaiseig's interior is filled with the type of furnishings that are equal to the grandeur of its grey, low-slung, crowstep gable exterior. (The gardens are interesting too, with a wide variety of different tree species.) Some rooms have canopy or four-poster beds, tremendous views of the loch and the surrounding mountains, with the kind of fixtures and fittings that make guests feel like they're part of a period movie. The latest addition to the accommodation is the contemporary and standalone Boatshed suite, bang on the water (yes, it was formerly a boatshed). All this together with a decent reputation for cooking (*see p392*) means Ardanaiseig has lately built a solid identity as a venue for romantic getaways.

It still manages a homely feel in terms of service, however. A guest who drops their mobile behind a radiator sees staff looking for long kitchen implements and inspiration rather than the number of a central heating engineer – an informality that puts people even more at ease.

ARDANAISEIG HOTEL
Loch Awe, Kilchrenan, nr Taynuilt, Argyll PA35 1HE (01866 833333/www.ardanaiseig.com). **Rates** £106-£316 double. **Credit** MC, V.

Mid Argyll & Bute

Tarbert Harbour

somewhat contemporary, boutique sensibility to the three B&B rooms, but it retains a quiet, distant and very relaxing atmosphere (it's on the side of Knapdale that looks over to Islay and Jura).

Kilfinan Hotel

Kilfinan, nr Tighnabruaich, Argyll PA21 2EP (01700 821201/www.kilfinan.com). **Lunch served** 12.30-2.30pm, **dinner served** 6.30-9.30pm daily. **Main courses** £6-£16. **Rates** £86-£106 double; £115 family room. **Credit** MC, V.

New owners Andrew and Helen Wyatt used to run a language school in Edinburgh. They moved west in summer 2006 to take over this 18th-century former coaching inn on the B8000, the road that runs up the south-west of the Cowal Peninsula. Helen is a self-taught chef and has received good notices for her menu (wild boar pâté to start, perhaps, then scallops with crispy bacon and sage, followed by chocolate fudge cake for pudding). The Wyatts also make an effort to source decent ingredients with seafood coming from Loch Fyne and meat from Bute. The rooms have a neat, polite look and public spaces are cosy. The hotel is situated next to Kilfinan parish church; the church burial vault houses ninth-century grave slabs and cross slabs that are worth investigating after breakfast.

Loch Fyne Hotel

Inveraray, Argyll PA32 8XT (0870 950 6270/ www.crerarhotels.com). **Lunch served** 11am-4.30pm, **dinner served** 6-8.45pm daily. **Main courses** £5.50-££12.95. **Set meal** £15.50 2 courses, £17.95 3 courses, £22.50 4 courses. **Rates** £90-£130 double; £150-£170 suite. **Credit** MC, V.

Part of the Crerar Hotels group, this establishment sits on the shore of Loch Fyne and has the kind of accommodation and facilities you might expect from somewhere a little more urban (contemporary rooms, plus a spa offering an outdoor hot tub, indoor swimming pool, sauna, steam room and treatments). Easy to spot on the main road just as you head south out of Inveraray, it's bigger than many other places around these parts (74 bedrooms), so could be a life-saver if you have left it late to confirm a stopover for the night.

Port Royal Hotel

37 Marine Road, Port Bannatyne, Isle of Bute PA20 0LW (01700 505073/www.butehotel. com). **Rates** £64 double. **Credit** AmEx, DC, MC, V.

Bute is celebrated for various things, including Mount Stuart (*see p392*), the island's history as a holiday spot for working-class Glaswegians, even for the quite astounding Victorian toilets at the pier in Rothesay. But interesting places to stay weren't among its notable features – until Dag and Olga Crawford took over the Port Royal in 2001. He's Norwegian and once worked for the BBC presenting *Farming Today*; she's a Russian palaeobiologist; Port Bannatyne, meanwhile, is a sleepy little village with a small harbour, around two miles north of Rothesay. The result is a fascinating collision of cultures. The Port Royal only has five rooms, so is more of a pub-restaurant with accommodation rather than a hotel but retains a great reputation for real ales and Russian food (*see p394*).

Stonefield Castle

Tarbert, Loch Fyne, Argyll PA29 6YJ (01880 820836/www.stonefieldcastle.co.uk). **Rates** £90-£120 double; £250 suite. **Credit** MC, V.

As you're in Scotland, it may well cross your mind to stay in a castle, and Stonefield is a castle in the true sense of dear old Caledonia's constructed national identity: it's a baronial-style mansion that was completed in the year Victoria came to the throne, rather than a medieval fortress. That said, it has a grandeur to it and the setting is splendid: around two miles north of Tarbert and set in 62 acres of gardens that will please any botanist (astounding rhododendrons) and with spectacular views of Loch Fyne. Staff are friendly and, though the decor is far from award-winning, this establishment is all about the exterior (the views, gardens, location) rather than the interior.

West Loch Hotel

Tarbert, Argyll PA29 6YF (01880 820283/ www.westlochhotel.co.uk). **Open** noon-11pm daily. **Meals served** noon-2pm, 6-9pm daily. **Main courses** £7.95-£14.95. **Rates** £70 double; £79 family room. **Credit** MC, V.
No more nor less than a roadside inn with seven rooms, a restaurant, bar (plus pool tables) and very handily sited for the ferry that goes over to Islay (it leaves from Kennacraig around four miles away). The West Loch Hotel sits at the back of Tarbert (or its west side) and if you're just looking to hole up for an evening, have a steak or a seafood pancake, and sink a couple of beers, it does just fine.

WHERE TO EAT & DRINK

Although the dining options in Mid Argyll and Bute are limited, visitors can eat very well indeed. The availability of fresh seafood (langoustines or scallops, for example) is high, and it's no accident that the original Loch Fyne Oyster Bar, progenitor of a chain of restaurants in England, still sits happily on the shore of its namesake in the heart of Mid Argyll. Some of the best restaurants come with rooms attached, which is testament to the difficulty of earning a living from a stand-alone eaterie in these parts.

When you're on Bute, West End Café (3 Gallowgate, Rothesay, 01700 503596) is the award-winning chippy to go to for fish and chips; no more, no less. Take away and eat as you walk along the seafront.

An Lochan

Tighnabruaich, Argyll PA21 2BE (01700 811239/www.anlochan.co.uk). **Lunch served** noon-2.30pm, **dinner served** 6.30-9pm daily. **Main courses** £22-£25. **Set dinner** £60 tasting menu. **Rates** £100-£190 double. **Credit** MC, V.
A family-run restaurant and hotel with Louise McKie in charge of the kitchen and dad Roger (also a talented chef) helping out, this has been one of the brighter culinary spots in Argyll for around a

BRING ME THE BED OF CITIZEN KANE

The Stuarts are an old, aristocratic family who can not only date their heritage to 11th-century Anglo-Normans, but have held the Lordship of Bute since around 1200. Although they had grand houses on the island before, it wasn't until an early 18th-century pile burned down in 1877 that John Crichton-Stuart, the third Marquess, in collaboration with celebrated architect Robert Rowand Anderson, went for broke to construct what would become today's Mount Stuart – set in extensive gardens five miles south of Rothesay. The third Marquess and Rowand Anderson never actually completed their very ambitious project, but, fortunately, the sixth Marquess started an ongoing programme of restoration in the 1980s, which has made a huge difference to what visitors can see today: an absolutely thrilling paradigm of Victorian Gothic. It opened to the public in 1995, and an award-winning visitors' centre, straight from the pages of a Scandinavian design magazine, was added nearby in 2001. This houses a restaurant, shop and small art gallery. In a parallel move, Mount Stuart has run a contemporary visual arts programme for the last few years (Mischa Haller, Anya Gallacio and Nathan Coley have all featured recently), as well as a performing arts programme that saw an open-air performance of *Twelfth Night* in summer 2006.

In the old pile itself, the Italian-marble Grand Hall is reminiscent of the atrium at Edinburgh's Scottish National Portrait Gallery (also by Rowand Anderson) but much more opulent, with astrological and astronomical decade. No tartan cliché here, the decor is up to date and so is the cooking. Good pub grub is available in the public bar (including tapas) while there are two more formal dining spaces to the front of the hotel: one woodier and warmer, the other more contemporary with light walls and complementary fabrics covering the chairs. There's a decent wine list, scallops are hand-dived, the venison comes from local shooting parties, and three typical courses could involve delicious smoked salmon on a potato scone with caper cream to start, shellfish platter with langoustines, scallops, oysters and lobster, and well-presented strawberry cheesecake for dessert.

Ardanaiseig Hotel by Loch Awe

Kilchrenan, nr Taynuilt, Argyll PA35 1HE (01866 833333/www.ardanaiseig.com). **Lunch served** noon-2pm, **dinner served** 7-8.45pm daily. **Main courses** (lunch) £3.50-£8.50. **Set dinner** £45 tasting menu. **Credit** AmEx, DC, MC, V.
Non-residents are welcome at Ardanaiseig but, given its location (*see p390*), most diners are

design themes. The Dining Room houses paintings by Reynolds and Gainsborough, among others, while the ceiling of the Horoscope Room is decorated with the positions of the stars and planets when the third Marquess was born. As if that wasn't enough, the Henry VIII Room has a four-poster bed bought by the fourth Marquess from Citizen Kane himself, William Randolph Hearst.

Outside, 300 acres of gardens were first laid out in 1717 by James Stuart, the second Earl of Bute, but developed and extended by the third Earl and others. They include a homage to the Via Dolorosa, Christ's route to crucifixion.

MOUNT STUART

Isle of Bute, PA20 9LR (01700 503877/www. mountstuart.com). **Open** Easter weekend, May-Sept) *House* 11am-3.45pm Mon-Fri, Sun; 10am-1.30pm Sat. *Gardens* 10am-6pm daily. **Admission** £7.50; £6 concessions; £3.50 5-16s; free under-5s. **Credit** MC, V.

staying over. If you really insist on popping in just for eats, make sure you book. Chef Gary Goldie serves a four-course set dinner menu, which could kick off with jerusalem artichoke soup, followed by ravioli of lobster with savoy cabbage. Best end of lamb with loads of French-style accoutrements is a typical main, although Goldie will give you cornfed chicken or sea bass as alternatives. In fact, discuss what you want in advance and he'll rustle it up. Finally, a prune and Armagnac soufflé might be served up for dessert. This is good food in a romantic setting, although it is far too easy to spend over £30 on a bottle of wine. Still, if you catch dinner on a clear night, then walk out on to the lawn to be greeted by a sky full of stars, you really won't care.

Glebe Cairn Restaurant

Kilmartin House Museum, Kilmartin, Argyll PA31 8RQ (01546 510278/www.kilmartin. org). **Lunch served** noon-3pm daily. **Dinner served** 7-9pm Thur-Sat. **Main courses** £4.95-£16. **Credit** MC, V.
Although this is the café attached to the estimable Kilmartin House Museum, the Glebe Cairn really does aim far higher than coffee and cake. Kitchen supremo Vanessa Lilof has been in charge since 2004 and offers a café menu during the day (classic soups, sandwiches, quiche, the odd hot dish), but from Thursday to Saturday the Glebe Cairn also does dinner. The venue is split into two spaces: a simple, stone-walled dining area with tables by the kitchen, then an attractive conservatory space downstairs, which is where the dinner guests are ushered for dishes such as goat's cheese and avocado salad, smoked haddock pancake with cheese sauce, fillet steak with haggis and whisky sauce, scallops with smoked bacon, and more. Freshly caught local shellfish is also a big feature. Pudding might be raspberry meringue or a Loch Fyne whisky posset. Vegetarians will find themselves well catered for and there are a couple of wines and good bottled beers to accompany the food.

Inver Cottage

Strathlachlan, Strachur, Argyll PA27 8BU (01369 860537/www.invercottage.co.uk). **Lunch served** *Apr-June, Sept* noon-2.30pm Tue-Sun. *July, Aug* noon-2.30pm daily. *Oct* noon-2pm Thur-Sun. **Dinner served** *Apr-June, Sept, Oct* 6-9pm Thur-Sat. *July, Aug* 6-9pm daily. **Main courses** £7-£16. **Credit** MC, V.
A coffeehouse and restaurant with craft shop (once a croft), Inver Cottage overlooks the ruins of the medieval Castle Lachlan on the east side of Loch Fyne around six miles south of Strachur. ('New' Castle Lachlan, dating from the 18th century, is about half a mile back up the strath.) Snacks and light meals are served during the day (houmous and roast red pepper baguette), while more elaborate cooking in the evening could involve dishes such as Loch Fyne scallops in garlic with a citrus salad, or local venison with rosemary potatoes and redcurrant jus; a comfort food option might be steak and Guinness pie with cheddar

mash. This is the kind of place you stumble across by accident, and then afterwards rave to your friends about the unexpected quality of the cooking out in the wilds. Inver Cottage is seasonal, though – open most days from April to September, curtailed hours in the autumn, then shut in the winter; phone ahead to check.

Kames Hotel

Kames, by Tighnabruaich, Argyll PA21 2AF (01700 811489/www.kames-hotel.com). **Meals served** *Bar* noon-9pm daily. *Restaurant* **Lunch served** noon-3pm Sun. **Dinner served** 6-10pm daily. **Main courses** £8-£20. **Set lunch** (Sun) £15 3 courses. **Rates** £85-£170 double. *Both* **Credit** MC, V.
Yes this is a hotel, yes it has a restaurant, and yes again, the place was actually refurbished a fair bit in 2006, but if there's one thing you don't want to miss here, it's the bar. Effortlessly relaxed, nautical and atmospheric (passing yachtsmen and women pop in as well as locals), you will want to settle down for the night, making only occasional excursions to buy another round (there's a good selection of whisky), or have a game of pool, as the Kyle of Bute glistens outside.

Kilberry Inn

Kilberry, nr Tarbert, Argyll PA29 6YD (01880 770223/www.kilberryinn.com). **Open** 11am-3pm, 6.30-10.30pm Tue-Sat; noon-3pm Sun.

Dinner served 7-8.30pm Tue-Sat. **Main courses** £11-£16. **Rates** £90 double. **Credit** MC, V.
A very small B&B (*see p389*) on the other side of Knapdale, the Kilberry also has a restaurant and your chef here is Clare Johnson, with David Wilson front of house (both formerly of the Anchorage in nearby Tarbert). The emphasis is much the same as it was at their old venue: good bistro cooking with plenty of seafood. At dinner, three courses could bring a puy lentil salad with tapenade toasts and soft-boiled egg to start; stir-fried monkfish with peppers and pak choi as a main; caramelised apple cakes with rum and raisin syrup, and Calvados crème fraiche for dessert. In summer the Kilberry is open five days a week, but in winter this is much curtailed, so phone ahead to check – but it's always worth the trip.

Loch Fyne Oyster Bar

Clachan, Cairndow, Argyll PA26 8BL (01499 600236/www.lochfyne.com). **Meals served** *Summer* 9am-9pm daily. *Winter* 9am-7pm daily. **Main courses** £5.95-£29.50. **Credit** AmEx, DC, MC, V.
Described as a 'sister business' to the namesake chain of Loch Fyne restaurants in England (it's not part of the limited company that operates them, though), this was the original that spawned the whole enterprise. It's also the closest to the raw materials, eco-conscious, and is actually owned by the staff who run it. The premises are

Loch Fyne

Argyll: get away from it all.

simple (whitewashed walls, wooden booths and tables) and although it may be too bright and busy for a romantic encounter, it's an ideal stopover for seafood-lovers. The menu breaks down into starters and light dishes (queen scallops with garlic butter, for example), mains (char-grilled Loch Duart salmon with lemon and ginger), specialities (Loch Fyne oysters on ice with hot sausage), or the daily specials. The seafood platter is spectacular (crab, oysters, langoustines, mussels, queen scallops, cockles, crevettes and clams) and there's an adjacent shop if you want to take anything home with you.

Russian Tavern

Port Royal Hotel, 37 Marine Road, Port Bannatyne, Isle of Bute PA20 0LW (01700 505073/www.butehotel.com). **Meals served** noon-10pm daily. **Main courses** £16-£24. **Credit** MC, V.

The catering wing of the friendly and offbeat Port Royal Hotel (*see p391*), the Russian Tavern is on a mission to bring authentic Russian dishes, and top-class Scottish ingredients to Bute. But before mentioning the food, it's important to note that the Port Royal is a really good pub as well: cask ale, proper cider, a brilliant range of vodkas and more (even a Moldovan merlot). As for the food, you could start with seafood blinis (small pancakes with marinated herring, smoked sprats, caviar and razor clams); follow up with a solid beef stroganoff, or maybe a simple plate of langoustines with mayonnaise, then a pavlova for dessert. Down the road in Rothesay, the tourist industry is used to catering at the cheap

'n' cheerful end of things, so when the bill per head here pushes towards £40 (without drinks) eyebrows are raised. If you can't run to dinner, just settle for a pint of ale.

Westward at the Crinan Hotel

Crinan by Lochgilphead, Argyll PA31 8SR (01546 830261/www.crinanhotel.com). **Meals served** *Bar* noon-2.30pm, 6-8.30pm daily. **Main courses** £11.45-£20.50. *Restaurant* **Dinner served** 7-8.30pm daily. **Set dinner** £47.50 4 courses. **Credit** MC, V.

The Crinan has been around as a hotel forever, and under its current ownership since the early 1970s (*see p389*). In that time you would expect changes, and in 2005 chef Ben Tish took his leave and replacement Scott Kennedy came along. But *plus ça change*, it's still regarded as one of Scotland's best destination dining experiences, especially for its high-quality seafood dishes. Its ground-floor Westward restaurant isn't cheap (a four-course dinner for two with wine sails easily over £100) but it is very good. You don't have to go with seafood all the way, however; you could start with rabbit, Stornoway black pudding, fennel and garlic cream; then comes a soup course (bisque perhaps, or something creamy with truffle oil); the huge Loch Crinan prawns as a main will have been landed that afternoon; then how about a white chocolate tart or a selection of fine Scottish cheeses and oatcakes to finish off? After dinner coffee is served with handmade chocolates. Crinan couldn't be in a more beautiful setting and the Westward provides the food to match.

Speyside

A distillation of nature.

If you strike out into Rothiemurchus forest early in the morning, before the other walkers have risen, there's a chance you could amble across a red deer foraging among the pines. Speyside presents such David Attenborough moments from time to time; its mountains, lochs and strath score high for outdoor attractions and activities. Alternatively, as the land flattens out and the Spey heads towards the Moray Firth, visitors can find the biggest concentration of whisky distilleries on the face of the planet. With only 30 miles separating the top of Cairn Gorm mountain (4,084 feet) and the home of Glenfiddich, however, it's easy to combine the big country and the *uisge beathe* ('water of life').

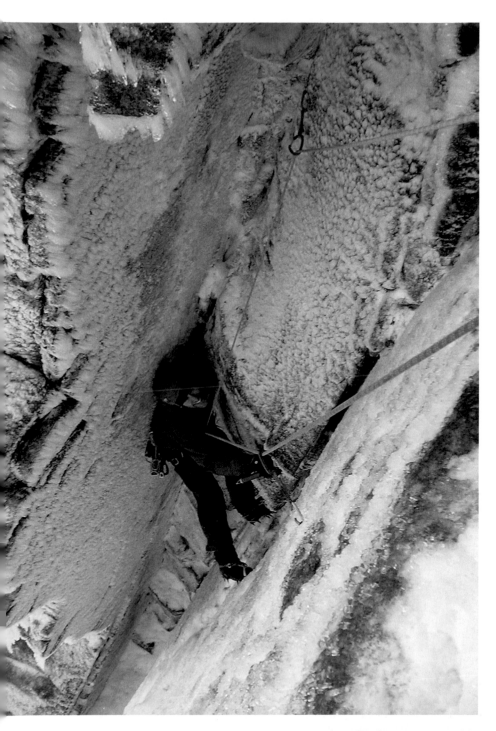

The River Spey rises from Loch Spey, a small body of water deep in the Monadhliath Mountains. From its source it heads roughly east through the hills to Newtonmore, then north-east via Kingussie and Aviemore towards Grantown on Spey. Around this stretch of the river, the two serious draws are wildlife and countryside. For more on wildlife, *see p368* **Wild thing**. Scenery ranges from wide-sky river valleys to epic mountains and extensive pine forests. The Abernethy Forest National Nature Reserve, for example, south of Nethy Bridge, has the biggest stretch of native pinewood left in Britain. Woodland aficionados also have the option of Glenmore Forest Park and Rothiemurchus, around Loch Morlich, east and south-east of Aviemore; Rothiemurchus, in particular,

is drop-dead gorgeous. Those who only want a short stroll with the smell of the pines could try a circumnavigation of scenic Loch an Eilean (two and a half miles south of Aviemore via Inverdruie).

South of Loch Morlich you're into the mountains – good for experienced walkers who want to get above the tree line. The Cairngorm plateau is a subarctic wilderness lording it over Speyside with lots of land more than 3,000 feet above sea level. It includes four of the five highest peaks in Britain (Ben Macdui, Braeriach, Cairn Toul and Cairn Gorm itself), as well as the commercial ski area on the mountain that gives its name to the district. There is a road up to the ski centre (01479 861261, www.cairngormmountain.com) and then a funicular railway to carry you from the centre's car park right up to its Ptarmigan Top Station, a shop and fairly ambitious restaurant not far from the summit. It's an entertaining excursion but, for solid safety and conservation reasons, funicular passengers cannot then wander off to the top of Cairn Gorm or elsewhere on the plateau. Booted and suited mountaineers can get into serious difficulty at these altitudes, especially in winter, let alone

Accommodation	★★★☆☆
Food & drink	★★☆☆☆
Nightlife	☆☆☆☆☆
Shopping	☆☆☆☆☆
Culture	★☆☆☆☆
Sights	★☆☆☆☆
Scenery	★★★★★

day trippers in T-shirts and flip-flops. If, however, you do want to learn the necessary outdoors skills to tackle this environment, one of the best places is Glenmore Lodge back down by Loch Morlich, Scotland's main national outdoors training centre. This has accommodation and a café-bar, perfect for the residential courses where instructors teach everything from winter mountain safety to first aid, rock climbing to kayaking (01479 861256, www.glenmorelodge.org.uk).

Continuing in a general outdoorsy spirit, there are also assorted activities such as sailing and windsurfing at Loch Insh Watersports, south of Aviemore by Kincraig (01540 651272, www.lochinsh.com).

Other attractions in this southern reach of Speyside include the ruins of Ruthven Barracks, just outside Kingussie (www.historic-scotland.gov.uk). The barracks was built by the British army a few years after the first Jacobite rebellion of 1715, and was caught up in the more celebrated rebellion of 1745-46 featuring Bonnie Prince Charlie. It's a fine place to wander and muse on the brutal political realities of 18th-century Britain. The Highland Folk Museum at Newtonmore and Kingussie offers more of a social history, however. Laid out over a large area, the Newtonmore site gives a taste of agriculture in the Highlands and includes a re-creation of rural life from the early 18th century to the early 20th; Kingussie is big on displays of farming artefacts, but also has an outdoors section with old buildings (both sites 01540 661307, www.highlandfolk.com).

The Strathspey Steam Railway is a much more Harry Potter-esque experience, (01479 810725, www.strathspeyrailway.co.uk). It chugs its way from Aviemore up to Boat of Garten, then on to the stop at Broomhill (possibly familiar to fans of BBC's *Monarch of the Glen* as home to Glenbogle Station). The railway's peak season is April to September, and aside from a few special trips around Christmas the trains tend to go into cold storage from November to March: more details available on the website.

Follow the Spey even further north-east, past Grantown on Spey, to Ballindalloch to discover an attraction best appreciated from a tulip-shaped tasting glass: Scotch whisky. From Ballindalloch up to Rothes via Charlestown-of-Aberlour, around Glenlivet and Dufftown, and on the roads towards the nearby towns of Keith and Elgin, lie the celebrated distilleries. Although most Scotch is still sold in the shape of popular blends (like Bell's, Famous Grouse, Teacher's and Grant's), since the 1970s there has been a well-documented upsurge in sales of single malts: whiskies of a certain age from individual distilleries.

These tend to be categorised by area and, in industry terms, the designation 'Speyside' extends beyond the banks of the Spey into adjacent glens and tributaries, even taking in relatively distant distilleries on rivers like the Findhorn in the west and the Deveron in the east. But you don't have to go that far to find famous names: Glenfarclas and Cragganmore are both made at Ballindalloch; Macallan at Craigellachie; Glenfiddich just by Dufftown; and Glenlivet at Glenlivet, of course. There are literally dozens of distilleries on and around this stretch of the Spey, and each has its own approach to visitors. Some will have a dedicated visitors' centre and offer tours all year; others are only open by appointment; some charge an entry fee; some don't. The one venue that has surely made the most of its public profile is Glenfiddich (*see p374* **Whisky a go go**). If you want to see several distilleries, the Malt Whisky Trail (www.maltwhiskytrail.com) is a tourist-friendly itinerary that includes Glenfiddich, Glenlivet, Cardhu and Glen Grant (all within a ten-mile radius of Charlestown-of-Aberlour), as well as Benromach and Dallas Dhu up by Forres, Glen Moray at Elgin, and Strathisla over the way at Keith.

Most distilleries with visitors' centres give guests every opportunity to buy their product. Otherwise, there is a great choice at the Whisky Shop in Dufftown (1 Fife Street, 01340 821097, www.whiskyshopdufftown.co.uk). It stocks all the popular varieties as well as some fine rare

TOURIST INFORMATION

Aviemore
Grampian Road, Aviemore, Inverness-shire PH22 1RH (08452 255121).
Dufftown
2 The Square, Dufftown, Banffshire AB55 4AD (01340 820501).
Grantown on Spey
54 High Street, Grantown on Spey, Inverness-shire PH26 3EH (08452 255121).
Kingussie
Highland Folk Museum, Duke Street, Kingussie, Badenoch PH21 1JG (08452 255121).
Nethy Bridge
Nethy Bridge Stores, Nethy Bridge, Inverness-shire PH25 3DA (08452 255121).
Newtonmore
Newtonmore Gallery, Main Street, Newtonmore, Badenoch PH20 1DA (08452 255121).
www.visitscotland.com
www.visithighlands.com
www.undiscoveredscotland.co.uk

WILD THING

Around Speyside there are all kinds of animals living wild in various habitats: red deer, roe deer, red squirrel, mountain hare, otter, wildcats, ptarmigan, and even reclusive capercaillie deep in the forests. You can make an effort to seek some of these out by hooking up with the ranger service at the Rothiemurchus Estate on a guided walk, or Land Rover tour (catch them at the Rothiemurchus Visitors' Centre, Inverdruie, clearly signposted a mile along the road from Aviemore to Coylumbridge, 01479 812345, www.rothiemurchus. net). Specialist company Speyside Wildlife (01479 812498, www. speysidewildlife.co.uk) also based at Inverdruie, offers evening tours in Rothiemurchus where it's more likely you will see the animals that move around after dark, particularly badger, pine marten and tawny owls.

As for the deeply impressive local ospreys, they merit a visitors' centre all of their own. These birds were persecuted out of existence in Scotland around the time of World War I, but in 1959 a pair reappeared at Loch Garten. Their presence was protected and encouraged, and now ospreys' talon-hold in these islands is much improved, although still fragile. Run by the Royal Society for the Protection of Birds (RSPB), the Loch Garten Osprey Centre (two and a half miles east of Boat of Garten village, 01479 821409, www.rspb.org.uk) is dedicated to the birds, and its visitors' centre is the best place to learn about

them. During the season (spring to late summer) a closed-circuit television camera is trained on the nest so people can view adult birds and their young. Ospreys are huge, with a wingspan of up to five and a half feet, and seeing one pull a fish from the loch is unforgettable.

Hard-core birdwatchers will also be interested in the RSPB site at Insh Marshes, just outside Kingussie on the B970 (01540 661518, www.rspb.org.uk), which is home to lapwings, redshanks and curlews in the spring, and whooper swans and greylag geese in winter.

As for animals in a more controlled environment, the Highland Wildlife Park at Kincraig (between Kingussie and Aviemore on the B9152, 01540 651270, www.highlandwildlifepark. org) provides a home for bigger mammals like European bison and elk as well as polecats, lynx, wolves, otters, beavers, and more. All kids love a reindeer, though, and the Cairngorm Reindeer Centre at Glenmore has quite a number of them (around seven miles east of Aviemore on the minor road for Loch Morlich, Glenmore Lodge and the Cairngorm ski area, 01479 861228, www.reindeer-company. demon.co.uk). Here you can get up close and personal with Santa's little helpers as well as taking a short trip up the slopes of Cairn gorm mountain to see them in the wild. The sight of a herd gradually looming into view out of the mist is really something special – especially across snow.

bottlings, and staff will even organise tastings. The best place to drink whisky on this part of Speyside – or virtually anywhere – is the Quaich Bar at the Craigellachie Hotel (*see p371*).

Finally, if you want to do Speyside under your own steam, then the Speyside Way is one of Scotland's four official, long-distance footpaths. It runs from Aviemore all the way to Spey Bay on the Moray Firth, then a few kilometres east to the fishing port of Buckie. There are spurs to Dufftown and Tomintoul, and plans for a southern extension to Newtonmore, but the core distance from Aviemore to Buckie is a shade over 60 miles. It's a good route for people who like to muddle along doing short, fairly flat meanders each day with the prospect of a decent-sized village at the end. For more details about the path, see www.speysideway.org.

WHERE TO STAY

When it comes to accommodation on Speyside, it's best to think small. Aside from the Aviemore Highland Resort (*see p370*) and a Hilton nearby at Coylumbridge, big names and big establishments are absent. The average hardy walker here to tramp the Cairngorms is more likely to kip in a tent or bunkhouse than a five-star hotel. Meanwhile, up in whisky country, distilleries are hardly labour intensive, the main villages are far from populous, and life tends to be fairly quiet. Accommodation reflects this: there are B&Bs everywhere but also a sprinkling of highly individual, small hotels that have managed to carve niches for themselves. One establishment that deserves a special mention, however, is Auchendean Lodge (Dulnain Bridge, near Grantown on Spey, Inverness-shire PH26 3LU, 01479 851347, www.auchendean.com), which has offered a very individual and hospitable experience on Speyside for 20 years. Sadly, it closes its doors as a hotel at the end of the 2007 season, although Auchendean's self-catering coach-house flat will remain open for business.

Archiestown Hotel

The Square, Archiestown, by Aberlour, Moray AB38 7QL (01340 810218/www.archiestown hotel.co.uk). **Rates** £120 double. **Credit** MC, V.
A small establishment (11 bedrooms) that's fairly out of the way, the Archiestown sits in the tiny village of the same name on the B9102 back road that runs up the west side of the Spey from Grantown on Spey. A solid, red granite building in the main square, it's hard to miss, and has been under the charge of Alan and Jane Hunter since late 2004. Some guests come for the fishing (in season), others just appreciate the peace and quiet, and the bistro cooking (*see p372*). Especially

handy for the Cardhu distillery (less than three miles away), it's traditionally furnished rather than contemporary, but is comfortable – and if you can get a room with a view south towards Ben Rinnes, you'll be a happy guest.

Aviemore Highland Resort

Aviemore, Inverness-shire PH22 1PN (08451 255455/www.macdonald-hotels.co.uk). **Rates** £69-£114 double; £109-£154 suite. **Credit** MC, V.
Bang in the middle of Aviemore there used to be something called the Centre. This was a misbegotten monstrosity of 1960s tourist development designed to cater to visiting skiers (winter) and climbers (summer) and thus boost the area's economy. Aiming for Alpine sophistication, the reality was plain tacky. In recent years various parties got together to try again, including Macdonald Hotels (a fairly big chain with more than 70 properties across the UK). The venture grew arms and legs until the new Aviemore Highland Resort had four Macdonald hotels cheek-by-jowl along with a cavernous retail centre, conference facilities doubling up as a theatre, lodges for let, and a leisure arena with swimming pool, gym and beauty spa. The complex actually dominates everything to the west side of the village's main street (and they even added the Spey Valley Championship Golf Course at Dalfaber, on the edge of Aviemore, in 2006). Accommodation-wise, the form and function of the hotels tends to change (according to the market and corporate strategy), but for the moment the pick of the bunch would be the Macdonald Four Seasons (for the mountain views from its upper floors looking east) and the Macdonald Highland,

Boathouse: seriously good food and a spectular view.

which is promoted as the jewel in the crown. All bedrooms have a dependable, contemporary style and give you modern urban comfort in Highland surroundings. There are on-site restaurants and bars, but remember that the fleshpots of Aviemore are only a couple of minutes' walk.

Boat

Boat of Garten, Inverness-shire PH24 3BH (01479 831258/www.boathotel.co.uk). **Rates** £133-£143 double; £184-£194 suite. **Credit** MC, V.
There's not a lot to Boat of Garten, a tiny village on the west bank of the Spey a few miles northeast of Aviemore. But it does have a small railway station where the steam trains stop; it's handy for Loch Garten and its ospreys – a short drive on the other side of the river; and it's home to the Boat hotel. It's a fairly ambitious establishment, granite-built, Victorian, which served as the station hotel when the village was connected to the main railway network. The dining room is among the best places to eat on Speyside (*see p372*), and combines old-school decor with some contemporary flourishes. Staff are friendly, and if you arrive on the steam train, it's very romantic indeed.

Cairngorm Hotel

Grampian Road, Aviemore, Inverness-shire PH22 1PE (01479 810233/www.cairngorm. com). **Rates** £80-£110 double. **Credit** MC, V.
An acceptable, often economical, and very handy hotel opposite Aviemore's railway station. You may well come to love Cairngorm for its pub grub and the conviviality of the bar (*see p373*), but its regular events and music mean there's no guarantee of a quiet night.

Corrour House

Rothiemurchus, nr Aviemore, Inverness-shire PH22 1QH (01479 810220/www.corrour househotel.co.uk). **Rates** £70-£100 double. **Credit** MC, V.
If Aviemore can be described as bustling – and sometimes it really can – then it's useful to find a peaceful haven of country-house respectability just a mile from the village centre. Head along the minor road towards Coylumbridge and before long you'll get to Corrour (signposted on the south side of the road before Inverdruie). A granite-built Victorian dower house with four acres of gardens and woodland, Corrour sits on the Rothiemurchus Estate and looks over to a dramatic cleft in the Cairngorms, the hill pass called the Lairig Ghru. Inside, decor is neat and polite; with only eight rooms it really feels like you have wandered into the private – if commodious – home of a Highland lady. Run by a couple, Carol and Robert Still, it doesn't offer metropolitan standards of service – so no elaborate sandwiches at 2am, then – but you can soak up the view from the garden of a summer evening before taking a good Speyside whisky up to bed.

Craigellachie Hotel

Craigellachie, Speyside, Banffshire AB38 9SR (01340 881204/www.craigellachie.com). **Rates** £135 double; £175 suite. DB&B £141.50-£187.50 double; £181.50-£227.50 suite. **Credit** MC, V.
The big white one on the hill. The Craigellachie Hotel is slap bang on the Speyside Way, and close to both the Macallan distillery (on the other side of the river) and the Speyside Cooperage Centre. It's the whisky country hotel par excellence and has the bar to prove it: the Quaich is not big, but it is very, very clever. It's a neatly appointed whisky nirvana with nearly 700 varieties, including Japanese brands as well as rare Scotch single malts. The more exclusive of these can set you back £15 to £275 per dram (fortunately, the majority are much more affordable). The Quaich will even cater to waifs and strays from the Speyside Way looking for an hour of bar lunch luxury – rucksacks can be left in the vestibule. In fact, walkers could be sorely tempted to brandish their credit cards and slump comfortably for the rest of the day. The Craigellachie also boasts a decent restaurant (*see p373*) and the general atmosphere is in keeping with its status as a late Victorian hotel (library, games room, old-fashioned look) – altogether quite a treat.

Cross

Tweed Mill Brae, Ardbroilach Road, Kingussie, Inverness-shire PH21 1LB (01540 661166/ www.thecross.co.uk). **Rates** £90-£220. **Credit** AmEx, MC, V.
Advertising itself as a 'restaurant with rooms' rather than a hotel, the Cross is one of the brighter stars in the Speyside hospitality firmament – run for some years now by David and Katie Young. Housed in a converted 19th-century tweed mill, with four acres of grounds, the interior has a modern-but-rustic chalet look (the eight attractive bedrooms, with their pale colours, are in a similar vein). Small but important touches are noticeable everywhere (good books and magazines to read, decent-sized beds, non-kitsch Scottish music), while the cooking just keeps gathering accolades (*see p373*). The small River Gynack burbling by outside completes an almost perfect picture. No disrespect to other hotels, or the Highland Folk Museum, but the Cross really is the best thing in Kingussie.

Heatherbrae

Dell Road, Nethy Bridge, Inverness-shire PH25 3DG (01479 821345/www.heatherbrae hotel.com). **Rates** £80 double; £100 family room. **Credit** MC, V.
It's all change at the basic but lovable Heatherbrae (though thankfully much has also remained the same). At the end of 2005, it was taken over by a Slovakian couple, Brano Gombarsky and Monika Butkajova, but they decided to make no radical departures. Red squirrels still gambol in the trees outside and the

happy clunk of pool balls still emanates from the bar. This small hotel (four bedrooms) is a short hike up Dell Road from the centre of the village, on the south side of the River Nethy. Housed in a sturdy old granite villa, it serves hearty food and is very handy for anyone who wants to head off just a few hundred yards further up the road and get lost (figuratively) on the tracks and paths of Abernethy Forest National Nature Reserve.

Minmore House

Glenlivet, Banffshire AB37 9DB (01807 590378/www.minmorehousehotel.com). **Rates** £128-£144 double; £192 suite. DB&B £206-£222 double; £270 suite. **Credit** AmEx, MC, V.
This is the only hotel in the world haunted by a calf called Ben Macdui, which, on reflection, is excellent news. One thinks of country-house spectres as the spirits of twisted old curmudgeons, hell-bent on devilment and revenge for ills suffered when alive. If you happen upon the ghost here, you're more likely to think, 'Aww, cute.' Minmore is run by the Janssen family, who used to be in the restaurant business in South Africa. Their current establishment is by the Glenlivet distillery on the minor roads north of Tomintoul (or only four miles south of Bridge of Avon on the main A95). Once the home of George Smith, who founded the distillery back in 1824, it has nine rooms (plus one suite), all with classic but fresh-looking country-house decor, four acres of landscaped gardens, good whisky, of course, and an engaging selection of South African wines. The food has a growing reputation (*see p375*).

Muckrach Lodge

Dulnain Bridge, by Grantown on Spey, Inverness-shire PH26 3LY (01479 851257/ www.muckrach.co.uk). **Rates** £140-£195 double; £160-£225 suite. **Credit** AmEx, MC, V.
A mid 19th-century sporting lodge that was transformed into a hotel in the 1960s, Muckrach is just outside Dulnain Bridge on the A938 towards Carrbridge – you will see the hotel sign on the road. It sits just a couple of miles from where the River Dulnain meets the Spey. With its Victorian exterior and classic Scottish reception space (tartan carpet, mounted stag horns) you might think you were in for Caledonian decor throughout, but the other public spaces, ten bedrooms and four suites have a more simple and classic hotel look. They take their food seriously here (*see p372* Where to Eat & Drink) and the owners (the Macfarlanes) are tremendously hospitable.

WHERE TO EAT & DRINK

Speyside is not crammed with major population centres. Newtonmore and Kingussie are pleasant villages, while Aviemore and Grantown on Spey are busier and have their share of populist bars and restaurants. But when it comes to good food, visitors will often – not always – find themselves heading for the dining rooms of the better hotels. This isn't a metropolitan centre and it can be hard to run a stand-alone restaurant that strikes a balance between the needs of the tourist market and the local people who fill tables over the winter. Unlikely, then, that you will find nitro-green tea and lime mousse, or crystallised seaweed on the menu around these parts (pace Mr Blumenthal). Good cooking on Speyside tends often, but not always, to mean an elevated Franco-Scots style with a reliance on quality local ingredients that, in context, can be very fine indeed. Then there is the odd venue that is damn good according to anyone's standards. Muckrach Lodge (*see above*) is one of these, boasting Grampian Chef of the Year Addy Daggert in the kitchen and fantastic Sunday lunches. Note, all smoking in enclosed public spaces was banned in Scotland in 2006 – this includes all restaurants, cafés and bars.

Archiestown Hotel

Archiestown, by Aberlour, Moray AB38 7QL (01340 810218/www.archiestownhotel.co.uk). **Lunch served** noon-2pm, **dinner served** 7-9pm daily. **Main courses** £8-£22. **Credit** MC, V.
A small ground-floor room looking out on to a walled garden operates as the hotel's bistro and it has been gaining momentum since the Hunters took over the reins here in 2004. Kick off with some own-smoked chicken on a potato pancake with tomato chutney; pan-fried collops of peppered pork fillet on charred polenta with rocket is a typical main. A likely dessert would be toffee apple tart with whisky custard. Priced more as a restaurant than as a bistro, it is the only show in town – and if you're staying in the hotel it would be a 35-mile round trip to Elgin for a bag of chips anyway. Treat yourself and eat in.

Boat

Boat of Garten, Inverness-shire PH24 3BH (01479 831258/www.boathotel.co.uk). **Lunch served** 12.30-2pm, **dinner served** 7-9pm daily. **Main courses** £5.85-£13.95. **Set dinner** £28.50 2 courses, £34.50 3 courses. **Credit** MC, V.
With its overwhelmingly blue decor and contemporary artworks, the main dining room at the Boat has a happily soothing effect, if a bolder look than you might have imagined in this Victorian building. The cooking is ambitious and could see three courses kick off with a parfait made of goose liver, chicken liver and pigeon, with a toasted hazelnut and sage brioche on the side. You could follow that with whisky and treacle-marinated venison on a prune and port jus, then finish with a pomegranate and orange pine nut tart. The beef, lamb and venison come from a local butcher, pork from Morayshire, while poultry, game and salmon are smoked and cured on site. If you're looking for

something more informal, the bar menu will run to venison and pork sausages (lunch) and more elaborate dishes in the evening such as roast loin of monkfish.

Boathouse

Loch Insh Watersports Centre, by Kincraig, Inverness-shire PH21 1NU (01540 651272/ www.lochinsh.com). **Meals served** 10am-6pm, 6.30-8.30pm daily. **Main courses** £5.85-£18.95. **Credit** MC, V.

Loch Insh, around halfway between Kingussie and Aviemore (on the B9152), is better known for sailing, canoeing and windsurfing than for haute cuisine. But all this outdoor activity can build up an appetite, and, cunningly, the water-sports centre includes a well-appointed canteen/restaurant that serves haddock and chips, filling burgers or good soup during the day (coffee and cakes too). It gets much more serious in the evenings, however, with duck terrine with black cherries, hazelnuts and spiced damson chutney a typical starter, and chicken breast stuffed with local haggis, wrapped in parma ham, with a Glayva and cracked pepper sauce as a possible main course. Catch it in the sunshine and you can sit on the balcony overlooking the loch.

Café Mambo

Units 12-13, Grampian Road, Aviemore, Inverness-shire PH22 1RB (01479 811670). **Meals served** noon-8.30pm daily. **Main courses** £4.95-£13.95. **Credit** MC, V.

Bringing style bar sensibility to Aviemore since 1998, this is a decent choice for drinks (coffees as well as the strong stuff) and classic burgers, steaks, pasta and nachos. During the day it's a chilled-out space to take the weight off, while a cocktail and shooter menu adds evening appeal. The owners also have a nightclub nearby if you're desperate for a late drink: the Vault, open Thursday to Saturday (01479 810508, www.thevaultaviemore.com).

Cairngorm Hotel

Grampian Road, Aviemore, Inverness-shire PH22 1PE (01479 810233/www.cairngorm. com). **Meals served** noon-9.30pm daily. **Main courses** £5.95-£16.95. **Credit** MC, V.

A big granite lump with fairy lights on the main street, the Cairngorm's chief selling points are its bar and its enormous menu. There's no poncing around with obscure wilted vegetables here – this is pure mince and tatties territory. Other options include liver, bacon and onions with mash and gravy, venison casserole or carb-heavy macaroni cheese with chips (served with bread and butter). On the drinks front, the lounge bar sports assorted football memorabilia, an accordionist on some evenings, a predominantly local clientele, and always has a single malt Scotch on special offer.

Craigellachie Hotel

Craigellachie, Banffshire AB38 9SR (01 881204/www.craigellachie.com). **Lunch served** noon-2pm, **dinner served** 6-9.30pm daily. **Main courses** (lunch) £7.65-£8.95. **Set dinner** £33.95 3 courses. **Credit** AmEx, DC, MC, V.

As a late Victorian hotel in the heart of whisky country, the Craigellachie leans on its history when it comes to decor, while it has long been a destination diner in the immediate locale and further afield. The restaurant is fairly cosy and three typical courses might involve terrine of mushroom and bacon with balsamic syrup and rocket to start; braised shank of local lamb cooked in a sage and red wine reduction as a main; iced malt whisky and honey parfait with forest fruit compote and cranachan for dessert. And to follow? Back upstairs to the Quaich Bar for another whisky, of course (*see p371*).

Cross

Tweed Mill Brae, Ardbroilach Road, Kingussie, Inverness-shire PH21 1LB (01540 661166/ www.thecross.co.uk). **Dinner served** 7-8.30pm Tue-Sat. **Set meals** £41-£45 4 courses. **Credit** AmEx, MC, V.

The dining room here is in keeping with the modern but rustic chalet style of the rest of the premises (*see p371*), and although it might not sound it, that's a compliment. Patio doors open from the restaurant on to a terrace overlooking the Gynack (a tributary of the Spey), which makes a perfect spot for a summer aperitif. Becca Henderson and David Young look after the kitchen and the menu is a real treat. In fact, the Cross currently stands as perhaps the best place to eat on Speyside. A typical three courses might involve seared Skye scallops with golden raisin purée and caper dressing, Gressingham duck with creamed savoy cabbage and chicory tarte tatin, and hot chocolate fondant with chilli ice-cream. Vegetarians present no problem but should call ahead. To complement this standard of food, the Cross also offers an impressive wine list.

La Faisanderie

2 Balvenie Street, Dufftown, Banffshire AB55 4AD (01340 821273/www.dufftown.co.uk/ lafaisanderie.htm). **Lunch served** noon-1.30pm, Mon, Thur-Sun, **dinner served** 6.30-8.30pm, Mon, Wed, Thur, Sun; 7-9pm Fri, Sat. **Main courses** £15.50-£18. **Set meals** 3 courses £24.50. **Credit** MC, V.

A genuine French restaurant run by a genuine Frenchman (Eric Obry), La Faisanderie is a small, simple space, with a no-frills style, bang in the middle of the village. It's the care taken over the food here that really grabs attention, though. The imaginative dishes use lots of prime local ingredients – try the lamb kidney tartlet, medallions of venison or lychee and passion fruit crème brûlée. An ideal place to stop if you've been visiting the nearby Glenfiddich distillery.

Speyside

WHISKY A GO GO

There is something deeply satisfying about the fact that while many whisky producers are owned by multinational conglomerates, Glenfiddich (which means 'valley of the deer') is still in the hands of the Grant family. The distillery was founded by William Grant in 1886; the distinctive triangular-shaped bottle first saw the light of day in 1957. The company was the first to market single malt Scotch in England (1963), the first to set up a visitors' centre (1969), and it created the prestigious Glenfiddich Food and Drink Awards in 1970. These days, 12-year-old Glenfiddich Special Reserve is the world's biggest-selling single malt Scotch, while the company's basic blended whisky (Grant's Family Reserve) featured in the 2007 edition of *Jim Murray's Whisky Bible* as standard blend of the year. This is serious stuff.

A basic distillery visit is free. It kicks off with a film about the company's history, followed by a tour following the whisky-making process from start to bottling, and is rounded off with a wee dram. If you've only ever sampled the ubiquitous 12-year-old drowned in ice, the intensity of a fresh sample in its natal surroundings will have the impact of a totally different drink.

In addition, the distillery runs special, more in-depth 'connoisseurs' tours (£20 per person), which include a tutored tasting session at the end; these are best booked in advance.

The Glenfiddich company also encourages contemporary art with its Artists in Residence scheme. Since 2002, invited artists have been able to live and work on site for three months during the summer; their work then goes on show. In 2006, nine artists were invited from all over the world including Wu Chi-Tsung, a film-maker from Taiwan; Annie Pootoogook, a painter from Arctic Canada; as well as Robert Bremner from rather closer to home

(a sculptor and recent graduate of Gray's School of Art in Aberdeen).

Those more interested in exploring the hands-on business of whisky production in all its many aspects will enjoy a visit to the Speyside Cooperage Centre (01340 871108, www.speysidecooperage.co.uk), around three miles from Glenfiddich up by Craigellachie. Around 100,000 whisky barrels are made or repaired here every year and its visitors' centre will tell you all about it.

Glenfiddich Distillery
Dufftown, Banffshire AB55 4AH (01340 820373/www.glenfiddich.com).

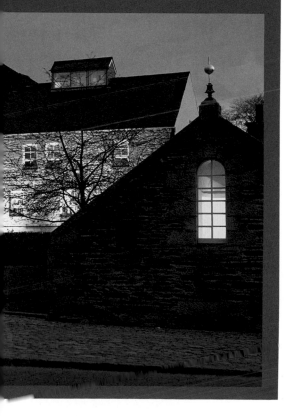

Minmore House
Glenlivet, Banffshire AB37 9DB (01807 590378/www.minmorehousehotel.com). **Lunch served** noon-2.30pm, **tea served** (bookings only) 4.30-5.30pm, **dinner served** (reserved set seating) 8pm daily. **Main courses** (lunch) £9.25-£18. **Set tea** £15. **Set dinner** £39 4 courses. **Credit** MC, V.
A small country-house hotel (*see p372*) near the Glenlivet distillery, your chef-proprietor is Victor Janssen who built his reputation in restaurants in South Africa before heading here. A typical four-course set menu for dinner could start with roasted red pepper soup, followed by own-made gravadlax. Next up might be supreme of guinea fowl (pan-fried then steamed on a bed of herbs) with red port wine sauce with redcurrants, rösti potatoes, red cabbage, and a carrot, parsnip and ginger mash, with a hot chocolate fondant for dessert. Unsurprisingly, Minmore House know its South African wines too.

Mountain Café
111 Grampian Road, Aviemore, Inverness-shire PH22 1RH (01479 812473/www.mountaincafe-aviemore.co.uk). **Meals served** 8.30am-5pm daily. **Main courses** £3.35-£8.95. **Credit** MC, V.
This is a first-floor café venue, above an outdoors shop in a wooden lodge on Aviemore's main street. Taken over by New Zealander Kirsten Gilmour at the end of 2004, its menu goes way beyond soup'n'sandwiches. If you just want coffee and cake, then the options here are first class (excellent coffee plus blueberry and lime drizzle cake, vegan berry flapjacks, Italian orange and almond cake, and much more besides). In the morning the menu runs to fruit porridge, full-on cooked breakfasts (vegetarian and meaty varieties), muffins and croissants; at lunch and all afternoon you could have seafood chowder, ham and eggs with fries, good salads (hot smoked salmon with roasted beets and green beans, for example), paninis, burgers and filled baguettes. This is simple but seriously good food and there's even a balcony for summer dining.

Old Bridge Inn
2 Dalfaber Road, Aviemore, Inverness-shire PH22 1PU (01479 811137/www.oldbridge inn.co.uk). **Lunch served** noon-2.30pm, **dinner served** 6-9pm Mon-Fri. **Meals served** noon-9pm Sat, Sun. **Main courses** £7.90-£16.70. **Credit** MC, V.
The Old Bridge Inn is a decent, old-school Highland bar with space for eats. It does good beer, a fine range of whiskies, a chargrill menu (Aberdeen Angus steak, perhaps) and specials and desserts on the blackboard (pork and mushroom casserole; poached pears in rose water) but can still run to starters and main courses off the menu like scallop and mussel bordelaise, then venison and pheasant platter respectively. The Inn has friendly staff, is patronised by locals, and is certainly worth seeking out even though it's not on the main street.

Strangford Lough

Wild and (tourist) free.

Designated as an Area of Outstanding Natural Beauty, Strangford Lough is nonetheless blissfully free of tourism. Instead, vast populations of migrant birds visit the large shimmering sand flats of its northern shores, while yachts and pleasure craft enjoy the challenges of this large intertidal playground, dotted with islands and natural harbours. Characterised by its unique drumlins – soft, undulating hills created by Ice Age glaciers – its shore is also defined by mature woodland, splendid stone-walled estates, pretty villages and sheep-strewn farmland.

Its southern entrance, or 'Narrows', is a deep channel with some of the fastest, strongest currents in Europe. These give rise to its Viking name, literally 'strong fjord', and make for dramatic ferry crossings and stunning scenery. Because of the area's subsequent raiders and settlers, there is no shortage of Viking forts, Anglo-Norman tower houses, early Christian monasteries, 18th-century stately homes, 19th-century linen mills and spine-tingling, head-clearing, ancient landscapes. The exceptionally mild and sunny microclimate allows palm trees to grow in even the most exposed areas, so you can enjoy a long season of outdoor activities. Don't forget an Ordnance Survey map, wellies, a pair of binoculars and swimming togs.

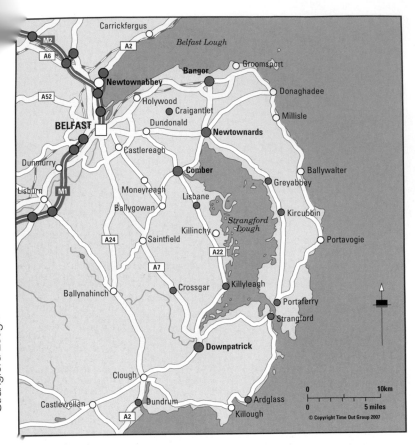

Newtownards to Grey Abbey

While the town centre of Newtownards, at the northern tip of the lough, holds no great draw, the prominent scraggy hill (a volcanic crag) locally known as Scrabo affords stupendous views. The panorama stretches the full 19 miles of the lough and beyond to the Mourne Mountains, the Isle of Man and, on a good day, Scotland. Turn to the north and you'll see Belfast. (Scrabo Country Park, 028 9181 1491, www.ehsni.gov.uk.)

Home to Stone Age and pre-Christian settlers, Triassic dinosaurs and great Irish deer over a period of 5,000 years, the hillside is a higgledy-piggledy network of pathways through gorse, whitethorn and dramatic disused quarries. It also boasts a golf course, albeit a rather wild and comical one, and a solid sandstone monument that was erected in 1859 to Charles William Vane-Stewart, third Marquess of Londonderry. The memorial commemorates his efforts to relieve the plight of tenant families during the famine.

When Scrabo Tower is open (Apr-late Sept, 10.30am-6pm Mon-Thur, Sat, Sun), you can check out the exhibition of pottery, flint arrows and stone axe heads. Sadly, the legendary Irish teas once provided by the Miss Millins, granddaughters of the tower's first caretaker and a local quarryman, are history too. However, Scrabo and the beech and hazel woods of Killynether provide lovely picnic spots and opportunities to stretch your legs. In the spring, the hillside bursts into flower and Killynether is carpeted with bluebells.

Here also is the reclaimed land of Ards Airport (028 9181 3327, www.ulsterflying club.com), home to the Ulster Flying Club and venue of a sporadic airshow. If Scrabo Hill has given you a taste for aerial views, then consider a surprisingly affordable 'air experience flight' (£70/40 mins). This will take you 'anywhere you want to go' in a four-seater plane at 2,500 feet. You can even take the controls, although the breathtaking views should satisfy the most demanding thrill seekers. This is also the spot for microlight flights (£75/ 60 mins, Gerry Snodden 028 9087 3244).

Sandstone quarried from Scrabo was shipped as far as Dublin and New York in the 18th century. It was also used for the original façade of Newtownards town hall, a fine, listed Georgian market house that now provides gallery space and craft studios. Rather tatty exhibitions can disappoint, and it is best to visit the profusion of artists and craftspeople in their home studios during August. For details, check out a beautifully illustrated publication, *The Creative Peninsula*, available from Ards Tourist Information Centre (*see below*) from June onwards.

Here you'll also find an extremely impressive set of brochures from the Armagh & Down regional tourist group (028 9182 2881, www.armaghdown tourism.com). If you're after active pursuits, the owners of Mike the Bike (53 Frances Street, 028 9181 1311), who kayak their way round the lough, are also a fantastic source of information on where best to windsurf, sail or fly. They also provide 'unsinkable' equipment, which they will deliver 'anywhere you like'.

Newtownards is a good place to stock up on picnic food (Homegrown, 66B East Street, 028 9181 8318), and if you really want to shop, Wardens, next to Knotts Cake & Coffee Shop (*see p384*), is a nice old family-run department store complete with hardware and haberdashery sections (45-47 High Street, 028 9181 2147, www.wardenbros.co.uk).

If you leave Newtownards, following signs to Portaferry, you will soon find yourself winding your way along the coastal road, right beside the lough. If the tide is out and the sparkling sand flats are exposed, horse riders, dog walkers, cockle pickers and a mass of migrant birds populate the beach. (Stop off at one of the many view and picnic points for a closer look.) When the tide is lapping the stony shores, year-round wind- and kitesurfers zip at exhilarating speed back and forth between islands across the shallow waters, best witnessed when the sea is whipped up to a white-edged, muddy froth. Clearsky Adventure Centre (028 4372 3933, www.clearsky-adventure.com) runs courses in kitesurfing, as well as plenty of other activities. Where the lough deepens, windsurfing and sailing are available at the friendly and unpretentious Newtownards Sailing Club (161 Portaferry Road, 028 9181 3426, www.newtownards sailingclub.co.uk). The club has now acquired some brand new GP14 dinghies and windsurfers that are for hire.

Accommodation	★★★☆☆
Food & drink	★★★☆☆
Nightlife	☆☆☆☆☆
Shopping	☆☆☆☆☆
Culture	★☆☆☆☆
Sights	★★☆☆☆
Scenery	★★★★★

If dry land is your preference, the neo-classical stately home Mount Stewart (Portaferry Road, 028 4278 8387, www.ntni.org.uk) is worth a visit. Don't miss out on its heavenly World Heritage Site gardens, five-acre lake and the hilltop banqueting house, Temple of the Winds. In the summer regular jazz weekends bring credible musicians and provide an excuse for civilised, wine-fuelled picnicking among the stunning, exotic plants and trees.

Fringed by impressive miles of old stone walls and wind-pruned deciduous woodland, the estate stops just short of Grey Abbey, a village of good antiques shops, tearooms and the enchanting ruins of Cistercian monastery Grey Abbey (028 9054 3037, www.ehsni.gov.uk). The first fully Gothic-style building in Ireland, it was founded in 1193 by Affreca, daughter of Godred, Viking king of the Isle of Man, and wife to Anglo-Norman conqueror John de Courcy. Tradition has it that the abbey was built as a gesture of thanksgiving for safe landing after a storm at sea. She is buried there and her stone effigy can still be seen. The abbey survived until the Dissolution of the Monasteries in 1541, and the ruins are now set in very attractive parkland with the backdrop of Grey Abbey House, a fine 18th-century mansion (private views for groups by appointment only, 028 4278 8666, www.greyabbeyhouse.com) – it's an intriguing place for a wander.

If you really want to stretch your legs, put on your wellies and head out from the car park just beyond Grey Abbey in the direction of the islands. These provided sanctuary for the United Irishmen hunted by Lord Castlereagh during the 1798 rebellion, including local hero Rev James Porter who was sent to the gallows in

TOURIST INFORMATION

Ards
31 Regent Street, Newtownards, County Down BT23 4AD (028 9182 6846/www.ards-council.gov.uk).
Down
53A Market Street, Downpatrick, County Down BT30 6LZ (028 4461 2233).
www.discovernorthernireland.com
www.strangfordlough.org

Grey Abbey. Nowadays, the beach is a magnet for sun-worshippers. You have to walk a fair distance into the surf to get any kind of depth, making it ideal for kids as well as paddlers.

Grey Abbey to Strangford

In Kircubbin – a significant harbour for the transport of kelp, brown (unbleached) linen and coal in the 19th century – you'll find another sailing club (Lough Road, 028 4273 8422) and a couple of excellent places to eat. Otherwise you'd be best advised to make tracks to Lisbane church, the tiny white 18th-century chapel that featured in the 1990 film of Sam Hanna Bell's *December Bride*.

The bird-filled estuary and Mourne Mountains backdrop are breathtakingly beautiful. So too are the views of Strangford from Castle Hill at Ardkeen. Named after the castle built by the knight William Baron Savage, this land was a reward for his part in the bloody Anglo-Norman conquest undertaken by John de Courcy. The hilly promontory is now marked with church ruins and crooked gravestones. It's particularly jaw-dropping at sunset, but so are the views all the way to Portaferry.

Take the Abbacy Road on the way out of Ardkeen Park – a ribbon of houses – and follow the winding road through drumlins, salt marshes and low-lying, flood-prone fields until you meet the coast again. This will give you a particularly stunning approach to Portaferry, past shipwrecks of wartime vessels, which mistook Strangford Lough for Belfast Lough, and the limpid, kelp-filled waters of boat moorings. This area is also popular with divers (DV Diving, 138 Mountstewart Road, 028 9146 4671, www.dvdiving.co.uk).

The town, once down at heel, is now a magnet for holiday homes with a mini-marina and harbour. It's here you can take the open-decked Strangford Ferry (028 4488 1637) across the swirling whirlpools of the Narrows, to the calm and very quaint village of Strangford.

Before you go, Strangford village and the natural beauty of the lough are best seen from the top of Portaferry's Windmill Hill. You should also have a look at the unusual L-shaped, 16th-century tower house built for the Savage family, or take a boat trip to see the seals or fish offshore. Ards Tourist Information Centre (*see p379*) arranges summer boat trips, or you can go with local men for bespoke jaunts (Des Rogers, 028 4272 8297 or John Murray, 028 4272 8414). Dress for the elements at the Port, an excellent shop for all-weather walking and sailing gear (14 Ferry Street, 028 4272 9666, www.theport ferrystreet.co.uk, summer season only).

Landlubbers may prefer to visit the aquarium and seal sanctuary (Exploris, The Rope Walk, Castle Street, 028 4272 8062, www.exploris.org.uk), just beside the castle. The flat country roads are perfect for cycling and walking as far as Quintin Castle. Wind-whipped, castellated and partially hidden by woodland on the exposed south shores of the peninsula, this is perfect *Famous Five* territory, with lighthouses, stories of ghosts and ever recurring rumours that Sean Connery is thinking of moving in.

Evenings should be spent at Fiddlers (10-12 Church Street, Portaferry, 028 4272 8393, www.fiddlersgreenportaferry.com), the hub for raucous music sessions and the centre of operations for the Portaferry Gala week float parade (www.portaferry gala.com). Thousands line the streets to

Experience the swirling whirlpools of the 'Narrows' on the dramatic Strangford Ferry crossing.

applaud the huge and spectacular creations fashioned from farm machinery by the fiercely competitive local teams.

Thought to have been founded by the Vikings, Strangford, with its sheltered harbour, was once a thriving port town. However, the absence of a rail link and the advent of steamships, which required deeper water, led to its decline. Nowadays many of its pretty properties belong to wealthy Belfast commuters. Take a detour along the coastal road to see the seals at Cloughy Rocks, the earliest datable tower house at Kilclief, the dramatic scenery at St John's Point lighthouse, or the picturesque harbour at Ardglass, the 19th-century headquarters of the herring trade, which employed more than 3,000 fishermen at its peak.

Alternatively, visit the calmer lough shores where the gardens and mature woodland of Castle Ward slope down to the sea (Strangford, 028 4488 1204, www.ntni.org.uk). With a Gothic west front and classical east front (both inside and out) this beguiling 18th-century mansion and pristinely preserved 19th-century farmyard is a charming setting for the opera that takes place every summer (028 9263 9545, www.castlewardopera.com).

Strangford to Killyleah

Next take the road to Downpatrick. Down Cathedral (028 4461 4922, www.down cathedral.org), a stunningly elegant and unostentatious cathedral, is poised ⸢ a cluster of trees and ancient graves, facing the Mourne Mountains on the Hill of Down. A place of Christian worship for an unbroken 1,500 years, it is said to be the resting place for St Patrick. His unmarked grave was commemorated with a stone laid by John de Courcy.

You can take in other local sites on board vintage passenger trains (028 4461 5779, www.downpatricksteamrailway.co.uk) on the original railway line that supported the linen trade between Belfast and Newcastle: Viking king Magnus Barefoot's grave, the limpid waters of the Quoile Pondage (a 450-acre freshwater bird sanctuary) and the 12th-century Cistercian monastery Inch Abbey (028 9054 3034, www.ehsni.gov.uk), built with money donated by John de Courcy, in atonement for his murderous conquest of Downpatrick.

Refreshments are best found, locals say, at the Daily Grind Coffee Shop (28 St Patrick's Avenue, 028 4461 7173) or Denvirs (14-16 English Street, 028 4461 2012), a 1642 coaching house and handy pit stop for the county gaol and museum. The Saint Patrick Centre (028 4461 9000, www.saintpatrickcentre.com) allows you to immerse yourself in an interactive history of Ireland's patron saint. However, you may prefer the natural beauty of nearby churches (Raholp and Saul) and numerous holy wells (including Struell Wells), which mark the progress of Christianity since St Patrick arrived on the shores of Strangford Lough in 461.

Killyleah castle

...ake the road over the Quoile Bridge, ...n the lovely drumlins to Killyleagh, a ...y village of multicoloured houses and a ...ately owned fairytale castle, where Van ...orrison holds the odd outdoor concert. A ...significant maritime port exporting cotton from the town mill and linen from Ireland's largest flax mill at Shrigley, the harbour is now the site for a sympathetic development of chi-chi second homes.

The focal point is a replica statue, erected by Prince Andrew, baron of Killyleagh, to physician and naturalist Sir Hans Sloane, former pupil of the 17th-century Killyleagh School of Philosophy and founder of the British Museum; Sloane Square, Sloane Street and Hans Place in London are all named after him. Not only do we have him to thank for the development of the smallpox vaccine, he also invented drinking chocolate; you can buy blocks of it, based on his original concoction, at Picnic (*see p384*).

For beverages of a more intoxicating kind, take a quick detour to Crossgar to the excellent wine merchant, James Nicholson (Killyleagh Street, 028 4483 0091, www.jnwine.com).

Killyleagh to Comber

Give yourself plenty of time and make sure you have a map to navigate the next leg of your journey, a breathtakingly beautiful stretch of the lough, densely dotted with islands. The sailing club at Ringhaddy (c/o Terry Anderson 028 9754 1044, www.ringhaddy.co.uk) has the air of a gated community, but if you're interested in boats you should be welcome here and at

Whiterock (Strangford Lough Yacht Club, Whiterock Bay, 028 9754 1883, www.strangford-lough-yacht-club.com), two of the centres for Strangford Race Week (028 4461 2233, www.slrw.org.uk). Even if you're not a sailor, it's still worth walking, cycling or driving along the causeway and country roads as they twist through and around seaweedy inlets, bird-filled salt marshes, Scots pine-covered islands and a manicured patchwork of hilly fields. Enjoy particularly panoramic views from hilltops on the Ballymorran Road and Ringhaddy Road, facing south.

To absorb the mystical, timeless quality of the landscape, visit Mahee Island and the ruins of Nendrum, a Benedictine settlement sacked and plundered repeatedly in Viking and Anglo-Norman raids. The lush, grassy knoll, topped with wind-gnarled trees and lichen-bleached ruins, is a spellbinding summer picnic spot with terrific all-round views of the lough. It's also worth visiting in the autumn when the shore is saturated by sea asters' blue, daisy-like flowers and displays of silver seed heads.

It's fascinating to see the profusion of wildlife and migrating birds in their natural habitat, but if you want to learn more, take the road to Comber to the stunningly situated and hugely informative Castle Espie (Ballydrain Road, Comber, 028 9187 4146, www.wwt.org.uk), a wildfowl and wetlands centre that hosts an equally laid-back and friendly Green Living Fair in September.

In Comber you should stop off briefly at Andrews Mill, a linen-spinning mill, which closed in 1997. Then continue

Bliss out with a warm welcome a lakeside views at Anna's House.

to Clatteringford, an unashamedly unfashionable linen outlet and mail-order company run by the Andrews' descendants on a very pretty family farm (51 Old Ballygowan Road, 028 9187 4545, www.clatteringford.com).

While the mill provided work for women, farms like this were created to provide employment for the men of the parish, to grow flax for the mill and food for the community. The Andrews family has an illustrious history, producing a prime minister, a lord chief justice and the designer of the Belfast-built *Titanic*. You can buy commemorative damask table linen with the same design and quality as that supplied to the doomed White Star liner.

Much of the town square in Comber has been demolished, but it's worth a trip to Pheasant's Hill (Unit 3, 10-12 Bridge Street, 028 9187 8470). A shop selling rare-breed meat and organic produce, it's an important outlet for the many hobby farmers in County Down. This includes Pheasant's Hill Farm, near Downpatrick (37 Killyleagh Road, 028 4461 7246), where you can go watch the pretty Tamworths enjoy a happy, outdoor life before they are turned into rather delicious sausages – an ideal present to take home.

WHERE TO STAY

Nestled in the green and pleasant land of the Craigantlet Hills, the quiet, tailored comfort of Victoria Brann's home and her discreet, reserved style will appeal to those who enjoy a sense of privacy: Beech Hill Country House (23 Ballymoney Road, Craigantlet, Newtownards, 028 9042 5892, www.beech-hill.net). For breakfast, Victoria cooks whatever takes your fancy on the Aga. Carriage House (71 Main Street, Dundrum, 028 4375 1635, www.carriagehousedundrum.com), meanwhile, is located in the village of Dundrum between Downpatrick and the Mourne Mountains. Bedrooms are homely and indulgent, with tasteful, treat-filled trays, powerful showers, and plump beds piled with soft pillows. Breakfast, served in the conservatory with views of the courtyard, is also a treat, with fresh fruit salads, star-anise-spiced plums, herby sausages and local breads. Edenvale House (130 Portaferry Road, Newtownards, 028 9181 4881, www.edenvalehouse.com) is a Georgian farmhouse run by Diane Whyte, who provides a warm and friendly welcome and makes as much effort for one guest at breakfast as for a full house, starting with hot stewed fruit and crème fraîche. In the morning you will enjoy glimpses of the sea. County Down's bistro Paul Arthurs (*see* p385) also has six comfortable en suite bedrooms.

Anna's House

35 Lisbarnett Road, Comber, County Down BT23 6AW (028 9754 1566/www.annashouse. com). **Rates** £70-£90 double. **Credit** MC, V.
There are few people who try as hard as Anna when it comes to providing a blissful B&B experience. Those who prefer the anonymity of a hotel really don't know what they're missing – from the cheery welcome at the door of your car to the cheery wave as you head down the drive, armed with the home-made scones or bread still warm from the oven. Breakfasts are particularly special. Of course, Anna is well practised in Ulster fries, but her forte is straying from the norm. Spiced stewed apple has a magic ingredient of elderflower syrup. Her omelettes – with just-picked herbs or heavenly mushrooms – would thrill a modern day Elizabeth David. You can also have delicious fishy things, such as kippers, kedgeree and Anna's signature mackerel patties, zesty and wholesome with toasted wheaten bread. What's more, all her ingredients are organic – Anna is the only landlady in Northern Ireland to have signed up to the Soil Association's code of conduct. She is also one of the few who bakes for coeliacs or allergy sufferers. All guests are wowed by the house – a County Down farmhouse conversion with a bold modern extension – all polished granite and glass with stupendous views over a private lake. You can also retreat to the low-ceilinged, firelit warmth of the old building, where every nook and cranny is stuffed with books and family possessions. Beds, with proper linen, are seriously comfortable, and the peace and tranquillity of the surrounding area will guarantee a good old snore. Anna's House is eco-friendly with underfloor heating powered on-site, and solar panelling.

Ballymote House

Killough Road, Downpatrick, County Down BT30 8BJ (028 4461 5500/www.ballymote house.com). **Rates** £70-£80 double. **Credit** MC, V.
A pink and pretty listed Georgian house set in a garden of huge mature trees, Ballymote is even more inviting on the inside. You're automatically welcomed to the large country kitchen, a well-used, relaxed space where landlady Nicola Manningham Buller exercises her passion for cooking, and where you'll probably eat breakfast – an excellent help-yourself affair that might include proper butcher's sausages, bacon and puddings, free-range eggs, breads from the local baker and so forth, all accompanied by rich roasted plunger coffee, freshly squeezed orange juice stewed fruits and cereals. Nicola makes something different every day so that long-stay guests don't get bored. If you're planning a trip in advance, you'd also be well advised to pre-order supper. This could range from a course of garlicky, butter-fried langoustines enjoyed around the kitchen table, to a full-on dinner party of local game, seafood and Irish cheeses in the serene dining room. Afternoon tea or pre- and post-dinner drinks by a roaring log fire, surrounded by books, fresh flowers and lovely

antiques make Ballymote a particularly restful spot, even before you head upstairs to comfortable bathrooms, luxurious beds and a long slumber.

WHERE TO EAT & DRINK

There are plenty of wonderful dining opportunities in and around the Strangford Lough area, including the Buck's Head (77 Main Street, Dundrum, 028 4375 1868), which fills its stunning dining room extension seven days a week. The set evening menu combines traditional favourites with global store-cupboard ingredients. A hand-picked selection of wines from local merchants makes this a special place for dinner, but it's also great for pub lunches and high teas. Curran's Bar (83 Strangford Road, Chapeltown, Ardglass, 028 4484 1332, www.curransbar.net) is on the road from Strangford to Ardglass, in the tiny settlement of Chapeltown, and was originally built in 1791. The snug and a porter-bottling room were replaced in a renovation that created the current conglomeration of firelit bars and opulent restaurant. An ambitiously lengthy menu serves roasts, pasta and risotto dishes. Fresh seafood from Ardglass and dry-hung steaks are the specialities, though.

Hoops Coffee Shop (7-9 Main Street, Grey Abbey, 028 4278 8541) is the place to garner strength over a good cup of tea and excellent own-baked cakes (try the orange drizzle) before you haggle in antiques shops around the courtyard. Another coffee stop is Knotts Cake & Coffee Shop (49 High Street, Newtownards, 028 9181 9098). Pass the bakery queues for unique griddle breads, sickly sweet 'wee buns' and fresh cream swiss rolls, and you'll join another fast-moving line for a self-service counter of country cooking. The Old Post Office (191 Killinchy Road, Lisbane, Comber, 028 9754 3335), dating from the mid 19th century, is a partially thatched warren of tearooms with exposed tree-trunk beams, creamy rough-cast plaster and flagstone floors. Stoves and open fires burning peat make it a cosy spot for winter months, while picnic benches and a garden provide a pleasant fair-weather setting.

Picnic (47 High Street, Killyleagh, 028 4482 8525) is a bustling all-day spot opposite the gates to Killyleagh Castle. All day, every day, locals pop into the cute shop, whose generously packed shelves, sturdy baskets, tiered cake stands and swinging blackboards lure customers with an irresistible choice of food. The passionate chef makes specials too, such as herby drop scones, served with mascarpone and roast red pepper, or the layered chilli beef and chickpea polenta pie.

Balloo House

1 Comber Road, Killinchy, County Down BT23 6PA (028 9754 1210/www.balloohouse.com). Bistro **Meals served** noon-9pm daily. **Main courses** £7.95-£11.95. *Restaurant* **Dinner served** 6-9pm Tue-Thur; 6-9.30pm Fri, Sat. **Main courses** £13.95-£18.95. **Credit** MC, V.
An exciting new restaurant and bistro pub in the remote but easily accessible County Down countryside, Balloo House, once purely a drinking institution, is rapidly making a name for itself as a food destination. It boasts one of Ireland's finest chefs and a savvy front of house team who've cut their teeth in slick, often starred, restaurants in Belfast and beyond. They're clearly relishing the more relaxed vibe of the countryside, so you get splendid service with lots of personality, as well as great food and fine wines. Although they've reluctantly had to beef up portion sizes to suit local appetites, the sophisticated dishes are otherwise uncompromised, benefiting enormously from a plethora of suppliers on the doorstep. A chunk of roast hake comes with a pleasant pickle of shallot in red wine, potato purée and buttery spinach. Spiced pork belly is happily paired with black pudding, roast scallops and butternut squash risotto. With warm chatter, soft lighting, natural stone and muted tapestries, it's also a lovely room, and you should make time for lounging in front of the fire in the equally civilised bar. When you're feeling more raucous Balloo's downstairs pub is always jammed with people enjoying big bowls of Strangford mussels, shepherd's pie made with local venison, or dishes such as crispy fried brie with apple chutney, walnuts and organic leaves. Desserts (say, creamy calvados rice pudding with spiced apple compote, or mandarin crème brûlèe) will also undoubtedly tantalise.

Bay Tree

118 High Street, Holywood, County Down BT18 9HW (028 9042 1419/www.baytree holywood.com). **Lunch served** noon-2.30pm Mon-Sat. **Dinner served** 7-9.30pm Fri. **Brunch served** 10am-2.45pm Sun. **Main courses** £9.50-£16.50. **Credit** MC, V.
'When my husband went to live in Australia for 18 months, he so missed this place that I sent him a framed Bay Tree postcard,' says Sonia Longridge, one of many adoring fans who pour their hearts out in the new Bay Tree cookbook. That this café has become a local institution is down to the unflagging energy of Sue Farmer and her team – instinctive, self-taught cooks, who produce consistently good food. From a tiny, larder-like kitchen comes a daily changing menu of earthy soups, abundant salads, immaculately prepared and well-sauced meat and fish, and indulgent sweet pastries and cakes. Best during the day, when the constant stream of customers has the kitchen at full tilt, the Bay Tree also does good food on Friday nights, and now to the delight of those who can't breakfast here during the week, it's also open for brunch on Sunday.

Strangford Lough

Balloo House

Poached eggs come with nutty, toasted wheaten bread, salmon and scrambled eggs with a glass of champagne. Sue's famous cinnamon scones, buttery, caramelised confections, will make your heart cartwheel.

Dufferin Arms

35 High Street, Killyleagh, County Down BT30 9QF (028 4482 1182). **Lunch served** noon-2.30pm, **dinner served** 5.30-8.30pm Mon-Thur. **Meals served** noon-9.30pm Fri, Sat; noon-7pm Sun. **Main courses** £9.95-£12.75. **Credit** MC, V.

In the colourful village of Killyleagh, you'll find this colourful pub, a hub for local and visiting gents since 1803 when it first opened as a coaching inn. Of course, it now extends a welcome to womenfolk and families, with a basement restaurant and weekend musical shindigs. But the Dufferin Arms is most famed for its cosy snugs, witty banter and pints of stout courtesy of long-serving barman Jarvis, who's apparently been pulling pints – and crowds – since his 14th birthday. The pub grub is good too, with legendary chowders, fresh seafood from Strangford Lough and excellent game from local estate farms, turned by a competent hand into hearty terrines, casseroles, pies and roasts.

Fontana

61A High Street, Holywood, County Down BT18 9AE (028 9080 9908). **Lunch served** noon-2.30pm Tue-Fri. **Dinner served** 5-9.30pm Tue-Fri; 6.30-10pm Sat. **Brunch served** 11am-3pm Sun. **Main courses** £11.50-£18.50. **Set lunch** £9 2 courses. **Set meal** (5-7pm Tue-Fri) £14 2 courses, £17.50 3 courses. **Credit** MC, V.

Fontana has a capable and inspired chef at the helm – Canadian Colleen Bennett, who followed celebrity schoolmate Jeanne Rankin to Northern Ireland to work at Roscoffs, and later Shanks. She runs a relaxed but enthusiastic team from an open kitchen. The recently updated restaurant is gorgeous – modern flock wallpaper, bold purple

orchids, Paul Smith-esque stripes and shimmering silks make for a smart, cool room that suits the easygoing sophistication of the menu and wine list. Fish cakes are petite patties of chunky seafood held together with a crisp batter and served with a crème fraîche tartare. Pink and tender haunch of venison comes with divine, rosemary-flecked polenta and meaty, slow-roasted tomatoes. Finish with coffee and cardamom crème brûlée or lemon panna cotta.

Paul Arthurs

66 Main Street, Kircubbin, County Down BT22 2SP (028 4273 8192/www.paul arthurs.com). **Lunch served** noon-2.30pm Sun. **Dinner served** 5-9pm Tue-Thur; 5-9.30pm Fri, Sat. **Main courses** £12.95-£16.50. **Credit** AmEx, DC, MC, V.

Paul Arthurs returned to his hometown five years ago to put down roots and open the kind of restaurant he would enjoy eating in. Since then he's created a small but perfectly formed empire including a smart chippy, an attractive beer garden for outdoor barbecues, six comfortable en suite bedrooms, and at its heart, a bistro that is undoubtedly worth the long and tortuous, if spectacularly scenic drive down the coast road between Newtownards and Portaferry. With a family background in farming and butchering, Paul offers first-rate meat and game dishes from beef short ribs, marinated in a salty sweet cure and served chargrilled to be eaten with your fingers, to whacking great steaks dripping with Café de Paris butter. For seafood fans the luxury of enormous creel-caught langoustines, lobster or healthy fat mussels, or prime fish from Strangford Lough and the local ports will be too much to resist. With serious, classical training and buckets of natural flair, Arthurs churns out simple, energetic salads, stocky, wine- and cream-laced soups, and flavour-charged grilled, baked and fried fish with bold but sophisticated sauces and dressings. Desserts – panna cotta with raspberries or bread and butter pudding with hot butterscotch, for example – are also equally irresistible.

Mid Kerry

Step back in time on the Irish riviera.

A nchored at its landward side by the town of Killarney, bordered on the north by Dingle Bay and on the south by the estuary of the Kenmare River, the wild, elemental landscapes of County Kerry's Iveragh Peninsula are simply breathtaking. Dubbed the 'Irish riviera', thanks to its fine summertime climate and sumptuous hotels, its southern shores still, thankfully, bear no resemblance to the cluttered, overdeveloped Mediterranean coastline. Rather, its natural beauty transports you to a simpler, more humble – though certainly glamorous – bygone era. The monumental blue-grey mountains stretching out to sea, and the bracken- and heather-carpeted heights of the pensinsula outdo any comparable coastline in Europe. Needless to say, the area – particularly Killarney – gets very busy in the summer season. Just to the south of Killarney is Kenmare, a village with a reputation for food and drink out of all proportion to its size.

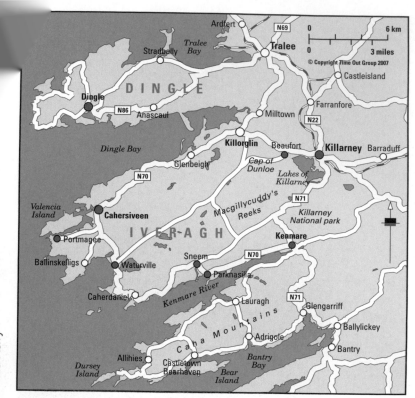

The peninsula is home to the highest range of hills in Ireland – Macgillycuddy's Reeks, topped out by the 3,414-foot Carrantuohill – and, adjacent to Killarney, the lakes and mountains of Killarney National Park (http://homepage.eircom. net/~knp). Here you'll find some of the most magnificent and rugged land in Ireland. At its core is the former Muckross Estate, which was gifted to the fledgling nation in 1932 by its American owners; this comprises Muckross House and 10,700 acres of land including the 'lake district' of Lough Leane, Muckross Lake (with the 1,655-foot Torc Mountain sitting directly above) and the Upper Lake. To the west behind Lough Leane are Tomies Mountain (2,411 feet) and Purple Mountain (2,730 feet). The combination of broken land, small islands in the lakes, varied waterscape and discrete high peaks is the kind of aesthetic package that you can look at all day. Hilltops aside, one of the best vantage points to take it all in is the Ladies' View on the N71 towards Kenmare (part of the Ring of Kerry). The road climbs up and away from the Upper Lake, heading south, until you come to a lay-by with the

inevitable café and shop, and a sign explaining that Queen Victoria's ladies-in-waiting were so impressed by the vista when they stopped here in 1861, it has been called the Ladies' View ever since. But keep going a few hundred yards up the road and there's another space to pull over, this time with no shop, café or sign.

The park proper is home to a wild herd of indigenous red deer, remnants of ancient oakwood and much else. There's a visitor's centre at Muckross House (064 31440, www.muckross-house.ie), which sits on the shores of Muckross Lake. Completed in 1843 for MP Henry Arthur Herbert, the pile is also worth visiting for its well-preserved Victorian interior, including a grand, stag-head-studded hall, a working kitchen and a library housing an eclectic collection of tomes. There is also an on-site restaurant, a garden centre and craft workshops. The ruins of the 15th-century Muckross Abbey are a short walk away. Another historic structure graces the shore of Lough Leane: Ross Castle is a 15th-century tower with later additions. From here, you can take a boat trip to Innisfallen Island on the lough, thought to be an important religious settlement from the seventh century, although the remains that can be seen today date from the tenth at the earliest.

While the Killarney–Kenmare axis is engrossing in itself, most people venture further – around the Ring of Kerry. The name can be misleading in a country with so many prehistoric sites. Is it a huge stone circle? An ancient fort? No, it's actually the route round the Iveragh Peninsula, but it's a gorgeous tour. The entire journey is over 100 miles if you go on the main roads and much more if you opt for the fun version, exploring the interior on minor ones. There are mountains, bays, beaches, rivers, wide panoramas and the big old North Atlantic running uninterrupted all the way to Newfoundland. At the western extent, Valentia Island – peppered with megalithic tombs and standing stones – is definitely worth a visit. Take the summer ferry from Reenard Point near Cahersiveen (€1.50; €5 with car, open 8.15am-10pm daily, Apr-end Sept, 066 9476141) or the bridge from Portmagee.

One thing about the Ring of Kerry, though: out of season, you can drive for ages and encounter very little that a city dweller would describe as 'traffic', so it doesn't matter if you do the route clockwise or anticlockwise. Summer is a different story. Organised coach tours set off in the morning and follow an anticlockwise route that makes life very hard for the contrarian motorist. It's much better to have a leisurely breakfast, give the coaches a decent head start, then set off at lunchtime. Doing the Ring that way, starting and finishing at Killarney, the last stretch of road is from Kenmare back to the main town. You climb up over the hill pass between the two, via the Ladies' View, then wind back past the Killarney lakes in an amazing finale to the day.

The Ring notwithstanding, the absolutely unmissable stretch of countryside around here is the Gap of Dunloe. This is a fabulously steep and dramatic hill pass between the massif of Macgillycuddy's Reeks to the west and the Purple and Tomies Mountains to the east. The numerous exposed outcrops, water tumbling off the rocks and small loughs give the impression that the glaciation that formed the Gap only finished a couple of weeks ago. In winter it makes for the

Accommodation	★★★★☆
Food & drink	★★★☆☆
Nightlife	★★★★★
Shopping	★★★★★
Culture	★★★★★
Sights	★★★★★
Scenery	★★★★★

most spectacular dr...
a haunt of the area's j...
(pony-and-trap rides for...
at the northern 'entrance...
Kate Kearney's Cottage, a...
the minor road up from Beau...
N72) and explore it on foot.

WHERE TO STAY

There are some utterly fabulous place...
to stay in Mid Kerry, but many of them...
close in the winter. The tourist business...
is so seasonal that even fairly major hotels...
can shut up shop for four to five months. We concentrate on establishments that open all year round, or if they do close, do so only for a few weeks after Christmas for an annual wash and brush-up. Fortunately, that still leaves quite a choice. Around Killarney, in particular, the number of new hotels that have sprung up in recent years (with spas attached) shows that the area's visitor-magnet status endures, while Kenmare hosts two of the best hotels in Ireland. The spa phenomenon is particularly handy if you've been doing the great outdoors and need a massage or the ministering jets of a hydrotherapy pool.

Meanwhile, if you do visit in summer and want more accommodation options, you could try Coolclogher House, a manor just outside Killarney (064 35996, www. coolclogherhouse.com). Otherwise, Killarney is stuffed with hotels, while Kenmare is more a centre for guesthouses, with some exceptions (see p390 and p391).

Aghadoe Heights Hotel & Spa (Lakes of Killarney, 064 31766, www.aghadoeheights. com) overlooks Lough Leane and the mountains. It's a contemporary and opulent pile, and makes a big deal of its Aveda Concept Resort Spa. The Brehon (Killarney, 064 30700, www.thebrehon.com) shouts, 'We're new and trendy and international.' The Thai-flavoured spa, Angsana, fits in nicely with the general theme.

Killarney Park Hotel (Town Centre, Killarney, 064 35555, www.killarney parkhotel.ie) is a prize-winning hotel and more contemporary on the inside than might be expected. The rooms are modern but retain a lush feel, while the spa extends to the likes of healing bath or stone ceremonies and indulgent 'spa ritual' packages tailored to men, pregnant women and jet-lagged travellers. The Parknasilla Hotel (Parknasilla, near Sneem, 064 45122, www.parknasillahotel.ie) lies west of Kenmare on the Kenmare River estuary. The hotel originally opened back in 1895 but has undergone refurbishment since then, not least the addition of six new luxury suites and a destination spa. The hotel reopens in July 2007 and will close again in late September for 'phase two'.

nmare Place,
www.killarneyplaza.
ozes contemporary
an aspirational, modern
luxury. There are three
ne Grand Pey restaurant,
ng room and Mentons bistro),
ton Brown spa has received
s for treatments. There are some
ed-and-fed deals for visitors who
o or three nights. Decor at the Park
Kenmare (Kenmare, 064 41200, www.
kkenmare.com), however, is more in
eeping with its late Victorian origins (with
some lovely antique pieces added in recent
years). Service is affable, the fine-dining
room is absolutely top class, and the Sàmas
spa is acclaimed as one of the top facilities
of its kind in Europe.

A recommended Kenmare B&B option
is Virginia's (064 41021, www.virginias-
kenmare.com), which is handily located
above Bruce Mulcahy's restaurant (*see
p392*). Virginia's is a friendly, unpretentious
option, and the breakfasts here are nothing
less than legendary.

Sheen Falls Lodge

*Kenmare, Kerry (064 41600/www.
sheenfallslodge.ie). Bistro* **Dinner served**
Easter-Nov 6-10pm daily. **Main courses**
€16-€27. *Restaurant* **Dinner served** 7-9.30pm
daily. **Main courses** €28-€38. **Set meal** €65
3 courses. **Rates** €300-€455 double; €515-
€1,860 suite. **Credit** AmEx, DC, MC, V.
The place to bring your wife and fall in love again
according to its Danish owner, who himself fell in
love with the Kerry countryside and made it the
location for his dream hotel. You can see why.
With the rugged beauty of a tumbling river,
jagged rock and wild flora on one side, and the
serene seascape of the bay on the other, there can
be few more beautiful places, even in Ireland. The
hotel – a new build in the 1980s – isn't the prettiest you'll ever see, designed to impress rather than
enchant. The upside of this is that bedrooms, or
rather suites, and communal spaces – even the
corridors – are generous in the extreme, allowing
privacy and contributing to its sense of hushed
exclusivity. The trappings of wealth and luxury
abound from the helipad and chauffeured Rolls-
Royce to tiered fountains and grass tennis courts outside. Indoors the hotel is equipped with well-padded

Killarney Park Hotel

libraries, club-like bars and a spa. In your private quarters vast beds and big flat-screens are only outdone by the view. Capacious showers and baths are characterised by floor-to-ceiling marble, endless high-pressure hot water and lots of nice smelly treats. With two restaurants offering high-brow French or conservative casual food, you could spend your whole time at the Sheen Falls, but you'd be wise to explore Kenmare, and the stunning scenery you can see out of every one of the hotel's windows.

Shelburne Lodge

Cork Road, Kenmare, Kerry (064 41013/www. shelburnelodge.com). **Open** mid Mar-Nov. **Rates** €100-€170 double. **Credit** MC, V.
A five-minute walk from Kenmare town centre, where Maura O'Connell Foley made her name as head chef at Packie's restaurant, you'll find Shelburne Lodge, a lovely old Georgian guesthouse. Foley's lifetime passion for food also shines through here – delicious aromas curl around the house in the evening if you arrive while she is cooking supper. And even if you have to wait until breakfast to experience her food, it is certainly worth the wait: perfect omelettes, porridge with

TOURIST INFORMATION
Dialling code from the UK: 00 353
Killarney
Beech Road, Killarney, County Kerry
(064 31633/www.corkkerry.ie).
Seasonal offices in **Cahersiveen** (066 9472589), **Kenmare** (064 41233) and **Waterville** (066 9474646).
www.killarneytown.com

honey and cream, ripe and scrumptious Irish cheeses, crab cakes, or smoked salmon with chive crème fraiche. It's all served at your table – in a civilised and pretty dining room – by family members and local helpers who are relaxed and ready to chat if you feel like it. The house has been restored and furnished with sensitivity and style: hissing log fires, piles of books and magazines, kilims, parquet floors, old mirrors, lamps and some stunning local art make for an enormously alluring winter sitting room. The summer appeal is equally great when the wisteria, formal kitchen gardens and orchards are in bloom. All the bedrooms are decorated individually, and share the covetable characteristics of polished wood floors, antique beds with deep mattresses and inviting linen, and Foley's signature arboreal sculptures – delicate branches of beech leaves plucked from her secluded garden to provide elegant decoration. The Shelburne Lodge is as good as it gets.

WHERE TO EAT & DRINK

Some of the best places to eat in Mid Kerry are in top hotels – notably the Park Hotel Kenmare (*see p390*), Sheen Falls Lodge (*see p390*), Aghadoe Heights (*see p389*) and Killarney Park (*see p389*) – but the listings below concentrate on interesting places outside a hotel environment.

Bustling Killarney offers quite a few year-round options. Kenmare, meanwhile, is famously said to have more restaurants than pubs, but since the village only comprises three streets (with eateries on all of them), it's not quite the boast it appears to be. On the Ring of Kerry, good restaurants are, understandably, more spread out and some places curtail their hours in the winter or hibernate altogether.

One such gem worth seeking out in the high season is the Lime Tree in Kenmare's Shelbourne Street (064 41225, www. limetreerestaurant.com, open Easter-Nov). Set back from the road in a 19th-century townhouse, and with an art gallery attached, it's one of the village's destination dining spots with a Modern European approach. Out on the western reaches of the Ring of Kerry, Paddyfrogs in Waterville (066 9478766, opposite the Waterville Craft Market) is open March to October, give or take a week or two. Launched in 2004, it's a Franco-Irish

KERRY SCENE

Mid Kerry

Although Kenmare is famed for its restaurant complement, a number of them are fairly informal places – more like pubs that have evolved into eateries thanks to the forces of tourist-driven natural selection. PF McCarthy (14 Main Street, 064 41516) is the modern example: a small and tidy blonde-wood affair with the bar area at the front and seating behind, where you could start with seafood chowder or broccoli and blue cheese soup, then try a simple baked lemon sole or salmon fritters with cider and apple sauce for mains. The Purple Heather (*see p394*), meanwhile, has been run by the same family, the O'Connells, since 1964 and has a long-standing reputation for the quality of its dishes. Its sister establishment a few doors along, Packie's (*see p394*) is more restaurant-like. Finally, the Horseshoe (3 Main Street, 064 41553) is a traditional-style venue with a friendly, rustic vibe. This is the place to go for a good honest beef and Guinness stew (although it does close for a couple of months after Christmas). Crowley's (26 Henry Street, 064 41472) is a must-visit Kenmare drinking pub; order a Guinness and get a taste of the true Kerry.

venture (hence the name) in a new building with a modern stone interior. It has outdoor seating at the back for summer.

The Club (Market Square, Kenmare, 064 42958, www.theclubrestaurant.com, closed mid Jan-mid Feb) is sister to the Cooperage in Killarney (*see below*), and is a relatively recent addition to Kenmare's main square. The kitchen offers some modern takes on traditional Irish dishes (starters like smoked haddock cooked in milk with onion and potato, topped with cheese), but its international leanings are dominant, whether reflected in a starter of frogs' legs in batter with mixed herb mayonnaise, or mains inspired by Hungary, Italy and elsewhere. The seafood specials are always worth considering too (pan-fried monkfish, butterfish or sea bass). The Cooperage (Old Market Lane, Killarney, 064 37716, www.cooperagerestaurant. com), opened in 1998, is another good choice and has established itself as one of the town's favourite contemporary eateries. It's a modern bistro with a bar area very much in the style-bar mould. Head here for dishes such as country-style seafood bisque, grilled sirloin with mushroom, chive and crispy bacon sauce, or perhaps poached fillet of salmon with a light muscadet sauce, chives and sweet pimientos.

Mulcahy's (36 Henry Street, Kenmare, 064 42383) has now moved further along Henry Street to bigger premises. Chef Bruce Mulcahy's new place also has a modern, designery feel, with plenty of bare brick and contemporary artworks, and he is still taking his cooking very seriously. His dishes demonstrate a definite international flair, which might mean a starter like spring roll of duck confit with Asian noodle salad and chilli jam; pan-fried black sole on the bone, warm potato salad, mascarpone and tomato and brown butter sauce as a main; and caramelised cashew nut crème brûlée for dessert. The two luxury hotels notwithstanding (Sheen Falls Lodge and the Park Hotel Kenmare), this is among the best two or three stand-alone establishments in the village. Mulcahy's restaurant is also attached to a very good bed and breakfast outfit (Virginia's, 064 41021, www.virginias-kenmare.com).

Around a mile south of the centre of Cahersiveen village on the N70, at the north-western extent of the Ring of Kerry, there's a turning to Reenard Point where the (seasonal) ferry chugs across to Valentia Island. Follow that minor road down its one and a half mile length to the end and there isn't anything here except a fantastic view (where the mainland meets the sea with Valentia Island and Beginish Island very close by), a seafood business and a pub: the Point Bar (Reenard Point, near Cahersiveen, 066 9472165). It's a light seaweed green and slate on the outside, wooden and neat on the inside, and gets very busy indeed in peak season when tourists head this way to make the ferry hop. Catch it when it's quieter, though, and it's a splendid place for a pint or some seafood-focused pub grub.

Another good choice is Treyvaud's (62 High Street, Killarney, 064 33062, www.treyvaudsrestaurant.com), which is easily identifiable by its predominantly yellow and red frontage. The restaurant runs to salads and light meals at lunchtime (fish cakes, a simple omelette) as well as full-on dinners in the evening when its sense of adventure becomes more apparent. That might mean shredded duck confit with Irish cream cheese and beetroot carpaccio to start, then pan-fried fillet of ostrich with caramelised shallots and red wine jus as a main.

Gaby's Seafood Restaurant

27 High Street, Killarney, Kerry (064 32519). **Dinner served** 6-10pm Mon-Sat. Closed Mon & Tue Feb, Mar. **Main courses** €24-€44. **Credit** AmEx, DC, MC, V.

A super-efficient restaurant with touristy rustic charm, Gaby's is best known for its fine seafood. Of course, there are alternatives: retro classics such as duet of melon or deep-fried brie with coulis are given smart, modern makeovers for starters, before meaty mains of steak au poivre or lamb. However, with daily landings of spanking fresh fish, you'd be mad not to try some o that are the real reasons for Gaby's 20-y. Stop off first in the cosy firelit bar fo. select your lobster from the tank, and served up in its shell with a rich house s cream, cognac and spices. Or enjoy one house platters of smoked salmon or wild r shellfish. Belgian chef Geert Maes expertly i duces modern notes to most of his dishes: salm comes with basil jus and a tropical salsa, or turb might arrive with caramelised apple and parsley glazed potato. For desserts it's back to the comfort of hand-me-down recipes, such as apple and raspberry crumble, honey-scented and served with crème anglaise and caramel ice-cream. An extensive list of exclusive – and rather pricey – fine wines will help you really splash out.

Jam

77 High Street, Killarney, Kerry (064 31441). **Open** 8am-5pm Mon-Sat. **Snacks** €5-€7. **Credit** DC, MC, V.

Supplied daily by a dedicated bakery, both branches of this shop have a loyal local following, but Jam is also ideal for holidaymakers jaded by restaurant food or in search of some easily acquired comfort. The counters teem with fresh-baked cakes and savouries that make it impossible to resist cravings for crisp, golden sausage rolls, or crusty sandwiches filled with Jam's own-made honey-glazed ham or peppered roast sirloin. Sit

Mid Kerry

Get high on life at the fabulously located Aghadoe Heights Hotel & Spa.

down amid the bustle of the shop and tuck into a wedge of jam sponge oozing cream and raspberry compote, a whiskey-laced bread and butter pudding or just a decent cup of coffee. On your way out you can stock up on sumptuous picnic fare such as chicken, pork and apricot terrine, smoked haddock and leek quiche or substantial salads (from mayo-lashed potato and spring onion to spiced chickpea). Jam is also good for those staying in self-catering accommodation – take the night off with one of the shop's stroganoffs, tagines or hearty pies.

Packie's

Henry Street, Kenmare, Kerry (064 41508).
Dinner served 6-10pm daily (Sat, Sun only in Dec). **Main courses** €13-€35. Closed 6wks Jan, Feb. **Credit** MC, V.
Whether you peek through the window, take a quick look at the menu, or open the door in anticipation, you'll definitely be sucked in to Packie's, – and disappointed if you haven't booked a table. Without being clamorous, the chatter here is infectious: you can tell everyone's enjoying the food, the vibe and the relaxed efficiency. This is a restaurant that feels warm and smells good. The walls might look like a badly iced Christmas cake, but your attention is soon diverted to the old antique tables, the candlelight and the general bonhomie. The menu is written with a confident hand and avoids flowery description: seafood sausage with beurre blanc, dover sole meunière, petit pot au chocolat. And there's no messing around in the kitchen either. Celeriac soup is rich, creamy and earthy. A chunk of fresh hake all but leaps off the plate. It may come with an over-sweetened red pepper chutney, but it's delicious as it is, or accompanied by lashings of colcannon.

The wine list is excellent too, and despite the profusion of other good restaurants in Kenmare, you could quickly become a regular here and live happily ever after.

Purple Heather Bistro & Lounge Bar

Henry Street, Kenmare, Kerry (064 41016).
Meals served 10.45am-6.30pm Mon-Sat.
Snacks €4-€15. **Credit** MC, V.
A great snack spot, especially after a long walk or on a cold afternoon, the Purple Heather is an interesting hybrid, combining pub and tearoom in one. Take away all the people and the tasty menu, and you'd be left with a cavernous old barn of a room, with patterned carpets, salvaged furniture, a few old Chianti bottles and a big ugly bar. Add great cooking, at very reasonable prices, and helpful staff, and you can be assured that you'll only notice the refreshing absence of interior design. The menu cleverly juxtaposes the downright plain (cheddar cheese sandwiches, bacon toasties and chicken salad) with slightly more elaborate dishes (pork sausages with green salad and apple chutney, a Purple Heather omelette of potato, onion, cheese and thyme, or a goat's cheese, toasted almond and seasonal fruit salad). Whatever you choose, it all tastes good and is definitely very fresh. There are plenty of cakes too – from rich Guinness fruit cake or wholemeal fruit crumble to indulgent hazelnut meringues or chocolate brownies. The only low point is the weak and astringent coffee, and over-frothed cappuccinos. Still, it's best to stick to what's local anyway: delicious pints of the black stuff, or a refreshingly down to earth pot of Barry's tea. Definitely worth a visit.

It's pure indulgence all the way at Jam.

Festivals & Events

Dates are given where available; for the latest information, see the relevant website.

JANUARY

London

New Year's Day Parade
(1 Jan)
If you like a good parade, the capital's New Year effort is a tough act to beat. Regally called a 'celebration of nations', it features more than 10,000 performers from 20 different countries strutting their stuff around central London.
www.londonparade.co.uk

Glasgow

Celtic Connections
(16 Jan-3 Feb 2008)
The UK's top Celtic music festival features well-known acts and the best new talent in a mix of concerts, ceilidhs, workshops and talks.
www.celticconnections.com

FEBRUARY

London

Chinese New Year Celebrations
(Sun after Chinese New Year)
A bright spectacle of dances, martial arts, music and costume fills the West End, centred around Leicester Square and Trafalgar Square.
www.chinatownchinese.co.uk

Bath

Bath Literature Festival
(23 Feb-2 Mar 2008)
With the city's literary history confirmed by Jane Austen's patronage, it seems odd that Bath's bookfest has only been running for 13 years. It's now a well-established nine days of literary happenings.
www.bathlitfest.org.uk

MARCH

Glasgow

Glasgow Comedy Festival
(Mid Mar)
Glasgow is very proud of its new comedy festival, which hosts almost 200 events throughout the city, including big-shot stand-up, sketch shows, film, drama and workshops.
www.glasgowcomedyfestival.com

APRIL

London

Flora London Marathon
(13 Apr 2008)
The starting point is Greenwich Park; the 13-mile halfway point is at the Tower of London and everyone grinds to a halt in St James's Park. This event attracts about 35,000 starters. It's a great spectacle, and a party atmosphere prevails along the route.
www.london-marathon.co.uk

Chelsea Art Fair
(24-27 Apr 2008)
For a few days, Chelsea Old Town Hall becomes home to one of the best collections of contemporary and 20th-century art in Europe. Roughly 40 well-known galleries show off paintings, ceramics, drawings and prints.
www.penman-fairs.com

Bury St Edmunds

East Anglian Beer Festival
(Last week of Apr)
With 80 different ales, this festival aims to provide beer from every brewery in East Anglia. Takes place in the Corn Exchange.
www.camra.org.uk

MAY

Padstow

'Obby 'Oss Day
(1 May)
Padstow's world-famous, 900-year-old 'Obby 'Oss Festival takes place on May Day. Two 'Osses, monstrous effigies made out of hoop-work, tarpaulin and horse hair, are paraded through the streets to the sound of wild singing, drumming and accordion music. Revellers keep going until midnight. It's a celebration of the onset of summer, and possibly linked to an ancient fertility rite.
www.padstow.com

Speyside

Speyside Whisky Festival
(Early May)
The festival brings out a quarter of a million drams of malt and single-malt whisky, plus a merry selection of entertainment.
www.spiritofspeyside.com

Bute, Scotland
Isle of Bute Jazz Festival
(First weekend in May)
Jazz sessions from morning till night (Thur-Mon). On the Saturday there are also marching bands, a street parade and jazz cruises.
www.butejazz.com

Bury St Edmunds
Bury St Edmunds Festival
(9-25 May 2008)
The Bury St Edmunds Festival is a major East Anglia event, with top classical, jazz, comedy and dance performers. There are theatre, walks, workshops and exhibitions too.
www.buryfestival.co.uk

Bath
Bath International Music Festival
(16 May-1 June 2008)
Inaugurated in 1948, the festival has become a highly regarded music event, which has many forms of the art covered, from orchestral, chamber and contemporary classical music to world and electronic sounds. The programme takes place mainly in city venues and also includes free outdoor events.
www.bathmusicfest.org.uk

Bath Fringe Festival
(23 May-8 June 2008)
Bath Fringe, an independently run jamboree of arts and entertainments across the city, is one of the oldest (it was started up 25 years ago) and largest in the country. There are usually about 200 events over its 17 days.
www.bathfringe.co.uk

London
Chelsea Flower Show
(20-24 May 2008)
Held on the 11-acre grounds of the Royal Hospital in Chelsea, this is the mother of all flower shows.
www.rhs.org.uk

Regent's Park Open Air Theatre
(Late May-mid Sept)
Sitting outdoors in Regent's Park watching Shakespeare and sipping wine is a gorgeous way to spend a summer evening in London. In 2007 the plays include *Macbeth* and *Fantastic Mr Fox*.
http://openairtheatre.org

Brecon Beacons
Hay Festival
(23 May-1 June 2008)
The pinnacle of British literary festivals, the Hay Festival is crammed with celebrity authors, influential critics, fine wines, storytelling and comedy. Hay is an idyllic market town with 41 bookshops for its population of 1,500. Tickets for the festival go on sale in April.
www.hayfestival.com

Tetbury
Annual Woolsack Races &
Traditional Street Fair
(Late May bank holiday)
Something you'd only ever find in the country – watch competitors race up and down Gumstool Hill carrying 60lb woolsacks.
www.tetburywoolsack.co.uk

JUNE
Isle of Wight
Isle of Wight Music Festival
(Early June)
An excellent non-nautical reason to come to the island in summer. The Isle of Wight music festival always scores several rock heavyweights.
www.isleofwightfestival.org

Old Gaffers Classic Boat Festival
(Early June)
The island is a boaties' paradise in the summer. Old Gaffers is a unique chance to inspect and delight in more than 100 gaff-rigged boats.
www.yarmoutholdgaffersfestival.co.uk

Isle of Wight's Round the Island
Yacht Race
(Late June)
This yacht race is one of the biggest of its kind in the world. Almost 2,000 yachts and 12,000 sailors set sail on a 50-nautical-mile chase west from Cowes.
www.roundtheisland.org.uk

Aldeburgh, Suffolk
Aldeburgh Festival
(Mid June)
Music combines the best of old and new classical, played by top musicians in a gorgeous setting. Tickets go on sale in March.
www.aldeburgh.co.uk

London
Meltdown, South Bank
(Mid June)
A celebrity artist curates the festival each year, choosing his or her own line-up. In 2007, Jarvis Cocker ran the show.
www.southbankcentre.co.uk

Wimbledon
(23 June-6 July 2008)
The grand slam to end all grand slams, as long as the rain stays away. Join the public ticket ballot or be prepared to queue.
www.wimbledon.org

Chichester

Chichester Festivities
(Late June-early July)
The festival, based around the city's Norman cathedral, features talks, walks, candlelit concerts, sculpture, classical music, jazz, comedy, street arts, fireworks and more.
www.chifest.org.uk

Glastonbury, Somerset

Glastonbury Festival
(Late June)
The UK's most famous festival. Tickets for 2007 sold out in under two hours. Pre-registration (essential to even be in with a chance of buying a ticket) starts in February.
www.glastonburyfestivals.co.uk

Goodwood

Festival of Speed
(Late June)
The world's biggest celebration of motor sport – loved by men and boys, in particular – is now in its 15th year. The theme for the 2007 festival was 'Spark of Genius – Breaking Records, Pushing Boundaries'.
www.goodwood.co.uk

Ludlow

Ludlow Festival
(Late June-early July)
Open-air Shakespeare in the grounds of the castle, plus opera, dance, poetry, music and a fireworks display.
www.ludlowfestival.co.uk

JULY

London

95.8 Capital FM Party in the Park
(Usually held in July)
Summer in the city is all about partying in parks. Here you can see the likes of Lenny Kravitz, Sugababes and Anastacia belting out tunes in Hyde Park. Book well in advance and check the website for exact dates.
www.capitalfm.com/pitp

Bognor Regis, Sussex

The Rox Festival
(July)
Rox is huge on the alternative music scene and features rock, punk, acoustic, blues, soul, reggae and hip hop.
www.the-rox.com

Cirencester

Cotswold Show & Country Fair
(Early July)
The Cotswolds' homespun charm is put on jolly (and large-scale) display – livestock, arts and crafts, gastronomic delights and much more. Be warned: the event attracts upwards of 35,000 people each summer.
www.cotswoldshow.co.uk

Harrogate

Harrogate Crime Writing Festival
(Mid July)
Runs in tandem with the International Festival. Speakers in 2007 included Frederick Forsyth, Lee Child and Val McDermid.
www.harrogate-festival.org.uk/crime

Harrogate International Festival
(Late July-Early Aug)
A celebration of classical, jazz and world music performed by contemporary stars.
www.harrogate-festival.org.uk

Isle of Wight

The New Forest & Hampshire County Show
(Mid July)
A big jamboree held in New Park every year, the show is one of the top ten agricultural and equestrian shows in Britain. There's livestock to admire, show-jumping to inspire, rare breeds and craft workers, food purveyors and entertainers.
www.newforestshow.co.uk

Sandringham, North Norfolk Coast

Sandringham Flower Show
(Mid July)
The Queen's Norfolk retreat is even more splendid than normal when it's ablaze with flowers. Check the website for other events on at Sandringham.
www.sandringhamestate.co.uk

Westonbirt, Tetbury

July concert/fireworks
(Mid July)
Westonbirt Arboretum hosts various events and festivals throughout the year. This is one of the finest.
www.forestry.gov.uk

AUGUST

Eastnor Castle, Herefordshire

Big Chill
(4-6 Aug 2007)
Held at Eastnor Castle in the Malvern Hills, the Big Chill is a rather grown-up festival featuring music, art, dance and film. It always sells out.
www.bigchill.net

Isle of Wight

Cowes Week
(4-11 Aug 2007)
August on the Isle of Wight is heralded by the longest-running, most prestigious and largest sailing regatta in the world.
www.skandiacowesweek.co.uk

Salcombe, Devon

Salcombe Yacht Club Regatta
(5-11 Aug 2007)
Salcombe Yacht Club organises regular dinghy racing, cadet sailing, cruiser races and rallies, but its big event is the Regatta, which attracts a fleet of boats and sailors as well as onlookers from all over the country. The Salcombe Town Regatta takes place the following week.
www.salcombeyc.org.uk

London

Great British Beer Festival
(7-11 Aug 2007)
Every year Earl's Court plays host to over 750 beers from all over the world drawing in more than 65,000 thirsty visitors.
www.gdbf.org

Notting Hill Carnival
(27-28 Aug 2007)
A vibrant highlight of the London summer, but be prepared for serious crowds.
www.rbkc.gov.uk/NottingHill

Brecon Beacons

Brecon International Festival of Jazz
(10-12 Aug 2007)
The Welsh market town swings every summer with big names and fresh talent, showing off their scat-and-sax skills at various venues. Previous events have featured the likes of Courtney Pine, Stan Tracey Big Band and Liane Carroll.
www.breconjazz.co.uk

Bognor Regis, Sussex

Hotham Park Country Fair
(11-12 Aug 2007)
This big and beautiful park is an ideal setting for a conglomeration of craft stalls, food tents, music and dancing.
www.arun.gov.uk

Totnes, Devon

Carnival & Orange Race
(12-19, 21 Aug 2007)
Oranges are the only fruit for this carnival, which sees this historic town all done up in its finery. The Orange Race on 21 August, organised by the Elizabethan Society, commemorates a visit to the town by Sir Francis Drake in the 1580s, when he gave a young boy some fruit. Contestants chase their oranges down the hill. Turn up and register on the day (the race starts at 11am). Oranges are provided.
www.totnesinformation.co.uk

Manchester

Manchester Gay Pride
(17-27 Aug 2007)
One of Europe's most splendid – you'd be hard pressed not to get caught up in the ten-day spate of parties and parades.
www.manchesterpride.com

Dunoon, Cowal

Cowal Highland Gathering
(23-25 Aug 2007)
These spectacular highland games have been going since 1894, and now boast 3,000 competitors and a crowd of 20,000 that flocks to see men dressed in tartan grunt as they hurl shot-puts, hammers and cabers.
www.cowalgathering.com

Arundel, Sussex

Arundel Festival
(24 Aug-2 Sept 2007)
The festival, held at Arundel Castle, attracts visitors from all over the world. In 2006 it witnessed performances by the great Humphrey Lyttelton, Katherine Jenkins and Texas. On 24-25 August there will be picnic concerts and fireworks in the grounds of Arundel Castle. The 26-27 August are reserved for pop acts (without the picnics). Other music and opera events take place inside the castle and the Fitzalan Chapel.
www.arundelfestival.co.uk

Grasmere, Windermere

Grasmere Sports & Show
(26 Aug 2007)
This historic and energetic Sports Day involves Cumberland wrestling, hound trails and the Fell Race, in which musclebound men who look as if they're made of steel and sinew run straight up the fellside. Then there are gundog and sheepdog displays, junior races, mountain bike dashes and a tug of war. You'll need the famous beer tents after that lot.
www.grasmeresportsandshow.co.uk

Dartmouth, Devon

Port of Dartmouth Royal Regatta
(30 Aug-1 Sept 2007)
This famous regatta, established in 1834, became royal when Queen Victoria sailed in unscheduled during some bad weather in 1856 and became a spontaneous patron. These days the event attracts much interest, for alongside the waterborne events, there's an air display,

fireworks, market stalls lining the embankment, music and dancing and fun events all week.
www.dartmouthregatta.co.uk

Edinburgh
Edinburgh International Festival
(10 Aug-2 Sept 2007)
Edinburgh Festival Fringe
(5-27 Aug 2007)
Edinburgh Film Festival
(15-26 Aug 2007)
Edinburgh becomes the envy of the world every August with its famous International Festival, of which one of its offshoots, the Fringe Festival, is the shining glory. Every possible type of theatre is on constant tap around town, with some 1,500 different shows.
www.edinburghfestivals.co.uk

SEPTEMBER
Bognor Regis, Sussex
Birdman 2007
(1-2 Sept 2007)
This is an annual flight competition for human-powered flying machines. Many flyers design machines to aim for the distance prizes – £25,000 is offered for the furthest flight over 100m. The attempt started in 1971 at the resort of Selsey, until the competition became too famous and defected to Bognor.
www.birdman.org.uk

Bristol
International Festival of Kites & Air Creations
(1-2 Sept 2007)
Up to 50,000 enthusiasts convene to see traditional, Chinese and funny-shaped kites let loose on the skies over the 850-acre Ashton Court Estate.
www.kite-festival.org

Organic Food Festival
(1-2 Sept 2007)
Britain's largest celebration of organic food and drink hosts over 300 exhibitors and gives visitors the chance to sample thousands of organic products. This year sees the introduction of an organic fashion show, relaxation zone and cookery workshops.
www.organicfoodfairs.co.uk

London
Regent Street Festival
(2 Sept 2007)
Food stalls, street performers and music events fill what is normally one of London's most traffic-congested areas, between Oxford Circus and Piccadilly Circus.
www.regentstreetonline.com

London Fashion Weekend
(26-30 Sept 2007)
Here is the ordinary mortal's chance to crash the glamour of London Fashion Week, as retailers and fashionistas set up shop at the Natural History Museum, SW7.
www.londonfashionweekend.co.uk

Ludlow
Ludlow Marches Food & Drink Festival
(7-9 Sept 2007)
Food-centric Ludlow's festival is not to be missed. There will be rare and speciality breed meat available, as well as local handmade cheese, game, cider, perry, ale and much more.
www.foodfestival.co.uk

Isle of Wight
Bestival
7-9 Sept 2007
One of the last festivals of the summer, Bestival is described as a 'boutique music festival' and is curated by Radio 1 DJ Rob da Bank. It takes place in an 88-acre park of natural woodland – Robin Hill on the Isle of Wight. You can bring your own tent, or hire a bivouac, tipi, yurt or beach hut.
www.bestival.net

Brighton
National Speed Trials
(8 Sept 2007)
Car enthusiasts should check out this traditional spectacle as vehicles old and new pack out Madeira Drive.

Beamish, nr Durham
Prize Leek Show & Harvest Festival
(8-9 Sept 2007)
The fattest leeks and marrows of the harvest season on display at the open-air Beamish Museum.
www.beamish.org.uk

Durham
Durham Literature Festival
(28 Sept-12 Oct 2007)
A wide range of readings, performances and lectures – last year's line-up included Vic Reeves, Simon Armitage and performances of *To Hell and Back*. Check the website for exact dates.
www.literaturefestival.co.uk

Frilford, Oxfordshire
Great British Cheese Festival
(29-30 Sept 2007)
Britain's largest cheese festival, with over 450 different cheeses laid out for your

...ation at Millets Farm Centre. Other
...ctions include a maze, landscaped
...ens and a fishing lake.
w.thecheeseweb.com

OCTOBER

Manchester
**Manchester Literature Festival
(4-14 Oct 2007)**
What was once the Manchester Poetry Festival
has expanded to become this extravaganza of
all things wordy.
www.manchesterliteraturefestival.co.uk

**Manchester Food & Drink Festival
(5-15 Oct 2007)**
Celebrating its tenth anniversary this year,
Manchester's food scene has more and more
to celebrate each year.
www.foodanddrinkfestival.com

**Manchester International
Film Festival
(26 Oct-4 Nov 2007)**
In 2007 this new biennial festival, born of the
success of the Manchester International Short
Film Festival, launches. The aim is to mix a
cutting-edge selection of features, shorts,
animation and documentary.
www.kinofilm.org.uk

Argyll, Scotland
**Cowalfest
(5-14 Oct 2007)**
Ramblers will be in heaven during this ten-
day event of over 80 walks around the Cowal
Peninsula. Art installations and exhibitions
are dotted about the area too.
www.cowalfest.org

Chichester
**Autumn Countryside Show
(6-7 Oct 2007)**
The Weald & Downland Museum reminds
all-comers of the way we used to plough the
fields and scatter in this mellow and fruitful
tribute to the harvest. Steam engines,
threshing boxes, plough horses and vintage
tractors are at work, and local craftspeople
display their skills. The 2007 event
incorporates the Wood Show.
www.wealddown.co.uk

Brighton
**Early Music Festival
(6-28 Oct 2007)**
Concerts of every genre (even medieval music)
take place throughout the month. This year's
theme is 'Improvisation and Transformation'
and the line-up so far includes Emma Kirkby,
Jakob Lindberg and I Fagiolini.
www.bremf.org.uk

Dartmouth
**Festival of Food
(11-13 Oct 2007)**
Dartmouth enters wholeheartedly into this
annual foodfest, which includes stalls from
local food producers, tasting sessions, food
education workshops and regular cookery
demonstrations. Local restaurants offer special
festival menus.
www.dartmouthfoodfestival.co.uk

NOVEMBER

Windermere
**Powerboat Record Attempts
(5-9 Nov 2007)**
The world's best powerboat racers zoom across
the lovely Lake Windermere. They set off from
the Low Wood Hotel and you can watch from
various lakeside outposts.
www.conistonpowerboatrecords.co.uk

London
**Lord Mayor's Show
(10 Nov 2007)**
This is when the newly elected Lord Mayor of
London (not Ken) is presented for approval to
the monarch or the monarch's justices. Amid a
procession of 66 floats, 21 marching bands and
6,000 people, the Lord Mayor leaves Mansion
House at 11am and proceeds to the Royal
Courts of Justice. The procession takes about
an hour and a quarter to pass, wherever you
stand. At 5pm fireworks are set off from a
Thames barge.
www.lordmayorsshow.org

**London Christmas Tree & Lights
(Late Nov)**
The Christmas lights (Oxford Street, Regent
Street, Trafalgar Square) are turned on by a
minor celeb around the end of November. In
Trafalgar Square a giant fir tree – a gift from
the Norwegian people in gratitude for Britain's
role in liberating their country from the Nazis
– is erected, and carols are sung around the
same time.
www.london.gov.uk

Ludlow
**Ludlow Medieval Christmas Fayre
(24-25 Nov)**
Vendors in medieval garb set up shop
outside Ludlow Castle. The event aims
to reconstruct a traditional Shropshire
Christmas.
www.ludlowcraftevents.co.uk

Edinburgh
**Capital Christmas
(Late Nov)**
Atmospheric Edinburgh pulls on its best
festive kilt in late November with the official

switch-on of the city's Christmas lights.
The fun continues for the entire month
with performances, fairground rides and
a profusion of markets.
www.edinburghschristmas.com

DECEMBER
Durham
Christmas Festival
(From mid Dec)
Durham fluffs out its feathers with this annual
Victorian festival – music, street entertainment
and market stalls light up the city centre.
www.discovercountydurham.com

Edinburgh
Edinburgh Hogmanay
(29 Dec-1 Jan 2007)
Edinburgh surges to the fore with its famous
New Year festivities. This is a four-day
extravaganza with non-stop concerts,
processions and a massive street party,
culminating in a concert and spectacular
fireworks display on New Year's Eve.
www.edinburghshogmanay.org

Tetbury
South Cotswold Christmas
Antiques Fair
(Usually mid Dec)
Tetbury is known for its antiques and this
fair at the Westonbirt School (of Arboretum
fame) has more than 80 stands, many aimed
at collectors. Still, the amateur need not fear
– there are plenty of bargains to be had.

London
New Year's Eve Celebrations
(31 Dec 2007)
Trafalgar Square becomes an alarmingly
crowded gathering point for revellers, but the
millions of pounds worth of fireworks let off
around the South Bank and the London Eye
are truly breathtaking.
www.london.gov.uk

Festivals & Events

Useful Addresses

HOTEL CHAINS

Alias
www.aliashotels.com
Best Western
www.bestwestern.com
Britannia Hotels
www.britanniahotels.com
City Inn
www.cityinn.com
Exclusive Hotels
www.exclusivehotels.co.uk
GoldenTulip
www.goldentulip.com
Hilton
www.hilton.com
Hotel du Vin
www.hotelduvin.com
Ibis Hotels
www.ibishotels.com
Intercontinental Hotels Group
www.ichotelsgroup.com
Jurys
www.jurysdoyle.com
Macdonald Hotels & Resorts
www.macdonald-hotels.co.uk
Malmaison
www.malmaison.com
Marriott
www.marriott.com
my hotel
www.myhotels.com
Novotel
www.novotel.com
Premier Travel Inn
www.premiertravelinn.com
Radisson
www.radisson.com
Small & Friendly Hotels and Inns
www.smallandfriendly.co.uk
Travelodge
www.travelodge.com
Von Essen
www.vonessenhotels.co.uk

CAR HIRE

Alamo
0870 400 4562/www.alamo.co.uk
Avis
0844 581 0147/www.avis.co.uk
Budget
0870 155 5656/www.budget.co.uk
easycar
www.easycar.com
Enterprise
0870 607 7757/www.enterprise.co.uk
Europcar
0870 607 5000/www.europcar.co.uk
Hertz
0870 599 6699/www.hertz.co.uk

Holiday Autos
0870 400 0099/www.holidayautos.co.uk
National Car Rental
0870 600 0044/www.nationalcar.co.uk

TRAIN BOOKING/ INFORMATION

National Rail Enquiries
0845 7484950/www.nationalrail.co.uk
The Train Line
www.thetrainline.com

COACHES

National Express
0870 580 8080/www.nationalexpress.co.uk

AIRLINES

Aer Lingus
0845 084 4444/www.aerlingus.com
bmi
0870 607 0555/www.flybmi.com
Bmibaby
0871 224 0224/www.bmibaby.com
British Airways
0870 850 9850/www.ba.com
easyjet
0905 821 0905 (65p/min)/www.easyjet.co.uk
Flybe
0871 700 0123/www.flybe.com
Ryanair
0871 246 0000/www.ryanair.com

TRAVEL/BOOKING WEBSITES

Expedia
www.expedia.co.uk
Hotel Link
www.hotellink.co.uk
lastminute.com
www.lastminute.com
Opodo
www.opodo.co.uk
Travel Intelligence
www.travelintelligence.net
Travelocity
www.travelocity.co.uk

DISABLED

Tourism for All
0845 124 9971/www.tourismforall.org.uk
Wheelchair Travel & Access Mini Buses
01483 233640/www.wheelchair-travel.co.uk

Index

Index

Numbers in **bold** indicate the key entry for the topic; numbers in *italics* indicate illustrations.

Index

Index

G

H

Index

R

S

T

RESTAURANTS, PUBS, CAFÉS & CLUBS

Index

Index

Advertisers' Index

Please refer to relevant sections for addresses/telephone numbers